C000068130

# The
# Yorkshire County
# Cricket Club Limited

Registered Number 28929R

## YEARBOOK
## 2016

## 118th EDITION

*Sponsors of*

**THE YORKSHIRE COUNTY CRICKET CLUB**

*Editor:*
DAVID WARNER

*Production Editor:*
JAMES M. GREENFIELD

*Records and Statistics*
*Yorkshire First Eleven:*
JOHN T POTTER

*Yorkshire Second Eleven:*
HOWARD CLAYTON

*Official Photographers:*
SIMON WILKINSON, ALEX WHITEHEAD
and ALLAN MCKENZIE. *SWpix.com*

*Published by*
THE YORKSHIRE COUNTY CRICKET CLUB LTD
HEADINGLEY CRICKET GROUND
LEEDS LS6 3BU
Tel: 0843 504 3099  Fax: 0113 278 4099
Internet: http://www.yorkshireccc.com
e-mail: cricket@yorkshireccc.com

*Solicitors:*
DLA PIPER UK LLP

*Auditors:*
KPMG Audit plc

Medical Officer: Dr NIGEL MAYERS, MBChB, MRCGP
Burley Park Medical Centre, 273 Burley Road, Leeds LS4 2EL

**The opinions expressed by contributors are not necessarily those of the Board.**

1

# TELEPHONE AND FAX NUMBERS

HEADINGLEY CRICKET GROUND — **Tel: 0843 504 3099**
Fax: 0113 278 4099

NORTH MARINE ROAD, SCARBOROUGH — **Tel: 01723 365625**
Fax: 01723 364287

BURNLEY ROAD, TODMORDEN — **Tel: 01706 813140**

SHIPTON ROAD, YORK — **Tel: 01904 623602**

BRADFORD & BINGLEY — **Tel: 01274 775441**
Wagon Lane, Bingley

STAMFORD BRIDGE — **Tel: 01759 371545**
Low Catton Road

© The Yorkshire County Cricket Club Ltd 2016

*Produced by:*

Great Northern Books
PO Box 213, Ilkley LS29 9WS
www.greatnorthernbooks.co.uk

ISBN: 978-0-9933447-5-6

# CONTENTS

*Colour Plates — Facing Pages 32 and 256*

3

# Officers for 2016

# JOHN HAMPSHIRE NOMINATED FOR YORKSHIRE PRESIDENCY

## By David Warner

After a gloriously successful two years as Yorkshire CCC President, "Dickie" Bird was due to step down at the Club's annual general meeting in March with John Hampshire, right, nominated to replace him.

No one is more deserving of the role than John, who can rightly claim a place in the very top category of Yorkshire batsmen. He made his first-class debut with his native county in 1961, and went on to become closely involved with virtually every facet of the professional game for well over half-a-century.

Born at Thurnscoe, near Rotherham, on February 10, 1941, the powerful right-hand batsman played in 456 first-class games for Yorkshire, scoring 21,979 runs at 46.16 and striking 34 centuries — a total exceeded by only 11 other players in the Club's history. Of those whose careers began after the Second World War only Geoffrey Boycott and Martyn Moxon exceeded John's tally of three-figure scores, and only Boycott and Brian Close accumulated more runs.

John was called up by England for eight Test matches, and on his debut against the West Indies at Lord's in 1969 he became the first English batsman to score a century at headquarters on his first Test appearance. He captained Yorkshire in 1979 and 1980 during a difficult period, and after the 1981 season he joined Derbyshire, where he played in 57 first-class matches over the next three years before retiring with an overall record of 28,059 first-class runs, which included 43 centuries.

He was among the cream of Yorkshire's batsmen in the one-day arena, often entertaining on a lavish scale while making his way to 6,296 List A runs at 31.63 with seven centuries and 36 half-centuries.

John's infrequently used leg-breaks brought him 30 first-class wickets, including a sensational haul of 7-52 against Glamorgan at Cardiff Arms Park in 1963. So quickly did he run through the Welsh batsmen that the game was all over by the time one cricket correspondent from a national newspaper arrived on the final morning expecting little to have happened!

As well as his various tours abroad John coached in Tasmania for many seasons, and was a member of the State side from 1967 to 1979.

With his playing days over he embarked on a successful career as a first-class umpire, officiating at international level, and later he was a member of the panel monitoring umpires in county matches.

Now John will be hoping that Yorkshire under his Presidency this summer can set the seal on a hat-trick of Championship titles.

Yorkshire won the Championship and then retained it during Dickie's two-year term of office — much to his great delight.

"I think John Hampshire is a good man for the job, and will make an excellent President," Dickie said.

Looking back at his time in office, Dickie added: "They

**JOHN HAMPSHIRE: Eyes set on a Championship hat-trick**
*(Photo: Ron Deaton Archive)*

have been an amazing two years, and I enjoyed every minute of them. I watched the team virtually at every match, home and away, and I was very proud of what they went on to achieve. I am confident the team have a bright future ahead of them, and I think they have a good enough squad of players to go on winning the Championship title for at least the next five seasons.

"That would put them level with Surrey's record-breaking run of seven consecutive Championships, and I wouldn't be surprised if Yorkshire went on to do even better than that. I will still be attending Yorkshire matches on a regular basis, and I am sure they will continue to give me as much pleasure as they have done over the past couple of years."

# Officials of the Yorkshire County Cricket Club

| President | Treasurer | Captain | Captain (Contd) |
|---|---|---|---|
| T R Barker 1863 | M J Ellison 1863-1893 | R Iddison 1863-1872 | P Carrick 1987-1989 |
| M J Ellison 1864-97 | M Ellison, jun 1894-1898 | J Rowbotham 1873 | M D Moxon 1990-1995 |
| Lord Hawke 1898-1938 | Chas Stokes 1899-1912 | L Greenwood 1874 | D Byas 1996-2001 |
| Rt Hon Sir F S Jackson 1939-1947 | R T Heselton 1913-1931 | J Rowbotham 1875 | D S Lehmann 2002 |
| T L Taylor 1948-1960 | A Wyndham Heselton 1932-1962 | E Lockwood 1876-1877 | A McGrath 2003 |
| Sir W A Worsley Bart 1961-1973 | M G Crawford 1963-1979 | T Emmett 1878-1882 | C White 2004-6 |
| Sir K Parkinson 1974-1981 | J D Welch 1980-1984 | Hon M B (Lord) Hawke 1883-1910 | D Gough 2007-8 |
| N W D Yardley 1981-1983 | P W Townend 1984-2002 | E J R H Radcliffe 1911 | A McGrath 2009 |
| The Viscount Mountgarret 1984-1989 | *Chairman* | Sir A W White 1912-1918 | A W Gale 2010- |
| Sir Leonard Hutton 1989-1990 | A H Connell, DL 1971-1979 | D C F Burton 1919-1921 | *Secretary* |
| Sir Lawrence Byford QPM, LLD, DL 1991-1999 | M G Crawford 1980-1984 | Geoff Wilson 1922-1924 | Geo Padley 1863 |
| R A Smith TD, LLB, DL 1999-2004 | H R Kirk 1984-1985 | A W Lupton 1925-1927 | J B Wostinholm 1864-1902 |
| David Jones CBE 2004-6 | B Walsh, QC 1986-1991 | W A Worsley 1928-1929 | F C (Sir Fredk.) Toone 1903-1930 |
| Robert Appleyard 2006-8 | Sir Lawrence Byford CBE, QPM, LLD, DL 1991-1998 | A T Barber 1930 | J H Nash 1931-1971 |
| Brian Close CBE 2008-10 | K H Moss MBE 1998-2002 | F E Greenwood 1931-1932 | J Lister 1972-1991 |
| Raymond Illingworth CBE 2010-12 | G A Cope 2002 | A B Sellers 1933-1947 | D M Ryder 1991-2002 |
| Geoffrey Boycott OBE 2012-13 | R A Smith TD, LLB, DL 2002-5 | N W D Yardley 1948-1955 | *Company Secretary* |
| Harold 'Dickie' Bird OBE 2014-15 | C J Graves 2005-15 | W H H Sutcliffe 1956-1957 | B Bouttell 2002-5 |
| | S J Denison 2015- | J R Burnet 1958-1959 | C Hartwell 2011-14 |
| | | J V Wilson 1960-1962 | P Hudson 2014- |
| | | D B Close 1963-1970 | *Chief Executive* |
| | | G Boycott 1971-1978 | C D Hassell 1991-2002 |
| | | J H Hampshire 1979-1980 | Colin J Graves 2002-5 |
| | | C M Old 1981-1982 | Stewart Regan 2006-10 |
| | | R Illingworth 1982-1983 | Colin J Graves 2012-13 |
| | | D L Bairstow 1984-1986 | Mark Arthur 2013- |

# IT'S NOT *JUST* CRICKET

## IT'S A GREAT DAY/NIGHT OUT AT HEADINGLEY

THURS 19 - MON 23 MAY 2016
**ENGLAND VS SRI LANKA**
· FIRST INVESTEC TEST

THURSDAY 1 SEPTEMBER 2016
**ENGLAND VS PAKISTAN**
4TH ROYAL LONDON ODI (D/N)

WE ARE
**ENGLAND CRICKET**

HEADINGLEY
CRICKET GROUND

BUY YOUR TICKETS:
**YORKSHIRECCC.COM/TICKETS**
**0843 504 3099**

THE YORKSHIRE
COUNTY CRICKET CLUB

# COUNTY FIXTURES — 2016

## PRE-SEASON FIRST CLASS

| Date | | Opponents | Venue |
|------|---|-----------|-------|
| Sun | 20-23 March | MCC XI . . . . . . . . . . . | Zayed Cricket Stadium, Abu Dhabi |

## LV COUNTY CHAMPIONSHIP — Division 1
### (All four-day matches)

| | | | | |
|---|---|---|---|---|
| **SUN** | **17-20** | **APRIL** | **HAMPSHIRE** . . . . . . . . . . . . . . . . . . | **HEADINGLEY** |
| Sun | 24-27 | April | Warwickshire . . . . . . . . . . . . . . . . . . | Edgbaston |
| Sun | 1-4 | May | Nottinghamshire . . . . . . . . . . . . . . | Trent Bridge |
| **SUN** | **8-11** | **MAY** | **SURREY** . . . . . . . . . . . . . . . . . . . . | **HEADINGLEY** |
| Sun | 15-18 | May | Somerset . . . . . . . . . . . . . . . . . . . . . | Taunton |
| **SUN** | **29-1** | **MAY/JUNE** | **LANCASHIRE** . . . . . . . . . . . . . . . . | **HEADINGLEY** |
| Mon | 20-23 | June | Durham . . . . . . . . . . . . . . . . . . . | Riverside |
| **SUN** | **3-6** | **JULY** | **MIDDLESEX** . . . . . . . . . . . . . . . | **SCARBOROUGH** |
| Mon | 11-14 | July | Surrey . . . . . . . . . . . . . . . . . . . . . | The Oval |
| **THU** | **4-7** | **AUGUST** | **WARWICKSHIRE** . . . . . . . . . . . . . | **HEADINGLEY** |
| Sat | 13-16 | August | Lancashire . . . . . . . . . . . . . . . . . . | Old Trafford |
| **TUE** | **23-26** | **AUGUST** | **NOTTINGHAMSHIRE** . . . . . . . . | **SCARBOROUGH** |
| Wed | 31-3 | August/September | Hampshire . . . . . . . . . . . . . . . . . . | Southampton |
| **TUE** | **6-9** | **SEPTEMBER** | **DURHAM** . . . . . . . . . . . . . . . . . . | **HEADINGLEY** |
| **MON** | **12-15** | **SEPTEMBER** | **SOMERSET** . . . . . . . . . . . . . . . . . . | **HEADINGLEY** |
| Tue | 20-23 | September | Middlesex . . . . . . . . . . . . . . . . . . | Lord's |

## ROYAL LONDON 50-OVER CUP

| | | | | |
|---|---|---|---|---|
| **TUE** | **7** | **JUNE** | **WORCESTERSHIRE** . . . . . . . . . . . . | **HEADINGLEY** |
| Sun | 12 | June | Derbyshire . . . . . . . . . . . . . . . . . . | Chesterfield |
| **TUE** | **14** | **JUNE** | **NORTHAMPTONSHIRE** . . . . . . | **SCARBOROUGH** |
| Wed | 15 | June | Lancashire . . . . . . . . . . . . . . . . . . | Old Trafford |
| Sun | 24 | July | Leicestershire . . . . . . . . . . . . . . . . | Leicester |
| **WED** | **27** | **JULY** | **NOTTINGHAMSHIRE** . . . . . . | **SCARBOROUGH** |
| Sun | 31 | July | Durham . . . . . . . . . . . . . . . . . . . | Riverside |
| **MON** | **1** | **AUGUST** | **WARWICKSHIRE** . . . . . . . . . . . . . | **HEADINGLEY** |
| Wed | 17-18 | August | Quarter-Finals . . . . . . . . . . . . . . . . | TBC |
| Sun | 28-29 | August | Semi-Finals . . . . . . . . . . . . . . . . . | TBC |
| Sat | 17 | September | Final . . . . . . . . . . . . . . . . . . . . . | Lord's |

## NATWEST T20 BLAST CUP

| | | | | |
|---|---|---|---|---|
| **FRI** | **27** | **MAY** | **LEICESTERSHIRE** . . . . . . . . . . . . | **HEADINGLEY** |
| Thu | 2 | June | Worcestershire . . . . . . . . . . . . . . . . | Worcester |
| Fri | 3 | June | Lancashire . . . . . . . . . . . . . . . . . . | Old Trafford |
| Fri | 10 | June | Birmingham . . . . . . . . . . . . . . . . . . | Edgbaston |
| **FRI** | **17** | **JUNE** | **NOTTINGHAMSHIRE** . . . . . . . . | **HEADINGLEY** |
| **SUN** | **19** | **JUNE** | **DERBYSHIRE** . . . . . . . . . . . . . . | **HEADINGLEY** |
| Fri | 24 | June | Durham . . . . . . . . . . . . . . . . . . . | Riverside |
| **FRI** | **1** | **JULY** | **LANCASHIRE** . . . . . . . . . . . . . . | **HEADINGLEY** |
| **FRI** | **8** | **JULY** | **BIRMINGHAM** . . . . . . . . . . . . . . | **HEADINGLEY** |
| Sun | 10 | July | Derbyshire . . . . . . . . . . . . . . . . . . | Chesterfield |
| Fri | 15 | July | Nottinghamshire . . . . . . . . . . . . . . | Trent Bridge |
| **WED** | **20** | **JULY** | **DURHAM** . . . . . . . . . . . . . . . . . . | **HEADINGLEY** |
| **FRI** | **22** | **JULY** | **NORTHAMPTONSHIRE** . . . . . . | **HEADINGLEY** |
| Fri | 29 | July | Northamptonshire . . . . . . . . . . . . . | Northampton |
| Mon | 8-11 | August | Quarter-Finals . . . . . . . . . . . . . . . . | TBC |
| Sat | 20 | August | Semi-Finals and Final . . . . . . . . . . . . | Edgbaston |

## OTHER MATCHES

| | | | | |
|---|---|---|---|---|
| **MON** | **11-13** | **APRIL** | **LEEDS/BRADFORD MCCU** . . . . . . | **HEADINGLEY** |

## TOUR MATCH

PAKISTAN A ...................HEADINGLEY

# INVESTEC TEST MATCHES

### (All five-day matches)

#### ENGLAND v. SRI LANKA

**THU 19-23 MAY** ......**HEADINGLEY**        Fri 27-31 May ..............Riverside
Thu   9-13   June   .......Lord's

#### ENGLAND v. PAKISTAN

Thu 14-18   July........Lord's        Fri  22-26 July ...........Old Trafford
Wed 3-7    August .....Edgbaston       Thu 11-15 August ............The Oval

## ROYAL LONDON ONE-DAY INTERNATIONALS

| | | | |
|---|---|---|---|
| Tue | 21 | June | England v. Sri Lanka ................Trent Bridge (Day/Night) |
| Fri | 24 | June | England v. Sri Lanka ................Edgbaston (Day/Night) |
| Sun | 26 | June | England v. Sri Lanka ...............................Bristol |
| Wed | 29 | June | England v. Sri Lanka ...............The Oval (Day/Night) |
| Sat | 2 | July | England v. Sri Lanka ..............................Cardiff |
| Wed | 24 | August | England v. Pakistan ........Southampton (Day/Night) |
| Sat | 27 | August | England v. Pakistan ...............................Lord's |
| Tue | 30 | August | England v. Pakistan ........Trent Bridge (Day/Night) |
| **THU** | **1** | **SEPTEMBER** | **ENGLAND V. PAKISTAN** .**HEADINGLEY (DAY/NIGHT)** |
| Sun | 4 | September | ...............................Cardiff |

## NATWEST INTERNATIONAL T20

| | | | |
|---|---|---|---|
| Tue | 5 | July | England v. Sri Lanka..........................Southampton |
| Wed | 7 | September | England v. Pakistan ..........................Old Trafford |

## SECOND ELEVEN CHAMPIONSHIP

| | | | |
|---|---|---|---|
| Tue | 7-9 | June | Warwickshire .........EFSG, Portland Road, Edgbaston |
| **MON** | **13-15** | **JUNE** | **LEICESTERSHIRE** .........................**YORK** |
| **TUE** | **21-23** | **JUNE** | **WORCESTERSHIRE** ............**SCARBOROUGH** |
| Mon | 4-6 | July | Lancashire...............................Todmorden |
| Tue | 19-21 | July | Nottinghamshire .............Trent College, Long Eaton |
| Tue | 26-28 | July | Derbyshire .......................Belper Meadows CC |
| Tue | 2-4 | August | Northamptonshire ..............Market Harborough CC |
| **TUE** | **9-11** | **AUGUST** | **DURHAM** ...............................**YORK** |
| **MON** | **15-17** | **AUGUST** | **MCC UNIVERSITIES** ........**STAMFORD BRIDGE** |
| Tues | 6-9 | September | Final ......................................TBC |

## SECOND ELEVEN TROPHY

| | | | |
|---|---|---|---|
| **TUE** | **3** | **MAY** | **UNICORNS** ..........................**BARNSLEY** |
| Mon | 6 | June | Warwickshire .......Knowle and Dorridge CC, Solihull |
| **THU** | **16** | **JUNE** | **LEICESTERSHIRE** ............**PUDSEY CONGS** |
| Thu | 7 | July | Lancashire ................Westhoughton CC, Bolton |
| Mon | 25 | July | Derbyshire ..........Alvaston and Boulton CC, Derby |
| **MON** | **8** | **AUGUST** | **DURHAM** ...............................**YORK** |
| Fri | 19 | August | Semi-Finals .................................TBC |
| Thu | 25 | August | Final ......................................TBC |

## SECOND ELEVEN TWENTY20 (TWO MATCHES IN THE SAME DAY)

| | | | |
|---|---|---|---|
| Mon | 16 | May | Northamptonshire .........Stowe School, Buckingham |
| Fri | 27 | May | Nottinghamshire ...........Trent College, Long Eaton |
| Tue | 31 | May | Durham ..............................Brandon CC |
| **WED** | **1** | **JUNE** | **DERBYSHIRE** ....................**HARROGATE** |
| **MON** | **20** | **JUNE** | **WORCESTERSHIRE** .......**MARSKE-BY-SEA CC** |
| Thu | 14 | July | Semi-Finals and Final ........................TBC |

## SECOND ELEVEN FRIENDLIES

| | | | | |
|---|---|---|---|---|
| Mon | 11-13 | April | Gloucestershire | Bristol |
| Tue | 19-21 | April | Lancashire | Old Trafford |
| Tue | 26-28 | April | Glamorgan | Cardiff |
| Mon | 9-12 | May | Kent | Beckenham |
| **WED** | **25** | **MAY** | **LANCASHIRE** | **YORK** |
| **MON** | **11-13** | **JULY** | **SOMERSET** | **HEADINGLEY** |
| **TUE** | **6-8** | **SEPTEMBER** | **SCOTLAND** | **HARROGATE** |
| **MON** | **12-14** | **SEPTEMBER** | **NOTTINGHAMSHIRE** | **SCARBOROUGH** |

## YORKSHIRE ACADEMY IN THE YORKSHIRE LEAGUE

| | | | | |
|---|---|---|---|---|
| Sat | 16 | April | Sheriff Hutton Bridge | Sheriff Hutton Bridge |
| **SAT** | **23** | **APRIL** | **DRIFFIELD** | **WEETWOOD** |
| Sat | 30 | April | Dunnington | Dunnington |
| Sat | 7 | May | Stamford Bridge | Stamford Bridge |
| **SAT** | **14** | **MAY** | **ACOMB** | **WEETWOOD** |
| **SAT** | **21** | **MAY** | **WOODHOUSE GRANGE** | **WEETWOOD** |
| Sat | 28 | May | Scarborough | Scarborough |
| **SAT** | **4** | **JUNE** | **CASTLEFORD** | **WEETWOOD** |
| **SAT** | **11** | **JUNE** | **HULL** | **WEETWOOD** |
| Sat | 18 | June | Harrogate | Harrogate |
| Sat | 25 | June | York | York |
| Sat | 2 | July | Driffield | Driffield |
| **SAT** | **9** | **JULY** | **SHERIFF HUTTON BRIDGE** | **WEETWOOD** |
| **SAT** | **16** | **JULY** | **DUNNINGTON** | **WEETWOOD** |
| **SAT** | **23** | **JULY** | **STAMFORD BRIDGE** | **WEETWOOD** |
| Sat | 30 | July | Acomb | Acomb Sports Club |
| Sat | 6 | August | Woodhouse Grange | Woodhouse Grange |
| **SAT** | **13** | **AUGUST** | **SCARBOROUGH** | **WEETWOOD** |
| **SAT** | **20** | **AUGUST** | **HARROGATE** | **WEETWOOD** |
| Sat | 27 | August | Castleford | Castleford |
| **SAT** | **3** | **SEPTEMBER** | **YORK** | **WEETWOOD** |
| Sat | 10 | September | Hull | Hull |

## YORKSHIRE ACADEMY IN THE YORKSHIRE LEAGUE CUP

| | | | | |
|---|---|---|---|---|
| Mon | 30 | May | Dunnington or Castleford | TBC |

## YORKSHIRE ACADEMY IN THE YORKSHIRE LEAGUE T20

| | | | | |
|---|---|---|---|---|
| Sun | 15 | May | York and Scarborough | York |

## YORKSHIRE ACADEMY FRIENDLIES

| | | | | |
|---|---|---|---|---|
| Sat | 9 | April | Keighley | Keighley CC |
| Mon | 19 | April | Durham Academy | Richmond CC |
| Thu | 5 | May | Sedbergh School | Sedbergh School |
| **TUE** | **5** | **JULY** | **SCOTLAND DEVELOPMENT XI** | **WEETWOOD** |
| **WED** | **6-7** | **JULY** | **SCOTLAND DEVELOPMENT XI** | **WEETWOOD** |
| Thu | 28 | July | YCCC Girls Big Bash XI | TBC |
| Tue | 9-11 | August | Durham | Away TBC |

## YORKSHIRE UNDER-17s in THREE-DAY CHAMPIONSHIP

| | | | | |
|---|---|---|---|---|
| **TUE** | **12-14** | **JULY** | **DERBYSHIRE** | **WEETWOOD** |
| Tue | 19-21 | July | Cheshire | Away |
| **TUE** | **26-28** | **JULY** | **LANCASHIRE** | **WEETWOOD** |
| Tue | 2-4 | August | Durham | Away |
| Tue | 9-11 | August | Semi-Final | Home Tie |
| Wed | 17-19 | August | Final | TBC |

## YORKSHIRE UNDER-17s in ONE-DAY CHAMPIONSHIP

| | | | | |
|---|---|---|---|---|
| Wed | 1 | June | Durham | Away |
| **SUN** | **5** | **JUNE** | **DERBYSHIRE** | **WEETWOOD** |
| **SUN** | **12** | **JUNE** | **LANCASHIRE** | **WEETWOOD** |
| Thu | 30 | June | Cheshire | Away |
| Wed | 17 | August | Semi-Final | Home Tie |
| Sun | 21 | August | Final | TBC |

# RETAINING CHAMPIONSHIP TITLE IS PART OF THE TEN-YEAR PLAN

## By Graham Hardcastle

The great Brian Close would have died a happy man in mid-September, knowing that the current crop of Yorkshire cricketers had won back-to-back LV=County Championship titles. When Andrew Gale lifted the trophy at Lord's after defeat against Middlesex — the only four-day reverse of the campaign — he became the first *White Rose* captain to retain the title since the revered Close in the late 1960s.

Gale *et al* have already been mentioned in the same breath as the great Yorkshire team of the 60s, and understandably so given the way they dominated the competition in 2015 as records tumbled. They secured a record points haul for either division of 286 since the Championship moved from one 18-team league in 2000. And when they beat Sussex at Headingley in their last match of the season they completed an 11th win — more than any team has done in the two-division era.

There was one statistic which summed up Yorkshire's dominance perfectly. They finished 68 points clear of second-placed Middlesex, who themselves finished 67 points clear of bottom-side Worcestershire.

The Yorkshire camp have spoken at length about wanting to create a dynasty. Batsman Alex Lees insisted that they will be training harder than ever ahead of this summer to try to make it three in a row, while former all-rounder and new coach Rich Pyrah said the Club were not content with winning two or three titles. They are gunning for a dominant 10 years: "We're going to have transitions over the next few years. Some of the senior lads are finishing, so it's important that we continue to feed the younger lads in at the right time," Pyrah said.

"We don't just want to be winning the Championship for two or three years. We want to have a successful 10 years now. We've definitely got the potential to do that."

To be labelled a truly great side Yorkshire must add limited-overs silverware to the cabinet. There were signs of improvement against the white ball last summer. Wins against the defending champions in both *T20* and List A one-day cricket, Birmingham and Durham, were significant achievements, while a host of young players progressed their games. Seamer Matthew Fisher was one of those, as was batsman Jack

Leaning and all-rounder Will Rhodes.

Ultimately, it was a season of disappointment in both of these competitions.

Yorkshire failed to get out of the North Division in *T20* for the third year running despite the addition to their squad of Australian batting superstars Aaron Finch and Glenn Maxwell, who both underwhelmed.

They were beaten semi-finalists in the Royal London One-day Cup by champions

**DAVID WILLEY: Can he ignite the one-day spark Yorkshire needs?**

Gloucestershire after crumbling from a great position with the bat.

Experienced Australian batsman Michael Klinger, the Gloucester skipper, gave the Vikings a lesson in how to construct a one-day innings — and how to anchor a chase — with a stunning century. Hopefully the signing of England limited-overs all-rounder David Willey can provide the spark this year. Willey arrives on the back of a jet-set winter with England and for Australian Big Bash *T20* team Perth Scorchers, where he came up against Jason Gillespie and the Adelaide Strikers.

Back to the Championship. This was a quite exceptional achievement. In many ways it was different to 2014. In many ways it was better.

Yorkshire did not have the foundation built by openers Lees and Adam Lyth, and had to rely on individuals sticking their hands up to get them out of a sticky situation or two. While Yorkshire's batsmen were exceptional the previous year this time it was the bowlers.

That is not to say that there were not some impressive returns. Jonny Bairstow's surge to 1,000 runs in only 13 innings meant that he was honoured by the Club's members and teammates at Yorkshire's end of season awards dinner. Bairstow, who won back his place in England's Test team for the second half of the *Ashes* series, took the Members' Player of the Year and the Players' Player of the Year awards.

Gale's 1,006 runs from 16 matches with three centuries and as many 50s is worth high praise. This summer's beneficiary certainly led from the front, and it was an emotional moment when he lifted the trophy at Lord's following the disappointment at the end of 2014.

Spearheaded again by leading wicket-taker Jack Brooks, the *White Rose* attack returned some inspiring performances. Warwickshire away springs to mind, when Ryan Sidebottom bagged 11 wickets in a match which saw the hosts blown away for 69 in the first innings. This came in a run of six successive wins through the middle of the season, and was a defining week, given that the Bears finished second in 2014.

So, were Yorkshire better than in 2014? Yes, better because they started the season without seven of their players due to England's Test tour of the Caribbean and Gale's ECB suspension for improper conduct.

The county had to get through the first three games with limited damage and kick on, and that is exactly what they did. They hammered Worcester by 10 wickets, with Steven Patterson capturing five cheap victims in the second innings. They then drew against close rivals Nottinghamshire at Trent Bridge and Warwickshire at Headingley before putting their foot on the accelerator and easing clear of the pack.

Rhodes stood in at the top of the order admirably for Lyth, while Leaning started a memorable summer like a house on fire with three centuries before the end of June. Patterson finished within five wickets of the first 50-wicket Championship campaign of his career, and may well have got there had he not been left out of the last match of the year.

Rolls Royce Sidebottom was exceptional again, despite missing 10 weeks with a torn calf as he moved beyond 700 First Class career wickets. That milestone was achieved during a sparkling first over of Yorkshire's match against Middlesex at Lord's in September when he weighed in with a triple-wicket maiden.

What about Tim Bresnan? After being eased out of the England reckoning he started the summer with a refined approach to the bowling crease and huge confidence with the bat.

Gale believes Bresnan could become one of county cricket's great all-rounders with a regular return of 50 Championship wickets and 800 runs. He finished five wickets away from the former but sailed beyond 800 runs to finish with 849. His standout contribution of the summer was a career-best 169 not out in the win at Durham.

All hail Yorkshire. We could be writing that for a few years to come!

**Graham Hardcastle writes on Yorkshire cricket**
**for the Bradford Telegraph & Argus,**
**The Press, York, and The Northern Echo**

# YORKSHIRE CLINCH TITLE
# AT LORD'S FOR FIRST TIME

### By Paul E Dyson

It was widely believed that after Yorkshire had won the Championship at Lord's on September 9 it was the first time they had done so at English cricket's headquarters. This is indeed so, and we can look at this and other aspects of Yorkshire's Championship-winning moments, the impetus having been provided by Nigel Pullan's article on the post-1945 successes in the 2015 edition of the *Yorkshire CCC Yearbook*.

The following list is of the venues, opponents and dates which relate to the clinching of each of the *White Rose* county's 32 Championship titles. The vital moment may have occurred during the match or been a direct consequence of the result achieved at the end of the game.

| | | | |
|---|---|---|---|
| 1893 | Sheffield (BL) | Kent | August 23 |
| 1896 | Hove | Sussex | August 22 |
| 1898 | Hove | Sussex | August 27 |
| 1900 | Taunton | Somerset | August 22 |
| 1901 | Canterbury | Kent | August 24 |
| 1902 | Cheltenham | Gloucs | August 16 |
| 1905 | Leyton | Essex | August 26 |
| 1908 | Cheltenham | Gloucs | August 22 |
| 1912 | Taunton | Somerset | August 28 |
| 1919 | Hove | Sussex | August 30 |
| 1922 | Leyton | Essex | September 1 |
| 1923 | Headingley | Hants | August 17 |
| 1924 | Hove | Sussex | September 1 |
| 1925 | Hove | Sussex | September 1 |
| 1931 | Headingley | Middlesex | August 18 |
| 1932 | Bournemouth | Hampshire | August 26 |
| 1933 | Bradford (PA) | Nottinghamshire | August 18 |
| 1935 | Worcester | Worcestershire | August 23 |
| 1937 | Bournemouth | Hampshire | August 30 |
| 1938 | Hove | Sussex | September 2 |
| 1939 | Bournemouth | Hampshire | August 29 |
| 1946 | Eastbourne | Sussex | August 26 |
| 1959 | Hove | Sussex | September 1 |
| 1960 | Harrogate | Worcestershire | August 30 |
| 1962 | Harrogate | Glamorgan | September 7 |
| 1963 | Leicester | Leicestershire | August 30 |

| 1966 | Harrogate | Kent | September 2 |
| 1967 | Harrogate | Gloucestershire | September 7 |
| 1968 | Hull (Circle) | Surrey | August 30 |
| 2001 | Scarborough | Glamorgan | August 24 |
| 2014 | Trent Bridge | Nottinghamshire | September 12 |
| 2015 | Lord's | Middlesex | September 9 |

In 1898, 1902, 1935 and 1939 the winning of the Championship was confirmed after the games outlined above, i.e. when Yorkshire were not actually playing. In these instances the dates given are when the Championship was actually won, not when the game was being played.

**The Championship has been won:**

Ten times in Yorkshire (Harrogate 4, Headingley 2, Bradford, Hull, Scarborough and Sheffield 1 each), eight times in Sussex (Hove 7, Eastbourne 1), three times in Hampshire (all Bournemouth), twice each in Essex (Leyton), Gloucestershire (Cheltenham) and Somerset (Taunton), once each in Kent (Canterbuy), Leicestershire (Leicester), Nottinghamshire (Trent Bridge), Worcestershire (Worcester) and once at Lord's against Middlesex

Yorkshire have never won the Championship in Derbyshire, Durham, Glamorgan, Lancashire, Northamptonshire, Surrey or Warwickshire

**The Championship has been won:**

Eight times against Sussex, four times against Hampshire, three times against each of Gloucestershire and Kent, twice against each of Essex, Glamorgan, Middlesex, Nottinghamshire, Somerset and Worcestershire, and once against each of Leicestershire and Surrey

Yorkshire have never won the Championship whilst playing against Derbyshire, Durham, Lancashire, Northamptonshire and Warwickshire.

**Earliest dates for winning the Championship:**

August 16, 1902; August 17, 1923; August 18th, 1931 and 1933

**Latest dates for winning the Championship:**

September 12, 2014; September 9, 2015; September 7, 1962 and 1967

**Yorkshire won the Championship:**

With five matches to spare in 1923, four to spare in 1933, three to spare in 1902, 1931 and 1935, two to spare in 1908, 1946, 2001 and 2015, and one to spare in 1893, 1896, 1900, 1905, 1912, 1925, 1932, 1939, 1960 and 2014. The title was won 13 times in Yorkshire's last match of its season in 1898, 1901, 1919, 1922, 1924, 1937, 1938, 1959, 1962, 1963, 1966, 1967 and 1968. The last four of these years were the four occasions when the county won the title under Brian Close.

Readers less familiar with Yorkshire's history will be surprised to note the prominence of counties situated in the South. This is because Yorkshire had a long-standing tradition of finishing their Championship season with a Southern tour. Hove was often the venue for the final match of the season, and five of Yorkshire's seven title victories at that ground have occurred when this has been the case.

# WHY SKIPPER WOULD RELISH PLAYING NOTTS AT LORD'S!

### By Andrew Bosi

There used to be a rumour that from time to time Eric Bedser would go out to bat in place of his brother, Alec, despite having already batted. No umpire or opposing captain would ever be the wiser.

One wonders whether Andrew Gale has, unbeknown to anyone else, an identical twin. How else can one explain the extraordinary fluctuations in his ability to combat the bowling? This phenomenon cannot be explained, as has been the case with others, on the condition of the wicket or the strength of the bowling.

In looking for an explanation one might observe that Gale has a particularly fine record against Nottinghamshire. However, as they turn up with a different attack every time we play them it is not a question of tucking in to the same bowler every time.

He also has a particularly good record at Lord's. His century in 2013 was the second of three successive hundreds, the smallest of the three but the most fluent. He scored 98 in what most observers regarded as his most fluent innings of 2015, but two matches out of 133 is insufficient for statistical significance. Gale has played only twice at headquarters, standing down in 2014 in the belief that others were more likely to make runs. He made another hundred on his return in the next match.

Only Sussex of the 2015 and 2016 first divisions have yet to concede a ton to Gale, and that looked likely to end at Hove until he was adjudged lbw, but in between fluent innings at Hove and Lord's came one of those floundering efforts, against Somerset, when seam and spin alike seemed alien to him.

Gale draws comparison with David Byas — a fellow left-hander also capable of scoring runs when no-one else could do so. An innings of 95 at Basingstoke, when no-one else reached 60, comes to mind. Byas was the first captain in the modern era to secure the Championship. Gale has become the second and the first to retain it. Their style of batting may have similarities, but their style of leadership has been very different.

In part this was of necessity, given the contrasting approaches of the Australian coaches with whom they worked. On the other hand team morale has never seemed better, even when the wealth of talent available

**FAVOURITE DISH: Captain Andrew Gale tucks into the Nottinghamshire attack with 148 as Yorkshire win by an innings at Headingley in June 2015**

has led to the exclusion of players who would walk into any other county side. Rarely has Gale had cause to regret his decision on winning the toss. The pitch in Hampshire did not play as expected, but thanks to the weather interruptions he found himself in pole position on the last day and ended up winning a match Yorkshire had scarcely deserved.

The first Championship was sullied for Gale by the response of the ECB to his misdemeanour at Old Trafford. Ignoring the premise that one should not be tried twice for the same offence, and over-riding and undermining the umpires in the process, the ECB must have given Gale an extra spur, if one were needed, to retain the Championship and to do so at the home of cricket. There was one positive move the ECB made, and the anger-management course stood the skipper in good stead at Hove when the aforementioned lbw verdict was delivered.

His benefit is sure to be popular with the Yorkshire public, and offers a welcome chance to keep county cricket in the public eye at a time when it faces an increasing threat from other sports.

## Lees named one-day captain

Yorkshire have announced that opening batsman Alex Lees, 22, has been officially appointed as Vikings' one-day captain for the 2016 season. He is the youngest player to hold the post. Last summer he led the team on eight occasions after Andrew Gale had stepped down as captain in limited-overs matches.

*Can Gale add his name to list of great achievers?*

# GEOFFREY WILSON — THE LESSER OF FOUR CHAMPIONSHIP EQUALS

### By Martin Howe

In leading Yorkshire to the County Championship in 2015 Andrew Gale is in a position to emulate the feat of four of his predecessors who led Yorkshire to three successive Championship titles. Three of those men were, without much argument, the most celebrated of all Yorkshire captains — Lord Hawke, Brian Sellers and Brian Close. The fourth is the less remembered Geoffrey Wilson.

Lord Hawke became Yorkshire's captain in 1883, but it was not for 10 years, by when he had transformed the team of unruly professionals he had inherited into a match-winning combination, that Yorkshire won their first Championship. By the time he gave up the captaincy in 1910 he had led them to eight titles, a record most unlikely to be bettered. The three consecutive successes were in 1900, 1901, and 1902.

Brian Sellers was appointed Yorkshire captain in 1933, and he held the position, aside from the interruption of the Second World War, until his retirement in 1947. In Sellers's nine seasons in charge Yorkshire won the title six times, an extraordinary proportion of successes. The hat-trick of Championships came in 1937,1938 and 1939 — and Sellers made it four in succession in the first season after the war.

Lord Hawke and Sellers were amateurs. While neither was a cricketer of the highest class they merited inclusion for their leadership qualities. Both were no nonsense, autocratic captains. No player would challenge their authority. Both would put in his place anyone who did not pull his weight or conduct himself in the manner expected of Yorkshire players.

Brian Close, as talented an all-round cricketer as ever wore Yorkshire's colours, became captain only after the retirement of Vic Wilson, the first professional to captain Yorkshire in modern times. Sellers, by then cricket-committee chairman would have preferred to revert to an amateur captain but, absent any suitable candidates, the clock could not be turned back. Close's reign was a short one, but in his eight seasons as captain he led Yorkshire to no fewer than four Championships, the three successive titles coming in 1966, 1967 and 1968. Close was an inspirational if mercurial captain, who earned the respect of his players for his ability, commitment to the Yorkshire cause and the fearless manner in which he played the game. Despite his record

— which also included Gillette Cup wins in 1965 and 1969 — Close was controversially sacked as captain after the 1970 season. His time as England captain was also brought to a premature end, even though England had won six of the seven Tests when he was in charge.

No more need be said about these three giants of Yorkshire cricket, but what about the fourth, Geoffrey Wilson, one of the eight amateurs to captain Yorkshire between the reigns of Lord Hawke and Brian Sellers? He was born in Leeds in 1895 — his father, a long-standing Yorkshire member, ran the family worsted clothing business, Joshua Wilson & Sons Ltd. A useful batsman and an outstanding cover-point fielder, Wilson made the Harrow First Eleven in the three years preceding the outbreak of the First World War and was captain in 1914.

He went up to Cambridge in 1914, but his university education was interrupted by the war in which he served with distinction in the Royal Marines Artillery. He returned to Cambridge, and in 1919 made his First Class debut for the university, obtained his Blue, and made his first appearance for Yorkshire. He played in seven successive matches for the county that season, doing reasonably well with a batting average of 26.00 and a top score of 70, but he played in few games, and with little success, in 1920. He then left university without completing his degree to work in the family business.

There seemed little prospect at this point of Wilson making any sort of mark in county cricket. He appeared three times for Yorkshire in 1921, reaching double figures once in his four innings, yet at the end of that season he was chosen to succeed D C L Burton as Yorkshire captain. Of no more than decent club cricket standard, Wilson's only qualification for the position was that he was an amateur and one who could devote himself full-time to the job — in contrast to his contemporary and namesake, Rockley Wilson, the Winchester schoolmaster, a much superior cricketer. Geoffrey must have been apprehensive about leading a side which included such sages as Wilfred Rhodes and Emmott Robinson, aggressive bowlers in Abram Waddington and George Macaulay, the dependable Edgar Oldroyd and other cricketers of international standing in Percy Holmes and Herbert Sutcliffe, Maurice Leyland and Roy Kilner. He was wise enough to lean heavily on Rhodes for advice, so much so that Robinson could observe: "He's a good captain. He allus does as Wilfred tells him!"

In 1922 Yorkshire finished fourth, but the following season they won the title, albeit by a whisker in the last game. Geoffrey had missed the last few games with appendicitis, Rockley Wilson taking his place. With an average for the season of 20.18, though only 18.37 in the Championship, Wilson had made a good enough impression to be included in the largely amateur MCC party captained by A.C. MacLaren that toured Australia and New Zealand in 1922-23. The tour was a disappointing one for Wilson, though he did make his only First Class century against Victoria at Melbourne.

In 1923 Yorkshire swept all before them, losing only one match out of 35, and that by only three runs, on their way to the title. In contrast Wilson had a wretched season.

He missed a number of games with a badly injured hand, and averaged only 7.04 in his 23 innings in the Championship, with a top score of 57, and 6.73 in all First Class matches.

With such a decline in his performance the captain's confidence must have taken a battering, and he must have begun to have doubts about his value to the side. Moreover, Yorkshire's success was not universally applauded outside the county.

A determination to win and, if that were not possible, to avoid defeat had long been characteristic of Yorkshire sides, sometimes leading to ill feeling. the criticisms were heightened by Yorkshire's spectacular success in

**GEOFFREY WILSON:
More of a figurehead
than a leader**
*(Photo: Mick Pope Archive)*

1923, when they came to be accused of a "win at all costs" approach, even slowing down over rates, roughing up the pitch, and sledging, as it would now be called. There was, as Derek Hodgson put it, "a growing conviction among some spectators and some players that success was an inherent right and failure a blasphemy against God and nature."

Imbued with the ethos of the English public schools, this was not how Wilson wanted his Yorkshire side to be seen. He was uncomfortable with the hostile remarks in the Press and elsewhere, and at the close of the 1923 season he conceded that some of the criticisms were justified, adding: "The Yorkshire team have been somewhat adversely criticised in the South of England during the past season for various alleged actions of an unsporting nature. I feel sure that no member of the team would deliberately do anything unsporting. Nevertheless, let us remember always to play the game as it should be played – in the most friendly spirit possible." This rather ambiguous statement does not suggest a captain wholly at ease in his position.

Any hope Wilson may have had of "a more friendly spirit" was blown away in 1924 when Yorkshire, while less dominant than in the previous summer, were champions again. Wilson was too mild a personality to change the way Rhodes and his fellow professionals went about their business. Complaints against Yorkshire continued, and relations with Middlesex, their closest rivals, deteriorated to such an extent that they threatened to drop their fixtures with Yorkshire in 1925.

A Middlesex side containing several amateurs and captained by Pelham Warner beat Yorkshire by an innings at Lord's early in the season, and it was in the return game at Bramall Lane in July that things came to a head. The umpires and the visitors were subjected to a barrage of barracking by the crowd, sparked by a number of decisions on which the Yorkshire players, Waddington in particular, made no attempt to conceal their dissent. The umpires reported the incidents to Lord's, and it was only after Waddington had been persuaded to write a letter of apology and some high-level mediation that the threat was withdrawn. Wilson was so disturbed that he offered to resign, or so it was rumoured. He saw out the season, but resigned after the final match, Yorkshire against the Rest of England, which Yorkshire lost by an innings. He returned to his business career. *Wisden's* harsh verdict was: "Mr Geoffrey Wilson did his best as captain, but he had not the force of will and character to control the discordant element in his team."

Wilson had had a wretched season. He scored only 283 runs in 36 innings, averaging 10.12 in the Championship and 9.43 in all First Class matches with a top score of 37, and quite probably would have "considered his position". Nevertheless he had the proud record of captaining Yorkshire to three Championships in succession in his four years in charge. As his successor Yorkshire chose Major Arthur W Lupton, a 45-year-old wine and spirits merchant who, if no better a cricketer, was more of a disciplinarian than Wilson could ever be. Whatever were the major's talents, he led Yorkshire to a fourth successive title in 1925.

The contrast between the playing records of Wilson and the three other captains with three successive championships to their name could not be starker. Wilson played in 92 matches for Yorkshire, and scored 983 runs at 12.28. Lord Hawke appeared in 510, scoring 13,133 at 20.26; Brian Sellers in 334 matches scored 8,949 at 23.18, and Close in 536 matches scored 22,650 runs at 31.94, taking 967 wickets at 24.29.

Maurice Leyland said of the 1920s: "I never counted the captain of the Yorkshire side – we won a few championships with the handicap of one." One does not have to be an outstanding player to be a good captain. Wilson was a thoughtful and fair-minded captain, but he lacked the know-how and forcefulness of Hawke, Sellers and Close. While they in their various ways contributed mightily to Yorkshire's success, the same could not be said of Wilson. He was more the figurehead than a leader.

# LYTH TON HELPS YORKSHIRE
# BEAT MCC IN ABU DHABI

### By Danny Reuben

Yorkshire continued their winning ways from 2014 with a thumping nine-wicket victory inside three days against the MCC as the Champions warmed up for the new season in the annual Champion County fixture in Abu Dhabi, UAE. The MCC included England captain Alastair Cook, who lasted six balls on his return to action, but he was then able to enjoy a first-hand view as Adam Lyth's unbeaten half-century set the cap on a successful opening day for the *White Rose* county.

Yorkshire provided six members of England's Test squad for the West Indies, and three of them lined up against Cook, who took his place in the MCC Eleven alongside several recent international teammates in Nick Compton, Michael Carberry and Graham Onions. Yorkshire were missing Joe Root, Gary Ballance and Liam Plunkett — but still put on a strong display, and gave a First Class debut to all-rounder Will Rhodes.

Ryan Sidebottom proved that he remained a force, even in his 38th year, by removing both MCC openers inside three overs. Compton and Cook opened for England 17 times in Tests, but they were separated after one delivery, MCC captain Compton caught behind off the first ball of the match.

Cook was then pinned lbw for three in Sidebottom's second over. MCC recovered from 7-2, firstly through Carberry and James Hildreth, who added 74 for the third wicket, and then Hildreth and Daryl Mitchell, whose stand of 79 seemed to have swung the balance. Both fell in the evening session — that is between lunch and tea, this match being played under lights with a pink ball — and Zafar Ansari was the only other batsman to make double-figures as the innings folded quickly.

Kent's Sam Billings joined Compton in making a duck as Jack Brooks, Adil Rashid and Rhodes matched Sidebottom in taking two wickets apiece. In reply Alex Lees fell for 11, and Jack Leaning made only 14, but Lyth guided the 2014 champions to the close.

On the second day in sweltering heat Lyth continued his impressive form as Yorkshire dominated the match. Lyth progressed from his overnight 53 to a 15th First Class century to help his side to a 151-run first-innings advantage. Cook, who had lasted only six balls on the first day, then had to weather a tricky five-over spell before the close, which included a strident lbw appeal from Jack Brooks.

Rhodes and dependable wicket-keeper Andrew Hodd put on 104 as Yorkshire opened up a sizeable lead. Rhodes and Hodd both posted 50s before falling to Chris Rushworth and Matt Dunn, but Yorkshire were eventually dismissed for 372.

The match was wrapped up on the third day. MCC began 138 runs in arrears, but Cook could manage only five to add to his first innings three. He lasted only 30 deliveries before his attempt to dispatch a short ball from Brooks went straight into the hands of Rashid at mid-wicket.

Rashid then took the ball to remove Mitchell for nine and Hildreth one short of a half-century, both lbw. Hildreth and Compton, the only player to go past a half-century in the second innings, steadied MCC with 45 for the third wicket.

Leg-spinner Rashid bagged four scalps as he used the conditions to his advantage, and the MCC's lower-order collapsed, the last five wickets going down for 27 runs.

Yorkshire were left with a chase of 70, and first innings centurion Lyth saw off the target with an unbeaten 46, finishing the match with successive boundaries.

**ADAM LYTH: 15th century as Yorkshire turn up heat**
(Photo: Getty Images)

**Danny Reuben is Yorkshire CCC Head of Media and Marketing**

# Champion County Match — First Class
## MCC v. Yorkshire

Played at Sheikh Zayed Cricket Stadium, Abu Dhabi, on March 22, 23 and 24, 2015
*Yorkshire won by nine wickets at 9.19pm on the Third Day*
Toss won by MCC

Close of play: First Day, Yorkshire 82-2 (Lyth 53*, Patterson 23*); Second Day, MCC 13-0 (Compton 7*, Cook 2*)

### MCC

| | First Innings | | Second innings | |
|---|---|--:|---|--:|
| * N R D Compton | c Bairstow b Sidebottom | 0 | c Bairstow b Rhodes | 74 |
| A N Cook | lbw b Sidebottom | 3 | c Rashid b Brooks | 5 |
| M A Carberry | c Lyth b Patterson | 36 | c Bresnan b Lyth | 23 |
| J C Hildreth | lbw b Bresnan | 89 | lbw b Rashid | 49 |
| D K H Mitchell | lbw b Rhodes | 54 | lbw b Rashid | 9 |
| Z S Ansari | not out | 24 | b Brooks | 15 |
| § S W Billings | b Brooks | 0 | c Bairstow b Brooks | 26 |
| C Rushworth | c Bairstow b Brooks | 0 | lbw b Patterson | 6 |
| G Onions | lbw b Rhodes | 1 | (11) c Rhodes b Rashid | 0 |
| A E N Riley | lbw b Rashid | 3 | (9) not out | 5 |
| M P Dunn | c Lyth b Patterson | 1 | (10) c Rhodes b Rashid | 0 |
| Extras | b 6, nb 4 | 10 | b 2, lb 6 | 8 |
| Total | | 221 | | 220 |

*FoW*: 1-0 (Compton), 2-7 (Cook), 3-81 (Hildreth), 4-160 (Mitchell), 5-185 (Mitchell),
1st 6-186 (Billings), 7-186 (Rushworth), 8-196 (Onions), 9-215 (Riley), 10-221 (Dunn)
*FoW*: 1-30 (Cook), 2-80 (Carberry), 3-125 (Compton), 4-140 (Mitchell), 5-176 (Ansari),
2nd 6-193 (Hildreth), 7-210 (Rushworth), 8-213 (Billings), 9-220 (Dunn), 10-220 (Onions)

| | O | M | R | W | | O | M | R | W |
|---|--:|--:|--:|--:|---|--:|--:|--:|--:|
| Sidebottom | 12 | 5 | 27 | 2 | Sidebottom | 8 | 1 | 17 | 0 |
| Brooks | 12 | 2 | 57 | 2 | Brooks | 13 | 6 | 22 | 3 |
| Bresnan | 10 | 2 | 33 | 1 | Patterson | 13 | 6 | 39 | 1 |
| Patterson | 12 | 4 | 31 | 1 | Bresnan | 4 | 1 | 21 | 0 |
| Rashid | 14.5 | 1 | 51 | 2 | Rashid | 22.5 | 3 | 72 | 4 |
| Lyth | 1 | 0 | 6 | 0 | Lyth | 10 | 2 | 29 | 1 |
| Rhodes | 6 | 3 | 10 | 2 | Rhodes | 6 | 0 | 12 | 1 |

### YORKSHIRE

| | First Innings | | Second Innings | |
|---|---|--:|---|--:|
| A Lyth | lbw b Riley | 113 | not out | 46 |
| * A Z Lees | c Billings b Dunn | 11 | c Billings b Riley | 8 |
| J A Leaning | c Mitchell b Ansari | 14 | not out | 13 |
| S A Patterson | b Riley | 36 | | |
| § J M Bairstow | lbw b Rushworth | 0 | | |
| W M H Rhodes | c Cook b Rushworth | 61 | | |
| A J Hodd | c Billings b Dunn | 57 | | |
| A U Rashid | lbw b Carberry | 42 | | |
| T T Bresnan | c Cook b Riley | 12 | | |
| R J Sidebottom | not out | 3 | | |
| J A Brooks | c Hildreth b Ansari | 2 | | |
| Extras | b 5, lb 14, nb 2 | 21 | lb 6 | 6 |
| Total | | 372 | Total (1 wkt) | 73 |

*FoW*: 1-39 (Lees), 2-79 (Leaning), 3-170 (Patterson), 4-173 (Bairstow), 5-195 (Lyth),
1st 6-299 (Hodd), 7-319 (Rhodes), 8-348 (Bresnan), 9-369 (Rashid), 10-372 (Brooks)
2nd 1-42 (Lees)

| | O | M | R | W | | O | M | R | W |
|---|--:|--:|--:|--:|---|--:|--:|--:|--:|
| Onions $ | 3.5 | 0 | 8 | 0 | Rushworth | 6 | 2 | 12 | 0 |
| Rushworth | 22 | 7 | 69 | 2 | Dunn | 6 | 2 | 13 | 0 |
| Dunn $ | 19.1 | 0 | 89 | 2 | Carberry | 3 | 1 | 6 | 0 |
| Riley | 31 | 4 | 90 | 3 | Riley | 4 | 0 | 28 | 1 |
| Ansari | 28.1 | 4 | 74 | 2 | Ansari | 1 | 0 | 8 | 0 |
| Mitchell | 8 | 1 | 23 | 0 | | | | | |
| Carberry | 2 | 2 | 0 | 1 | | | | | |

*$ Onions was unable to finish his fourth over, which waas completed by Dunn.*

Umpires: M J D Bodenham and P J Hartley          Scorers: J T Potter and A B Jones

# RASHID IS THE HIGH FLYER
# IN EMIRATES AIRLINE WIN

### By Danny Reuben

More silverware found its way to Headingley when Yorkshire Vikings won the Emirates Airline *T20* competition in Dubai, hammering defending champions Sussex by 74 runs. Vikings secured their place in the final after defeating Lancashire Lightning in the semi-final by 21 runs.

Andrew Hodd and Jack Leaning starred with the bat in the final as Yorkshire posted 176-4, having elected to bat first. It was biggest total of the day. The fifth-wicket pair shared an unbroken stand of 99 in swashbuckling style, helping Yorkshire to recover from some peril at 10-3 after two overs, Matt Hobden claiming all three in an over.

Both Hodd and Leaning played some excellent shots after the early loss of Adam Lyth, captain Alex Lees and Jonny Bairstow. Ex-Sussex wicket-keeper/batsman Hodd finished unbeaten on 79 and Leaning 51 not out. Jack Brooks then struck twice before the spin of Lyth and Adil Rashid proved key through the middle of the innings, as they picked up wickets in their first overs.

Sussex slipped to 58-5, and they never recovered. Rashid finished with stunning figures of 4-16 as his spin ripped through the heart of the Sharks, who were bowled out for 102. The Hove side had won this competition for three years, so this was a notable success for the Vikings.

**QUICK SILVER: Alex Lees lifts the Emirates Airline *T20* Trophy on Yorkshire's pre-season trip to Dubai.**
(Photo: Getty Images)

# STRONG BOOKENDS BUT SOME WEAK STUFF IN BETWEEN

### By Howard Clayton

The season resembled a pair of bookends. It began and ended strongly with victories against Glamorgan and Lancashire in three-day friendlies but, in between, once the Championship, Trophy and *T20* competitions had kicked in defeats followed thick and fast.

The Championship illustrated perfectly the inconsistencies in performances. Against Northamptonshire at York and Derbyshire at Scarborough things clicked and the games were won handsomely, but four defeats and two draws followed these early successes.

Ryan Gibson hit an unbeaten 137 at York in a stand of 223 with Mosun Hussain, who made 104, his maiden Second Eleven century. This enabled the home side to declare on 404-5, and thanks to Ben Coad's career-best second five-wicket haul of the

**BEN COAD: Thumping win**

game and match figures of 10-79 to complete a thumping win by an innings and 101 runs. The next game at Scarborough against Derbyshire was won by eight wickets as Alex Lees and Glenn Maxwell saw their side home, but those two matches were the highlight of an otherwise disappointing season in the premier format. Too often, the batting did not do its job and, especially when batting first, paltry totals meant that the side was on the backfoot for the rest of the game. Whenever a good stand had been built one wicket meant two, and something like 120-2 would become 128-4 with two new batsmen in but yet to score. And so momentum, so carefully constructed, was destroyed in an instant.

Gibson led the way with 416 Championship runs, and Coad with 17 wickets and Matt Fisher, with 15, led the bowlers.

The final game of the season, a friendly against Lancashire at Scarborough, was badly affected by the weather, but it saw the best two performances of the summer by Academy players in the Second Eleven. James Logan returned 8-76 with his slow left-arm as Lancashire chased 365 for victory, and Matthew Waite hit a magnificent 143 from 156 deliveries with 12 boundaries and seven maximums, two of which landed on the pavilion roof. That innings won for Matthew the Second Eleven Performance of the Year Trophy at the Gala Dinner in October.

Harry Brook from Burley-in-Wharfedale got into the side at the end of the season, and showed that he could form a valuable part of second-team planning for the foreseeable future. Jonathan Read made his debut behind the stumps and pouched 11 catches. He had played in the Under-17s side, as had seam bowler Matthew Taylor, who took four wickets on his debut against the MCC Universities at Weetwood. Yaaser Imtiaz from Huddersfield also appeared at the end of the season.

Two Second Eleven players, Mosun Hussain and Eliot Callis, travelled to Australia for the winter to further their cricket education, and the Club looks to them to produce runs more consistently in 2016.

In the Trophy competition some restructuring had taken place as fixtures were reduced from nine to six to accommodate an increased *T20* programme. The Trophy was the most disappointing part of the season with only one win, against Warwickshire, recorded in the six games as Yorkshire finished bottom in the Northern group. No centuries were made and only four players hit 50s — Maxwell, 77, Richard Pyrah, 69, Gibson, 52, and Waite, 50. Coad led the way with five wickets.

So to the *T20*, 12 games in 2015. The weather played its part at the start with one game against Lancashire and both Derbyshire fixtures washed out without a ball bowled. Only three wins were recorded and Yorkshire finished eighth. Dan Hodgson, 249, and Gibson, 230, led the batsmen and Carver's nine wickets, the best return by a bowler, included an analysis of 5-20 against Worcestershire, the best in Second Eleven *T20* for Yorkshire and the second best in the competition nationally.

It would seem that the Second Eleven white-ball competitions have succumbed to the national fervour for increased exposure to these formats. This is the way of modern cricket, but the longer game can still teach skills that can be transferred more easily to the white-ball game than vice-versa.

**\*Howard Clayton is the Yorkshire CCC Second Eleven Scorer**

# BLACK SHEEP WIN CROWNS
# ANOTHER GREAT SEASON

A very successful 2014 was followed by a 2015 season which started quite slowly with a number of losses. With the team losing four quality players in Will Rhodes, Josh Shaw, Ryan Gibson and Matt Fisher — who all moved on from the Academy — and Barney Gibson, who "retired", it was always going to be a good challenge for the younger players coming in.

After a couple of close games against Harrogate and Driffield, which were narrowly lost, our fortunes changed, and we started playing good, consistent cricket following our win against league leaders Rotherham. We had spoken a lot in team talks about showing courage and fight when we were behind, and this game sticks in my mind as when we began to take this on board. Rotherham managed to bowl us out for 202, and then progressed swiftly to 111-2, but with a fine spell of bowling from James Logan, who took 4-32 in 13 overs, and Jared Warner with 3-29 from 10 we managed to turn the game and bowl them out for 153.

The season as a whole was still very successful, the team winning two trophies and finishing third in the Yorkshire League behind strong York and Barnsley sides. To win the league cup in successive years was a massive highlight of the season. The team loved playing in coloured kit with a pink ball, and that showed in our performances as we beat Appleby Frodingham and Barnsley on the way to the final against York.

In the final York got off to a flyer, making their way to 38-0 off six overs, but with our fighting spirit we pegged them back to 69-5, and ended up bowling them out for 160. But with runs on the board in a final and a good bowling attack the game was still in the balance. An opening stand of 83 between Mosun Hussain and Eliot Callis helped to calm the nerves, and we went on to win by eight wickets with Callis 50 not out.

The most impressive cricket we played came in the Black Sheep competition, which involves the champions of each league in Yorkshire from the previous year competing against one another. Our first game was a trip to Hoylandswaine — the Huddersfield League champions — and this turned out to be the most unbelievable match I think I have been involved in. Hoylandswaine came hard at us with both the ball and verbally, but Ryan Gibson and Callis went back twice as hard with an immediate run rate of nine an over as we raced to 131 from 15 overs!

Gibson and Hussain went on to make incredible centuries, and Jordan

Thompson finished on 98 not out off about 40 balls, claiming 11 sixes out of 27 that we hit as a team! We finished our 50 overs with a ground record-breaking 463-6, and then bowled Hoylandswaine out for 300 to round off an extremely enjoyable win in front of a hostile crowd!

We moved on to the semi-final against a very strong Treeton side, this time without Ryan Gibson and Matthew Fisher. We fell to 26-3 in the first nine overs, and the game was not looking too promising until another amazing innings from Thompson, who scored 94 well assisted by Jared Warner and Karl Carver, got us up to 249-9. Warner then came out and bowled a great spell to remove both of their dangerous openers. The Academy went on to win by 42 runs and headed to the final at Elsecar against my home club, Methley.

The final went down to the last over to decide the champions of Yorkshire League cricket. Thankfully, man-of-the match Mosun Hussain, who hit 82 not out, took a cheeky single to bring home the victory. It was an amazing way to end another fantastic Academy season.

*(Photos by Coach Richard Damms appear in our colour pages.)*

## YORKSHIRE ACADEMY BATTING IN LEAGUE AND CUP MATCHES

| Player | M. | I. | N.O. | Runs | H.S. | Avge | 100s | 50s | Run Rate | ct/st |
|--------|----|----|------|------|------|------|------|-----|----------|-------|
| R Gibson | 3 | 3 | 0 | 224 | 102 | 74.67 | 1 | 1 | 226.26 | 1 |
| E Callis | 29 | 30 | 5 | 988 | 164* | 39.52 | 1 | 9 | 64.66 | 15 |
| J Thompson | 29 | 21 | 5 | 616 | 98* | 38.50 | 0 | 5 | 97.93 | 17 |
| M Hussain | 27 | 26 | 5 | 771 | 127 | 36.71 | 1 | 4 | 70.67 | 6 |
| B Ainsley | 23 | 23 | 4 | 651 | 87 | 34.26 | 0 | 3 | 59.24 | 8 |
| J Logan | 26 | 11 | 7 | 130 | 33* | 32.50 | 0 | 0 | 62.80 | 5 |
| D Hussain | 3 | 3 | 0 | 90 | 53 | 30.00 | 0 | 1 | 45.69 | 0 |
| M Fisher | 7 | 6 | 2 | 114 | 31* | 28.50 | 0 | 0 | 82.01 | 1 |
| M Waite | 27 | 23 | 4 | 517 | 83 | 27.21 | 0 | 4 | 86.45 | 5 |
| J Warner | 23 | 12 | 2 | 248 | 73 | 24.80 | 0 | 1 | 79.49 | 11 |
| K Carver | 18 | 12 | 2 | 196 | 44* | 19.60 | 0 | 0 | 85.22 | 2 |
| J Read | 28 | 13 | 7 | 115 | 31* | 19.17 | 0 | 0 | 54.25 | 28/6 |
| Y Imtiaz | 23 | 16 | 3 | 240 | 57* | 18.46 | 0 | 1 | 58.25 | 4 |
| E Barnes | 6 | 2 | 0 | 36 | 29 | 18.00 | 0 | 0 | 75.00 | 1 |
| H Brook | 15 | 12 | 1 | 116 | 24 | 10.55 | 0 | 0 | 49.57 | 10 |
| N Firn | 18 | 11 | 2 | 58 | 17* | 6.44 | 0 | 0 | 53.21 | 7 |
| M Rafique | 11 | 4 | 3 | 5 | 2* | 5.00 | 0 | 0 | 35.71 | 1 |
| W Rhodes | 1 | 1 | 0 | 0 | 0 | 0.00 | 0 | 0 | 0.00 | 2 |
| B Birkhead | 1 | 0 | 0 | 0 | — | — | 0 | 0 | 0.00 | 0 |

## YORKSHIRE ACADEMY BOWLING IN LEAGUE AND CUP MATCHES

| Player | Overs | Mdns | Runs | Wkts | Avge | Best | 5wI | Econ. | Strike Rate |
|--------|-------|------|------|------|------|------|-----|-------|-------------|
| J Logan | 245 | 49 | 800 | 65 | 12.31 | 7-15 | 3 | 3.27 | 23.15 |
| R Gibson | 8.3 | 0 | 29 | 2 | 14.50 | 1-10 | 0 | 3.41 | 26.50 |
| E Barnes | 41 | 4 | 171 | 9 | 19.00 | 4-28 | 0 | 4.17 | 28.33 |
| Y Imtiaz | 76.5 | 7 | 279 | 14 | 19.93 | 5-71 | 1 | 3.63 | 34.29 |
| J Warner | 180.4 | 23 | 738 | 36 | 20.50 | 5-24 | 2 | 4.08 | 32.47 |
| M Waite | 184.3 | 15 | 797 | 34 | 23.44 | 4-23 | 0 | 4.32 | 34.38 |
| J Thompson | 93.4 | 12 | 379 | 16 | 23.69 | 4-28 | 0 | 4.05 | 36.38 |
| M Fisher | 58.3 | 11 | 247 | 9 | 27.44 | 4-15 | 0 | 4.22 | 41.00 |
| N Firn | 82 | 3 | 429 | 14 | 30.64 | 3-46 | 0 | 5.23 | 38.21 |
| M Rafique | 37.1 | 5 | 134 | 4 | 33.50 | 2-10 | 0 | 3.61 | 57.75 |
| K Carver | 167 | 18 | 660 | 19 | 34.74 | 5-36 | 1 | 3.95 | 53.11 |
| W Rhodes | 10 | 0 | 62 | 1 | 62.00 | 1-62 | 0 | 6.20 | 60.00 |
| B Ainsley | 6 | 0 | 32 | 0 | — | 0-6 | 0 | 5.33 | — |

**GALE'S GLORY:** Yorkshire captain Andrew Gale, proudly holds the LV=County Championship Trophy which his side retained last season, not least through his own efforts in scoring over 1,000 runs in the Competition. Now Andrew is hoping that under his command this summer Yorkshire will be able to make it a hat-trick of title wins for the first time since 1966-1968.

**CHAMPIONS 2015:** Back Row, left to right: Tony Pickersgill, Age Group Coach; Blaine Clancy, Strength and Conditioning Coach; Karl Carver, Dan Hodgson, Josh Shaw, Ben Coad, James Wainman, Moin Ashraf, Jonathan Tattersall, Chris Liversidge, Second Eleven Physiotherapist, and Anthony McGrath, Coaching Consultant. Middle row: Ian Dews, Director of Cricket Development and Second Eleven Coach; Ian Fisher, Head Strength and Conditioning Coach; Jack Brooks, Alex Lees, Jack Leaning, Andrew Hodd, Matthew Fisher, Will Rhodes, Kunwar Bansil, Club Physiotherapist, and Richard Damms, Academy Head Coach. Front row: Ian Dews, Director of Cricket Development and Second Eleven Coach; Tim Bresnan, Cheteshwar Pujara, Ryan Sidebottom, Adam Lyth, Richard Pyrah, Andrew Gale (captain), Joe Root, Gary Ballance, Adil Rashid, Jonathan Bairstow, Steven Patterson and Martyn Moxon, Director of Cricket.

**MY TURN NEXT:** Andy Hodd takes a celebratory draught from the LV=County Championship Trophy crowd before handing it over to fellow wicket-keeper/batsman, Jonathan Bairstow.

**JUST CHAMPION:** Yorkshire captain, Andrew Gale, holds aloft the LV=County Championship Trophy surrounded by his ecstatic teammates before the Headingley crowd.

## YORKSHIRE AT THE PALACE

**ROYAL RECOGNITION: Y**orkshire's trophy-winning men's and women's teams visited Buckingham Palace in mid-October to receive their silverware from Prince Philip, the Duke of Edinburgh. Yorkshire captain Andrew Gale is holding The Lord's Taverners ECB Trophy which his side retained for winning the LV=County Championship, while Yorkshire Women's captain, Lauren Winfield, has the Lady Taverners ECB Trophy which her team received for lifting the Royal London One-Day Cup.

**SPLENDID SECOND SPELL:** Former Yorkshire off-spinner James Middlebrook, who played for his native county from 1998 to 2001 before moving to Essex, returned last season as replacement cover for Adil Rashid. He slipped effortlessly into the role, and claimed 17 wickets in six Championship appearances, kicking off with eight in his first match against Warwickshire at Headingley. His contribution in helping Yorkshire to retain the Championship title was warmly applauded by Director of Cricket Martyn Moxon.

**MAIDEN TEST TON:** Adam Lyth celebrates completing his maiden Test century on his home ground at Headingley during the Test match against New Zealand which England went on to lose by an innings and 199 runs. Adam hit 107 off 212 balls with 15 boundaries before being run out. He and his captain, Alastair Cook, had piled up 177 together for the first wicket.

# YORKSHIRE'S 2015 ENGLAND HEROES

**ACTION MEN:** Yorkshire all-rounder Liam Plunkett is fully focussed as he prepares to send down a delivery in the Fourth Royal London One-Day international against Australia at Headingley. Plunkett grabbed a couple of wickets and scored 17 runs as England won by three wickets.

*******

**HARD IN:** A difficult return for Yorkshire wicket-keeper J o n a t h a n Bairstow, who chipped in with 31 runs and a catch in the Headingley O n e - D a y International.

**ON PARADE:** Yorkshire fans got an early view of new signing David Willey in the fourth Royal London One-Day international between England and Australia at Headingley, the former Northamptonshire all-rounder bagging 3-51 and scoring 12 in England's three-wicket victory.

# UNBEATEN 13s RACK UP
# A FESTIVAL HAT-TRICK

## By Chris Hassell

It was another eventful season with plenty to celebrate. The 15s battled their way through to the ECB finals at Kibworth to finish third. The 14s won their Taunton Festival unbeaten. The 13s enjoyed a brilliant season undefeated, and won their Taunton Festival for the third year as well as the England Schools Cricket Association Northern Counties Championship. The 11s won their Taunton Festival for the fourth time, and lost only two matches by close margins.

15 A – P15 W8 L5 D2. This was an enjoyable and indeed successful year with 23 boys featuring through the season – a marvellous advertisement for cricket development. A sound performance in the opening cup match against Durham was followed by two salutary lessons with defeats by Lancashire and Cheshire. That wake-up call produced excellent victories over Nottingham twice, Cheshire and Durham. The final group match against Lancashire confirmed their superiority, and in the Royal London ECB Cup final they overcame Surrey.

As Northern runners up Yorkshire were drawn against West winners Wales in the quarter-final, and won with a convincing performance at Pontypool to reach the Kibworth finals and a semi-final against Surrey: a score of 222-6 in difficult conditions was not quite enough as the match swung one way and the other with victory snatched from us by a *Duckworth/Lewis* calculation. We took third place in the play-off with a clear victory over Essex. Our two-day matches against Wales and Durham were both drawn. Team manager: Andy Rowsell; coaches: James Wiggan, Andrew Chadwick and Bob Wincer.

15 B – P19 W13 L3 Ab3. The team enjoyed a splendid year with 23 boys given the opportunity of developing their skills. By the end of the season the squad had gelled into a fine side. Most interestingly, some of the newcomers were playing only at district level in the early part of the season. The three matches lost to Lancashire, Warwickshire and Cumbria were close affairs with our boys in winning positions each time. Several batsmen excelled, left-handers Lewis Pike (Oakwood HS) and Rory France (Shelley Coll) forcing their way into the A side, which reached the ECB finals day at Kibworth. Wahab Mirza (Samuel Lister) quickly established himself as an opening bowler to be reckoned with, and was soon promoted to the A side where he stayed. Billy Whitford (Bingley GS) showed himself a valuable all rounder and leading wick-

33

et-taker with 20 along with valuable runs. Ben Shufflebotham (Shelley Coll) bowled his left-arm spin with great enthusiasm, and took the bowling award. The side was beautifully led by Adarsh Vani (QEGS) who showed excellent potential. Team manager: Bob Wincer; coaches Peter Hepworth and Graham Orange.

14 A – P23 W14 L5 Ab2 C2. A successful season in certain respects, but with five defeats some questions need to be answered. There were numerous injuries and unavailability, resulting in 24 players being used. Bowling generally was our strength, although extras contributed to our downfall in some matches. The pace attack was good with Dominic Leech (Nunthorpe Academy) George Hill (Sedbergh) Vikram Sharma (Grammar School at Leeds) and Dan Ward (Ryedale) accumulating 62 wickets. The spin department of Harry Sullivan (Temple Moor) Harry Harding (Stokesley) and Craig Robinson (Harrogate GS) did a fine job in taking a further 62 wickets. The batting was held together by James Wharton (Holmfirth HS) 761 runs, Elliot Audsley (Grammar School at Leeds) 416, George Hill 379 and Louis Horsfield (Ermysted's GS) 377. Many boys got good starts but failed to go on to bigger totals. The highnote was retention of the winners' shield at the Taunton Festival with four victories – fifth-day abandoned through rain. Captain James Wharton showed good understanding and knowledge of the game. Team manager/coach Tony Pickersgill; coaches Jack Bethel and Jim Love.

14 B – P19 W11 L7 Ab1. The season started with a series of matches against other squads (15b, 14a, 13a) which proved extremely valuable in assessing capabilities. The first county match against Lancashire was won in convincing style with fine performances all round. The team continued to play good cricket with excellent returns. Our two matches against Lincolnshire A, who move up to the ECB 15 A group next year, were lost but by narrow margins. The Scarborough Festival was a highlight, our boys reaching the final against North Yorkshire on the main square at North Marine Road, which will have been a great experience for all 22 Yorkshire boys. The outstanding performers were Sam Winter (Richmond School) leading run-scorer, Harrison Wood (Lady Lumleys) with 20 wickets for the bowling award, and Oliver Riley (Tadcaster GS) performance award. Captain Will Hutchinson (Lady Lumley's) led the side well. Team manager/coach James Wiggan; coach Bren Terry.

13 A – P18 W18. An outstand season saw a talented and resourceful side sweep aside all others, winning both the Taunton Festival and the Northern Counties Championship. To go through a season with 18 games undefeated is a record. Harry Anderson (Brigshaw HS) Matthew Revis (Ilkley GS) and Finlay Bean (Ripon GS) each scored over 500 runs, another record. Three bowlers took over 20 wickets, a similar record. Three bowlers took over 20 wickets, a similar record. Lewis O'Donnell (Ripon GS) took 25 as did Harry Sullivan (Temple Moor HS) who set a new high for an under 12-playing up. Chris Wood (St Peter's, York) took 32, a total only two others have ever surpassed. Harry Anderson held 16 outfield catches, seven more than anyone previously.

# RYDER STILL HAS KEY ROLE
# TO PLAY AT HEADINGLEY

### By David Warner

A driving force at Headingley since 1975 in the running of Yorkshire County Cricket Club, David Ryder retired from full-time employment at the end of last season, but he will remain actively connected on a part-time basis until well into 2019.

David, 65 on April 3 this year, joined the Club as assistant secretary to Joe Lister. He was a member of a staff of four which grew into double figures in 1991, when Chris Hassell arrived as YCCC's first Chief Executive following the unexpected death of Mr Lister.

From that point on, David adapted extremely well to the different job titles he was given, but his duties remained chiefly financial until 2008, when he moved to Operations and was responsible for managing a stadium which was undergoing rapid redevelopment to retain its Test status, and also to enhance facilities for Yorkshire members and supporters.

So valued was David's work that Chief Executive Mark Arthur last summer persuaded him to stay on in a part-time role through to the completion of the new cricket/rugby stand and the *Ashes* Test and World Cup matches to be staged at Headingley in 2019.

David's arrival at Headingley in 1975 coincided with the start of my own role as Yorkshire Cricket Correspondent for the *Bradford Telegraph & Argus*, and I have been able to observe over the years what a reliable and steady hand he has had on the tiller. Even when ploughing through stormy waters he would remain outwardly calm and in control— qualities which have served him well, and will continue to do so.

Outside Headingley's walls David has long enjoyed his own cricket career as a wicket-keeper/batsman, and he remains on active service. He began a long association with Colton Cricket Club in 1966, when he turned out for the Under-17s before progressing through the Second XI and becoming a regular first-team player in 1972. Over the next 20 years he captained the side in two spells for a total of seven years.

He helped his team to reach four Hepworth Cup finals, lifting the trophy once, and on three occasions his side were league champions. David represented the Leeds League v. the Bradford League in the White Rose Trophy final at Headingley in 1975. He later had spells as captain of

Colton's Third XI and the Second XI, where he led them for his last five years at the club before moving to Thorp Arch and Boston Spa in 2013.

Cricket is only one of several sports which David has participated in. He was a Rugby Union fullback with Roundhegians in Leeds from 1970 to 1985, making a few first-team appearances before moving to Leeds YMCA for three seasons, and he played soccer for Manston Park Avenue in the Leeds Sunday Combination League premier division for 10 years up to the club folding in 1983. Now, as well as his cricket, he is a member of Leeds Golf Club, and he bowls twice a week for Colton.

Born in Bramley, David also has a passion for Rugby League, his father taking him to his first game at the Old Barley Mow ground when he was only three. The family moved to Crossgates two years later, and he has lived in Leeds 15 ever since.

Educated at Manston Church of England Junior School and then Temple Moor Grammar School, he followed the same education path as his friend Geoff Cope, the former Yorkshire and England off-spinner, who still has a strong working connection with the *White Rose* club.

Although David will remain very much focussed on the redevelopment of Headingley Cricket Stadium until at least 2019, he will still find sufficient time to carry on his much-valued work as honorary treasurer of the Yorkshire CCC Players' Association. He may also manage to spend a little more time with his supportive wife, Andrea.

---

# Home attendances grow

Home crowd figures in Yorkshire showed a sharp rise in 2015, both for domestic and international matches. The Investec Test in May, when England played New Zealand, attracted a total of 44,522 spectators, an increase of 8,223 over the previous year's game against Sri Lanka. There was a full house of 16,500 in September for the one-day international between England and Australia – as there had been in 2014 for England v. India.

Domestic-cricket attendances across all three formats showed a year-on-year increase of 38,064 — a 39 per cent rise on 2014. The biggest growth area was in the LV=County Championship, where 59,000 supporters enjoyed watching Yorkshire retain the title — up 19,099 on the previous year.

With the advent of floodlights and later start times for the *NatWest T20 Blast* competition the aggregate tournament total reached an all-time high of 55,655 — up 19 per cent on 2014.

# PYRAH RETIRES BUT IS STILL VERY MUCH AT HOME

### By David Warner

**RICHARD PYRAH: Devoted servant who gave his all**

Yorkshire's regular followers were sad to hear in late September that Richard Pyrah had retired as a player.

At the same time they were delighted with the news that he was joining the Club's coaching staff and that he would be working across all teams from age-group cricket to the senior side.

Richard, last year's beneficiary, has been a popular figure ever since making his First Class debut in 2004, and his 100 per cent loyalty to Yorkshire has never been in doubt.

Had he moved to another county, he would unquestionably have enjoyed more regular first-team cricket and have picked up more runs and taken more wickets. But he was happy with his lot, uncomplaining when left out of the action and giving his all when duty called.

Richard may have played less than he would have liked, but he still made his mark in more ways than one. He was up there with the best as a fielder, particularly around point, and his groundwork and catching were outstanding and true testimony to his athleticism. He was also one of county cricket's most successful *Twenty20* bowlers, becoming the first English-born player to capture 100 wickets in the domestic form of the game, and he ended up with 108 at a cost of 21.43 runs apiece.

His 5-16 against Derbyshire at Scarborough in 2011 remains Yorkshire's best analysis in the competition, and Richard features in

**BIRD ON THE WING: Richard in full flight to catch Worcestershire's Vikram Solanki off Tim Bresnan in the Friends Provident League at Headingley in 2007.**

three of the county's top seven returns, enjoying figures of 4-20 against Durham at Headingley in 2008 and 4-21 against Worcestershire on the same ground two years later.

Richard also turned in some excellent List A bowling performances, which brought him a very respectable 140 wickets in 118 matches at an average of 26.21 including five four-wicket hauls.

A genuine all-rounder, Richard was an attractive strokeplayer who would have made more than his tally of 1,621 runs from 51 matches had he been given greater opportunities higher up the order. He hit three centuries, two of them against Loughborough MCCU, but it was his 117 in the *Roses* match at Headingley in 2011 that provided him with the highlight of his career and will never be forgotten by those who saw it.

Replying to Lancashire's 328, Yorkshire were 44-7 when Pyrah came in and 44-8 with the departure of Anthony McGrath, but Richard then lashed the ball to all parts during a record ninth-wicket partnership for Headingley of 154 with Ryan Sidebottom, who fell for 52 with Pyrah on 97. Iain Wardlaw would have been last in if Tim Bresnan had not driven from the England camp at Lord's in time to make it to the crease, and he helped to add another 40 before Pyrah was dismissed, having hit 12 fours and three sixes. It was one of Yorkshire's greatest innings with the chips down, and in the end Lancashire squeezed home by only 23 runs.

Now Richard is part of the strong coaching team which is building Yorkshire's future. The experience and advice he passes on to the younger players should prove invaluable.

## Moin Ashraf

Just as the fans held Pyrah in their affections, the same can be said of Moin Ashraf, who always gave of his best and showed great promise when he burst on the Championship scene in the last two games of 2010.

On debut against Champions-elect Nottinghamshire at Trent Bridge he began by bowling Australian Adam Voges with an out-swinger, and then had Samit Patel caught behind without scoring to return first-innings figures of 6-4-11-2.

**MOIN ASHRAF: Nearly made Yorkshire 2010 Champions**

Second time round he sent back opener Alex Hales, Yorkshire going on to win by five wickets. In a dramatic finale to the season Yorkshire could have been crowned Champions if they had not collapsed inexplicably to Kent, but Ashraf again caught the eye with a first-innings 5-32, his side's best of the season. In the two games he took 9-106 at 11.77.

In 2012 Moin played a leading role in seeing Yorkshire to the *t20* Finals Day for their first and only time, losing by 10 runs to Hampshire in the final. He, Australian Mitchell Starc and Pyrah were the chief wicket-takers, Starc collecting 21 victims and the other two 15 apiece.

Injuries and losses of form blocked Moin's way to the regular first-team place everyone expected would be his one day, but he is still young enough to make an impact elsewhere, and he left with everyone's best wishes for the future.

## Dan Hodgson

A capable wicket-keeper and clean-hitting batsman who drove attractively, Dan Hodgson made his First Class debut for Yorkshire in 2014 against Leeds-Bradford MCCU, for whom he had formerly played, scoring 64 on debut against Surrey at The Oval two years earlier. With Jonny Bairstow back in the England fold and Andrew Hodd likely to be standing in regularly for him this summer, it was perhaps surprising that

Yorkshire should announce Dan's departure in September.

Dan featured regularly in List A and *t20* matches in 2013, often with considerable success and rarely letting the side down.

In five Yorkshire Bank 40 innings he made 190 runs at an average of 39.40, hitting his top score of 90 in the last match against Glamorgan, when he added 100 for the third wicket with Kane Williamson and 55 for the fourth with Adam Lyth.

He played in all 10 Friends Life *t20* North Group matches, only Gary Ballance topping his 177 runs, including an unbeaten 52 against Leicestershire at

**DAN HODGSON: Job done**

Headingley, or finishing with a better average than his 19.66.

Dan was prominent in Yorkshire's 2012 Champions League appearance in South Africa, where he kept wicket in the absence of Bairstow and Hodd. Although he was out of the first team last summer, he was a mainstay of the Second Eleven and captained them a number of times.

Yorkshire also released former England Under-19s batsman Jonny Tattersall, now 21, and wicket-keeper/batsman Barney Gibson, who was 20 on March 31.

Jonny made one List A appearance for Yorkshire in 2013 when he opened the innings against Glamorgan at Headingley, but he was bowled by Michael Hogan's second legitimate delivery after he had started up with three wides. A splendid fielder, Jonny was called upon by England for 12th man duties in Headingley internationals. In 2014 he represented England Under 19s at the ICC World Cup in the UAE, and helped them to reach the semi-finals.

Barney, below, had one moment of fame, hitting the sporting headlines in the summer of 2011 when he was selected by Yorkshire against

Durham MCCU, and so becoming at 15 years and 27 days the youngest E n g l i s h - b o r n cricketer to play a First Class match.

# RICHARD MICHAEL PYRAH

## FIRST CLASS CRICKET FOR YORKSHIRE 2004 TO 2015

Right-hand batsman.     Right-arm medium-pace bowler
Born: Dewsbury            November 1, 1982
Debut for Yorkshire:   v. Glamorgan at Colwyn Bay     August 24, 2004
Last played:           v. Nottinghamshire at Nottingham   April 19, 2015

### BATTING AND FIELDING

| Season | M | I | NO | Runs | HS | Avge | 100s | 50s | Ct |
|---|---|---|---|---|---|---|---|---|---|
| 2004 | 4 | 7 | 1 | 158 | 39 | 26.33 | 0 | 0 | 0 |
| 2005 | 2 | 3 | 0 | 78 | 78 | 26.00 | 0 | 1 | 1 |
| 2007 | 1 | 1 | 0 | 106 | 106 | 106.00 | 1 | 0 | 0 |
| 2008 | 5 | 6 | 0 | 96 | 51 | 16.00 | 0 | 1 | 5 |
| 2009 | 3 | 4 | 1 | 59 | 50* | 19.66 | 0 | 1 | 3 |
| 2010 | 7 | 7 | 2 | 304 | 134* | 60.80 | 1 | 1 | 4 |
| 2011 | 11 | 16 | 1 | 376 | 117 | 25.06 | 1 | 1 | 2 |
| 2012 | 4 | 4 | 0 | 9 | 9 | 2.25 | 0 | 0 | 0 |
| 2013 | 5 | 3 | 1 | 70 | 55 | 35.00 | 0 | 1 | 5 |
| 2014 | 6 | 6 | 2 | 161 | 62 | 40.25 | 0 | 1 | 2 |
| 2015 | 3 | 4 | 0 | 204 | 84 | 51.00 | 0 | 1 | 0 |
| | 51 | 61 | 8 | 1621 | 134* | 30.58 | 3 | 8 | 22 |

### BOWLING

| Seasons | Overs | Mdns | Runs | Wkts | Avge | Best | 5wI |
|---|---|---|---|---|---|---|---|
| 2004 | 6 | 4 | 2 | 0 | — | — | 0 |
| 2005 | 10 | 2 | 34 | 3 | 11.33 | 1-4 | 0 |
| 2007 | 12 | 2 | 41 | 1 | 41.00 | 1-3 | 0 |
| 2008 | 56 | 11 | 201 | 1 | 201.00 | 1-14 | 0 |
| 2009 | 60 | 7 | 213 | 4 | 53.25 | 2-53 | 0 |
| 2010 | 84.4 | 16 | 326 | 7 | 46.57 | 2-8 | 0 |
| 2011 | 266.4 | 54 | 956 | 29 | 32.96 | 5-58 | 1 |
| 2012 | 38 | 9 | 128 | 2 | 64.00 | 1-9 | 0 |
| 2013 | 77 | 19 | 244 | 2 | 122.00 | 1-45 | 0 |
| 2014 | 99 | 26 | 309 | 6 | 51.50 | 3-37 | 0 |
| 2015 | 21 | 3 | 73 | 0 | — | — | 0 |
| | 730.2 | 153 | 2527 | 55 | 45.94 | 5-58 | 1 |

### Centuries (3)

| 2007 | 106 | v. Loughborough UCCE | at Leeds |
|---|---|---|---|
| 2010 | 134* | v. Loughborough MCCU | at Leeds |
| 2011 | 117 | v. Lancashire | at Leeds |

### 5 wickets in an innings (1)

| 2011 | 5-58 | v. Nottinghamshire | at Leeds |
|---|---|---|---|

## LIST A CRICKET FOR YORKSHIRE 2004 TO 2015

Yorkshire Cricket Board debut: v. Northamptonshire CB at Northampton   May 15, 2001
Yorkshire debut:   totesport league     v. Leicestershire at Leicester     August 18, 2004
Last played: Royal London One-Day Cup v.Gloucestershire at Leeds September 6, 2015

## BATTING AND FIELDING

| Season | M | I | NO | Runs | HS | Avge | 100s | 50s | Ct |
|--------|---|---|----|------|----|------|------|-----|-----|
| 2004 | 2 | 2 | 0 | 44 | 42 | 22.00 | 0 | 0 | 0 |
| 2005 | 10 | 10 | 2 | 90 | 28* | 11.25 | 0 | 0 | 3 |
| 2006 | 3 | 3 | 0 | 88 | 32 | 29.33 | 0 | 0 | 2 |
| 2007 | 17 | 10 | 2 | 98 | 24 | 12.25 | 0 | 0 | 5 |
| 2008 | 18 | 9 | 4 | 83 | 26* | 16.60 | 0 | 0 | 10 |
| 2009 | 15 | 12 | 5 | 233 | 67 | 33.28 | 0 | 1 | 3 |
| 2010 | 13 | 3 | 0 | 33 | 29 | 11.00 | 0 | 0 | 3 |
| 2011 | 7 | 6 | 2 | 93 | 69 | 23.25 | 0 | 1 | 2 |
| 2012 | 4 | 3 | 0 | 62 | 44 | 20.66 | 0 | 0 | 3 |
| 2013 | 12 | 10 | 2 | 90 | 34 | 11.25 | 0 | 0 | 2 |
| 2014 | 9 | 4 | 3 | 57 | 29* | 57.00 | 0 | 0 | 1 |
| 2015 | 4 | 3 | 0 | 7 | 5 | 2.33 | 0 | 0 | 1 |
| | 114 | 75 | 20 | 978 | 69 | 17.78 | 0 | 2 | 35 |

## BOWLING

| Seasons | Overs | Mdns | Runs | Wkts | Avge | Best | 5wI |
|---------|-------|------|------|------|------|------|-----|
| 2004 | 5 | 0 | 17 | 2 | 8.50 | 2-17 | 0 |
| 2005 | 12 | 0 | 107 | 1 | 107.00 | 1-41 | 0 |
| 2006 | 14 | 0 | 97 | 2 | 48.50 | 2-51 | 0 |
| 2007 | 107.2 | 5 | 533 | 22 | 24.22 | 3-22 | 0 |
| 2008 | 105.2 | 4 | 585 | 24 | 24.37 | 4-35 | 1 |
| 2009 | 90 | 3 | 538 | 22 | 24.45 | 4-54 | 1 |
| 2010 | 81 | 1 | 484 | 20 | 24.20 | 4-24 | 2 |
| 2011 | 34 | 1 | 213 | 7 | 30.42 | 3-41 | 0 |
| 2012 | 17 | 0 | 106 | 3 | 35.33 | 2-55 | 0 |
| 2013 | 82 | 3 | 481 | 15 | 32.06 | 4-43 | 1 |
| 2014 | 66.4 | 3 | 333 | 15 | 22.20 | 4-51 | 1 |
| 2015 | 18 | 1 | 78 | 0 | — | — | 0 |
| | 632.2 | 21 | 3572 | 133 | 26.85 | 4-24 | 6 |

### 4 wickets in an innings (6)

| | | | |
|--|--|--|--|
| 2008 | 4-35 | v. Kent | at Scarborough |
| 2009 | 4-54 | v. Gloucestershire | at Leeds |
| 2010 | 4-24 | v. Netherlands | at Rotterdam |
| 2010 | 4-43 | v. Gloucestershire | at Leeds |
| 2013 | 4-43 | v. Glamorgan | at Colwyn Bay |
| 2014 | 4-51 | v. Durham | at Leeds |

## ALL LIST A MATCHES
### BATTING, FIELDING AND BOWLING

| M | I | NO | Runs | HS | Avge | 100s | 50s | Ct | Overs | M | Runs | Wkts | Avge | Best | 4wI |
|---|---|----|------|----|------|------|-----|-----|-------|---|------|------|------|------|-----|
| 118 | 79 | 20 | 1084 | 69 | 18.37 | 0 | 2 | 37 | 649.2 | 22 | 3670 | 140 | 26.21 | 5-50 | 7 |

## TWENTY20 CRICKET FOR YORKSHIRE 2005 TO 2015

| Debut for Yorkshire: | v. Lancashire at Leeds | June 22, 2005 |
|----------------------|------------------------|---------------|
| Last played: | v. Warwickshire at Leeds | July 25, 2015 |

## BATTING AND FIELDING

| Season | M | I | NO | Runs | HS | Avge | 100s | 50s | Ct |
|--------|---|---|----|------|----|------|------|-----|-----|
| 2005 | 8 | 7 | 3 | 100 | 33* | 25.00 | 0 | 0 | 3 |
| 2007 | 8 | 4 | 0 | 10 | 6 | 2.50 | 0 | 0 | 2 |
| 2008 | 9 | 5 | 2 | 16 | 8 | 5.33 | 0 | 0 | 6 |
| 2009 | 6 | 5 | 1 | 35 | 26* | 8.75 | 0 | 0 | 0 |
| 2010 | 16 | 10 | 3 | 89 | 22* | 12.71 | 0 | 0 | 8 |
| 2011 | 15 | 10 | 3 | 62 | 17* | 8.85 | 0 | 0 | 5 |
| 2012 | 12 | 9 | 3 | 94 | 35 | 15.66 | 0 | 0 | 2 |
| 2013 | 10 | 9 | 2 | 104 | 42 | 14.85 | 0 | 0 | 5 |
| 2014 | 11 | 6 | 3 | 48 | 16* | 16.00 | 0 | 0 | 4 |
| 2015 | 10 | 6 | 1 | 35 | 13* | 7.00 | 0 | 0 | 5 |
| | 105 | 71 | 21 | 593 | 42 | 11.86 | 0 | 0 | 40 |

## BOWLING

| Seasons | Overs | Mdns | Runs | Wkts | Avge | Best | 4wI |
|---------|-------|------|------|------|------|------|-----|
| 2005 | 3 | 0 | 26 | 0 | — | — | 0 |
| 2007 | 9 | 0 | 65 | 6 | 10.83 | 2-8 | 0 |
| 2008 | 30 | 0 | 209 | 14 | 14.92 | 4-20 | 1 |
| 2009 | 16 | 0 | 136 | 2 | 68.00 | 1-28 | 0 |
| 2010 | 58 | 0 | 408 | 21 | 19.42 | 3-12 | 0 |
| 2011 | 53 | 0 | 417 | 21 | 19.85 | 5-16 | 2 |
| 2012 | 45 | 0 | 359 | 15 | 23.93 | 3-21 | 0 |
| 2013 | 32 | 1 | 192 | 9 | 21.33 | 3-15 | 0 |
| 2014 | 36 | 0 | 274 | 13 | 21.07 | 3-19 | 0 |
| 2015 | 31 | 0 | 229 | 7 | 32.71 | 2-13 | 0 |
| | 313 | 1 | 2315 | 108 | 21.43 | 5-16 | 3 |

### 4 wickets in an innings (3)

| | | | |
|------|-------|---------------------|------------------|
| 2008 | 4-20 | v. Durham | at Leeds |
| 2011 | 4-21 | v. Worcestershire | at Leeds |
| 2011 | 5-16 | v. Durham | at Scarborough |

# MOIN AQEEB ASHRAF

## FIRST CLASS CRICKET FOR YORKSHIRE 2010 TO 2013

Right-hand batsman.  Right-arm fast-medium-pace bowler
Born: Bradford  January 5, 1992
Debut for Yorkshire:  v. Loughborough MCCU at Leeds  May 10, 2010
Last played:  v. Nottinghamshire at Scarborough  June 5, 2013

### BATTING AND FIELDING

| Season | M | I | NO | Runs | HS | Avge | 100s | 50s | Ct |
|--------|---|---|----|------|----|------|------|-----|-----|
| 2010 | 4 | 4 | 0 | 15 | 10 | 3.75 | 0 | 0 | 1 |
| 2011 | 7 | 9 | 1 | 27 | 8* | 3.37 | 0 | 0 | 0 |
| 2012 | 8 | 6 | 4 | 14 | 6* | 7.00 | 0 | 0 | 1 |
| 2013 | 2 | 0 | 0 | 0 | — | — | 0 | 0 | 0 |
| | 21 | 19 | 5 | 56 | 10 | 4.00 | 0 | 0 | 2 |

## BOWLING

| Seasons | Overs | Mdns | Runs | Wkts | Avge | Best | 5wI |
|---|---|---|---|---|---|---|---|
| 2010 | 75 | 20 | 212 | 11 | 19.27 | 5-32 | 1 |
| 2011 | 158 | 28 | 561 | 11 | 51.00 | 3-71 | 0 |
| 2012 | 117.5 | 27 | 376 | 17 | 22.11 | 4-36 | 0 |
| 2013 | 38.3 | 13 | 119 | 4 | 29.75 | 3-60 | 0 |
| | 389.2 | 88 | 1268 | 43 | 29.48 | 5-32 | 1 |

### 5 wickets in an innings (1)

2010　5-32　v. Kent　　　　　　　at Leeds

## LIST A CRICKET FOR YORKSHIRE 2011 TO 2013

List A debut:　For England Players Dev XI　v. Sri Lanka at Manchester August 8, 2011
Yorkshire debut:　Clydesdale Bank 40　v. Derbyshire at Chesterfield　August 14, 2011
Last played:　　Yorkshire Bank 40　v. Glamorgan at Leeds　　August 26, 2013

### BATTING AND FIELDING

| Season | M | I | NO | Runs | HS | Avge | 100s | 50s | Ct |
|---|---|---|---|---|---|---|---|---|---|
| 2011 | 3 | 0 | 0 | 0 | — | — | 0 | 0 | 1 |
| 2012 | 10 | 3 | 3 | 3 | 3* | — | 0 | 0 | 1 |
| 2013 | 9 | 3 | 1 | 0 | 0* | 0.00 | 0 | 0 | 2 |
| | 22 | 6 | 4 | 3 | 3* | 1.50 | 0 | 0 | 4 |

### BOWLING

| Seasons | Overs | Mdns | Runs | Wkts | Avge | Best | 4wI |
|---|---|---|---|---|---|---|---|
| 2011 | 17.5 | 0 | 129 | 2 | 64.50 | 1-29 | 0 |
| 2012 | 69 | 2 | 362 | 11 | 32.90 | 2-36 | 0 |
| 2013 | 62.1 | 1 | 404 | 10 | 40.40 | 3-38 | 0 |
| | 149 | 3 | 895 | 23 | 38.91 | 3-38 | 0 |

## ALL LIST A MATCHES
### BATTING AND FIELDING

| Matches | Innings | Not Out | Runs | Highest Score | Avge | 100s | 50s | Ct |
|---|---|---|---|---|---|---|---|---|
| 23 | 6 | 4 | 3 | 3* | 1.50 | 0 | 2 | 4 |

### BOWLING

| Overs | Maidens | Runs | Wickets | Average | Best | 4wI |
|---|---|---|---|---|---|---|
| 155 | 3 | 920 | 25 | 36.80 | 3-38 | 0 |

## TWENTY20 CRICKET FOR YORKSHIRE 2012 TO 2013

Debut for Yorkshire:　v. Durham　　at Leeds　　June 15, 2012
Last played:　　　v. Leicestershire　at Leicester　July 28, 2013

### BATTING AND FIELDING

| Seasons | M | I | NO | Runs | HS | Avge | 100s | 50s | Ct |
|---|---|---|---|---|---|---|---|---|---|
| 2012 | 12 | 0 | 0 | 0 | — | — | 0 | 0 | 1 |
| 2012/3 | 4 | 0 | 0 | 0 | — | — | 0 | 0 | 0 |
| 2013 | 1 | 1 | 0 | 4 | 4 | 4.00 | 0 | 0 | 0 |
| | 17 | 1 | 0 | 4 | 4 | 4.00 | 0 | 0 | 1 |

## BOWLING

| Seasons | Overs | Mdns | Runs | Wkts | Avge | Best | 4wI |
|---------|-------|------|------|------|------|------|-----|
| 2012 | 47 | 0 | 359 | 15 | 23.93 | 4-18 | 1 |
| 2012/3 | 8.3 | 0 | 75 | 2 | 37.50 | 2-29 | 0 |
| 2013 | 2 | 0 | 28 | 0 | — | — | 0 |
| | 57.3 | 0 | 462 | 17 | 27.17 | 4-18 | 1 |

**4 wickets in an innings (1)**

2012   4-18  v. Derbyshire        at Derby

# DANIEL (Dan) MARK HODGSON

## FIRST CLASS CRICKET FOR YORKSHIRE 2014 TO 2015

|  |  |  |
|--|--|--|
| Right-hand batsman. | Wicket-keeper | |
| Born: Northallerton | February 26, 1990 | |

| | | |
|--|--|--|
| First Class Debut: | For Leeds/Bradford MCCU  v. Surrey  at The Oval  March 31, 2012 | |
| Yorkshire Debut: | v. Leeds/Bradford MCCU | at Leeds | April 27, 2014 |
| Last played: | v. Leeds/Bradford MCCU | at Leeds | April 7, 2015 |

### YORKSHIRE BATTING AND FIELDING

| Season | M | I | NO | Runs | HS | Avge | 100s | 50s | Ct |
|--------|---|---|----|------|-----|------|------|-----|-----|
| 2014 | 1 | 1 | 0 | 18 | 18 | 18.00 | 0 | 0 | 1 |
| 2015 | 1 | 2 | 0 | 54 | 35 | 27.00 | 0 | 0 | 1 |
| | 2 | 3 | 0 | 72 | 35 | 24.00 | 0 | 0 | 2 |

### ALL FIRST CLASS MATCHES

| Matches | Innings | NO | Runs | HS | Avge | 100s | 50s | Ct/St |
|---------|---------|----|------|-----|------|------|-----|-------|
| 13 | 24 | 2 | 504 | 94* | 22.90 | 0 | 4 | 35/1 |

### LIST A CRICKET FOR YORKSHIRE 2012 TO 2014

| | | |
|--|--|--|
| Yorkshire Debut: | Clydesdale Bank 40   v. Unicorns | at Leeds | August 12, 2012 |
| Last played: | v. Sri Lanka A | at Leeds | July 31, 2014 |

### BATTING AND FIELDING

| Season | M | I | NO | Runs | HS | Avge | 100s | 50s | Ct/St |
|--------|---|---|----|------|-----|------|------|-----|-------|
| 2012 | 4 | 3 | 1 | 19 | 9 | 9.50 | 0 | 0 | 3/1 |
| 2013 | 7 | 6 | 0 | 202 | 90 | 33.66 | 0 | 2 | 5/1 |
| 2014 | 1 | 1 | 0 | 51 | 51 | 51.00 | 0 | 1 | 2/0 |
| | 12 | 10 | 1 | 272 | 3* | 30.22 | 0 | 3 | 10/2 |

### ALL LIST A MATCHES

| Matches | Innings | NO | Runs | HS | Avge | 100s | 50s | Ct/St |
|---------|---------|----|------|-----|------|------|-----|-------|
| 14 | 11 | 1 | 296 | 90 | 29.60 | 0 | 3 | 14/3 |

### TWENTY20 CRICKET FOR YORKSHIRE 2012 TO 2013

| | | |
|--|--|--|
| Yorkshire Debut: | v. UVA Next | at Johannesburg | October 9, 2012 |
| Last played: | v. Leicestershire | at Leicester | July 28, 2013 |

| Season | M | I | NO | Runs | HS | Avge | 100s | 50s | Ct/St |
|--------|---|---|----|------|-----|-------|------|-----|-------|
| 2012/3 | 6 | 4 | 1 | 36 | 18 | — | 0 | 0 | 0/0 |
| 2013 | 10 | 10 | 1 | 177 | 52* | 19.66 | 0 | 1 | 5/1 |
| | 16 | 14 | 2 | 213 | 52* | 17.75 | 0 | 1 | 5/1 |

**ALL TWENTY20 MATCHES**

| Matches | Innings | NO | Runs | HS | Avge | 100s | 50s | Ct/St |
|---------|---------|----|------|-----|-------|------|-----|-------|
| 17 | 15 | 2 | 225 | 52* | 17.30 | 0 | 1 | 10/1 |

# Nothing to write home about!

In the first Warwickshire innings of 69 at Birmingham last season six batsmen were dismissed without scoring. This was the 13th time there have been six 0s in an innings against Yorkshire.

The most recent before that was in 1970 versus Essex at the Garrison Ground, Colchester. Essex were all out for 121. Yorkshire had batted first and made 450-4 declared — Geoffrey Boycott making an unbeaten 260, his highest score for the county.

There have been seven 0s on three occasions — and one where no fewer than eight batsmen failed to trouble the scorers.

This was versus Lancashire at Old Trafford in 1894. Lancashire lost their first four wickets before a run had been scored, and were 17-7 and eventually 50 all out. Although Yorkshire could manage only 152 they won by an innings and four runs. This match was for Johnny Briggs's benefit, and 15,000 were present on the first day

*Roy D Wilkinson*

# Bookstall brings in £4,800

The second-hand bookstall at Headingley, run by Vivien Stone, Geoff Holmes and Jeremy Wimbush, raised £4,800 last summer for the John Featherstone Foundation with proceeds going to Yorkshire Schools' Cricket Association. Since the bookstall started up 17 years ago it has raised £106,675.

# YORKSHIRE CAP STILL WORTH MORE THAN MONEY CAN BUY

### By Paul Edwards

It is kissed in moments of joyful achievement. It is hurled to the ground in explosions of rage-fuelled disappointment. Its presentation to a cricketer is so significant that the task is generally entrusted to a respected former player. It is frequently the last thing sent to the auction house, and it is often the lot which commands the highest prices. Which manages to be both odd and not surprising, given that few items are more commonly described as "beyond price".

If it is faded, a little tatty and stained with the sweat of many summers so much the better. An old book may be more valuable if it is in excellent condition, but this object is more valued for having been worn and used. Pictures of it adorn the dust jackets of countless cricket books. Sometimes it is placed reverently in the coffin at funerals. It is, of course, a cricket cap.

These things are deeply subjective, but I reckon the most famous caps are those of England, Australia, Yorkshire and Lancashire. That is a Northern-Anglocentric point of view, of course, and it almost certainly underestimates the claims of other counties, other countries and equally passionate cricketers. Yet when I watched the late Richie Benaud hand over a cap to the latest Australian debutant the event seemed charged with a multiplicity of powerful meanings far beyond the two individuals. It is the cap that matters, and the full measure of devotion it represents.

Yet these are strange times for cricket caps. They are never worn by batsmen, who therefore have to kiss the badge on their helmets when they reach a century, an action which seems roughly comparable to the winner of a grand prix planting a smacker on his front bumper. Some counties have done away with the practice of a player earning a cap because they believe it creates division within a team which should be united by a common purpose.

In Australia, almost by contrast, the stature of "the baggy green" has grown: it was the name of a journal, is the title of at least one book and has been incorporated into a cherished heritage. But as Gideon Haigh points out in his excellent article *Baggy Green Dreaming* the Australian cap has not always been either baggy or green and does not even feature the country's coat of arms. "In short," writes Haigh, "we are moving in the realm of Hobsbawm's concept of 'invented tradition': a set of practices that 'seek to inculcate certain values and norms of behaviour by repetition, which automatically implies continuity with the past'".

To judge from the testimony of Martyn Moxon and Geoff Cope it would seem that such creativity has not been necessary in Yorkshire. Moxon, the Director of Cricket, was awarded his cap in 1984. "It was the best moment of my life," he said. "I can't tell you how good it felt to have those three bands on my sweater, and to have the full rose on my cap was such a great moment. I think that still holds now.

"There's an argument as to whether you should have a capping system or not. Some counties don't because of the team ethos. Our view is that it's still nice for the players to have to aspire to that First Eleven cap, and the pride that being capped gives to them is worth preserving. I was really taken by the pride felt by Jack Brooks and Liam Plunkett when we capped them quite recently. It showed what Yorkshire cricket is about."

Just as powerful is Geoff Cope's story of his Yorkshire caps. "All I wanted was a Yorkshire cap," he said, "and I remember one occasion which occurred when I was an uncapped player who had been picked for the first team.

"One lunchtime I came back into the dressing room, made sure there was nobody there, locked both doors and actually put a Yorkshire cap on. I looked at myself in the mirror and said: 'I want one of those', but to this day I still feel guilty because it wasn't my property. It wasn't my cap and I was wrong to do it...but I had this ambition to be a capped player. I got my cap in 1970, and I rang my Dad to tell him.

"I just said: 'Dad, they've given me it'. I didn't need to say the word 'cap'. He knew what I was talking about, and I knew what it meant to him. There was a silence, because he couldn't speak to me. He had to ring me back later because he was so overjoyed."

And since this is the *Yorkshire Yearbook*, perhaps it is fitting to conclude this piece with the story of a Lancashire cricketer. It took ages for that fine seam bowler Kyle Hogg to be awarded his cap. One evening he admitted, mostly in jest, that he was thinking of buying one from a shop.

But when a back injury forced Hogg to retire in 2014 he tweeted a photograph of his sun-bleached and battered cap with the simple caption: "This is what I played for". Hogg's sentiment is one which Cope or Moxon would understand only too well. It might also serve as a reminder that the fierce *Roses* rivalry is rooted in similarity not difference. Maybe we should all remember that when the fur is flying at Headingley and Old Trafford this summer.

**Paul Edwards is a freelance cricket journalist**
**who frequently reports from Headingley**

# TWO WILSON HAT-TRICKS SEND YORKSHIRE SPINNING TO TITLE

### By Anthony Bradbury

The County Championship of 1966 has two similarities with 2016. Yorkshire will be seeking a hat-trick of Championships, just as Worcestershire were doing in 1966, having won the competition in 1964 and 1965. When the last matches of the 1966 season started Worcestershire were six points behind Yorkshire, and the momentum in recent games had all been with the Midlands county. The excitement became intense, and the outcome is set out below.

The second similarity is with the gloom that always seems to surround the future of the Championship and the constant urgings of the game's governing body for change. In the Notes by the Editor for *Wisden* 1967 this was written about the 1966 season: "The standard of English first-class cricket has never been so low...the County Championship cannot last much longer in its present form without public support, which has dwindled to next to nothing...Even members, though still paying their subscriptions, do not appear with any regularity...The prevalence of medium-fast bowling has brought about the almost complete disappearance of the genuine leg-spin bowler and the left-arm slow bowler...For the past 20 years we have had one change after another and the final abomination, the limit of 65 overs for the first innings in some matches in 1966."

The limit of 65 overs in the first innings of a Championship match, adopted for only some matches, was an idea of the Clark Report, set up by the Advisory County Cricket Committee, and which was published in March 1966. It was intended to combat slow scoring, often of less than two runs per over and then prevalent throughout the game. While the use of the limit did encourage some increase in the pace of scoring by the early batsmen it also inhibited middle-order batsmen — often the new arrivals in a team — from learning the art of building a score. This experiment was abandoned after 1966. It had certainly not been popular.

Also noteworthy was a long-standing Championship format which might have been reintroduced for 2016 – whereby some opponents were played twice and others only once – 17 counties in 1966 each playing 28 games. There were 10 points for a win, none for a draw – save in certain unusual circumstances – and two points for a lead on first innings. The concept of batting and bowling bonus points had not yet arrived. Yorkshire, with 15 wins in their 28 matches and 17 leads on first innings amassed 184 points, and all in three-day matches on uncovered pitches.

The Clark Report threw up another idea enormously radical at the time, a Championship whereby each county played each other once — 16 three-day matches — and of a further 16 one-day matches against each county, all 32 matches to constitute either a single Championship or a pair of Championships.

The First Class counties rejected such a format 16-4, which the journalist Charles Bray wrote in *Wisden* was "a majority so emphatic that the counties may have signed their own death warrant."

The 1960s were for Yorkshire an era to compare with earlier decades. They

**DON WILSON: Championship snatcher at the last ditch**
*(Photo: Ron Deaton Archive)*

had won the Championship in 1960, 1962 and 1963, and in the other years were never lower than fifth. So what was their strength in 1966?

As a starter they had a wonderfully courageous and innovative captain in Brian Close. He had led the team to success in 1963, and by the end of 1966 was to be captain of England in a scintillating innings win against the might of the West Indies at The Oval.

Yorkshire had a remarkable core of Test players. Geoffrey Boycott, Raymond Illingworth and Close played for England that year; Fred Trueman, still a fast bowling maestro; Philip Sharpe, Jimmy Binks, Don Wilson and Doug Padgett already had England caps, and John Hampshire, Richard Hutton, Geoff Cope and Chris Old would do so in future years. Chris Balderstone became an England player when later with Leicestershire. That left only Tony Nicholson, very close to an England cap, and fast bowler John Waring without England colours.

50

This combination was formidable and with the combined experience necessary for a wide range of playing circumstances. The 1966 season brought a wet summer, and when pitches dried out Yorkshire had the players to take advantage of such conditions. No county team found batting easy, and generally the bowlers prevailed. Boycott did score four centuries at a Championship average of 39.17, and Close scored two centuries. Only those two averaged more than 30 runs per innings. Illingworth topped the bowling averages with 85 wickets at 14.51, and Nicholson, Wilson and Trueman took a further 293 wickets between them at a combined average of less than 17 runs apiece. On 10 occasions other counties were bowled out for less than 100 runs.

The Championship season started in early May, and Yorkshire were riding high by mid-June, having won six of their first eight games without a loss. Wilson took nine wickets against Gloucestershire in the opening match, and Close with 105 and Illingworth 98 not out did well in the return fixture a week later. Illingworth showed his versatility with 11 wickets against Leicestershire at Leicester, a county to which he was to go in time as captain. Yet the early highlight must have been John Waring's 10 wickets for 63 runs against Lancashire at Headingley. Lancashire were bowled out for 57 in their first innings, and Yorkshire won by 10 wickets. It was the highlight of Waring's career, yet he was released at the end of the season. He later played once for Warwickshire, and had several years with Cumberland. Perhaps he was due to be overtaken by Chris Old, who in 1966 played his first Championship match.

The first setback came with the home defeat by Sussex in late June. Sussex, no doubt to their chagrin, had their first innings forcefully terminated at 231-4 by the 65-over rule, but were good enough to bowl out Yorkshire twice, winning at 7.12pm on the second day. Yorkshire in 1966 took part in five matches that ended in two days. The only match played against reigning champions Worcestershire was drawn with Worcester doing much the better in the first two days. A drawn match against Sussex (Boycott 164) included Yorkshire's highest innings total that season of 383-8 declared. So there was nothing in excess of 400 in 1966, a great contrast with more modern times.

All 40 wickets were lost at Headingley in the Northampton game, each innings by the two sides being between 123 and 190 runs. The sturdy Albert Lightfoot took 7-25 in 14 overs in Yorkshire's first innings, and Yorkshire lost. Lightfoot took only three more wickets all season. Yorkshire recovered from that hiccup by defeating Nottinghamshire at Sheffield, with Boycott scoring a century in each innings. In the first innings Boycott was run out while batting with Doug Padgett, and in the second Padgett was run out while batting with Boycott. It would be 17 years before Boycott again scored two centuries in a single Yorkshire match, and that "double double" has only otherwise been achieved in

**YORKSHIRE 1966. Back row, left to right: John Waring, Philip Sharpe, Jimmy Binks, Don Wilson, Richard Hutton, John Hampshire, Doug Padgett and Geoffrey Boycott. Front row: Raymond Illingworth, Brian Close (captain) Freddie Trueman and Ken Taylor.**

*(Photo: Ron Deaton Archive)*

Yorkshire Championship matches by Ted Lester and Len Hutton. Yorkshire then beat Middlesex by taking eight wickets in an hour on the last afternoon. In the next game Yorkshire again beat Nottinghamshire, this time at Worksop, with Wilson taking a hat-trick towards the end of the third day. It must have been unusual even in the 60s for these teams to play each other twice without going to Headingley or Trent Bridge.

In early August Yorkshire were 40 points clear at the head of the Championship table. They had just beaten Lancashire for the second time in 1966, and now at Old Trafford. They did so by taking advantage of another new Championship rule: rain had washed out nearly all of the first two days, so Yorkshire were still in their first innings when they declared at 146-7 at lunch on the third day. Lancashire came out to bat as they were obliged to do under match regulations, scored one run in one over and declared. Yorkshire were not obliged to bat — it being permitted to forfeit a second innings. Lancashire came out again, and were bowled out for 133, leaving Yorkshire winners by 12 runs. The last wicket came off the last permitted ball of the match with leg-spinner Tommy Greenhough lbw to Illingworth. That was brave umpiring at Old Trafford by either Sid Buller or Tom Spencer.

Now came an unexpected Yorkshire slump. Draws against Hampshire and Essex were followed by a loss to Surrey at Bradford Park Avenue, the margin of defeat being 21 runs. Yorkshire had been 74 adrift on first innings, but had pulled themselves back by bowling Surrey out for 98. Surrey clung on, and bowled out Yorkshire for 151 to take the victory. A thriller at Scarborough followed against Glamorgan, no side scoring 150 and Yorkshire clinging on at 105-8 to win by two wickets. These low-scoring matches were a feature of 1966. Two more consecutive games were lost – Northamptonshire (again) and Warwickshire, and then there was a draw at The Oval, with Surrey just ahead. Meantime, Worcestershire were winning their games and making up ground. The difference between Yorkshire and Worcestershire became six points.

So to the grand finale, Wednesday to Friday, August 31 and September 1 and 2. Worcestershire at home to Sussex, and Yorkshire at Harrogate against Kent. If Worcester won Yorkshire would need to win to become Champions. Rain fell in both games. The turf needed to dry, and bowlers took advantage. At Worcester 20 wickets fell on the first day, Sussex were all out for 145, and then in a bitter blow for home supporters Worcester were bowled out for 77. Yorkshire had the better of their first day, 210 all out (Boycott 80) and Kent losing early wickets (Colin Cowdrey lbw Trueman 1).

Next day Worcester fought back, with Sussex out for 113 and time lost to rain. There was more bad weather at Harrogate, but Derek Underwood took seven successive wickets as Yorkshire with a first innings lead of 91 were out for 109.

At one point on the third day Worcester, needing 182 to win, had reached 114-4, and rain had prevented a start at Harrogate. A draw would not be enough for Yorkshire if Worcester won. The anxiety in the North was severe. The fortunes changed. As a drying pitch at Harrogate led to a restart and Kent were reaching 143-4 Worcester collapsed. The strain had told. They lost by 31 runs. Yorkshire became Champions, but they wanted to win in style: Kent wickets were spun away by Illingworth and Wilson, who took his second hat-trick of the season. The last Kent wicket fell in the last half hour at 4.55pm. Yorkshire had won the match by 24 runs and the Championship by 16 points.

Nothing else then mattered. Yorkshire, Gillette Cup winners over Surrey in 1965, had long ago been eliminated in 1966 in their first match in May, when they lost to Somerset by 40 runs, scoring just 150 well within their allotted 60 overs. That setback could now be forgiven.

Off the field Sir Leonard Hutton became an Honorary Life Member of Yorkshire County Cricket Club, joining Sir Donald Bradman, Wilfred Rhodes and Herbert Sutcliffe. The *Yearbook*, for many years devoid of photographs, now showed one of the newly appointed Patroness of the Club, HRH the Duchess of Kent, daughter of President Sir William Worsley Bart., himself a former captain from the 1920s. This year the Duchess of Kent will have been Patroness for 50 years.

# YORKSHIRE'S FIRST CLASS HIGHLIGHTS OF 1966

**Win by an innings (1)**

Yorkshire (258-6) defeated Derbyshire (89 and 154) by an innings and 15 runs at Chesterfield

**Wins by 10 wickets (3)**

Lancashire (57 and 144) lost to Yorkshire (196-9 and 6-0) at Leeds
Derbyshire (85 and 65) lost to Yorkshire (149 and 2-0) at Sheffield
Nottinghamshire (204 and 124) lost to Yorkshire (332-8 dec and 9-0) at Worksop

**Win by over 200 runs (1)**

Yorkshire (234-9 and 243-4 dec) defeated Nottinghamshire (163-8 and 85) by 229 runs at Sheffield

**Totals of 400 and over (0)**

Many of the County Championship matches had a first-innings restriction of 65 overs

**Opponents dismissed for under 100 (11)**

| | | |
|---|---|---|
| 57 Lancashire at Leeds | 85 Derbyshire at Sheffield | |
| 64 Hampshire at Portsmouth | | (1st innings) |
| 65 Derbyshire at Sheffield | 85 Nottinghamshire at Sheffield | |
| (2nd innings) | 89 Derbyshire at Chesterfield | |
| 69 Gloucestershire at Middlesbrough | 91 Glamorgan at Scarborough | |
| 70 Somerset at Taunton | 98 Surrey at Bradford | |
| 81 Cambridge University at Cambridge | | |

**Century Partnerships (8)**

**For the 1st wicket (5)**

| | | |
|---|---|---|
| 177 | G Boycott and K Taylor | v. MCC at Lord's |
| 144 | G Boycott and D B Close | v. Derbyshire at Chesterfield |
| 135 | G Boycott and K Taylor | v. Sussex at Hove |
| 135 | G Boycott and P J Sharpe | v. Nottinghamshire at Sheffield |
| 123 | G Boycott and K Taylor | v. Leicestershire at Leicester |

**For the 2nd wicket (1)**

| | | |
|---|---|---|
| 190 | G Boycott and D E V Padgett | v. Warwickshire at Birmingham |

**For the 5th wicket (1)**

| | | |
|---|---|---|
| 119 | D B Close and P J Sharpe | v. Nottinghamshire at Worksop |

**For the 7th wicket (1)**

| | | |
|---|---|---|
| 104 | R Illingworth and J C Balderstone | v. Gloucestershire at Bristol |

**Centuries (9)**

G Boycott (5)

| | |
|---|---|
| 164 | v. Sussex at Hove |
| 136* | v. Warwickshire at Birmingham |
| 123 | v. MCC at Lord's |
| 105 | v. Nottinghamshire at Sheffield (2nd innings) |
| 103 | v. Nottinghamshire at Sheffield (1st innings) |

D B Close (3)

| | |
|---|---|
| 115* | v. Nottinghamshire at Worksop |
| 105 | v. Gloucestershire at Bristol |
| 103 | v. Cambridge University at Cambridge |

K Taylor (1)

| | |
|---|---|
| 106 | v. MCC at Lord's |

**5 wickets in an innings (22)**

R Illingworth (8)

| | |
|---|---|
| 6-30 | v. Leicestershire at Leicester (2nd innings) |
| 6-66 | v. Warwickshire at Birmingham |
| 5-33 | v. Lancashire at Manchester |
| 5-42 | v. Sussex at Leeds |
| 5-54 | v. Nottinghamshire at Worksop |
| 5-55 | v. Kent at Harrogate |
| 5-75 | v. Gloucestershire at Bristol |
| 5-96 | v. Leicestershire at Leicester (1st innings) |

D Wilson (5)

| | |
|---|---|
| 6-15 | v. Gloucestershire at Middlesbrough |
| 6-22 | v. Middlesex at Sheffield |
| 5-40 | v. Somerset at Taunton |
| 5-46 | v. Nottinghamshire at Worksop |
| 5-59 | v. Essex at Leyton |

A G Nicholson (4)

| | |
|---|---|
| 6-32 | v. Essex at Bradford |
| 5-12 | v. Derbyshire at Sheffield |
| 5-60 | v. Worcestershire at Worcester |
| 5-83 | v. Northamptonshire at Northampton |

D B Close (2)

| | |
|---|---|
| 6-27 | v. Surrey at The Oval |
| 6-47 | v. Surrey at Bradford |

F S Trueman (2)

| | |
|---|---|
| 8-37 | v. Essex at Bradford |
| 5-18 | v. Lancashire at Leeds |

J S Waring (1)

| | |
|---|---|
| 7-40 | v. Lancashire at Leeds |

### 10 wickets in a match (3)

R Illingworth (1)

    11-126   (5-96 and 6-30)   v. Leicestershire at Leicester

F S Trueman (1)

    10-67   (8-37 and 2-30)   v. Essex at Bradford

J S Waring (1)

    10-63   (3-23 and 7-40)   v. Lancashire at Leeds

### 3 catches in an innings (11)

J G Binks (6)

    4      v. Worcestershire at Worcester
    3      v. MCC at Lord's
    3      v. Middlesex at Lord's
    3      v. Derbyshire at Chesterfield (1st innings)
    3      v. Derbyshire at Chesterfield (2nd innings)
    3      v. Nottinghamshire at Sheffield

D B Close (2)

    4      v. Essex at Leyton
    3      v. Nottinghamshire at Worksop

R Illingworth (1)

    3      v. Nottinghamshire at Sheffield

P J Sharpe (1)

    3      v. West Indies at Bradford

### 3 dismissals in an innings (1)

J G Binks (1)

    3 (2ct, 1st) v. Essex at Bradford

### 5 catches in a match (2)

J G Binks (1)

    6 (3 + 3)   v. Derbyshire at Chesterfield

D B Close (1)

    5 (3 + 2)   v. Nottinghamshire at Worksop

### 5 dismissals in a match (1)

J G Binks (1)

    5 (4ct, 1st) v. Essex at Bradford

### Debut (3)

**In First Class cricket:** G A Cope, B Leadbeater and C M Old

# 50 YEARS AGO

## YORKSHIRE AVERAGES 1966

### ALL FIRST-CLASS MATCHES

Played 32    Won 16    Lost 6    Drawn 10    Abandoned 1

County Championship: Played 28    Won 15    Lost 5    Drawn 8

## BATTING AND FIELDING *(Qualification 10 completed innings)*

| Player | M. | I. | N.O. | Runs | H.S. | Avge | 100s | 50s | ct/st |
|---|---|---|---|---|---|---|---|---|---|
| G Boycott | 22 | 39 | 3 | 1388 | 164 | 38.55 | 5 | 6 | 11 |
| D B Close | 30 | 50 | 9 | 1259 | 115* | 30.70 | 3 | 6 | 44 |
| D E V Padgett | 31 | 52 | 5 | 1194 | 79 | 25.40 | 0 | 6 | 16 |
| K Taylor | 25 | 45 | 3 | 1044 | 106 | 24.85 | 1 | 5 | 10 |
| R Illingworth | 25 | 36 | 8 | 666 | 98* | 23.78 | 0 | 2 | 20 |
| J H Hampshire | 30 | 52 | 4 | 1105 | 78 | 23.02 | 0 | 5 | 25 |
| P J Sharpe | 32 | 49 | 5 | 988 | 72 | 22.45 | 0 | 3 | 45 |
| J G Binks | 32 | 42 | 11 | 517 | 60* | 16.67 | 0 | 1 | 55/10 |
| D Wilson | 31 | 42 | 6 | 578 | 52 | 16.05 | 0 | 1 | 13 |
| J C Balderstone | 11 | 13 | 1 | 183 | 64 | 15.25 | 0 | 1 | 4 |
| F S Trueman | 31 | 41 | 4 | 431 | 43 | 11.64 | 0 | 0 | 22 |
| A G Nicholson | 29 | 28 | 16 | 130 | 41 | 10.83 | 0 | 0 | 3 |

### Also batted

| Player | M. | I. | N.O. | Runs | H.S. | Avge | 100s | 50s | ct/st |
|---|---|---|---|---|---|---|---|---|---|
| J S Waring | 13 | 13 | 8 | 95 | 26 | 19.00 | 0 | 0 | 7 |
| R A Hutton | 3 | 6 | 1 | 40 | 16 | 8.00 | 0 | 0 | 0 |
| B Leadbeater | 2 | 4 | 0 | 14 | 7 | 3.50 | 0 | 0 | 0 |
| G A Cope | 3 | 5 | 1 | 6 | 3 | 1.50 | 0 | 0 | 3 |
| C M Old | 2 | 2 | 0 | 3 | 3 | 1.50 | 0 | 0 | 3 |

## BOWLING *(Qualification 10 wickets)*

| Player | Overs | Mdns | Runs | Wkts | Avge | Best | 5wI | 10wM |
|---|---|---|---|---|---|---|---|---|
| A G Nicholson | 879.3 | 297 | 1752 | 113 | 15.50 | 6-32 | 4 | 0 |
| R Illingworth | 767.1 | 292 | 1515 | 96 | 15.78 | 6-30 | 8 | 1 |
| F S Trueman | 810.2 | 197 | 1852 | 107 | 17.30 | 8-37 | 2 | 1 |
| D Wilson | 851 | 341 | 1753 | 100 | 17.53 | 6-15 | 5 | 0 |
| D B Close | 502.3 | 192 | 1118 | 54 | 20.70 | 6-27 | 2 | 0 |
| J S Waring | 206.2 | 49 | 542 | 25 | 21.68 | 3-39 | 0 | 0 |

### Also bowled

| Player | Overs | Mdns | Runs | Wkts | Avge | Best | 5wI | 10wM |
|---|---|---|---|---|---|---|---|---|
| R A Hutton | 63 | 15 | 176 | 8 | 22.00 | 7-40 | 1 | 1 |
| J C Balderstone | 28.1 | 6 | 84 | 3 | 28.00 | 2-18 | 0 | 0 |
| K Taylor | 24 | 7 | 46 | 1 | 46.00 | 1-24 | 0 | 0 |
| G A Cope | 36 | 16 | 98 | 0 | — | — | 0 | 0 |
| J H Hampshire | 30 | 5 | 111 | 0 | — | — | 0 | 0 |
| G Boycott | 12 | 5 | 25 | 0 | — | — | 0 | 0 |
| C M Old | 8 | 1 | 8 | 0 | — | — | 0 | 0 |

# 50 YEARS AGO

## YORKSHIRE AVERAGES 1966

### LIST A KNOCKOUT COMPETITION — GILLETTE CUP

Played 1        Lost 1

#### BATTING AND FIELDING

| Player | M. | I. | N.O. | Runs | H.S. | Avge | 100s | 50s | ct/st |
|---|---|---|---|---|---|---|---|---|---|
| D B Close ......... | 1 | 1 | 0 | 29 | 29 | 29.00 | 0 | 0 | 0 |
| K Taylor ........... | 1 | 1 | 0 | 27 | 27 | 27.00 | 0 | 0 | 0 |
| G Boycott ........... | 1 | 1 | 0 | 21 | 21 | 21.00 | 0 | 0 | 0 |
| D E V Padgett ....... | 1 | 1 | 0 | 15 | 15 | 15.00 | 0 | 0 | 0 |
| J H Hampshire ....... | 1 | 1 | 0 | 14 | 14 | 14.00 | 0 | 0 | 1 |
| P J Sharpe .......... | 1 | 1 | 0 | 10 | 10 | 10.00 | 0 | 0 | 2 |
| D Wilson ........... | 1 | 1 | 0 | 3 | 3 | 3.00 | 0 | 0 | 0 |
| F S Trueman ........ | 1 | 1 | 0 | 0 | 0 | 0.00 | 0 | 0 | 0 |
| J G Binks ........... | 1 | 1 | 0 | 0 | 0 | 0.00 | 0 | 0 | 1 |
| A G Nicholson ....... | 1 | 1 | 0 | 0 | 0 | 0.00 | 0 | 0 | 0 |
| R Illingworth ........ | 1 | 1 | 1 | 29 | 29* | — | 0 | 0 | 0 |

#### BOWLING

| Player | Overs | Mdns | Runs | Wkts | Avge | Best | 4wI | RPO |
|---|---|---|---|---|---|---|---|---|
| D Wilson ........... | 9 | 1 | 38 | 2 | 19.00 | 2-38 | 0 | 4.22 |
| D B Close .......... | 12 | 6 | 22 | 1 | 22.00 | 1-22 | 0 | 1.83 |
| A G Nicholson ...... | 12 | 6 | 23 | 1 | 23.00 | 1-23 | 0 | 1.91 |
| R Illingworth ....... | 7 | 1 | 23 | 1 | 23.00 | 1-23 | 0 | 3.28 |
| Trueman ............ | 12 | 1 | 39 | 0 | — | — | 0 | 3.25 |
| K Taylor ........... | 5 | 0 | 26 | 0 | — | — | 0 | 5.20 |
| G Boycott ........... | 3 | 0 | 12 | 0 | — | — | 0 | 4.00 |

---

# Floods Appeal launched

Yorkshire CCC, in conjunction with the Yorkshire Cricket Board and the Yorkshire Cricket Foundation, launched the Yorkshire Cricket Floods Taskforce to work with the region's cricket clubs which were badly affected by the Boxing Day floods. A Yorkshire CCC Floods Appeal was set up, and in February the Yorkshire CCC Players' Association made a £5,000 donation to take the amount raised at that time to around the £15,000 mark.

# TED LESTER MEMORABILIA AMONG ITEMS ACQUIRED

### By J C David Allan

Once again the Archives Committee enjoyed an extremely busy year with many new items of Yorkshire memorabilia received through purchase, donation or loan as well as a steady stream of queries from cricket enthusiasts being investigated and answered.

In addition to finding new items of interest for the museum at Headingley and for the show cases in the Long Room we added considerably to the volume of items stored in the West Yorkshire Archives at Morley, which was visited regularly by myself, Brian Sanderson and Chris Hardy and occasionally by Brian Warne.

One of the biggest influx of items followed the death last March of the then doyen of Yorkshire cricket, Ted Lester, who had served Yorkshire as player and scorer for half a century and whose obituary is featured in this publication. Ted's family generously gave all of his memorabilia gathered over many years including caps, blazers, yearbooks and other personal items, plus much correspondence. So extensive is the collection that former Archives Committee member Ron Deaton has spent part of the winter sorting and scheduling everything.

In appreciation of this gift Yorkshire invited Ted's widow, Mary, son Kevin and daughter Maureen to lunch at Headingley on the day of a Championship match, and they thoroughly enjoyed their visit.

Ted's death was preceded by that of Bob Appleyard, one of Yorkshire and England's greatest players and a former President of Yorkshire CCC. Material from Bob's splendid collection had earlier been loaned for an exhibition in the museum, and since that was on show talks have been ongoing with Bob's family over the future of many other items.

We also had a visit from Anne Smithson, G A Smithson's (Yorkshire 1946-50) widow and from his daughter to deposit his clothing from his career with Yorkshire, Leicestershire and England on long-term loan. They were also entertained to a day's play and lunch.

Among the many items which came into the committee's possession through various ways were an empty champagne bottle donated by John Brayford and signed by David Byas and Darren Lehmann from Scarborough, 2001, when Yorkshire clinched the Championship by beating Glamorgan; a framed print of Len Hutton; a Huddersfield League

Centenary brochure, and video tapes from 1994-2001 by courtesy of Martyn Moxon.

Also received were *Yorkshire Post* cuttings from Roy D Wilkinson for several seasons in the 1960s, cricket match tokens in brass, copper and silver from the 19th Century; Fred Trueman's plain Australian tour blazer 1962-63 in frame; J T Brown 1904 letter; Maurice Leyland cap; lapel pins for Herbert Sutcliffe and Maurice Leyland; Geoffrey Boycott cap 1982; Herbert Sutcliffe items including a silver cigarette box given by Rowntrees, a ball given to him upon becoming the first batsman to score two centuries in a Test match, his personal silver cigarette case with initials H S, and coloured ink characters of himself; Yorkshire v. Essex signed bat 1978; Yorkshire v. West Indies bat 1950, and a Yorkshire edition of Stephen Chalke's book *Summer's Crown* donated by the author.

Ron Deaton is also to be thanked for listing and scheduling the donated collection of the late Maurice Dover.

The committee discussed the provision of blue plaques in memory of some of Yorkshire's legendary players, including the Hon Sir F S Jackson, Bob Appleyard, Maurice Leyland and Willie Watson. Roy Wilkinson is seeking more information from local authorities.

With the publishers of *Wisden Cricketers' Almanack* no longer providing county clubs with complimentary copies one or two gaps had appeared in Yorkshire's collection, but these have now been filled.

The committee dealt with 30 postal enquiries during the year. Some of these concerned the possible donation and/or valuation of signed bats and other memorabilia, while others were concerned with research. Topics included pre-1992 non-Yorkshire-born county players, the first *Roses* match in 1867, W Holmes, who played in one Second Eleven match in 1903, and Schofield Haigh, one of Yorkshire's best bowlers.

An effort was made to improve relations with the Yorkshire Cricket Foundation, the charitable arm of Yorkshire CCC, and we invited the Foundation's chairman, David Gent, to our May meeting. Our members introduced themselves to him before he outlined the work and aims of the Foundation. Will Saville, the Foundation's development manager, was then invited to address our August meeting.

Our four meetings throughout the year were all extremely constructive, and in May we warmly welcomed our two new members — Philip E Dunn, who had replaced Howard Clayton as secretary when Howard stood down from the committee at the end of 2014, and Chris Hardy, both of whom were highly valued. I thank all members for their time and constructive enthusiasm for all we undertake and their support for the cause

**\* David Allan is Chairman of the Yorkshire Foundation Cricket Archives Committee**

# HOW WHITE ROSE BITS AND PIECES BECAME FINE OBJETS D'ART

"Could you take on the chairmanship of the Archives Committee from Harold North?"

Little did I know where this request from Robin Smith, then Yorkshire CCC President, would lead.

The idea of a Yorkshire CCC Archives Committee was the inspiration of Robin during the first year of his Chairmanship and Presidency following the establishment of the Club's Management Board in 2002.

He had recognised that since the death of Tony Woodhouse the collection of county memorabilia had drifted aimlessly. Items were spread among cupboards, drawers, under the stands and in garages with little understanding by anyone of what we had, and even less where

**By David Hall
CBE TD**

it might be! Tony had even removed some items for safekeeping to his home. Towards the end of his life he had met Robin to tell him of his holdings, which included the remarkable *Jubilee Book of Cricket* by K S Ranjitsinhje, complete with original manuscript letters from many of the personalities featured in the book. I subsequently arranged for this to be auctioned at Christie's in London for over £50,000 net, the decision having been made that it was not relevant to Yorkshire cricket.

Harold North was asked by Robin initially to form the committee and bring some order to a chaotic situation. At the same time Chris Hassell, as part of fulfilling the remainder of his contract, was asked to take on the secretarial responsibilities. These were to include the start of listing the entire collection we owned. Arrangements were made with Yorkshire Archives Services to store the memorabilia in purpose accommodation at Morley, as no space existed at Headingley.

The records element, comprising mainly minute books, scorebooks etc from the Club's formation in 1863, are held in their Public Records Office and are available for public viewing.

Having assumed the chairmanship I quickly realised that we had a liquorice-allsorts collection of memorabilia gathered at random over the years which needed rationalising. The decision was taken to concentrate on items relating to the history and heritage of Yorkshire cricket. The considerable collection of non-Yorkshire related items was sold at auctions in the UK, Australia, and on e-Bay. The sums raised have been used to acquire items specifically related to Yorkshire cricket as they become available, and for other heritage projects such as a blue plaque at the birthplace of Hedley Verity in Leeds.

It was decided that our inventories needed to be more detailed. The overseeing of this task was initially undertaken by Ron Deaton with the assistance of committee members, Ron's considerable knowledge of the subject matter proving invaluable. This is an ongoing operation with new items arriving and memorabilia being withdrawn for displays in the museum, Long Room, around Headingley and elsewhere, generating a constant in-and-out scenario.

While this work was ongoing and always will be, many other projects were being progressed. In 2006 the Test Match Honours Boards were installed in the Long Room, recording all the players in Headingley Tests who have scored centuries, taken 10 wickets in a match, five wickets in an innings or achieved a hat-trick. These are updated as required during each Headingley Test match. In the same year cabinets were placed in the Long Room to feature memorabilia and events. These are changed regularly and represent another opportunity to display the Club's memorabilia collection.

A memorial plaque to Yorkshire players killed in military action was unveiled in 2007 next to the Hutton Gates by the then Yorkshire President, Bob Appleyard, and Field Marshal Lord Inge, who had served with Hedley Verity's regiment, The Green Howards. The cost of the plaque was met by donations.

In 2008 we marked the 70th anniversary of Sir Leonard Hutton's record Test innings of 364 at The Oval in 1938. Through the kindness of Richard and John Hutton we were able to supplement our collection of Hutton memorabilia with some personal items from the collection they hold for a special display in the Long Room. We were able to borrow from MCC, with the Hutton family agreement, the portrait of Sir Leonard which normally hangs in the Pavilion at Lord's. During its tenure at Headingley it was agreed that we could copy it, and canvas prints now hang in the museum and the Taverners' Suite at Headingley.

As part of the task to record the history of the Club 13 DVDs have been produced, recording the experiences of Yorkshire players. These are available for purchase in the Club shop and museum.

With the generous assistance of author and publisher Stephen Chalke two booklets were produced — *A Summer of Plenty*, the story of George Hirst's remarkable 1906 season, and *555*, the Holmes and Sutcliffe record stand in 1932. This booklet was nominated for an award.

For many years a museum had been an aspiration of the Club, but money and space had not been available. When the decision was taken to build the Carnegie Pavilion and move the offices from the East Stand into the pavilion space became available, but where was the finance to come from? Dr Keith Howard, chairman of the Emerald Foundation, stepped into the breach with a gift of £300,000.

The substantial task of assembling the appropriate collection of memorabilia, facts and stats began. I added Twickenham, Wimbledon and Arsenal to my previous museum visits to pick a few brains.

It was decided that the museum should have a broad appeal, and would not be exclusively for cricket anoraks. The younger generation should find it interesting. Interactivity was to be a feature and easy understanding of the history by dividing it into zones and puzzle points. Screens were to be set into the zones with related film sequences, and a small cinema was to be created with a film of the history of Yorkshire cricket replaying every 15 minutes, which we entitled *Yorksview*. Each zone was to have its own display cabinet of related memorabilia.

We selected Mather & Co to work with us to create the museum. The work progressed steadily over a year and the opening was performed by Dr Howard in March 2011 before a distinguished gathering of Yorkshire's ex-players and notables. We continue to adapt and improve the presentations. It has proved popular with visitors, who frequently tell us they need more than one visit to absorb the presentations. Schoolchildren come as part of our *Cricket in the Classroom* scheme.

In 2013, following a successful Lottery Fund application for £30,000, we were able to design and build a mobile museum. We used the design of Army Recruiting trailers as a basis for the construction and layout. The display panels tell the story of Yorkshire cricket and a screen is inset with a 15-minute history film, as in the main museum. The mobile visits shows in Yorkshire and the Scarborough Cricket Festival annually.

The challenge for me throughout my term of office has been to provide interesting and attractive displays to illustrate the historical facts and figures of Yorkshire cricket. It has been a pleasure to be involved, and I would like to thank the numerous people who have assisted me in the various projects undertaken over the years.

This is the story so far. The rich heritage of Yorkshire cricket will continue to be a source of future developments.

# BRIAN CLOSE CBE — THE TRUE CAPTAIN COURAGEOUS

### By David Warner

Tributes from far and wide poured in following the death at his Baildon home on September 14 of former Yorkshire and England captain Brian Close CBE, who had deservedly earned the reputation of being one of cricket's great leaders — and the most courageous.

Brian, aged 84, had been ill for some months, and his death came as no great surprise, but his passing was mourned by all who knew him personally as well as those who simply marvelled at his bravery on the field of play.

He had a rare and natural talent for every sport he turned his hand to — they included almost any you can think of — but it was cricket at every level that he loved the most, and which made him a much loved and respected figure wherever the game is played.

Born and brought up in Rawdon, only a few miles from Baildon, Brian became a true legend of the game. No sportsman who ever lived was the subject of more stories and anecdotes, almost all of them having more than a grain of truth about them.

To me, however, his greatest attribute was that he was loved by virtually all who played under him. He was revered by his teammates and talked about with a fondness that few other captains have been able to experience. He was his own man, and he knew his own mind, but at the same time he was able to remain "one of the boys" among those who made up that great Yorkshire team of the 1960s.

Educated at Aireborough Grammar School where, unsurprisingly, he was captain of both cricket and football, Brian at 11 years of age played for Rawdon Cricket Club where the likes of Hedley Verity and Bryan Stott also made their mark. He was in the same Yorkshire Federation side as Fred Trueman and Raymond Illingworth, and he made his Yorkshire debut as an 18-year-old against Cambridge University at

Fenner's in 1949, Trueman and Frank Lowson, who also went on to play for England, also making their first appearances in that game.

So rich was Brian's talent that he scored 1,098 First Class runs and claimed 113 wickets in that initial season, and in the same summer he made his England Test debut against New Zealand at Old Trafford. He was 18 years and 149 days old, and his record of being England's youngest ever Test player still stands. At Melbourne in 1950-1951 he became the youngest to represent England against Australia, aged 19 years and 301 days.

Brian succeeded Vic Wilson as Yorkshire captain in 1963, and was immediately successful in retaining the County Championship title. He had taken the reins during a golden period of Yorkshire cricket, and his side went on to notch a hat-trick of title wins from 1966 to 1968.

Most fittingly, in the days immediately after his death, Yorkshire were playing Hampshire at Southampton, and current skipper Andrew Gale scored a splendid century which enabled his side to win the match. They had already retained the Championship title for the first time since Brian's team had done so in the 60s. Although Brian did not favour the introduction of one-day cricket to the county calendar he fought just as hard in the limited-overs arena as in any First Class battle, and he led Yorkshire to Gillette Cup triumphs at Lord's in 1965 and 1969.

It was his perceived attitude to one-day cricket, however, that caused him to fall out of favour with cricket chairman Brian Sellers, who captained the great Yorkshire side leading up to the 1939-45 war. Sellers unwisely sacked Brian at the end of the 1970 season, with Geoffrey Boycott taking over the captaincy. It was an act Sellers came to regret, and Close later told me that he was so upset when he was given the news at Headingley that he was physically sick while driving to his home.

Brian departed Yorkshire for Somerset, where he became a cult figure in that county also, and he mentored several of their leading young players including Ian Botham, who became a firm friend, as did the great Viv Richards. He made his debut for Somerset against Leicestershire at Grace Road in 1971, and under his captaincy they went on to enjoy one of their most fruitful periods. He was there until the end of the 1977 season, playing in 142 matches and topping 1,000 runs on five occasions.

Brian loved his time at Somerset, but his heart was always in his native Yorkshire, for whom he played in 536 First Class matches, scoring 22,650 runs with 33 centuries and capturing 967 wickets at 24.29 apiece. Perhaps the greatest and most fearless of all short-leg fielders, he held on to 564 catches, many of them only a few feet from the bat.

His highest score for Yorkshire was an unbeaten 198 against Surrey at The Oval in 1960, and his best bowling figures were 8-41 against Kent at Headingley in 1959. He scored 1,000-plus runs for Yorkshire in

13 seasons, his best being 1,821 in 1961.

But for courting controversy with the authorities Brian would have played in more than 22 Test matches for England — in seven of which he was their captain and from which he emerged with the outstanding record of six wins and a draw.

Perhaps he will best be remembered internationally for being recalled by England in 1976 at the age of 45 for the Old Trafford Test and heroically fending off the West Indies' fearsome attack for 162 minutes before returning to the pavilion with his body a mass of bruises.

England lost heavily, but Close's bravery against brutal bowling was never forgotten.

When he retired from all forms of First Class cricket after captaining his own XI against the New Zealanders at Scarborough in 1986 he was 55. His overall record read: 34,994 runs at 33.26 with 52 centuries, and 1,171 wickets at 26.42, plus 813 catches and one stumping.

**GOLDEN DAYS: Brian in his hey-day as Championship-winning Yorkshire captain and captain of England in 1967. *(Mick Pope Archive.)***

It is probably true to say that his distinguished record could never have been achieved without the constant support of his dear wife, Vivien, who stood by him faithfully through thick and thin.

Brian excelled at whatever sport took his fancy, and he was on Leeds United's books before transferring to Arsenal, later playing a few games for Bradford City until retirement was forced upon him by a knee injury.

An England cricket selector for a while, Brian became actively involved with Yorkshire again once his First Class career was over, and it was typical of the man that he should spend a season captaining the Club's young Academy side at the age of 60, one of the up-and-coming young players being Ryan Sidebottom.

A Bradford representative on the Yorkshire Committee, he served as cricket chairman for a time during the difficult days of the early 1980s, when the Club was split down the middle over the Geoffrey Boycott controversy. He was an early President of Yorkshire CCC Players' Association, and he was a proud man when he was elected Club President for the years 2008 and 2009.

Players past and present were deeply saddened by Brian's death, none more so than his old friend and teammate Doug Padgett, who played alongside him throughout Brian's Yorkshire career, and went on to become the Club's first-team coach during half-a-century of service.

"Brian was a terrific competitor who never knew when he was beaten, and he was the sort of bloke you wanted in your side," Doug said. "He was an exceptional all-round cricketer with tremendous enthusiasm and a not-to-be beaten attitude. He was a magnificent character to play cricket with and very unselfish — a great team man who didn't think of personal things, but was 100 per cent for the team and 100 per cent Yorkshire."

Former England captain Raymond Illingworth also paid warm tribute to his close friend and county captain, as did virtually every other *White Rose* cricketer who had the privilege to play alongside him.

There was a packed congregational for a Service of Thanksgiving for Brian, which was held at St Chad's Parish Church, Far Headingley. Tributes were paid by his former teammate Bryan Stott, Sir Ian Botham and Colin Graves, chairman of the England and Wales Cricket Board. Readings were given by Brian and Vivien's son and daughter, Lance and Lyn, and Dr Ingrid Roscoe, Lord Lieutenant of West Yorkshire.

**Dennis Brian Close**     **Born: February 24, 1931**
**Died: September 14, 2015**

## DENNIS BRIAN CLOSE

**FIRST-CLASS CRICKET FOR YORKSHIRE 1949 TO 1970**
**FIRST-CLASS CRICKET FOR SOMERSET 1971 TO 1977**

| | | |
|---|---|---|
| Left-hand batsman | Right-arm pace and off-break bowler | |
| Born: Rawdon, Leeds | February 24, 1931 | |
| Died: Baildon | September 14, 2015 | |
| First Class Debut for Yorkshire | v. Cambridge University at Fenners | May 11, 1949 |
| Last played for Yorkshire: | v. Somerset at Hull | September 12, 1970 |
| First Class Debut for Somerset | v. Leicestershire at Leicester | May 1, 1971 |
| Last played for Somerset: | v. Worcestershire at Worcester | September 7, 1977 |
| Final First Class: | | |
| for D B Close's XI | v. New Zealanders at Scarborough | August 31, 1986 |
| | Yorkshire Cap: August 31, 1949 | |

# FIRST-CLASS MATCHES FOR YORKSHIRE
## BATTING AND FIELDING

| Season | M | I | NO | Runs | HS | Avge | 100s | 50s | Ct |
|--------|-----|-----|-----|-------|------|-------|------|-----|-----|
| 1949 | 26 | 42 | 8 | 958 | 88* | 28.17 | 0 | 3 | 16 |
| 1950 | 1 | 2 | 0 | 39 | 22 | 19.50 | 0 | 0 | 0 |
| 1951 | 2 | 4 | 0 | 64 | 39 | 16.00 | 0 | 0 | 0 |
| 1952 | 33 | 45 | 9 | 1192 | 87* | 33.11 | 0 | 8 | 27 |
| 1953 | 2 | 2 | 1 | 14 | 10 | 14.00 | 0 | 0 | 1 |
| 1954 | 30 | 41 | 7 | 1287 | 164 | 37.85 | 2 | 7 | 23 |
| 1955 | 28 | 45 | 5 | 1131 | 143 | 28.27 | 2 | 4 | 35 |
| 1956 | 27 | 37 | 5 | 802 | 88 | 25.06 | 0 | 3 | 23 |
| 1957 | 29 | 48 | 3 | 1315 | 120 | 29.22 | 3 | 4 | 32 |
| 1958 | 32 | 49 | 4 | 1335 | 120 | 29.66 | 1 | 7 | 30 |
| 1959 | 31 | 54 | 3 | 1740 | 154 | 34.11 | 4 | 8 | 32 |
| 1960 | 36 | 51 | 3 | 1699 | 198 | 35.39 | 3 | 8 | 44 |
| 1961 | 34 | 58 | 7 | 1821 | 132 | 35.70 | 5 | 8 | 44 |
| 1962 | 28 | 45 | 6 | 1438 | 142* | 36.87 | 3 | 7 | 29 |
| 1963 | 24 | 36 | 3 | 1145 | 161 | 34.69 | 1 | 7 | 24 |
| 1964 | 33 | 50 | 7 | 1281 | 100* | 29.79 | 1 | 7 | 46 |
| 1965 | 30 | 46 | 7 | 1127 | 117* | 28.89 | 3 | 2 | 31 |
| 1966 | 30 | 50 | 9 | 1259 | 115* | 30.70 | 3 | 6 | 44 |
| 1967 | 15 | 20 | 2 | 643 | 98 | 35.72 | 0 | 8 | 21 |
| 1968 | 25 | 31 | 7 | 599 | 77* | 24.95 | 0 | 3 | 32 |
| 1969 | 20 | 27 | 4 | 812 | 146 | 35.30 | 1 | 4 | 10 |
| 1970 | 20 | 28 | 2 | 949 | 128 | 36.50 | 1 | 6 | 20 |
| | 536 | 811 | 102 | 22650 | 198 | 31.94 | 33 | 110 | 564 |

## Centuries (33)

| | | | |
|------|------|------------------------|------------------|
| 1954 | 123* | v. Somerset | at Sheffield |
| | 164 | v. Combined Services | at Harrogate |
| 1955 | 114 | v. Cambridge University | at Cambridge |
| | 143 | v. Somerset | at Taunton |
| 1957 | 108 | v. Derbyshire | at Bradford |
| | 120 | v. Derbyshire | at Chesterfield |
| | 103 | v. Sussex | at Hove |
| 1958 | 120 | v. Glamorgan | at Swansea |
| 1959 | 144 | v. Oxford University | at Oxford |
| | 154 | v. Nottinghamshire | at Nottingham |
| | 128 | v. Lancashire | at Sheffield |
| | 128 | v. Somerset | at Bath |
| 1960 | 102 | v. Hampshire | at Portsmouth |
| | 198 | v. Surrey | at The Oval |
| | 184 | v. Nottinghamshire | at Scarborough |
| 1961 | 132 | v. Surrey | at The Oval |
| | 111 | v. Lancashire | at Manchester |
| | 103 | v. Glamorgan | at Leeds |
| | 103 | v. Somerset | at Hull |
| | 100 | v. Cambridge University | at Cambridge |
| 1962 | 121* | v. Somerset | at Taunton |
| | 140* | v. Warwickshire | at Sheffield |
| | 142* | v. Essex | at Sheffield |
| 1963 | 161 | v. Northamptonshire | at Northampton |
| 1964 | 100* | v. Surrey | at Bradford |
| 1965 | 115 | v. New Zealanders | at Bradford |
| | 117* | v. South Africans | at Bradford |
| | 101* | v. Surrey | at Bradford |
| 1966 | 103 | v. Cambridge University | at Cambridge |

|      | 105  | v. Gloucestershire   | at Bristol       |
|------|------|----------------------|------------------|
|      | 115* | v. Nottinghamshire   | at Worksop       |
| 1969 | 146  | v. New Zealanders    | at Bradford      |
| 1970 | 128  | v. Northamptonshire  | at Northampton   |

## BOWLING

| Seasons | Matches | Overs  | Mdns | Runs  | Wkts | Avge  | Best  | 5wI | 10wM |
|---------|---------|--------|------|-------|------|-------|-------|-----|------|
| 1949    | 26      | 1089   | 291  | 2703  | 105  | 25.74 | 6-47  | 6   | 0    |
| 1950    | 1       | 50.2   | 14   | 132   | 7    | 18.85 | 4-66  | 0   | 0    |
| 1951    | 2       | 39     | 16   | 74    | 2    | 37.00 | 1-22  | 0   | 0    |
| 1952    | 33      | 1107.4 | 331  | 2746  | 114  | 24.08 | 6-69  | 6   | 0    |
| 1953    | 2       | 45     | 19   | 105   | 3    | 35.00 | 2-61  | 0   | 0    |
| 1954    | 30      | 519    | 136  | 1428  | 66   | 21.63 | 6-38  | 4   | 0    |
| 1955    | 28      | 804.4  | 244  | 2002  | 90   | 22.24 | 7-62  | 5   | 0    |
| 1956    | 27      | 266.5  | 75   | 674   | 24   | 28.08 | 4-27  | 0   | 0    |
| 1957    | 29      | 259    | 84   | 682   | 30   | 22.73 | 5-29  | 1   | 0    |
| 1958    | 32      | 324.1  | 82   | 856   | 32   | 26.75 | 4-30  | 0   | 0    |
| 1959    | 31      | 726.2  | 206  | 2031  | 81   | 25.07 | 8-41  | 5   | 0    |
| 1960    | 36      | 611.3  | 207  | 1493  | 64   | 23.32 | 8-43  | 3   | 0    |
| 1961    | 34      | 568.2  | 214  | 1426  | 58   | 24.58 | 6-49  | 2   | 0    |
| 1962    | 28      | 392.5  | 156  | 885   | 29   | 30.51 | 3- 4  | 0   | 0    |
| 1963    | 24      | 388.2  | 127  | 1038  | 42   | 24.71 | 6-55  | 1   | 1    |
| 1964    | 33      | 539.5  | 195  | 1243  | 52   | 23.90 | 6-29  | 1   | 0    |
| 1965    | 30      | 527.2  | 202  | 1217  | 58   | 20.98 | 6-49  | 4   | 1    |
| 1966    | 30      | 502.3  | 192  | 1118  | 54   | 20.70 | 6-27  | 2   | 0    |
| 1967    | 15      | 250.1  | 96   | 565   | 18   | 31.38 | 3-28  | 0   | 0    |
| 1968    | 25      | 316    | 136  | 694   | 29   | 23.93 | 4-87  | 0   | 0    |
| 1969    | 20      | 115    | 47   | 282   | 7    | 40.28 | 1-4   | 0   | 0    |
| 1970    | 20      | 34     | 10   | 95    | 2    | 47.50 | 1-15  | 0   | 0    |
|         | 536     | 9476.5 | 3080 | 23489 | 967  | 24.29 | 8-41  | 40  | 2    |

### 10 wickets in a match (2)

| 1963 | 10-74 (6-55 and 4-19) | v. Glamorgan | at Sheffield   |
|------|-----------------------|--------------|----------------|
| 1965 | 11-119 (6-52 and 5-67)| v. Kent      | at Gillingham  |

### 5 wickets in an innings (40)

| 1949 | 5-58  | v. Essex            | at Leeds        |
|------|-------|---------------------|-----------------|
|      | 7-47  | v. Worcester        | at Worcester    |
|      | 5-73  | v. Sussex           | at Leeds        |
|      | 6-87  | v. Surrey           | at Bradford     |
|      | 6-130 | v. Lancashire       | at Leeds        |
|      | 6-105 | v. Gloucestershire  | at Huddersfield |
| 1952 | 5-64  | v. MCC              | at Lord's       |
|      | 5-40  | v. Oxford University| at Oxford       |
|      | 5-36  | v. Lancashire       | at Leeds        |
|      | 6-69  | v. Nottinghamshire  | at Nottingham   |
|      | 5-24  | v. Leicestershire   | at Leicester    |
|      | 6-94  | v. Hampshire        | at Scarborough  |
| 1954 | 6-68  | v. Gloucestershire  | at Bristol      |
|      | 6-45  | v. Gloucestershire  | at Sheffield    |
|      | 6-38  | v. Northamptonshire | at Bradford     |
|      | 5-32  | v. Hampshire        | at Bournemouth  |
| 1955 | 5-32  | v. Kent             | at Hull         |
|      | 5-88  | v. Northamptonshire | at Northampton  |
|      | 5-95  | v. Nottinghamshire  | at Nottingham   |
|      | 7-62  | v. Essex            | at Bradford     |
|      | 6-63  | v. Derbyshire       | at Bradford     |

| | | | |
|---|---|---|---|
| 1957 | 5-29 | v. Cambridge University | at Cambridge |
| 1959 | 5-12 | v. Warwickshire | at Sheffield |
| | 5-75 | v. Middlesex | at Scarborough |
| | 8-41 | v. Kent | at Leeds |
| | 6-87 | v. Somerset | at Bath |
| | 5-47 | v. The Rest | at The Oval |
| 1960 | 5-64 | v. Sussex | at Middlesbrough |
| | 6-59 | v. Derbyshire | at Chesterfield |
| | 8-43 | v. Essex | at Leeds |
| | 5-36 | v. Somerset | at Hull |
| | 6-49 | v. Kent | at Dover |
| 1963 | 6-55 | v. Glamorgan | at Sheffield |
| 1964 | 6-29 | v. Kent | at Bradford |
| 1965 | 5-69 | v. New Zealanders | at Bradford |
| | 6-52 | v. Glamorgan | at Swansea |
| | 5-67 | v. Kent | at Gillingham (1st innings) |
| | 6-49 | v. Kent | at Gillingham (2nd innings) |
| 1966 | 6-47 | v. Surrey | at Bradford |
| | 6-27 | v. Surrey | at The Oval |

# FIRST-CLASS MATCHES FOR SOMERSET

## BATTING AND FIELDING

| Season | M | I | NO | Runs | HS | Avge | 100s | 50s | Ct |
|---|---|---|---|---|---|---|---|---|---|
| 1971 | 25 | 41 | 10 | 1388 | 116* | 44.77 | 5 | 6 | 33 |
| 1972 | 19 | 31 | 5 | 1299 | 135 | 49.96 | 3 | 6 | 17 |
| 1973 | 21 | 32 | 5 | 1096 | 153 | 40.59 | 3 | 3 | 21 |
| 1974 | 23 | 38 | 7 | 1099 | 114 | 35.45 | 1 | 5 | 23 |
| 1975 | 21 | 36 | 6 | 1276 | 138* | 42.53 | 1 | 8 | 14 |
| 1976 | 17 | 28 | 4 | 971 | 88 | 40.45 | 0 | 7 | 13 |
| 1977 | 16 | 25 | 2 | 438 | 87 | 19.04 | 0 | 2 | 19 |
| | 142 | 231 | 39 | 7567 | 153 | 39.41 | 13 | 37 | 140 |

## Centuries (13)

| | | | |
|---|---|---|---|
| 1971 | 104* | v. Leicestershire | at Leicester |
| | 116* | v. Northamptonshire | at Northampton |
| | 102 | v. Yorkshire | at Taunton |
| | 114 | v. Surrey | at Taunton |
| | 103* | v. Indians | at Taunton |
| 1972 | 108 | v. Glamorgan | at Swansea |
| | 108 | v. Warwickshire | at Weston-super-Mare |
| 1972 | 135 | v. Gloucestershire | at Taunton |
| 1973 | 114 | v. Essex | at Taunton |
| | 153 | v. Middlesex | at Lord's |
| | 108 | v. Glamorgan | at Neath |
| 1974 | 114 | v. Leicestershire | at Weston-super-Mare |
| 1975 | 138* | v. Gloucestershire | at Bristol |

## BOWLING

| Seasons | Matches | Overs | Mdns | Runs | Wkts | Avge | Best | 5wI | 10wM |
|---|---|---|---|---|---|---|---|---|---|
| 1971 | 25 | 32 | 9 | 124 | 4 | 31.00 | 3-20 | 0 | 0 |
| 1972 | 19 | 35 | 10 | 128 | 3 | 42.66 | 2-77 | 0 | 0 |
| 1973 | 21 | 159.5 | 29 | 560 | 10 | 56.00 | 2-3 | 0 | 0 |
| 1974 | 23 | 97 | 29 | 255 | 13 | 19.61 | 5-70 | 1 | 0 |
| 1975 | 21 | 290.1 | 87 | 906 | 29 | 31.24 | 4-22 | 0 | 0 |
| 1976 | 17 | 163.1 | 36 | 605 | 15 | 40.33 | 3-35 | 0 | 0 |
| 1977 | 16 | 0.2 | 0 | 8 | 0 | — | — | 0 | 0 |
| | 142 | 777.3 | 200 | 2586 | 74 | 34.94 | 5-70 | 1 | 0 |

1974    5-70    v. Lancashire at Taunton

## TEST MATCHES

### BATTING AND FIELDING

| Season | Versus | M | I | NO | Runs | HS | Avge | 100s | 50s | Ct |
|---|---|---|---|---|---|---|---|---|---|---|
| 1949 | New Zealand | 1 | 1 | 0 | 0 | 0 | 0.00 | 0 | 0 | 0 |
| 1950-51 | Australia | 1 | 2 | 0 | 1 | 1 | 0.50 | 0 | 0 | 1 |
| 1955 | South Africa | 1 | 2 | 0 | 47 | 32 | 23.50 | 0 | 0 | 0 |
| 1957 | West Indies | 2 | 3 | 0 | 89 | 42 | 29.66 | 0 | 0 | 2 |
| 1959 | India | 1 | 1 | 0 | 27 | 27 | 27.00 | 0 | 0 | 4 |
| 1961 | Australia | 1 | 2 | 0 | 41 | 33 | 20.50 | 0 | 0 | 2 |
| 1963 | West Indies | 5 | 10 | 0 | 315 | 70 | 31.50 | 0 | 3 | 2 |
| 1966 | West Indies | 1 | 1 | 0 | 4 | 4 | 4.00 | 0 | 0 | 1 |
| 1967 | India and Pakistan | 6 | 9 | 1 | 197 | 47 | 24.62 | 0 | 0 | 8 |
| 1976 | West Indies | 3 | 6 | 1 | 166 | 60 | 33.20 | 0 | 1 | 4 |
| | | 22 | 37 | 2 | 887 | 70 | 25.34 | 0 | 4 | 24 |

### BOWLING

| Seasons | Matches | Overs | Mdns | Runs | Wkts | Avge | Best | 5wI | 10wM |
|---|---|---|---|---|---|---|---|---|---|
| 1949 | 1 | 42 | 14 | 85 | 1 | 85.00 | 1-39 | 0 | 0 |
| 1950-51 | 1 | 9.2 | 1 | 28 | 1 | 28.00 | 1-20 | 0 | 0 |
| 1957 | 2 | 2 | 1 | 8 | 0 | — | — | 0 | 0 |
| 1959 | 1 | 16 | 1 | 53 | 5 | 10.60 | 4-35 | 0 | 0 |
| 1961 | 1 | 8 | 1 | 33 | 0 | — | — | 0 | 0 |
| 1963 | 5 | 25 | 5 | 88 | 0 | — | — | 0 | 0 |
| 1966 | 1 | 12 | 3 | 28 | 1 | 28.00 | 1-21 | 0 | 0 |
| 1967 | 6 | 87.4 | 30 | 209 | 10 | 20.90 | 4-68 | 0 | 0 |
| | 18 | 202 | 56 | 532 | 18 | 29.55 | 4-35 | 0 | 0 |

## ALL FIRST-CLASS MATCHES

| Matches | Innings | NO | Runs | HS | Avge | 100s | 50s | Ct/St |
|---|---|---|---|---|---|---|---|---|
| 786 | 1225 | 173 | 34994 | 198 | 33.26 | 52 | 171 | 813/1 |

| Overs | Maidens | Runs | Wkts | Avge | Best | 5Wi | 10Wm |
|---|---|---|---|---|---|---|---|
| 11661.5 | 3602 | 30947 | 1171 | 26.42 | 8-41 | 43 | 3 |

## LIST A: YORKSHIRE 1963 TO 1970 AND SOMERSET 1971 TO 1977

| | | |
|---|---|---|
| Yorkshire debut: | Gillette Cup v. Nottinghamshire at Middlesbrough | May 22, 1963 |
| Last played: | John Player League v. Somerset at Harrogate | September 13, 1970 |
| Somerset debut: | John Player League v. Leicestershire at Leicester | May 2, 1971 |
| Last played: | John Player League v. Gloucestershire at Taunton | August 28, 1977 |

### YORKSHIRE BATTING AND FIELDING

| Season | M | I | NO | Runs | HS | Avge | 100s | 50s | Ct |
|---|---|---|---|---|---|---|---|---|---|
| 1963 | 2 | 2 | 1 | 58 | 29* | 58.00 | 0 | 0 | 0 |
| 1964 | 1 | 1 | 0 | 1 | 1 | 1.00 | 0 | 0 | 1 |
| 1965 | 4 | 4 | 1 | 128 | 79 | 42.66 | 0 | 1 | 1 |
| 1966 | 1 | 1 | 0 | 29 | 29 | 29.00 | 0 | 0 | 0 |
| 1967 | 1 | 1 | 0 | 1 | 1 | 1.00 | 0 | 0 | 1 |
| 1968 | 1 | 1 | 0 | 10 | 10 | 10.00 | 0 | 0 | 0 |
| 1969 | 12 | 12 | 0 | 263 | 96 | 21.91 | 0 | 2 | 8 |
| 1970 | 10 | 9 | 0 | 141 | 28 | 15.66 | 0 | 0 | 3 |
| | 32 | 31 | 2 | 631 | 96 | 21.75 | 0 | 3 | 14 |

## YORKSHIRE BOWLING

| Seasons | Matches | Overs | Mdns | Runs | Wkts | Avge | Best | 5wI |
|---|---|---|---|---|---|---|---|---|
| 1963 | 2 | 30 | 3 | 102 | 6 | 17.00 | 4-60 | 1 |
| 1964 | 1 | 11 | 1 | 35 | 2 | 17.50 | 2-35 | 0 |
| 1965 | 4 | 17 | 6 | 47 | 2 | 23.50 | 1-12 | 0 |
| 1966 | 1 | 12 | 6 | 22 | 1 | 22.00 | 1-22 | 0 |
| 1967 | 1 | 2 | 0 | 8 | 2 | 4.00 | 2-8 | 0 |
| 1968 | 1 | 12 | 1 | 30 | 0 | — | — | 0 |
| 1969 | 12 | 48 | 11 | 162 | 7 | 23.14 | 3-36 | 0 |
| 1970 | 10 | 20 | 3 | 69 | 3 | 23.00 | 3-27 | 0 |
| | 32 | 152 | 31 | 475 | 23 | 20.65 | 4-60 | 1 |

### 4 wickets in an innings (1)

1963    4-60    v. Sussex    at Hove

## SOMERSET BATTING AND FIELDING

| Season | M | I | NO | Runs | HS | Avge | 100s | 50s | Ct |
|---|---|---|---|---|---|---|---|---|---|
| 1971 | 16 | 15 | 4 | 467 | 89* | 42.45 | 0 | 3 | 2 |
| 1972 | 20 | 20 | 1 | 484 | 88 | 25.47 | 0 | 2 | 8 |
| 1973 | 18 | 17 | 1 | 313 | 76 | 19.56 | 0 | 1 | 6 |
| 1974 | 24 | 24 | 0 | 630 | 131 | 26.25 | 2 | 0 | 2 |
| 1975 | 23 | 21 | 0 | 308 | 55 | 14.66 | 0 | 1 | 9 |
| 1976 | 19 | 18 | 1 | 391 | 69 | 23.00 | 0 | 1 | 8 |
| 1977 | 6 | 4 | 1 | 65 | 28* | 21.66 | 0 | 0 | 2 |
| | 126 | 119 | 8 | 2658 | 131 | 23.94 | 2 | 8 | 37 |

### Centuries (2)

| 1974 | 128 | v. Gloucestershire | at Bristol |
|---|---|---|---|
| | 131 | v. Yorkshire at Bath | |

## SOMERSET BOWLING

| Seasons | Overs | Mdns | Runs | Wkts | Avge | Best | 5wI |
|---|---|---|---|---|---|---|---|
| 1971 | 55 | 8 | 206 | 11 | 18.72 | 3-17 | 0 |
| 1972 | 66.4 | 10 | 273 | 11 | 24.81 | 3-25 | 0 |
| 1973 | 96.4 | 5 | 440 | 19 | 23.15 | 4-9 | 1 |
| 1975 | 3 | 0 | 21 | 0 | — | — | 0 |
| | 221.2 | 23 | 940 | 41 | 22.92 | 4-9 | 1 |

### 4 wickets in an innings (1)

1973    4-9    v. Glamorgan    at Taunton

## ENGLAND BATTING AND FIELDING

| Season | M | I | NO | Runs | HS | Avge | 100s | 50s | Ct |
|---|---|---|---|---|---|---|---|---|---|
| 1972 | 3 | 3 | 0 | 49 | 43 | 16.33 | 0 | 0 | 1 |

## ENGLAND BOWLING

| Season | Matches | Overs | Mdns | Runs | Wkts | Avge | Best | 5wI |
|---|---|---|---|---|---|---|---|---|
| 1972 | 3 | 3 | 0 | 21 | 0 | — | — | 0 |

## ALL LIST A MATCHES
### BATTING, FIELDING AND BOWLING

| M | I | NO | Runs | HS | Avge | 100s | 50s | Ct | Overs | M | Runs | Wkts | Avge | Best |
|---|---|---|---|---|---|---|---|---|---|---|---|---|---|---|
| 164 | 156 | 11 | 3458 | 131 | 23.84 | 2 | 11 | 53 | 376.3 | 54 | 1436 | 66 | 21.75 | 4-9 |

# BOB APPLEYARD MBE

## By Stephen Chalke

Bob Appleyard never gave up. On the cricket field, in the committee room, whatever he took on, he was a battler who refused to accept defeat. His approach was not always comfortable for those around him, certainly not for those whose views he opposed, but that never deterred him.

His cricket career was an extraordinary one. A Bradford League medium-pace bowler, he did not play for Yorkshire till he was 26. Yet in 1951, his first full season, he not only filled the gap left by opening bowler Alec Coxon, but he also became the county's off-spinner in the absence of Brian Close, who was away on National Service. Always wanting the ball in his hands, he got through an exhausting 1,323 overs and took 200 wickets. It was an achievement that became all the more astonishing when in May the following year he was diagnosed with advanced tuberculosis; he had been bowling with the whole top half of his left lung missing.

Few gave him any chance of returning to cricket. He underwent major surgery and had to learn to walk again after 11 months in bed. Yet back he came in 1954, and he confounded all expectations, taking 154 wickets and winning his first Test cap. Bob always said that he was more proud of his return that summer than he was of the 200 wickets. His success gave inspiration to fellow TB sufferers.

He could have done with a winter's rest but, instead, he was on the boat to Australia, winning selection ahead of Jim Laker on Len Hutton's triumphant Ashes-winning tour. The eight-ball overs, the heat and the unsuitable pitches were fresh challenges, but Bob was a thinking bowler and he adapted. The headlines were won by the fast bowlers, Frank Tyson and Brian Statham, but he took vital wickets, all of them top-six batsmen, and he topped the bowling averages. Then at Auckland, at the end of the six-month tour, he was the principal destroyer when England bowled out New Zealand for 26.

Injuries plagued his career thereafter, and he retired in 1958. His final

First Class bowling figures – 708 wickets at 15.48 each – have been bettered since the First World War by only Hedley Verity.

He went into business, as a salesman in the packaging industry, and he made a great success of that.

Then in 1984 he joined the Yorkshire committee. It was a time of turmoil, and soon enough he became an implacable foe of the Boycott camp.

But despite the debilitating arguments he brought back from Australia the idea of an Academy for promising young players, and he drew on his commercial experience to raise funds for its establishment.

**FIGHTER AND VISIONARY: Bob overcame tuberculosis to go on the 1954-55 Ashes tour,and later pioneered the drive to found and finance Yorkshire Academy.**
*(Mick Pope Archive.)*

That was Bob at his best: visionary, full of single-minded determination, seeing obstacles only as challenges to overcome, committed to improving the world for future generations. How fitting that he lived to see a Yorkshire team, almost all of whom had come through the Academy, crowned champions in 2014. He had turned down offers to write a book in 1955, feeling that he was too young and knew too little, and the detail of his remarkable story was almost lost to history. By the time Derek Hodgson started work with him in the late 1990s there were no longer any publishers interested. "Who's Bob Appleyard?" they asked.

I was brought in to take over the project. Initially, I was unsure whether he and I would hit it off; he did not sound my type of person at all. How wrong I was! Yes, he was exhausting at times. He insisted that we never wasted a minute during my stays at his house, and he went through every word of each submitted chapter with painstaking rigour. But at the heart of it all was a perfectionism – second-best was never good enough for Bob – and that suited me well. Also, more than any other cricketer I have worked with, he was keen to know about all the stages of the book, right through to the printing and the selling. It was the same curiosity that led him as a cricketer to learn yoga techniques and to develop a theory of peak concentration.

He was reluctant to include the tragedies of his childhood. He had bottled up the worst of them for more than half a century, not even sharing the trauma with his family, and that created a dilemma for me. So much of his personality, not least his unflinching Christian faith, was moulded by those experiences and, thankfully, after some persuasion, he approved the chapter. In the event he was relieved by the unburdening, especially when he discovered that his family had known all along.

We called the book *No Coward Soul* from the last poem written by Emily Bronte before her death from tuberculosis, and it was named as the *Wisden* Book of the Year. It brought Bob back into the spotlight, and nothing gave him greater pride than his appointment as Yorkshire President in 2006. He was now in his 80s, caring for his wife Connie, but he undertook all his duties with typical conscientiousness. He hoped, of course, that as President he might influence the future direction of the Club – he was still burning "to put things right" – but that was not to be.

In the 1980s, if the waters had been less choppy, he might have made an outstanding Chief Executive of Yorkshire. He had the business acumen, the cricketing knowledge, the vision, and he was never one who was stuck in the past. He knew that cricket had to adapt to new challenges, just as he had done throughout his life.

Bob was a special man: devoted to his family, loyal to his friends, committed to his faith and to his sense of right and wrong. I originally suggested calling the book *A Bloody-Minded Yorkshireman* – it was what the rogue tycoon Robert Maxwell had called him during a court case that Bob won – but then I came up with *No Coward Soul*.

**'No coward soul is mine, No trembler in the world's storm-troubled sphere.'**

That was perfect for Bob's story.

*There was a packed congregation for a service of Thanksgiving and Celebration of the life of Bob at The Priory Church of St Mary and St Cuthbert, Bolton Abbey, on March 31.

The Welcome and Opening Prayer were said by the Rector, the Rev. Simon Cowling, who also preached the sermon, and the prayers were led by the Rev. James Turnbull, who also paid a tribute. The readings were given by Mike Vineall and Sidney Fielden, a Vice-President of Yorkshire CCC and a close friend of Bob's.

| Bob Appleyard | Born: June 27, 1924 |
|---|---|
| | Died: March 17, 2015 |

# ROBERT (Bob) APPLEYARD

## FIRST CLASS CRICKET FOR YORKSHIRE 1950 TO 1958

Right-hand batsman.     Right-arm off-break bowler and medium pace bowler
Born: Wibsey, Bradford   June 27, 1924
Died: Harrogate       March 17, 2015
Debut:       v. Scotland       at Edinburgh  July 12, 1950
Last played: v. Northamptonshire  at Bradford   June 7, 1958
Yorkshire Cap: August 13, 1951

### BATTING AND FIELDING

| Season | M | I | NO | Runs | HS | Avge | 100s | 50s | Ct |
|--------|-----|-----|-----|------|-----|-------|------|-----|-----|
| 1950 | 3 | 3 | 2 | 16 | 8* | 16.00 | 0 | 0 | 0 |
| 1951 | 31 | 22 | 4 | 104 | 21* | 5.77 | 0 | 0 | 11 |
| 1952 | 1 | 0 | 0 | 0 | — | | 0 | 0 | 1 |
| 1954 | 27 | 27 | 11 | 161 | 34* | 10.06 | 0 | 0 | 15 |
| 1955 | 15 | 16 | 9 | 54 | 9 | 7.71 | 0 | 0 | 6 |
| 1956 | 25 | 25 | 8 | 86 | 28 | 5.05 | 0 | 0 | 19 |
| 1957 | 22 | 22 | 8 | 179 | 63 | 12.78 | 0 | 1 | 14 |
| 1958 | 9 | 7 | 1 | 79 | 21* | 13.16 | 0 | 0 | 4 |
| | 133 | 122 | 43 | 679 | 63 | 8.59 | 0 | 1 | 70 |

### BOWLING

| Seasons | Matches | Overs | Mdns | Runs | Wkts | Avge | Best | 5wI | 10wM |
|---------|---------|-------|------|------|------|------|------|-----|------|
| 1950 | 3 | 83.4 | 18 | 177 | 11 | 16.09 | 4-47 | 0 | 0 |
| 1951 | 31 | 1323.2 | 394 | 2829 | 200 | 14.14 | 8-76 | 20 | 9 |
| 1952 | 1 | 16 | 4 | 28 | 1 | 28.00 | 1-28 | 0 | 0 |
| 1954 | 27 | 928 | 293 | 2018 | 141 | 14.31 | 7-16 | 14 | 4 |
| 1955 | 15 | 511 | 171 | 1028 | 83 | 12.38 | 7-29 | 9 | 3 |
| 1956 | 25 | 839.4 | 250 | 1883 | 110 | 17.11 | 7-46 | 7 | 1 |
| 1957 | 22 | 613.5 | 152 | 1568 | 74 | 21.18 | 6-35 | 3 | 0 |
| 1958 | 9 | 151.2 | 43 | 372 | 22 | 16.90 | 5-23 | 1 | 0 |
| | 133 | 4466.1 | 1325 | 9903 | 642 | 15.42 | 8-76 | 54 | 17 |

### 10 wickets in a match(17)

| | | | | |
|------|--------|----------|------|------|
| 1951 | 10-110 | (5-71 and 5-39) | v. Worcestershire | at Huddersfield |
| | 11-131 | (7-84 and 4-47) | v. Gloucestershire | at Bradford |
| | 12-94 | (6-59 and 6-35) | v. Somerset | at Taunton |
| | 10-174 | (5-81 and 5-93) | v. Surry | at Leeds |
| | 12-93 | (5-36 and 7-57) | v. Leicestershire | at Leicester |
| | 12-43 | (6-17 and 6-26) | v. Essex | at Bradford |
| | 10- 87 | (4-55 and 6-32) | v. Hampshire | at Leeds |
| | 11-127 | (5-43 and 6-84) | v. Northamptonshire | at Northampton |
| | 11-181 | (8-76 and 3-105) | v. MCC | at Scarborough |
| 1954 | 12-88 | (5-72 and 7-16) | v. Somerset | at Taunton |
| | 10-54 | (3-19 and 7-35) | v. Hampshire | at Bradford |
| | 10-103 | (6-62 and 4-41) | v. Middlesex | at Leeds |
| | 11-124 | (7-44 and 5-80) | v. MCC | at Scarborough |
| 1955 | 11-48 | (6-25 and 5-23) | v. Northamptonshire | at Bradford |
| | 10-110 | (4-19 and 6-91) | v. Gloucestershire | at Bradford |
| | 10-80 | (5-51 and 5-29) | v. Derbyshire | at Chesterfield |
| 1956 | 12-106 | (6-37 and 6-69) | v. Derbyshire | at Chesterfield |

**5 wickets in an innings** *(not included in above)* **(26). Total 54**

| 1951 | 6-38 | v. South Africans | at Bradford |
|------|------|-------------------|-------------|
| | 5-51 | v. Essex | at Brentwood |
| | 5-44 | v. Glamorgan | at Leeds |
| | 5-42 | v. Derbyshire | at Harrogate |
| | 5-31 | v. Sussex | at Hove |
| 1954 | 6-32 | v. Warwickshire | at Coventry |
| | 6-71 | v. Derbyshire | at Chesterfield |
| | 5-51 | v. Essex | at Romford |
| | 5-24 | v. Northamptonshire | at Northampton |
| | 5-53 | v. Worcestershire | at Sheffield |
| | 7-33 | v. Lancashire | at Manchester |
| | 6-36 | v. Essex | at Scarborough |
| | 6-12 | v. Hampshire | at Bournemouth |
| 1955 | 5-21 | v. Sussex | at Leeds |
| | 5-45 | v. Sussex | at Hove |
| | 7-29 | v. Surrey | at The Oval |
| | 6-51 | v. Middlesex | at Lord's |
| 1956 | 5-78 | v. Gloucestershire | at Sheffield |
| | 6-31 | v. Surrey | at The Oval |
| | 7-48 | v. Warwickshire | at Bradford |
| | 5-69 | v. Hampshire | at Hull |
| | 5-49 | v. Nottinghamshire | at Nottingham |
| 1957 | 6-60 | v. Middlesex | at Lord's |
| | 6-35 | v. Leicestershire | at Hull |
| | 5-18 | v. Glamorgan | at Cardiff |
| 1958 | 5-23 | v. Cambridge University | at Cambridge |

# TEST MATCHES

## BATTING AND FIELDING

| Season | Versus | M | I | NO | Runs | HS | Avge | 100s | 50s | Ct |
|--------|--------|---|---|----|------|-----|------|------|-----|----|
| 1954 | Pakistan | 1 | 0 | 0 | 0 | — | — | 0 | 0 | 0 |
| 1954-55 | Australia | 4 | 5 | 3 | 44 | 19* | 22.00 | 0 | 0 | 4 |
| 1954-55 | New Zealand | 2 | 2 | 1 | 6 | 6 | 6.00 | 0 | 0 | 0 |
| 1955 | South Africa | 1 | 1 | 1 | 0 | 0* | — | 0 | 0 | 0 |
| 1956 | Australia | 1 | 1 | 1 | 1 | 1* | — | 0 | 0 | 0 |
| | | 9 | 9 | 6 | 51 | 111 | 17.00 | 0 | 0 | 4 |

## BOWLING

| Seasons | Matches | Overs | Mdns | Runs | Wkts | Avge | Best | 5wI | 10wM |
|---------|---------|-------|------|------|------|------|------|-----|------|
| 1954 | 1 | 47.4 | 13 | 123 | 7 | 17.57 | 5-51 | 1 | 0 |
| 1954-55 | 4 | 105.2 | 22 | 224 | 11 | 20.36 | 3-13 | 0 | 0 |
| 1954-55 | 2 | 36 | 12 | 80 | 9 | 8.88 | 4-7 | 0 | 0 |
| 1955 | 1 | 47 | 13 | 78 | 2 | 39.00 | 2-46 | 0 | 0 |
| 1956 | 1 | 30 | 10 | 49 | 2 | 24.50 | 2-17 | 0 | 0 |
| | 9 | 266 | 70 | 554 | 31 | 17.87 | 5-51 | 1 | 0 |

## ALL FIRST-CLASS MATCHES

| Matches | Innings | NO | Runs | HS | Avge | 100s | 50s | Ct/St |
|---------|---------|-----|------|-----|------|------|-----|-------|
| 152 | 145 | 54 | 776 | 63 | 8.52 | 0 | 1 | 80 |

| Overs | Maidens | Runs | Wkts | Avge | Best | 5Wi | 10Wm |
|-------|---------|------|------|------|------|-----|------|
| 4994.4 | 1470 | 10965 | 708 | 15.48 | 8-76 | 57 | 17 |

# TED LESTER

Ted Lester, left, at 92 the doyen of Yorkshire County Cricket Club's capped players, died on March 23, 2015, in his home town of Scarborough where he had lived all his life. An honorary life member of Yorkshire CCC, Ted gave almost half a century of loyal and continuous service to his county.

He was a hard-hitting right-hand batsman for the Club between 1945 and 1956, after which he became second-team captain in 1958 before taking over as first-team scorer. He did the job full time until current scorer John Potter filled in for away matches from 1989 onwards, and he put away his pencil at the end of the 1992 season.

He remained very much in touch with how the team were faring, and he was a familiar figure on his old stamping ground at North Marine Road whenever Yorkshire were playing at Scarborough.

He set many batting records for Scarborough Cricket Club, and whether he was playing for club or county his attacking style was much appreciated by spectators who knew they were in for an entertaining time while he was at the crease.

In the golden summer of 1947 Ted finished third in the national averages to the great Middlesex and England pair, Denis Compton and Bill Edrich, who each scored over 3,000 First Class runs. Ted turned out in only 11 first-team matches that season, but he still averaged 73, which was exactly the same as he did in the second team. That season he plundered a century in each innings against Northamptonshire at Wantage Road, and the following year he performed the feat again, this time against Lancashire at Old Trafford — an achievement no other Yorkshire batsman has equalled since in a *Roses* encounter.

He played in 232 matches for Yorkshire, scoring 10,616 runs and hitting 24 centuries, six of them in 1952, when he hammered out 1,786 runs and averaged 49.61. Ted was in even better form in 1949, when he totalled 1,801 runs and hit his career-best score of 186 against Warwickshire on his home ground at Scarborough.

Just after the Second World War had finished Ted made his debut for Yorkshire in a two-day game arranged against Lancashire at Old Trafford, and he was selected for only one First Class game that season. It was at Scarborough, and it turned out to be the last match in the illustrious career of the great Herbert Sutcliffe.

Ted went on to bat with another Yorkshire and England "great", Len Hutton, and one of his most treasured memories was of when he played against his boyhood hero, Don Bradman, for Yorkshire against the Australians at Bramall Lane, Sheffield. "The Don" scored 54 and 86 while Ted managed 31 and five not out, the game ending in a draw.

Some of Ted's happiest and most satisfying moments during his playing career came when he was appointed second-team captain, and in 1958, his first season in that role, he led them with great pride to the Minor Counties' title with such promising young players as Philip Sharpe, Brian Bolus, Jackie Birkenshaw, Mel Ryan, Don Wilson, Bob Platt, Doug Padgett and "Dickie" Bird.

Yearbook Editor and Yorkshire Vice-President David Warner said: "I have very happy memories of Ted Lester going back to 1975, when I first started covering Yorkshire cricket for the Bradford Telegraph & Argus, The Evening Press at York and the Northern Echo. Ted, my cricket-writing colleague, John Callaghan, and myself, travelled the country to Yorkshire matches together, and we had some marvellous times.

"I learned a great deal about First Class cricket from Ted, who knew the game inside out. He was always happy to pass on his great knowledge, but he was extremely modest about his own career, and would only speak about it if pressed to do so. He was respected by players past and present, and his death is a tremendous loss to Yorkshire cricket."

Ted was a natural at many other sports, including football and table tennis. He was a goalkeeper with Scarborough AFC and he signed amateur forms with Bradford City and Bradford Park Avenue. He knew the Bradford area well, having played cricket for Undercliffe and Keighley at various times during the 1939-45 War.

A service of Celebration and Thanksgiving for Ted was held at Queen

Street Methodist Central Hall, Scarborough. The service was conducted by the Rev. Robert Amos, who gave the eulogy, and tributes were paid by John Callaghan and David Warner.

Ted's widow, Mary, and their family later donated Ted's extensive collection of cricket memorabilia to the Archives section of Yorkshire County Cricket Club, and as a token of the Club's appreciation the family were invited to Headingley for a day during a Championship fixture.

**Edward Ibson Lester**    **Born: February 18, 1923**
**Died: March 23, 2015**

# EDWARD (Ted) IBSON LESTER

## FIRST CLASS CRICKET FOR YORKSHIRE 1945 TO 1956

Right-hand batsman.    Right-arm off-break bowler
Born: Scarborough    February 18, 1923
Died: Scarborough    March 23, 2015
Debut:    v. RAF    at Scarborough  August 29, 1945
Last played: v. Scotland  at Hull    May 16, 1956
Yorkshire Cap: May 13, 1948

### BATTING AND FIELDING

| Season | M | I | NO | Runs | HS | Avge | 100s | 50s | Ct |
|--------|-----|-----|-----|-------|-----|-------|------|-----|-----|
| 1945 | 1 | 1 | 0 | 12 | 12 | 12.00 | 0 | 0 | 0 |
| 1946 | 2 | 3 | 0 | 54 | 47 | 18.00 | 0 | 0 | 0 |
| 1947 | 7 | 11 | 2 | 657 | 142 | 73.00 | 3 | 3 | 1 |
| 1948 | 30 | 45 | 3 | 1256 | 149 | 29.90 | 4 | 4 | 15 |
| 1949 | 30 | 49 | 3 | 1774 | 186 | 38.56 | 4 | 8 | 7 |
| 1950 | 28 | 43 | 2 | 1015 | 89 | 24.75 | 0 | 5 | 21 |
| 1951 | 29 | 35 | 2 | 925 | 118 | 28.03 | 1 | 7 | 12 |
| 1952 | 26 | 42 | 6 | 1786 | 178 | 49.61 | 6 | 8 | 14 |
| 1953 | 29 | 44 | 4 | 1380 | 137 | 34.50 | 2 | 9 | 13 |
| 1954 | 29 | 43 | 5 | 1330 | 163 | 35.00 | 4 | 2 | 17 |
| 1955 | 16 | 22 | 0 | 410 | 54 | 18.63 | 0 | 3 | 5 |
| 1956 | 1 | 1 | 0 | 17 | 17 | 17.00 | 0 | 0 | 0 |
| | 228 | 339 | 27 | 10616 | 186 | 34.02 | 24 | 49 | 105 |

### BOWLING

| Seasons | Overs | Mdns | Runs | Wkts | Avge | Best | 5wI |
|---------|-------|------|------|------|-------|------|-----|
| 1947 | 16 | 2 | 55 | 1 | 55.00 | 1-7 | 0 |
| 1948 | 13 | 3 | 41 | 1 | 41.00 | 1-10 | 0 |
| 1949 | 15 | 6 | 26 | 0 | — | — | 0 |
| 1950 | 2 | 0 | 7 | 0 | — | — | 0 |
| 1953 | 6 | 1 | 21 | 0 | — | — | 0 |
| 1955 | 3 | 1 | 10 | 1 | 10.00 | 1-10 | 0 |
| | 55 | 13 | 160 | 3 | 53.33 | 1-7 | 0 |

| | | | |
|---|---|---|---|
| 1947 | 127 | v. Derbyshire | at Scarborough |
| | 126 | v. Northamptonshire | at Northampton (1st innings) |
| | 142 | v. Northamptonshire | at Northampton (2nd innings) |
| 1948 | 149 | v. Oxford University | at Oxford |
| | 110 | v. Gloucestershire | at Bristol |
| | 125* | v. Lancashire | at Manchester (1st innings) |
| | 132 | v. Lancashire | at Manchester (2nd innings) |
| 1949 | 112 | v. Sussex | at Leeds |
| | 102 | v. Essex | at Colchester |
| | 140* | v. Derbyshire | at Bradford |
| 1950 | 186 | v. Warwickshire | at Scarborough |
| 1951 | 118 | v. Nottinghamshire | at Sheffield |
| 1952 | 130* | v. Leicestershire | at Sheffield |
| | 101* | v. Nottinghamshire | at Sheffield |
| | 178 | v. Nottinghamshire | at Nottingham |
| | 110* | v. Indians | at Sheffield |
| | 109 | v. Hampshire | at Scarborough |
| | 130* | v. Surrey | at Leeds |
| 1953 | 157 | v. Cambridge University | at Hull |
| | 103* | v. Surrey | at Leeds |
| 1954 | 150 | v. Oxford University | at Oxford |
| | 121* | v. Derbyshire | at Chesterfield |
| | 163 | v. Essex | at Romford |
| | 142 | v. Surrey | at The Oval |

**ALL FIRST-CLASS MATCHES**

| Matches | Innings | NO | Runs | HS | Avge | 100s | 50s | Ct/St |
|---|---|---|---|---|---|---|---|---|
| 232 | 347 | 28 | 10912 | 186 | 34.20 | 25 | 50 | 108 |

| Overs | Maidens | Runs | Wkts | Avge | Best | 5Wi |
|---|---|---|---|---|---|---|
| 55 | 13 | 160 | 3 | 53.33 | 1-71 | 0 |

**ONLY LIST A MATCH**

v. Middlesex at Lord's    May 27, 1964    Score 0    Catches 0    Did not bowl

# MEL RYAN

Melville (Mel) Ryan, the Huddersfield-born-and-bred fast bowler who played in four of Yorkshire's Championship-winning seasons, died in Kirkland Hospice, Kirklees, on November 16, 2015, aged 82.

Mel played in 150 First Class matches for Yorkshire between 1954 and 1965, capturing 423 wickets at 22.92 runs apiece with a best return of 7-45 against Warwickshire at Edgbaston in 1958. He claimed five wickets in an innings 12 times, and twice took 10 in a match.

A tall, willing and hard-working pace-man, Mel shared the new ball with Fred Trueman on many occasions. Although he first played in 1954, he did not gain a regular first-team place until 1960. He did, however, take 21 Championship wickets in 1959 when Yorkshire, under Ronnie Burnet, lifted the title to end Surrey's record run of seven consecutive Championship successes.

Mel went on to play in three further Championship-winning seasons, taking 37 wickets in 1960, 74 in 1962 and 63 in 1963. After retiring from First Class cricket he joined the Yorkshire Committee as a Huddersfield district member in 1974, and served until 1982. He was on the cricket committee from 1975 to 1980.

Together with his elder brother, Granville, Mel was a partner in the Huddersfield-based family news agency chain, Ryan's. The business ran for more than a century, having been set up by his father, John, and mother, Cora. Mel, who lived in Almondbury, Huddersfield, left a widow, June, a daughter, Clare, and three grandchildren. Mel and June also had a son, James, who died in a skiing accident in the Italian Alps in March 2010.

Former Yorkshire players who attended the funeral service at Fixby Crematorium were Bob Platt, Bryan Stott, Geoff Cope, Richard Hutton and Keith Gillhouley.

| | |
|---|---|
| **Melville Ryan** | **Born: June 23, 1933** |
| | **Died: November 16, 2015** |

## MELVILLE (Mel) RYAN

### FIRST-CLASS CRICKET FOR YORKSHIRE 1954 TO 1965

Right-hand batsman.  Right-arm pace bowler.
Born: Huddersfield  June 23, 1933
Died: Huddersfield  November 16, 2015
Debut:  v. Combined Services  at Harrogate  July 21, 1954
Last played:  v. Northamptonshire  at Leeds  June 19, 1965
Yorkshire Cap: April 18, 1962

### BATTING AND FIELDING

| Season | M | I | NO | Runs | HS | Avge | 100s | 50s | Ct |
|---|---|---|---|---|---|---|---|---|---|
| 1955 | 5 | 6 | 4 | 26 | 10 | 13.00 | 0 | 0 | 7 |
| 1956 | 6 | 7 | 1 | 6 | 3 | 1.00 | 0 | 0 | 1 |
| 1957 | 3 | 4 | 1 | 17 | 7* | 5.66 | 0 | 0 | 0 |
| 1958 | 8 | 10 | 1 | 32 | 8 | 3.55 | 0 | 0 | 2 |
| 1959 | 7 | 6 | 4 | 42 | 17 | 21.00 | 0 | 0 | 3 |
| 1960 | 15 | 17 | 4 | 82 | 23 | 6.30 | 0 | 0 | 3 |
| 1961 | 23 | 17 | 10 | 53 | 17* | 7.57 | 0 | 0 | 11 |
| 1962 | 24 | 23 | 10 | 83 | 15* | 6.38 | 0 | 0 | 13 |
| 1963 | 32 | 33 | 11 | 217 | 26* | 9.86 | 0 | 0 | 12 |
| 1964 | 23 | 23 | 11 | 112 | 21 | 9.33 | 0 | 0 | 7 |
| 1965 | 3 | 3 | 1 | 12 | 11 | 6.00 | 0 | 0 | 0 |
| | 150 | 149 | 58 | 682 | 26* | 7.49 | 0 | 0 | 59 |

## BOWLING

| Seasons | Matches | Overs | Mdns | Runs | Wkts | Avge | Best | 5wI | 10wM |
|---|---|---|---|---|---|---|---|---|---|
| 1954 | 1 | 23 | 6 | 84 | 3 | 28.00 | 3-84 | 0 | 0 |
| 1955 | 5 | 124.3 | 25 | 330 | 16 | 20.62 | 4-44 | 0 | 0 |
| 1956 | 6 | 165 | 38 | 369 | 19 | 19.42 | 4-32 | 0 | 0 |
| 1957 | 3 | 94 | 19 | 293 | 10 | 29.30 | 3-13 | 0 | 0 |
| 1958 | 8 | 193.4 | 47 | 436 | 25 | 17.44 | 7-45 | 1 | 0 |
| 1959 | 7 | 261.4 | 77 | 640 | 30 | 21.33 | 5-45 | 1 | 0 |
| 1960 | 15 | 421.5 | 122 | 974 | 46 | 21.17 | 7-57 | 2 | 0 |
| 1961 | 23 | 680.5 | 161 | 1707 | 70 | 24.38 | 6-47 | 4 | 1 |
| 1962 | 24 | 767.1 | 189 | 1962 | 81 | 24.22 | 6-33 | 2 | 1 |
| 1963 | 32 | 704.2 | 194 | 1547 | 63 | 24.55 | 4-13 | 0 | 0 |
| 1964 | 23 | 418.3 | 102 | 1006 | 44 | 22.86 | 5-38 | 2 | 0 |
| 1965 | 3 | 44 | 10 | 118 | 6 | 19.66 | 2-28 | 0 | 0 |
| | 150 | 3894 | 990 | 9466 | 413 | 22.92 | 7-45 | 12 | 2 |

### 10 wickets in a match(2)

| 1961 | 10-94 (4-47 and 6-47) | v. Northamptonshire | at Middlesbrough |
|---|---|---|---|
| 1962 | 10-77 (4-44 and 6-33) | v. Leicestershire | at Bradford |

### 5 wickets in an innings (12)

| 1958 | 7-45 | v. Warwickshire | at Birmingham |
|---|---|---|---|
| 1959 | 5-45 | v. Nottinghamshire | at Nottingham |
| 1960 | 6-40 | v. Gloucestershire | at Gloucester |
| | 5-50 | v. Lancashire | at Manchester |
| 1961 | 6-47 | v. Northamptonshire | at Middlesbrough |
| | 6-57 | v. Northamptonshire | at Northampton |
| | 5-55 | v. Sussex | at Bradford |
| | 5-58 | v. Lancashire | at Sheffield |
| 1962 | 6-33 | v. Leicestershire | at Bradford |
| | 5-35 | v. Leicestershire | at Leicester |
| 1964 | 5-72 | v. Leicestershire | at Bradford |
| | 5-38 | v. Hampshire | at Portsmouth |

## LIST A CRICKET FOR YORKSHIRE 1963 TO 1964

| Debut: | Gillette Cup v. Nottinghamshire at Middlesbrough | May 22, 1963 |
|---|---|---|
| Last played: | Gillette Cup v. Middlesex at Lord's | May 27, 1964 |

### BATTING, FIELDING AND BOWLING

| Season | M | I | NO | Runs | HS | Avge | 100s | 50s | Ct | O | M | Runs | W | Avge | Best |
|---|---|---|---|---|---|---|---|---|---|---|---|---|---|---|---|
| 1963 | 2 | 1 | 1 | 6 | 6* | — | 0 | 0 | 3 | 30 | 1 | 117 | 3 | 39.00 | 2-31 |
| 1964 | 1 | 1 | 0 | 1 | 1 | 1.00 | 0 | 0 | 0 | 13 | 2 | 32 | 2 | 16.00 | 2-32 |
| | 3 | 2 | 1 | 7 | 6* | 7.00 | 0 | 0 | 3 | 43 | 3 | 149 | 5 | 29.80 | 2-31 |

# BILL FOORD

Former Yorkshire fast-medium bowler Bill Foord died at his Scarborough home on July 8, 2015, aged 91. Bill played in 51 First Class matches for Yorkshire between 1947 and 1953, claiming 126 wickets at 27.07 runs apiece, and he was one of the first of the great Fred Trueman's bowling partners with the county.

He will always be remembered as one of Scarborough Cricket Club's most loyal servants — and one of their greatest bowlers. In a career at North Marine Road spanning 30 years from 1941 to 1971 he captured 1,071 wickets at 15.07. Until the end of his life Bill was passionately interested in the development of young Scarborough cricketers. He coached them himself for many years, and about 20 years ago he founded and funded the Bill Foord Cricket Coaching Scholarship Scheme, a three-year course which, at the time of his death, had over 40 young players on its books. Bill was an honorary life member of Scarborough Cricket Club as well as being their senior vice-president.

A single and unassuming man, Bill had lived alone since the death of his sister, Betty, over 20 years ago. His association with Scarborough CC had begun at a very early age — the family home was on the corner of Dean Road and Clifton Street, a stone's throw from the ground.

A splendidly accurate bowler who wasted little energy in his short run-up, Bill had the ability to move the ball both ways, and he may well have enjoyed a longer career with Yorkshire had he not decided to continue his teaching career rather than try to attain professional status with his county. He taught for most of his working life at Friaridge Infants and Primary School in Scarborough, and his work commitments prevented him from turning out for Yorkshire on a regular basis.

On his debut against Hampshire he took 1-67 while Bill Bowes captured 5-52, and in the second innings he claimed 3-67. Six years later the sides met at Bournemouth in the last Championship match of the season, and this time Bill enjoyed his career-best return of 6-63, Yorkshire going on to win by an innings and 45 runs. It proved to be Bill's last match in what was his most successful season with 62 wickets at 25.83. During his career he took five wickets or more in an innings five times.

Scarborough CC secretary Colin Adamson, said: "Bill, like Ted Lester who died earlier in the year, was a Scarborough man through and through, and had been closely associated with our club since boyhood. He will be very much missed."

Scarborough CC chairman and Yorkshire CCC Vice-President Bill Mustoe said: "Bill was a great cricketer with the club and a wonderful champion of youngsters playing cricket in the area. He was known and respected as a very good cricketer but, above all, as a true gentleman. He embodied cricket as some still remember it being played in the 1940s and 1950s — as a social event with a code of conduct."

**Charles William (Bill) Foord**     **Born: June 11, 1924**
                                     **Died: July 8, 2015**


# CHARLES WILLIAM (Bill) FOORD

## FIRST CLASS CRICKET FOR YORKSHIRE 1947 TO 1953

Right-hand batsman.     Right-arm fast-medium bowler
Born: Scarborough     June 11, 1924
Died: Scarborough     July 8, 2015

| | | | | |
|---|---|---|---|---|
| First Class Debut | For North v. South | at Harrogate | August 27, 1947 |
| First Class debut for Yorkshire: | v. Hampshire | at Bournemouth | August 30, 1947 |
| Last played: | v. MCC | at Scarborough | September 2, 1953 |

### BATTING AND FIELDING

| Season | M | I | NO | Runs | HS | Avge | 100s | 50s | Ct |
|---|---|---|---|---|---|---|---|---|---|
| 1947 | 1 | 0 | 0 | 0 | — | — | 0 | 0 | 0 |
| 1948 | 4 | 4 | 3 | 0 | 0* | 0.00 | 0 | 0 | 2 |
| 1949 | 6 | 5 | 4 | 13 | 6* | 13.00 | 0 | 0 | 0 |
| 1950 | 1 | 0 | 0 | 0 | — | — | 0 | 0 | 0 |
| 1951 | 6 | 4 | 2 | 22 | 20 | 11.00 | 0 | 0 | 5 |
| 1952 | 7 | 5 | 2 | 9 | 5 | 3.00 | 0 | 0 | 3 |
| 1953 | 26 | 16 | 5 | 70 | 35 | 6.36 | 0 | 0 | 9 |
| | 51 | 34 | 16 | 114 | 35 | 6.33 | 0 | 0 | 19 |

### BOWLING

| Seasons | Matches | Overs | Mdns | Runs | Wkts | Avge | Best | 5wI | 10wM |
|---|---|---|---|---|---|---|---|---|---|
| 1947 | 1 | 40.4 | 9 | 115 | 4 | 28.75 | 3-46 | 0 | 0 |
| 1948 | 4 | 118 | 28 | 264 | 12 | 22.00 | 4-67 | 0 | 0 |
| 1949 | 6 | 185.5 | 31 | 520 | 16 | 32.50 | 5-35 | 1 | 0 |
| 1950 | 1 | 33 | 10 | 74 | 1 | 74.00 | 1-56 | 0 | 0 |
| 1951 | 6 | 117.2 | 32 | 238 | 8 | 29.75 | 3-37 | 0 | 0 |
| 1952 | 7 | 251 | 62 | 599 | 23 | 26.04 | 4-21 | 0 | 0 |
| 1953 | 26 | 622.4 | 165 | 1602 | 62 | 25.83 | 6-63 | 4 | 0 |
| | 51 | 1368.3 | 337 | 3412 | 126 | 27.07 | 6-63 | 5 | 0 |

### 5 wickets in an innings (5)

| | | | |
|---|---|---|---|
| 1949 | 5-35 | v. Gloucestershire | at Huddersfield |
| 1953 | 5-88 | v. Glamorgan | at Cardiff |
| | 4-38 | v. Gloucestershire | at Sheffield |
| 1953 | 5-61 | v. Surrey | at Leeds |
| | 6-63 | v. Hampshire | at Bournemouth |

## ALL FIRST-CLASS MATCHES

| Matches | Innings | NO | Runs | HS | Avge | 100s | 50s | Ct/St |
|---|---|---|---|---|---|---|---|---|
| 52 | 36 | 16 | 125 | 35 | 6.25 | 0 | 0 | 19 |

| Overs | Maidens | Runs | Wkts | Avge | Best | 5Wi | 10Wm |
|---|---|---|---|---|---|---|---|
| 1388.3 | 338 | 3469 | 128 | 27.10 | 6-63 | 5 | 0 |

# KEN SMALES

Ken Smales, an off-spinner who played in 13 games for Yorkshire but went on to make a bigger name for himself with Nottinghamshire, died on March 10, 2015, aged 87. Born in Horsforth on September 15, 1927, Ken was educated at Aireborough Grammar School, and made his First Class debut for Yorkshire against Oxford University at The Parks in 1948, scoring 45 — his highest for the county — and adding 146 for the fifth wicket with Ted Lester, who blasted 149.

Although he was a capable batsman, it was chiefly as an off-spin bowler that he made his mark, playing for Horsforth CC before moving to Bradford League club Keighley, where he took 31 wickets at 21.38. He soon came to the attention of Yorkshire, but with so much spin talent at their disposal he was not called upon at all in 1949 and, despite capturing 5-44 and 2-29 on a spinner's pitch at Bradford Park Avenue against the West Indies in 1950 he was not chosen again.

He moved to Nottinghamshire the following summer, and in eight seasons on mainly unresponsive pitches he claimed 117 wickets, his greatest achievement being all 10 in an innings against Gloucestershire in June 1956. This was the first Championship game to be played on the Erinoid ground at Stroud, but despite Ken's heroic effort Nottinghamshire still lost by nine wickets inside two days.

In 1958 Ken began to work for Nottingham Forest, and became club secretary, a post he held for 30 years during which time the team enjoyed great success during Brian Clough's reign.

|  |  |
|---|---|
| **Ken Smales** | **Born: September 15, 1927** |
|  | **Died: March 10, 2015** |

## KENNETH (KEN) SMALES
### FIRST CLASS CRICKET FOR YORKSHIRE 1948 TO 1950

Right-hand batsman.       Right-arm off-break bowler
Born: Horsforth            September 15, 1927
Died: Torpoint, Cornwall March 10, 2015

| | | |
|---|---|---|
| First Class debut for Yorkshire: | v. Oxford University | at The Parks May 8, 1948 |
| Last played for Yorkshire: | v. West Indies | at Bradford May 10, 1950 |
| First Class debut | | |
| for Nottinghamshire | v. Kent | at Gillingham May 5, 1951 |
| Last played for Nottinghamshire | v. Leicestershire | at Nottingham August 9, 1958 |

### BATTING AND FIELDING

| Season | M | I | NO | Runs | HS | Avge | 100s | 50s | Ct |
|---|---|---|---|---|---|---|---|---|---|
| 1948 | 10 | 13 | 3 | 149 | 45 | 14.90 | 0 | 0 | 4 |
| 1950 | 3 | 6 | 0 | 16 | 7 | 2.66 | 0 | 0 | 0 |
| | 13 | 19 | 3 | 165 | 45 | 10.31 | 0 | 0 | 4 |

## BOWLING

| Seasons | Matches | Overs | Mdns | Runs | Wkts | Avge | Best | 5wI | 10wM |
|---------|---------|-------|------|------|------|------|------|-----|------|
| 1948 | 10 | 222.4 | 56 | 546 | 12 | 45.50 | 5-65 | 1 | 0 |
| 1950 | 3 | 92 | 29 | 220 | 10 | 22.00 | 5-44 | 1 | 0 |
| | 13 | 314.4 | 85 | 766 | 22 | 34.81 | 5-44 | 2 | 0 |

### 5 wickets in an innings (2

| | | | | |
|---|---|---|---|---|
| 1948 | 5-65 | v. Surrey | at The Oval |
| 1950 | 5-44 | v. West Indies | at Bradford |

### NOTTINGHAMSHIRE BATTING AND FIELDING

| Season | M | I | NO | Runs | HS | Avge | 100s | 50s | Ct |
|--------|---|---|----|------|-----|------|------|-----|-----|
| 1951-58 | 148 | 210 | 52 | 2347 | 64 | 14.85 | 0 | 4 | 56 |

### BOWLING

| Seasons | Matches | Overs | Mdns | Runs | Wkts | Avge | Best | 5wI | 10wM |
|---------|---------|-------|------|------|------|------|------|-----|------|
| 1951-58 | 148 | 4541.5 | 1505 | 11180 | 367 | 30.46 | 10-66 | 18 | 5 |

### ALL FIRST-CLASS MATCHES

| Matches | Innings | NO | Runs | HS | Avge | 100s | 50s | Ct/St |
|---------|---------|-----|------|-----|------|------|-----|-------|
| 161 | 229 | 55 | 2512 | 64 | 14.43 | 0 | 4 | 60 |

| Overs | Maidens | Runs | Wkts | Avge | Best | 5Wi | 10Wm |
|-------|---------|------|------|------|------|-----|------|
| 4856.3 | 1590 | 11946 | 389 | 30.70 | 10-66 | 20 | 5 |

# PHILIP HODGSON

Philip Hodgson, the tallest of Yorkshire's armoury of fast bowlers in the mid-1950s, died on March 30, 2015, aged 79. Philip, who was born in Todmorden and had lived in Hornsea for many years, stood 6ft 8in tall and played in 13 matches for Yorkshire between 1954 and 1960.

He would probably have had a much longer career for his county had he not faced strong competition from a battery of talented bowlers including Fred Trueman, Bob Appleyard, Brian Close, Mike Cowan, Bob Platt and Mel Ryan. Nevertheless, Philip was able to recall several notable achievements in what was a very happy time for him, and he remembered those days with pride throughout his life.

In Yorkshire's match against the Pakistanis at Bramall Lane in June 1954 he twice claimed the considerable scalp of Hanif Mohammad — and caught by Norman Yardley — after sharing the new ball with Close. Yorkshire went on to win by seven wickets, the tourists being made to follow-on after Close had hit an unbeaten 123 in the first innings.

Philip made his debut for Yorkshire in the previous game against Essex at Romford, which the visitors won by eight wickets. He opened the bowling with Appleyard, claiming 3-43 in the first innings while his more experienced partner captured 3-58, and followed up with 5-51. Ted Lester thrashed 163 in Yorkshire's 386-9 before Essex followed on. Sadly, Appleyard, Lester and Hodgson were all to die within a month of each other. There was a notable end to Philip's county career when in his last match against Kent in August 1956 he clean bowled Colin Cowdrey for eight in a rain-hit draw. His best bowling return was 5-41 against Sussex at Hove in 1954.

Philip, who had served in the RAF, also turned out for Combined Services, and at Cardiff Arms Park in 1956 he took 4-29 in Glamorgan's first innings. He played league cricket with Sheffield United from 1951, and also enjoyed spells with Pudsey St Lawrence, Almondbury, York and Hull up to his retirement from the game in 1982.

He was a teacher for many years in the Hornsea and Hull areas, and his pastimes included building model aeroplanes.

|  |  |
|---|---|
| **Philip Hodgson** | **Born: September 21, 1935** |
| | **Died: March 30, 2015** |

# PHILIP HODGSON
## FIRST CLASS CRICKET FOR YORKSHIRE 1954 TO 1956

Right-hand batsman. Right-arm fast-medium bowler
Born: Todmorden September 21, 1935
Died: March 30, 2015

| | | | |
|---|---|---|---|
| First Class debut for Yorkshire: | v. Essex | at Romford | June 23, 1954 |
| Last played for Yorkshire: | v. Kent | at Scarborough | August 1, 1956 |
| Last First Class Match: | | | |
| for Combined Services | v. Warwickshire | at Birmingham | August 14, 1957 |

### BATTING AND FIELDING

| Season | M | I | NO | Runs | HS | Avge | 100s | 50s | Ct |
|---|---|---|---|---|---|---|---|---|---|
| 1954 | 7 | 1 | 0 | 8 | 8 | 8.00 | 0 | 0 | 2 |
| 1955 | 2 | 2 | 0 | 6 | 6 | 3.00 | 0 | 0 | 2 |
| 1956 | 4 | 3 | 2 | 19 | 8* | 19.00 | 0 | 0 | 2 |
| | 13 | 6 | 2 | 33 | 8* | 8.25 | 0 | 0 | 6 |

### BOWLING

| Seasons | Matches | Overs | Mdns | Runs | Wkts | Avge | Best | 5wI | 10wM |
|---|---|---|---|---|---|---|---|---|---|
| 1954 | 7 | 123.3 | 32 | 363 | 17 | 21.35 | 5-41 | 1 | 0 |
| 1955 | 2 | 52.4 | 7 | 173 | 2 | 86.50 | 1-39 | 0 | 0 |
| 1956 | 4 | 51 | 13 | 112 | 3 | 37.33 | 2- 6 | 0 | 0 |
| | 13 | 227.1 | 52 | 648 | 22 | 29.45 | 5-41 | 1 | 0 |

#### 5 wickets in an innings (1

| | | | |
|---|---|---|---|
| 1954 | 5-41 | v. Sussex | at Hove |

### ALL FIRST-CLASS MATCHES

| Matches | Innings | NO | Runs | HS | Avge | 100s | 50s | Ct/St |
|---|---|---|---|---|---|---|---|---|
| 17 | 11 | 4 | 65 | 26 | 9.28 | 0 | 0 | 7 |

| Overs | Maidens | Runs | Wkts | Avge | Best | 5Wi | 10Wm |
|---|---|---|---|---|---|---|---|
| 348.5 | 83 | 946 | 39 | 24.25 | 5-41 | 1 | 0 |

# BRIAN TURNER

**LIKE FATHER, LIKE SON: Cyril Turner puts son Brian through his paces in the indoor nets.**
*(Ron Deaton Archive)*

Brian Turner, who died on December 27, aged 77, played in only two First Class matches for Yorkshire, but he was from a family with strong links to the *White Rose* county and he retained a keen interest in the Club and its former players.

Born in Sheffield on July 25, 1938, Brian was a left-hand bat and right-arm medium-fast bowler.

He made his Yorkshire debut against the South Africans at Bramall Lane in 1960, and in 1961 he played at Bristol against Gloucestershire. He made seven runs in four innings, but he captured four wickets at 11.75, and held two catches.

In 1961 he informed Yorkshire that he would be unavailable for further matches because he was studying engineering. He became a senior lecturer and head of mechanical science at Rotherham Technical College.

In 1964 and 1965 he topped the Yorkshire League averages, helping Sheffield United to win the league championship before joining Golcar as professional in 1968. His distinguished career in the Huddersfield League brought him 1,144 wickets at an average of 11.09, and he scored over 3,000 runs in his aggressive style. Brian's father, Cyril, played in 200 matches for Yorkshire between 1925 and 1946, and went on to become the Club's first-team scorer, while his elder brother, Irvine — Brian's uncle — played seven times for the county. Brian was an enthusiastic member of Yorkshire CCC Players' Association.

**Brian Turner**

**Born: July 25, 1938**
**Died: December 27, 2015**

89

# ROBIN FEATHER

Robin Feather, left, a Keighley woolman who captained Yorkshire's Second Eleven and went on to give long service as a Bradford representative on the Club's General Committee, died in Harrogate on July 28, 2015, 82.

Christened Robert Leigh Feather, but known generally as Robin, he was also a Vice-President of Yorkshire County Cricket Club.

He was a former chairman of the finance subcommittee as well as sitting on the cricket subcommittee, but he said in January 1984 that he would not defend his Bradford seat if Geoffrey Boycott were reinstated as a player at the Club's special general meeting. That is exactly what happened, and Robin was as good as his word, former Yorkshire and England bowler Bob Appleyard replacing him without being opposed.

A native of Keighley, he lived at his parents' house on Bradford Road before moving to Braes Castle, Harden, in the early 1960s. He was the son of Leigh Feather, a partner in the Keighley firm of Henderson and Feather, wool merchants and topmakers, on Dalton Lane.

After National Service in the Army he went to Oxford, where he obtained a BA degree studying law, and then went to work with his father in the wool trade, later becoming a director of the firm. He played a lot of cricket in Oxford and in the Army, and he made his debut for Yorkshire Seconds under Ted Lester's captaincy in 1958, when they won the Minor Counties Championship.

He took over the second-team captaincy in 1962, when outstanding young players like Geoffrey Boycott and John Hampshire were beginning to make their mark, and he led the side for four seasons before standing down for business reasons. Also in 1962, he was talked of in some quarters as a possible Yorkshire captain when it was announced in July that Vic Wilson would retire at the end of the season, but the job went to Brian Close, who led the county through a golden period.

Robin was elected to the Yorkshire Committee in 1967, when a vacancy occurred in Bradford District because Herbert Sutcliffe had been made a vice-president, and he gave continuous service until his resignation in 1984. He enjoyed long spells on both the cricket and finance subcommittees, and was chairman of finance in 1982 and 1983, when he also served on the executive committee.

An enthusiastic amateur, Robin enjoyed his batting with the Second Eleven, but was never consistently successful, his highest score being 53 against Durham at Middlesbrough in 1960. He was captain of Harrow School in 1952, leading them to victory by seven wickets over Eton College at Lord's, when he opened the batting and scored 38 and 16.

# PHILIP AKROYD

Yorkshire CCC Vice-President Philip Akroyd, who gave many years of outstanding service on the former General Committee, died on January 5, aged 80. Elected a Vice-President in 2006, he had also been actively involved in Yorkshire Cricket Association Council and then Yorkshire Cricket Board when it was formed in 1996.

Philip and his devoted wife, Patsy, from Mirfield, were among Yorkshire's most loyal supporters, travelling widely to watch their team and never happier than when soaking up the atmosphere from the balcony at Scarborough's North Marine Road.

Philip joined the Yorkshire Committee as a Dewsbury district representative in 1984 following fresh elections as a consequence of the Geoffrey Boycott controversy. He served Dewsbury until the committee was revamped in 1993, when he was returned as a West District representative on the 12-strong body. He served on the Finance and Marketing subcommittee before gaining a place on the Cricket subcommittee in 1995, where he remained until 2001.

A man of strong principles, he then resigned his West District seat because of cuts which had been made to the playing staff. He remained active, and was particularly prominent in encouraging young cricketers from an ethnic background. He served on several YCB subcommittees, including coaching, senior cricket, Centre of Cricket Excellence, disability, women's cricket and BME subcommittees or forums. Always loyal to his roots, he acted as secretary to Heavy Woollen Area Cricket Council in 2002-2003 when no-one else put themselves forward.

Philip's greatest committee commitment was to the Black Minority Ethnic Cricket Forum, where he represented YCA and YCB from 1990 to 2003, seeing the formation and development of all the BME Cricket Development Centres. He developed a particularly close association with the progressive Mount Cricket Club at Batley, where he regularly spoke at their prize presentation nights. Only last year Philip and Patsy were invited to be chief guests at the Club's open day for boys and girls.

Philip was also president of the prestigious Joe Lumb Competition for Under-17 teams from 2003 to 2007, and then a vice-president until his death. A fine batsman in his playing days, Philip was actively connected with Hanging Heaton Cricket Club, and also played for Yorkshire Owls.

# JEWELS GALORE IN MAJESTIC STORY OF COUNTY CRICKET

**By Nigel Pullan**

**SUMMER'S CROWN: The Story of Cricket's County Championship**                                          **Stephen Chalke**
**(Fairfield Books, www.fairfieldbooks.org.uk £20).**

This is an excellent book that I enjoyed reading more than any cricket book I can remember. It is an account of the development of the County Championship from 1890, admittedly a controversial date, but the consensus favours that year. When Stephen Chalke announced the project I wondered how such a familiar subject would be treated. I have a high opinion of his cricket-writing from when I first read his books about Championship matches — *Runs in the Memory* and *Caught in the Memory* — and his biographies of Bob Appleyard, written with Derek Hodgson, and of Geoffrey Howard who managed Len Hutton's Australian tour in 1954-1955. This book is just as good as these.

It is beautifully produced with an abundance of illustrations, and divided into three main sections. First, there is a two-page compact history of each of the 18 counties and some statistics. Colour photographs of a ground for each county show a large crowd at Queen's Park in Chesterfield looking towards the crooked spire, the school buildings at Cheltenham and then, by contrast in black and white, Tivoli Road in Hornsey, where Middlesex played one match, and Kettering, where Bill Bowes took 16-35 in the 1935 game. Stephen lists all the Championship grounds used by each county — a total now at 170. In 1961 cricket was played at 81 Championship venues. This section also gives you all of the counties' Championship positions.

The main section is a history of the Championship decade by decade. A short summary is followed by profiles of five or six players from Bobby Abel, the diminutive batsman from the dock area of Rotherhithe in the 1890s, to Aneurin Donald, currently starting at Glamorgan. The author excels in his stories about players, matches and significant events. Some are in a miscellany of unusual incidents like Andy Ducat running seven, more whippetish than Adam Lyth apparently, or Josiah Coulthurst, the only player never to set foot on the field in his only appearance, if that is the right word, for Lancashire.

He discusses Herbert Sutcliffe's rejection of the Yorkshire captaincy in some detail and who supported him — Major Lupton and Jack Hobbs

— and who opposed him — Lord Hawke and Wilfred Rhodes. He describes Harold Gimblett's debut at Frome, when he missed the bus from Bicknoller and had to hitch a lift in a lorry before making a century at No. 8, and Glamorgan's first Championship success at Dean Park – did umpire Dai Davies really say: "That's out, and we've won the Championship"?

There is a profile of Derek Randall. When Stephen went to meet him during the winter at home he was wearing cricket pads "just to break them in", and so was Mrs Randall. Each county that has had periods of success receives recognition, for example Warwickshire's wonderful year of 1911 under the mercurial Frank Foster, whose later life was so tragic. Post war there are tributes to Essex's travelling caravan pictured in 1949 alongside the county secretary's Rolls Royce. Sussex's years of success and the rise of Durham are also discussed.

*Summer's Crown* is a tribute to those who have played in the Championship over 125 years. The author shows his understanding of character and his range of stories and anecdotes, but above all his affection for the players and the first-class game in all its variety. He writes so well about Lord Hawke, Herbert Sutcliffe and Brian Close as well as loyal county players like Roly Jenkins. The profile of Mike Brearley and his Middlesex side is a good example, and ends with his story of Fred Titmus, aged 49, wearing Radley's flannels and Brearley's socks and boots after being persuaded to play on a day off from his Post Office.

The enjoyment of this book is much enhanced by the illustrations. There are so many, and they are so well chosen. There are simple portraits of players whose names we have heard like Charlie Parker in his wide-brimmed hat and Arthur Booth in triplicate. As Stephen says, if Booth had been picked for Australia in 1946 he might not have caught rheumatic fever in that bitter winter and been forced to retire. There is a lovely picture of Sachin Tendulkar trying on his new Yorkshire cap.

Bradford Park Avenue is shown, packed to the rafters, perhaps not literally, on Whit Monday 1926, and the Blackpool ground in 1908 showing rows and rows of men, all wearing hats and only two women visible on a day when the *Manchester Guardian* reported: "You have skylarks singing immediately above the pitch." Surrey's great team are shown on pre-season training in the Long Room, and there are pictures of Ilford on May 11,1966, when the first day of Sunday play took place. I was there, fearing thunderbolts, alongside the Lord's Day Observance Society. You paid a voluntary donation to enter.

The third section is called The Appendix, and has 14 headings. They include Champion Counties and their captains, a discussion of which was the greatest side — Surrey wins, just — whether batting or bowling is the more important, and stories about umpires, scorers and secretaries of counties. I am particularly interested in the section on grounds, because what I enjoyed about county cricket was the variety of venues.

Of the 170 grounds 28 at least are not now used for cricket. Some have disappeared like the Erinoid at Stroud, where Ken Smales took all 10, the Angel at Tonbridge, where Frank Woolley started, Hoffman's Social Club at Chelmsford which is now houses, and the old Priory Ground at Hastings, where Yorkshire did not play to the chagrin of visiting members. Yorkshire have lost five: Dewsbury, Fartown, Hull Circle, Bramall Lane and Wigginton Road, now part of York Hospital.

I have emphasised Stephen Chalke's portrayal of character, description of incidents and even-handed discussion of controversial matters, but there is a compendious presentation of statistics, neat, accurate, reasonably concise and readily accessible. Philip Mead made the most runs in a career and in one season, and similarly Tich Freeman took most wickets with 252 in 1933 – how did he do it? For statistical detail you must go to *Wisden* or the *Yorkshire Yearbook*.

I would strongly recommend this book, not only to antediluvian buffers like your reviewer who may wish to reminisce and recall wet days at Lydney, but more especially to anyone younger who would appreciate a clear, well researched, interesting and often humorous account of the players and matches over 125 years of the County Championship which is, after all, the foundation of first-class cricket in this country and the basis from which Test cricketers are produced.

# ENGLAND CAPTAIN IN WAITING SALUTES HIS YORKSHIRE ROOTS

**By James Greenfield**

**Bringing Home The Ashes    Joe Root with Richard Gibson (Hodder and Stoughton, www.hodder.co.uk £20)**

This, the first autobiography of England Vice-Captain Joe Root, will not be the last. Already the Yorkshire superstar is spoken of in the same breath as that mighty triumvirate of Herbert Sutcliffe, Sir Leonard Hutton and Geoffrey Boycott. Will he be even greater than these? Sutcliffe and Hutton retired years before List A had been even heard of, let alone *Twenty20*. Boycott played List A, although like the ill treated Brian Close before him one always suspected that it was not his preference. By the time of *T20* Geoffrey was esconced in the commentary box, but Joe is a man apart — truly a master of all trades, so much so that after the last *Ashes* Test of 2015 England coach Trevor Bayliss had to bar him from the mouth-watering one-dayers against the old enemy: otherwise he would have had no rest at all before the hard winter ahead.

This is the thinking man's cricket book. The chapters on last year's home Test matches read like an express train, yet as you are waiting for the next man to come in Joe goes off into a teach-in: an early backlift gets your hands higher and out in front sooner to combat the pace of Mitchell Johnson; you cannot get a full stride in against a 90mph missile, so concentrate on getting your head and weight over the ball; standing at slip you see Ben Stokes apparently swing the ball away from the Australian left-handers...only for it to jag back in again. How does he do that? Probably even Ben does not know, which must be the secret.

It is as though you are standing at slip alongside Joe to hear the machinations: Steve Smith will want to cut through point, so tell Stokes to sidle round from a gully in a ball or two without making a fuss. He does, and the catch is held. Joe is self-effacing about his own catching, but the adage of "catches win matches" strikes home. This is why Bayliss and his boys like "holidays" away: to bond and practise catching not only as individuals, but as a cordon. Light years from the days before central contracts when a player was called up without knowing who all the others were, let alone how they would learn inter-dependence.

It is a story of pain. Starting when the Root family of mother Helen, Grandpa Don, young brother Billy and Joe would tag along to see father Matt playing for Sheffield Collegiate – Michael Vaughan's club – in the Yorkshire League on Saturday afternoons. Joe and Billy would find a quiet corner of the ground to play their own "Tests", but they had no DRS and one day the umpires had to stop play at Scarborough when Billy, unable to take yes for an answer, was seen chasing Joe round the boundary with his bat. The pain became official when Joe at 12, a Yorkshire scholarship winner, met coach Kevin Sharp at Headingley for the first time. Joe watched Anthony McGrath netting against the short stuff before insisting that he had some of the same. It was that day that Kevin told Ian Dews that he had met a lad who would bat for Yorkshire.

Joe took his peppering, and after England's disastrous whitewash tour of Australia in 2013-14 he spent numerous sessions with Mark Ramprakash hurling bucketloads of indoor cricket balls at him from his side-arm contraption. Joe teamed up with Jos Buttler after England's 2015 setback at Lord's, this time taking over an AstroTurf strip at Joe's beloved Collegiate, soaking it with a binful of water to make the ball skid, and knuckling down to more self-inflicted barrages. The blows to the body were worth it as Joe moved from ducking and weaving to the hook that would put Johnson to the fence.

Players and coaches are put under the microscope. Joe is kind but always comes to the point. The departure of England coaches Andy Flower and Peter Moores is noted with gratitude for all they did for him, but he cheers the turnaround under stand-in Paul Farbrace and Trevor Bayliss, who arrived in time for the 2015 *Ashes*. He thanks Kevin Pietersen for all his help, but dismisses the lobbying for his Test recall as irrelevant. He wants more of the return to batting and captaincy form of Alastair Cook, the man he is expected to succeed...R-O-O-O-O-O-T!

# The Players

### Andrew William GALE

Left-hand batsman
*Born:* Dewsbury, November 28, 1983

**First-Class cricket:**
*Debut:* v. Somerset at Scarborough, 2004
*Highest score:* 272 v. Nottinghamshire
at Scarborough, 2013
*Best bowling:* 1-33 v. Loughborough UCCE
at Leeds, 2007

**One-Day:**
*Highest score:* 125* v. Essex at Chelmsford, 2010

**t20:**
*Highest score:* 91 v. Nottinghamshire
at Leeds, 2009

### Joe Edward ROOT

Right-hand batsman, right-arm off-spin bowler
*Born:* Sheffield, December 30, 1990
**First-Class cricket:**
*Debut:* v. Loughborough MCCU at Leeds, 2010
*Highest Score:* 236 v. Derbyshire at Leeds, 2013
*Best bowling:* 3-33 v. Warwickshire
at Birmingham, 2011
**One-Day:**
*Highest Score:* 121 for England v. Sri Lanka
at Wellington, 2015
*Hiighest for Yorkshire:* 63 v. Essex at Leeds, 2009
*Best bowling:* 2-10 for England Lions v. Bangladesh A
at Sylhet, 2011/12
*For Yorkshire:* 2-14 v. Kent at Leeds, 2012
**t20:**
*Highest score:* 90* for England v. Australia
at Southampton, 2013
*For Yorkshire:* 65 v. Worcestershire at Leeds, 2012
*Best bowling:* 1-12 v.Warwickshire at Leeds, 2011

### Gary Simon BALLANCE

Left-hand batsman, leg-break bowler
*Born:* Harare, Zimbabwe, November 22, 1989

**First-Class Cricket:**
*Debut:* v Kent at Canterbury, 2008
*Highest score:* 210 for Mid-West Rhinos v.
Southern Rocks at Masvingo, Zimbabwe, 2011-12
*For Yorkshire:* 174 v. Northamptonshire
at Leeds, 2014

**One-Day:**
*Highest score:* 139 v. Unicorns at Leeds, 2013

**t20:**
*Highest score:* 68 v Durham
at Chester-le-Street, 2013

**Alexander Zak LEES**

Left-hand batsman
*Born:* Halifax, April 14, 1993

**First-Class Cricket:**
*Debut:* India A at Leeds, 2010
*Highest score:* 275* v Derbyshire
at Chesterfield, 2013
*Best bowling:* 0-14 v. Nottinghamshire
at Scarborough 2013

**One-Day:**
*Highest score:* 102 v. Northamptonshire
at Northampton, 2014

**t20:**
*Highest score:* 67* v. Derbyshire
at Chesterfield ,2014

**Jonathan Marc BAIRSTOW**

Right-hand batsman, wicket-keeper
*Born:* Bradford, September 26, 1989

**First-Class Cricket:**
*Debut:* v Somerset at Leeds, 2009
*Highest score:* 219* v. Durham
at Chester-le-Street, 2015

**One-Day:**
*Highest score:* 123 for England Lions
v. New Zealand A at Bristol, 2014
*Highest score:* 114 v. Middlesex at Lord's, 2011

**t20:**
*Highest score:* 102* v. Durham
at Chester-le-Street, 2014

**Ryan Jay SIDEBOTTOM**

Left-hand bat, left-arm fast-medium bowler
*Born:* Huddersfield, January 15, 1978
**First-Class cricket:**
*Debut:* v. Leicestershire at Leicester, 1997
*Highest score:* 61 v. Worcestershire
at Worcester, 2011
*Best bowling:* 7-37 v. Somerset at Leeds 2011
**One-Day:**
*Highest score:* 32 for Nottinghamshire v. Middlesex
at Nottingham, 2005
*Highest score for Yorkshire:* 30* v. Glamorgan
at Leeds, 2002
*Best bowling:* 6-40 v. Glamorgan at Cardiff, 1998
**t20:**
*Highest score for Yorkshire:* 16* v. Worcestershire
at Worcester, 2011
*Best bowling:* 4-25 v. Durham
at Chester-le-Street, 2012

**Adil Usman RASHID**

Right-hand batsman, leg-break bowler
*Born:* Bradford, February 17, 1988

**First-Class cricket:**

*Debut:* v. Warwickshire at Scarborough, 2006
*Highest score:* 180 v Somerset at Leeds, 2013
*Best bowling:* 7-107 v. Hampshire
at Southampton, 2008

**One-Day:**

*Highest score:* 71 v. Gloucestershire at Leeds, 2014
*Best bowling:* 5-33 v. Hampshire
at Southampton, 2014

**t20:**

*Highest score:* 36* v Uva Next
at Johannesburg, 2012/3
*Best bowling:* 4-20 v. Leicestershire at Leeds, 2010

**Adam LYTH**

Left-hand batsman, right-arm medium bowler
*Born:* Whitby, September 25, 1987

**First-Class cricket:**

*Debut:* v. Loughborough UCCE at Leeds, 2007
*Highest score:* 251 v. Lancashire
at Manchester, 2014
*Best bowling:* 2-15 v. Somerset at Taunton, 2013

**One-Day:**

*Highest score:* 109* v. Sussex
at Scarborough, 2009
*Best bowling:* 1-6 v Middlesex at Leeds, 2013

**t20:**

*Highest score:* 78 v. Derbyshire at Leeds, 2012
*Best bowling:* 2-5 v. Derbyshire
at Chesterfield, 2014

**Steven Andrew PATTERSON**

Right-hand batsman, right-arm medium-fast bowler
*Born:* Beverley, October 3, 1983

**First-Class cricket:**

*Debut:* v. Bangladesh 'A' at Leeds, 2005
*Highest score:* 53 v. Sussex at Hove, 2011
*Best bowling:* 5-11 v. Worcestershire
at Worcester, 2015

**One-Day:**

*Highest score:* 25* v. Worcestershire at Leeds, 2006
*Best bowling:* 6-32 v. Derbyshire at Leeds, 2010

**t20:**

*Highest score:* 3* v. Derbyshire at Leeds, 2010
*Best bowling:* 4-30 v. Lancashire at Leeds, 2010

**Kane Stuart WILLIAMSON**
Right-hand batsman, right-arm off-break bowler
*Born:* Tauranga, August 8, 1990
**First-Class cricket:**
*Debut:* Northern Districts v. Auckland
at Auckland, 2007/8
*Debut for Yorkshire:* Nottinghamshire
at Nottingham, 2013
*Highest score:* 284* for Northern Districts
v. Wellington at Lincoln, 2011/12
*For Yorkshire:* 189 v. Sussex at Scarborough, 2014
*Best bowling:* 5-75 for Northern Districts
v. Canterbury at Christchurch, 2008-9
*For Yorkshire:* 2-44 v. Sussex at Hove, 2013
**One-Day:**
*Highest score:* 145* for New Zealand
v. South Africa at Kimberley, 2012/13

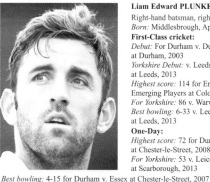

*For Yorkshire:* 70 v. Lancashire at Manchester, 2014
*Best bowling:* 5-51 for Northern Districts v. Auckland at Auckland, 2009/10
*For Yorkshire:* 1-42 v Glamorgan at Leeds, 2013
**t20:**
*Highest score:* 101* for Northern Districts v. Cape Cobras at Raipur, India, 2014
*For Yorkshire:* 41 v. Derbyshire at Chesterfield, 2014
Best bowling: 3-33 for Northern Districts v. Wellington at Wellington, 2011/12
*For Yorkshire:* 2-26 v. Derbyshire at Chesterfield, 2014

**Liam Edward PLUNKETT**
Right-hand batsman, right-arm fast-medium bowler
*Born:* Middlesbrough, April 6, 1985
**First-Class cricket:**
*Debut:* For Durham v. Durham UCCE
at Durham, 2003
*Yorkshire Debut:* v. Leeds/Bradford MCCU
at Leeds, 2013
*Highest score:* 114 for England Lions v. S Lanka A
Emerging Players at Colombo, 2013/14
*For Yorkshire:* 86 v. Warwickshire at Leeds, 2014
*Best bowling:* 6-33 v. Leeds/Bradford MCCU
at Leeds, 2013
**One-Day:**
*Highest score:* 72 for Durham v. Somerset
at Chester-le-Street, 2008
*For Yorkshire:* 53 v. Leicestershire
at Scarborough, 2013
*Best bowling:* 4-15 for Durham v. Essex at Chester-le-Street, 2007
*For Yorkshire:* 3-40 v. Durham at Chester-le-Street, 2015
**t20:**
*Highest score:* 41 for Durham v. Lancashire at Manchester, 2011
*For Yorkshire:* 36 v. Northamptonshire at Leeds, 2014
*Best bowling:* 5-31 for Durham v. Lancashire at Chester-le-Street, 2011
*For Yorkshire:* 3-49 v. Worcestershire at Leeds, 2015

**Jack Alexander BROOKS**

Right-hand batsman, right-arm medium-fast bowler
*Born:* Oxford, June 4, 1984
**First-Class Cricket:**
*Debut:* For Northamptonshire v. Australia
at Northampton, 2009
*Debut for Yorkshire:* v. Leeds/Bradford MCCU
at Leeds, 2013
*Highest score:* 53 for Northamptonshire
v. Gloucestershire at Bristol, 2010
*For Yorkshire:* 50* v. Middlesex at Lord's, 2015
*Best bowling:* 5-23 for Northamptonshire
v. Leicestershire at Leicester, 2011
*For Yorkshire:* 5-35 v. Somerset at Leeds, 2015
**One-Day:**
*Highest score:* 10 for Northamptonshire
v. Middlesex at Uxbridge, 2009
*Highest score for Yorkshire:* 6 v. Somerset at Scarborough, 2015
*Best bowling:* 3-30 v. Hampshire at Southampton, 2014
**t20:**
*Highest score:* 33* for Northamptonshire v. Warwickshire at Birmingham, 2011
*For Yorkshire:* Has not batted
*Best bowling:* 5-21 v Leicestershire at Leeds, 2013

**Timothy Thomas BRESNAN**

Right-hand batsman, right-arm medium-fast bowler
*Born:* Pontefract, February 28, 1985
**First-Class cricket:**
*Debut:* v. Northamptonshire at Northampton, 2003
*Highest score:* 169* v. Durham
at Chester-le-Street, 2015
*Best bowling:* 5-42 v. Worcestershire
at Worcester, 2005
**One-Day:**
*Highest score:* 80 for England v. Australia
at Centurion Park, 2009
*For Yorkshire:* 61 v. Leicestershire at Leeds, 2003
*Best bowling:* 4-25 v. Somerset at Leeds, 2005
**t20:**
*Highest score:* 51 v. Lancashire

at Manchester, 2015
*Best bowling:* 3-10 England v. Pakistan at Cardiff, 2010
*Best bowling for Yorkshire:* 3-21 v. Durham at Chester-le-Street, 2006

**Andrew John HODD**

Right-hand batsman, wicket keeper
*Born:* Chichester, January 12, 1984
**First-Class cricket:**
*Debut:* Sussex v. Zimbabwe at Hove, 2003
*Debut for Yorkshire:* v. Derbyshire at Leeds, 2012
*Highest score:* 123 for Sussex v. Yorkshire
at Hove, 2007
*Highest score for Yorkshire:* 68* v. Somerset
at Taunton, 2013
**One-Day:**
*Highest score:* 91 for Sussex v. Lancashire
at Hove, 2010
*For Yorkshire:* 69* v. Leicestershire
at Leicester, 2014
**t20:**
*Highest score:* 70 v. Nottinghamshire
at Leeds, 2015

**Jack Andrew LEANING**

Right-hand batsman, right-arm medium
and off-break bowler
*Born:* Bristol, October 18, 1993

**First-Class cricket:**
*Debut:* v. Surrey at Leeds, 2013
*Highest score:* 123 v. Somerset at Taunton, 2015
*Best bowling:* 1-12 v. Nottinghamshire
at Nottingham, 2015

**One-Day:**
*Highest score:* 111* v. Essex at Scarborough, 2014
*Best bowling:* 5-22 v. Unicorns at Leeds, 2013

**t20:**
*Highest score:* 60* v. Worcestershire at Leeds, 2015
*Best bowling:* 0-12 v. Derbyshire at Leeds, 2014

**David Jonathan WILLEY**

Left-hand batsman, left-arm fast-medium
*Born:* Northampton, February 28, 1990
Awaiting Yorkshire debut
**First-Class cricket:**
*Debut:* for Northamptonshire v. Leicestershire
at Leicester, 2009
*Highest score:* 104* for Northamptonshire
v. Gloucestershire at Northampton, 2015
*Best bowling:* 5-29 for Northamptonshire
v. Gloucestershire at Northampton, 2011
**One-Day:**
*Highest score:* 167 for Northamptonshire
v. Warwickshire at Birmingham, 2013
*Best bowling:* 5-62 for England Lions
v. New Zealand A at Bristol, 2014
**t20:**
*Highest score:* 100 for Northamptonshire v. Sussex
at Hove, 2015

*Best bowling:* 4-9 for Northamptonshire v. Surrey at Cardiff, 2013

**Karl CARVER**

Left-hand batsman, slow left-arm orthodox bowler
*Born:* Northallerton, March 26, 1996
**First-Class Cricket:**
*Debut for Yorkshire:* v. Warwickshire
at Birmingham, 2014
*Highest score:* 16 v. Leeds/Bradford MCCU
at Leeds, 2015
*Best bowling:* 2-6 v. Leeds/Bradford MCCU
at Leeds, 2015

**One-Day:**
*Highest score:* 35* v. Somerset
at Scarborough, 2015
*Best bowling:* 2-40 v. Surrey at The Oval, 2015

**t20:**
*Highest score:* 2 v. Worcestershire at Leeds, 2015
*Best bowling:* 0-30 v. Worcestershire at Leeds, 2015

**William Michael Harry RHODES**

Left-hand batsman, right-arm medium fast
*Born:* Nottingham, March 2, 1995
**First-Class Cricket:**
*Debut:* v. MCC at Abu Dhabi, 2015
*Highest score:* 79 v. Warwickshire
at Birmingham, 2015
*Best bowling:* 3-42 v. Middlesex at Leeds, 2015

**One-Day:**
*Highest score:* 46 v. Leicestershire at Leeds, 2015
*Best bowling:* 2-22 v. Essex at Chelmsford, 2015

**t20:**
*Highest score:* 13 v. Nottinghamshire
at Nottingham, 2015
*Best bowling:* 3-27 v. Warwickshire at Leeds, 2015

**Matthew David FISHER**

Right-hand batsman, right-arm fast-medium bowler
*Born:* York, November 9, 1997
**First-Class Cricket:**
*Debut:* v. Nottinghamshire at Nottingham, 2015
*Highest score:* 0* v. Warwickshire at Leeds, 2015
*Best bowling:* 2-61 v. Hampshire
at West End, Southampton, 2015

**One-Day:**
*Highest score:* 34 v. Somerset at Scarborough, 2015
*Best bowling:* 3-32 v. Leicestershire at Leeds, 2015

**t20:**
*Highest score:* 0* v. Worcestershire at Leeds, 2015
*Best bowling:* 5-21 v. Derbyshire at Leeds, 2015

# YORKSHIRE'S FIRST-CLASS HIGHLIGHTS OF 2015

### Wins by an innings (3)

Somerset (110 and 155) lost to Yorkshire (391) by an innings and 126 runs at Leeds

Yorkshire (557-6 dec) defeated Durham (208 and 302) by an innings and 47 runs at Chester-le-Street

Nottinghamshire (224 and 198) lost to Yorkshire (430) by an innings and 8 runs at Leeds

### Win by 10 wickets (1)

Worcestershire (311 and 100) lost to Yorkshire (307 and 105-0) by 10 wickets at Worcester

### Win by over 200 runs (1)

Yorkshire (370 and 305-4 dec) defeated Hampshire (227 and 143) by 305 runs at Leeds

### Totals of 400 and over (8)

| | |
|---|---|
| 557-5 dec | v. Durham at Chester-le-Street |
| 494 | v. Sussex at Hove |
| 441 | v. Nottinghamshire at Nottingham |
| 440 | v. Durham at Scarborough |
| 438 | v. Somerset at Taunton (1st innings) |
| 430 | v. Nottinghamshire at Leeds |
| 430 | v. Worcestershire at Scarborough |
| 419 | v. Somerset at Taunton (2nd innings) |

### Opponents dismissed for under 100 (1)

69  v. Warwickshire at Birmingham

### Century Partnerships (17)

#### For the 1st wicket (1)

| 105* | A Z Lees and W M H Rhodes | v. Worcestershire at Worcester |
|---|---|---|

#### For the 2nd wicket (1)

| 116 | A Z Lees and C A Pujara | v. Nottinghamshire at Nottingham |
|---|---|---|

#### For the 3rd wicket (1)

| 108 | A Z Lees and R M Pyrah | v. Worcestershire at Worcester |
|---|---|---|

#### For the 4th wicket (5)

| 255 | A W Gale and J A Leaning | v. Nottinghamshire at Leeds |
|---|---|---|
| 254 | A W Gale and J M Bairstow (1st innings) | v. Worcestershire at Scarborough |
| 190 | A W Gale and J A Leaning | v. Hampshire at West End, Southampton |
| 130 | C A Pujara and J M Bairstow | v. Hampshire at Leeds |
| 113* | A Z Lees and J M Bairstow (2nd innings) | v. Worcestershire at Scarborough |

#### For the 5th wicket (2)

| 155 | J M Bairstow and J A Leaning | v. Hampshire at Leeds |
|---|---|---|
| 111 | J A Leaning and R M Pyrah | v. Nottinghamshire at Nottingham |

## Century Partnerships *(Continued)*

### For the 6th wicket (4)

| | | |
|---|---|---|
| 248 | G J Maxwell and A U Rashid | v. Durham at Scarborough |
| 117 | J M Bairstow and A U Rashid | v. Somerset at Taunton |
| 116 | R M Pyrah and A J Hodd | v. Leeds/Bradford MCCU at Leeds |
| 104 | W M H Rhodes and A J Hodd | v. MCC at Abu Dhabi |

### For the 7th wicket (3)

| | | |
|---|---|---|
| 366* | J M Bairstow and T T Bresnan | v. Durham at Chester-le-Street |
| | *(Yorkshire record)* | |
| 119 | J A Leaning and T T Bresnan | v. Somerset at Taunton |
| 197 | G S Ballance and T T Bresnan | v. Sussex at Hove |

## Centuries (19)

J M Bairstow (5)

| | |
|---|---|
| 219* | v. Durham at Chester-le-Street |
| 139 | v. Worcestershire at Scarborough |
| 125* | v. Middlesex at Leeds |
| 108 | v. Warwickshire at Birmingham |
| 102 | v. Hampshire at Leeds |

A W Gale (3)

| | |
|---|---|
| 164 | v. Worcestershire at Scarborough |
| 148 | v. Nottinghamshire at Leeds |
| 125 | v. Hampshire at West End, Southampton |

J A Leaning (3)

| | |
|---|---|
| 123 | v. Somerset at Taunton |
| 116 | v. Nottinghamshire at Nottingham |
| 110 | v. Nottinghamshire at Leeds |

T T Bresnan (2)

| | |
|---|---|
| 169* | v. Durham at Chester-le-Street |
| 100* | v. Somerset at Taunton |

G S Ballance (1)

| | |
|---|---|
| 165 | v. Sussex at Hove |

A Z Lees (1)

| | |
|---|---|
| 100 | v. Nottinghamshire at Nottingham |

A Lyth (1)

| | |
|---|---|
| 113 | v. MCC at Abu Dhabi |

G J Maxwell (1)

| | |
|---|---|
| 140 | v. Durham at Scarborough |

C A Pujara (1)

| | |
|---|---|
| 133* | v. Hampshire at Leeds |

A U Rashid (1)

| | |
|---|---|
| 127 | v. Durham at Scarborough |

## 5 wickets in an innings (10)

J A Brooks (3)

| | |
|---|---|
| 5-35 | v. Somerset at Leeds |
| 5-44 | v. Middlesex at Leeds |
| 5-56 | v Worcestershire at Worcester |

R J Sidebottom (3)

| | |
|---|---|
| 6-34 | v. Warwickshire at Birmingham (1st innings) |
| 5-18 | v. Middlesex at Lord's |
| 5-42 | v. Warwickshire at Birmingham (2nd innings) |

**5 wickets in an innings** *(Continued)*

S A Patterson (2)

    5-11    v. Worcestershire at Worcester

    5-70    v. Somerset at Taunton

T T Bresnan (1)

    5-85    v. Warwickshire at Leeds

J D Middlebrook (1)

    5-82    v. Warwickshire at Leeds

## 10 wickets in a match (1)

R J Sidebottom (1)

    11-76    (6-34 and 5-42)    v. Warwickshire at Birmingham

## 3 catches in an innings (13)

J M Bairstow (6)

    4    v. Sussex at Leeds

    3    v Hampshire at Leeds

    3    v. Somerset at Taunton

    3    v. Durham at Chester-le-Street (1st innings)

    3    v. Durham at Chester-le-Street (2nd innings)

    3    v. Somerset at Leeds

A J Hodd (5)

    4    v. Nottinghamshire at Nottingham

    4    v. Hampshire at West End, Southampton

    3    v. Leeds/Bradford MCCU at Leeds

    3    v. Worcestershire at Worcester

    3    v. Middlesex at Lord's

A Z Lees (1)

    3    v. Nottinghamshire at Nottingham

A Lyth (1)

    3    v. Somerset at Leeds

## 5 catches in a match (3)

J M Bairstow (2)

    6 (3+3)    v. Durham at Chester-le-Street

    6 (4+2)    v Sussex at Leeds

A Lyth (1)

    5 (3+2)    v. Somerset at Leeds

## 5 dismissals in a match (1)

A J Hodd (1)

    5 (4ct+1st)    v. Hampshire at West End, Southampton

## Debuts (4)

**In first-class cricket:** M D Fisher and W M H Rhodes

**In first-class cricket for Yorkshire:** G J Maxwell and C A Pujara

# LV CHAMPIONSHIP FACTFILE

## Compiled by John T Potter

### Versus MCC at Abu Dhabi

1. Yorkshire's first First Class match at this venue and their first day/night fixture with a pink ball
2. They last played MCC in 1987 at Scarborough
3. P J Hartley, who played in that match, umpired at Abu Dhabi
4. W M H Rhodes made his First Class debut
5. S A Patterson passed 1,000 First Class career runs

### Versus LEEDS/BRADFORD MCCU at Headingley

1. S F G Bullen made his First Class debut
2. T T Bresnan took his 400th First Class wicket

### Versus WORCESTERSHIRE at Worcester

1. C A Pujara made his First Class debut for Yorkshire
2. W M H Rhodes made his Championship debut
3. S A Patterson took his First Class career-best analysis of 5-11 in Worcestershire's second innings
4. Patterson's last three wickets came in four balls

### Versus NOTTINGHAMSHIRE at Nottingham

1. M D Fisher made his First Class debut
2. A D Hales's 236 was his maiden First Class double-century, and the highest home score for Nottinghamshire against Yorkshire, beating R T Robinson's 220* at Trent Bridge in 1990
3. This century by A D Hales was Nottinghamshire's 50th against Yorkshire in Nottinghamshire
4. J A Leaning's 116 was his maiden First Class century
5. A Z Lees (100 against Nottinghamshire and 87 and 52* against Worcestershire) had scored over 50 in the first three innings of the Championship season. The last Yorkshire player to do this was D S Lehmann (95 v. Derbyshire at Headingley, 85 v. Hampshire at Headingley and 133 v. Derbyshire at Derby) in 2000. The first two matches were won by an innings. The last Yorkshire batsman to score three half-centuries in the first three innings of the first two matches was D Byas in 1998 (101 and 52 v. Somerset at Headingley and 103 v. Derbyshire at Headingley)
6. T T Bresnan took his 300th First Class wicket for Yorkshire

# LV CHAMPIONSHIP FACTFILE *(Continued)*

## Versus WARWICKSHIRE at Headingley

1. J D Middlebrook last played for Yorkshire at Bath against Somerset, the match starting on June 13, 2001
2. T T Bresnan (5-85) took his 300th Championship wicket
3. A W Gale passed 6,000 Championship runs
4. W B Rankin's 6-55 was his First Class career-best

## Versus HAMPSHIRE at Headingley

1. Yorkshire's fifth-wicket partnership of 155 by J M Bairstow and J A Leaning was their highest against Hampshire in Yorkshire
2. J A Brooks took his 250th First Class career wicket
3. C A Pujara's 133* was his maiden First Class century for Yorkshire
4. Yorkshire's winning margin of 305 was their ninth highest by runs
5. It was their second highest margin in runs at Headingley, the best being 370 in 1904 also against Hampshire

## Versus SOMERSET at Taunton

1. G J Maxwell made his First Class debut for Yorkshire
2. J A Leaning's 123 was a First Class career-best
3. T T Bresnan's 100* was his first century since his 101* against Warwickshire at Scarborough in August 22-24, 2007
4. It was Yorkshire's 100th century against Somerset
5. S A Patterson took his 250th First Class wicket

## Versus MIDDLESEX at Headingley

1. A Lyth passed 6,000 Championship runs
2. J M Bairstow passed 6,500 First Class career runs

## Versus NOTTINGHAMSHIRE at Headingley

1. A W Gale passed 7,000 First Class career runs
2. Yorkshire's fourth wicket partnership of 255 by A W Gale and J A Leaning was their highest against Nottinghamshire, and it was the third highest by Yorkshire at Headingley
3. J A Leaning's 110 gave him a century at home and away against Nottinghamshire in 2015
4. R J Sidebottom took his 550th Championship wicket

# LV CHAMPIONSHIP FACTFILE (Continued)

## Versus DURHAM at Chester-le-Street

1. J M Bairstow's 219* was his First Class career-best, and it was the fourth-highest score at Riverside
2. Bairstow's innings took him passed 5,000 First Class runs for Yorkshire
3. T T Bresnan's 169* was his First Class career-best
4. Yorkshire's undefeated seventh-wicket partnership of 366 was their highest for this wicket
5. It was the highest for any wicket other than the opening partnership, which has exceeded it four times
6. This was the best stand for any wicket for and against Durham in a First Class match
7. It was the third-highest seventh-wicket partnership in First Class cricket, 460 by Bhupinder Singh Jun. and P Dharmani for Punjab v. Delhi in 1994-95 and 371 by Mitchell Marsh and Sam Whiteman for Australia A v. India A at Brisbane in 2014 being higher
8. It was the highest seventh-wicket partnership in the history of the County Championship
9. This was Yorkshire's first victory by an innings in Durham

## Versus WARWICKSHIRE at Birmingham

1. S A Patterson played his 100th First Class match for Yorkshire
2. J M Bairstow passed 5,000 Championship runs
3. W M H Rhodes's 79 was a First Class career-best
4. J A Brooks took his 250th Championship wicket
5. Warwickshire's first innings total of 69 was their sixth lowest against Yorkshire at Edgbaston

## Versus WORCESTERSHIRE at Scarborough

1. This was Yorkshire's 250th First Class match at Scarborough
2. J M Bairstow passed 7,000 First Class career runs
3. J M Brooks took his 50th First Class wicket of the season
4. Yorkshire's fourth-wicket first-innings partnership of 254 between A W Gale and J M Bairstow was their highest against Worcestershire, beating the undefeated 210 by A Mitchell and M Leyland at Worcester in 1933
5. Yorkshire's two fourth-wicket partnerships added a total of 367 runs
6. Yorkshire completed the 2015 double against Worcestershire

# LV CHAMPIONSHIP FACTFILE *(Continued)*

## Versus DURHAM at Scarborough

1. J T A Burnham made his First Class debut
2. AU Rashid took his 400th First Class career wicket
3. G Onions took his 500th First Class career wicket
4. G J Maxwell's 140 was his maiden First Class century for Yorkshire
5. Yorkshire's sixth-wicket second-innings partnership of 248 by G J Maxwell and A U Rashid was Yorkshire's highest against Durham and their fourth highest in all
6. It was a record for the sixth wicket in First Class matches at Scarborough
7. Yorkshire did the double against Durham for the first time
8. This was Yorkshire's fourth win in a row at Scarborough. The last time this was done the dates were August 19, 1978 (Nottinghamshire), September 6, 1978 (Gloucestershire), July 28, 1979 (Middlesex) and September 5, 1979 (Essex)

## Versus SUSSEX at Hove

1. R J Sidebottom passed 2,500 First Class career runs
2. S A Patterson took his 250th Championship wicket
3. Yorkshire's seventh-wicket partnership of 197 by G S Ballance and T T Bresnan was Yorkshire's highest against Sussex. Bresnan had also set the previous record with K S Williamson (157) at Scarborough in 2014
4. This was Yorkshire's fourth-highest stand for this wicket
5. Yorkshire's run of six consecutive wins came to an end

## Versus SOMERSET at Headingley

1. J M Bairstow passed 1,000 Championship runs for the season
2. J A Brooks took his 50th Championship wicket of the season

# LV CHAMPIONSHIP FACTFILE *(Continued)*

## Versus MIDDLESEX at Lord's

1. A Lyth played his 100th First Class match for Yorkshire
2. R J Sidebottom took his 700th First Class wicket with the third ball of the match. By the end of the over he had 702 wickets
3. 3.10pm on the first day it was announced that Nottinghamshire had been bowled out by Durham, so Yorkshire had retained the Championship
4. J A Brooks's 50* was his maiden First Class 50 for Yorkshire
5. Middlesex's second-innings total of 573-8 dec was their highest against Yorkshire, surpassing their 527 at Huddersfield in 1887 and 488 at Lord's in 1899
6. T S Roland-Jones's 103* was his maiden First Class century
7. Middlesex's second-innings ninth-wicket unbroken stand of 146 was their highest against Yorkshire

## Versus HAMPSHIRE at West End, Southampton

1. Yorkshire's second innings of 305-5 was their joint 11th-highest fourth-innings total to win a match
2. A W Gale passed 7,000 First Class runs for Yorkshire
3. Yorkshire completed the double over Hampshire. The last time they did this was in 2000
4. J D Middlebrook played his last game of the season for Yorkshire. Little did he think that after being released by Northamptonshire in September 2014 he would be visiting Buckingham Palace for a second time to collect a Championship winners' medal

## Versus SUSSEX at Headingley

1. A W Gale passed 1,000 First Class runs for the season
2. T T Bresnan passed 4,000 First Class runs for Yorkshire and 5,000 First Class career runs
3. A U Rashid passed 5,000 First Class runs for Yorkshire
4. With his final wicket of the season J A Brooks took his total of First Class wickets to 300
5. This win gave Yorkshire a victory against all the counties in Division 1
6. Yorkshire's 11th win of the season and 286 points were the best achieved since the two-division Championship began
7. Yorkshire's points lead over Middlesex in second place was 68. The points difference between Middlesex and the bottom county was 67
8. Yorkshire recorded seven home wins for the first time since 1968

# LV Championship
# Division 1, 2015

Captain: A W Gale

*Captain

§ Wicket-Keeper

Figures in brackets ( ) indicate position in 2nd Innings batting order,
where different from 1st Innings.

DETAILS OF PLAYERS WHO APPEARED FOR YORKSHIRE IN 2015
(ALL FIRST-CLASS MATCHES)

| Player | Date of Birth | Birthplace | First-Class debut for Yorkshire | Date Capped |
|---|---|---|---|---|
| A W Gale | November 28, 1983 | Dewsbury | July 21, 2004 | Sept. 18, 2008 |
| R J Sidebottom | January 15, 1978 | Huddersfield | July 2, 1997 | July 23, 2000 |
| T T Bresnan | February 28, 1985 | Pontefract | May 14, 2003 | July 19, 2006 |
| A U Rashid | February 17, 1988 | Bradford | July 19, 2006 | Sept. 18, 2008 |
| A Lyth | September 25, 1987 | Whitby | May 16, 2007 | Aug. 22, 2010 |
| R M Pyrah | November 1, 1982 | Dewsbury | August 24, 2004 | Aug. 22 ,2010 |
| J M Bairstow | September 26, 1989 | Bradford | June 11, 2009 | Aug. 17, 2011 |
| S A Patterson | October 3, 1983 | Beverley | August 3, 2005 | May 16, 2012 |
| G S Ballance | November 22, 1989 | Harare, Zim | July 11, 2008 | Sept 4, 2012 |
| J A Brooks | June 4, 1984 | Oxford | April 5, 2013 | Aug. 2, 2013 |
| L E Plunkett | April 6, 1985 | Middlesbrough | April 5, 2013 | Aug. 2, 2013 |
| A J Finch | November 17, 1986 | Colac, Australia | May 31, 2014 | May 31, 2014 |
| A Z Lees | April 14, 1993 | Halifax | June 5, 2010 | Sept 23, 2014 |
| C A Pujara | January 25, 1988 | Rajkot, India | April 12, 2015 | Apr. 12, 2015 |
| G J Maxwell | October 14, 1988 | Kew, Melbourne | May 24, 2015 | May 24, 2015 |
| J D Middlebrook | May 13, 1977 | Leeds | June 27, 1998 | — |
| A J Hodd | January 12, 1984 | Chichester | August 15, 2012 | — |
| J A Leaning | October 18, 1993 | Bristol | June 21, 2013 | — |
| D M Hodgson | February 26, 1990 | Northallerton | April 1, 2014 | — |
| K Carver | March 26, 1996 | Northallerton | June 22, 2014 | — |
| W M H Rhodes | March 2, 1995 | Nottingham | March 22, 2015 | — |
| M D Fisher | November 9, 1997 | York | April 19, 2015 | — |

## Match-By-Match Reports      NIGEL PULLAN

# LV County Championship Division 1
## Worcestershire v. Yorkshire

Played at New Road, Worcester, on April 12, 13 and 14, 2015
*Yorkshire won by 10 wickets at 3.41pm on the Third Day*

Toss won by Worcestershire     Yorkshire 22 points, Worcestershire 6 points
Close of play: First Day, Worcestershire 264-8 (Andrew 42*, Senanayake 0*); Second Day, Yorkshire 298-9 (Bresnan 78*, Sidebottom 10*)

| | First Innings | WORCESTERSHIRE | Second innings | |
|---|---|---|---|---|
| * D K H Mitchell, c Leaning b Brooks | | 4 | c Lees b Brooks | 8 |
| R K Oliver, c Hodd b Brooks | | 0 | lbw b Bresnan | 1 |
| M M Ali, c Hodd b Bresnan | | 62 | c Leaning b Brooks | 4 |
| T C Fell, c Hodd b Bresnan | | 114 | c Lees b Patterson | 14 |
| A P R Gidman, lbw b Bresnan | | 7 | c Hodd b Brooks | 4 |
| T Kohler-Cadmore, b Brooks | | 3 | c Patterson b Brooks | 24 |
| § O B Cox, c Bresnan b Sidebottom | | 9 | lbw b Patterson | 0 |
| G M Andrew, c Lees b Brooks | | 59 | c Brooks b Patterson | 16 |
| J D Shantry, lbw b Patterson | | 15 | not out | 15 |
| S M S M Senanayake, c Rhodes b Brooks | | 13 | c Rhodes b Patterson | 9 |
| C J Morris, not out | | 8 | lbw b Patterson | 0 |
| Extras b 4, lb 11, nb 2 | | 17 | Extras b 1, nb 4 | 5 |
| Total | | 311 | Total | 100 |

Bonus points — Worcestershire 3, Yorkshire 3

FoW: 1-2 (Oliver), 2-11 (Mitchell), 3-129 (Ali), 4-159 (Gidman), 5-171 (Kohler-Cadmore),
1st 6-195 (Cox), 7-216 (Fell), 8-255 (Andrew), 9-298 (Senanayake). 10-311 (Morris)
FoW: 1-3 (Oliver), 2-10 (Ali), 3-15 (Mitchell), 4-21 (Gidman), 5-48 (Fell), 6-48 (Cox),
2nd 7-65 (Kohler-Cadmore), 8-90 (Andrew), 9-100 (Senanayake). 10-100 (Morris)

| | O | M | R | W | | O | M | R | W |
|---|---|---|---|---|---|---|---|---|---|
| Sidebottom | 22 | 5 | 77 | 1 | Bresnan | 13 | 4 | 44 | 1 |
| Brooks | 21.3 | 7 | 56 | 5 | Brooks | 10 | 3 | 28 | 4 |
| Bresnan | 16 | 2 | 48 | 3 | Patterson | 7.3 | 3 | 11 | 5 |
| Patterson | 19 | 8 | 40 | 1 | Rhodes | 5 | 1 | 16 | 0 |
| Pyrah | 3 | 2 | 14 | 0 | | | | | |
| Carver | 6 | 0 | 36 | 0 | | | | | |
| Rhodes | 5 | 1 | 19 | 0 | | | | | |
| Leaning | 1 | 0 | 6 | 0 | | | | | |

| | First Innings | YORKSHIRE | Second Innings | |
|---|---|---|---|---|
| * A Z Lees, lbw b Andrew | | 87 | not out | 52 |
| W M H Rhodes, c Mitchell b Morris | | 0 | not out | 45 |
| C A Pujara, c Fell b Andrew | | 0 | | |
| R M Pyrah, c Mitchell b Shantry | | 43 | | |
| J A Leaning, lbw b Shantry | | 10 | | |
| § A J Hodd, c Mitchell b Andrew | | 30 | | |
| T T Bresnan, c Fell b Andrew | | 83 | | |
| S A Patterson, b Shantry | | 0 | | |
| R J Sidebottom, not out | | 14 | | |
| J A Brooks, c Cox b Andrew | | 26 | | |
| K Carver, c Oliver b Shantry | | 5 | | |
| Extras b 1, lb 6, nb 2 | | 9 | Extras b 8 | 8 |
| Total | | 307 | Total (0 wkts) | 105 |

*R J Sidebottom retired hurt on 10\**

Bonus points — Yorkshire 3, Worcestershire 3

FoW: 1-2 (Rhodes), 2-3 (Pujara), 3-111 (Pyrah), 4-127 (Leaning), 5-172 (Lees),
1st 6-186 (Hodd), 7-193 (Patterson), 7-217 (Sidebottom rh), 8-274 (Brooks), 9-293
 (Carver), 10-307 (Bresnan)

| | O | M | R | W | | O | M | R | W |
|---|---|---|---|---|---|---|---|---|---|
| Andrew | 21.1 | 4 | 85 | 5 | Andrew | 4 | 0 | 25 | 0 |
| Morris | 14 | 3 | 70 | 1 | Morris | 4 | 1 | 14 | 0 |
| Shantry | 23 | 5 | 65 | 4 | Shantry | 3 | 0 | 19 | 0 |
| Senanayake | 18 | 2 | 47 | 0 | Senanayake | 4 | 0 | 24 | 0 |
| Ali | 9 | 0 | 33 | 0 | Ali | 2 | 0 | 15 | 0 |

Umpires: J H Evans and J W Lloyds    Scorers: J T Potter and D E Pugh

# Patterson's career-best haul

Yorkshire began their Championship season as early as April 12 with Worcester Cathedral prominent behind leafless trees and a distinct chill in the air.

They were without six players in the West Indies — Bairstow, Ballance, Lyth, Plunkett, Rashid and Root.

Gale was still suspended, and Sidebottom was injured on the second evening. After two even days Yorkshire produced an outstanding performance on the third day to win by 10 wickets.

Worcestershire made 264-8 on Sunday after a century from Fell and 62 from Moeen Ali, who was playing to prove his fitness to rejoin the England side. Ali demonstrat-

**STEVEN PATTERSON: Pace with disconcerting bounce**

ed his class with fine off-side strokes. Good catches were taken, none better than when Hodd dived left-handed at full stretch to dismiss Fell. Brooks took early wickets and Bresnan had Moeen, Fell and Gidman.

The second day saw Yorkshire work hard to reach parity. Andrew continued to hit, so Worcestershire reached 311. He and Morris reduced Yorkshire to 3-2 but Lees, captaining the side in Gale's absence, played a most responsible innings. Sideways on and playing very straight, his impeccable timing and placement found gaps in the off-side field, although he did thump Senanayake for six over extra-cover in his first over in county cricket. Lees had resolute support from Pyrah, justifiably promoted to No 4. Shantry, an awkward left-armer, and Andrew bowled well, so it was left to Bresnan to steer Yorkshire towards 307, supported by Sidebottom who returned virtually immobile after a calf tear.

Yorkshire bowled Worcestershire out for exactly 100 on Tuesday. No batsman could contend with the pace of Brooks and the skill of Patterson. Brooks had a fine match as a penetrative quick bowler, moving the ball away bat with pace and lift. Patterson took a career best 5-11, his accuracy and disconcerting bounce accounting for the rest of the batsmen. Rhodes came in with Lees, and they hit off the 105 required.

# LV County Championship Division 1
## Nottinghamshire v. Yorkshire

Played at Trent Bridge, Nottingham, on April 19, 20, 21 and 22, 2015

*Match drawn at 4.50pm on the Fourth Day*

Toss won by Yorkshire      Yorkshire 11 points, Nottinghamshire 11 points

Close of play, First Day, Nottinghamshire 393-7 (Hales 222*); Second Day, Yorkshire 226-3 (Gale 13*, Leaning 3*); Third Day, Nottinghamshire 74-3 (J W A Taylor 7*, Gidman 7*)

| First Innings | NOTTINGHAMSHIRE | Second innings | |
|---|---|---|---|
| S J Mullaney, lbw b Patterson | 27 | lbw b Fisher | 20 |
| B R M Taylor, c Lees b Fisher | 27 | b Brooks | 32 |
| A D Hales, b Patterson | 236 | c Hodd b Bresnan | 2 |
| J W A Taylor, c Lees b Brooks | 59 | c sub ( M A Ashraf) b Rhodes | 35 |
| S R Patel, c Lees b Brooks | 4 | (6) c Hodd b Rhodes | 76 |
| M H Wessels, c Leaning b Rhodes | 18 | (7) c Hodd b Leaning | 43 |
| * § C M W Read, lbw b Bresnan | 7 | (8) not out | 83 |
| W R S Gidman, c Lees b Patterson | 8 | (5) c Hodd b Patterson | 13 |
| V D Philander, c Leaning b Brooks | 7 | (9) not out | 38 |
| J T Ball, b Bresnan | 14 | | |
| H F Gurney, not out | 0 | | |
| Extras b 9, lb 7, w 1, nb 4 | 21 | Extras b 2, lb 6, nb 4 | 12 |
| Total | 428 | Total (7 wkts dec) | 354 |

Bonus points — Nottinghamshire 5, Yorkshire 3

FoW: 1-37 (Mullaney, 2-77 (B R M Taylor), 3-248 (J W A Taylor), 4-252 (Patel), 5-324 (Wessels),
1st   6-344 (Read), 7-393 (Gidman), 8-414 (Philander), 9-414 (Hales), 10-428 (Ball)
FoW: 1-46 (Mullaney), 2-52 (Hales), 3-58 (B R M Taylor), 4-92 (Gidman), 5-134 (J W A Taylor)
2nd   6-213 (Patel), 7-245 (Wessels)

| | O | M | R | W | | O | M | R | W |
|---|---|---|---|---|---|---|---|---|---|
| Bresnan | 21.2 | 4 | 85 | 2 | Bresnan | 21 | 6 | 77 | 1 |
| Brooks | 27 | 5 | 99 | 3 | Brooks | 21 | 5 | 67 | 1 |
| Patterson | 29 | 10 | 78 | 3 | Fisher | 16 | 3 | 34 | 1 |
| Fisher | 15 | 3 | 68 | 1 | Patterson | 15 | 4 | 32 | 1 |
| Pyrah | 7 | 0 | 26 | 0 | Rhodes | 15 | 4 | 42 | 2 |
| Rhodes | 6 | 0 | 28 | 1 | Leaning | 14 | 2 | 82 | 1 |
| Leaning | 3 | 0 | 28 | 0 | Lees | 3 | 0 | 12 | 0 |

### YORKSHIRE

| | | |
|---|---|---|
| A Z Lees, c Read b Gidman | | 100 |
| W M H Rhodes, c Patel b Gurney | | 41 |
| C A Pujara, c sub (B M Kitt) b Patel | | 57 |
| * A W Gale, c Wessels b Gurney | | 13 |
| J A Leaning, st Read b Patel | | 116 |
| R M Pyrah, c Mullaney b Patel | | 37 |
| § A J Hodd, b Philander | | 6 |
| T T Bresnan, c Mullaney b Patel | | 34 |
| S A Patterson, not out | | 12 |
| J A Brooks, c Gidman b Gurney | | 5 |
| M D Fisher, lbw b Patel | | 0 |
| Extras b 3, lb 12, w 5 | | 20 |
| Total | | 441 |

Bonus points — Yorkshire 3, Nottinghamshire1      Score at 110 overs: 320-4

FoW: 1-68 (Rhodes), 2-182 (Pujara), 3-215 (Lees), 4-235 (Gale), 5-346 (Pyrah),
6-353 (Hodd), 7-422 (Bresnan), 8-427 (Leaning), 9-438 (Brooks), 10-441 (Fisher)

| | O | M | R | W |
|---|---|---|---|---|
| Philander | 26 | 9 | 51 | 2 |
| Ball | 24 | 6 | 66 | 0 |
| Gurney | 28.4 | 7 | 90 | 3 |
| Gidman | 25 | 8 | 75 | 1 |
| Mullaney | 11.2 | 1 | 42 | 0 |
| Patel | 32.5 | 9 | 102 | 4 |

*Gurney was unable to complete his 29th over, which was was finished by Mullaney*

Umpires: R J Bailey and R J Evans      Scorers: J T Potter and R Marshall

# Leaning raps maiden century

**JACK LEANING**
**Quality strokes**

The hosts had much the better of the first day after being put in to bat on a windy, cloudy morning.

Hales played a career-best innings of 236, displaying his strength and power of stroke, but otherwise they did not bat particularly well despite a dogged 59 from James Taylor, and on the second morning the bowlers broke through the lower order.

Fisher made his debut at 17 years 161 days. He was encouraged by the wicket of Brendan Taylor with his seventh ball, but he then encountered Hales in full flight. Yorkshire perhaps bowled a little too short in helpful conditions, but the few chances were not really catchable.

Having conceded advantage, Yorkshire batted with stern concentration, initially to ensure that there would be no follow-on and the game could be saved. Lees was a solid, reliable opener well deserving his century, and Rhodes gained in assurance.

It was good to see Pujara, a late replacement for Younus Khan, make a maiden 50 for Yorkshire in his calm, composed manner. Leaning took over from Lees, and made the maiden century that had been in prospect for some time. He comes from York, although born in Bristol, where his father was keeping goal at Ashton Gate. He is an Academy player with good temperament and quality shots. The bowlers were led by South African Test player Philander. Gurney, once of Leeds/Bradford UCCE, took three wickets, but went off injured. It was the left-arm Patel who took most wickets as Yorkshire led by 13.

Nottinghamshire ended the third day on 74-3, so there was still a possibility that Yorkshire might win, and at 134-5 this remained a reality. Patel, Read, Wessels and Philander were obdurate, and it became apparent that a match so important to both sides would have to be drawn. Read made 83 not out, and having brilliantly stumped Leaning he now steered Nottinghamshire to safety to demonstrate that he is still one of the best county cricketers.

# LV County Championship Division 1
## Yorkshire v. Warwickshire

Played at Headingley, Leeds, on April 26, 27, 28 and 29, 2015
*Match drawn at 6.11pm on the Fourth Day*

Toss won by Warwickshire
Warwickshire 11 points, Yorkshire 2 points
Close of play: First Day, Warwickshire 270-4 (Westwood 151*, McKay 17*); Second Day, Yorkshire 128-3 (Gale 17*, Leaning 17*); Third Day, Warwickshire 108-2 (Westwood 48*, Evans 15*)

| WARWICKSHIRE | | | |
|---|---|---|---|
| | First Innings | | Second innings |
| * V Chopra, c Hodd b Bresnan | 0 | lbw b Bresnan | 10 |
| I J Westwood, lbw b Middlebrook | 196 | lbw b Middlebrook | 84 |
| W T S Porterfield, c Hodd b Bresnan | 35 | c Pujara b Middlebrook | 30 |
| L J Evans, lbw b Patterson | 14 | lbw b Bresnan | 15 |
| S R Hain, lbw b Bresnan | 50 | b Middlebrook | 24 |
| § P McKay, b Bresnan | 17 | st Hodd b Middlebrook | 5 |
| R Clarke, lbw b Fisher | 39 | c Fisher b Middlebrook | 36 |
| K H D Barker, b Middlebrook | 27 | not out | 1 |
| J S Patel, c Patterson b Bresnan | 31 | | |
| C J C Wright, not out | 10 | | |
| W B Rankin, lbw b Middlebrook | 3 | | |
| Extras lb 13 | 13 | Extras b 1, lb 5, nb 8 | 14 |
| Total | 435 | Total (7 wkts dec) | 219 |

Bonus points — Warwickshire 3, Yorkshire1
Score at 110 overs: 309-5

*FoW:* 1-0 (Chopra), 2-95 (Porterfield), 3-136 (Evans), 4-229 (Hain), 5-278 (McKay),
1st 6-360 (Westwood), 7-380 (Clarke), 8-404 (Barker), 9-426 (Patel), 10-435 (Rankin)
*FoW:* 1-12 (Chopra), 2-64 (Porterfield), 3-114 (Evans), 4-157 (Westwood), 5-167 (McKay),
2nd 6-202 (Hain), 7-219 (Clarke)

| | O | M | R | W | | O | M | R | W |
|---|---|---|---|---|---|---|---|---|---|
| Bresnan | 30 | 10 | 85 | 5 | Bresnan | 13 | 2 | 39 | 2 |
| Brooks | 25 | 7 | 66 | 0 | Brooks | 9 | 2 | 35 | 0 |
| Patterson | 29 | 11 | 64 | 1 | Patterson | 14 | 1 | 47 | 0 |
| Fisher | 17 | 2 | 70 | 1 | Fisher | 2 | 0 | 10 | 0 |
| Middlebrook | 31.3 | 6 | 96 | 3 | Middlebrook | 16.3 | 1 | 82 | 5 |
| Rhodes | 10 | 2 | 36 | 0 | | | | | |
| Pujara | 1 | 0 | 5 | 0 | | | | | |

| YORKSHIRE | | | |
|---|---|---|---|
| | First Innings | | Second innings |
| A Z Lees, lbw b Patel | 19 | c McKay b Clarke | 21 |
| W M H Rhodes, c Rankin b Patel | 46 | lbw b Patel | 29 |
| C A Pujara, c McKay b Rankin | 23 | lbw b Patel | 33 |
| * A W Gale, c Hain b Rankin | 96 | c McKay b Patel | 28 |
| J A Leaning, c Hain b Rankin | 41 | not out | 35 |
| § A J Hodd, b Porterfield b Rankin | 4 | not out | 54 |
| T T Bresnan, b Patel | 2 | | |
| J D Middlebrook, run out (Clarke/Patel) | 2 | | |
| S A Patterson, c McKay b Rankin | 11 | | |
| J A Brooks, c Evans b Rankin | 21 | | |
| M D Fisher, not out | 0 | | |
| Extras b 8, lb 7, w 2, nb 13 | 30 | Extras b 4, lb 9, nb 8 | 21 |
| Total | 303 | Total (4 wkts) | 221 |

Bonus points — Yorkshire 3, Warwickshire 3

*FoW:* 1-41 (Lees), 2-88 (Rhodes), 3-88 (Pujara), 4-185 (Leaning), 5-207 (Hodd),
1st 6-222 (Bresnan), 7-224 (Middlebrook), 8-249 (Patterson), 9-303 (Brooks, 10-303 (Gale)
2nd 1-48 (Lees), 2-82 (Rhodes), 3-129 (Pujara), 4-136 (Gale)

| | O | M | R | W | | O | M | R | W |
|---|---|---|---|---|---|---|---|---|---|
| Barker | 22 | 4 | 74 | 0 | Barker | 9 | 4 | 25 | 0 |
| Wright | 18 | 1 | 63 | 0 | Wright | 7 | 0 | 30 | 0 |
| Clarke | 12 | 4 | 19 | 0 | Patel | 28 | 8 | 70 | 3 |
| Patel | 31 | 9 | 77 | 3 | Clarke | 11 | 0 | 48 | 1 |
| Rankin | 15,3 | 0 | 55 | 6 | Rankin | 8 | 0 | 26 | 0 |
| | | | | | Westwood | 1 | 0 | 9 | 0 |

Umpires: S A Garratt and J W Lloyds
Scorers: J T Potter and M D Smith

# Captain's knock from Gale

Chopra fell third ball, but Westwood and Porterfield batted until lunch on a docile wicket, and Westwood went on to a career-best 196 before he was out on the second morning.

He played some fine shots, although he appeared to have been run out on 118. Hain, a young player born in Hong Kong of English parents and raised in Australia, looked an accomplished batsman, and there was support for the indefatigable Westwood all down the order.

Bresnan, bowling off a straighter run and closer to the stumps, was Yorkshire's best, and should have stayed on to claim a sixth wicket. Middlebrook, recalled after being released by Northamptonshire, performed the role of containing off-spinner, taking three wickets. It was his first game for Yorkshire since 2001.

Yorkshire owed most to Gale, whose captain's innings ended controversially on 96. Gale expected a no-ball to be called as Rankin's delivery was very high. There was also dispute about whether Pujara was caught low by the wicket-keeper.

It was Rankin with a career-best 6-55 who ensured that Yorkshire fell over 100 behind. The 6ft 8in Irishman from Derry/Londonderry, who played one Test at Sydney, has a good, high action and can be very quick, but is prone to inaccuracy.

Middlebrook was needlessly run out, but Rankin with some assistance from Patel, one of *Wisden's* Five Cricketers of the Year, accounted for the lower order.

Warwickshire added 219 runs as

**JAMES MIDDLEBOOK**
**First game since 2001**

Westwood almost made a second century — a feat not achieved on this ground. Diligent Middlebrook took five more wickets. Warwickshire, having batted cautiously, would have to bowl well to take 10 wickets, but when Leaning and Hodd came together any prospect of a result disappeared. Yorkshire, with six players on England duty and Sidebottom injured, had done well in their results to date.

# LV County Championship Division 1
## Yorkshire v. Hampshire

Played at Headingley, Leeds, on May 10, 11, 12 and 13, 2015
*Yorkshire won by 305 runs at 2.41pm on the Fourth Day*

Toss won by Yorkshire          Yorkshire 23 points, Hampshire 4 points
Close of play: First Day, Yorkshire 333-7 (Leaning 77*, Bresnan 23*); Second Day, Hampshire 223-8 (McManus 10*|); Third Day, Hampshire 37-4 (Smith 18*, Tomlinson 0*)

| | First Innings | | | | Second innings | |
|---|---|---|---|---|---|---|
| A Lyth, c McManus b Adams | | 53 | | c McManus b Edwards | | 23 |
| A Z Lees, lbw b Tomlinson | | 1 | | b Berg | | 16 |
| C A Pujara, c Ervine b Tomlinson | | 18 | | not out | | 133 |
| * A W Gale, c Carberry b Adams | | 30 | | c Tomlinson b Edwards | | 12 |
| § J M Bairstow, c McManus b Adams | | 102 | | c Ervine b Dawson | | 59 |
| J A Leaning, lbw b Tomlinson | | 82 | | not out | | 43 |
| A U Rashid, c Edwards b Berg | | 0 | | | | |
| W M H Rhodes, c Ervine b Berg | | 4 | | | | |
| T T Bresnan, c Smith b Tomlinson | | 28 | | | | |
| S A Patterson, not out | | 17 | | | | |
| J A Brooks, c McManus b Edwards | | 9 | | | | |
| Extras b 1, lb 17, nb 8 | | 26 | | Extras b 4, lb 2, w 1, nb 12 | | 19 |
| Total | | 370 | | Total (4 wkts dec) | | 305 |

Bonus points — Yorkshire 4, Hampshire 3        Score at 110 overs: 359-9

FoW: 1-9 (Lees), 2-57 (Pujara), 3-109 (Lyth), 4-114 (Gale), 5-269 (Bairstow),
1st 6-274 (Rashid), 7-279 (Rhodes), 8-343 (Bresnan), 9-254 (Leaning), 10-370 (Brooks)
2nd 1-35 (Lyth), 2-57 (Lees), 3-80 (Gale), 4-210 (Bairstow)

| | O | M | R | W | | O | M | R | W |
|---|---|---|---|---|---|---|---|---|---|
| Tomlinson | 34 | 10 | 86 | 4 | Tomlinson | 9 | 2 | 33 | 0 |
| Edwards | 15.3 | 1 | 77 | 1 | Edwards | 17 | 4 | 96 | 2 |
| Adams | 30 | 9 | 68 | 3 | Berg | 12 | 2 | 42 | 1 |
| Berg | 19 | 4 | 49 | 2 | Adams | 12 | 1 | 34 | 0 |
| Dawson | 5 | 0 | 30 | 0 | Dawson | 12 | 0 | 63 | 1 |
| Ervine | 9 | 1 | 42 | 0 | Smith | 7 | 0 | 31 | 0 |

| | First Innings | | | | Second Innings | |
|---|---|---|---|---|---|---|
| S P Terry, lbw b Bresnan | | 0 | | c Bresnan b Brooks | | 1 |
| L A Dawson, c Leaning b Rhodes | | 40 | | lbw b Rashid | | 16 |
| M A Carberry, c Pujara b Rashid | | 97 | | c Bairstow b Brooks | | 0 |
| * J M Vince, lbw b Brooks | | 6 | | c Lyth b Brooks | | 2 |
| W R Smith, c Lyth b Brooks | | 0 | | not out | | 64 |
| S M Ervine, c Patterson b Brooks | | 48 | | (7) c Bairstow b Bresnan | | 5 |
| § L D McManus, lbw b Brooks | | 10 | | (8) c Bairstow b Rhodes | | 28 |
| G K Berg, c Lyth b Rashid | | 10 | | (9) c Brooks b Rashid | | 12 |
| A R Adams, c Gale b Rashid | | 8 | | (10) c Bresnan b Rashid | | 0 |
| J A Tomlinson, lbw b Rashid | | 2 | | (6) b Rashid | | 3 |
| F H Edwards, not out | | 2 | | c Lees b Patterson | | 1 |
| Extras lb 2, nb 2 | | 4 | | Extras b 5, lb 4, nb 2 | | 11 |
| Total | | 227 | | Total | | 143 |

Bonus points — Hampshire 1, Yorkshire 3

FoW: 1-8 (Terry), 2-83 (Dawson), 3-109 (Vince), 4-109 (Smith), 5-195 (Carberry),
1st 6-199 (Ervine), 7-215 (Berg), 8-223 (Adams), 9-223 (McManus), 10-227 (Tomlinson)
FoW: 1-1 (Terry), 2-1 (Carberry), 3-11 (Vince), 4-36 (Dawson), 5-54 (Tomlinson),
2nd 6-67 (Ervine), 7-123 (McManus), 8-138 (Berg), 9-138 (Adams), 10-143 (Edwards)

| | O | M | R | W | | O | M | R | W |
|---|---|---|---|---|---|---|---|---|---|
| Bresnan | 17 | 7 | 33 | 1 | Bresnan | 12 | 3 | 25 | 1 |
| Brooks | 18 | 5 | 57 | 4 | Brooks | 17 | 7 | 31 | 3 |
| Patterson | 17 | 9 | 35 | 0 | Patterson | 10.3 | 4 | 16 | 1 |
| Rhodes | 8 | 2 | 29 | 1 | Rashid | 26 | 9 | 48 | 4 |
| Rashid | 18 | 0 | 70 | 4 | Lyth | 2 | 0 | 8 | 0 |
| Lyth | 2 | 1 | 1 | 0 | Rhodes | 7 | 5 | 6 | 1 |

Umpires: M J D Bodenham and R A Kettleborough     Scorers: J T Potter and K R Baker

# Bairstow a class apart

On a cold, windy morning Yorkshire's batsmen had to contend with a moving ball skilfully manipulated by Tomlinson and Adams.

They lost four wickets including Lyth for a creditable 53 on his return from the West Indies.

Many spectators had to contend with traffic disruption caused by the Leeds Marathon, but they were rewarded with a Bairstow century. When he is in such fine fettle Jonathan is a class apart — immaculate timing and shot selection, cover and straight-driving and three leg-side sixes off Edwards, a Test player on debut for Hampshire, were all a pleasure to watch.

**JONATHAN BAIRSTOW: Shot selection, timing and bix sixes**

Leaning again demonstrated his ability to step in to sustain an innings as Yorkshire reached 370 next morning. Tomlinson's left arm trajectory, Adams's away swing and Berg's accuracy kept some control while Edwards improved notably in the second innings.

Hampshire's batting was disappointing, and only Carberry made any serious impact. His patient application and range of strokes impressed until he lost concentration and hit a simple catch to mid-wicket on 97. Brooks removed Vince and Smith cheaply, and Rashid disposed of the tail as Hampshire finished 143 behind. Pujara showed what a good batsman he is on a profitable third day for Yorkshire with a fine century, and he was pushed forward to lead the team off at the end of his last match here. With support from Bairstow and Leaning, showing his attacking shots this time, Pujara ensured that Yorkshire had an impregnable lead. Brooks then had one of his inspired spells, leaving Hampshire on 37-4 including Carberry first ball and a second failure by Vince, the captain.

The last day was a formality, but the end was delayed by Smith's obdurate 64 not out and a good innings from McManus, a young wicket-keeper/batsman from Bournemouth. Rhodes played because Plunkett had been disciplined for failure to attend the practice and photo session.

# LV County Championship Division 1
## Somerset v. Yorkshire

Played at The County Ground, Taunton, on May 24, 25, 26 and 27, 2015
*Match drawn at 5pm on the Fourth Day*

Toss won by Somerset

Yorkshire 13 points, Somerset 12 points

Close of play: First Day, Yorkshire 345-8 (Bresnan 56*); Second Day, Somerset 309-4 (Cooper 55*, Thomas 4*); Third Day, Yorkshire 171-5 (Bairstow 33*, Rashid 23*)

| YORKSHIRE | First Innings | | Second innings | |
|---|---|---|---|---|
| A Z Lees, lbw b Trego | 34 | c Barrow b Trego | 1 |
| W M H Rhodes, c Cooper b J Overton | 28 | c Allenby b Myburgh | 40 |
| J A Leaning, b Trego | 123 | c Hildreth b C Overton | 52 |
| * A W Gale, c Allenby b Trego | 22 | c Trescothick b C Overton | 12 |
| § J M Bairstow, c Trescothick b C Overton | 54 | c Barrow b Thomas | 66 |
| G J Maxwell, c Abell b C Overton | 0 | b C Overton | 2 |
| A U Rashid, b Thomas | 9 | c Thomas b Myburgh | 99 |
| T T Bresnan, not out | 100 | lbw b Myburgh | 29 |
| L E Plunkett, lbw b Thomas | 0 | run out (J Overton/Barrow) | 21 |
| S A Patterson, c Barrow b Trego | 42 | not out | 44 |
| J A Brooks, c Barrow b C Overton | 0 | c Barrow b Abell | 24 |
| Extras b 10, lb 18, nb 2 | 30 | Extras b 10, lb 12, w 1, nb 6 | 29 |
| Total | 438 | Total | 419 |

Bonus points — Yorkshire 5, Somerset 2

Score at 110 overs: 412-8

*FoW:* 1-55 (Lees), 2-79 (Rhodes), 3-118 (Gale), 4-211 (Bairstow), 5-211 (Maxwell),
1st    6-225 (Rashid), 7-344 (Leaning), 8-345 (Plunkett), 9-437 (Patterson), 10-438 (Brooks)
*FoW:* 1-5 (Lees), 2-82 (Rhodes), 3-108 (Leaning), 4-109 (Gale), 5-117 (Maxwell),
2nd    6-234 (Bairstow), 7-323 (Bresnan), 8-331 (Rashid), 9-355 (Plunkett), 10-419 (Brooks)

| | O | M | R | W | | O | M | R | W |
|---|---|---|---|---|---|---|---|---|---|
| Thomas | 26 | 7 | 90 | 2 | Thomas | 18 | 3 | 57 | 1 |
| J Overton | 18 | 4 | 78 | 1 | Trego | 19 | 3 | 57 | 1 |
| Trego | 19 | 6 | 73 | 4 | C Overton | 24 | 3 | 73 | 3 |
| C Overton | 22.2 | 4 | 74 | 3 | J Overton | 21 | 4 | 60 | 0 |
| Allenby | 22 | 5 | 61 | 0 | Allenby | 19 | 6 | 36 | 0 |
| Myburgh | 3 | 0 | 18 | 0 | Myburgh | 28 | 10 | 57 | 3 |
| Cooper | 4 | 0 | 16 | 0 | Cooper | 13 | 1 | 46 | 0 |
| | | | | | Abell | 4.4 | 0 | 11 | 1 |

| SOMERSET | First Innings | | Second Innings | |
|---|---|---|---|---|
| * M E Trescothick, c Bairstow b Patterson | 56 | c Plunkett b Maxwell | 4 |
| T B Abell, c Bresnan b Rashid | 62 | not out | 1 |
| J G Myburgh, lbw b Patterson | 41 | not out | 1 |
| J C Hildreth, c and b Rashid | 82 | | |
| T L W Cooper, c Bairstow b Plunkett | 99 | | |
| A C Thomas, b Plunkett | 4 | | |
| J Allenby, b Patterson | 31 | | |
| P D Trego, b Patterson | 10 | | |
| § A W R Barrow, c Bairstow b Patterson | 0 | | |
| C Overton, not out | 31 | | |
| J Overton, c Bresnan b Rashid | 50 | | |
| Extras b 4, lb 2, w 1, nb 12 | 19 | Extras | 0 |
| Total | 485 | Total (1 wkt) | 6 |

Bonus points — Somerset 5, Yorkshire 3

*FoW:* 1-84 (Trescothick), 2-163 (Abell), 3-165 (Myburgh), 4-294 (Hildreth), 5-311 (Thomas),
1st    6-369 (Allenby), 7-387 (Trego), 8-389 (Barrow), 9-409 (Cooper), 10-485(J Overton)
2nd    1-5 (Trescothick)

| | O | M | R | W | | O | M | R | W |
|---|---|---|---|---|---|---|---|---|---|
| Bresnan | 11 | 1 | 69 | 0 | Bresnan | 1 | 0 | 4 | 0 |
| Brooks | 19 | 4 | 88 | 0 | Maxwell | 1 | 0 | 2 | 1 |
| Plunkett | 23 | 4 | 101 | 2 | | | | | |
| Patterson | 23 | 10 | 70 | 5 | | | | | |
| Rashid | 20.4 | 0 | 121 | 3 | | | | | |
| Rhodes | 4 | 1 | 13 | 0 | | | | | |
| Maxwell | 2 | 0 | 17 | 0 | | | | | |

Umpires: P W Baldwin and D J Millns

Scorers: J T Potter and G A Stickley

## Somerset v. Yorkshire

# Rashid halts twin challenge

This small ground is where batsmen prosper and bowlers perspire. There were three totals over 400, two centuries and two 99s.

Trescothick asked Yorkshire to bat on a cloudy Spring Bank Holiday Sunday, and although Trego and the Overton twins took wickets Leaning went on to his second century of the summer.

The solid Leaning received stolid support from Bresnan, who reached an undefeated hundred next morning, his first for eight years.

Somerset responded

**ADIL RASHID: Battling 99 helped to see Yorkshire out of danger.**

with 485 against some indifferent bowling, made more quickly than Yorkshire's 438, but credit must go to Patterson for his economy despite the Overton onslaught and five-hard earned wickets. Taunton young player Abell showed promise; the consistent Hildreth made 82, but top scorer was Australian Cooper, who made an attractive 99.

Then came the Overton twins, Craig and Jamie from the North Devon club at Instow. They made 76 for the 10th wicket in 5.5 overs, Jamie hitting 50 off 19 balls with seven fours and three sixes, and Craig 31 off 25. Craig hit four boundaries in a Patterson over, probably unprecedented, and Jamie four off a Rashid over. It was a remarkable stand between identical twins, recalling memories of A D E and A E S Rippon opening for Somerset – how often did Eric and Alec Bedser bat together?

Somerset had a lead of 47, and the Overtons were not finished yet. Yorkshire were reduced to 117-5 as Craig removed Leaning, Gale and Maxwell, and were only 70 ahead. Good batting from Bairstow and especially Rashid, who made 99, and sensible application from the lower order, including Patterson's 44 not out, ended any prospect of a positive result. Somerset had deregistered Rehman in order to have two other overseas players for a *T20* game, but makeshift spinner Myburgh took 3-57. They did miss an experienced spin bowler on the last day.

# LV County Championship Division 1
## Yorkshire v. Middlesex

Played at Headingley, Leeds, on June 7, 8 and 9, 2015
*Yorkshire won by 4 wickets at 6.24pm on the Third Day*

Toss won by Middlesex — Yorkshire 20 points, Middlesex 4 points
Close of play: First Day, Yorkshire 96-4 (Bairstow 25*, Leaning 20*); Second Day, Middlesex 127 -4 (Malan 33*, Franklin 26*)

| First Innings | MIDDLESEX | | Second innings | |
|---|---|---|---|---|
| S D Robson, b Brooks | 41 | | (2) lbw b Patterson | 34 |
| J A Burns, lbw b Brooks | 4 | | (1) c Lyth b Brooks | 20 |
| N R D Compton, c Leaning b Brooks | 70 | | lbw b Brooks | 0 |
| D J Malan, c Bairstow b Patterson | 9 | | c Bresnan b Lyth | 35 |
| N J Dexter, c Bairstow b Brooks | 0 | | lbw b Bresnan | 2 |
| * J E C Franklin, c Leaning b Maxwell | 3 | | not out | 55 |
| § J A Simpson, lbw b Maxwell | 0 | | b Bresnan | 15 |
| O P Rayner, b Maxwell | 20 | | c Ballance b Patterson | 28 |
| J A R Harris, c Ballance b Brooks | 22 | | lbw b Rhodes | 5 |
| T S Roland-Jones, lbw b Patterson | 11 | | c Ballance b Rhodes | 4 |
| T J Murtagh, not out | 17 | | b Rhodes | 13 |
| Extras b 12, lb 3 | 15 | | Extras b 8, lb 4, nb 6 | 18 |
| Total | 212 | | Total | 229 |

Bonus points — Middlesex 1, Yorkshire 3

*FoW:* 1st: 1-6 (Burns), 2-68 (Robson), 3-83 (Malan), 4-92 (Dexter), 5-119 (Franklin), 6-119 (Simpson), 7-147 (Rayner), 8-171 (Compton), 9-188 (Roland-Jones), 10-212 (Harris)
*FoW:* 2nd: 1-51 (Burns), 2-51 (Compton), 3-65 (Robson), 4-72 (Dexter), 5-130 (Malan), 6-159 (Simpson), 7- 206 (Rayner), 8-211 (Harris), 9-215 (Roland-Jones), 10-229 (Murtagh)

| | O | M | R | W | | O | M | R | W |
|---|---|---|---|---|---|---|---|---|---|
| Bresnan | 15 | 6 | 36 | 0 | Bresnan | 17 | 5 | 51 | 2 |
| Brooks | 18.5 | 4 | 44 | 5 | Brooks | 16 | 2 | 51 | 2 |
| Patterson | 19 | 7 | 42 | 2 | Patterson | 23 | 12 | 33 | 2 |
| Rhodes | 5 | 1 | 20 | 0 | Rhodes | 9.5 | 0 | 42 | 3 |
| Maxwell | 11 | 1 | 55 | 3 | Maxwell | 4 | 0 | 19 | 0 |
| | | | | | Lyth | 10 | 1 | 21 | 1 |

| First Innings | YORKSHIRE | | Second innings | |
|---|---|---|---|---|
| A Lyth, c Rayner b Roland - Jones | 17 | | c Simpson b Rayner | 67 |
| A Z Lees, c Rayner b Murtagh | 11 | | lbw b Franklin | 10 |
| G S Ballance, lbw b Murtagh | 1 | | st Simpson b Rayner | 29 |
| * A W Gale, lbw b Harris | 18 | | b Murtagh | 37 |
| § J M Bairstow, not out | 125 | | c Rayner b Roland-Jones | 0 |
| J A Leaning, lbw b Roland-Jones | 20 | | c Rayner b Harris | 25 |
| G J Maxwell, c Simpson b Roland-Jones | 0 | | not out | 23 |
| W M H Rhodes, c Simpson b Murtagh | 11 | | not out | 10 |
| T T Bresnan, c Rayner b Harris | 4 | | | |
| S A Patterson, b Roland-Jones | 12 | | | |
| J A Brooks, c Simpson b Rayner | 6 | | | |
| Extras b 1, lb 3 | 4 | | Extras b 4, lb 8, nb 2 | 14 |
| Total | 229 | | Total (6 wkts) | 215 |

Bonus points — Yorkshire 1, Middlesex 3

*FoW:* 1st: 1-29 (Lyth), 2-29 (Lees), 3-36 (Ballance), 4-52 (Gale), 5-96 (Leaning), 6-96 (Maxwell), 7-131 (Rhodes), 8-142 (Bresnan), 9-170 (Patterson), 10-229 (Brooks)
*FoW:* 2nd: 1-27 (Lees), 2-98 (Ballance), 3-129 (Lyth), 4-132 (Bairstow), 5-169 (Leaning), 6-189 (Gale)

| | O | M | R | W | | O | M | R | W |
|---|---|---|---|---|---|---|---|---|---|
| Murtagh | 21 | 4 | 62 | 3 | Murtagh | 13 | 3 | 36 | 1 |
| Roland-Jones | 23 | 5 | 78 | 4 | Roland-Jones | 16 | 5 | 32 | 1 |
| Harris | 15 | 0 | 47 | 2 | Harris | 12.4 | 2 | 56 | 1 |
| Dexter | 11 | 2 | 19 | 0 | Franklin | 4 | 1 | 19 | 1 |
| Rayner | 2.5 | 0 | 19 | 1 | Rayner | 17 | 6 | 52 | 2 |
| | | | | | Dexter | 3 | 0 | 8 | 0 |

Umpires: J H Evans and M J Saggers          Scorers: J T Potter and D K Shelley

# Bairstow at his brilliant best

**JONATHAN BAIRSTOW: 125 was surely one of his finest innings**

A keenly contested, evenly balanced match ended late on the third day with a win for Yorkshire.

It featured an outstanding innings from Bairstow, solid contributions from Compton and Franklin and some remarkable catching, but batting was never assured on a lively, initially greenish pitch.

Robson was out just before lunch, and then the Middlesex middle-order succumbed mainly to an exuberant Brooks, but the profligate Maxwell took three wickets in four overs despite conceded five consecutive boundaries to Rayner. Brooks well deserved his 5-44, but by the Sunday close Yorkshire were 96-4 as Murtagh, Rowland-Jones and Harris all bowled well. All the more credit to Bairstow, whose unbeaten 125 was surely one of his best innings with no imperfections after he had lost Leaning first ball on Monday. The cover and straight-driving, four splendid sixes and his timing and composure will long live in the memory. Murtagh and Rowland-Jones took wickets, but Patterson and Brooks stayed with Bairstow long enough to give Yorkshire a narrow lead that had seemed unattainable at 142-8.

Middlesex started their second innings well, but lost Burns and then Compton first ball. Lyth, opening the bowling next morning, dismissed left-hander Malan, and Middlesex could only equal Yorkshire's 229. Their New Zealand captain, Franklin, regained his form with an unbeaten 55, but Rhodes, replacing Sidebottom, finished off the innings with three wickets. Yorkshire had to get 215, which was never going to be straightforward. Lyth made a good 67, and Ballance and Gale helped, but at 169-5 it was anybody's game. The Middlesex seamers and Rayner, a very tall off-spinner, looked as if they might win the match. But Yorkshire survived and Maxwell hit the winning six.

A special feature of the match was the superb catching: Compton caught at third slip by Leaning, Burns by a diving Lyth miraculously at second slip, Rayner smartly at cover by Ballance. Rayner himself held five slip catches including a beauty to dismiss Leaning.

# LV County Championship Division 1
## Yorkshire v. Nottinghamshire

Played at Headingley, Leeds, on June 22, 23 and 24, 2015
*Yorkshire won by an innings and 8 runs at 5.25pm on the Third Day*

Toss won by Yorkshire

Yorkshire 24 points, Nottinghamshire 3 points

Close of play: First Day, Nottinghamshire 169-8 (Wood 19*, Hilfenhaus 1*); Second Day, Yorkshire 302-3 (Gale 144*, Leaning 107*)

### NOTTINGHAMSHIRE

| | First Innings | | Second innings | |
|---|---|---|---|---|
| S J Mullaney, c Hodd b Sidebottom | 28 | c Bairstow b Sidebottom | 9 |
| B R M Taylor, c Lees b Patterson | 29 | c Middlebrook b Sidebottom | 0 |
| M J Lumb, lbw b Bresnan | 7 | lbw b Bresnan | 47 |
| * J W A Taylor, c Hodd b Patterson | 0 | lbw b Patterson | 6 |
| § M H Wessels, lbw b Sidebottom | 33 | c Bairstow b Bresnan | 16 |
| S R Patel, lbw b Brooks | 4 | c Lees b Sidebottom | 4 |
| W R S Gidman, lbw b Brooks | 4 | c Ballance b Brooks | 0 |
| S C J Broad, c Leaning b Bresnan | 34 | c Gale b Middlebrook | 50 |
| L Wood, b Brooks | 38 | b Sidebottom | 12 |
| B W Hilfenhaus, not out | 28 | not out | 17 |
| J T Ball, b Brooks | 0 | c Sidebottom b Middlebrook | 6 |
| Extras b 8, lb 5, nb 6 | 19 | Extras b 8, lb 16, w 1, nb 6 | 31 |
| Total | 224 | Total | 198 |

Bonus points — Nottinghamshire 1, Yorkshire 3

FoW: 1-43 (B R M Taylor), 2-52 (Lumb), 3-53 (J W A Taylor), 4-80 (Mullaney), 5-87 (Patel),
1st   6-109 (Gidman), 7-133 (Wessels), 8-159 (Broad), 9-224 (Wood), 10-224 (Ball)
FoW: 1-1 (B R M Taylor), 2-20 (Mullaney), 3-40 (J W A Taylor), 4-79 (Wessels), 5-84 (Lumb),
2nd   6-88 (Gidman), 7-108 (Patel), 8-126 (Wood), 9-186 (Broad), 10-198 (Ball)

| | O | M | R | W | | O | M | R | W |
|---|---|---|---|---|---|---|---|---|---|
| Sidebottom | 13 | 4 | 41 | 2 | Sidebottom | 11 | 3 | 39 | 4 |
| Brooks | 14.5 | 2 | 56 | 4 | Brooks | 11 | 2 | 49 | 1 |
| Patterson | 14 | 2 | 59 | 2 | Bresnan | 10 | 3 | 40 | 2 |
| Bresnan | 15 | 6 | 49 | 2 | Patterson | 7 | 0 | 34 | 1 |
| Middlebrook | 3 | 1 | 6 | 0 | Middlebrook | 3.3 | 2 | 12 | 2 |

### YORKSHIRE

| | |
|---|---|
| A Lyth, lbw b Broad | 0 |
| A Z Lees, b Broad | 15 |
| G S Ballance, c Patel b Hilfenhaus | 14 |
| * A W Gale, lbw b Broad | 148 |
| J A Leaning, b Broad | 110 |
| § J M Bairstow, b Wood | 15 |
| T T Bresnan, not out | 52 |
| J D Middlebrook, c Mullaney b Hilfenhaus | 13 |
| S A Patterson, c Wessels b Broad | 23 |
| J A Brooks, c B R M Taylor b Broad | 8 |
| R J Sidebottom, lbw b Broad | 0 |
| Extras b 10, lb 10, nb 12 | 32 |
| Total | 430 |

*§ J M Bairstow replaced A J Hodd before play on the Third Day*

Bonus points — Yorkshire 5, Nottinghamshire 2

Score at 110 overs: 418-7

FoW: 1-0 (Lyth), 2-28 (Ballance), 3-51 (Lees), 4-306 (Gale), 5-325 (Leaning), 6-325
(Bairstow), 7-368 (Middlebrook), 8-418 (Patterson), 9-430 (Brooks), 10-430 (Sidebottom)

| | O | M | R | W |
|---|---|---|---|---|
| Broad | 26.4 | 5 | 84 | 7 |
| Wood | 18 | 3 | 73 | 1 |
| Hilfenhaus | 23 | 5 | 75 | 2 |
| Ball | 19 | 2 | 77 | 0 |
| Gidman | 7 | 1 | 28 | 0 |
| Patel | 18 | 2 | 60 | 0 |
| Mullaney | 3 | 0 | 13 | 0 |

Umpires: G D Lloyd and D J Millns

Scorers: J T Potter and R Marshall

## Yorkshire v. Nottinghamshire
# Gale spoils Broad's party

A smiling Gale led his side off the field at the end having deployed his bowlers intelligently over two innings, taken a stunning catch in the covers and played a match-winning innings.

The game was transformed by a partnership of 255 between Gale and Leaning for the fourth wicket after it had seemed that it would be a close contest with modest totals on a greenish wicket.

The pair ensured that Yorkshire had a lead of 206, so the visitors sec-

**ANDREW GALE: The right tactics, captain's innings and great catch**

ond innings was in a hopeless cause. It was cold and windy when Yorkshire won the toss. They used this advantage to put Nottinghamshire in to bat and take early wickets, once they had broken through Brendan Taylor and Mullaney. As has become customary all Yorkshire's seam bowlers contributed to the sustained pressure with their accuracy and movement, and wickets were shared around.

Yorkshire lost three early wickets as Broad, Wood, a promising 19-year-old from Worksop, and Hilfenhaus all bowled well, but Gale was then joined by Leaning and each made centuries. Gale showed tenacity and resolution, but he played with aggression when offered the opportunity. Leaning was solid and imperturbable, but also demonstrated the power of his shots. On the last morning Yorkshire soon lost both batsmen, but Bresnan hit a valuable 52 not out. Bairstow replaced Hodd and suffered an unexpected failure.

Broad had an energetic 29th birthday on a rare county appearance, his 16th Championship match in eight years. He has a smooth run-up and a good high arm action, and achieved sufficient movement to claim 7-84. He then made a rapid 50 in a losing cause. Nottinghamshire had to survive almost two days, and it proved beyond them. Sidebottom dismissed both openers, and wickets fell around Lumb, who defied his former county. Patel's misfortunes continued as Lees took a remarkable high catch at first slip. It was over when Sidebottom caught Ball at long-off.

125

# LV County Championship Division 1
## Durham v. Yorkshire

Played at Durham ICG, Chester-le Street, on June 28, 29 and 30 and July 1, 2015

*Yorkshire won by an innings and 47 runs at 12.22pm on the Fourth Day*

Toss won by Durham          Yorkshire 23 points, Durham 3 points

Close of play: First Day, Yorkshire 329-6 (Bairstow 102*, Bresnan 66*); Second Day, Durham 140-5 (Borthwick 35*, Pringle 34*); Third Day, Durham 2nd 244-4 (Stoneman 116*, Muchall 21*)

### YORKSHIRE

| | | |
|---|---|---:|
| A Z Lees, c Richardson b Onions | | 40 |
| W M H Rhodes, b Harrison | | 24 |
| J A Leaning, b Harrison | | 28 |
| * A W Gale, c Collingwood b Hastings | | 22 |
| § J M Bairstow, not out | | 219 |
| A J Finch, c Borthwick b Hastings | | 10 |
| A U Rashid, c Collingwood b Rushworth | | 21 |
| T T Bresnan, not out | | 169 |
| S A Patterson | | |
| J A Brooks | Did not bat | |
| R J Sidebottom | | |
| Extras b 2, lb 13, w 1, nb 8 | | 24 |
| Total (6 wkts dec) | | 557 |

Bonus points — Yorkshire 4, Durham 2       Score at 110 overs: 378-6

*FoW:* 1-56 (Rhodes), 2-82 (Lees), 3-124 (Leaning), 4-130 (Gale), 5-152 (Finch), 6-191 (Rashid)

| | O | M | R | W |
|---|---:|---:|---:|---:|
| Rushworth | 30 | 10 | 70 | 1 |
| Onions | 26 | 5 | 98 | 1 |
| Harrison | 23 | 1 | 77 | 2 |
| Hasting | 31 | 8 | 122 | 2 |
| Collingwood | 13 | 3 | 36 | 0 |
| Pringle | 8 | 0 | 47 | 0 |
| Borthwick | 12 | 1 | 65 | 0 |
| Stoneman | 2 | 0 | 13 | 0 |
| Jennings | 3 | 0 | 14 | 0 |

### DURHAM

| First Innings | | Second innings | |
|---|---:|---|---:|
| M D Stoneman, b Patterson | 25 | lbw b Sidebottom | 131 |
| K K Jennings, c Bresnan b Rashid | 12 | c Lees b Rashid | 41 |
| S G Borthwick, c Bairstow b Bresnan | 54 | c Bairstow b Patterson | 11 |
| * P D Collingwood, lbw b Patterson | 0 | c Bairstow b Rashid | 20 |
| § M J Richardson, lbw b Sidebottom | 31 | c Bairstow b Brooks | 29 |
| G J Muchall, b Bresnan | 0 | b Patterson | 26 |
| R D Pringle, not out | 69 | c sub (R Gibson) b Brooks | 22 |
| J W Hastings, c Bairstow b Bresnan | 0 | b Sidebottom | 7 |
| J Harrison, b Brooks | 11 | lbw b Brooks | 2 |
| C Rushworth, c Bairstow b Brooks | 2 | c Bairstow b Brooks | 3 |
| G Onions, lbw b Rashid | 0 | not out | 0 |
| Extras lb 2, nb 2 | 4 | Extras b 2, lb 6, nb 2 | 10 |
| Total | 208 | Total | 302 |

Bonus points — Durham 1, Yorkshire 3

*FoW:* 1-37 (Jennings), 2-41 (Stoneman), 3-41 (Collingwood), 4-80 (Richardson), 5-81 (Muchall),
1st 6-169 (Borthwick), 7-169 (Hastings), 8-193 (Harrison), 9-195 (Rushworth), 10-208 (Onions)

*FoW:* 1-116 (Jennings), 2-129 (Borthwick), 3-168 (Collingwood), 4-213 (Richardson), 5-251
2nd (Muchall), 6-275 (Stoneman), 7-289 (Hastings), 8-299 (Pringle), 9-299 (Harrison),
10-312 (Rushworth)

| | O | M | R | W | | O | M | R | W |
|---|---:|---:|---:|---:|---|---:|---:|---:|---:|
| Sidebottom | 15 | 4 | 57 | 1 | Brooks | 18.4 | 2 | 66 | 4 |
| Brooks | 10 | 1 | 59 | 2 | Patterson | 14 | 1 | 48 | 2 |
| Patterson | 18 | 11 | 20 | 2 | Rashid | 31 | 2 | 90 | 2 |
| Rashid | 12.1 | 3 | 30 | 2 | Sidebottom | 12 | 1 | 41 | 2 |
| Bresnan | 10 | 2 | 40 | 3 | Bresnan | 12 | 1 | 40 | 0 |
| | | | | | Rhodes | 3 | 0 | 9 | 0 |

Umpires: P K Baldwin and S J O'Shaughnessy     Scorers: J T Potter and B Hunt

## Durham v. Yorkshire
# Records fall as 2 Bs buzz

**TIM BRESNAN: Career-best with 27 boundaries**

An undefeated stand of 366 for the seventh wicket broke many records. Bairstow's 219 and Bresnan's 169 took the Yorkshire score from 191-6 to 557-6.

It broke Yorkshire's seventh-wicket record compiled at Saville Town in 1919 by 112 runs and then the Championship record that had stood since 1902, replacing Prince Ranjitsinhji and Billy Newham's stand at Leyton after 113 years.

For much of the first day it was a competitive contest with runs hard earned against steady bowlers after Collingwood had asked Yorkshire to bat.

Soon after he took a remarkable catch running back from slip, and it was 191-6 and evenly balanced. Then came the stand that turned the match. On the first day they put on 138 at a much accelerated pace as Bairstow reached his century, and Bresnan was just as prolific.

On Monday they batted until the declaration in mid-afternoon, both making career-best scores. Bairstow batted beautifully. He timed the ball so well, showed such impressive footwork and quick hands, and looked as good as any Yorkshire player in my recollection. Bresnan excelled with 27 boundaries and later on a good slip catch and a perfect yorker for Muchall as he topped the Yorkshire wicket-takers with three.

When Durham batted on Monday they had their backs to the wall, and lost six wickets. They eventually reached 208 with a solid contribution from Pringle, but Yorkshire dismissed both Collingwood and Muchall for ducks. So all the home side could do was to try to stave off the inevitable. Stoneman led the way with a defiant 131, and when he and Jennings were batting salvation seemed a possibility.

Brooks had other ideas, and on the final morning the six wickets needed were soon taken. The bowlers worked together, and their ability to take 20 wickets was a crucial factor in Yorkshire's success. It had been a good performance against a side second in the table, and was so well attended that one had to join a long queue on Sunday morning.

# LV County Championship Division 1
## Warwickshire v. Yorkshire

Played at Edgbaston, Birmingham, on July 5, 6, 7 and 8, 2015
*Yorkshire won by 174 runs at 4.49pm on the Fourth Day*

Toss won by Yorkshire      Yorkshire 20 points, Warwickshire 3 points

Close of play: First Day, Warwickshire 11-2 (Westwood 8*, Trott 2*); Second Day, Yorkshire 125-1 (Rhodes 53*, Leaning 28*); Third Day, Warwickshire 43-1 (Leaning 17*, Trott 25*)

| | First Innings | YORKSHIRE | | Second innings | |
|---|---|---|---|---|---|
| A Z Lees, st McKay b Patel | | | 18 | c Chopra b Clarke | 28 |
| W M H Rhodes, b Wright | | | 10 | c sub (TR Ambrose) b Hannon-Dalby | 79 |
| J A Leaning, c Patel b Wright | | | 4 | c sub (TR Ambrose) b Rankin | 46 |
| * A W Gale, c Chopra b Hannon-Dalby | | | 1 | (5) b Patel | 1 |
| § J M Bairstow, b Wright | | | 108 | (6) c Westwood b Hannon-Dalby | 23 |
| A J Finch, lbw b Clarke | | | 28 | (4) not out | 73 |
| T T Bresnan, c McKay b Clarke | | | 10 | run out (Clarke/sub TR Ambrose) | 1 |
| J D Middlebrook, c Clarke b Hannon-Dalby | | | 5 | c Hain b Hannon-Dalby | 2 |
| S A Patterson, c McKay b Wright | | | 11 | not out | 10 |
| J A Brooks, b Wright | | | 8 | | |
| R J Sidebottom, not out | | | 2 | | |
| Extras b 1, lb 4, w 1, nb 2 | | | 8 | Extras b 16, lb 9, w 1 | 26 |
| Total | | | 213 | Total (7 wkts dec) | 289 |

Bonus points — Yorkshire 1 point, Warwickshire 3

FoW: 1-17 (Rhodes), 2-21 (Leaning), 3-26 (Gale), 4-55 (Lees), 5-129 (Finch), 6-153 (Bresnan),
1st   7-170 (Middlebrook), 8-195 (Patterson), 9-208 (Bairstow), 10-213 (Brooks)
FoW: 1-58 (Lees), 2-152 (Leaning), 3-219 (Rhodes), 4-222 (Gale), 5-259 (Bairstow),
2nd   6-263 (Bresnan), 7-267 (Middlebrook)

| | O | M | R | W | | O | M | R | W |
|---|---|---|---|---|---|---|---|---|---|
| Wright | 16.2 | 4 | 40 | 5 | Wright | 15 | 1 | 46 | 0 |
| Hannon-Dalby | 22 | 4 | 60 | 2 | Hannon-Dalby | 21 | 4 | 80 | 3 |
| Clarke | 13 | 1 | 49 | 2 | Patel | 18 | 3 | 53 | 1 |
| Rankin | 11 | 3 | 50 | 1 | Clarke | 10 | 3 | 18 | 1 |
| Patel | 4 | 0 | 9 | 1 | Rankin | 11 | 0 | 54 | 1 |
| | | | | | Trott | 5 | 0 | 13 | 0 |

| | First Innings | WARWICKSHIRE | | Second innings | |
|---|---|---|---|---|---|
| * V Chopra, b Sidebottom | | | 0 | lbw b Sidebottom | 0 |
| I J Westwood, b Sidebottom | | | 14 | lbw b Sidebottom | 40 |
| C J C Wright, lbw b Sidebottom | | | 0 | (9) b Brooks | 6 |
| I J L Trott, c Leaning b Brooks | | | 18 | (3) b Sidebottom | 29 |
| L J Evans, b Sidebottom | | | 2 | (4) lbw b Sidebottom | 0 |
| S R Hain, c Leaning b Sidebottom | | | 0 | (5) lbw b Bresnan | 106 |
| § P McKay, b Sidebottom | | | 0 | (6) c Finch b Patterson | 2 |
| R Clarke, b Patterson | | | 28 | (7) c Leaning b Middlebrook | 18 |
| J S Patel, c Bairstow b Brooks | | | 0 | (8) c Rhodes b Brooks | 13 |
| W B Rankin, c Lees b Brooks | | | 0 | (11) not out | 9 |
| O J Hannon-Dalby, not out | | | 5 | (10) b Sidebottom | 8 |
| Extras lb 2 | | | 2 | Extras b 16, lb 10, nb 2 | 28 |
| Total | | | 69 | Total | 259 |

Bonus points — Yorkshire 3

FoW: 1-0 (Chopra), 2-0 (Wright), 3-29 (Westwood), 4-35 (Evans), 5-35 (Hain),
1st   6-35 (McKay), 7-35 (Trott), 8-35 (Patel), 9-37 (Rankin), 10-69 (Clarke)
FoW: 1-0 (Chopra), 2-58 (Trott), 3-58 (Evans), 4-109 (Westwood), 5-123 (McKay),
2nd   6-170 (Clarke), 7-189 (Patel), 8-203 (Wright), 9-219 (Hannon-Dalby), 10-259 (Hain)

| | O | M | R | W | | O | M | R | W |
|---|---|---|---|---|---|---|---|---|---|
| Sidebottom | 12 | 6 | 34 | 6 | Sidebottom | 19 | 6 | 42 | 5 |
| Brooks | 11 | 4 | 14 | 3 | Brooks | 20 | 4 | 72 | 2 |
| Bresnan | 3 | 0 | 13 | 0 | Patterson | 12 | 4 | 30 | 1 |
| Patterson | 2.1 | 0 | 6 | 1 | Bresnan | 14.5 | 3 | 43 | 1 |
| | | | | | Middlebrook | 15 | 4 | 34 | 1 |
| | | | | | Rhodes | 3 | 0 | 11 | 0 |
| | | | | | Finch | 2 | 1 | 1 | 0 |

Umpires: M Burns and A G Wharf      Scorers: J T Potter and M D Smith

# Eleven scalps for Ryan

**RYAN SIDEBOTTOM: Deadly nagger who did not need his catchers**

A meagre 213, sustained almost entirely by Bairstow's 108, looked inadequate until the Yorkshire bowlers got to work.

Wright led the Warwickshire attack with 5-40, assisted by former Yorkshire bowler Hannon-Dalby and Clarke.

No one else but Finch made a score, so Bairstow's dominance was crucial. He showed both firm resolution and fluent stroke play.

Warwickshire managed only 69 in their reply, saving the follow-on which might have been enforced in view of a dubious weather forecast. There was a remarkable mid innings collapse. At 29-3 recovery was possible, but it became 35-8 and at 37-9 all hope was extinguished. After the dismissal of Westwood left-armer Sidebottom bowled Evans at 35, had Hain caught at slip, and McKay, deputising for Ambrose as he had at Headingley, lbw.

Straight away Brooks struck, having Trott caught by Leaning. Then he removed Patel, still at 35, coincidentally the score at Abbeydale in 1979 when Graham Stevenson took 6-14 and Ryan's father, Arnie, bowled one over to claim the last wicket. Warwickshire lost Rankin at 37, but Hannon-Dalby stayed with Clarke to add 32 for the 10th wicket.

It was good to see Rhodes reach a career-best 79 in Yorkshire's second innings after he had assumed the opener's role in emergency and Finch make an unbeaten 73. Yorkshire led by 434, and their win on the last day was inspired by Sidebottom, who took 5-42 to give him match figures of 11-76. He bowled over the wicket with nagging accuracy on or outside off stump, bowling five and trapping five lbw. Brooks bowled with characteristic exuberance and the rest helped as required.

Warwickshire were indebted to Hain, 19, who made a battling century when all around him failed after they had lost the adhesive Westwood.

129

# LV County Championship Division 1
## Yorkshire v. Worcestershire

Played at North Marine Road, Scarborough, on July 19, 20, 21 and 22, 2015
*Yorkshire won by 7 wickets at 2.54pm on the Fourth Day*

Toss won by Yorkshire — Yorkshire 24 points, Worcestershire 5 points

Close of play: First Day, Yorkshire 357-5 (Gale 127*, Bresnan 17*); Second Day, Worcestershire 195-6, Clarke 76*, Leach 13*); Third Day, Worcestershire f/o 221-6 (Whiteley 65*, Leach 14*)

| First Innings | YORKSHIRE | | Second innings | |
|---|---|---|---|---|
| A Z Lees, c Whiteley b Leach | 12 | | not out | 58 |
| W M H Rhodes, c Whiteley b Leach | 9 | | c Shantry b Saeed Ajmal | 12 |
| J A Leaning, lbw b Leach | 17 | | lbw b Morris | 4 |
| * A W Gale, c Mitchell b Shantry | 164 | | run out (Fell/Saeed Ajmal) | 4 |
| § J M Bairstow, c Fell b d'Oliveira | 139 | | not out | 74 |
| A U Rashid, c Mitchell b Saeed Ajmal | 6 | | | |
| T T Bresnan, c Whiteley b Leach | 28 | | | |
| L E Plunkett, c Cox b Morris | 10 | | | |
| S A Patterson, b Morris | 1 | | | |
| J A Brooks, c Whiteley b Morris | 0 | | | |
| R J Sidebottom, not out | 8 | | | |
| Extras b 4, lb 10, nb 22 | 36 | | Extras lb 1, nb 4 | 5 |
| Total | 430 | | Total (3 wkts) | 157 |

Bonus points — Yorkshire 5, Worcestershire 3

*FoW:* 1-18 (Rhodes), 2-33 (Lees), 3-57 (Leaning), 4-311 (Bairstow) 5-322 (Rashid), 6-368
1st (Bresnan), 7-385 (Plunkett), 8-387 (Patterson), 9-391 (Brooks), 10-430 (Patterson)
2nd 1-34 (Rhodes), 2-40 (Leaning), 3-44 (Gale),

| | O | M | R | W | | O | M | R | W |
|---|---|---|---|---|---|---|---|---|---|
| Morris | 30 | 4 | 90 | 3 | Morris | 9 | 1 | 49 | 1 |
| Leach | 27 | 3 | 139 | 4 | Leach | 3 | 0 | 24 | 0 |
| Shantry | 19.2 | 2 | 84 | 1 | Saeed Ajmal | 11.2 | 3 | 50 | 1 |
| D'Oliveira | 8 | 2 | 28 | 1 | Shantry | 2 | 0 | 14 | 0 |
| Saeed Ajmal | 21 | 3 | 61 | 1 | D'Oliveira | 2 | 0 | 19 | 0 |
| Whiteley | 3 | 0 | 14 | 0 | | | | | |

| First Innings | WORCESTERSHIRE | | Second innings | |
|---|---|---|---|---|
| * D K H Mitchell, lbw b Patterson | 14 | | c Lees b Brooks | 25 |
| R K Oliver, c Plunkett b Brooks | 18 | | lbw b Bresnan | 14 |
| T C Fell, c Leaning b Plunkett | 30 | | c Bairstow b Brooks | 23 |
| J M Clarke, c Lees b Sidebottom | 88 | | b Rashid | 21 |
| B L d'Oliveira, c Bairstow b Patterson | 13 | | c Brooks b Plunkett | 37 |
| R A Whiteley, c Leaning b Patterson | 6 | | lbw b Sidebottom | 101 |
| § O B Cox, c Rashid b Brooks | 15 | | c Leaning b Plunkett | 4 |
| J Leach, lbw b Rashid | 27 | | c Plunkett b Patterson | 27 |
| J D Shantry, c Lees b Rashid | 17 | | b Brooks | 8 |
| Saeed Ajmal, b Bresnan | 37 | | not out | 12 |
| C A J Morris, not out | 3 | | b Sidebottom | 11 |
| Extras b 1, lb 5, nb 6 | 12 | | Extras b 1, lb 10, w 2, nb 10 | 23 |
| Total | 280 | | Total | 306 |

Bonus points — Worcestershire 2, Yorkshire 3

*FoW:* 1-32 (Oliver), 2-53 (Mitchell), 3-66 (Fell), 4-109 (d'Oliveira), 5-119 (Whiteley),
1st 6-175 (Cox), 7-221 (Clarke), 8-225 (Leach). 9-242 (Shantry), 10-280 (Ajmal)
*FoW:* 1-18 (Oliver), 2-65 (Fell), 3-93 (Mitchell), 4-95 (Clarke), 5-195 (d'Oliveira),
2nd 6-201 (Cox), 7-252 (Leach), 8-280 (Shantry), 9-280 (Whiteley), 10-306 (Morris)

| | O | M | R | W | | O | M | R | W |
|---|---|---|---|---|---|---|---|---|---|
| Sidebottom | 16 | 5 | 41 | 1 | Sidebottom | 12.4 | 2 | 37 | 2 |
| Brooks | 15 | 2 | 65 | 2 | Bresnan | 14 | 2 | 48 | 1 |
| Bresnan | 10.3 | 4 | 34 | 1 | Patterson | 17 | 4 | 55 | 1 |
| Patterson | 13 | 2 | 34 | 3 | Plunkett | 11 | 0 | 26 | 2 |
| Plunkett | 11 | 0 | 61 | 1 | Brooks | 15 | 0 | 41 | 3 |
| Rashid | 10 | 1 | 39 | 2 | Rashid | 21 | 3 | 88 | 1 |

Umpires: R J Evans and D J Millns    Scorers: J T Potter and D E Pugh

# Fans stand for Bairstow

**JONATHAN BAIRSTOW**
**213 for once out**

Yorkshire won without playing to their full potential, still suffering top-order failures and not bowling as incisively as of late.

Worcestershire batted well in their second innings, and there were promising individual performances from Clarke and Whiteley. What made the difference was the batting of Gale and Bairstow: Gale solid and tenacious, but with plenty of good shots, and Bairstow at his exhilarating best.

Leach took three early wickets, but once Bairstow joined Gale in a stand of 254 Yorkshire were dominant. When D'Oliveira dismissed Bairstow for 139 everyone rose in tribute to another superb innings.

Gale was last out as Morris led the destruction of the Yorkshire tail, and the captain recorded his second highest score after his 272, also at Scarborough.

Worcestershire ended the second day on 195-6 as the bowlers worked in tandem, Patterson taking most wickets. Clarke, 19 years of age, caught the eye with a fine innings and was looking to a maiden century when he edged Sidebottom to Lees at first slip. The catch of the day was Plunkett's flyer at fourth slip to dismiss Oliver. Worcestershire missed saving the follow-on by one run. It looked as if they would make it as Plunkett conceded boundaries, but at 280 Bresnan unexpectedly bowled Ajmal. How often have a team been exactly 150 behind?

Worcestershire were more defiant in their second innings, making Yorkshire bat again. The outstanding contribution came from Whiteley, Sheffield-born, Repton-educated, who made his third century with a more sedate innings than his recent *T20* contribution. Requiring as many as 157 and aware of a dubious weather forecast, Yorkshire were 44-3 after Gale was run out. Lees called, Gale responded with alacrity, but only to find that Lees had turned back. Lees batted very well, hitting Leach for a massive six in the second over, but again it was Bairstow who transformed the innings with some wonderful hitting and sixes to all parts of the ground. He has fully deserved his recall by England.

# LV County Championship Division 1
## Yorkshire v. Durham

Played at North Marine Road, Scarborough, on August 7, 8 and 9, 2015
*Yorkshire won by 183 runs at 4.44pm on the Third Day*

Toss won by Yorkshire                                    Yorkshire 19 points, Durham 3 points

Close of play: First Day, Yorkshire 10-0 (Hodd 2*, Lees 6*); Second Day, Yorkshire 420-9 (Patterson 18*, Sidebottom 1*)

| | First Innings | YORKSHIRE | | Second innings | |
|---|---|---|---|---|---|
| § A J Hodd, lbw b Harrison | | 9 | c Richardson b Onions | | 21 |
| A Z Lees, b Rushworth | | 2 | c Richardson b Rushworth | | 19 |
| J A Leaning, c Muchall b Hastings | | 16 | c Stoneman b Harrison | | 13 |
| * A W Gale, c Borthwick b Rushworth | | 12 | c Richardson b Onions | | 1 |
| G S Ballance, c Muchall b Onions | | 6 | b Harrison | | 5 |
| G J Maxwell, c Richardson b Onions | | 36 | c Clarke b Pringle | | 140 |
| A U Rashid, c Burnham b Onions | | 4 | c Clark b Rushworth | | 127 |
| T T Bresnan, b Harrison | | 47 | c Borthwick b Rushworth | | 28 |
| L E Plunkett, c Muchall b Rushworth | | 1 | lbw b Pringle | | 27 |
| S A Patterson, c Pringle b Rushworth | | 0 | b Onions | | 36 |
| R J Sidebottom, not out | | 17 | not out | | 1 |
| Extras lb 4, nb 8 | | 12 | Extras lb 15, w 1, nb 6 | | 22 |
| Total | | 162 | Total | | 440 |

Bonus points — Durham 3

*FoW:* 1-13 (Hodd), 2-15 (Lees), 3-27 (Gale), 4-46 (Leaning), 5-54 (Ballance),
1st 6-91 (Maxwell), 7-94 (Rashid), 8-95 (Plunkett), 9-95 (Patterson), 10-162 (Bresnan)
*FoW:* 1-35 (Lees), 2-62 (Leaning), 3-66 (Hodd), 4-73 (Ballance), 5-79 (Gale),
2nd 6-327 (Maxwell), 7-369 (Rashid), 8-377 (Bresnan), 9-416 (Plunkett), 10-440 (Patterson)

| | O | M | R | W | | O | M | R | W |
|---|---|---|---|---|---|---|---|---|---|
| Rushworth | 13 | 4 | 37 | 4 | Rushworth | 23 | 8 | 53 | 3 |
| Harrison | 9 | 0 | 42 | 2 | Harrison | 24 | 3 | 103 | 2 |
| Onions | 11 | 0 | 41 | 3 | Onions | 23.2 | 3 | 95 | 2 |
| Hastings | 10 | 2 | 38 | 1 | Hastings | 9 | 2 | 47 | 0 |
| | | | | | Pringle | 10 | 2 | 46 | 2 |
| | | | | | Borthwick | 12 | 0 | 74 | 0 |
| | | | | | Muchall | 2 | 0 | 7 | 0 |

| | First Innings | DURHAM | | Second innings | |
|---|---|---|---|---|---|
| * M D Stoneman, c Bresnan b Patterson | | 17 | c and b Bresnan | | 37 |
| G Clark, c Balance b Bresnan | | 6 | lbw b Plunkett | | 36 |
| S G Borthwick, lbw b Sidebottom | | 19 | c Maxwell b Plunkett | | 31 |
| G J Muchall, lbw b Patterson | | 0 | c Hodd b Plunkett | | 15 |
| § M J Richardson, c Hodd b Patterson | | 24 | lbw b Bresnan | | 48 |
| J T A Burnham, b Plunkett | | 4 | c Gale b Plunkett | | 50 |
| R D Pringle, c Rashid b Sidebottom | | 40 | c Ballance b Rashid | | 4 |
| J W Hastings, c Lees b Sidebottom | | 13 | (9) lbw b Rashid | | 16 |
| J Harrison, lbw b Rashid | | 0 | (8) run out (Gale/Hodd) | | 0 |
| C Rushworth, c Maxwell b Sidebottom | | 6 | c Plunkett b Rashid | | 0 |
| G Onions, not out | | 8 | not out | | 18 |
| Extras b 4, lb 10, w 1, nb 8 | | 23 | Extras b 1, lb 3, nb 4 | | 8 |
| Total | | 156 | Total | | 263 |

Bonus points — Yorkshire 3

*FoW:* 1-29 (Clark), 2-29 (Stoneman), 3-29 (Muchall), 4-65 (Richardson), 5-66 (Burnham),
1st 6-91 (Borthwick), 7-131 (Hastings), 8-132 (Harrison), 9-148 (Pringle), 10-156 (Rushworth)
*FoW:* 1-54 (Stoneman), 2-107 (Clark), 3-108 (Borthwick), 4-143 (Muchall), 5-196 (Richardson),
2nd 6-209 (Pringle), 7-209 (Harrison), 8-235 (Hastings), 9-235 (Rushworth), 10-263 (Burnham)

| | O | M | R | W | | O | M | R | W |
|---|---|---|---|---|---|---|---|---|---|
| Sidebottom | 13.2 | 3 | 44 | 4 | Sidebottom | 11 | 1 | 54 | 0 |
| Bresnan | 10 | 1 | 50 | 1 | Bresnan | 11 | 1 | 35 | 2 |
| Patterson | 11 | 5 | 16 | 3 | Patterson | 14 | 6 | 35 | 0 |
| Plunket | 6 | 4 | 8 | 1 | Plunkett | 16.1 | 4 | 61 | 4 |
| Rashid | 3 | 0 | 24 | 1 | Rashid | 14 | 2 | 66 | 3 |
| | | | | | Maxwell | 2 | 0 | 8 | 0 |

Umpires: N G B Cook and J W Lloyds                    Scorers: J T Potter and B Hunt

## Yorkshire v. Durham

# Big stand follows slumps

It looked like a closely contested low-scoring game at the end of the first day when 20 wickets had fallen and up to lunchtime on the second.

A sixth-wicket stand of 248 in Yorkshire's second innings between Maxwell and Rashid transformed the situation, and the hosts won with some ease. It was the third such stand in recent matches, all with different participants.

Gale won the toss on a green pitch with some movement and lively

**GLENN MAXWELL: 248 stand with Rashid transformed the match**

bounce, and the Durham seam bowlers dominated the first morning. Yorkshire were 94-7 at lunch, and they soon lost two more wickets. Then Bresnan and Sidebottom added 67 for the last wicket. Rushworth bowled beautifully from the Trafalgar Square end with an easy action and natural away movement, and Onions was more incisive than at Riverside, so wickets fell regularly. Sidebottom, who is having such a fine season, now led the attack as Yorkshire fought back, while Patterson took three good wickets at little cost, including Muchall first ball.

Yorkshire gained a narrow lead, but they had lost five second-innings wickets by lunch on Saturday, and Onions had his 500th First Class wicket. Maxwell now took control, playing a responsible innings with a judicious mixture of defence and characteristically uninhibited strokes. Rashid provided stability with his best innings for some time.

Durham, set an impossible 447 to win, had to survive virtually two days. They made a good start, but they had lost five second-innings wickets either side of lunch, helped by Maxwell's magnificent catch and followed by his dismissal of Muchall, were decisive. Durham-born Burnham, only 18 and making his debut in place of Collingwood, batted well for his 50, but Plunkett and Rashid ensured that there would be no more surprises.

The large crowds over three days, especially on the first when there were long queues at the turnstiles, were a tribute to the attraction of cricket at North Marine Road.

# LV County Championship Division 1
## Sussex v. Yorkshire

Played at The County Ground, Hove, on August 21, 22, 23 and 24, 2015

*Match drawn at 12.15pm on the Fourth Day*

Toss won by Yorkshire        Sussex 12 points, Yorkshire 11 points

Close of play: First Day, Yorkshire 346-6 (Ballance 98*, Bresnan 44 *); Second Day, Sussex 175-4 (Yardy 7*, Robinson 0*); Third Day, Sussex 493-7 (Brown 106*, Jordan 9*)

### YORKSHIRE

| | |
|---|---|
| § A J Hodd, c Jordan b Robinson | 11 |
| A Z Lees, b Robinson | 69 |
| J A Leaning, c and b Jordan | 0 |
| * A W Gale, lbw b Jordan | 39 |
| G S Ballance, b Liddle | 165 |
| G J Maxwell, c Jordan b Robinson | 43 |
| A U Rashid, c Brown b Jordan | 7 |
| T T Bresnan, run out (Nash/Liddle) | 78 |
| L E Plunkett, run out (Joyce) | 28 |
| S A Patterson, c Brown b Liddle | 0 |
| R J Sidebottom, not out | 17 |
| Extras b 8, lb 12, w 4, nb 13 | 37 |
| Total | 494 |

Bonus points — Yorkshire 4, Sussex 2       Score at 110 overs: 393-6

*FoW:* 1-21 (Hodd), 2-22 (Leaning), 3-110 (Gale), 4-134 (Lees), 5-203 (Maxwell), 6-252 (Rashid), 7-449 (Ballance), 8-454 (Bresnan), 9-459 (Patterson), 10-494 (Plunkett)

| | O | M | R | W |
|---|---|---|---|---|
| Magoffin | 30 | 5 | 91 | 0 |
| Robinson | 30 | 11 | 72 | 3 |
| Jordan | 24 | 3 | 87 | 3 |
| Liddle | 24 | 0 | 119 | 2 |
| Wells | 23.3 | 4 | 77 | 0 |
| Nash | 5 | 0 | 28 | 0 |

### SUSSEX

| | |
|---|---|
| * E C Joyce, c Leaning b Rashid | 100 |
| L W P Wells, b Rashid | 43 |
| M W Machan, c Leaning b Rashid | 0 |
| C D Nash, lbw b Plunkett | 18 |
| M H Yardy, lbw b Sidebottom | 124 |
| O E Robinson, c Maxwell b Plunkett | 48 |
| L J Wright, b Patterson | 23 |
| § B C Brown, not out | 106 |
| C J Jordan, not out | 9 |
| S J Magoffin | |
| C J Liddle | Did not bat |
| Extras b 12, lb 10 | 22 |
| Total (7 wkts) | 493 |

Bonus points — Sussex 5, Yorkshire 2       Score at 110 overs: 420-6

*FoW:* 1-110 (Wells), 2-110 (Machan), 3-139 (Nash), 4-175 (Joyce), 5-272 (Robinson), 6-326 (Wright), 7-461 (Yardy)

| | O | M | R | W |
|---|---|---|---|---|
| Sidebottom | 15 | 3 | 39 | 1 |
| Bresnan | 20 | 5 | 66 | 0 |
| Patterson | 19 | 6 | 63 | 1 |
| Plunkett | 24 | 4 | 90 | 2 |
| Rashid | 33 | 5 | 159 | 3 |
| Maxwell | 9 | 1 | 43 | 0 |
| Leaning | 3 | 1 | 11 | 0 |

Umpires: N L Bainton and P J Hartley       Scorers: J T Potter and M J Charman

## Sussex v. Yorkshire
# Ballance provides ballast

There were two high-scoring first innings and no time for any more as rain and a moribund pitch led to an inevitable draw.

On the first day Hodd, on his return to Hove, and Leaning were soon out, but an improving Lees and Gale steadied the ship.

Magoffin always bowls well and was accurate, but he took no wickets. Jordan is lively and quick, and

**GARY BALLANCE: Invaluable 165 and stand with Bresnan worth 197**

Robinson, a revelation this year, has done well on his return south after leaving Headingley after the 2014 season. He bowled Lees for 69, but Ballance provided the ballast to the Yorkshire innings as he proceeded to an invaluable 165 from being 98 overnight. Bresnan, who has never batted better than he has this season, made 78 as he put on 197 with him in another characteristic Yorkshire mid-innings recovery.

Sussex, who were determined not to lose this important game, hit three centuries in an innings that fell one short of the visitors, but they were marginally faster to gain full batting points. Joyce, an Irishman who captains Sussex, made exactly 100 as opener. Yardy, who is shortly to retire after an exemplary career with his native county and who has frequently batted well against Yorkshire, made 124, his fifth century against the *White Rose*.

Enterprising wicket-keeper Brown enjoyed himself with a rapid 106 not out. The Yorkshire bowlers worked hard, not least Rashid, whose three wickets were expensive but were the top three in the order.

It rained on Monday, and prevented any further play. It would have been impossible to arrange any competitive declaration, so spectators were saved a tedious final day and supporters could start the long journey back north or stop off at Chelmsford. The team had not managed a seventh successive victory, but they remained in a strong position in the Championship with a game in hand on their main challengers.

# LV County Championship Division 1
## Yorkshire v. Somerset

Played at Headingley, Leeds, on September 1, 2 and 3, 2015
*Yorkshire won by an innings and 126 runs at 12.30pm on the Third Day*

Toss won by Yorkshire                                    Yorkshire 22 points, Somerset 2 points

Close of play: First Day, Yorkshire 138-3 (Ballance 49*, Patterson 2*); Second Day, Somerset 44-2 (Cooper 12*, Hildreth 18*)

### SOMERSET

| | First Innings | | | Second innings | |
|---|---|---|---|---|---|
| * M E Trescothick, b Sidebottom | | 5 | lbw b Sidebottom | | 5 |
| T B Abell, c Lees b Brooks | | 2 | c Finch b Brooks | | 4 |
| T L W Cooper, c Lyth b Brooks | | 5 | c Bairstow b Patterson | | 28 |
| J C Hildreth, b Lyth b Sidebottom | | 3 | c Lyth b Brooks | | 57 |
| J Allenby, b Brooks | | 0 | c Finch b Patterson | | 12 |
| P D Trego, c Bairstow b Bresnan | | 19 | c Bairstow b Patterson | | 13 |
| § L Ronchi, c Bresnan b Brooks | | 25 | c Bairstow b Sidebottom | | 22 |
| L Gregory, lbw b Brooks | | 24 | c Lyth b Bresnan | | 2 |
| C Overton, c Bresnan b Patterson | | 10 | b Sidebottom | | 4 |
| T D Groenewald, not out | | 15 | c Ballance b Bresnan | | 1 |
| M J Leach, c Lyth b Patterson | | 2 | not out | | 0 |
| Extras | | 0 | Extras lb 3, nb 4 | | 7 |
| Total | | 110 | Total | | 155 |

Bonus points — Yorkshire 3

*FoW:* 1-6 (Abell), 2-8 (Trescothick), 3-14 (Cooper), 4-14 (Allenby), 5-20 (Hildreth),
1st  6-36 (Trego), 7-74 (Gregory), 8-85 (Overton), 9-101 (Ronchi), 10-110 (Leach)
*FoW:* 1-6 (Abell), 2-10 (Trescothick), 3-87 (Cooper), 4-105 (Allenby), 5-111 (Hildreth),
2nd  6-137 (Trego), 7-148 (Ronchi), 8-152 (Overton), 9-154 (Gregory), 10-155 (Groenewald)

| | O | M | R | W | | O | M | R | W |
|---|---|---|---|---|---|---|---|---|---|
| Sidebottom | 8 | 3 | 17 | 2 | Sidebottom | 11 | 2 | 32 | 3 |
| Brooks | 12 | 1 | 35 | 5 | Brooks | 13 | 4 | 49 | 2 |
| Bresnan | 5 | 1 | 16 | 1 | Bresnan | 12.1 | 5 | 28 | 2 |
| Patterson | 10 | 1 | 42 | 2 | Patterson | 11 | 3 | 43 | 3 |

### YORKSHIRE

| | | |
|---|---|---|
| A Lyth, c Gregory b Allenby | | 62 |
| A Z Lees, lbw b Overton | | 10 |
| G S Ballance, c Trescothick b Overton | | 91 |
| * A W Gale, b Leach | | 5 |
| S A Patterson, c Ronchi b Overton | | 44 |
| § J M Bairstow, b Gregory | | 91 |
| A J Finch, lbw b Overton | | 13 |
| T T Bresnan, b Groenewald | | 18 |
| J D Middlebrook, c Trego b Gregory | | 23 |
| J A Brooks, b Gregory | | 11 |
| R J Sidebottom, not out | | 0 |
| Extras b 4, lb 19 | | 23 |
| Total | | 391 |

Bonus points — Yorkshire 3, Somerset 2                    Score at 110 overs: 305-7

*FoW:* 1-46 (Lees), 2-111 (Lyth), 3-133 (Gale), 4-223 (Ballance), 5-236 (Patterson), 6-258
(Finch), 7-304 (Bresnan), 8-364 (Middlebrook), 9-390 (Brooks), 10-391 (Bairstow)

| | O | M | R | W |
|---|---|---|---|---|
| Gregory | 30.2 | 7 | 75 | 3 |
| Groenewald | 26 | 1 | 74 | 1 |
| Overton | 28 | 10 | 64 | 4 |
| Trego | 8 | 1 | 42 | 0 |
| Allenby | 22 | 8 | 46 | 1 |
| Leach | 14 | 2 | 67 | 1 |

Umpires: S A Garratt and I J Gould                    Scorers: J T Potter and G A Stickley

# Brooks leads pace assault

**VITAL BREAK: Bresnan runs to congratulate Brooks on the second-innings wicket of Somerset's Hildreth**

Yorkshire won in less than three days by twice bowling Somerset out cheaply and batting solidly against some good bowling.

An excellent opening spell by Brooks and Sidebottom left Somerset on 20-5. Brooks, recalled to the side under the rotation system, took three as Abell and Cooper were caught in the slips and Allenby was bowled after an injudicious leave.

Sidebottom took crucial wickets when he bowled Trescothick and then had the prolific Hildreth caught by Lyth. Somerset were 80-8 at lunch and all out shortly after a rain break. An exuberant Brooks finished with a career best 5-32.

By the close on Tuesday the hosts had made 138-3, Lyth partially rehabilitated with 62 but well caught at slip by Gregory.

Next morning Ballance and nightwatchman Patterson batted very sensibly, but Ballance fell for 91 just before lunch. Patterson became an afternoon watchman, going on to a dogged if occasionally fortunate 44.

Bairstow took command with a beautifully struck 91 to give him 1,071 Championship runs from 13 innings and an average of 107. It is not so much the average as the quality of strokes and timing that have made his batting so memorable. Craig Overton, whose identical twin, Jamie, withdrew after an injury before the start, bowled very well. Tall, strong, quick, accurate and irascible, he looked a Test player.

Yorkshire have won matches because of their varied pace attack with five bowlers to be supplemented next year by David Willey from Northamptonshire and young Fisher, not forgetting leg-spinner Rashid. Here, fast bowlers shared the wickets at regular intervals. Yorkshire's 22 points put them in a strong position to retain the title at Lord's.

# LV County Championship Division 1
## Middlesex v. Yorkshire

Played at Lord's Cricket Ground on September 9, 10, 11 and 12, 2015
*Middlesex won by 246 runs at 3.07pm on the Fourth Day*

Toss won by Yorkshire

Middlesex 19 points, Yorkshire 5 points

Close of play: First Day, Yorkshire 238-9 (Brooks 12*, Sidebottom 9*); Second Day, Middlesex 274-5 (Compton 86*, Franklin 60*); Third Day, Middlesex 573-8 (Harris 67*, Roland-Jones 103*)

| First Innings | MIDDLESEX | Second innings | |
|---|---|---|---|
| P R Stirling, lbw b Sidebottom | 0 | (2) b Middlebrook | 34 |
| S D Robson, c Lees b Bresnan | 26 | (1) b Bresnan | 53 |
| N R D Compton, c Hodd b Sidebottom | 0 | lbw b Middlebrook | 149 |
| D J Malan, b Sidebottom | 0 | lbw b Middlebrook | 0 |
| S S Eskinazi, c Lyth b Sidebottom | 4 | b Patterson | 22 |
| N J Dexter, c Hodd b Bresnan | 18 | c and b Brooks | 13 |
| * J E C Franklin, c Leaning b Bresnan | 12 | lbw b Sidebottom | 63 |
| § J A Simpson, c Hodd b Middlebrook | 28 | lbw b Lyth | 47 |
| J A R Harris, not out | 0 | not out | 67 |
| T S Roland-Jones, lbw b Bresnan | 0 | not out | 103 |
| T J Murtagh, b Sidebottom | 3 | | |
| Extras lb 4, nb 2 | 6 | Extras b 6, lb 8, nb 8 | 22 |
| Total | 106 | Total (8 wkts dec) | 573 |

Bonus points — Yorkshire 3

FoW: 0-1 (Stirling), 0-2 (Compton), 0-3 (Malan), 4-14 (Eskinazi), 5-44 (Dexter),
1st 6-55 (Robson), 7-92 (Simpson), 8-95 (Franklin), 9-95 (Roland-Jones), 10-106 (Murtagh)
FoW: 1-87 (Robson), 2-87 (Stirling), 3-87 (Malan), 4-128 (Eskinazi), 5-143 (Dexter),
2nd 6-293 (Franklin), 7-380 (Compton), 8-427 (Simpson)

| | O | M | R | W | | O | M | R | W |
|---|---|---|---|---|---|---|---|---|---|
| Sidebottom | 12 | 5 | 18 | 5 | Sidebottom | 28 | 7 | 70 | 1 |
| Brooks | 6 | 0 | 39 | 0 | Brooks | 27 | 3 | 122 | 1 |
| Patterson | 6 | 2 | 11 | 0 | Patterson | 33 | 8 | 96 | 1 |
| Bresnan | 8 | 1 | 30 | 4 | Bresnan | 37 | 13 | 108 | 1 |
| Middlebrook | 1 | 0 | 4 | 1 | Middlebrook | 40 | 7 | 130 | 3 |
| | | | | | Lyth | 8 | 0 | 19 | 1 |
| | | | | | Leaning | 2 | 0 | 14 | 0 |

| First Innings | YORKSHIRE | Second innings | |
|---|---|---|---|
| A Lyth, lbw b Roland-Jones | 25 | c Simpson b Harris | 14 |
| A Z Lees, lbw b Stirling | 39 | c Malan b Roland-Jones | 62 |
| G S Ballance, lbw b Roland-Jones | 0 | lbw b Harris | 0 |
| * A W Gale, c Robson b Dexter | 98 | lbw b Dexter | 17 |
| J A Leaning, lbw b Dexter | 9 | c Robinson b Roland-Jones | 4 |
| T T Bresnan, lbw b Dexter | 11 | c Simpson b Harris | 9 |
| § A J Hodd, b Murtagh | 20 | c Simpson b Roland-Jones | 0 |
| J D Middlebrook, c Simpson b Roland-Jones | 4 | c Malan b Roland-Jones | 0 |
| S A Patterson, c Simpson b Murtagh | 0 | b Murtagh | 9 |
| J A Brooks, not out | 50 | c Eskinazi b Roland-Jones | 2 |
| R J Sidebottom, c and b Murtagh | 28 | not out | 6 |
| Extras b 2, lb 1, w 2, nb 10 | 15 | Extras lb 7, nb 4 | 11 |
| Total | 299 | Total | 134 |

Bonus points — "Yorkshire 2, Middlesex3

FoW: 1-45 (Lyth), 2-51 (Lees), 3-119 (Ballance), 4-163 (Leaning), 5-187 (Bresnan), 6-198,
1st (Gale), 7-217 (Hodd), 8-217 (Patterson), 9-221 (Middlebrook), 10-299 (Sidebottom)
FoW: 1-28 (Lyth), 2-28 (Ballance), 3-92 (Gale), 4-106 (Lees), 5-111 (Leaning),
2nd 6-111 (Hodd), 7-115 (Bresnan), 8-115 (Middlebrook), 9-117 (Brooks), 10-134 (Patterson)

| | O | M | R | W | | O | M | R | W |
|---|---|---|---|---|---|---|---|---|---|
| Murtagh | 18 | 1 | 81 | 3 | Murtagh | 7 | 3 | 18 | 1 |
| Roland-Jones | 25 | 5 | 93 | 3 | Roland-Jones | 21 | 10 | 27 | 5 |
| Harris | 12 | 0 | 67 | 0 | Harris | 14 | 6 | 37 | 3 |
| Franklin | 5 | 1 | 18 | 0 | Franklin | 4 | 2 | 7 | 0 |
| Stirling | 4 | 1 | 13 | 1 | Stirling | 4 | 2 | 7 | 0 |
| Dexter | 8 | 2 | 24 | 3 | Dexter | 8 | 2 | 31 | 1 |

Umpires: S J O'Shaughnessy and R T Robinson

Scorers: J T Potter and D K Shelley

138

# Match lost, title won

**RYAN SIDEBOTTOM: Began with a three-wicket maiden over**

Yorkshire won the Championship at Lord's on the first day, but it was confirmed statistically at Nottingham.

Six points were needed. By bowling out Middlesex for 106 Yorkshire gained three as Middlesex lost five batting points.

It was still necessary for Nottinghamshire to concede one more point. This happened when they were all out at Trent Bridge at about 3 o'clock, so the dignity of the upper tier of the pavilion was disturbed by members' celebrations, and the players' balcony erupted.

It had been a remarkable morning's cricket. Fortunate to win the toss in misty conditions, Yorkshire put Middlesex in and Sidebottom began with a three-wicket maiden over. Stirling was lbw, Compton caught by Hodd and Malan was comprehensively bowled. Eskinazi soon followed, and then Bresnan took over, claiming four wickets. Yorkshire ended the day on 231-9, Gale making a brave 98.

Then the match was transformed as Middlesex took command. Roland-Jones had a game to remember, and Yorkshire suffered a miserable defeat that had seemed inconceivable at the end of the first day. A stand of 78 between Brooks and Sidebottom took the visitors to 299. Middlesex batted with greater resolution to compile a total of 573-8 based on a long, patient innings from Compton and a partnership of 146 for the ninth-wicket in which Roland-Jones made his first century and Harris 67 not out.

Yorkshire had a day to save the match, and at lunch had lost only two wickets. After the interval they subsided, with Roland-Jones and Harris again responsible. Tall and strong, bowling off a long run, Roland-Jones looked a fine cricketer, and Harris is now fulfilling his promise.

There can be few, if any, Yorkshire matches when a side has recovered from such a disastrous first day to win by over 200 runs, so great credit to Middlesex. But there have been no more dramatic and significant overs than that bowled by Sidebottom on Wednesday morning. At the end of the game Andrew Gale was able to receive the trophy to compensate for his tribulations last year at Trent Bridge.

# LV County Championship Division 1
## Hampshire v. Yorkshire

Played at The Rose Bowl, Southampton, on September 14, 15, 16 and 17, 2015
*Yorkshire won by 5 wickets at 5.30pm on the Fourth Day*

Toss won by Yorkshire                                    Yorkshire 19 points, Hampshire 6 points

Close of play: First Day, Hampshire 219-4 (Dawson 47*, Ervine 26*); Second Day, Yorkshire 82-4 (Lees 31*, Bresnan 4*); Third Day, Yorkshire 97-4 (Lees 37*, Bresnan 12*)

*Hampshire forfeited their Second Innings*

### HAMPSHIRE

| | | |
|---|---|---|
| M A Carberry, c Hodd b Brooks | . . . . . . . . . . . . . . . . . . . . | 28 |
| J H K Adams, c Lees b Patterson | . . . . . . . . . . . . . . . . . . . . | 52 |
| * J M Vince, b Bresnan | . . . . . . . . . . . . . . . . . . . . . . . . . | 3 |
| W R Smith, c Hodd b Brooks | . . . . . . . . . . . . . . . . . . . . | 46 |
| L A Dawson, c Hodd b Middlebrook | . . . . . . . . . . . . . . | 140 |
| S M Ervine, st Hodd b Middlebrook | . . . . . . . . . . . . . . | 43 |
| § A J A Wheater, c Gale b Brooks | . . . . . . . . . . . . . . . . | 7 |
| R McLaren, c Leaning b Fisher | . . . . . . . . . . . . . . . . . . | 23 |
| G K Berg, not out | . . . . . . . . . . . . . . . . . . . . . . . . . . . . | 27 |
| R A Stevenson, c Hodd b Fisher | . . . . . . . . . . . . . . . . . | 4 |
| F H Edwards | Did not bat | |
| Extras b 8, lb 9, nb 10 | . . . . . . . . . . . . . . . . . . . . | 27 |
| Total (9 wkts dec) | . . . . . . . . . . . . . . . . . . . . . . | 400 |

Bonus points — Hampshire 5, Yorkshire 3

*FoW:* 1-74 (Carberry), 2-77 (Vince), 3-109 (Adams), 4-181 (Smith), 5-305 (Ervine), 6-320 (Wheater), 7-368 (McLaren), 8-374 (Dawson), 9-400 (Stevenson)

| | O | M | R | W |
|---|---|---|---|---|
| Brooks | . . . . . . . . . . . . . . . . . | 22 | 4 | 97 | 3 |
| Fisher | . . . . . . . . . . . . . . . . . | 23.5 | 10 | 61 | 2 |
| Patterson | . . . . . . . . . . . . . . . . . | 24 | 8 | 68 | 1 |
| Bresnan | . . . . . . . . . . . . . . . . . | 22 | 7 | 69 | 1 |
| Middlebrook | . . . . . . . . . . . . . . | 16 | 1 | 77 | 2 |
| Lyth | . . . . . . . . . . . . . . . . . . . . | 1 | 0 | 11 | 0 |

### YORKSHIRE

| First Innings | | Second innings | |
|---|---|---|---|
| A Lyth, c Vince b Edwards . . . . . . . . . . . . . . | 0 | run out (Adams) . . . . . . . . . . . . . . | 12 |
| A Z Lees, not out . . . . . . . . . . . . . . | 37 | b Edwards . . . . . . . . . . . . . . | 5 |
| G S Ballance, c Berg b Stevenson . . . . . . . . . | 30 | c Wheater b Berg . . . . . . . . . . . . . | 17 |
| * A W Gale, c Wheater b McLaren . . . . . . . . | 3 | c Adams b Edwards . . . . . . . . . . | 125 |
| J A Leaning, c Ervine b McLaren . . . . . . . . | 3 | c Wheater b Edwards . . . . . . . . . | 76 |
| T T Bresnan, not out . . . . . . . . . . . . . . | 12 | not out . . . . . . . . . . . . . . | 35 |
| § A J Hodd | | not out . . . . . . . . . . . . . . | 17 |
| J D Middlebrook | | | |
| S A Patterson | Did not bat | | |
| J A Brooks | | | |
| M D Fisher | | | |
| Extras lb 3, w 5, nb 4 . . . . . . . . . | 12 | Extras lb 8, w 1, nb 9 . . . . . . . . | 18 |
| Total (4 wkts dec) . . . . . . . . . . . | 97 | Total (5 wkts) . . . . . . . . . . . | 305 |

Bonus points — Hampshire 1

*FoW:* 1st   1-0 (Lyth), 2-51 (Ballance), 3-58 (Gale), 4-62 (Leaning)
*FoW:* 2nd   1-13 (Lees), 2-18 (Lyth), 3-37 (Ballance), 4-227 (Leaning), 5-264 (Gale)

| | O | M | R | W | | O | M | R | W |
|---|---|---|---|---|---|---|---|---|---|
| Edwards | 13 | 3 | 26 | 1 | Edwards | 20 | 1 | 74 | 3 |
| McLaren | 14.4 | 3 | 33 | 2 | McLaren | 21 | 0 | 81 | 0 |
| Berg | 7 | 2 | 15 | 0 | Berg | 10 | 0 | 41 | 0 |
| Stevenson | 7 | 0 | 20 | 1 | Stevenson | 10 | 3 | 26 | 0 |
| | | | | | Dawson | 25.2 | 7 | 63 | 0 |
| | | | | | Smith | 5 | 2 | 12 | 0 |

Umpires: P J Hartley and R T Robinson                    Scorers: J T Potter and K R Baker
Third Umpire: N G C Cowley

# Weather assists Yorkshire

**JACK LEANING: Justified his award with match-clinching 76**

Play began late and finished early on the first day, and was twice disrupted, but the hosts made a steady start as Adams and Carberry added 74 after Gale had put Hampshire in.

Dawson was still there at the close, and went on to an invaluable 140. Yorkshire wore black armbands in honour of Brian Close.

Hampshire's objective was to gain full batting points, and some enterprising play enabled them to do so. The excellent Dawson was the mainstay, assisted by Ervine who pushed the score along and Berg who hit four consecutive boundaries off Middlebrook.

The spinner ended with the wickets of both Dawson and Ervine. The bowlers worked hard. Fisher, still 17 until November, was marginally more economical than Patterson, the master of economy, and was rewarded with two late wickets. The fragility of Yorkshire's top order was again evident as four wickets fell in the evening, although Lees remained undefeated.

The weather intervened, and day three was a virtual washout. It was especially important for Hampshire to win points to escape from relegation, so they conceded their second innings and left Yorkshire to score a relatively modest 304 on the last day but giving themselves a full day to take 10 wickets. They seemed justified as Yorkshire lost Lyth, Lees and Ballance for only 37 runs. They relied on Edwards, a West Indian Test bowler, with experienced players like McLaren and Berg to back him up, but once again Yorkshire's middle-order batted well as Gale and Leaning put on 190 for the fourth wicket.

Gale played another responsible captain's innings, and Leaning, chosen as the Cricket Writers' Young Cricketer of the Year, justified the accolade with an accomplished 76. Both fell to Edwards, but Bresnan and Hodd saw Yorkshire home to their 10th win of the season.

141

# LV County Championship Division 1
## Yorkshire v. Sussex

Played at Headingley, Leeds, on September 22, 23, 24 and 25, 2015
*Yorkshire won by 100 runs at 3.10pm on the Fourth Day*

Toss won by Sussex — Yorkshire 21 points, Sussex 4 points

Close of play: First Day, Yorkshire 241-7 (Bresnan 13*, Plunkett 2*); Second Day, Yorkshire 55-1 (Lyth 16*, Balance 39*); Third Day, Yorkshire 298-9 (Bresnan 50*)

| First Innings | YORKSHIRE | | Second innings | |
|---|---|---|---|---|
| A Lyth, lbw b Jordan | 3 | b Hatchett | | 39 |
| A Z Lees, lbw b Hatchett | 29 | c and b Jordan | | 0 |
| G S Ballance, c Joyce b Liddle | 55 | b Magoffin | | 45 |
| * A W Gale, b Magoffin | 31 | c Jordan b Liddle | | 67 |
| § J M Bairstow, c Brown b Magoffin | 1 | lbw b Jordan | | 36 |
| J A Leaning, c Jordan b Hatchett | 36 | c Jordan b Liddle | | 9 |
| A U Rashid, c Brown b Liddle | 53 | lbw b Magoffin | | 21 |
| T T Bresnan, c Jordan b Magoffin | 16 | c Hatchett b Magoffin | | 55 |
| L E Plunkett, c Joyce b Magoffin | 5 | c Machan b Jordan | | 4 |
| J A Brooks, c Yardy b Jordan | 1 | c Brown b Hatchett | | 14 |
| R J Sidebottom, not out | 0 | not out | | 2 |
| Extras b, lb 7, nb 10 | 21 | Extras lb 9, nb 4 | | 13 |
| Total | 251 | Total | | 305 |

Bonus points — Yorkshire 2, Sussex 3

*FoW:* 1-3 (Lyth), 2-55 (Lees), 3-106 (Gale), 4-108 (Bairstow), 5-140 (Ballance), 1st 6-212 (Leaning), 7-238 (Rashid), 8-250 (Bresnan), 9-251 (Brooks), 10-251 (Sidebottom).

*FoW:* 1-0 (Lees), 2-65 (Ballance), 3-123 (Lyth), 4-190 (Bairstow), 5-202 (Leaning), 2nd 6-217 (Gale), 7-238 (Rashid), 8-255 (Plunkett), 9-298 (Brooks), 10-305 (Bresnan).

| | O | M | R | W | | O | M | R | W |
|---|---|---|---|---|---|---|---|---|---|
| Magoffin | 24.2 | 6 | 57 | 4 | Magoffin | 22.3 | 7 | 57 | 3 |
| Jordan | 20 | 3 | 85 | 2 | Jordan | 24 | 3 | 73 | 3 |
| Hatchett | 20 | 5 | 47 | 2 | Hatchett | 21 | 4 | 66 | 2 |
| Liddle | 15 | 4 | 44 | 2 | Liddle | 18 | 1 | 62 | 2 |
| Ashar Zaidi | 4 | 1 | 7 | 0 | Ashar Zaidi | 19 | 6 | 38 | 0 |

| First Innings | SUSSEX | | Second innings | |
|---|---|---|---|---|
| * E C Joyce, c Bairstow b Brooks | 2 | b Brooks | | 1 |
| C J Jordan, c and b Sidebottom | 1 | lbw b Brooks | | 20 |
| M W Machin, c Bairstow b Brooks | 26 | c Bairstow b Brooks | | 16 |
| C D Nash, c Bairstow b Bresnan | 16 | b Bresnan | | 17 |
| L J Wright, c Lees b Plunkett | 21 | c Bairstow b Bresnan | | 2 |
| M H Yardy, b Brooks | 70 | c Lees b Bresnan | | 41 |
| § B C Brown, c Sidebottom b Bresnan | 39 | c Leaning b Rashid | | 42 |
| Ashar Zaidi, lbw b Rashid | 26 | lbw b Lyth | | 47 |
| S J Magoffin, c Bairstow b Plunkett | 0 | lbw b Rashid | | 3 |
| L J Hatchett, c Bresnan b Lyth | 25 | not out | | 8 |
| C J Liddle, not out | 10 | lbw b Rashid | | 0 |
| Extras b 5, lb 4, w 1, nb 2 | 12 | Extras b 7, lb 4 | | 11 |
| Total | 248 | Total | | 208 |

Bonus points — Sussex 1, Yorkshire 3

*FoW:* 1-3 (Joyce), 2-3 (Jordan), 3-35 (Machin), 4-68 (Nash), 5-70 (Wright), 1st 6-134 (Brown), 7-187 (Zaidi), 8-188 (Magoffin), 9-211 (Yardy), 10-248 (Hatchett).

*FoW:* 1-3 (Joyce), 2-36 (Jordan), 3-39 (Machan), 4-56 (Nash), 5-61 (Wright), 2nd 6-142 (Yardy), 7-148 (Brown), 8-154 (Magoffin), 9-199 (Zaidi), 10-208 (Liddle).

| | O | M | R | W | | O | M | R | W |
|---|---|---|---|---|---|---|---|---|---|
| Brooks | 12 | 2 | 55 | 3 | Brooks | 11 | 1 | 39 | 3 |
| Bresnan | 9 | 2 | 55 | 2 | Plunkett | 14 | 1 | 53 | 0 |
| Plunkett | 10 | 0 | 59 | 2 | Bresnan | 12 | 5 | 30 | 3 |
| Rashid | 12 | 4 | 34 | 1 | Rashid | 11.3 | 2 | 44 | 3 |
| Lyth | 1.5 | 0 | 4 | 1 | Lyth | 3 | 1 | 12 | 1 |

Umpires: M A Gough and D J Millns        Scorers: J T Potter and M J Charman

## Yorkshire v. Sussex

# Champs net record points

**GAME'S UP: Michael Yardy top-edges Tim Bresnan to Lees and ends Sussex's chances of saving the game**

Sussex put Yorkshire in on a lively wicket and run-scoring was never simple against Magoffin, competitive and accurate, supported by Jordan and two left-arm seamers in Hatchett and Yorkshire-born Liddle.

Ballance was the mainstay early on and Rashid's 53 in the latter part of a rain-interrupted day achieved parity.

Yorkshire's third batting bonus point, gained from a leg-bye, gave them a record points total in any division of the Championship. Their bowlers soon disrupted Sussex, and it was Yardy mainly and Brown who enabled the visitors to match Yorkshire. Brown had an impressive match as wicket-keeper and batsman, but fell next ball after a beautiful six over extra-cover.

Yorkshire dug in to make 305 in their second innings as Sussex again bowled well. Gale reached his 1,000 runs for the summer, making 67 when he needed 61. He received support from an uncharacteristically subdued Lyth, from Ballance and from Bresnan who made 55. Sussex by now expected Hampshire to win at Trent Bridge, so they had to survive for a draw to stay in Division One.

Batting for a full fourth day against the Yorkshire attack proved to be beyond Sussex despite sound contributions from Yardy, Brown and Zaidi. Yorkshire won their 11th Championship match out of 16. Yardy has played so well for Sussex since 2000, but this was his last innings, and every Yorkshire player shook his hand. The crowd stood to applaud.

On the first morning there had been a tribute to Brian Close, who died on September 14, aged 84, as the family, both sets of players and many officials led a minute's applause. Many of us will remember the years of his captaincy with admiration, respecting his skill and courage as a player, his insight as motivator and tactician and the personal qualities which have inspired so much affection. Andrew Gale has a team of comparable quality to Brian's, playing the game so differently now, but Andrew has captained two successive Championship-winning sides.

# LV COUNTY CHAMPIONSHIP 2015

## DIVISION 1

| | P | W | L | D | BAT | BOWL | Pen. | Points |
|---|---|---|---|---|---|---|---|---|
| | | | | | **Bonus Points** | | | |
| **1 Yorkshire (Div 1, 1)** ............ | **16** | **11** | **1** | **4** | **45** | **45** | **0.0** | **286.0** |
| 2 Middlesex (Div 1, 7) ............ | 16 | 7 | 2 | 7 | 29 | 43 | 1.0 | 218.0 |
| 3 Nottinghamshire (Div 1, 4) ....... | 16 | 6 | 5 | 5 | 45 | 45 | 0.0 | 211.0 |
| 4 Durham (Div1, 5) .............. | 16 | 7 | 8 | 1 | 26 | 45 | 0.0 | 188.0 |
| 5 Warwickshire (Div 1, 2) ......... | 16 | 5 | 5 | 6 | 31 | 45 | 0.0 | 186.0 |
| 6 Somerset (Div1, 6) ............ | 16 | 4 | 6 | 6 | 46 | 43 | 0.0 | 183.0 |
| 7 Hampshire (Div 2, 1) .......... | 16 | 4 | 6 | 6 | 31 | 38 | 0.0 | 163.0 |
| 8 Sussex (Div1, 3) * .............. | 16 | 4 | 8 | 4 | 36 | 41 | 0.0 | 161.0 |
| 9 Worcestershire (Div 2, 2) * ....... | 16 | 3 | 10 | 3 | 44 | 44 | 0.0 | 151.0 |

*Pen.* 1 point deducted for each over short in a match based on a rate of 16 overs per hour

\* Relegated to Division 2 for 2016

## DIVISION 2

| | P | W | L | D | BAT | BOWL | Pen. | Points |
|---|---|---|---|---|---|---|---|---|
| | | | | | **Bonus Points** | | | |
| 1 Surrey (Div 2, 5) * ............. | 16 | 8 | 1 | 7 | 56 | 45 | 0.0 | 264.0 |
| 2 Lancashire (Div 1, 8) * .......... | 16 | 7 | 1 | 8 | 58 | 44 | 0.0 | 254.0 |
| 3 Essex (Div 2, 3) ............... | 16 | 6 | 5 | 5 | 37 | 42 | 0.0 | 200.0 |
| 4 Glamorgan (Div 2, 8) ........... | 16 | 4 | 4 | 8 | 42 | 37 | 0.0 | 183.0 |
| 5 Northamptonshire (Div 1, 9) ...... | 16 | 3 | 3 | 10 | 38 | 46 | 2.0 | 180.0 |
| 6 Gloucestershire (Div 2, 7) ........ | 16 | 5 | 5 | 6 | 31 | 36 | 0.0 | 177.0 |
| 7 Kent (Div 2, 6) ................ | 16 | 4 | 7 | 5 | 28 | 44 | 0.0 | 161.0 |
| 8 Derbyshire (Div 2, 4) ........... | 16 | 3 | 7 | 6 | 34 | 42 | 1.0 | 153.0 |
| 9 Leicestershire (Div 2, 9) ......... | 16 | 2 | 9 | 5 | 36 | 41 | 16.0 | 118.0 |

*Pen.* 1 point deducted for each over short in a match based on a rate of 16 overs per hour
    Leicestershire's penalty of 16 points was for disciplinary reasons

\* Promoted to Division 1 for 2016.

*(2014 positions in brackets)*

---

# McGrath takes on Essex role

Former Yorkshire captain Anthony McGrath gave up his part-time coaching job with the county in February to take on the role of assistant coach at Essex CCC, where the head coach is Anthony's former *White Rose* teammate, Chris Silverwood.

# YORKSHIRE AVERAGES 2015

## LV COUNTY CHAMPIONSHIP

Played 16      Won 11      Lost 1      Drawn 4

### BATTING AND FIELDING

*(Qualification 10 completed innings)*

| Player | M. | I. | N.O. | Runs | H.S. | 100s | 50s | Avge | ct/st |
|--------|----|----|------|------|------|------|-----|------|-------|
| J M Bairstow | 9 | 15 | 3 | 1108 | 219* | 5 | 5 | 92.33 | 29 |
| T T Bresnan | 16 | 22 | 5 | 849 | 169* | 2 | 4 | 49.94 | 13 |
| A W Gale | 15 | 25 | 0 | 1006 | 164 | 3 | 3 | 40.24 | 4 |
| J A Leaning | 15 | 25 | 2 | 922 | 123 | 3 | 3 | 40.08 | 19 |
| G S Ballance | 8 | 13 | 0 | 458 | 165 | 1 | 2 | 35.23 | 7 |
| A U Rashid | 7 | 10 | 0 | 347 | 127 | 1 | 2 | 34.70 | 3 |
| A Z Lees | 16 | 27 | 3 | 795 | 100 | 1 | 5 | 33.12 | 20 |
| W M H Rhodes | 9 | 15 | 2 | 388 | 79 | 0 | 1 | 29.84 | 3 |
| A Lyth | 7 | 12 | 0 | 315 | 67 | 0 | 3 | 26.25 | 10 |
| S A Patterson | 15 | 17 | 4 | 272 | 44* | 0 | 0 | 20.92 | 3 |
| J A Brooks | 14 | 15 | 1 | 185 | 50* | 0 | 1 | 13.21 | 4 |

**Also played**

| C A Pujara | 4 | 6 | 1 | 264 | 133* | 1 | 1 | 52.80 | 2 |
| R J Sidebottom | 10 | 12 | 10 | 95 | 28 | 0 | 0 | 47.50 | 3 |
| A J Finch | 3 | 4 | 1 | 124 | 73* | 0 | 1 | 41.33 | 4 |
| G J Maxwell | 4 | 7 | 1 | 244 | 140 | 1 | 0 | 40.66 | 3 |
| R M Pyrah | 2 | 2 | 0 | 80 | 43 | 0 | 0 | 40.00 | 0 |
| A J Hodd | 8 | 10 | 2 | 180 | 54* | 0 | 1 | 22.50 | 21/2 |
| L E Plunkett | 5 | 8 | 0 | 96 | 28 | 0 | 0 | 12.00 | 4 |
| J D Middlebrook | 6 | 7 | 0 | 49 | 23 | 0 | 0 | 7.00 | 1 |
| K Carver | 1 | 1 | 0 | 5 | 5 | 0 | 0 | 5.00 | 0 |
| M D Fisher | 3 | 2 | 1 | 0 | 0* | 0 | 0 | 0.00 | 1 |

### BOWLING

*(Qualification 10 wickets)*

| Player | Overs | Mdns | Runs | Wkts | Avge | Best | 5wI | 10wM |
|--------|-------|------|------|------|------|------|-----|------|
| R J Sidebottom | 248 | 65 | 734 | 41 | 17.90 | 6-34 | 3 | 1 |
| J A Brooks | 420.5 | 83 | 1480 | 65 | 22.76 | 5-35 | 3 | 0 |
| S A Patterson | 431.1 | 142 | 1128 | 45 | 25.06 | 5-11 | 2 | 0 |
| J D Middlebrook | 126.3 | 22 | 441 | 17 | 25.94 | 5-82 | 1 | 0 |
| A U Rashid | 212.2 | 31 | 813 | 29 | 28.03 | 4-48 | 0 | 0 |
| T T Bresnan | 422.5 | 112 | 1390 | 45 | 30.88 | 5-85 | 1 | 0 |
| L E Plunkett | 115.1 | 17 | 459 | 14 | 32.78 | 4-61 | 0 | 0 |

**Also bowled**

| A Lyth | 27.5 | 3 | 76 | 4 | 19.00 | 1-4 | 0 | 0 |
| W M H Rhodes | 80.5 | 17 | 271 | 8 | 33.87 | 3-42 | 0 | 0 |
| G J Maxwell | 29 | 2 | 144 | 4 | 36.00 | 3-55 | 0 | 0 |
| M D Fisher | 73.5 | 18 | 243 | 5 | 48.60 | 2-61 | 0 | 0 |
| J A Leaning | 23 | 3 | 141 | 1 | 141.00 | 1-82 | 0 | 0 |
| R M Pyrah | 10 | 2 | 40 | 0 | — | 0-14 | 0 | 0 |
| K Carver | 6 | 0 | 36 | 0 | — | 0-36 | 0 | 0 |
| A Z Lees | 3 | 0 | 12 | 0 | — | 0-12 | 0 | 0 |
| A J Finch | 2 | 1 | 1 | 0 | — | 0-1 | 0 | 0 |
| C A Pujara | 1 | 0 | 5 | 0 | — | 0-5 | 0 | 0 |

# MCC University Match (First-Class)
# Yorkshire v. Leeds/Bradford MCCU

Played at Headingley, Leeds, on April 7, 8 and 9, 2015
*Match drawn at 5pm on the Third Day*
Toss won by Leeds/Bradford MCCU

Close of play: First day, Leeds/Bradford MCCU 46-0 (Bullen 21*, Thompson 21*); Second Day, Yorkshire 126-6 (Pyrah 1*, Bresnan 6*)

## YORKSHIRE

| | First Innings | | Second Innings | |
|---|---|---|---|---|
| A Z Lees, c Wakefield b Pratt | | 63 | lbw b Lilley | 8 |
| W M H Rhodes, c Wakefield b Watkinson | | 1 | b Ellis-Grewell | 19 |
| D M Hodgson, b Rouse | | 35 | lbw b Ellis-Grewell | 19 |
| * A W Gale, lbw b Pratt | | 7 | c Weston b Rouse | 32 |
| J A Leaning, b Lilley | | 8 | c Scott b Rouse | 31 |
| R M Pyrah, lbw b Lilley | | 84 | c Weston b Ellis-Grewell | 40 |
| § A J Hodd, lbw b Lilley | | 54 | lbw b Ellis-Grewell | 5 |
| T T Bresnan, c Weston b Ellis-Grewell | | 8 | c Thompson b Watkinson | 38 |
| S A Patterson, b Lilley | | 41 | c Weston b Pratt | 30 |
| K Carver, not out | | 7 | c Wakefield b Rouse | 16 |
| J A Brooks, not out | | 0 | not out | 38 |
| Extras lb 5, w 3, nb 13 | | 21 | Extras b 11, lb 5, w 1 | 17 |
| Total (9 wkts dec) | | 329 | Total | 293 |

*FoW:* 1-4 (Rhodes), 2-76 (Hodgson), 3-87 (Gale), 4-121 (Leaning), 5-148 (Lees),
1st 6-264 (Hodd), 7-275 (Pyrah), 8-297 (Bresnan), 9-326 (Patterson)
*FoW:* 1-8 (Lees), 2-47 (Rhodes), 3-48 (Hodgson), 4-102 (Gale), 5-115 (Leaning), 6-120
2nd (Hodd), 7-197 (Pyrah), 8-199 (Bresnan), 9-243 (Carver), 10-293 (Patterson)

| | O | M | R | W | | O | M | R | W |
|---|---|---|---|---|---|---|---|---|---|
| Lilley | 20 | 4 | 65 | 4 | Lilley | 13 | 2 | 42 | 1 |
| Watkinson | 14 | 2 | 52 | 1 | Watkinson | 10 | 2 | 32 | 1 |
| Pratt | 15 | 1 | 51 | 2 | Rouse | 13 | 1 | 45 | 3 |
| Rouse | 14 | 2 | 60 | 1 | Pratt | 18.2 | 6 | 40 | 1 |
| Scott | 7 | 1 | 54 | 0 | Ellis-Grewell | 33 | 2 | 118 | 4 |
| Ellis-Grewell | 12 | 2 | 42 | 1 | | | | | |

## LEEDS/BRADFORD MCCU

| | First Innings | | Second innings | |
|---|---|---|---|---|
| S F G Bullen, b Brooks | | 36 | lbw b Carver | 25 |
| H L Thompson, lbw b Bresnan | | 21 | c Leaning b Bresnan | 3 |
| W T Root, b Patterson | | 18 | b Brooks | 6 |
| L P Weston, c Hodd b Brooks | | 4 | c Hodgson b Carver | 7 |
| G F B Scott, b Hodd b Carver | | 11 | not out | 1 |
| H P Rouse, c Hodd b Rhodes | | 23 | not out | 5 |
| § C F Wakefield, lbw b Brooks | | 7 | | |
| L Watkinson, lbw b Patterson | | 20 | | |
| * A E Lilley, run out (Brooks) | | 6 | | |
| J S E Ellis-Grewell, c Bresnan b Carver | | 42 | | |
| D T P Pratt, not out | | 2 | | |
| Extras b 7, lb 4, nb 4 | | 15 | Extras lb 1 | 1 |
| Total | | 202 | Total (4 wkts) | 48 |

*FoW:* 1-62 (Thompson), 2-64 (Bullen), 3-66 (Weston), 4-89 (Root), 5-115 (Scott), 6-123
1st (Rouse), 7-130 (Wakefield), 8-141 (Lilley), 9-172 (Watkinson), 10-202 (Ellis-Grewell)
2nd 1-3 (Thompson), 2-10 (Root), 3-33 (Weston), 4-42 (Bullen)

| | O | M | R | W | | O | M | R | W |
|---|---|---|---|---|---|---|---|---|---|
| Bresnan | 15 | 5 | 35 | 1 | Bresnan | 6 | 3 | 3 | 1 |
| Brooks | 14 | 5 | 41 | 3 | Brooks | 6 | 1 | 14 | 1 |
| Patterson | 15 | 6 | 38 | 2 | Carver | 10 | 8 | 6 | 2 |
| Pyrah | 8 | 0 | 27 | 0 | Rhodes | 2 | 1 | 12 | 0 |
| Carver | 15 | 8 | 33 | 2 | Patterson | 5 | 2 | 6 | 0 |
| Rhodes | 4 | 2 | 6 | 1 | Pyrah | 3 | 1 | 6 | 0 |
| Leaning | 3 | 1 | 11 | 0 | Lees | 1 | 1 | 0 | 0 |

Umpires: P J Hartley and T Lungley          Scorers: J T Potter and C N Rawson

# Pyrah leads recovery

**RICHARD PYRAH: Adam Lyth on his way to 140**

Yorkshire started with a First Class match against Leeds/Bradford MCCU, for which the sun shone brightly — some of the time.

The University side included Billy Root, Joe's brother, and Liam Watkinson, son of Mike of Lancashire and England. Alex Lilley, who captained them, had played one game for Yorkshire in 2011.

This was more of a contest than most University games. Yorkshire lost their first five wickets for 148, including a sound 63 from Lees, who was captaining the team.

Pyrah and Hodd started a recovery, Pyrah going on to 84, but left-armer Lilley then took three wickets, and Yorkshire ended on 329. Bullen and Thompson survived the first evening. Bullen, making his First Class debut, had played with Somerset Second Eleven, and Thompson with all the Lancashire age-group teams. Ellis-Grewal, born in Walthamstow like Harry Kane, and who had impressed with his left-arm spin, hit an adventurous 41, so the University reached 202.

They then reduced Yorkshire to a precarious 126-6 by the close on Wednesday. There followed a recovery, again led by Pyrah, assisted by Bresnan and Brooks, but Ellis-Grewal and Sheffield born Rouse, a product of Kingswood School in Bath, took four and three wickets, and the match ended in a draw. It was by no means a one-sided affair, but a good number of university games with counties have been.

The first two matches for each university are regarded as First Class. Some consider that the current standard of university cricket does not merit this, but it enables those who take a degree to play against more experienced opposition. The best university players may already be contracted to counties or be given contracts on completing their degree, which may offer them wider career opportunities. They play in a university league incorporating the six together with Exeter and Solent.

# YORKSHIRE AVERAGES 2015

## ALL FIRST-CLASS MATCHES

Played 18          Won 12          Lost 1          Drawn 5

### BATTING AND FIELDING

*(Qualification 10 completed innings)*

| Player | M. | I. | N.O. | Runs | H.S. | 100s | 50s | Avge | ct/st |
|---|---|---|---|---|---|---|---|---|---|
| J M Bairstow | 10 | 16 | 3 | 1108 | 219* | 5 | 5 | 85.23 | 33 |
| T T Bresnan | 18 | 25 | 5 | 907 | 169* | 2 | 4 | 45.35 | 15 |
| A W Gale | 16 | 27 | 0 | 1045 | 164 | 3 | 3 | 38.70 | 4 |
| J A Leaning | 17 | 29 | 3 | 988 | 123 | 3 | 3 | 38.00 | 20 |
| A Lyth | 8 | 14 | 1 | 474 | 113 | 1 | 3 | 36.46 | 12 |
| A U Rashid | 8 | 11 | 0 | 389 | 127 | 1 | 2 | 35.36 | 4 |
| G S Ballance | 8 | 13 | 0 | 458 | 165 | 1 | 2 | 35.23 | 7 |
| A Z Lees | 18 | 31 | 3 | 885 | 100 | 1 | 6 | 31.60 | 20 |
| W M H Rhodes | 11 | 18 | 2 | 469 | 79 | 0 | 2 | 29.31 | 5 |
| A J Hodd | 10 | 13 | 2 | 296 | 57 | 0 | 3 | 26.90 | 24/2 |
| S A Patterson | 17 | 20 | 4 | 379 | 44* | 0 | 0 | 23.68 | 3 |
| J A Brooks | 16 | 18 | 1 | 225 | 50* | 0 | 1 | 13.23 | 4 |
| **Also played** | | | | | | | | | |
| C A Pujara | 4 | 6 | 1 | 264 | 133* | 1 | 1 | 52.80 | 2 |
| R M Pyrah | 3 | 4 | 0 | 204 | 84 | 0 | 1 | 51.00 | 0 |
| R J Sidebottom | 11 | 13 | 11 | 98 | 28 | 0 | 0 | 49.00 | 3 |
| A J Finch | 3 | 4 | 1 | 124 | 73* | 0 | 1 | 41.33 | 3 |
| G J Maxwell | 4 | 7 | 1 | 244 | 140 | 1 | 0 | 40.66 | 3 |
| D M Hodgson | 1 | 2 | 0 | 54 | 35 | 0 | 0 | 27.00 | 1 |
| K Carver | 2 | 3 | 1 | 28 | 16 | 0 | 0 | 14.00 | 0 |
| L E Plunkett | 5 | 8 | 0 | 96 | 28 | 0 | 0 | 12.00 | 4 |
| J D Middlebrook | 6 | 7 | 0 | 49 | 23 | 0 | 0 | 7.00 | 1 |
| M D Fisher | 3 | 2 | 1 | 0 | 0* | 0 | 0 | 0.00 | 1 |

### BOWLING

*(Qualification 10 wickets)*

| Player | Overs | Mdns | Runs | Wkts | Avge | Best | 5wI | 10wM |
|---|---|---|---|---|---|---|---|---|
| R J Sidebottom | 268 | 71 | 778 | 43 | 18.09 | 6-34 | 3 | 1 |
| J A Brooks | 465.5 | 97 | 1614 | 74 | 21.81 | 5-35 | 3 | 0 |
| S A Patterson | 476.1 | 160 | 1242 | 49 | 25.34 | 5-11 | 2 | 0 |
| W M H Rhodes | 98.5 | 23 | 311 | 12 | 25.91 | 3-42 | 0 | 0 |
| J D Middlebrook | 126.3 | 22 | 441 | 17 | 25.94 | 5-82 | 1 | 0 |
| A U Rashid | 250 | 35 | 936 | 35 | 26.74 | 4-48 | 0 | 0 |
| T T Bresnan | 457.5 | 123 | 1482 | 48 | 30.87 | 5-85 | 1 | 0 |
| L E Plunkett | 115.1 | 17 | 459 | 14 | 32.78 | 4-61 | 0 | 0 |
| **Also bowled** | | | | | | | | |
| K Carver | 31 | 16 | 75 | 4 | 18.75 | 2-6 | 0 | 0 |
| A Lyth | 38.5 | 5 | 111 | 5 | 22.20 | 1-4 | 0 | 0 |
| G J Maxwell | 29 | 2 | 144 | 4 | 36.00 | 3-55 | 0 | 0 |
| M D Fisher | 73.5 | 18 | 243 | 5 | 48.60 | 2-61 | 0 | 0 |
| J A Leaning | 26 | 4 | 152 | 1 | 152.00 | 1-82 | 0 | 0 |
| R M Pyrah | 21 | 3 | 73 | 0 | — | 0-6 | 0 | 0 |
| A Z Lees | 4 | 1 | 12 | 0 | — | 0-0 | 0 | 0 |
| A J Finch | 2 | 1 | 1 | 0 | — | 0-1 | 0 | 0 |
| C A Pujara | 1 | 0 | 5 | 0 | — | 0-5 | 0 | 0 |

# Second Investec Test Match
# England v. New Zealand

Played at Headingley, Leeds, on May, 29, 30 and 31 and June 1 and 2, 2015
*New Zealand won by 199 runs at 4.56pm on the Fifth Day*

Toss won by England

Close of play: First Day, New Zealand, 297-8 (Craig 16*, Henry 14*); Second Day, England 253-5 (Bell 12*, Buttler 6*); Third Day, New Zealand 338-6 (Watling 100*, Craig 15*); Fourth Day, England 44-0 (Lyth 24*, Cook 18*)

| First Innings | NEW ZEALAND | Second innings | |
|---|---|---|---|
| M J Guptill, c Bell b Anderson | 0 | (2) c Root b Broad | 3 |
| T W M Latham, c Root b Broad | 84 | (1) c Buttler b Wood | 70 |
| K S Williamson, c Buttler b Anderson | 0 | c Buttler b Broad | 6 |
| L R P L Taylor, lbw b Broad | 20 | c Stokes b Wood | 48 |
| * B B McCullum, c Wood b Stokes | 41 | lbw b Wood | 55 |
| B J Watling, b Wood | 14 | c Root b Anderson | 120 |
| § L Ronchi, c Anderson b Broad | 88 | c Buttler b Anderson | 31 |
| M D Craig, not out | 41 | not out | 58 |
| T G Southee, c Lyth b Wood | 1 | c Anderson b Ali | 40 |
| M J Henry, c Buttler b Broad | 27 | not out | 12 |
| T A Boult, c Lyth b Broad | 15 | | |
| Extras b 4, lb 14, nb 1 | 19 | Extras b 4, lb 6, w 1 | 11 |
| Total | 350 | Total (8 wkts dec) | 454 |

*FoW:* 1-2 (Guptill), 2-2 (Williamson), 3-68 (Taylor), 4-123 (McCullum), 5-144 (Watling),
1st 6-264 (Latham), 7-265 (Ronchi), 8-281 (Southee), 9-310 (Henry), 10-350 (Boult)
*FoW:* 1-15 (Latham), 2-23 (Williamson), 3-122 (Taylor), 4-141 (Guptill), 5-262 (McCullum),
2nd 6-315 (Ronchi), 7-368 (Watling), 8-435 (Southee)

| | O | M | R | W | | O | M | R | W |
|---|---|---|---|---|---|---|---|---|---|
| Anderson | 13 | 3 | 43 | 2 | Anderson | 23 | 4 | 96 | 2 |
| Broad | 17.1 | 0 | 109 | 5 | Broad | 16 | 1 | 94 | 2 |
| Wood | 14 | 4 | 62 | 2 | Wood | 19 | 2 | 97 | 3 |
| Stokes | 17 | 4 | 70 | 1 | Stokes | 12 | 1 | 61 | 0 |
| Ali | 11 | 3 | 48 | 0 | Ali | 16 | 0 | 73 | 1 |
| | | | | | Root | 5 | 0 | 23 | 0 |

| First Innings | ENGLAND | Second innings | |
|---|---|---|---|
| A Lyth, run out (Boult/Ronchi) | 107 | c Ronchi b Boult | 24 |
| * A N Cook, lbw b Craig | 75 | lbw b Williamson | 56 |
| G S Ballance, b Boult | 29 | b Boult | 6 |
| I R Bell, c Craig b Southee | 12 | c Williamson b Craig | 1 |
| J E Root, c Ronchi b Southee | 0 | c Latham b Craig | 0 |
| B A Stokes, c Craig b Boult | 6 | c Ronchi b Williamson | 29 |
| § J C Buttler, c Taylor b Southee | 10 | lbw b Craig | 73 |
| M M Ali, c Guptill b Southee | 4 | b Henry | 2 |
| S C J Broad, b Henry | 46 | b Williamson | 23 |
| M A Wood, c Ronchi b Craig | 19 | c Craig b Southee | 17 |
| J M Anderson, not out | 10 | not out | 8 |
| Extras b 19, lb 5, w 5, nb 5 | 34 | Extras b 12, lb 2, w 2 | 16 |
| Total | 350 | Total | 255 |

*FoW:* 1-177 (Cook), 2-215 (Lyth), 3-238 (Ballance), 4-239 (Root), 5-247 (Stokes),
1st 6-257 (Bell), 7-266 (Buttler), 8-267 (Ali), 9-318 (Wood), 10-350 (Broad)
*FoW:* 1-47 (Lyth), 2-61 (Ballance), 3-62 (Bell), 4-62 (Root), 5-102 (Stokes),
2nd 6-141 (Cook), 7-153 (Ali), 8-188 (Broad), 9-230 (Wood), 10-255 (Buttler)

| | O | M | R | W | | O | M | R | W |
|---|---|---|---|---|---|---|---|---|---|
| Boult | 30 | 7 | 98 | 2 | Boult | 23 | 4 | 61 | 2 |
| Southee | 30 | 5 | 83 | 4 | Southee | 18 | 7 | 43 | 1 |
| Henry | 20.2 | 4 | 92 | 1 | Craig | 31.5 | 12 | 73 | 3 |
| Craig | 26 | 12 | 48 | 2 | Henry | 12 | 2 | 49 | 1 |
| Williamson | 2 | 1 | 5 | 0 | Williamson | 7 | 1 | 15 | 3 |

Man of the Match: B J Watling

Umpires: S Ravi and R J Tucker      Scorers: J T Potter and H Clayton
Third Umpire: M Erasmus    Fourth Umpire: N A Mallender    Match Referee: D C Boon

# ROYAL LONDON ONE-DAY CUP
# HIGHLIGHTS OF 2015

WINNERS

**Gloucestershire**, who defeated Surrey by 6 runs

**Win by 100 or more runs (1)**

Yorkshire (345-6) beat Worcestershire (212) by 133 runs at Worcester

**Totals of 250 and over (5)**

| | | |
|---|---|---|
| 345-6 | v. Worcestershire | at Worcester (won) |
| 277-9 | v. Leicestershire | at Leeds (won) |
| 263-9 | v. Gloucestershire | at Leeds (lost) |
| 259-7 | v. Surrey | at The Oval (lost) |
| 252-9 | v. Essex | at Chelmsford (won) |

**Match aggregates of 450 and over (5)**

| | |
|---|---|
| 557 | Yorkshire (345-6) beat Worcestershire (212) by 133 runs at Worcester |
| 530 | Yorkshire (263-9) lost to Gloucestershire (267-2) by 8 wickets at Leeds |
| 524 | Surrey (265-8) beat Yorkshire (259-7) by 6 runs at The Oval |
| 523 | Yorkshire (277-9) beat Leicestershire (246) by 31 runs at Leeds |
| 484 | Yorkshire (252-9) beat Essex (232) by 20 runs at Chelmsford |

**Century Partnerships (3)**

**For the 1st wicket (1)**

103    A Lyth and A Z Lees           v. Gloucestershire at Leeds

**For the 3rd wicket (1)**

105    G J Maxwell and G S Ballance  v. Worcestershire at Worcester

**For the 6th wicket (1)**

102    J A Leaning and A U Rashid     v. Worcestershire at Worcester

**Century (1)**

G J Maxwell (1)

111    v. Worcestershire at Worcester

**4 wickets in an innings (1)**

S A Patterson (1)

5-24    v. Worcestershire at Worcester

**3 catches in an innings (3)**

A J Hodd (2)

3           v. Durham at Chester-le-Street
3           v. Somerset at Scarborough

L E Plunkett (1)

3           v. Surrey at The Oval

**4 victims in an innings (1)**

A J Hodd (1)

4 (3ct + 1st) v. Durham at Chester-le-Street

**Debuts (2)**

**List A cricket:** K Carver
**For Yorkshire:** G J Maxwell

| **Match-By-Match Reports** | **DAVE CALDWELL** |
|---|---|

# Royal London One-Day Cup — Group A
## Yorkshire v. Gloucestershire

Played at North Marine Road, Scarborough, on July 26, 2015
*No result*

Toss won by Yorkshire                    Yorkshire 1 point, Gloucestershire 1 point

### YORKSHIRE

| | | |
|---|---|---:|
| A Z Lees, c Roderick b Fuller | .................... | 14 |
| * A W Gale, c Roderick b Miles | ................. | 16 |
| G J Maxwell, c Jones b Fuller | .................... | 33 |
| G S Ballance, c Roderick b Noema-Barnett | ........ | 31 |
| J A Leaning, b Fuller | .......................... | 0 |
| W M H Rhodes, c Klinger b Miles | .............. | 32 |
| § A J Hodd, c Smith b Miles | .................... | 7 |
| T T Bresnan, c Dent b Smith | .................... | 43 |
| L E Plunkett, c Roderick b Miles | ................. | 0 |
| S A Patterson, lbw b Smith | ..................... | 24 |
| M D Fisher, not out | ........................... | 4 |
| Extras lb 5, w 10, nb 8 | ..................... | 23 |
| Total (50 overs) | ....................... | 227 |

*FoW:* 1-24 (Lees), 2-34 (Gale), 3-82 (Maxwell), 4-82 (Leaning), 5-128 (Ballance), 6-148 (Rhodes), 7-151 (Hodd), 8-151 (Plunkett), 9-208 (Patterson), 10-227 (Bresnan)

| | O | M | R | W |
|---|---:|---:|---:|---:|
| Payne ................. | 10 | 1 | 41 | 0 |
| Fuller ................. | 8 | 0 | 45 | 3 |
| Miles ................. | 9 | 2 | 29 | 4 |
| Howell ................. | 4 | 0 | 24 | 0 |
| Taylor ................. | 7 | 0 | 30 | 0 |
| Noema-Barnett .......... | 4 | 0 | 19 | 1 |
| Smith ................. | 8 | 0 | 34 | 2 |

### GLOUCESTERSHIRE

| | | |
|---|---|---:|
| * M Klinger, not out | .......................... | 4 |
| C D J Dent, not out | ........................... | 0 |
| § G H Roderick | | |
| B A C Howell | | |
| G O Jones | | |
| K Noema-Barnett | | |
| J M R Taylor | | |
| J K Fuller | | |
| C N Miles | | |
| T M J Smith | | |
| D A Payne | | |
| Extras lb 1 | ......................... | 1 |
| Total (0 wkts, 2 overs) | ................. | 5 |

| | O | M | R | W |
|---|---:|---:|---:|---:|
| Bresnan ................. | 1 | 1 | 0 | 0 |
| Fisher ................. | 1 | 0 | 4 | 0 |

Umpires: N L Bainton and J W Lloyds          Scorers: J T Potter and A J Bull

152

# Happy to make a point

**Close call: Yorkshire's Maxwell just makes his ground against Roderick**

Yorkshire can look back on a point gained after they had struggled with the bat before rain curtailed proceedings only two overs into the visitors' reply.

To make it worse for Gloucestershire in pursuit of a barely adequate 227 they needed to make only 20 without loss after 10 overs to take home the spoils. With the exception of Leaning all of the top Yorkshire six got starts, but none went on to make a telling score.

The tall seam bowler Miles impressed with the ball as he generated good control and a degree of bounce on a typically good Scarborough wicket. Lees and Gale were the first to fall, both to regulation catches behind the wicket, before a stand of 48 between Maxwell and Ballance got the Vikings back into the contest.

Maxwell was looking in ominous form despite having a slice or two of luck in his 38-ball 33. He was caught off a no-ball and then spilled by Jones before the same fielder swiftly atoned for his error and had the Australian caught at mid-wicket off the next delivery.

Leaning fell to his first ball in the 19th over before Ballance and Rhodes set about a restoration mission. Ballance's vigil ended after 55 deliveries as he tried to late-cut Noema-Barnett, only to feather the ball to the wicket-keeper for 31. Miles then struck three times in 11 balls as Rhodes — who had impressed during his 32 — Hodd and Plunkett all departed, leaving Yorkshire on 151-8 in the 37th over.

A ninth-wicket stand of 57 between Bresnan and Patterson brought some cheer to the home crowd before Patterson was trapped in front for 24. Bresnan added some valuable blows before he was last man out for 43, taken on the leg-side boundary from the last ball of the innings.

The weather closed in rapidly, and Gloucestershire had reached 5-0 in reply before proceedings were abandoned for the day after only 12 deliveries.

# Royal London One-Day Cup — Group A
## Derbyshire v. Yorkshire

Played at The County Ground, Derby, on July 27, 2015
*Yorkshire won by 7 runs (D/L method)*

Toss won by Derbyshire          Yorkshire 2 points, Derbyshire 0 points

### YORKSHIRE

| | |
|---|---|
| A Z Lees, c Cotton b Thakor ..................... | 14 |
| * A W Gale, lbw b Footitt ........................ | 37 |
| G J Maxwell, c Footitt b A L Hughes ............. | 16 |
| G S Ballance, c Poynton b Cotton ............... | 69 |
| J A Leaning, c Critchley b Footitt ............... | 42 |
| T T Bresnan, c A L Hughes b Thakor .......... | 16 |
| L E Plunkett, not out ............................ | 17 |
| W M H Rhodes, not out ........................ | 4 |
| § A J Hodd | |
| S A Patterson       Did not bat | |
| J A Brooks | |
| Extras b 2, lb 9, w 8, nb 5 ................. | 24 |
| Total (6 wkts, 42 overs) ................ | 239 |

*FoW*: 1-37 (Lees), 2-60 (Maxwell, 3-91 (Gale), 4-174 (Leaning), 5-210 (Bresnan), 6-213 (Ballance)

| | O | M | R | W |
|---|---|---|---|---|
| Footitt ................ | 9 | 0 | 45 | 2 |
| Cotton ................ | 9 | 0 | 42 | 1 |
| Thakor ................ | 8 | 0 | 57 | 2 |
| A L Hughes ........... | 8 | 0 | 51 | 1 |
| Durston ............... | 4 | 0 | 15 | 0 |
| Critchley ............. | 4 | 0 | 18 | 0 |

### DERBYSHIRE
*(Target to win : 197 runs off 29 overs)*

| | |
|---|---|
| B A Godleman, c Hodd b Plunkett ............... | 45 |
| W J Durston, c Balance b Brooks ............... | 1 |
| * W L Madsen, b Patterson ...................... | 22 |
| S J Thakor, run out (Plunkett/Gale) ............ | 14 |
| H D Rutherford, c Maxwell b Patterson .......... | 56 |
| A L Hughes, c Maxwell b Patterson ........... | 14 |
| C F Hughes, c Hodd b Bresnan ................. | 9 |
| § T Poynton, not out ........................... | 20 |
| M J J Critchley, b Brooks ...................... | 1 |
| B D Cotton, c Lees b Brooks ................... | 0 |
| M H A Footitt, not out ........................ | 0 |
| Extras lb 4, w 1, nb 2 ................... | 7 |
| Total (9 wkts, 29 overs) ............... | 189 |

*FoW*: 1-17 (Durston), 2-66 (Madsen), 3-74 (Godleman), 4-85 (Thakor), 5-132 (A L Hughes), 6-153 (C F Hughes), 7-181 (Rutherford), 8-183 (Critchley), 9-183 (Cotton)

| | O | M | R | W |
|---|---|---|---|---|
| Brooks ................ | 6 | 0 | 40 | 3 |
| Bresnan ............... | 6 | 0 | 36 | 1 |
| Plunkett .............. | 6 | 0 | 34 | 1 |
| Patterson ............. | 6 | 0 | 37 | 3 |
| Rhodes ............... | 3 | 1 | 20 | 0 |
| Maxwell .............. | 2 | 0 | 18 | 0 |

Umpires: M R Benson and S A Garratt      Scorers: J T Potter and J M Brown

## Derbyshire v. Yorkshire

# Ballance back to his best

Gary Ballance made a much needed return to form in this rain-affected day-night fixture as Yorkshire scraped home by the Duckworth-Lewis method.

The combative left-hander top-scored in a dour struggle as both sides battled against a slow surface and inclement weather.

After a 90-minute delay and the match reduced to 42 overs Yorkshire were asked to bat in conditions favouring the bowlers. Runs were at a premium, with Gale and Lees restricted to 31 in the first nine overs.

Lees and Maxwell were out cheaply, but Gale and Ballance added 31 in just under six overs before the skipper was trapped in front by left-arm paceman Footitt for 37 from 59 balls.

This left the Vikings on 91-3 from 20 overs before the key partnership between Ballance and Leaning ensured that the bowlers would have enough to

**GARY BALLANCE: 69 just what the doctor ordered**

defend on a helpful pitch and sluggish outfield. Derbyshire's disciplined attack and tight out-cricket made the batsmen work hard for their runs. Leaning fell at 174, having made 42 from 50 balls, when he top-edged a short one from Footitt. This paved the way for Ballance and Bresnan to strike 36 in 25 balls before Bresnan was caught by Alex Hughes. Ballance's 69 from 70 balls was just what the doctor ordered. Yorkshire closed on 239-8, with Plunkett adding valuable boundaries at the death.

Further rain fell as Derbyshire's target was revised to 196 in 29 overs. Brooks quickly removed Durston, but Godleman was striking the ball cleanly, ably assisted by Madsen. The two departed in quick succession, Patterson thwarting Madsen's scoop shot and Godleman was caught behind for 45 from 38 balls. Rutherford's 48-ball 56 looked to have won the game until Maxwell caught him at long-off. Maxwell had earlier accounted for Alex Hughes with a superb one-handed catch.

The last over arrived with the Falcons needing 16 to win, but they lost two wickets to Brooks, enabled Yorkshire to claim their first win.

# Royal London One-Day Cup — Group A
## Surrey v. Yorkshire

Played at The Oval on July 29, 2015
*Surrey won by 6 runs*

Toss won by Surrey                    Surrey 2 points, Yorkshire 0 points

### SURREY

| | | |
|---|---|---|
| J J Roy, c Plunkett b Patterson | | 15 |
| S M Davies, b Patterson | | 39 |
| K C Sangakkara, c Gale b Carver | | 23 |
| § G C Wilson, c Fisher b Carver | | 10 |
| B T Foakes, c Plunkett b Maxwell | | 44 |
| Z S Ansari, not out | | 66 |
| J E Burke, c and b Fisher | | 1 |
| * G J Batty, c Plunkett b Maxwell | | 12 |
| T K Curran, b Fisher | | 44 |
| S M Curran, not out | | 4 |
| J W Dernbach | Did not bat | |
| Extras b 3, lb 2, w 2 | | 7 |
| Total (8 wkts, 50 overs) | | 265 |

*FoW:* 1-52 (Davies), 2-59 (Roy), 3-80 (Wilson), 4-107 (Sangakkara), 5-153 (Foakes), 6-160 (Burke), 7-187 (Batty), 8-253 (T K Curran).

| | O | M | R | W |
|---|---|---|---|---|
| Bresnan | 6 | 0 | 28 | 0 |
| Fisher | 7 | 0 | 55 | 2 |
| Patterson | 10 | 0 | 44 | 2 |
| Maxwell | 9 | 0 | 61 | 2 |
| Carver | 10 | 0 | 40 | 2 |
| Plunkett | 8 | 0 | 32 | 0 |

### YORKSHIRE

| | | |
|---|---|---|
| * A W Gale, lbw b S M Curran | | 3 |
| A Z Lees, c Roy b Ansari | | 28 |
| G J Maxwell, c Wilson b Ansari | | 55 |
| G S Ballance, c Foakes b Ansari | | 77 |
| J A Leaning, c Dernbach b Batty | | 29 |
| § A J Hodd, c Batty b T K Curran | | 25 |
| T T Bresnan, c Roy b Dernbach | | 16 |
| L E Plunkett, not out | | 9 |
| S A Patterson, not out | | 1 |
| M D Fisher | | |
| K Carver | Did not bat | |
| Extras b 1, lb 6, w 7, nb 2 | | 16 |
| Total (7 wkts, 50 overs) | | 259 |

*FoW:* 1-7 (Gale), 2-74 (Lees), 3-110 (Maxwell), 4-175 (Leaning), 5-216 (Hodd), 6-244 (Ballance), 7-249 (Bresnan).

| | O | M | R | W |
|---|---|---|---|---|
| Dernbach | 9 | 0 | 54 | 1 |
| S M Curran | 8 | 0 | 33 | 1 |
| Burke | 4 | 0 | 27 | 0 |
| Ansari | 10 | 0 | 58 | 3 |
| Batty | 10 | 0 | 44 | 1 |
| T K Curran | 9 | 0 | 36 | 1 |

Umpires: M J D Bodenham and M J Saggers        Scorers: J T Potter and K R Booth

# Yorkshire fall just short

**KARL CARVER: Fine debut**

Ballance struck his second half-century in three days, but it was not enough to force a successful run chase as the *White Rose* fell an agonising seven runs short in this high-scoring affair.

In pursuit of 266 Ballance looked to have provided his side with the perfect platform as his partnerships with Maxwell, Leaning and Hodd left Yorkshire in pole position after the early loss of Gale.

Lees and Maxwell offered a stable combination for the second wicket, Maxwell beginning to impress as he passed 50 for the second time in a Viking shirt. Lees fell to Ansari for 28, and the same bowler took the vital wicket of Maxwell, who was caught by Foakes for a 59-ball 55 containing four boundaries and a maximum.

Ballance and Leaning looked well set until Leaning perished at 175 in the 37th over. Ballance continued past his half-century, while Hodd added some lusty blows to keep Yorkshire up with the asking rate. Tom Curran dismissed Hodd, but the stage seemed set for Ballance to take his side home. Ansari, who earlier had provided fireworks with the bat, now proved decisive with the ball as Ballance swept him into the hands of Foakes, leaving the Vikings on 244-6 midway through the 48th over.

Ballance's 77 off 97 balls had been measured in expert fashion, but his dismissal was a pivotal moment as Yorkshire failed to negotiate the 22 runs required from 16 balls. Tom Curran bowled a lovely final over, from which Yorkshire needed 14 runs but only made seven.

Surrey's innings had looked as if it might hit the buffers as they struggled to 187-7 in 42 overs after some excellent bowling by debutant Carver backed up by the more experienced Plunkett and Patterson, but Ansari and Tom Curran added 66 from the final seven overs, giving the hosts a decent total to defend. Left-hander Carver took the key wickets of Wilson and Sangakkara to finish with the highly respectable figures of 2-40 off his 10 overs.

# Royal London One-Day Cup — Group A
## Worcestershire v. Yorkshire

Played at New Road, Worcester, on July 30, 2015
*Yorkshire won by 133 runs*

Toss won by Yorkshire        Yorkshire 2 points, Worcestershire 0 points

### YORKSHIRE

| | | |
|---|---|---:|
| § A J Hodd, c Kohler-Cadmore b Barnard | | 18 |
| * A Z Lees, st Cox b Saeed Ajmal | | 67 |
| G J Maxwell, c Cox b Barnard | | 111 |
| G S Ballance, c Saeed Ajmal b Morris | | 28 |
| J A Leaning, not out | | 58 |
| W M H Rhodes, c Cox b Barnard | | 0 |
| A U Rashid, c Cox b Morris | | 41 |
| L E Plunkett, not out | | 7 |
| S A Patterson | | |
| K Carver | Did not bat | |
| J A Brooks | | |
| Extras b 2, lb 3, w 8, nb 2 | | 15 |
| Total (6 wkts, 50 overs) | | 345 |

*FoW:* 1-61 (Hodd), 2-122 (Lees), 3-227 (Ballance), 4-236 (Maxwell), 5-236 (Rhodes), 6-338 (Rashid)

| | O | M | R | W |
|---|---:|---:|---:|---:|
| Morris | 10 | 1 | 61 | 2 |
| Leach | 10 | 1 | 72 | 0 |
| Barnard | 10 | 0 | 59 | 3 |
| Saeed Ajmal | 10 | 0 | 67 | 1 |
| d'Oliveira | 8 | 0 | 64 | 0 |
| Mitchell | 2 | 0 | 17 | 0 |

### WORCESTERSHIRE

| | | |
|---|---|---:|
| * D K H Mitchell, run out (Lees) | | 32 |
| R K Oliver, run out (Patterson) | | 2 |
| T C Fell, c Carver b Patterson | | 14 |
| B L d'Oliveira, c Hodd b Plunkett | | 42 |
| T Kohler-Cadmore, c Rhodes b Rashid | | 18 |
| R A Whiteley, c Leaning b Patterson | | 77 |
| § O B Cox, c Rashid b Plunkett | | 6 |
| J Leach, c Ballance b Patterson | | 7 |
| E G Barnard, lbw b Patterson | | 0 |
| Saeed Ajmal, c Rhodes b Patterson | | 6 |
| C A J Morris, not out | | 0 |
| Extras lb 1, w 7 | | 8 |
| Total (41.3 overs) | | 212 |

*FoW:* 1-3 (Oliver), 2-32 (Fell), 3-60 (Mitchell), 4-95 (Kohler-Cadmore), 5-137 (d'Oliveira), 6-153 (Cox), 7-184 (Leach), 8-185 (Barnard), 9-212 (Ajmal), 10-212 (Whiteley)

| | O | M | R | W |
|---|---:|---:|---:|---:|
| Brooks | 6 | 0 | 21 | 0 |
| Patterson | 7.3 | 1 | 24 | 5 |
| Plunkett | 10 | 0 | 51 | 2 |
| Rhodes | 6 | 0 | 29 | 0 |
| Rashid | 8 | 0 | 67 | 1 |
| Maxwell | 4 | 0 | 19 | 0 |

Umpires: S C Gale and A G Wharf      Scorers: J T Potter and D E Pugh

# Maxwell's dazzling 'Nelson'

**GLENN MAXWELL: Scintillating**

A scintillating century by Maxwell ensured that Yorkshire would claim their second victory of this season's tournament in a one-sided fixture.

Maxwell smashed an uncompromising 111 from 76 balls with four fours and four sixes. Hodd, deputising at the top of the order for the injured Gale, added 61 for the first wicket with acting captain Lees.

Hodd was caught at slip by Kohler-Cadmore for 18, giving Barnard his first List A wicket in his first over. Lees accelerated while his World Cup partner, Maxwell, took control, and Lees reached 67 from 83 balls before Ajmal deceived him with his flight.

From this point it was all Maxwell. Ballance played anchor as his partner flayed the bowling to all points, but Ballance fell for 28, caught by Ajmal off Morris. The total was 227-3 as Maxwell completed his century in 71 balls, his second 50 spanning only 25 balls. Maxwell finally miscued to mid-on, and Rhodes fell to Barnard's next ball before Rashid and Leaning made sure that Worcestershire would have to chase their biggest List A total to win. Leaning remained undefeated on 58 while Rashid contributed a quickfire 41, the pair adding 101 in 11 overs to leave Yorkshire loftily placed at 235-8.

Worcestershire got off to a poor start as Oliver was run out for two by Patterson, who then grabbed the wicket of Fell, reducing the hosts to 32-2 in the 10th over. A useful partnership developed between Mitchell and D'Oliveira before the Worcestershire skipper became the second run-out victim. Rashid accounted for Kohler-Cadmore, and the game seemed over as D'Oliveira was caught behind off Plunkett for 42. Worcestershire 137-5, but not for the first time this season Yorkshire-born Whiteley proved a thorn in the side of the *White Rose*. His 77 came from 51 balls before Patterson produced an outstanding spell, claiming four wickets in 15 balls and 5-24 from 7.3 overs. Worcestershire finished 133 runs light as they were dismissed in the 42nd over.

# Royal London One-Day Cup — Group A
## Durham v. Yorkshire

Played at Durham ICG, Chester-le-Street, on August 2, 2015
*Yorkshire won by 32 runs (D/L method)*

Toss won by Yorkshire      Yorkshire 2 points, Durham 2 points

### DURHAM

| | |
|---|---|
| * M D Stoneman, c Maxwell b Bresnan | 16 |
| § P Mustard, c Hodd b Plunkett | 32 |
| S G Borthwick, c Leaning b Plunkett | 32 |
| G Clark, c Maxwell b Plunkett | 42 |
| P D Collingwood, st Hodd b Rashid | 17 |
| R D Pringle, c Hodd b Bresnan | 30 |
| G J Muchall, not out | 35 |
| J W Hastings, c Hodd b Patterson | 2 |
| K K Jennings, not out | 11 |
| U Arshad | |
| C Rushworth      Did not bat | |
| Extras lb 3, w 4 | 7 |
| Total (7 wkts, 43 overs) | 224 |

*FoW:* 1-23 (Stoneman), 2-80 (Mustard), 3-84 (Borthwick), 4-128 (Collingwood), 5-158 (Clark), 6-189 (Pringle), 7-198 (Hastings)

| | O | M | R | W |
|---|---|---|---|---|
| Patterson | 9 | 2 | 32 | 1 |
| Bresnan | 9 | 0 | 51 | 2 |
| Fisher | 7 | 0 | 49 | 0 |
| Plunkett | 9 | 1 | 40 | 3 |
| Rashid | 6 | 0 | 38 | 1 |
| Rhodes | 3 | 0 | 11 | 0 |

### YORKSHIRE

| | |
|---|---|
| § A J Hodd, c Mustard b Borthwick | 20 |
| * A Z Lees, run out (Pringle) | 9 |
| G J Maxwell, not out | 65 |
| G S Ballance, not out | 26 |
| J A Leaning | |
| A U Rashid | |
| T T Bresnan | |
| L E Plunkett      Did not bat | |
| W M H Rhodes | |
| S A Patterson | |
| M D Fisher | |
| Extras lb 6, w 4 | 10 |
| Total (2 wkts, 24.3 overs) | 130 |

*(Par score: 98-2)*

FoW: 1-14 (Lees), 2-80 (Hodd)

| | O | M | R | W |
|---|---|---|---|---|
| Hastings | 8.3 | 0 | 29 | 0 |
| Rushworth | 6 | 2 | 20 | 0 |
| Collingwood | 2 | 0 | 15 | 0 |
| Borthwick | 3 | 0 | 36 | 1 |
| Arshad | 3 | 0 | 11 | 0 |
| Pringle | 2 | 0 | 13 | 0 |

Umpires: M A Gough and R T Robinson      Scorers: J T Potter and B Hunt

# Plunkett plays major role

**STEVEN PATTERSON**
**Outstanding control**

A rejuvenated Maxwell led the way with his third consecutive major contribution as the Vikings comfortably won this weather-affected contest by 32 runs.

Chasing 225 to win from 43 overs on a miserable day Yorkshire kept an eye on the *Duckworth-Lewis* target, but with Maxwell and Ballance together the result never looked in doubt.

Yorkshire had bowled with reasonable discipline, and never let their hosts completely get away from them. Patterson bowled with outstanding control as Durham managed only 13 from the first five overs.

It was the introduction of Plunkett that brought the wickets column into play. Bowling at searing pace, just short of a length, the former Durham pace-man proved to be a menace.

Stoneman fell first, taken at backward-point low down by Maxwell off Bresnan. A subdued Mustard was caught at the wicket trying to late-cut Plunkett, who then induced a false shot from Borthwick to be taken by Leaning on the mid-wicket boundary. A series of short partnerships followed as Durham tried to gain a stranglehold, with a late flurry from Muchall, who was unbeaten on 35 from 26 balls. Plunkett returned an excellent 3-40 in nine overs, while Patterson also impressed with a typically economical 1-32.

Yorkshire lost Lees in the sixth over as the acting captain attempted a quick single to Pringle at mid-off and fell short of his ground. Durham skipper Stoneman turned to Borthwick to regain the initiative, but Maxwell had other ideas: the dynamic Australian went straight for the jugular as Borthwick's three overs cost 36 runs, 28 to Maxwell, although the leg-spinner did dismiss Hodd. Maxwell's half century came up in 35 balls, and the arrival of Ballance only accelerated Durham's downfall. The constant drizzle became heavier, and the players left the field with Yorkshire 130-2 off 24.3 overs before the rain set in.

# Royal London One-Day Cup — Group A
## Yorkshire v. Leicestershire

Played at Headingley, Leeds, on August 3, 2015
*Yorkshire won by 31 runs*

Toss won by Leicestershire        Yorkshire 2 points, Leicestershire 0 points

### YORKSHIRE

| | | |
|---|---|--:|
| § A J Hodd, run out (Eckersley) | | 36 |
| * A Z Lees, b Taylor | | 75 |
| G J Maxwell, c Ali b Sayer | | 28 |
| W M H Rhodes, b Raine | | 46 |
| J A Leaning, c Robson b Taylor | | 0 |
| A U Rashid, c Burgess b Raine | | 20 |
| T T Bresnan, c Ali b McKay | | 23 |
| M J Waite, not out | | 11 |
| R M Pyrah, c Sayer b McKay | | 5 |
| S A Patterson, b McKay | | 12 |
| M D Fisher | Did not bat | |
| Extras b 4, lb 11, w 6 | | 21 |
| Total (9 wkts, 50 overs) | | 277 |

*FoW:* 1-80 (Hodd), 2-129 (Maxwell), 3-198 (Lees), 4-198 (Leaning), 5-220 (Rhodes), 6-234 (Rashid), 7-253 (Bresnan), 8-264 (Pyrah), 9-277 (Patterson)

| | O | M | R | W |
|---|--:|--:|--:|--:|
| Sheikh | 8 | 0 | 45 | 0 |
| McKay | 10 | 1 | 47 | 3 |
| Raine | 9 | 0 | 48 | 2 |
| Taylor | 7 | 0 | 43 | 2 |
| Sayer | 10 | 0 | 52 | 1 |
| Ali | 6 | 0 | 27 | 0 |

### LEICESTERSHIRE

| | | |
|---|---|--:|
| A J Robson, c Lees b Rhodes | | 90 |
| * M J Cosgrove, b Fisher | | 23 |
| E J H Eckersley, b Maxwell | | 14 |
| A M Ali, c Patterson b Rashid | | 28 |
| § N J O'Brien, b Rhodes | | 2 |
| M G K Burgess, b Fisher | | 25 |
| B A Raine, c Lees b Bresnan | | 20 |
| R M L Taylor, c Pyrah b Patterson | | 18 |
| R J Sayer, c Hodd b Bresnan | | 4 |
| C J McKay, c Bresnan b Fisher | | 5 |
| A Sheikh, not out | | 3 |
| Extras lb 5, w 7, nb 2 | | 14 |
| Total (49.5 overs) | | 246 |

*FoW:* 1-49 (Cosgrove), 2-87 (Eckersley), 3-159 (Ali), 4-166 (Robson), 5-167 (O'Brien), 6-212 (Raine), 7-212 (Burgess), 8-219 (Sayer), 9-241 (McKay), 10-246 (Taylor)

| | O | M | R | W |
|---|--:|--:|--:|--:|
| Patterson | 8.5 | 0 | 32 | 1 |
| Bresnan | 7 | 0 | 49 | 2 |
| Fisher | 7 | 1 | 32 | 3 |
| Pyrah | 6 | 1 | 21 | 0 |
| Maxwell | 5 | 0 | 23 | 1 |
| Rashid | 10 | 0 | 42 | 1 |
| Waite | 2 | 0 | 17 | 0 |
| Rhodes | 4 | 0 | 25 | 2 |

Umpires: M Burns and J H Evans        Scorers: J T Potter and P J Rogers

# Openers set right tempo

Yorkshire picked up a priceless win to strengthen their grip on a top-two finish.

The Foxes asked Yorkshire to bat first, and a promising opening stand flourished between Lees and Hodd.

The pair added 80 in 10 overs before Hodd tried to steal a single to mid-wicket, only to

**Narrow squeak: Yorkshire's Rhodes fields from his own bowling as he catches Raine out of his crease**

see Eckersley's direct hit find him short of his ground after he had made 36 from 40 deliveries. Maxwell arrived in typically belligerent mood before his 24-ball cameo was ended on 28, caught in the deep by Ali.

The key partnership between Lees and Rhodes began to blossom as the Vikings captain passed his 50 in 76 balls. The two left-handers added 69 before Lees was bowled by Taylor for 75 from 110 deliveries. Two balls later a leading edge from Leaning reduced the hosts to 198-4, but the total had advanced to 220 when Rhodes was castled by Raine for 46. Leicestershire continued to keep a lid on Yorkshire's advances with McKay taking key wickets in the final stages. Hopes of reaching 300 were thwarted as the Vikings were all out for 277 in the last over.

An opening partnership between Robson and Cosgrove gave the Foxes impetus before Fisher's second delivery breached the defences of Leicestershire's skipper for 23. Maxwell accounted for Eckersley with the score on 87, but Ali and Robson provided some entertaining stroke-play in a stand worth 72. Robson offered Maxwell a low chance which was not taken before passing his half-century in 71 balls.

At 159 Rashid made the key breakthrough as Patterson took a catch at third-man from a horrible miscue by Ali. Then Rhodes took the wicket of Robson, caught by Lees for 90. O'Brien fell one run later, and the Foxes' valiant chase was run to earth. The Vikings completed their victory in the last over as Leicestershire finished 31 runs adrift. Fisher with 3-32 and Patterson 1-32 were the pick of the attack.

# Royal London One-Day Cup — Group A
## Yorkshire v. Somerset

Played at North Marine Road, Scarborough, on August 5, 2015
*Somerset won by 6 wickets*

Toss won by Yorkshire

Somerset 2 points, Yorkshire 0 points

### YORKSHIRE

| | |
|---|---|
| § A J Hodd, lbw b Davey | 0 |
| * A Z Lees, c Barrow b Davey | 1 |
| G J Maxwell, c Leach b Overton | 4 |
| G S Ballance, b Overton | 6 |
| J A Leaning, c Abell b Trego | 40 |
| W M H Rhodes, b Leach | 37 |
| T T Bresnan, c Allenby b Trego | 0 |
| R M Pyrah, c Barrow b Trego | 1 |
| K Carver, not out | 35 |
| J A Brooks, c Hildreth b Leach | 6 |
| M D Fisher, b Trego | 34 |
| Extras lb 6, w 5 | 11 |
| Total (49.5 overs) | 175 |

*FoW:* 1-0 (Hodd), 2-7 (Maxwell), 3-7 (Lees), 4-22 (Ballance), 5-92 (Rhodes), 6-93 (Bresnan), 7-94 (Leaning), 8-97 (Pyrah), 9-108 (Brooks), 10-175 (Fisher)

| | O | M | R | W |
|---|---|---|---|---|
| Davey | 9 | 2 | 37 | 2 |
| Overton | 10 | 2 | 19 | 2 |
| Groenewald | 10 | 2 | 43 | 0 |
| Allenby | 2 | 0 | 16 | 0 |
| Leach | 10 | 1 | 25 | 2 |
| Trego | 8.5 | 2 | 29 | 4 |

### SOMERSET

| | | |
|---|---|---|
| A J Hose, c Hodd b Bresnan | | 19 |
| T B Abell, c Hodd b Rhodes | | 80 |
| P D Trego, c Hodd b Fisher | | 19 |
| T L W Cooper, c Ballance b Fisher | | 13 |
| J C Hildreth, not out | | 23 |
| * J Allenby, not out | | 11 |
| C Overton | | |
| § A W R Barrow | | |
| J H Davey | Did not bat | |
| M J Leach | | |
| T D Groenewald | | |
| Extras lb 5, w 2, nb 6 | | 13 |
| Total (4 wkts, 38.1 overs) | | 178 |

*FoW:* 1-29 (Hose), 2-61 (Trego), 3-91 (Cooper), 4-162 (Abell)

| | O | M | R | W |
|---|---|---|---|---|
| Bresnan | 6 | 1 | 20 | 1 |
| Brooks | 7 | 1 | 35 | 0 |
| Rhodes | 4.1 | 0 | 19 | 1 |
| Fisher | 5 | 0 | 29 | 2 |
| Pyrah | 7 | 0 | 29 | 0 |
| Carver | 6 | 1 | 18 | 0 |
| Maxwell | 3 | 0 | 23 | 0 |

Umpires: R J Bailey and N A Mallender          Scorers: J T Potter and G A Stickley

## Yorkshire v. Somerset
# Last pair salvage pride

This unconvincing reversal in front of an expectant 5,000 crowd left Yorkshire still on course for a quarter-final berth.

Somerset came through comfortably by six wickets with more than 11 overs remaining, yet their victory could have been even more emphatic had a thor-

**That's entertainment: Karl Carver shows top order how it is done**

oughly entertaining 10th-wicket stand of 67 between Carver and Fisher not salvaged something from a disastrous batting display.

Yorkshire lost Hodd, trapped in front to the fourth ball for a duck, and never got their innings out of freefall. The in-form Maxwell went with the total on seven, closely followed by Lees, who was caught at the wicket. By the time Ballance had been dismissed by Chris Overton the Vikings had stumbled to 22-4 in the eighth over. Rhodes and Leaning added some grit to the proceedings in almost 20 overs, contributing 70 runs before another clatter of wickets took the scoreboard from 92-4 to 97-8 as the experienced Trego did the damage.

Brooks was dismissed at 108-9, but then an excellent partnership between the two young players in just over 10 overs brought the crowd to their feet. Trego removed Fisher for 34, not surprisingly a career-best, made from 38 balls with four fours and a six, but Carver finished unbeaten on a personal best 35 made from 38 balls.

Somerset had 21-year-old Abell to thank for making relatively short work of their task as he struck an assured career-best 80 in 112 deliveries. The early wickets Yorkshire strived for never materialised, although Hose was caught off Bresnan for 19, and Trego also departed as his attempted pull shot found the top edge and the waiting hands of Hodd off Fisher after a lively 17-ball stay at the crease.

The total became 91-3 when Fisher grabbed his second wicket as Cooper, who had been dropped twice, found Ballance at mid-wicket. Only one more wicket fell, the assured Abell's innings ending as Rhodes found the edge, but Somerset were as good as home. They reached their target with no further alarms.

**The match between Yorkshire and Northamptonshire scheduled to be played at Headingley on August 18 was abandoned without a ball bowled. The official teamsheet appears at the end of this section.**

# Royal London One-Day Cup — Quarter-Final
## Essex v. Yorkshire

Played at The County Ground, Chelmsford, on August 27, 2015
*Yorkshire won by 20 runs*
Toss won by Essex

### YORKSHIRE

| | |
|---|---|
| A Lyth, b Porter | 36 |
| * A Z Lees, c Foster b Topley | 18 |
| J A Leaning, c Nijjar b Topley | 72 |
| § J M Bairstow, c Foster b Ryder | 19 |
| G S Ballance, c Foster b Bopara | 32 |
| W M H Rhodes, c Nijjar b Bopara | 9 |
| A U Rashid, b ten Doeschate | 0 |
| T T Bresnan, c Nijjar b Topley | 7 |
| L E Plunkett, not out | 49 |
| S A Patterson, b Topley | 1 |
| M D Fisher, not out | 5 |
| Extras lb 3, w 1 | 4 |
| Total (9 wkts, 50 overs) | 252 |

*FoW:* 1-33 (Lees), 2-64 (Lyth), 3-96 (Bairstow), 4-163 (Ballance), 5-183 (Rhodes), 6-187 (Rashid), 7-195 (Leaning), 8-199 (Bresnan), 9-202 (Patterson)

| | O | M | R | W |
|---|---|---|---|---|
| Topley | 10 | 0 | 56 | 4 |
| Masters | 10 | 0 | 29 | 0 |
| Porter | 8 | 0 | 64 | 1 |
| Ryder | 5 | 0 | 20 | 1 |
| Nijjar | 5 | 0 | 27 | 0 |
| Bopara | 10 | 1 | 46 | 2 |
| ten Doeschate | 2 | 0 | 7 | 1 |

### ESSEX

| | |
|---|---|
| M L Pettini, run out (Bresnan) | 2 |
| N L J Browne, c Plunkett b Rashid | 37 |
| T Westley, b Plunkett | 54 |
| R S Bopara, c Bairstow b Plunkett | 17 |
| J D Ryder, b Plunkett | 3 |
| * R N ten Doeschate, c Bresnan b Rhodes | 52 |
| § J S Foster, c Leaning b Rhodes | 30 |
| A S S Nijjar, lbw b Bresnan | 21 |
| D D Masters, lbw b Patterson | 7 |
| R J W Topley, b Bresnan | 0 |
| J A Porter, not out | 5 |
| Extras lb 3, w 1 | 4 |
| Total (47.5 overs) | 232 |

*FoW:* 1-3 (Pettini), 2-95 (Westley), 3-95 (Browne), 4-100 (Ryder), 5-129 (Bopara), 6-189 (Foster), 7-206 (ten Doeschate), 8-227 (Masters), 9-227 (Nijjar), 10-232 (Topley)

| | O | M | R | W |
|---|---|---|---|---|
| Bresnan | 8.5 | 0 | 41 | 2 |
| Patterson | 9 | 0 | 37 | 1 |
| Plunkett | 10 | 1 | 58 | 3 |
| Fisher | 5 | 0 | 26 | 0 |
| Rashid | 10 | 0 | 45 | 1 |
| Rhodes | 5 | 0 | 22 | 2 |

*Man of the Match: L E Plunkett*

Umpires: S J O'Shaughnessy and R T Robinson     Scorers: J T Potter and A E Choat
Third Umpire: A G Wharf

# Plunkett's fire-cracker

**LIAM PLUNKETT:** Man-of-the-Match who was to be vital to England's one-day win against Australia at Headingley

Liam Plunkett provided the fireworks with bat and ball in a man-of-the-match performance to take Yorkshire to the semi-finals with an excellent victory.

A *White Rose* side packed with internationals back from Test duty played a curious innings. Many got themselves in, only to depart to a combination of poor shots and inventive bowling.

Leaning moved smoothly through the gears, raising his half-century with a vicious strike over mid-wicket, and he found Ballance an able ally. The total was 163 in the 34th over before Ballance gave Foster his third catch.

Yorkshire's innings subsided almost without trace, and in the 45th over was 202-9. Plunkett, with Fisher in almost silent support, produced an innings of zeal and purpose, his unbeaten 49 from 32 balls taking them to an unlikely par score of 252, the last pair adding 50.

Pettini was run out at the non-striker's end by Bresnan's deflection, but a stand of 92 between Browne and Westley looked to put Essex in the box seat. Plunkett then ripped out Westley's off-stump for a run-a-ball 54 and Browne fell to Rashid for 37.

The key wicket of Ryder followed as Plunkett found the ball of the day to jag back in and crash into the Kiwi's timbers. Bopara was Plunkett's next victim, caught behind, and much credit must go to acting captain Lees as he let Plunkett bowl his overs in one spell.

ten Doeschate and Foster gave the home crowd some hope with a 60 partnership, but the vital wicket of Foster, taken by Leaning off Rhodes, turned the game again. Rhodes induced a false stroke from the well set ten Doeschate, and Yorkshire held their nerve.

167

# Royal London One-Day Cup Semi-Final
## Yorkshire v. Gloucestershire

Played at Headingley, Leeds, on September 6, 2015
*Gloucestershire won by 8 wickets*
Toss won by Gloucestershire

### YORKSHIRE

| | |
|---|---:|
| A Lyth, c Payne b Fuller | 96 |
| * A Z Lees, c and b Howell | 21 |
| J A Leaning, lbw b Howell | 8 |
| § J M Bairstow, lbw b Norwell | 34 |
| G S Ballance, c and b Howell | 27 |
| W M H Rhodes, c Fuller b Taylor | 4 |
| T T Bresnan, c Klinger b Payne | 27 |
| R M Pyrah, c Klinger b Smith | 1 |
| S A Patterson, run out (Dent/Roderick) | 9 |
| M D Fisher, not out | 9 |
| K Carver | Did not bat |
| Extras b 8, lb 12, w 7 | 27 |
| Total (9 wkts, 50 overs) | 263 |

*FoW:* 1-103 (Lees), 2-127 (Leaning), 3-159 (Lyth), 4-198 (Bairstow), 5-208 (Rhodes), 6-226 (Ballance), 7-245 (Bresnan), 8-249 (Pyrah), 9-263 (Patterson)

| | O | M | R | W |
|---|---:|---:|---:|---:|
| Fuller | 7 | 0 | 52 | 1 |
| Payne | 9 | 0 | 32 | 1 |
| Norwell | 9 | 0 | 46 | 1 |
| Taylor | 10 | 0 | 46 | 1 |
| Howell | 10 | 0 | 37 | 3 |
| Smith | 5 | 0 | 30 | 1 |

### GLOUCESTERSHIRE

| | |
|---|---:|
| C J D Dent, b Fisher | 28 |
| * M Klinger, not out | 137 |
| § G H Roderick, c Leaning b Rhodes | 18 |
| H J H Marshall, not out | 78 |
| B A C Howell | |
| G O Jones | |
| J M R Taylor | |
| J K Fuller | Did not bat |
| T M J Smith | |
| D A Payne | |
| L C Norwell | |
| Extras lb 2, w 4 | 6 |
| Total (2 wkts, 46.5 overs) | 267 |

*FoW:* 1-56 (Dent), 2-90 (Roderick)

| | O | M | R | W |
|---|---:|---:|---:|---:|
| Patterson | 8 | 0 | 52 | 0 |
| Bresnan | 7 | 0 | 40 | 0 |
| Fisher | 9.5 | 0 | 50 | 1 |
| Rhodes | 8 | 0 | 29 | 1 |
| Carver | 6 | 0 | 50 | 0 |
| Pyrah | 5 | 0 | 28 | 0 |
| Lyth | 3 | 0 | 16 | 0 |

*Man of the Match: M Klinger*

Umpires: J W Lloyds and N A Mallender                    Scorers: J T Potter and A J Bull
Third Umpire: D J Millns

## Yorkshire v Gloucestershire

# Stunned by record stand

A record List A partnership for any wicket for Gloucestershire against Yorkshire between Michael Klinger, 137 not out, and Hamish Marshall, 78 not out, ended the Vikings' hopes of a Lord's final.

They crashed to a comprehensive eight-wicket defeat as the two batsmen added an unbroken 177 from 170 balls after Yorkshire had capitulated from 189-2 to 263-9 in their 50 overs.

Gloucestershire put Yorkshire in, and Lyth and Lees started confidently. Lyth hit his straps early with a flurry of boundaries, carving Fuller repeatedly through the off side, and when Fuller was removed from the attack his three-over spell had cost 28 runs.

Yorkshire's 50 arrived in the eighth over, Lees contributing only two, and Lyth advanced to his half-century from 41 balls. The century partnership came in emphatic fashion — Lees lofting a lovely drive over mid-off in the 18th over.

Two balls later, however, he almost apologetically pushed back to the medium pace of Howell, and Yorkshire's skipper was on his way for 21 from 48 balls. Leaning's innings never really caught fire, but Bairstow's appearance reaped instant dividends as the run rate accelerated.

**ADAM LYTH: Carved up the attack with his 96**

Just as the Vikings were looking ominous Lyth fell, agonisingly close to his second List A century as he swivelled a pull straight to the diving Payne at long-leg for 96. His innings spanned 88 balls, and contained 10 fours and a six. Bairstow, on 34, pushed a simple catch back to Norwell...who dropped it while throwing the ball up in celebration...but the bowler got his man lbw in his next over.

169

**WILL RHODES**
**Tight spell and a wicket**

**JONATHAN BAIRSTOW**
**Caught, dropped, lbw**

The 200 arrived in the 36th over, but runs dried up as Norwell and Taylor kept the pressure on. Rhodes fell to a lofted drive on the long-off fence, and a total of 300 looked some way off. The important wicket of Ballance fell in the 43rd over, and Gloucestershire maintained a firm grip as the Vikings limped to an unsatisfactory 263-9.

Gloucestershire's riposte was positive, Klinger and Dent both driving through the off-side in lordly fashion. At 56, Fisher made the breakthrough by dismissing Dent for 28, and Rhodes's accurate spell was rewarded with the wicket of Broderick, a poor stroke lofted to mid-on with the total on 90. Both the 100 and Klinger's half-century came in the 21st over, and from there on Gloucestershire were in command.

Klinger and Marshall added a century partnership with minimal discomfort as the game was allowed to drift. Marshall brought up his 50 at just under a run a ball, and Klinger completed a wonderful chanceless century in 177 deliveries, his fourth in this year's competition. Both batsmen continued on their merry way to their 150 partnership. Marshall was dropped by Lees on 77 in the 46th over, and the game was wrapped up with a huge six from Klinger with 19 balls to spare.

# Royal London One-Day Cup — Group A
## Yorkshire v. Northamptonshire

Played at Headingley, Leeds, on August 18, 2015
*No Result*
*No play was possible after the toss because of rain*

Toss won by Yorkshire                    Yorkshire 1 point, Northamptonshire 1 point

### NORTHAMPTONSHIRE

J J Cobb
D J Willey
R E Levi
§ B M Duckett
* A G Wakely
R I Keogh
K J Coetzer
R K Kleinveldt
B W Sanderson
S P Crook
M Azharullah

### YORKSHIRE

* A Z Lees
§ A J Hodd
G J Maxwell
G S Ballance
J A Leaning
W M H Rhodes
R M Pyrah
T T Bresnan
K Carver
S A Patterson
M D Fisher

Umpires: S C Gale and J H Evans                    Scorers: J T Potter and A C Kingston
Third Umpire: G D Lloyd

# Royal London One-Day Cup

## FINAL TABLES 2015

### GROUP A

| | | P | W | L | T | NR/A | PTS | NRR |
|---|---|---|---|---|---|---|---|---|
| 1 | **Surrey (B 9) \*** .................... | **8** | **6** | **1** | **0** | **1** | **13.00** | **1.079** |
| 2 | Gloucestershire (A 3) \* ............. | 8 | 5 | 2 | 0 | 0 | 11.00 | 0.069 |
| 3 | **Yorkshire Vikings (A 1) \*** .......... | **8** | **4** | **2** | **0** | **2** | **10.00** | **0.536** |
| 4 | Durham (B 4) \* .................... | 8 | 4 | 3 | 0 | 1 | 9.00 | 0.402 |
| 5 | Northamptonshire Steelbacks (A 6) .... | 8 | 4 | 3 | 0 | 1 | 9.00 | -0.458 |
| 6 | Somerset (B 6) .................... | 8 | 4 | 4 | 0 | 0 | 8.00 | 0.814 |
| 7 | Derbyshire Falcons (A 4) ............ | 8 | 4 | 4 | 0 | 0 | 8.00 | 0.151 |
| 8 | Worcestershire (A 7) ............... | 8 | 1 | 6 | 0 | 1 | 3.00 | -0.629 |
| 9 | Leicestershire Foxes ( A 8) .......... | 8 | 0 | 7 | 0 | 1 | 1.00 | -1.914 |

### GROUP B

| | | P | W | L | T | NR/A | PTS | NRR |
|---|---|---|---|---|---|---|---|---|
| 1 | Nottinghamshire Outlaws (A 1) \* ...... | 8 | 5 | 1 | 0 | 2 | 12.00 | 0.755 |
| 2 | Essex Eagles (A 2) \* ................ | 8 | 4 | 2 | 0 | 2 | 10.00 | 0.480 |
| 3 | Hampshire Royals (A 9) \* ........... | 8 | 4 | 3 | 0 | 1 | 9.00 | 0.554 |
| 4 | Kent Spitfires (B 2) \* ............... | 8 | 3 | 3 | 0 | 2 | 8.00 | 0.031 |
| 5 | Lancashire Lightning (A 8) .......... | 8 | 3 | 3 | 0 | 2 | 8.00 | -0.034 |
| 6 | Warwickshire Bears (B 3) ............ | 8 | 3 | 3 | 0 | 2 | 8.00 | -0.765 |
| 7 | Middlesex Panthers (B 7) ............ | 8 | 3 | 4 | 0 | 1 | 7.00 | -0.224 |
| 8 | Glamorgan (B 5) ................... | 8 | 2 | 3 | 0 | 3 | 3.00 | 0.160 |
| 9 | Sussex Sharks (B 8) ................ | 8 | 0 | 5 | 0 | 3 | 3.00 | -1.063 |

\* Qualified for Quarter-Finals

Glamorgan were deducted 2 points for a poor pitch in 2014 against Durham and 2 points for a poor pitch against Hampshire in 2015. The 2015 match was awarded to Hampshire

*(2014 group positions in brackets)*

# YORKSHIRE AVERAGES 2015

## ROYAL LONDON ONE-DAY CUP

Played 10    Won 5    Lost 3    No Result 2

### BATTING AND FIELDING

*(Qualification 4 completed innings)*

| Player | M. | I. | N.O. | Runs | H.S. | 100s | 50s | Avge | ct/st |
|--------|----|----|------|------|------|------|-----|------|-------|
| G J Maxwell ........ | 8 | 7 | 1 | 312 | 111 | 1 | 2 | 52.00 | 4 |
| G S Ballance ........ | 9 | 8 | 1 | 296 | 77 | 0 | 2 | 42.28 | 3 |
| J A Leaning ........ | 10 | 8 | 1 | 249 | 72 | 0 | 2 | 35.57 | 4 |
| A Z Lees ........... | 10 | 9 | 0 | 247 | 75 | 0 | 2 | 27.44 | 3 |
| W M H Rhodes ...... | 9 | 7 | 1 | 132 | 46 | 0 | 0 | 22.00 | 2 |
| T T Bresnan ........ | 9 | 7 | 0 | 132 | 43 | 0 | 0 | 18.85 | 2 |
| A J Hodd ........... | 8 | 6 | 0 | 106 | 36 | 0 | 0 | 17.66 | 10/1 |
| S A Patterson ........ | 9 | 5 | 1 | 47 | 24 | 0 | 0 | 11.75 | 1 |

#### Also played

| | | | | | | | | | |
|--------|----|----|------|------|------|------|-----|------|-------|
| L E Plunkett ......... | 6 | 5 | 4 | 82 | 49* | 0 | 0 | 82.00 | 4 |
| A Z Lyth ............ | 2 | 2 | 0 | 132 | 96 | 0 | 1 | 66.00 | 0 |
| M D Fisher .......... | 8 | 4 | 3 | 52 | 34 | 0 | 0 | 52.00 | 2 |
| J M Bairstow ........ | 2 | 2 | 0 | 53 | 34 | 0 | 0 | 26.50 | 1 |
| A U Rashid .......... | 4 | 3 | 0 | 61 | 41 | 0 | 0 | 20.33 | 1 |
| A W Gale ........... | 3 | 3 | 0 | 56 | 37 | 0 | 0 | 18.66 | 1 |
| J A Brooks .......... | 3 | 1 | 0 | 6 | 6 | 0 | 0 | 6.00 | 0 |
| R M Pyrah .......... | 4 | 3 | 0 | 7 | 5 | 0 | 0 | 2.33 | 1 |
| K Carver ........... | 5 | 1 | 1 | 35 | 35* | 0 | 0 | — | 1 |
| M J Waite ........... | 1 | 1 | 1 | 11 | 11* | 0 | 0 | — | 0 |

### BOWLING

*(Qualification 4 wickets)*

| Player | Overs | Mdns | Runs | Wkts | Avge | Best | 4wI | RPO |
|--------|-------|------|------|------|------|------|-----|-----|
| S A Patterson ....... | 58.2 | 3 | 258 | 13 | 19.84 | 5-24 | 1 | 4.42 |
| L E Plunkett ......... | 43 | 2 | 215 | 9 | 23.88 | 3-40 | 0 | 5.00 |
| W M H Rhodes ...... | 33.1 | 1 | 155 | 6 | 25.83 | 2-22 | 0 | 4.67 |
| M D Fisher .......... | 41.5 | 1 | 245 | 8 | 30.62 | 3-32 | 0 | 5.85 |
| T T Bresnan ........ | 50.5 | 2 | 265 | 8 | 33.12 | 2-41 | 0 | 5.21 |
| A U Rashid .......... | 34 | 0 | 192 | 4 | 48.00 | 1-38 | 0 | 5.64 |

#### Also bowled

| | | | | | | | | |
|--------|-------|------|------|------|------|------|-----|-----|
| J A Brooks .......... | 19 | 1 | 96 | 3 | 32.00 | 3-40 | 0 | 5.05 |
| G J Maxwell ......... | 23 | 0 | 144 | 3 | 48.00 | 2-61 | 0 | 6.26 |
| K Carver ........... | 22 | 1 | 108 | 2 | 54.00 | 2-40 | 0 | 4.90 |
| R M Pyrah .......... | 18 | 1 | 78 | 0 | — | 0-21 | 0 | 4.33 |
| A Lyth .............. | 3 | 0 | 16 | 0 | — | 0-16 | 0 | 5.33 |
| M J Waite ........... | 2 | 0 | 17 | 0 | — | 0-17 | 0 | 8.50 |

# Fourth Royal London One-Day International
## England v. Australia

Played at Headingley, Leeds, on September 11, 2015
*England won by 3 wickets*

Toss won by Australia

### AUSTRALIA

| | |
|---|---|
| J A Burns, c Willey | 2 |
| A J Finch, c Bairstow b Willey | 15 |
| * S P D Smith, lbw b Willey | 5 |
| G J Bailey, c and b Plunkett | 75 |
| G J Maxwell, b Ali | 85 |
| M R Marsh, c Willey b Plunkett | 17 |
| § M S Wade, not out | 50 |
| M P Stoinis, c Rashid b Ali | 4 |
| J W Hastings, not out | 34 |
| P J Cummins | |
| J L Pattinson | Did not bat |
| Extras lb 8, w 3, nb 1 | 12 |
| Total (7 wkts, 50 overs) | 299 |

*FoW:* 1-14 (Burns), 2-25 (Smith), 3-30 (Finch), 4-167 (Maxwell), 5-210 (Marsh), 6-210 (Marsh), 7-215 (Stoinis).

| | O | M | R | W |
|---|---|---|---|---|
| Willey | 8 | 0 | 51 | 3 |
| Wood | 9 | 0 | 65 | 0 |
| Plunkett | 8 | 0 | 47 | 2 |
| Stokes | 5 | 0 | 25 | 0 |
| Rashid | 10 | 0 | 63 | 0 |
| Ali | 10 | 0 | 40 | 2 |

### ENGLAND

| | |
|---|---|
| J J Roy, c Finch b Cummins | 36 |
| A D Hales, lbw b Cummins | 0 |
| J W A Taylor, c Wade b Marsh | 41 |
| * E J G Morgan, c Maxwell b Cummins | 92 |
| B A Stokes, b Marsh | 41 |
| § J M Bairstow, c Wade b Maxwell | 31 |
| M M Ali, not out | 21 |
| L E Plunkett, c Maxwell b Cummins | 17 |
| D J Willey, not out | 12 |
| A U Rashid | |
| M A Wood | Did not bat |
| Extras lb 3, w 8, nb 2 | 13 |
| Total (7 wkts, 48.2overs) | 304 |

*FoW:* 1-1 (Hales), 2-73 (Roy), 3-89 (Taylor), 4-180 (Stokes), 5-238 (Morgan), 6-261 (Bairstow), 7-282 (Plunkett).

| | O | M | R | W |
|---|---|---|---|---|
| Pattinson | 9 | 0 | 73 | 0 |
| Cummins | 10 | 0 | 49 | 4 |
| Hastings | 6.2 | 0 | 56 | 0 |
| Marsh | 9 | 0 | 52 | 2 |
| Maxwell | 10 | 0 | 54 | 1 |
| Stoinis | 4 | 0 | 17 | 0 |

Man of the Match: E J G Morgan

Umpires: H D P K Dharmasena and M A Gough    Scorers: D M White and H Clayton
Third Umpire J S Wilson    Fourth: R A Kettleborough    Match Referee: J J Crowe

# NATWEST T20 BLAST
# HIGHLIGHTS OF 2015

### WINNERS

**Lancashire,** who beat Northamptonshire by 13 runs

### Totals of 150 and over (6)

209-4    v. Nottinghamshire at Leeds (won)
202-8    v. Lancashire at Manchester (lost)
194-5    v. Durham at Leeds (won)
185-8    v. Lancashire at Leeds (lost)
176-8    v. Durham at Chester-le-Street (lost)
153-7    v. Northamptonshire at Northampton (lost)

### Match aggregates of 350 and over (5)

433    Lancashire (231-4) beat Yorkshire (202-8) by 29 runs at Manchester
385    Durham (191-6) lost to Yorkshire (194-5) by 5 wickets at Leeds
378    Yorkshire (209-4) beat Nottinghamshire (169-6) by 40 runs at Leeds
371    Yorkshire (185-8) lost to Lancashire (186-6) by 4 wickets at Leeds
358    Durham (182-4) beat Yorkshire (176-8) by 6 runs at Chester-le-Street

### Century Partnerships (2)

**For the 2nd wicket (1)**

104    A Z Lees and J A Leaning          v. Warwickshire at Leeds

**For the 3rd wicket (1)**

101    A J Hodd and G J Maxwell          v. Nottinghamshire at Leeds

### 4 wickets in an innings (1)

M D Fisher (1)

    5-33    v. Derbyshire at Leeds

### 3 catches in an innings (1)

R M Pyrah (1)

    3          v. Derbyshire at Leeds

### Debuts (8)

**t 20 cricket:** K Carver, B O Coad, M D Fisher, R Gibson, J Shaw and M D Waite
**For Yorkshire:** G J Maxwell and J D Middlebrook

## Match-By-Match Reports          DAVE CALDWELL

# NatWest T20 BLAST — North Group
## Yorkshire v. Derbyshire

Played at Headingley, Leeds, on May 15, 2015
*Yorkshire won by 7 wickets*

Toss won by Yorkshire

Yorkshire 2 points, Derbyshire 0 points

### DERBYSHIRE

| | |
|---|---|
| H M Amla, c Gale b Pyrah | 29 |
| * W J Durstan, c Rashid b Bresnan | 8 |
| C F Hughes, c Pyrah b Fisher | 27 |
| S J Thakor, lbw b Fisher | 4 |
| B A Godleman, c and b Pyrah | 2 |
| A L Hughes, c and b Fisher | 11 |
| S L Elstone, c Pyrah b Rashid | 3 |
| § T Poynton, c Bairstow b Fisher | 27 |
| D J Wainwright, c Bairstow b Plunkett | 5 |
| B D Cotton, c and b Fisher | 8 |
| M H A Footitt, not out | 0 |
| Extras lb 3, w 1 | 4 |
| Total (18.2 overs) | 128 |

*FoW:* 1-27 (Durston), 2-66 (C F Hughes), 3-70 (Amla), 4-72 (Thakor), 5-78 (Godleman), 6-81 (Elstone), 7-108 (A L Hughes), 8-115 (Poynton), 9-119 (Wainwright), 10-128 (Cotton)

| | O | M | R | W |
|---|---|---|---|---|
| Brooks | 2 | 0 | 21 | 0 |
| Bresnan | 3 | 0 | 18 | 1 |
| Plunkett | 3 | 0 | 25 | 1 |
| Rashid | 3 | 0 | 26 | 1 |
| Pyrah | 4 | 0 | 13 | 2 |
| Fisher | 3.2 | 0 | 22 | 5 |

### YORKSHIRE

| | |
|---|---|
| * A W Gale, c Poynton b Cotton | 41 |
| A J Hodd, b Cotton | 0 |
| A Z Lees, c Amla b Footitt | 23 |
| § J M Bairstow, not out | 40 |
| J A Leaning, not out | 19 |
| A U Rashid | |
| T T Bresnan | |
| L E Plunkett | Did not bat |
| J A Brooks | |
| R M Pyrah | |
| M D Fisher | |
| Extras lb 4, nb 4 | 8 |
| Total (3 wkts, 16.4 overs) | 131 |

*FoW:* 1-1 (Hodd), 2-31 (Lees), 3-100 (Gale)

| | O | M | R | W |
|---|---|---|---|---|
| Cotton | 4 | 0 | 19 | 2 |
| Thakor | 2.4 | 0 | 13 | 0 |
| Footitt | 4 | 0 | 42 | 1 |
| A L Hughes | 2 | 0 | 16 | 0 |
| Wainwright | 3 | 0 | 29 | 0 |
| Elstone | 1 | 0 | 8 | 0 |

*Man of the Match: M D Fisher*

Umpires: R J Evans and G D Lloyd

Scorers: J T Potter and J M Brown

# Fisher's high-fives debut

A stunning *T20* debut by Matthew Fisher gave Yorkshire an opening victory as the 17-year-old pacemen became only the third *White Rose* bowler to claim a five-wicket haul in the shortest format.

**STUNNING: Bairstow leads the players' applause for Fisher**

Fisher's 5-22 from only 20 deliveries kept Derbyshire well in check, and they were despatched for 128 in the 19th over. The visitors started confidently enough. Durston and Amla shared a first-wicket stand of 27 before Durston was taken by Rashid off Bresnan for eight. Progress continued without too many alarms, Amla and Chesney Hughes taking the total to 66 in the ninth over before the wheels came off in fairly rapid fashion.

Fisher nipped in with his first wicket, Pyrah taking the catch to dismiss Hughes for 27. The key wicket of Amla followed for a 22-ball 29, Gale taking the catch in the cover region off Pyrah, and the two bowlers continued to provide the perfect balance as they shared two more wickets. Thakor was trapped in front by a quicker ball from Fisher, and Pyrah took a smart return catch to remove Godleman.

By the time Rashid had accounted for Elstone the Falcons had slipped from 66-1 to a less imposing 81-6. There was a brief recovery as Alex Hughes and Poynton added 27 for the seventh wicket, but Hughes offered a caught-and-bowled chance which Fisher gratefully accepted. Fisher's fourth wicket arrived in the 17th over as Poynton, who had moved to 27, was caught at the wicket. The innings subsided as Fisher took his second return catch — running to short cover to remove Cotton — leaving Yorkshire to chase a relatively small target.

Despite losing Hodd to a first-ball duck, clean bowled by Cotton, Yorkshire recovered well enough to ensure no further alarms. Gale and Lees took no undue risks in pursuit of the below-par target, putting on 30 for the second wicket before Lees fell for 23, carving to Amla at third-man off Footitt. Bairstow joined his skipper, the pair combining to great effect as poor balls were punished and singles scampered. The target loomed large. They put on 69 before Gale was caught behind for 41. Bairstow, 40 not out, and Leaning, 19 not out, completed the job with 20 balls remaining.

# NatWest T20 BLAST — North Group
## Nottinghamshire v. Yorkshire

Played at Trent Bridge, Nottingham, on May 22, 2015

*Yorkshire won by 6 wickets*

Toss won by Yorkshire        Yorkshire 2 points, Nottinghamshire 0 points

### NOTTINGHAMSHIRE

| | | |
|---|---|---:|
| M H Wessels, c Fisher b Bresnan | | 13 |
| G P Smith, c Plunkett b Pyrah | | 27 |
| § B R M Taylor, c Fisher b Plunkett | | 8 |
| S R Patel, c Bairstow b Rashid | | 41 |
| * J W A Taylor, c Bairstow b Plunkett | | 3 |
| S J Mullaney, run out (Maxwell/Bairstow) | | 38 |
| S K W Wood, run out (Bairstow) | | 8 |
| W R S Gidman, not out | | 2 |
| J T Ball | | |
| L J Fletcher | Did not bat | |
| H F Gurney | | |
| Extras b 1, lb 1, w 1 | | 3 |
| Total (7 wkts, 20 overs) | | 143 |

*FoW:* 1-19 (Wessels), 2-31 ( B R M Taylor), 3-75 (Smith), 4-80 (J W A Taylor), 5-112 (Patel), 6-128 (Wood), 7-143 (Mullaney).

| | O | M | R | W |
|---|---|---|---|---|
| Maxwell | 4 | 0 | 31 | 0 |
| Bresnan | 4 | 0 | 31 | 1 |
| Plunkett | 4 | 0 | 18 | 2 |
| Fisher | 2 | 0 | 22 | 0 |
| Rashid | 4 | 0 | 23 | 1 |
| Pyrah | 2 | 0 | 16 | 1 |

### YORKSHIRE

| | | |
|---|---|---:|
| * A W Gale, not out | | 68 |
| A J Hodd, c J W A Taylor b Patel | | 22 |
| A Z Lees, c J W A Taylor b Mullaney | | 2 |
| § J M Bairstow, c B R M Taylor b Mullaney | | 10 |
| G J Maxwell, c Mullaney b Wood | | 20 |
| J A Leaning, not out | | 9 |
| A U Rashid | | |
| T T Bresnan | | |
| L E Plunkett | Did not bat | |
| R M Pyrah | | |
| M D Fisher | | |
| Extras b 5, lb 7, w 3 | | 15 |
| Total (4 wkts, 18.5 overs) | | 146 |

*FoW:* 1-61 (Hodd), 2-70 (Lees), 3-92 (Bairstow), 4-127 (Maxwell).

| | O | M | R | W |
|---|---|---|---|---|
| Gurney | 4 | 1 | 22 | 0 |
| Ball | 3 | 0 | 25 | 0 |
| Fletcher | 2 | 0 | 23 | 0 |
| Patel | 4 | 0 | 26 | 1 |
| Mullaney | 4 | 0 | 27 | 2 |
| Wood | 1.5 | 0 | 11 | 1 |

*Man of the Match: A W Gale*

Umpires: P K Baldwin and S A Garratt      Scorers: J T Potter and R Marshall

# Gale blows away Outlaws

**ANDREW GALE: Led run chase with great authority**

Yorkshire continued their positive start with an excellent all-round display before a near 10,000 crowd.

Gale had little hesitation in inserting the hosts, and after a brief flurry in the early skirmishes Wessels fell to Bresnan with the score on 19. The in-form Brendan Taylor was next to go, the excellent Plunkett inducing a false stroke from the Zimbabwean.

Smith and Patel began to restore the innings with a lively stand, and young Fisher was brought back down to earth after the previous week's heroics, his two overs costing 22 runs.

The Outlaws had reached 75 at the half-way point when Pyrah picked up the vital wicket of Smith, caught by Plunkett for 27. Skipper James Taylor swiftly made his exit, Plunkett grabbing his second wicket courtesy of a fine diving catch behind the stumps by Bairstow. Plunkett's spell proved decisive, his four overs costing a mere 18 runs with 13 dot balls. The Vikings' disciplined bowling continued to contain as wickets fell at key times, none more so than Patel, whose sprightly 27-ball 41 was ended by some tidy work from Bairstow off leg-spinner Rashid. The Outlaws closed on 143-7, and Yorkshire made little mistake in reaching their target.

Gale and Hodd began the reply in commanding fashion, combining well judged runs and lusty blows to reach 61 in the ninth over before Hodd and Lees fell in quick succession. James Taylor caught both on the off-side, Lees being completely outfoxed by a fine slower ball from Mullaney. Gale showed great authority and leadership in ensuring that Yorkshire made the target without any undue alarms, despite losing Bairstow to a real steepler from a top edge for 10 and debutant Maxwell for a rapid 20. Gale saw the job through with an unbeaten 68 from 55 balls with five boundaries — and his only six proved to be the match-winning hit, straight down the ground to take his side home with seven balls remaining.

# NatWest T20 BLAST — North Group
## Durham v. Yorkshire

Played at Durham ICG, Chester-le-Street, on May 29, 2015

*Durham won by 6 runs*

Toss won by Yorkshire        Durham 2 points, Yorkshire 0 points

### DURHAM

| | | |
|---|---|--:|
| * M D Stoneman, c Lees b Plunkett | | 20 |
| § P Mustard, c Rashid b Maxwell | | 39 |
| C S MacLeod, c Bresnan b Rashid | | 8 |
| P D Collingwood, b Plunkett | | 31 |
| G J Muchall, not out | | 34 |
| J W Hasting, not out | | 37 |
| R D Pringle | | |
| U Arshad | | |
| K K Jennings | Did not bat | |
| S G Borthwick | | |
| P Coughlin | | |
| Extras lb 2, w 3, nb 8 | | 13 |
| Total (4 wkts, 20 overs) | | 182 |

*FoW:* 1-30 (Stoneman), 2-72 (MacLeod), 3-75 (Mustard), 4-123 (Collingwood)

| | O | M | R | W |
|---|--:|--:|--:|--:|
| Bresnan | 4 | 0 | 51 | 1 |
| Fisher | 3 | 0 | 29 | 0 |
| Plunkett | 4 | 0 | 29 | 2 |
| Pyrah | 3 | 0 | 21 | 0 |
| Rashid | 3 | 0 | 22 | 1 |
| Maxwell | 3 | 0 | 28 | 1 |

### YORKSHIRE

| | | |
|---|---|--:|
| A J Hodd, lbw b Coughlin | | 2 |
| * A W Gale, hit wicket b Collingwood | | 41 |
| A Z Lees, c MacLeod b Arshad | | 9 |
| § J M Bairstow, b Jennings | | 27 |
| G J Maxwell, lbw b Jennings | | 8 |
| J A Leaning, c Pringle b Jennings | | 16 |
| R M Pyrah, c Pringle b Jennings | | 5 |
| T T Bresnan, not out | | 30 |
| L E Plunkett, b Arshad | | 17 |
| A U Rashid, not out | | 8 |
| M D Fisher | Did not bat | |
| Extras b 8, lb 3, w 2 | | 13 |
| Total (8 wkts, 20 overs) | | 176 |

*FoW:* 1-7 (Hodd), 2-25 (Lees), 3-75 (Bairstow), 4-93 (Maxwell), 5-97 (Gale), 6-104 (Pyrah), 7-124 (Leaning), 8-154 (Plunkett)

| | O | M | R | W |
|---|--:|--:|--:|--:|
| Pringle | 2 | 0 | 12 | 0 |
| Coughlin | 2 | 0 | 23 | 1 |
| Hastings | 4 | 0 | 38 | 0 |
| Arshad | 4 | 0 | 33 | 2 |
| Collingwood | 4 | 0 | 22 | 1 |
| Jennings | 4 | 0 | 37 | 4 |

*Man of the Match: J W Hastings*

Umpires: N G B Cook and G D Lloyd      Scorers: T J Kempson, J M Williamson and B Hunt

## Durham v. Yorkshire
# Bresnan blast is too late

A first defeat for Yorkshire marked the opening of Durham's permanent floodlights — thanks to the most unlikely of match-winners with the ball.

Jennings's medium pace accounted for four Vikings batsmen and proved the deciding factor in a six-run margin.

After a delayed start Stoneman and Mustard made great strides, plundering 30 runs in the first three overs before Stoneman was caught by Lees off Plunkett for 20.

Mustard was joined by Macleod, whose timing was eluding him, and Plunkett and Pyrah made the explosive left-hander work hard for his runs.

Both fell in quick succession as Yorkshire began to claw back the initiative. The scoring rate slowed considerably in the middle overs, and Collingwood's

**TIM BRESNAN: Last-ball six**

unconvincing knock ended on 31, when he was cleaned up by a rampant Plunkett. At 123-4 in the 17th Yorkshire hoped to contain their hosts to around 160, but this notion was blown out of the water as Muchall and Hastings lashed out, Hastings finishing on 37 from 16 balls and Muchall 34 from 24. Bresnan went for 51 in four wicketless overs.

Yorkshire's reply hit the buffers early as Hodd was trapped in front by Coughlin for two, while Lees continued his patchy form with nine before he was caught on the drive, leaving Vikings on 25-2 in the fourth. Bairstow repaired the damage with Gale, who was striking the ball in fine fashion, before Jennings bowled Yorkshire's wicket-keeper as he aimed across the line, for 27. The pair had added 50 in six overs.

Two key wickets followed. Maxwell was lbw to Jennings aiming to leg and, more curiously, Gale on 41 went for a big leg-side blow, only for his back foot to slip and disturb the bails. Further wickets fell, and Vikings needed 21 from the last over. Despite some valiant strikes from Bresnan, including the last ball sailing for six, the asking rate had been too much for too long. Jennings finished with a career-best 4-37.

# NatWest T20 BLAST — North Group
## Yorkshire v. Lancashire

Played at Headingley, Leeds, on June 5, 2015
*Lancashire won by 4 wickets*

Toss won by Lancashire

Lancashire 2 points, Yorkshire 0 points

### YORKSHIRE

| | | |
|---|---|---:|
| G J Maxwell, c Davies b Edwards | | 18 |
| * A W Gale, b Faulkner | | 6 |
| J E Root, c Bailey b Faulkner | | 55 |
| § J M Bairstow, c Brown b Lilley | | 18 |
| G S Ballance, c Brown b Lilley | | 31 |
| J A Leaning, c Buttler b Faulkner | | 22 |
| T T Brenan, b Edwards | | 12 |
| R M Pyrah, run out (Edwards) | | 4 |
| L E Plunkett, not out | | 9 |
| A U Rashid | | |
| M D Fisher | Did not bat | |
| Extras lb 6, w 4 | | 10 |
| Total (8 wkts, 20 overs) | | 185 |

FoW: 1-20 (Maxwell), 2-25 (Gale), 3-65 (Root), 4-128 (Ballance), 5-155 (Root),
6-172 (Bresnan), 7-174 (Leaning), 8-185 (Pyrah)

| | O | M | R | W |
|---|---|---|---|---|
| Croft | 2 | 0 | 29 | 0 |
| Edwards | 4 | 0 | 29 | 2 |
| Faulkner | 4 | 0 | 27 | 3 |
| Bailey | 2 | 0 | 16 | 0 |
| Parry | 4 | 0 | 33 | 0 |
| Lilley | 4 | 0 | 45 | 2 |

### LANCASHIRE

| | | |
|---|---|---:|
| A G Prince, lbw b Maxwell | | 32 |
| L S Livingstone, c Rashid b Maxwell | | 27 |
| K R Brown, c Ballance b Maxwell | | 21 |
| § J C Buttler, not out | | 71 |
| * S J Croft, c Pyrah b Plunkett | | 15 |
| J P Faulkner, c Maxwell b Fisher | | 8 |
| A L Davies, lbw b Fisher | | 0 |
| A M Lilley, not out | | 1 |
| T E Bailey | | |
| S D Parry | Did not bat | |
| G A Edwards | | |
| Extras lb 1, w 8, nb 2 | | 11 |
| Total (6 wkts, 20 overs) | | 186 |

FoW: 1-41 (Livingstone), 2-82 (Brown), 3-89 (Prince), 4-141 (Croft), 5-155 (Faulkner),
6-169 (Davies)

| | O | M | R | W |
|---|---|---|---|---|
| Fisher | 3 | 0 | 35 | 2 |
| Bresnan | 4 | 0 | 51 | 0 |
| Plunkett | 4 | 0 | 33 | 1 |
| Maxwell | 3 | 0 | 15 | 3 |
| Pyrah | 2 | 0 | 18 | 0 |
| Rashid | 4 | 0 | 33 | 0 |

*Man of the Match:* J C Buttler

Umpires: R J Bailey and N A Mallender          Scorers: J T Potter and D M White
Third Umpire: N L Bainton

# Buttler serves up whine

Yorkshire lost a thrilling contest in front of a capacity crowd as a stunning 35-ball unbeaten 71 from Jos Buttler proved the difference.

Lightning grabbed 17 runs from the final over to reach 186-6 and take the spoils on the last ball.

Livingstone was dropped by Fisher on 27 off Maxwell, but next ball he offered a simple catch to Rashid at fly gully. The power play brought Lancashire to 53-1 as they kept up with the required rate.

Gale shuffled his bowlers with imagination as the asking rate crept over 10 an over. Maxwell was again the crucial wicket-taker as Brown slapped a full toss straight to long-on at 82 with 10 overs remaining.

Maxwell trapped Prince for 32, and the rate spiralled towards 14 with six overs to go. Buttler and Croft were key, and their stand was worth 52 when Plunkett had Croft caught at long-off. They needed 32 from the last two overs.

Fisher bowled the 19th, and held his nerve to take the wicket of Faulkner. Buttler then struck two huge sixes before a fine yorker despatched Davies first ball.

**PARTING SORROW: Joe Root's bat flies through the air as he is caught by Bailey off Faulkner**

Buttler struck 14 from Bresnan's first three deliveries of the last over. One ball to go, one run needed...Buttler dug out a yorker...the ball went straight to Maxwell, whose throw from close range missed the stumps.

Yorkshire had got off to a spectacular start as Maxwell reverse-swept Croft's first ball for six and took 18 off the over. Maxwell was caught by Davies off a skier, and Gale was castled by a lovely yorker from Faulkner. Bairstow and Root steadied the ship with a pro-active stand of 40 before Bairstow thrashed Lilley's off-spin to Brown at deep mid-wicket. Root and Ballance set about the attack with calculated efficiency, taking the total to 128 in the 14th before Ballance miscued Lilley to Brown. Root cracked on to a 35-ball 55 before he lost his bat and his wicket to Faulkner. Yorkshire managed a more than useful 185-8.

# NatWest T20 BLAST — North Group
## Yorkshire v. Northamptonshire

Played at Headingley, Leeds, on June 14, 2015
*Northamptonshire won by 8 wickets (D/L method)*

Toss won by Northamptonshire          Northamptonshire 2 points, Yorkshire 0 points

### YORKSHIRE

| | | |
|---|---|---:|
| A J Finch, c Kleinveldt b Stone | | 5 |
| G J Maxwell, c Crook b Kleinveldt | | 2 |
| * A W Gale, c Cobb b Azharullah | | 7 |
| § J M Bairstow, c Keogh b Azharullah | | 23 |
| G S Ballance, c Cobb b Shahid Afridi | | 16 |
| J A Leaning, lbw b Shahid Afridi | | 0 |
| T T Bresnan, not out | | 14 |
| R M Pyrah, b Shahid Afridi | | 7 |
| J D Middlebrook, not out | | 4 |
| S A Patterson | | |
| J A Brooks | Did not bat | |
| Extras b 1, lb 1, w2 | | 4 |
| Total (7 wkts, 12 overs) | | 82 |

*FoW:* 1-7 (Finch), 2-9 (Maxwell), 3-20 (Gale), 4-55 (Bairstow), 5-55 (Ballance), 6-55 (Leaning), 7-66 (Pyrah).

| | O | M | R | W |
|---|---|---|---|---|
| Kleinveldt | 2 | 0 | 8 | 1 |
| Stone | 2 | 0 | 11 | 1 |
| Azharullah | 3 | 0 | 24 | 2 |
| Crook | 2 | 0 | 22 | 0 |
| Shahid Afridi | 3 | 0 | 15 | 3 |

### NORTHAMPTONSHIRE
*(D/L target: 83 off 12 overs)*

| | | |
|---|---|---:|
| R E Levi, lbw b Middlebrook | | 35 |
| * J J Cobb, c Finch b Bresnan | | 1 |
| § B M Duckett, not out | | 31 |
| Shahid Afridi, not out | | 14 |
| R I Newton | | |
| R I Keogh | | |
| S P Crook | | |
| R K Kleinveldt | Did not bat | |
| G G White | | |
| Azharullah | | |
| O P Stone | | |
| Extras lb 3, w 1 | | 4 |
| Total (2 wkts, 7.4 overs) | | 85 |

*FoW:* 1-6 (Cobb), 2-56 (Levi)

| | O | M | R | W |
|---|---|---|---|---|
| Brooks | 2 | 0 | 22 | 0 |
| Bresnan | 1 | 0 | 8 | 1 |
| Patterson | 1 | 0 | 18 | 0 |
| Pyrah | 2 | 0 | 13 | 0 |
| Middlebrook | 1.4 | 0 | 21 | 1 |

*Man of the Match: Shahid Afridi*

Umpires: R J Evans and P J Hartley          Scorers: J T Potter and A C Kingston

# Heavy defeat adds to gloom

**JONATHAN BAIRSTOW**
**Top-scorer on poor day**

A rain-reduced affair gave Yorkshire's home support little to cheer as the Steelbacks made light work of chasing down 83 in 7.4 of the 12 overs available.

Put in under leaden skies, Yorkshire lost the returning Finch to an indeterminate shot to mid-wicket. Maxwell was then caught in the cover region, and Gale fell with a miscue to leg.

The first five overs had Vikings struggling on 20-3 before further rain reduced the allocation from 14 overs to 12. The disruption clearly had an effect on Yorkshire's batting.

Bairstow, who top-scored with an 18-ball 23, fell to the bowling of Azharullah, and this started a collapse as further wickets went down off the next two balls from Afridi. Ballance and Leaning's departures made it 55-6.

Yorkshire's strong-looking batting line-up closed on an insufficient total, with only six fours and two sixes. Afridi took 3-15 in his three-over stint.

The early wicket of Cobb, taken by Finch in the slips off Bresnan, gave Vikings a fillip before Levi and Duckett combined to put the game firmly in Northamptonshire's grasp. There was little to comfort Yorkshire as the belligerent pair found the fence all too easily. Levi, although dropped on 26, looked in an uncompromising mood until he was trapped in front my former teammate Middlebrook for 35 from 21 balls. Afridi arrived at the crease in his usual uncompromising mood, smacking his first delivery for six as Steelbacks cruised to victory. Duckett remained unbeaten on 31 from 13 deliveries, Northamptonshire winning by eight wickets with 27 balls to spare to leave Yorkshire's home form a serious cause for concern.

# NatWest T20 BLAST — North Group
## Yorkshire v. Nottinghamshire

Played at Headingley, Leeds, on June19, 2015

*Yorkshire won by 40 runs*

Toss won by Nottinghamshire       Yorkshire 2 points, Nottinghamshire 0 points

### YORKSHIRE

| | | |
|---|---|---:|
| * A W Gale, c Patel b Fletcher | | 20 |
| A J Finch, b Ball | | 6 |
| § A J Hodd, c J W A Taylor b Patel | | 70 |
| G J Maxwell, not out | | 92 |
| G S Ballance, b Gurney | | 9 |
| J A Leaning, not out | | 0 |
| T T Bresnan | | |
| R M Pyrah | | |
| J D Middlebrook | Did not bat | |
| S A Patterson | | |
| M D Fisher | | |
| Extras b 2, lb 7, w 3 | | 12 |
| Total (4 wkts, 20 overs) | | 209 |

*FoW:* 1-11 (Finch), 2-49 (Gale), 3-150 (Hodd), 4-196 (Ballance)

| | O | M | R | W |
|---|---|---|---|---|
| Gurney | 4 | 0 | 44 | 1 |
| Ball | 4 | 0 | 38 | 1 |
| Christian | 4 | 0 | 38 | 0 |
| Fletcher | 2 | 0 | 24 | 1 |
| Mullaney | 2 | 0 | 17 | 0 |
| Patel | 4 | 0 | 39 | 1 |

### NOTTINGHAMSHIRE

| | | |
|---|---|---:|
| M H Wessels, c Hodd b Bresnan | | 5 |
| M J Lumb, c and b Maxwell | | 0 |
| § B R M Taylor, c Hodd b Fisher | | 2 |
| S R Patel, not out | | 90 |
| * J W A Taylor, c Maxwell b Middlebrook | | 32 |
| D T Christian, c and b Middlebrook | | 6 |
| S J Mullaney, c Ballance b Maxwell | | 20 |
| S K W Wood, not out | | 9 |
| J T Ball | | |
| L J Fletcher | Did not bat | |
| H F Gurney | | |
| Extras b 1, lb 1, w 3 | | 5 |
| Total (6 wkts, 20 overs) | | 169 |

*FoW:* 1-1 (Lumb), 2-5 (Wessels), 3-10 (B R M Taylor), 4-68 (J W A Taylor), 5-82 (Christian), 6-132 (Mullaney)

| | O | M | R | W |
|---|---|---|---|---|
| Maxwell | 4 | 0 | 31 | 2 |
| Bresnan | 3 | 0 | 30 | 1 |
| Fisher | 3 | 0 | 21 | 1 |
| Patterson | 4 | 0 | 29 | 0 |
| Pyrah | 3 | 0 | 25 | 0 |
| Middlebrook | 3 | 0 | 31 | 2 |

*Man of the Match: G J Maxwell*

Umpires: J H Evans and M J Saggers      Scorers: J T Potter and R Marshall

## Yorkshire v. Nottinghamshire

# In-form Maxwell raps 92

Glenn Maxwell found the perfect time to hit some form with the bat as he smashed an unbeaten 92 to help his side to a much needed victory in front of an 8,000-plus crowd.

Yorkshire lost Finch early in the second over, playing on to Ball.

Hodd, only getting the call to play a few hours earlier, and skipper Gale

**GLENN MAXWELL: Shrugged off bad trot to smash scintillating 92**

added a useful partner ship for the second wicket before Gale fell to a catch on the long-on fence by Patel off Fletcher with the score handily placed at 49-2 inside six overs.

This brought Maxwell to the wicket, desperate for a score after several failures in all forms of the game. Hodd and Maxwell, in their contrasting styles, allowed the Outlaws no let-up as the run rate began to nudge 10 per over. The fence was cleared with alarming regularity, the highlight of which was a sumptuous straight-drive for six by Hodd off Fletcher. The partnership had just passed the century from 58 deliveries when Hodd rather meekly ended his innings with a simple catch to James Taylor off Patel for a superb 70 from 39 balls.

Maxwell took matters into his own hands, two lovely reverse-sweeps from the expensive Gurney delighting the partisan crowd. He dashed the Vikings to 209-4 with his last 47 runs coming from a paltry 17 balls.

The Outlaws response to this formidable total came unstuck with two early dismissals, Lumb offering a return catch to a buoyant Maxwell in the first over and Bresnan producing a beauty to find the edge of Wessels's bat in the next. The total became 10-3 as Fisher persuaded Brendan Taylor to edge, and despite a recovery of sorts between James Taylor and Patel the Outlaws pretty much subsided with a double scalp for Middlebrook: the veteran off-spinner claimed the wicket of James Taylor, who was looking in ominously good form, and Christian with a tidy return catch, thus leaving Patel to plough a lone, yet ultimately fruitless furrow. Patel finished unbeaten on a superb 90 from 55 balls, but the required run rate became unmanageable and the Outlaws surrendered effectively 40 runs short.

# NatWest T20 BLAST — North Group
## Warwickshire v. Yorkshire

Played at Edgbaston, Birmingham, on June21, 2015
*Warwickshire won by 6 wickets*

Toss won by Yorkshire          Warwickshire 2 points, Yorkshire 0 points

### YORKSHIRE

| | | |
|---|---|---:|
| * A W Gale, c Ambrose b Clarke | | 9 |
| A J Finch, b Poysden | | 30 |
| § A J Hodd, c Clarke b Hannon-Dalby | | 2 |
| A Z Lees, c Ambrose b Gordon | | 4 |
| G J Maxwell, c Evans b Gordon | | 0 |
| J A Leaning, c Clarke b Gordon | | 45 |
| T T Bresnan, c Ambrose b Hannon-Dalby | | 16 |
| R M Pyrah, not out | | 13 |
| J D Middlebrook | | |
| S A Patterson | Did not bat | |
| M D Fisher | | |
| Extras lb 7, w 2, nb 4 | | 13 |
| Total (7 wkts, 20 overs) | | 132 |

*FoW*: 1-17 (Gale), 2-20 (Hodd), 3-36 (Lees), 4-36 (Maxwell), 5-79 (Finch), 6-118 (Bresnan), 7-132 (Leaning).

| | O | M | R | W |
|---|---|---|---|---|
| Clarke | 4 | 1 | 18 | 1 |
| Hannon-Dalby | 4 | 0 | 27 | 2 |
| Gordon | 4 | 0 | 30 | 3 |
| Patel | 4 | 0 | 21 | 0 |
| Barker | 1 | 0 | 14 | 0 |
| Poysden | 3 | 0 | 15 | 1 |

### WARWICKSHIRE

| | | |
|---|---|---:|
| I R Bell, b Maxwell | | 5 |
| * V Chopra, c Finch b Maxwell | | 3 |
| W T S Porterfield, c Leaning b Middlebrook | | 42 |
| § T R Ambrose, b Patterson | | 46 |
| L J Evans, not out | | 32 |
| R Clarke, not out | | 4 |
| R O Gordon | | |
| K H D Barker | | |
| J S Patel | Did not bat | |
| O J Hannon-Dalby | | |
| J E Poysden | | |
| Extras w 2, nb 2 | | 4 |
| Total (4 wkts, 18.4 overs) | | 136 |

*FoW*: 1-6 (Bell), 2-15 (Chopra), 3-66 (Porterfield), 4-132 (Ambrose).

| | O | M | R | W |
|---|---|---|---|---|
| Maxwell | 4 | 0 | 26 | 2 |
| Bresnan | 3 | 0 | 32 | 0 |
| Fisher | 2 | 0 | 15 | 0 |
| Patterson | 2.4 | 0 | 23 | 1 |
| Pyrah | 4 | 0 | 24 | 0 |
| Middlebrook | 3 | 0 | 16 | 1 |

*Man of the Match: R O Gordon*

Umpires: N G C Cowley and J H Evans          Scorers: J T Potter and M D Smith
Third Umpire: R J Bailey

# Vikings hit rough water

Vikings opted to bat, but simply could not get going against a hugely impressive Bears outfit, which provided discipline and precision to thwart the visitors.

Gale was first to go after a couple of off-side boundaries. Attempting a third, he could only edge behind off Clarke. Hodd's curious innings was ended with an indeterminate heave to mid-on.

Lees, also struggling for form, edged Gordon behind and Yorkshire were in a perilous position at 36-3 in the power-play overs. Maxwell was deceived by Gordon's slower ball and taken by Evans in the deep for a duck, and a total of 120 looked a long way from reality.

Leaning and Finch brought some calm to the proceedings with the need to pre-serve wickets during the middle overs. Finch was just starting to go through the gears when he was bowled by the leg-spin of Poysden, having made 30 from 36 balls, and with that went Yorkshire's hopes of a competitive total.

Leaning manfully stuck to his task against some impressive bowling. Careful shot selection was the key allied to good support from Bresnan. The pair put on 39, but were separated when Bresnan was

**AARON FINCH: Key to hopes of a target**

taken by wicket-keeper Ambrose off Hannon-Dalby for 16. Leaning was out to the last ball of the innings for an excellent 45 from 44 balls, Yorkshire closing on what seemed an inadequate 132.

Inadequate it was despite the boost of two early wickets to Maxwell's off-spin, which breached Bell's defences and had Chopra caught by Finch at wide mid-off. Bears needed a partnership to settle themselves, and Porterfield and Ambrose provided it. Porterfield peppered the off-side boundary with his trademark drives before falling to Middlebrook — the pick of the attack — on the mid-wicket fence for 42. Ambrose and Evans took the game away from Yorkshire's slippery grasp, and when Ambrose was bowled by Patterson for 46 the game was practically won. Evans ended unbeaten on 32 as Bears romped home by six wickets.

# NatWest T20 BLAST — North Group
## Leicestershire v. Yorkshire

Played at Grace Road, Leicester, on June 26, 2015

*Match tied*

Toss won by Yorkshire                    Leicestershire 1 point, Yorkshire 1 point

### LEICESTERSHIRE

| | | |
|---|---|---:|
| E J H Eckersley, b Pyrah | | 28 |
| * M J Cosgrove, c Leaning b Fisher | | 4 |
| K J O'Brien, c Maxwell b Rhodes | | 10 |
| G D Elliott, c and b Rashid | | 3 |
| § N J O'Brien, run out (Bairstow) | | 25 |
| A P Agathangelou, run out (Pyrah/Fisher/Bairstow) | | 40 |
| T J Wells, c Pyrah b Patterson | | 0 |
| B A Raine, not out | | 2 |
| C J McKay, not out | | 10 |
| J K H Naik | | |
| O H Freckingham | Did not bat | |
| Extras b 1, lb 5, w 14 | | 20 |
| Total (7 wkts, 20 overs) | | 142 |

*FoW:* 1-11 (Cosgrove), 2-31 (K J O'Brien), 3-45 (Elliott), 4-69 (Eckersley), 5-114 (N J O'Brien), 6-119 (Wells), 7-125 (Agathangelou).

| | O | M | R | W |
|---|---|---|---|---|
| Patterson | 4 | 0 | 25 | 1 |
| Fisher | 4 | 0 | 22 | 1 |
| Pyrah | 4 | 0 | 26 | 1 |
| Rhodes | 2 | 0 | 21 | 1 |
| Rashid | 4 | 0 | 27 | 1 |
| Maxwell | 2 | 0 | 15 | 0 |

### YORKSHIRE

| | | |
|---|---|---:|
| * A W Gale, c N J O'Brien b K J O'Brien | | 23 |
| A J Finch, lbw b McKay | | 2 |
| A J Hodd, lbw b Raine | | 2 |
| § J M Bairstow, b Raine | | 37 |
| G J Maxwell, c Naik b Freckingham | | 10 |
| J A Leaning, not out | | 48 |
| W M H Rhodes, c Naik b Freckingham | | 11 |
| R M Pyrah, c Wells b Elliott | | 3 |
| A U Rashid, lbw b Raine | | 3 |
| S A Patterson | | |
| M D Fisher | Did not bat | |
| Extras lb 1, w 2 | | 3 |
| Total (8 wkts, 20 overs) | | 142 |

*FoW:* 1-5 (Finch), 2-12 (Hodd), 3-64 (Bairstow), 4-75 (Maxwell), 5-79 (Gale), 6-105 (Rhodes), 7-127 (Pyrah), 8-142 (Rashid).

| | O | M | R | W |
|---|---|---|---|---|
| Raine | 4 | 0 | 23 | 3 |
| McKay | 4 | 0 | 29 | 1 |
| Freckingham | 4 | 0 | 21 | 2 |
| K J O'Brien | 4 | 0 | 27 | 1 |
| Naik | 1 | 0 | 14 | 0 |
| Elliott | 3 | 0 | 27 | 1 |

*Man of the Match: J A Leaning*

Umpires: G D Lloyd and A G Wharf          Scorers: J T Potter and P J Rogers

# Leaning the best in tie

Yorkshire squandered the chance to gain two vital points when this game was sensationally tied as Rashid was trapped in front by the last ball with the scores level.

They restricted the Foxes to a more than manageable 142 on a slow, low pitch, but regularly tripped themselves up in pursuit. Finch and Hodd both fell early, and then Gale and Bairstow seemed to have the hosts on the rack.

Bairstow enjoyed sumptuous blows on both sides of the wicket, but he was clean bowled by Raine for 37 and Maxwell and Gale went in quick succession as the Foxes began to take a hold.

Vikings were struggling on 79-5 in the 12th. Leaning and Rhodes provided some backbone, but Rhodes drove straight to cover on 11, and it was 105-6 in the 16th.

Leaning struck a towering six off McKay, leaving Yorkshire needing 24 from the last three overs. Pyrah departed, but Leaning continued undaunted with two further boundaries.

A controversial decision to let a Raine bouncer go unpunished in

**JACK LEANING: Undaunted**

the last over proved pivotal, Raine claiming the vital wicket with the last ball. Leaning remained unbeaten on a career-best 48 from 30 balls.

The Yorkshire bowlers had performed admirably. They reduced Foxes to 45-3 in the eighth over, and it was only a late onslaught from Agathangelou, who smacked 40 before being run out by Fisher, that ensured a competitive total. All the top-order batsmen struggled against accurate bowling, and a run-a-ball was a good as it seemed to get. Niall O'Brien provided a combative foil for Agathangelou as they increased the rate after 12 overs. O'Brien's inning's ended when he tried to scurry a single to Bairstow behind the stumps after the pair had added 45. All the bowlers contributed, only Rhodes receiving some rough treatment.

# NatWest T20 BLAST — North Group
## Lancashire v. Yorkshire

Played at Old Trafford, Manchester, on July 3, 2015
*Lancashire won by 29 runs*

Toss won by Yorkshire              Lancashire 2 points, Yorkshire 0 points

### LANCASHIRE

| | | |
|---|---|--:|
| A G Prince, c Bairstow b Pyrah | | 59 |
| P J Horton, c Gale b Maxwell | | 27 |
| K R Brown, c Maxwell b Finch | | 69 |
| § A L Davies, c Bresnan b Fisher | | 22 |
| * S J Croft, not out | | 27 |
| L S Livingstone, not out | | 13 |
| J Clark | | |
| A M Lilley | | |
| T E Bailey | Did not bat | |
| S D Parry | | |
| K M Jarvis | | |
| Extras b 5, lb 3, w 4, nb 2 | | 14 |
| Total (4 wkts, 20 overs) | | 231 |

*FoW:* 1-76 (Horton), 2-104 (Prince), 3-169 (Brown), 4-187 (Davies)

| | O | M | R | W |
|---|--:|--:|--:|--:|
| Maxwell | 3 | 0 | 26 | 1 |
| Fisher | 3 | 0 | 25 | 1 |
| Patterson | 4 | 0 | 49 | 0 |
| Bresnan | 2 | 0 | 29 | 0 |
| Pyrah | 3 | 0 | 52 | 1 |
| Middlebrook | 4 | 0 | 33 | 0 |
| Finch | 1 | 0 | 9 | 1 |

### YORKSHIRE

| | | |
|---|---|--:|
| * A W Gale, run out (Lilley) | | 35 |
| A J Finch, c Lilley b Parry | | 33 |
| G J Maxwell, c Davies b Parry | | 1 |
| § J M Bairstow, b Croft | | 26 |
| A J Hodd, c Croft b Parry | | 0 |
| J A Leaning, c Croft b Lilley | | 16 |
| T T Bresnan, c Prince b Lilley | | 51 |
| R M Pyrah, c Jarvis b Lilley | | 3 |
| J D Middlebrook, not out | | 29 |
| S A Patterson, not out | | 1 |
| M D Fisher | Did not bat | |
| Extras lb 4, w 3 | | 7 |
| Total (8 wkts, 20 overs) | | 202 |

*FoW:* 1-64 (Finch), 2-67 (Maxwell), 3-91 (Gale), 4-93 (Hodd), 5-102 (Bairstow), 6-121 (Leaning), 7-140 (Pyrah), 8-194 (Bresnan)

| | O | M | R | W |
|---|--:|--:|--:|--:|
| Jarvis | 4 | 0 | 44 | 0 |
| Bailey | 2 | 0 | 27 | 0 |
| Clark | 2 | 0 | 17 | 0 |
| Parry | 4 | 0 | 29 | 3 |
| Lilley | 4 | 0 | 31 | 3 |
| Croft | 4 | 0 | 50 | 1 |

*Man of the Match: S D Parry*

Umpires: R J Evans and S C Gale      Scorers: J T Potter and D M White
Third Umpire: B V Taylor

# Records and Vikings tumble

**TIM BRESNAN: Hit 24-ball 50**

A record-breaking night provided more *Roses* anguish as the Yorkshire bowlers were put to the sword on a batting strip that gave bowlers very little of assistance.

Lancashire were put into bat, but got off to a superb start, the 50 arriving early in the fifth over as Prince and Horton took the game by the scruff of the neck.

Gale shuffled his bowlers around with limited success, five of them being used in the power-play alone. The scoreboard raced to 76 with minimum fuss before Horton drove a full toss from Maxwell hard to Gale at short cover after striking 27 from 17 balls.

Prince brought up his half-century with a maximum over deep square-leg from 26 balls, and Lightning raced on. The 100 came up in the 10th over, and a total well in excess of 200 looked likely. Pyrah claimed the vital scalp of Prince for 59, his marvellous innings ending as he skied a slower ball and wicket-keeper Bairstow held a steeper.

Brown continued the assault on the hapless attack, smashing 50 from 25 balls, including 27 runs from a solitary Pyrah over. A much-needed breakthrough came with the introduction of Finch, who picked up the wicket of Brown for 69, caught on the long-on fence to end an innings spanning a mere 35 deliveries. The run rate slowed slightly as Fisher showed fine discipline at the death. Records tumbled. It was Lancashire's highest score in *T20* cricket and the highest conceded by Yorkshire in the competition.

Yorkshire's 50 came up in the fifth over as they manfully stayed with the rate, Finch and Gale scoring equally. Gale on 24 offered a catch to short-third-man, but Parry spilled a simple chance. Finch became the first of two Parry wickets in the seventh over, caught at long-off, while Maxwell was taken brilliantly at the wicket by Davies. Gale and Bairstow repaired the damage, taking the score to 91 before Gale was run out by a direct throw from Lilley. Hodd departed in the next over without scoring, and the game was effectively over.

Bairstow made a sprightly 26 and Bresnan a 24-ball half-century, but the required rate became completely unmanageable by the half-way point. Vikings finished 29 runs light, Lilley claiming three wickets.

# NatWest T20 BLAST — North Group
## Yorkshire v. Durham

Played at Headingley, Leeds, on July 10, 2015
*Yorkshire won by 5 wickets*

Toss won by Durham                    Yorkshire 2 points, Durham 0 points

### DURHAM

| | | |
|---|---|---:|
| § P Mustard, c Leaning b Maxwell | | 4 |
| * M D Stoneman, c Bresnan b Maxwell | | 1 |
| G Clark, not out | | 91 |
| P D Collingwood, c Bresnan b Rhodes | | 5 |
| M J Richardson, c and b Rashid | | 8 |
| G J Muchall, st Bairstow b Rashid | | 18 |
| U Arshad, c Bairstow b Fisher | | 10 |
| J W Hasting, not out | | 43 |
| R D Pringle | | |
| S G Borthwick | Did not bat | |
| C Rushworth | | |
| Extras lb 2, w 9 | | 11 |
| Total (6 wkts, 20 overs) | | 191 |

*FoW:* 1-4 (Mustard), 2-11 (Stoneman), 3-39 (Collingwood), 4-49 (Richardson), 5-105 (Muchall), 6-134 (Arshad)

| | O | M | R | W |
|---|---|---|---|---|
| Maxwell | 4 | 0 | 28 | 2 |
| Shaw | 4 | 0 | 42 | 0 |
| Fisher | 4 | 0 | 53 | 1 |
| Rhodes | 3 | 0 | 25 | 1 |
| Rashid | 4 | 0 | 26 | 2 |
| Finch | 1 | 0 | 15 | 0 |

### YORKSHIRE

| | | |
|---|---|---:|
| A J Finch, c Borthwick b Hastings | | 0 |
| * A W Gale, c Mustard b Hastings | | 9 |
| A Z Lees, c Mustard b Arshad | | 7 |
| § J M Bairstow, c Collingwood b Arshad | | 92 |
| G J Maxwell, b Borthwick | | 16 |
| J A Leaning, not out | | 39 |
| T T Bresnan, not out | | 24 |
| W M H Rhodes | | |
| M D Fisher | Did not bat | |
| A U Rashid | | |
| J Shaw | | |
| Extras lb 2, w 3, nb 2 | | 7 |
| Total (5 wkts, 18.5 overs) | | 194 |

*FoW:* 1-0 (Finch), 2-10 (Gale), 3-28 (Lees), 4-66 (Maxwell), 5-163 (Bairstow)

| | O | M | R | W |
|---|---|---|---|---|
| Hastings | 3 | 0 | 25 | 2 |
| Rushworth | 4 | 0 | 40 | 0 |
| Arshad | 3.5 | 0 | 42 | 2 |
| Collingwood | 4 | 0 | 42 | 0 |
| Borthwick | 2 | 0 | 20 | 1 |
| Pringle | 1 | 0 | 13 | 0 |
| Clark | 1 | 0 | 10 | 0 |

*Man of the Match: J M Bairstow*

Umpires: P K Baldwin and D J Millns                    Scorers: J T Potter and B Hunt

# Jonny comes marching home

A destructive 92 from only 42 balls by Jonny Bairstow suggested that Yorkshire could still make their way into the knockout stages.

They chased down a formidable 191 with seven deliveries left in front of an excellent crowd under the Headingley lights.

Gale opted to field first, and his men were soon in the ascendancy, Mustard

**JONATHAN BAIRSTOW: Took game by the scruff in scintillating display**

and Stoneman both falling foul of Maxwell's off-spin. Opening the bowling with the Aussie all-rounder was debutant Josh Shaw, whose first two overs were accurate and with no little pace. Collingwood scratched around before Rhodes had him caught by Bresnan, and Richardson also fell cheaply, caught and bowled by Rashid as Durham slumped to 49-4 in the seventh over. A partnership of 56 between Muchall and the impressive young Graham Clark, who was appearing in only his third *T20* match, provided a much-needed fillip for the visitors before the Muchall was superbly stumped by Bairstow off Rashid for 18. Rashid's spell was hugely impressive, his analysis reading 4-0-26-2.

Arshad was caught at the wicket off Fisher. The not insignificant frame of Hastings joined Clark, and the pair provided more devastating striking than had been seen for some time. The last four overs bled 69 as Clark raced to an unbeaten 91, while Hastings contributed 43 from 12 deliveries with five fours and three sixes. Fisher and Shaw bore the brunt of the punishment, but Clark really captured the hearts of the crowd.

Finch went first ball, taken on the mid-wicket fence, and when Gale and Lees also fell on their swords the omens could not have looked much worse. Durham had not reckoned on Bairstow, who almost single-handedly took the game by the scruff of the neck. The key wicket of Maxwell fell at 66, but after hitting his first ball to the boundary Bairstow cracked on. His half-century came from 24 balls as he and Leaning added 97 in 54 deliveries before Bairstow was caught by Collingwood of Arshad. Bresnan hit 24 from eight balls, and the game was won with consecutive sixes off Arshad, Leaning unbeaten on 39.

# NatWest T20 BLAST — North Group
## Derbyshire v. Yorkshire

Played at Queen's Park, Chesterfield, on July 12, 2015
*Derbyshire won by 4 wickets*

Toss won by Derbyshire                    Derbyshire 2 points, Yorkshire 0 points

### YORKSHIRE

| | | |
|---|---|---:|
| A U Rashid, st Poynton b Durston | | 7 |
| * A W Gale, b Durston | | 5 |
| A Z Lees, b Durston | | 1 |
| § J M Bairstow, c Rimmington b Cork | | 22 |
| G J Maxwell, b Thakor | | 45 |
| J A Leaning, lbw b Thakor | | 37 |
| T T Bresnan, c Knight b Rimmington | | 4 |
| L E Plunkett, c sub (S L Elstone) b Thakor | | 17 |
| W M H Rhodes, run out (Thakor) | | 0 |
| J Shaw, not out | | 0 |
| M D Fisher | Did not bat | |
| Extras lb 4, w 2, nb 2 | | 8 |
| Total (9 wkts, 20 overs) | | 146 |

*FoW:* 1-10 (Rashid), 2-12 (Lees), 3-16 (Gale), 4-80 (Bairstow), 5-88 (Maxwell), 6-103 (Bresnan), 7-140 (Leaning), 8-140 (Rhodes), 9-146 (Plunkett)

| | O | M | R | W |
|---|---|---|---|---|
| Durston | 4 | 0 | 14 | 3 |
| Cork | 4 | 0 | 32 | 1 |
| Thakor | 4 | 0 | 34 | 3 |
| A L Hughes | 4 | 0 | 29 | 0 |
| Rimmington | 4 | 0 | 33 | 1 |

### DERBYSHIRE

| | | |
|---|---|---:|
| * W J Durston, b Fisher | | 11 |
| H D Rutherford, c and b Plunkett | | 40 |
| C F Hughes, lbw b Maxwell | | 8 |
| S J Thakor, run out (Fisher/Bairstow) | | 10 |
| W L Madsen, c Bairstow b Bresnan | | 41 |
| B A Godleman, run out (Bresnan) | | 14 |
| A L Hughes, not out | | 19 |
| § T Poynton, not out | | 0 |
| T C Knight | | |
| G T C Cork | Did not bat | |
| N J Rimmington | | |
| Extras w 7 | | 7 |
| Total (6 wkts, 18.5 overs) | | 150 |

*FoW:* 1-17 (Durston), 2-40 (C F Hughes), 3-72 (Rutherford), 4-89 (Thakor), 5-130 (Madson), 6-130 (Godleman)

| | O | M | R | W |
|---|---|---|---|---|
| Maxwell | 4 | 0 | 33 | 1 |
| Fisher | 2.5 | 0 | 30 | 1 |
| Shaw | 1 | 0 | 19 | 0 |
| Rashid | 4 | 0 | 17 | 0 |
| Plunkett | 4 | 0 | 32 | 1 |
| Rhodes | 2 | 0 | 14 | 0 |
| Bresnan | 1 | 0 | 5 | 1 |

*Man of the Match: W J Durston*

Umpires: N L Bainton and R A Kettleborough          Scorers: J T Potter and J M Brown

# Hopes left in tatters

**ADIL RASHID: Four overs of flight, guile, variation**

A below-par Yorkshire were left to rue a poor start with the bat and sloppy fielding.

They were inserted, and Durston cut through the top order with some fine off-spin. Rashid, promoted to opener, aimed an agricultural mow only to be stumped smartly by Poynton.

Lees came and went, bowled while cutting at Durston's quicker ball, and Gale became Durston's third victim, again deceived by the quicker one.

The first four arrived in the fifth over as the power-play period ended, Vikings teetering on 27-3.

Bairstow and Maxwell began to repair the damage, the score advancing quietly to 38 from the first eight overs before Bairstow struck the first maximum in the ninth, a drive over deep-extra-cover. There were 12 runs from the 10th as Maxwell began to take a hold of proceedings, and the out-cricket became ragged. The stand was worth 64 when Bairstow put a paddle-sweep off Cork into the hands of Rimmington for 22, and Maxwell had struck an entertaining 29-ball 45 when he tried one reverse-sweep too many. A flurry from Leaning and Plunkett propelled Yorkshire to 146-9.

The Falcons' thin-looking line-up would be best served by going for the total quickly rather than letting Vikings in. There were two early wickets, Durston losing his leg stump to Fisher and Chesney Hughes lbw sweeping at Maxwell, but runs bled far too freely with loose balls aplenty. Shaw's opening over went for 19 and Derbyshire after six overs were 68-2. Rashid bowled a lovely four-over spell, full of flight, guile and variation and costing only 17 runs. Two more wickets fell, Rutherford to a sharp return catch by Plunkett for 40 and Thakor inexplicably run out stealing a single to backward-point.

Falcons needed less than seven per over, but Madsen was caught behind off Bresnan for 41 and Godleman was out going for a suicidal single. 130-6 with four overs to go. Hughes and Poynton finished it with seven balls to spare, leaving Yorkshire's qualification hopes in tatters.

# NatWest T20 BLAST — North Group
## Yorkshire v. Worcestershire

Played at Headingley, Leeds, on July 14, 2015
*Worcestershire won by 74 runs*

Toss won by Worcestershire        Worcestershire 2 points, Yorkshire 0 points

### WORCESTERSHIRE

| | |
|---|---|
| * D K H Mitchell, b Plunkett | 49 |
| R K Oliver, c Bresnan b Plunkett | 13 |
| T Kohler-Cadmore, c Lees b Fisher | 8 |
| C Munro, c Bairstow b Rhodes | 8 |
| B L d'Oliveira, c Carver b Rhodes | 4 |
| R A Whiteley, not out | 91 |
| § O B Cox, c Bairstow b Plunkett | 10 |
| J Leach, not out | 1 |
| E G Barnard | |
| Saeed Ajmal       Did not bat | |
| J D Shantry | |
| Extras b 1, lb 1, w 5 | 7 |
| Total (6 wkts, 20 overs) | 191 |

*FoW:* 1-23 (Oliver), 2-33 (Kohler-Cadmore), 3-51 (Munro), 4-63 (d'Oliveira), 5-124 (Mitchell), 6-152 (Cox).

| | O | M | R | W |
|---|---|---|---|---|
| Maxwell | 2 | 0 | 21 | 0 |
| Fisher | 4 | 0 | 34 | 1 |
| Plunkett | 4 | 0 | 49 | 3 |
| Bresnan | 1 | 0 | 8 | 0 |
| Carver | 4 | 0 | 30 | 0 |
| Rhodes | 4 | 0 | 30 | 2 |
| Gibson | 1 | 0 | 17 | 0 |

### YORKSHIRE

| | |
|---|---|
| A Z Lees. c Shantry b Saeed Ajmal | 20 |
| * A W Gale. c Saeed Ajmal b d'Oliveira | 24 |
| W M H Rhodes, run out (Mitchell/Cox) | 10 |
| § J M Bairstow, c Barnard b Mitchell | 4 |
| G J Maxwell, c Kohler-Cadmore b d'Oliveira | 0 |
| J A Leaning, run out (Shantry) | 27 |
| T T Bresnan, c Whiteley b d'Oliveira | 4 |
| L E Plunkett, c Leach b Saeed Ajmal | 9 |
| R Gibson, c Whiteley b Shantry | 14 |
| K Carver, c Cox b Shantry | 2 |
| M D Fisher, not out | 0 |
| Extras lb 2, w 1 | 3 |
| Total (17 overs) | 117 |

*FoW:* 1-27 (Lees), 2-43 (Rhodes), 3-60 (Bairstow), 4-60 (Maxwell), 5-60 (Gale), 6-69 (Bresnan), 7-97 (Plunkett), 8-101 (Leaning), 9-108 (Carver), 10-117 (Gibson).

| | O | M | R | W |
|---|---|---|---|---|
| Shantry | 4 | 0 | 26 | 2 |
| Leach | 2 | 0 | 17 | 0 |
| Saeed Ajmal | 4 | 0 | 21 | 2 |
| Barnard | 1 | 0 | 11 | 0 |
| d'Oliveira | 4 | 0 | 29 | 3 |
| Mitchell | 2 | 0 | 11 | 1 |

*Man of the Match: R A Whiteley*

Umpires: N G B Cook and R J Evans       Scorers: J T Potter and D E Pugh
Third Umpire: P K Baldwin

# Whiteley is smash hit

A ruthless batting display by Ross Whiteley, unbeaten on 91, coupled with abject batting by Yorkshire, allowed the rampant Rapids to confirm their quarter-final berth while eliminating their more illustrious hosts.

A 74-run defeat was a bitter pill for Yorkshire skipper Gale to swallow as his young bowlers, including two debutants, were given few positives to take away.

A notable exception was Will Rhodes, who bowled with great skill for his 2-30 while chaos surrounded him. Karl Carver, a debutant in this format, bowled admirably in the middle overs.

Oliver was dismissed by Plunkett after a bright start, and

**WILL RHODES: Great skill**

when Kohler-Cadmore and Munro left cheaply the Rapids were wobbling on 51-3. Rhodes grabbed the fourth wicket, that of D'Oliveira, and at 63-4 in the 10th it was Yorkshire who had a firm grip on proceedings.

Mitchell and Whiteley combined to add 61 for the fifth wicket before Worcestershire's skipper was cleaned up by the expensive Plunkett. It was all Whiteley from this junction, as the Sheffield-born middle-order man wreaked havoc on the beleaguered attack. The West stand was located regularly with clean and powerful hitting, debutant Ryan Gibson's solitary over costing 17. Whiteley's half-century came in 24 balls and his next 41 runs in only 10. The total increased from 124 after 16 overs to 191, quite remarkable even by present-day standards.

Yorkshire's response never looked like troubling their opponents after a breezy start from Lees and Gale was halted by the wily Ajmal, Lees caught by Shantry for 20. Rhodes was next to go after a mixup with Gale, run out by Mitchell for 10. Bairstow offered little resistance and there was even less from Maxwell, who holed out first ball to the leg-spin of D'Oliveira. Gale's somewhat painful vigil ended on 24 in the ninth over, and with that a great many spectators saw fit to head for the exit gates. There was a typically well measured 27 from Leaning, but Yorkshire's innings ended swiftly in the 17th over, still an ocean away from the victory target. D'Oliveira, Shanty and Ajmal were all outstanding with the ball.

## NatWest T20 BLAST — North Group
## Northamptonshire v. Yorkshire

Played at Wantage Road, Northampton, on July 17, 2015
*Northamptonshire won by 6 wickets*

Toss won by Northamptonshire        Northamptonshire 2 points, Yorkshire 0 points

### YORKSHIRE

| | | |
|---|---|---:|
| A Z Lees, c and b White | | 46 |
| W M H Rhodes, c Duckett b Willey | | 0 |
| J A Leaning, run out (Cobb) | | 0 |
| * § J M Bairstow, c Duckett b Cobb | | 21 |
| G J Maxwell, c Willey b Crook | | 17 |
| L E Plunkett, b Azharullah | | 23 |
| R Gibson, c Levi b Kleinveldt | | 18 |
| M J Waite, not out | | 14 |
| B O Coad, not out | | 2 |
| K Carver | | |
| M D Fisher | Did not bat | |
| Extras lb 2, w 8, nb 2 | | 12 |
| Total (7 wkts, 20 overs) | | 153 |

*FoW:* 1-1 (Rhodes), 2-11 (Leaning), 3-57 (Bairstow), 4-87 (Lees), 5-97 (Maxwell), 6-124 (Plunkett), 7-136 (Gibson)

| | O | M | R | W |
|---|---|---|---|---|
| Willey | 4 | 1 | 24 | 1 |
| Kleinveldt | 3 | 0 | 26 | 1 |
| Crook | 4 | 0 | 33 | 1 |
| Azharullah | 4 | 0 | 31 | 1 |
| White | 3 | 0 | 23 | 1 |
| Cobb | 2 | 0 | 14 | 1 |

### NORTHAMPTONSHIRE

| | | |
|---|---|---:|
| R E Levi, run out (Plunkett) | | 30 |
| D J Willey, c Waite b Fisher | | 34 |
| J J Cobb, c Leaning b Coad | | 0 |
| * A G Wakely, c Maxwell b Coad | | 46 |
| B M Duckett, not out | | 40 |
| S P Crook, not out | | 1 |
| § A M Rossington | | |
| R I Keogh | | |
| R K Kleinveldt | Did not bat | |
| G G White | | |
| M Azharullah | | |
| Extras lb 3, nb 2 | | 5 |
| Total (4 wkts, 19 overs) | | 156 |

*FoW:* 1-39 (Levi), 2-40 (Cobb), 3-102 (Willey), 4-146 (Wakely)

| | O | M | R | W |
|---|---|---|---|---|
| Plunkett | 3 | 0 | 36 | 0 |
| Fisher | 4 | 0 | 33 | 1 |
| Coad | 3 | 0 | 24 | 2 |
| Rhodes | 2 | 0 | 9 | 0 |
| Maxwell | 1 | 0 | 10 | 0 |
| Waite | 4 | 0 | 28 | 0 |
| Gibson | 2 | 0 | 13 | 0 |

*Man of the Match: D J Willey*

Umpires: P J Hartley and G D Lloyd        Scorers: J T Potter and A C Kingston

# Coad and Waite impress

Two further debuts were handed to promising graduates of the Yorkshire Academy, this time Ben Coad and Matthew Waite, as the Vikings went down in a spirited display at Wantage Road.

Yorkshire lost Rhodes to his second ball, driving into the covers off Willey, and Leaning also failed to get off the mark, run out by Cobb with a direct hit.

**MATTHEW WAITE: Spirited debut**

A stand of 46 between acting skipper Bairstow and Lees in a little over seven overs brought some cheer, both batsmen operating at a run a ball as the innings began to take shape. Bairstow departed for 21, taken on the leg-side boundary off the bowling of Cobb, and Lees was fourth out for a top score of 46 from 42 deliveries when he gave a return catch to the off-spin of White.

The Vikings' lower order all contributed, Maxwell, Gibson, Plunkett and Waite each managing boundaries as Yorkshire finished on 153-7. The bowling had been disciplined throughout and the wickets shared.

With such an inexperienced bowling attack it was always going to be a challenge for Yorkshire to restrict their opponents, and so it proved initially as Levi and Willey got off to a flier. By the time Levi was run out by Plunkett for 30 from only 14 deliveries Northamptonshire were going at well over 10 runs per over. Cobb was taken in the deep off Coad, but the normally explosive Willey opted for a more cautious approach, as did his new partner, Wakeley.

The rate was always under control, so Willey and Wakeley ensured that no undue risks were taken. They brought up the 100 in the 12th over before Willey went for 34 to Fisher, but an unbeaten 40 from 26 balls from Duckett killed off any threat of an upset for the hosts, who reached their target with an over to spare.

Waite, Coad and Fisher all performed admirably with the ball, backed up by some livewire out-cricket. The experience will no doubt have stood these young cricketers in good stead.

# NatWest T20 BLAST — North Group
## Yorkshire v. Warwickshire

Played at Headingley, Leeds, on July 24, 2015
*Yorkshire won by 8 wickets*

Toss won by Warwickshire
Yorkshire 2 points, Warwickshire 0 points

### WARWICKSHIRE

| | |
|---|---|
| T P Lewis, c Leaning b Plunkett | 4 |
| B B McCullum, b Fisher | 6 |
| § T R Ambrose, c Hodd b Coad | 19 |
| R Clarke, c Lees b Coad | 21 |
| L J Evans, c Hodd b Rhodes | 25 |
| C R Woakes, c Fisher b Pyrah | 6 |
| A Javid, c Lees b Fisher | 22 |
| * J S Patel, c Leaning b Pyrah | 4 |
| R O Gordon, c Gibson b Rhodes | 18 |
| O J Hannon-Dalby, b Rhodes | 1 |
| J E Poysden, not out | 1 |
| Extras b 4, lb 5, w 9 | 18 |
| Total (18.4 overs) | 145 |

*FoW:* 1-4 (Lewis), 2-11 (McCullum), 3-50 (Ambrose), 4-57 (Clarke), 5-77 (Woakes), 6-92 (Evans), 7-101 (Patel), 8-131 (Gordon), 9-135 (Hannon-Dalby), 10-145 (Javid)

| | O | M | R | W |
|---|---|---|---|---|
| Plunkett | 4 | 1 | 20 | 1 |
| Fisher | 2.4 | 0 | 21 | 2 |
| Coad | 4 | 0 | 30 | 2 |
| Pyrah | 4 | 0 | 21 | 2 |
| Rhodes | 3 | 0 | 27 | 3 |
| Waite | 1 | 0 | 17 | 0 |

### YORKSHIRE

| | |
|---|---|
| * A Z Lees, lbw b Patel | 63 |
| W M H Rhodes, c Poysden b Clarke | 5 |
| J A Leaning, not out | 60 |
| § A J Hodd, not out | 15 |
| R M Pyrah | |
| L E Plunkett | |
| R Gibson | |
| M J Waite | Did not bat |
| B O Coad | |
| K Carver | |
| M D Fisher | |
| Extras lb 3, w 2 | 5 |
| Total (2 wkts, 19.3 overs) | 148 |

*FoW:* 1-16 (Rhodes), 2-120 (Lees)

| | O | M | R | W |
|---|---|---|---|---|
| Clarke | 4 | 0 | 22 | 1 |
| Hannon-Dalby | 4 | 0 | 35 | 0 |
| Gordon | 3.3 | 0 | 28 | 0 |
| Poysden | 4 | 0 | 30 | 0 |
| Patel | 4 | 0 | 30 | 1 |

*Man of the Match: J A Leaning*

Umpires: N L Bainton and P J Hartley
Scorers: J T Potter and M D Smith

## Yorkshire v. Warwickshire

# Skipper Lees pleases

This fixture was immaterial to the final standings, but it still brought a heartening win for a Yorkshire side which included five players aged 22 years or under.

Supporters had been rocked by the news that Maxwell would be dropped for disciplinary reasons, but this did not detract from a fine win against a Bears outfit already through to the knockout stages.

Spearheaded by the excellent Plunkett, who delivered the Vikings' only maiden of the season, the young attack all played their part in dismissing the Bears for 145 in 18.4 overs.

Plunkett struck in the first over before Fisher bowled McCullum in the next, reducing the visitors to 11-2. Ambrose and Clarke played within their capabilities to prevent further damage, but seamer Coad bagged them both in six balls.

Ambrose edged behind for 19 and Clarke was neatly taken by Lees for 21. That made the score 57-4, which became 57-5 as Pyrah found the edge of Evans's bat.

Wickets continued to fall as the Bears failed to gain impetus against a disciplined attack backed by fine

**ALEX LEES: A winning captain and top-scorer**

fielding. Fisher and Pyrah, each 2-21, and Coad 2-30, all impressed, Rhodes weighing in with three to conclude a hugely satisfactory effort.

Vikings lost Rhodes in the third over when he lobbed a catch to mid-on, but Lees and Leaning made light work of the chase. Lees took the newly acquired captaincy seriously as he played a watchful innings, seizing upon anything loose yet clearly intent on seeing his side over the line. The pair began to accelerate, keeping up with the required rate almost to the decimal. Lees was the main aggressor as he reached his first half-century of an inconsistent season off 38 balls, and the century partnership came up before Lees was trapped in front for an excellent 60. With 26 still needed Leaning, unbeaten on 60, and Hodd saw it out.

# NatWest T20 BLAST in 2015

## NORTH GROUP

| | | P | W | L | T | NR/A | PTS | NRR |
|---|---|---|---|---|---|---|---|---|
| 1 | Birmingham Bears (N 4) * | 14 | 10 | 4 | 0 | 0 | 20.00 | 0.200 |
| 2 | Worcestershire Rapids (N 3) * | 14 | 9 | 4 | 0 | 1 | 19.00 | 0.682 |
| 3 | Northamptonshire Steelbacks (N 7) * | 14 | 7 | 5 | 0 | 2 | 16.00 | 0.115 |
| 4 | Lancashire Lightning (N 1) * | 14 | 7 | 6 | 0 | 1 | 15.00 | 0.469 |
| 5 | Nottinghamshire Outlaws (N 2) | 14 | 7 | 6 | 0 | 1 | 15.00 | 0.018 |
| 6 | Durham Jets (N 6) | 14 | 5 | 8 | 0 | 1 | 11.00 | -0.149 |
| 7 | Leicestershire Foxes (N 8) | 14 | 4 | 7 | 1 | 2 | 11.00 | -0.304 |
| **8** | **Yorkshire Vikings (N 5)** | **14** | **5** | **8** | **1** | **0** | **11.00** | **-0.324** |
| 9 | Derbyshire Falcons (N 9) | 14 | 4 | 10 | 0 | 0 | 8.00 | -0.662 |

## SOUTH GROUP

| | | P | W | L | T | NR/A | PTS | NRR |
|---|---|---|---|---|---|---|---|---|
| 1 | Kent Spitfires (S 6) * | 14 | 9 | 4 | 0 | 1 | 19.00 | 0.166 |
| 2 | Sussex Sharks (S 7) * | 14 | 7 | 5 | 0 | 2 | 16.00 | 0.206 |
| 3 | Hampshire Royals (S 3) * | 14 | 8 | 6 | 0 | 0 | 16.00 | -0.120 |
| 4 | Essex Eagles (S 1) * | 14 | 7 | 6 | 0 | 1 | 15.00 | 0.208 |
| 5 | Gloucestershire (S 8) | 14 | 7 | 7 | 0 | 0 | 14.00 | 0.354 |
| 6 | Glamorgan (S 4) | 14 | 7 | 7 | 0 | 0 | 14.00 | -0.522 |
| 7 | Surrey (S 2) | 14 | 5 | 6 | 0 | 3 | 13.00 | -0.145 |
| 8 | Somerset (S 7) | 14 | 4 | 8 | 0 | 2 | 10.00 | -0.184 |
| 9 | Middlesex Panthers (S 9) | 14 | 4 | 9 | 0 | 1 | 9.00 | 0.030 |

\* Qualified for the Quarter-Finals

*(2014 group positions in brackets)*

# Bairstow signs new deal

While Jonny Bairstow was preparing to help to steer England to their Test series triumph over South Africa in December Yorkshire announced that the wicket-keeper/batsman had signed a new three-year contract, which will keep him at Headingley until at least the end of 2018. Last summer Bairstow blasted 1,108 Championship runs at an average of 92.33, hitting five centuries and making a career-best 219 not out against Durham at Chester-le-Street.

# YORKSHIRE AVERAGES 2015

## NATWEST T20 BLAST

Played 14   Won 5   Lost 8   Tied 1

### BATTING AND FIELDING

*(Qualification 4 completed innings)*

| Player | M. | I. | N.O. | Runs | H.S. | 100s | 50s | Avge | ct/st |
|---|---|---|---|---|---|---|---|---|---|
| J A Leaning | 14 | 14 | 6 | 338 | 60* | 0 | 1 | 42.25 | 6 |
| J M Bairstow | 11 | 11 | 1 | 320 | 92 | 0 | 1 | 32.00 | 9/1 |
| T T Bresnan | 11 | 8 | 3 | 155 | 51 | 0 | 1 | 31.00 | 5 |
| A W Gale | 12 | 12 | 1 | 288 | 68* | 0 | 1 | 26.18 | 2 |
| G J Maxwell | 12 | 12 | 1 | 229 | 92* | 0 | 1 | 20.81 | 6 |
| A Z Lees | 9 | 9 | 0 | 175 | 63 | 0 | 1 | 19.44 | 4 |
| L E Plunkett | 8 | 5 | 1 | 75 | 23 | 0 | 0 | 18.75 | 2 |
| A J Hodd | 8 | 8 | 1 | 113 | 70 | 0 | 1 | 16.14 | 40 |
| A J Finch | 6 | 6 | 0 | 76 | 33 | 0 | 0 | 12.66 | 2 |
| R M Pyrah | 10 | 6 | 1 | 35 | 13* | 0 | 0 | 7.00 | 5 |
| W M H Rhodes | 6 | 5 | 0 | 26 | 11 | 0 | 0 | 5.20 | 0 |
| *Also played* | | | | | | | | | |
| J E Root | 1 | 1 | 0 | 55 | 55 | 0 | 1 | 55.00 | 0 |
| G S Ballance | 3 | 3 | 0 | 56 | 31 | 0 | 0 | 18.66 | 2 |
| R Gibson | 3 | 2 | 0 | 32 | 18 | 0 | 0 | 16.00 | 1 |
| A U Rashid | 7 | 3 | 1 | 18 | 8* | 0 | 0 | 9.00 | 5 |
| K Carver | 3 | 1 | 0 | 2 | 2 | 0 | 0 | 2.00 | 1 |
| J D Middlebrook | 4 | 2 | 2 | 33 | 29* | 0 | 0 | — | 1 |
| M J Waite | 2 | 1 | 1 | 14 | 14* | 0 | 0 | — | 1 |
| B O Coad | 2 | 1 | 1 | 2 | 2* | 0 | 0 | — | 0 |
| S A Patterson | 5 | 1 | 1 | 1 | 1* | 0 | 0 | — | 0 |
| J Shaw | 2 | 1 | 1 | 0 | 0* | 0 | 0 | — | 0 |
| M D Fisher | 13 | 1 | 1 | 0 | 0* | 0 | 0 | — | 5 |
| J A Brooks | 2 | 0 | 0 | 0 | — | 0 | 0 | — | 0 |

### BOWLING

*(Qualification 4 wickets)*

| Player | Overs | Mdns | Runs | Wkts | Avge | Best | 4wI | RPO |
|---|---|---|---|---|---|---|---|---|
| B O Coad | 7 | 0 | 54 | 4 | 13.50 | 2-24 | 0 | 7.71 |
| W M H Rhodes | 16 | 0 | 126 | 7 | 18.00 | 3-27 | 0 | 7.87 |
| G J Maxwell | 34 | 0 | 264 | 12 | 22.00 | 3-15 | 0 | 7.76 |
| L E Plunkett | 30 | 1 | 242 | 11 | 22.00 | 3-49 | 0 | 8.06 |
| M D Fisher | 40.5 | 0 | 362 | 16 | 22.62 | 5-22 | 1 | 8.86 |
| J D Middlebrook | 11.4 | 0 | 101 | 4 | 25.25 | 2-31 | 0 | 8.65 |
| A U Rashid | 26 | 0 | 174 | 6 | 29.00 | 2-26 | 0 | 6.69 |
| R M Pyrah | 31 | 0 | 229 | 7 | 32.71 | 2-13 | 0 | 7.38 |
| T T Bresnan | 26 | 0 | 263 | 5 | 52.60 | 1-5 | 0 | 10.11 |
| *Also bowled* | | | | | | | | |
| A J Finch | 2 | 0 | 24 | 1 | 24.00 | 1-9 | 0 | 12.00 |
| S A Patterson | 15.4 | 0 | 144 | 2 | 72.00 | 1-23 | 0 | 9.19 |
| R Gibson | 3 | 0 | 30 | 0 | — | 0-17 | 0 | 10.00 |
| K Carver | 4 | 0 | 30 | 0 | — | 0-30 | 0 | 7.50 |
| J A Brooks | 4 | 0 | 43 | 0 | — | 0-21 | 0 | 10.75 |
| M J Waite | 5 | 0 | 45 | 0 | — | 0-17 | 0 | 9.00 |
| J Shaw | 5 | 0 | 61 | 0 | — | 0-19 | 0 | 12.20 |

# Second Eleven 2015

PLAYERS WHO APPEARED FOR YORKSHIRE SECOND ELEVEN IN 2015
*(excluding First Eleven capped players)*

| Player | Date of Birth | Birthplace | Type |
|---|---|---|---|
| M A Ashraf * | January 5, 1992 | Bradford | RHB/RF |
| K Carver * | March 26, 1996 | Northallerton | LHB/SLA |
| B O Coad * | January 10, 1994 | Harrogate | RHB/RM |
| M D Fisher* | November 9, 1997 | York | RHB/RMF |
| D M Hodgson * | February 26, 1990 | Northallerton | RHB/WK |
| A J Hodd * | January 12, 1984 | Chichester | RHB/WK |
| J A Leaning * | October 18, 1993 | Bristol | RHB/OB |
| W M H Rhodes * | March 2, 1995 | Nottingham | LHB/RM |
| J Shaw * | January 3, 1996 | Wakefield | RHB/RMF |
| J A Tattersall * | December 15, 1994 | Knaresborough | RHB/LB |
| B L Ainsley | November 19, 1997 | Middlesbrough | RHB /OB |
| H C Brook | February 22, 1999 | Keighley | RHB /RM |
| E Callis | November 8, 1994 | Doncaster | RHB |
| T R Craddock | July 13, 1989 | Huddersfieldd | RHB /LB |
| A J Finch | November 17, 1986 | Colac, Victoria, Aus | RHB/SLA |
| N J Firn | October 9, 1995 | York | RHB /RM |
| R Gibson | January 22, 1996 | Middlesbrough | RHB/RM |
| M Hussain | March 27, 1997 | Leeds | RHB/RM |
| Y Imtiaz | March 9, 1998 | Huddersfield | RHB/OB |
| J E G Logan | October 12, 1997 | Wakefield | LHB/SLA |
| G J Maxwell | October 14, 1998 | Kew, Melbourne, Aus | RHB/OB |
| J Read | February 2, 1998 | Scarborough | RHB/WK |
| M A Taylor | December 18, 1997 | Wakefield | RHB/RMF |
| J A Thompson | October 9, 1996 | Leeds | LHB/ RMF |
| J C Wainman | January 25, 1993 | Harrogate | RHB/LFM |
| M J Waite | December 24, 1995 | Leeds | RHB/RMF |
| J D Warner | November 14, 1996 | Wakefield | RHB /RFM |

* Second Eleven cap

# SECOND ELEVEN HIGHLIGHTS OF 2015

## CHAMPIONSHIP

**Century partnerships (4)**

**For the 2nd wicket (1)**

   180    G J Maxwell and A Z Lees    v Derbyshire at Scarborough

**For the 3rd wicket (1)**

   116*   A J Finch and H C Brook    v Nottinghamshire at Stamford Bridge

**For the 5th wicket (1)**

   223    R Gibson and M Hussain    v Northamptonshire at York

*This is the highest-ever fifth-wicket parternship for Yorkshire against Northamptonshire in the Second Eleven Championship*

**For the 8th wicket (1)**

   115*   W M H Rhodes and K Carver    v. Derbyshire at Scarborough

**For the 9th wicket (1)**

   100    T R Craddock and K Carver    v Leicestershire at Hinckley

*This is the highest-ever ninth-wicket stand for Yorkshire against Leicestershire in the Second Eleven Championship*

**Centuries (3)**

  R Gibson (1)

     137*   v Northamptonshire at York

  W M H Rhodes (1)

     124*   v Derbyshire at Scarborough

  M Hussain (1)

     104    v Northamptonshire at York

**10 wickets in a match (1)**

  B O Coad (1)

     10-79    (5-41 and5-38)    v Northamptonshire at York

**Five wickets in an innings (2)**

  B O Coad (2)

     5-38   v Northamptonshire at York

     5-41   v Northamptonshire at York

**Five victims in an innings (1)**

  J Read (1)

     5 (5ct)    v. MCC Universities at Weetwood

### CHAMPIONSHIP MILESTONES IN 2015

Moin Ashraf reached an aggregate of 50 wickets. Ben Coad`s match return of 10-79 against Northamptonshire included his maiden five-wicket haul.

## TROPHY

**Century Partnerships:** None

**Centuries:** None

**5 wickets in an innings (1)**

  M D Fisher (1)

     5-35  Warwickshire at York.

*These are the best figures ever recorded by a Yorkshire bowler against Warwickshire in the Second Eleven Trophy.*

**Five victims in an innings:** None

## T20 COMPETITION

**Century Partnerships:** None

**5 wickets in an innings (1)**

K Carver (1)

5-20   v Worcestershire at Barnt Green.

*These are the best figures ever recorded by a Yorkshire bowler against all opposition in the Second Eleven T20 competition.*

**Four victims in an innings:** None

## Debuts (5)

B L Ainsley, N J Firn, J E G Logan, M J Waite and J D Warner

### T20 MILESTONE FOR 2016

Will Rhodes needs a further 97 runs to become the Club's leading scorer in the competition.

# Second Eleven Championship
## Leicestershire v. Yorkshire

Played at Hinckley Town CC on April 28, 29 and 30, 2015
*Leicestershire won by an innings and 37 runs at 5.30pm on the Third Day*

Toss won by Leicestershire                    Leicestershire 24 points, Yorkshire 2 points
Close of play: First Day. Leicestershire 485-6 (Ali 65, Sykes 5, 104 overs); Second Day, Yorkshire
(2) 134-4 (Gibson 16, 44.3 overs)

### LEICESTERSHIRE

| | | |
|---|---|---:|
| M G Pardoe, c Craddock b Wainman | ...................... | 144 |
| * MA G Boyce, c Wainman b Craddock | ............... | 161 |
| M H Cross, b Thompson | ...................... | 37 |
| A M Ali, c Waite b Craddock | ............... | 84 |
| § L J Hill, lbw b Ashraf | ...................... | 20 |
| R M L Taylor, b Ashraf | ...................... | 7 |
| J K H Naik, lbw b Craddock | ...................... | 1 |
| J S Sykes, c Hodgson b Ashraf | ...................... | 5 |
| Z J Chappell, not out | ...................... | 41 |
| J C Pearson, st Hodgson b Craddock | ............... | 8 |
| A C F Wyatt | | |
| D O D Hampton | Did not bat | |
| Extras 10 b, 6 lb, 6 nb | ...................... | 22 |
| Total (9 wkts dec. 113.2 overs) | ............... | 530 |

*FoW:* 1-263 (Pardoe), 2-333 (Cross), 3-377 (Boyce), 4-427 (Hill), 5-441 (Taylor),
6-448 (Naik), 7-461 (Sykes), 8-501 (Ali), 9-530 (Pearson)

| | O | M | R | W |
|---|---|---|---|---|
| Wainman | 15 | 3 | 69 | 1 |
| Coad | 18 | 3 | 80 | 0 |
| Ashraf | 22 | 3 | 100 | 3 |
| Waite | 15 | 2 | 71 | 0 |
| Thompson | 11 | 2 | 48 | 1 |
| Craddock | 26.2 | 4 | 101 | 4 |
| Carver | 6 | 0 | 45 | 0 |

### YORKSHIRE

| First Innings | | Second Innings | |
|---|---:|---|---:|
| J A Tattersall, b Hampton | 31 | c Hill b Sykes | 57 |
| B L Ainsley, lbw b Pearson | 8 | b Pearson | 1 |
| § D M Hodgson, lbw b Naik | 29 | c Sykes b Taylor | 35 |
| * R M Pyrah, c Pardoe b Naik | 12 | c Hill b Sykes | 11 |
| R Gibson, c Hill b Taylor | 5 | c Hill b Sykes | 53 |
| M J Waite, c Pardoe b Naik | 2 | b Naik | 13 |
| J A Thompson, c Boyce b Naik | 4 | c Hill b Naik | 10 |
| T R Craddock, c Sykes b Naik | 6 | b Naik | 95 |
| J C Wainman, b Naik | 0 | b Naik | 6 |
| K Carver, not out | 10 | b Sykes | 38 |
| B O Coad, b Naik | 7 | not out | 17 |
| M A Ashraf | Did not bat | | |
| Extras 1 b, 8 nb | 9 | Extras 18 b, 12 lb, 4 nb | 34 |
| Total (44.1 overs) | 123 | Total (143.3 overs) | 370 |

*FoW:* 1-24 (Ainsley), 2-62 (Tattersall), 3-76 (Pyrah), 4-87 (Gibson), 5-91 (Hodgson),
1st  6-99 (Thompson), 7-104 (Waite), 8-104 (Wainman), 9-107 (Craddock), 10-123 (Coad)
*FoW:* 1-3 (Ainsley), 2-61 (Hodgson), 3-80 (Pyrah), 4-134 (Tattersall), 5-169 (Waite),
2nd  6-199 (Gibson), 7-199 (Thompson), 8-213 (wainman), 9-313 (Carver), 10-370 (Craddock)

| | O | M | R | W | | O | M | R | W |
|---|---|---|---|---|---|---|---|---|---|
| Wyatt | 7 | 1 | 26 | 0 | Pearson | 20 | 6 | 65 | 1 |
| Pearson | 6 | 0 | 23 | 1 | Chappell | 12 | 3 | 29 | 0 |
| Hampton | 5 | 0 | 23 | 1 | Sykes | 44 | 12 | 108 | 4 |
| Taylor | 10 | 6 | 9 | 1 | Taylor | 10 | 3 | 23 | 1 |
| Naik | 11.1 | 2 | 29 | 7 | Hampton | 11 | 2 | 45 | 0 |
| Sykes | 5 | 1 | 12 | 0 | Naik | 27.3 | 13 | 39 | 4 |
| | | | | | Ali | 12 | 4 | 21 | 0 |
| | | | | | Pardoe | 7 | 1 | 10 | 0 |

Umpires: P K Baldwin and N Pratt                    Scorers: P N Johnson and J R Virr

# Second Eleven Championship
## Yorkshire v. Northamptonshire

Played at York CC on June 8, 9 and 10, 2015

*Yorkshire won by an innings and 101 runs at 3pm on the Third Day*

Toss won by Yorkshire      Yorkshire 24 points, Northamptonshire 2 points

Close of play: First Day, Northamptonshire 126-9 (Fawcett 12, Richardson 2, 36 overs); Second Day, Northamptonshire (2) 14-0 (Zaib 1, Plater 13, 9 overs)

### NORTHAMPTONSHIRE

| | First Innings | | Second Innings | |
|---|---|---|---|---|
| A Patel, | lbw b Shaw | 46 | (2) c Tattersall b Coad | 39 |
| S A Zaib, | lbw b Ashraf | 4 | (1) c Waite by Gibson | 27 |
| K J Coetzer, | b Coad | 22 | c Tattersall b Coad | 0 |
| * § D Murphy, | lbw b Coad | 22 | b Carver | 45 |
| J D Fawcett, | not out | 13 | b Ashraf | 0 |
| A S T West, | c Carver b Coad | 8 | c Hussain b Carver | 14 |
| M J Plater, | lbw b Coad | 0 | (8) c Gibson b Coad | 7 |
| T B Sole, | c Hodgson b Gibson | 9 | (7) c Tattersall b Carver | 22 |
| M A Chambers, | b Gibson | 0 | c Hodd b Coad | 3 |
| D A Burton, | b Gibson | 0 | lbw b Coad | 2 |
| D P Richardson, | c Hodgson b Coad | 2 | not out | 4 |
| G G White | Did not bat | | | |
| | Extras 1 lb | 1 | Extras 9 lb, 4 nb | 13 |
| | Total (36.4 overs) | 127 | Total (58.4 overs) | 176 |

*FoW:* 1-12 (Zaib), 2-56 (Coetzer), 3-90 (Patel), 4-94 (Murphy), 5-102 (West),
1st 6-102 (Plater), 7-113 (Sole), 8-115 (Chambers), 9-115 (Burton), 10-127 (Richardson)
*FoW:* 1-55 (Patel), 2-55 (Coetzer), 3-100 (Zaib), 4-101 (Fawcett), 5-126 (West),
2nd 6-139 (Murphy), 7-160 (Plater), 8-170 (Chambers), 9-170 (Sole), 10-176 (Burton)

| | O | M | R | W | | O | M | R | W |
|---|---|---|---|---|---|---|---|---|---|
| Shaw | 8 | 2 | 25 | 1 | Coad | 15.4 | 5 | 41 | 5 |
| Ashraf | 10 | 3 | 34 | 1 | Ashraf | 16 | 3 | 48 | 1 |
| Waite | 5 | 1 | 28 | 0 | Sidebottom | 8 | 4 | 16 | 0 |
| Coad | 8.4 | 2 | 38 | 5 | Shaw | 5 | 1 | 27 | 0 |
| Gibson | 5 | 4 | 1 | 3 | Gibson | 4 | 2 | 5 | 1 |
| | | | | | Carver | 10 | 2 | 30 | 3 |

### YORKSHIRE

| | | |
|---|---|---|
| E Callis, | c Murphy b Burton | 16 |
| J A Tattersall, | b Chambers | 7 |
| § A J Hodd, | c Plater b Chambers | 57 |
| * D M Hodgson, | c Coetzer b Sole | 30 |
| M Hussain, | c Patel b Burton | 104 |
| R Gibson, | not out | 137 |
| M J Waite, | not out | 34 |
| K Carver | | |
| R J Sidebottom | | |
| J Shaw | Did not bat | |
| M A Ashraf | | |
| B O Coad | | |
| | Extras 4 b, 7 lb, 8 nb | 19 |
| | Total (5 wkts dec, 90 overs) | 404 |

*FoW:* 1-23 (Tattersall), 2-27 (Callis), 3-115 (Hodd), 4-118 (Hodgson), 5-341 (Hussain

| | O | M | R | W |
|---|---|---|---|---|
| Chambers | 21 | 5 | 56 | 2 |
| Burton | 20 | 3 | 102 | 2 |
| Coetzer | 18 | 1 | 66 | 0 |
| Richardson | 12 | 1 | 71 | 0 |
| Sole | 8 | 0 | 52 | 1 |
| Zaib | 11 | 1 | 46 | 0 |

Umpires: S J Malone and P R Pollard      Scorers: H Clayton and M E Woolley

# Second Eleven Championship
## Yorkshire v. Derbyshire

Played at North Marine Road, Scarborough, on June 16, 17 and 18, 2015

*Yorkshire won by 8 wickets at 4.29pm on the Third Day*

Toss won by Derbyshire

Yorkshire 23 points, Derbyshire 5 points

Close of play: First Day, Yorkshire 72-3 (Rhodes 29, Hodgson 3, 31 overs); Second Day, Derbyshire (2) 125-5 (Hosein 36, Cork 34, 53 overs)

|  | First Innings | DERBYSHIRE | Second Innings |  |
|---|---|---|---|---|
| * J L Clare, | c Lyth b Sidebottom | 9 | (4) c Maxwell b Sidebottom | 5 |
| T A Wood, | c Maxwell b Sidebottom | 8 | b Ashraf | 13 |
| Rahib Ali, | c and b Coad | 7 | c Lyth b Ashraf | 17 |
| A L Hughes, | c Maxwell b Rhodes | 26 | (1) lbw b Ashraf | 1 |
| R Bramwell, | c Maxwell b Coad | 44 | lbw b Sidebottom | 13 |
| § H R Hosein, | c Hodgson b Sidebottom | 20 | c Hodgson b Wainman | 57 |
| G T G Cork, | b Shaw | 10 | c Hodd b Carver | 65 |
| M J J Critcheley, | lbw b Maxwell | 35 | c Lyth b Maxwell | 9 |
| D J Wainwright, | not out | 34 | lbw b Ashraf | 11 |
| R P Hemmings, | c Hodgson b Maxwell | 1 | c Gibson b Coad | 20 |
| H J White, | lbw b Ashraf | 3 | not out | 0 |
| W S Davis | Did not bat | | | |
| | Extras 14 b, 17 lb | 31 | Extras 11 lb | 11 |
| | Total (72.4 overs) | 228 | Total (86.4 overs) | 222 |

*FoW:* 1-14 (Clare), 2-17 (Wood), 3-24 (Rahib Ali), 4-69 (Hughes), 5-113 (Hosein), 6-141 1st (Bramwell), 7-150 (Cork), 8-209 (Critcheley), 9-215 (Hemmings), 10-218 (White)

*FoW:* 1-5 (Hughes), 2-32 (Wood), 3-37 (Clare), 4-39 (Rahib Ali), 5-69 (Bramwell), 6-157 2nd (Hosein); 7-181 (Cork); 8-187 (Critcheley); 9-218 (Wainright); 10-222 (Hemmings)

| | O | M | R | W | | O | M | R | W |
|---|---|---|---|---|---|---|---|---|---|
| Sidebottom | 12 | 4 | 30 | 3 | Sidebottom | 17 | 3 | 41 | 2 |
| Ashraf | 8.4 | 1 | 25 | 1 | Ashraf | 19 | 5 | 36 | 4 |
| Shaw | 11 | 2 | 41 | 1 | Coad | 9.4 | 2 | 32 | 1 |
| Coad | 15 | 0 | 46 | 2 | Gibson | 2 | 0 | 10 | 0 |
| Rhodes | 7 | 2 | 11 | 1 | Maxwell | 9 | 3 | 28 | 1 |
| Carver | 9 | 2 | 30 | 0 | Carver | 17 | 4 | 45 | 1 |
| Maxwell | 10 | 2 | 14 | 2 | Rhodes | 4 | 2 | 6 | 0 |
| | | | | | Lyth | 3 | 1 | 5 | 0 |
| | | | | | Wainman | 6 | 2 | 8 | 1 |

|  | First Innings | YORKSHIRE | Second Innings |  |
|---|---|---|---|---|
| A Lyth, | c Hughes b White | 9 | c and b White | 0 |
| A Z Lees, | c Hosein b Cork | 11 | not out | 78 |
| * W M H Rhodes, | not out | 124 | (4) not out | 4 |
| A J Hodd, | lbw b David | 17 | | |
| § D M Hodgson, | c Critcheley b Davis | 7 | | |
| G J Maxwell, | c Clare b White | 0 | (3) b Davis | 97 |
| R Gibson, | c Hosein b White | 0 | | |
| J Shaw, | retired hurt | 1 | | |
| R J Sidebottom, | c and b Clare | 22 | | |
| K Carver, | not out | 53 | | |
| M A Ashraf | | | | |
| B O Coad | Did not bat | | | |
| | Total (7 wkts dec, 80 overs) | 255 | Total (2 wkts; 30.2 overs) | 196 |

*FoW:* 1-10 (Lyth), 2-44 (Lees), 3-67 (Hodd), 4-87 (Hodgson), 5-90 (Maxwell), 1st 6-90 (Gibson), 7-140 (Sidebottom)

2nd 1-0 (Lyth), 2-180 (Maxwell)

| | O | M | R | W | | O | M | R | W |
|---|---|---|---|---|---|---|---|---|---|
| White | 15 | 4 | 50 | 3 | White | 8.2 | 2 | 39 | 1 |
| Hemmings | 10 | 1 | 44 | 0 | Davis | 12 | 2 | 67 | 1 |
| Davis | 18 | 4 | 34 | 2 | Cork | 3 | 0 | 23 | 0 |
| Cork | 14 | 7 | 23 | 1 | Critcheley | 2 | 0 | 32 | 0 |
| Clare | 8 | 0 | 33 | 1 | Clare | 3 | 0 | 17 | 0 |
| Hughes | 5 | 2 | 11 | 0 | Hemmings | 2 | 0 | 6 | 0 |
| Wainwright | 7 | 0 | 42 | 0 | | | | | |
| Critcheley | 3 | 0 | 15 | 0 | | | | | |

*J C Wainman replaced R J Sidebottom in the second innings. Shaw was hit on the head by a bouncer in Yorkshire's first innings. He was discharged from hospital, but took no further part in the match.*

Umpires: I J Dixon and R J Warren

Scorers: Sarah R Smith and Jane E M Hough

## Second Eleven Championship
## Worcestershire v. Yorkshire

Played at Barnt Hill CC on June 22, 23 and 24, 2015
*Worcestershire won by an innings and 40 runs at 12.11pm on the Third Day*

Toss won by Yorkshire      Worcestershire 24 points, Yorkshire 3 points
Close of play: First Day, Worcestershire 187-4 (Kohler-Cadmore 100, Barnard 1, 58 overs);
Second Day, Yorkshire (2) 130-6 (Fisher 16, Wainman 0, 42 overs)

### YORKSHIRE

| | First Innings | | Second Innings | |
|---|---|---|---|---|
| * J A Tattersall, c and b Russell | 0 | c Dodd b Russell | 6 |
| M Hussain, c Kohler-Cadmore b Russell | 5 | (4) c G H Rhodes b Hepburn | 28 |
| § D M Hodgson, c Dodd b Russell | 3 | c d'Oliveira b Barnard | 7 |
| A J Finch, retired hurt | 19 | Did not bat | |
| R Gibson, c Dodd b Hepburn | 66 | c Dodd b Hepburn | 28 |
| M J Waite, c Dodd b Russell | 20 | lbw b d'Oliveira | 27 |
| W M H Rhodes, lbw b Hepburn | 9 | (2) lbw b Barnard | 4 |
| M D Fisher, lbw b Russell | 4 | (7) not out | 36 |
| J C Wainman, lbw b Hepburn | 16 | (8) lbw b Barnard | 8 |
| K Carver, not out | 7 | (9) c Woods b Hepburn | 1 |
| B O Coad, c Woods b Hepburn | 4 | b Barnard | 12 |
| J D Warner | Did not bat | (10) c Kohler-Cadmore b Barnard | 0 |
| Extras b 2, lb 3, nb 2, w 4 | 11 | Extras b 4, lb 10 | 14 |
| Total (43.2 overs) | 164 | Total (61.5 overs) | 171 |

*FoW:* 1-0 (Tattersall), 2-4 (Hodgson), 3-16 (Hussain), 4-113 (Waite), 5-127 (Gibson),
1st 6-137 (Fisher), 7-137 (W M H Rhodes), 8-156 (Wainman), 9-164 (Coad)
*FoW:* 1-10 (W M H Rhodes), 2-10 (Tattersall), 3-28 (Hodgson), 4-76 (Hussain), 5-87 (Gibson),
2nd 6-125 (Waite), 7-145 (Wainman), 8-148 (Carver), 9-153 (Warner), 10-171 (Coad)

| | O | M | R | W | | O | M | R | W |
|---|---|---|---|---|---|---|---|---|---|
| Russell | 12 | 1 | 52 | 5 | Russell | 4 | 1 | 13 | 1 |
| Barnard | 14 | 2 | 40 | 0 | Barnard | 21.5 | 3 | 67 | 5 |
| Whiteley | 5 | 0 | 24 | 0 | Hepburn | 21 | 9 | 48 | 4 |
| Hepburn | 12.2 | 4 | 43 | 4 | Whiteley | 5 | 0 | 12 | 0 |
| | | | | | Choudhry | 6 | 0 | 11 | 0 |
| | | | | | d'Oliveira | 4 | 1 | 6 | 0 |

### WORCESTERSHIRE

| | | |
|---|---|---|
| T Kohler-Cadmore, c Wainman b Warner | | 153 |
| B L d'Oliveira, lbw b Wainman | | 14 |
| G H Rhodes, c Coad b W M H Rhodes | | 18 |
| A N Kervezee, c Coad b Carver | | 15 |
| R A Whiteley, lbw b Fisher | | 21 |
| E G Barnard, c Gibson b Coad | | 60 |
| A Hepburn, c Warner b Carver | | 23 |
| * S H Choudhry, b Fisher | | 14 |
| W A R Fraine, not out | | 10 |
| § J M H Dodd, c Hodgson b Carver | | 4 |
| C J Russell, c Wainman b Carver | | 4 |
| A J Woods | Did not bat | |
| Extras b 4, lb 2, nb 22, w 11 | | 39 |
| Total (119.5 overs) | | 375 |

*FoW:* 1-51 (d'Oliveira), 2-102 (G H Rhodes), 3-132 (Kervezee), 4-179 (Whiteley), 5-297
(Kohler-Cadmore), 6-324 (Barnard), 7-340 (Hepburn), 8-362 (Choudhry), 9-369 (Dodd),
10-375 (Russell)

| | O | M | R | W |
|---|---|---|---|---|
| Fisher | 25 | 2 | 85 | 2 |
| Wainman | 18 | 5 | 56 | 1 |
| Warner | 13 | 2 | 35 | 1 |
| Coad | 24 | 7 | 48 | 1 |
| Rhodes | 17 | 5 | 60 | 1 |
| Carver | 22.5 | 1 | 85 | 4 |

Umpires: M Burns and D J Gower      Scorers: P M Mellish and J R Virr

# Second Eleven Championship
## Yorkshire v. Lancashire

Played at Headingley, Leeds, on July 6, 7 and 8, 2015
*Match drawn at 2.02pm on the Third Day*

Toss won by Lancashire                                   Yorkshire 9 points, Lancashire 9 points

Close of play: First Day, Lancashire 233-4 (Jones 40, Parry 4, 63.1 overs); Second Day, no play

## LANCASHIRE
*(Second Innings forfeited)*

| | | |
|---|---|---:|
| A J Mellor, c Hodd b Fisher | .................... | 3 |
| H Hameed, lbw b Shaw | .................... | 34 |
| L A Procter, c Tattersall b Maxwell | .................... | 115 |
| L S Livingstone, lbw b Shaw | .................... | 27 |
| R P Jones, c Hodd b Fisher | .................... | 40 |
| * S D Parry, b Shaw | .................... | 11 |
| D J Lamb, c Hodd b Fisher | .................... | 1 |
| § A M Gowers, c Hodd b Fisher | .................... | 36 |
| S C Kerrigan, b Coad | .................... | 11 |
| G T Griffiths, b Craddock | .................... | 0 |
| M W Parkinson, not out | .................... | 9 |
| S Mahmood | Did not bat | |
| Extras b 2, lb 12, w 1w | .................... | 15 |
| Total (88.2 overs) | .................... | 302 |

*FoW:* 1-8 (Mellor), 2-80 (Hameed), 3-146 (Livingstone), 4-222 (Procter), 5-234 (Jones), 6-242 (Lamb), 7-242 (Parry), 8-262 (Kerrigan), 9-263 (Griffiths), 10-302 (Gowers).

| | O | M | R | W |
|---|---|---|---|---|
| Fisher | 23.2 | 6 | 66 | 4 |
| Shaw | 23 | 7 | 72 | 3 |
| Waite | 5 | 1 | 29 | 0 |
| Coad | 21 | 3 | 52 | 1 |
| Carver | 4 | 0 | 21 | 0 |
| Craddock | 9 | 0 | 39 | 1 |
| Maxwell | 3 | 0 | 9 | 1 |

## YORKSHIRE
*(First Innings forfeited)*

| | | |
|---|---|---:|
| § A J Hodd, not out | .................... | 7 |
| J A Tattersall, lbw b Mahmood | .................... | 2 |
| * D M Hodgson, not out | .................... | 0 |
| G J Maxwell | | |
| R Gibson | | |
| M J Waite | | |
| J A Thompson | | |
| J Shaw | Did not bat | |
| K Carver | | |
| T R Craddock | | |
| M D Fisher | | |
| B O Coad | | |
| Extras b 1, lb 5 | .................... | 6 |
| Total (1 wkt, 5 overs) | .................... | 15 |

*FoW:* 1-14 (Tattersall)

| | O | M | R | W |
|---|---|---|---|---|
| Griffiths | 3 | 1 | 3 | 0 |
| Mahmood | 2 | 0 | 6 | 1 |

Umpires: I J Dixon and R P Medland           Scorers: H Clayton and C Rimmer

# Second Eleven Championship
## Yorkshire v. Warwickshire

Played at Harrogate CC on July 21, 22 and 23, 2015

*Warwickkhire won by 4 wickets at 5.18pm on the Third Day*

Toss won by Yorkshire      Yorkshire 6 points, Warwickshire 20 points

Close of play: First Day, Yorkshire (2) 5-0 (Hodd 1, Callis 2, 1 over), Second Day, Warwickshire (2) 10-0 (Umeed 10, Lambert 0, 6 overs)

| First Innings | YORKSHIRE | Second Innings | |
|---|---|---|---|
| § A J Hodd, run out (Thomason) | 25 | lbw b Milnes | 27 |
| E Callis, lbw b Adair | 6 | c Sukhjit Singh b Adair | 18 |
| G J Maxwell, c and b Thomason | 77 | c Banton b Panayi | 5 |
| * D M Hodgson, lbw b Adair | 4 | c Banton b Panayi | 8 |
| R Gibson, c Coleman b Thomason | 3 | b Panayi | 22 |
| M J Waite, c Adair b Thomason | 3 | c Webb b Sukhjit Singh | 32 |
| J A Thompson, lbw b Milnes | 61 | c Webb b Brookes | 15 |
| K Carver, b Milnes | 24 | lbw b Sukhjit Singh | 9 |
| T R Craddock, c Thomason b Brookes | 6 | c Banton b Milnes | 6 |
| M D Fisher, lbw b Brookes | 1 | not out | 21 |
| J C Wainman, not out | 14 | not out | 7 |
| B O Coad | Did not bat | | |
| Extras b 5, lb 4, nb 6 | 15 | Extras b 7, lb 9, nb 4 | 20 |
| Total (58.5 overs) | 230 | Total (9 wkts dec, 53 overs) | 190 |

FoW: 1-16 (Callis), 2-49 (Hodd), 3-79 (Hodgson), 4-102 (Gibson), 5-106 (Waite),
1st   6-145 (Maxwell), 7-209 (Thompson), 8-214 (Carver), 9-217 (Fisher), 10-230 (Craddock)

FoW: 1-47 (Hodd), 2-57 (Maxwell), 3-59 (Callis), 4-65 (Hodgson), 5-106 (Gibson),
2nd   6-132 (Thompson), 7-144 (Waite), 8-149 (Carver), 9-167 (Craddock)

| | O | M | R | W | | O | M | R | W |
|---|---|---|---|---|---|---|---|---|---|
| Milnes | 20 | 4 | 80 | 2 | Adair | 11 | 4 | 32 | 1 |
| Adair | 13 | 5 | 38 | 2 | Milnes | 10 | 1 | 41 | 2 |
| Thomason | 10 | 0 | 50 | 3 | Panayi | 7 | 1 | 31 | 3 |
| Panayi | 7 | 1 | 35 | 0 | Thomason | 2 | 0 | 7 | 0 |
| Brookes | 8.5 | 0 | 18 | 2 | Sukhjit Singh | 14 | 3 | 35 | 2 |
| | | | | | Brookes | 9 | 1 | 28 | 1 |

| First Innings | WARWICKSHIRE | Second Innings | |
|---|---|---|---|
| A R I Umeed, c Hodd b Fisher | 0 | lbw b Fisher | 21 |
| S J W Lambert, lbw b Coad | 2 | c Hodgson b Wainman | 31 |
| * F R J Coleman, c Hodd b Fisher | 5 | b Waite | 118 |
| J P Webb, lbw b Wainman | 3 | lbw b Carver | 92 |
| A D Thomason, c Maxwell b Fisher | 0 | not out | 24 |
| L Banks, c Fisher b Waite | 16 | b Waite | 9 |
| T P Milnes, b Fisher | 30 | | |
| § T Banton, lbw b Coad | 21 | (7) lbw b Carver | 1 |
| M R Adair, c Gibson b Craddock | 4 | (8) not out | 24 |
| G D Panayi, not out | 0 | | |
| B L Brookes, c Maxwell b Carver | 0 | | |
| Sukhjit Singh | Did not bat | | |
| Extras b 4b | 4 | Extras b 5, lb 10, nb 2 | 17 |
| Total (42 overs) | 85 | Total (6 wkts, 87.2 overs) | 337 |

FoW: 1-2 (Umeed), 2-2 (Lambert), 3-12 (Coleman), 4-12 (Thomason), 5-30 (Webb),
1st   6-40 (Banks), 7-73 (Milnes), 8-85 (Banton), 9-85 (Adair), 10-85 (Brookes)

FoW: 1-44 (Umeed), 2-66 (Lambert), 3-272 (Coleman), 4-272 (Webb), 5-287 (Banks),
2nd   6-292 (Banton)

| | O | M | R | W | | O | M | R | W |
|---|---|---|---|---|---|---|---|---|---|
| Fisher | 13 | 6 | 23 | 4 | Fisher | 16 | 2 | 69 | 1 |
| Coad | 13 | 6 | 23 | 2 | Coad | 14.2 | 5 | 34 | 0 |
| Waite | 7 | 4 | 12 | 1 | Maxwell | 1 | 1 | 0 | 0 |
| Wainman | 7 | 3 | 23 | 1 | Waite | 13 | 1 | 40 | 2 |
| Craddock | 1 | 1 | 0 | 1 | Wainman | 12 | 1 | 54 | 1 |
| Carver | 1 | 1 | 0 | 1 | Craddock | 9 | 0 | 63 | 0 |
| | | | | | Gibson | 3 | 1 | 5 | 0 |
| | | | | | Carver | 19 | 7 | 57 | 2 |

Umpires: S A Garrett and I Marland      Scorers: H Clayton and S Smith

# Second Eleven Championship
## Durham v. Yorkshire

Played at Durham ICG, Chester-le-Street, on August 11, 12 and 13, 2015
*Durham won by 40 runs at 12.52pm on the Third Day*

Toss won by Durham    Durham 23 points, Yorkshire 4 points
Close of play: First Day, Yorkshire (1) 116-4 (Waite 16, 33 overs); Second Day, Yorkshire (2) 122-6 (Rhodes 22, Thompson 40 overs)

|  | First Innings | DURHAM | Second Innings |  |
|---|---|---|---|---|
| * K K Jennings, c Thompson b Fisher | | 20 | lbw b Rhodes | 24 |
| P Mustard, c Rhodes b Carver | | 144 | c Read b Shaw | 15 |
| C S MacLeod, b Fisher | | 0 | Did not bat | |
| J A Tattersall, lbw b Rhodes | | 32 | (3) c Thompson b Waite | 3 |
| § S W Poynter, c Read b Rhodes | | 9 | (4) c Fisher b Waite | 9 |
| W J Weighell, c Read b Waite | | 5 | (5) c Thompson b Rhodes | 7 |
| A C Simpson, b Fisher | | 2 | (6) c Read b Fisher | 3 |
| J Coughlin, c Gibson b Imtiaz | | 6 | (7) c Thompson b Rhodes | 4 |
| G S Randhawa, b Thompson | | 4 | (8) c Read b Shaw | 33 |
| B J McCarthy, not out | | 14 | (9) c Read b Rhodes | 5 |
| G T Main, run out (Callis) | | 0 | (10) c Imtiaz b Waite | 3 |
| G H I Harding | Did not bat | | (11) not out | 3 |
| Extras b 2, lb 10, nb 6 | | 18 | Extras b 5, lb 1, nb 2 | 8 |
| Total (71 overs) | | 252 | Total (46.1 overs) | 117 |

FoW: 1-30 (Jennings), 2-32 (MacLeod), 3-128 (Tattersall), 4-152 (Poynter), 5-165 (Weighell),
1st  6-172 (Simpson), 7-203 (Coughlin), 8-226 (Randhawa), 9-242 (Mustard), 10-252 (Main)
FoW: 1-28 (Mustard), 2-45 (Tattersall), 3-55 (Poynter), 4-55 (Jennings), 5-62 (Weighell),
2nd  6-70 (Coughlin), 7-70 (Simpson), 8-79 (McCarthy), 9-98 (Main), 10-117 (Randhawa)

|  | O | M | R | W |  | O | M | R | W |
|---|---|---|---|---|---|---|---|---|---|
| Fisher | 14 | 2 | 39 | 3 | Fisher | 13 | 5 | 32 | 1 |
| Ashraf | 3 | 0 | 13 | 0 | Shaw | 10.1 | 1 | 33 | 2 |
| Shaw | 11 | 1 | 39 | 0 | Rhodes | 11 | 5 | 18 | 4 |
| Rhodes | 16 | 1 | 50 | 2 | Waite | 9 | 2 | 22 | 3 |
| Waite | 8 | 1 | 34 | 1 | Carver | 3 | 0 | 6 | 0 |
| Carver | 8 | 1 | 19 | 1 | | | | | |
| Imtiaz | 7 | 2 | 30 | 1 | | | | | |
| Thompson | 4 | 0 | 16 | 1 | | | | | |

|  | First Innings | YORKSHIRE | Second Innings |  |
|---|---|---|---|---|
| E Callis, c Poynter b Weighell | | 19 | c Simpson b Jennings | 29 |
| * W M H Rhodes, c Poynter b Weighell | | 6 | (4) lbw b McCarthy | 31 |
| M Hussain, c Poynter b Main | | 17 | b Main | 0 |
| R Gibson, b Randhawa | | 52 | (5) c Simpson b Randhawa | 4 |
| M J Waite, b Weighell | | 16 | (3) c Poynter b Weighell | 7 |
| B L Ainsley, c Jennings b Main | | 6 | (2) c Mustard b Main | 26 |
| Y Imtiaz, c Tattersall b Weighell | | 1 | c Tattersall b Weighell | 4 |
| J A Thompson, lbw b Weighell | | 0 | b Main | 33 |
| J Shaw, b Randhawa | | 0 | lbw b Randhawa | 31 |
| M D Fisher, lbw b Randhawa | | 0 | not out | 30 |
| K Carver, not out | | 0 | b Randhawa | 0 |
| M A Ashraf | | | | |
| § J Read | Did not bat | | | |
| Extras b 4, lb 6 | | 10 | Extras b 4, lb 3 | 7 |
| Total (47.1 overs) | | 127 | Total (74.5 overs) | 202 |

FoW: 1-17 (Rhodes), 2-26 (Callis), 3-65 (Hussain), 4-116 (Gibson), 5-116 (Waite),
1st  6-122 (Imtiaz), 7-124 (Thompson), 8-125 (Shaw), 9-127 (Fisher), 10-127 (Ainsley)
FoW: 1-62 (Ainsley), 2-62 (Hussain), 3-62 (Callis), 4-75 (Gibson), 5-84 (Waite),
2nd  6-88 (Imtiaz), 7-139 (Thompson), 8-141 (Rhodes), 9-202 (Shaw), 10-202 (Carver)

|  | O | M | R | W |  | O | M | R | W |
|---|---|---|---|---|---|---|---|---|---|
| Weighell | 17 | 6 | 32 | 5 | Weighell | 13 | 4 | 39 | 2 |
| McCarthy | 7 | 1 | 34 | 0 | McCarthy | 14 | 2 | 47 | 1 |
| Main | 5.1 | 0 | 30 | 2 | Jennings | 7 | 0 | 27 | 1 |
| Jennings | 6 | 1 | 11 | 0 | Main | 12 | 4 | 37 | 3 |
| Randhawa | 12 | 7 | 10 | 3 | Randhawa | 19.5 | 9 | 30 | 3 |
| | | | | | Harding | 9 | 1 | 15 | 0 |

Umpires: P R Gardner and M A Gough    Scorers: R V Hilton and Sarah R Smith

# Second Eleven Championship
## MCC Universities v. Yorkshire

Played at Weetwood, Leeds, on August 17, 18 and 19, 2015

*Match drawn at 5.37pm on the Third Day*

Toss won by MCC Universities      MCC Universities 9 points, Yorkshire 9 points

Close of play: First Day, Yorkshire 48-1 (Hussain 29, Gibson 8, 17 overs); Second Day, no play

| | First Innings | | MCC UNIVERSITIES | Second Innings | |
|---|---|---|---|---|---|
| Hasan Azad, c Read b Gibson | | 54 | b Wainman | | 2 |
| H L Thompson, c Read b Shaw | | 16 | c Ainsley b Shaw | | 3 |
| I A Karim, c Read b Shaw | | 4 | not out | | 45 |
| * S F G Bullen, b Imtiaz  b Taylor | | 31 | c Logan b Shaw | | 2 |
| H R C Ellison, b Imtiaz | | 68 | c Shaw b Wainman | | 2 |
| L Watkinson, lbw b Logan | | 26 | c Brook b Taylor | | 22 |
| § J W Tetley, c Firn b Taylor | | 71 | not out | | 9 |
| J N McIver, c Read b Taylor | | 15 | | | |
| M E Milnes, c Read b Wainman | | 16 | | | |
| J S E Ellis-Grewal, c Hussain b Wainman | | 15 | | | |
| J O Grundy, not out | | 14 | | | |
| D T P Pratt | Did not bat | | | | |
| Extras b 4, lb 8, nb 10, w 1 | | 23 | Extras nb 2 | | 2 |
| Total (86.1 overs) | | 353 | Total (5 wkts dec, 10 overs) | | 87 |

*FoW:* 1-33 (Thompson), 2-47 (Karim), 3-110 (Hasan Azad), 4-118 (Bullen), 5-169 (Watkinson),
1st    6-244 (Ellison), 7-289 (McIver), 8-316 (Tetley), 9-322 (Milnes), 10-353 (Ellis-Grewal)
2nd: 1-5 (Hasan Azad), 2-13 (Thompson), 3-15 (Bullen), 4-38 (Ellison), 5-70 (Watkinson)

| | O | M | R | W | | O | M | R | W |
|---|---|---|---|---|---|---|---|---|---|
| Shaw | 13 | 1 | 55 | 2 | Shaw | 4 | 0 | 39 | 2 |
| Wainman | 18.1 | 3 | 67 | 2 | Wainman | 4 | 0 | 19 | 2 |
| Firn | 5 | 1 | 43 | 0 | Taylor | 1 | 0 | 16 | 1 |
| Gibson | 11 | 3 | 32 | 1 | Logan | 1 | 0 | 13 | 0 |
| M A Taylor | 10 | 1 | 48 | 3 | | | | | |
| Logan | 19 | 6 | 53 | 1 | | | | | |
| Imtiaz | 10 | 3 | 43 | 1 | | | | | |

| | First Innings | | YORKSHIRE | Second Innings | |
|---|---|---|---|---|---|
| B L Ainsley, lbw b Grundy | | 11 | c Milnes b Pratt | | 0 |
| M Hussain, not out | | 29 | c Tetley b Grundy | | 0 |
| * R Gibson, not out | | 8 | (4) c Grundy b Milnes | | 38 |
| H C Brook | | | (3) lbw b McIver | | 51 |
| Y Imtiaz | | | lbw b Grundy | | 0 |
| J A Thompson | | | (7) c Grundy b Pratt | | 5 |
| N J Firn | Did not bat | | | | |
| J Shaw | | | (6) not out | | 38 |
| J C Wainman | | | (8) not out | | 4 |
| § J Read | | | | | |
| J E G Logan | | | | | |
| M A Taylor | | | | | |
| Extras | | 0 | Extras b 12, nb 2, w 2 | | 16 |
| Total (1 wkt dec, 17 overs) | | 48 | Total (6 wkts, 45 overs) | | 152 |

*FoW:* 1st   1-39 (Ainsley)
2nd: 1-1 (Ainsley), 2-1 (Hussain), 3-76 (Gibson), 4-84 (Imtiaz), 5-119 (Brook),
     6-124 (Thompson)

| | O | M | R | W | | O | M | R | W |
|---|---|---|---|---|---|---|---|---|---|
| Pratt | 9 | 2 | 25 | 0 | Pratt | 13 | 5 | 31 | 2 |
| Grundy | 8 | 3 | 23 | 1 | Grundy | 12 | 3 | 62 | 2 |
| | | | | | Milnes | 11 | 2 | 31 | 1 |
| | | | | | McIver | 9 | 2 | 16 | 1 |

*Although played at Weetwood the match counted as a home fixture for the Universities*

Umpires: N G C Cowley & A Davies      Scorers: H Clayton and C N Rawson

Played at Stamford Bridge CC on August 24, 25 and 26, 2015
*Match drawn at 5pm on the Third Day*

Toss won by Nottinghamshire          Yorkhire 6 points, Nottinghamshire 13 points
Close of play: First Day, Nottinghamshire 65-0 (Smith 51, Libby 12, 14.3 overs); Second Day, Yorkshire (2) 9-0 (Callis 5, Hussain 3, 5 overs)

## YORKSHIRE

| First Innings | | Second Innings | |
|---|---|---|---|
| E Callis, c Moores b Gidman | 0 | c Moores b Gidman | 6 |
| M Hussain, b Kitt | 0 | c Kitt b Walton | 20 |
| A J Finch, lbw b Kitt | 60 | not out | 104 |
| H C Brook, b Walton | 19 | not out | 36 |
| * R Gibson, lbw b Carter | 0 | | |
| M J Waite, lbw b Tillcock | 13 | | |
| J A Thompson, c Gidman b Kitt | 8 | | |
| J Shaw, c Moores b Gidman | 1 | | |
| J C Wainman, c Moores b Kitt | 0 | | |
| J D Warner, lbw b Kitt | 0 | | |
| K Carver, not out | 2 | | |
| § J Read | Did not bat | | |
| Extras b 2, lb 1 | 3 | Extras b 2, lb 3 | 5 |
| Total (43.5 overs) | 106 | Total (2 wkts, 52 overs) | 171 |

*FoW:* 1-0 (Callis), 2-6 (Hussain), 3-51 (Brook), 4-52 (Gibson), 5-87 (Waite),
1st   6-103 (Finch), 7-104 (Thompson), 8-104 (Wainman), 9-104 (Shaw), 10-106 (Warner)
2nd   1-16 (Callis), 2-55 (Hussain)

| | O | M | R | W | | O | M | R | W |
|---|---|---|---|---|---|---|---|---|---|
| Gidman | 12 | 2 | 32 | 2 | Carter | 13 | 2 | 37 | 0 |
| Kitt | 10.5 | 3 | 21 | 5 | Kitt | 12 | 1 | 31 | 0 |
| Carter | 11 | 1 | 28 | 1 | Tillcock | 8 | 1 | 30 | 0 |
| Walton | 6 | 1 | 15 | 1 | Gidman | 8 | 2 | 34 | 1 |
| Tillcock | 4 | 0 | 7 | 1 | Walton | 4 | 0 | 9 | 1 |
| | | | | | Webster | 4 | 1 | 15 | 0 |
| | | | | | Wood | 3 | 1 | 10 | 0 |

## NOTTINGHAMSHIRE

| | |
|---|---|
| * G P Smith, b Wainman | 51 |
| J D Libby, not out | 152 |
| S K W Wood, lbw b Wainman | 5 |
| W T Root, c Thompson b Wainman | 60 |
| W R S Gidman, not out | 79 |
| § T J Moores | |
| A Dal | |
| A D Tillcock | |
| S W Webster | Did not bat |
| M Carter | |
| B M Kitt | |
| S D Walton | |
| Extras nb 6 | 6 |
| Total (3 wkts dec, 87.5 overs) | 353 |

*FoW:* 1-65 (Smith), 2-75 (Wood), 3-164 (Root)

| | O | M | R | W |
|---|---|---|---|---|
| Shaw | 15 | 3 | 68 | 0 |
| Wainman | 17.5 | 3 | 86 | 3 |
| Waite | 14 | 4 | 31 | 0 |
| Warner | 11 | 1 | 44 | 0 |
| Carver | 19 | 3 | 81 | 0 |
| Gibson | 6 | 0 | 29 | 0 |
| Finch | 2 | 0 | 10 | 0 |
| Thompson | 3 | 1 | 4 | 0 |

Umpires: I D Blackwell and J D Middlebrook          Scorers: H Clayton and Mrs A Cusworth

# SECOND ELEVEN CHAMPIONSHIP 2015

## FINAL

Middlesex (254 and 264) lost to **Nottinghamshire** (331 and 188-6) by four wickets

### NORTHERN GROUP FINAL TABLE

| | | P | W | L | D | Tied | Aban. | Bat | Bowl | Ded | Points |
|---|---|---|---|---|---|---|---|---|---|---|---|
| 1 | Nottinghamshire (2) .... | 9 | 4 | 0 | 5 | 0 | 0 | 19 | 34 | 0 | 142 |
| 2 | Durham (8) .......... | 9 | 4 | 1 | 4 | 0 | 0 | 29 | 28 | 0 | 141 |
| 3 | Lancashire (3) ........ | 9 | 3 | 1 | 5 | 0 | 0 | 25 | 30 | 0 | 128 |
| 4 | Leicestershire (1) ...... | 9 | 3 | 2 | 4 | 0 | 0 | 20 | 34 | 0 | 122 |
| 5 | Warwickshire (6) ...... | 9 | 3 | 1 | 3 | 0 | 2 | 14 | 24 | -2 | 112 |
| 6 | Derbyshire (5) ......... | 9 | 2 | 2 | 5 | 0 | 0 | 19 | 23 | 0 | 99 |
| **7** | **Yorkshire (4) ........** | **9** | **2** | **4** | **3** | **0** | **0** | **10** | **29** | **0** | **86** |
| 8 | Worcestershire (10) ..... | 9 | 1 | 4 | 4 | 0 | 0 | 20 | 27 | -0.5 | 82.5 |
| 9 | MCC Universities (-) ... | 9 | 0 | 2 | 6 | 0 | 1 | 22 | 20 | 0 | 77 |
| 10 | Northamptonshire (-) ... | 9 | 1 | 6 | 2 | 0 | 0 | 14 | 32 | -1.5 | 70.5 |

### SOUTHERN GROUP FINAL TABLE

| | | P | W | L | D | Tied | Aban. | Bat | Bowl | Ded | Points |
|---|---|---|---|---|---|---|---|---|---|---|---|
| 1 | Middlesex (3) ........ | 9 | 6 | 2 | 1 | 0 | 0 | 22 | 32 | -1.5 | 153.5 |
| 2 | Somerset (2) .......... | 9 | 4 | 3 | 2 | 0 | 0 | 25 | 32 | -1.5 | 129.5 |
| 3 | Kent (6) ............. | 9 | 3 | 2 | 4 | 0 | 0 | 24 | 35 | 0 | 127 |
| 4 | Surrey (4) ............ | 9 | 4 | 4 | 1 | 0 | 0 | 26 | 29 | 0 | 124 |
| 5 | Gloucestershire (7) ..... | 9 | 4 | 4 | 1 | 0 | 0 | 25 | 26 | -2 | 120 |
| 6 | Hampshire (9) ......... | 9 | 3 | 2 | 3 | 0 | 1 | 24 | 27 | -0.5 | 119 |
| 7 | Sussex (5) ............ | 9 | 3 | 3 | 3 | 0 | 0 | 26 | 29 | 0 | 118 |
| 8 | Essex (1) ............. | 9 | 2 | 3 | 3 | 0 | 1 | 27 | 26 | 0 | 105 |
| 9 | Glamorgan (-) ......... | 9 | 2 | 4 | 3 | 0 | 0 | 16 | 21 | 0 | 84 |
| 10 | MCC Young Cricketers (-) | 9 | 0 | 4 | 5 | 0 | 0 | 25 | 24 | 0 | 74 |

*Ded.* Points deducted for slow over-rates

*(2014 group positions in brackets)*

# SECOND ELEVEN CHAMPIONS

In the seasons in which Yorkshire have competed. The Championship has been split into two groups since 2009, the group winners playing off for the Championship. These groups were deemed North and South from the 2012 season.

| Season | Champions | Yorkshire's Position | Season | Champions | Yorkshire's Position |
|--------|-----------|---------------------|--------|-----------|---------------------|
| 1959 | Gloucestershire | 7th | 1995 | Hampshire | 5th |
| 1960 | Northamptonshire | 14th | 1996 | Warwickshire | 4th |
| 1961 | Kent | 11th | 1997 | Lancashire | 2nd |
| 1975 | Surrey | 4th | 1998 | Northamptonshire | 9th |
| 1976 | Kent | 5th | 1999 | Middlesex | 14th |
| **1977** | **Yorkshire** | **1st** | 2000 | Middlesex | 5th |
| 1978 | Sussex | 5th | 2001 | Hampshire | 2nd |
| 1979 | Warwickshire | 3rd | 2002 | Kent | 3rd |
| 1980 | Glamorgan | 5th | **2003** | **Yorkshire** | **1st** |
| 1981 | Hampshire | 11th | 2004 | Somerset | 8th |
| 1982 | Worcestershire | 14th | 2005 | Kent | 10th |
| 1983 | Leicestershire | 2nd | 2006 | Kent | 3rd |
| **1984** | **Yorkshire** | **1st** | 2007 | Sussex | 10th |
| 1985 | Nottinghamshire | 12th | 2008 | Durham | 5th |
| 1986 | Lancashire | 5th | 2009 | Surrey | A 2nd |
| **1987** | **Yorkshire** and Kent | **1st** | 2010 | Surrey | A 8th |
| 1988 | Surrey | 9th | 2011 | Warwickshire | A 10th |
| 1989 | Middlesex | 9th | 2012 | Kent | North 9th |
| 1990 | Sussex | 17th | 2013 | Lancashire & Middlesex | |
| **1991** | **Yorkshire** | **1st** | | | (North) 4th |
| 1992 | Surrey | 5th | 2014 | Leicestershire | (North) 4th |
| 1993 | Middlesex | 3rd | 2015 | Nottinghamshire | (North) 7th |
| 1994 | Somerset | 2nd | | | |

# SECOND ELEVEN CHAMPIONSHIP
## AVERAGES 2015

Played 9　　Won 2　　Lost 4　　Drawn 3

## BATTING AND FIELDING
*(Qualification 5 innings)*

| Player | M. | I. | N.O. | Runs | H.S. | Avge | 100s | 50s | ct/st |
|---|---|---|---|---|---|---|---|---|---|
| W M H Rhodes | 5 | 6 | 2 | 178 | 124* | 44.50 | 1 | 0 | 1 |
| R Gibson | 9 | 13 | 2 | 416 | 137* | 37.81 | 1 | 3 | 5 |
| M D Fisher | 4 | 6 | 3 | 92 | 36* | 30.66 | 0 | 0 | 2 |
| K Carver | 8 | 10 | 5 | 144 | 53* | 28.80 | 0 | 1 | 1 |
| M Hussain | 5 | 9 | 1 | 203 | 104 | 25.37 | 1 | 0 | 2 |
| J Shaw | 6 | 5 | 2 | 71 | 38* | 23.66 | 0 | 0 | 1 |
| M J Waite | 7 | 10 | 1 | 167 | 34* | 18.55 | 0 | 0 | 2 |
| J A Tattersall | 4 | 6 | 0 | 103 | 57 | 17.16 | 0 | 1 | 4 |
| J A Thompson | 6 | 8 | 0 | 136 | 61 | 17.00 | 0 | 1 | 5 |
| D M Hodgson | 6 | 9 | 1 | 123 | 35 | 15.37 | 0 | 0 | 8/1 |
| E Callis | 4 | 7 | 0 | 94 | 29 | 13.42 | 0 | 0 | 0 |
| J C Wainman | 6 | 8 | 3 | 46 | 16 | 9.20 | 0 | 0 | 3 |
| B L Ainsley | 3 | 6 | 0 | 26 | 26 | 8.66 | 0 | 0 | 1 |

### Also played

| Player | M. | I. | N.O. | Runs | H.S. | Avge | 100s | 50s | ct/st |
|---|---|---|---|---|---|---|---|---|---|
| A J Finch | 2 | 3 | 2 | 183 | 104* | 183.00 | 1 | 1 | 0 |
| A Z Lees | 1 | 2 | 1 | 89 | 78* | 89.00 | 0 | 1 | 1 |
| H C Brook | 2 | 3 | 1 | 106 | 51 | 53.00 | 0 | 2 | 1 |
| G J Maxwell | 3 | 4 | 0 | 179 | 97 | 44.75 | 0 | 1 | 6 |
| A J Hodd | 4 | 5 | 1 | 133 | 57 | 33.25 | 0 | 1 | 8 |
| T R Craddock | 3 | 4 | 0 | 113 | 95 | 28.25 | 0 | 1 | 1 |
| R J Sidebottom | 2 | 1 | 0 | 22 | 22 | 22.00 | 0 | 0 | 0 |
| B O Coad | 6 | 4 | 1 | 40 | 17* | 13.33 | 0 | 0 | 3 |
| R M Pyrah | 1 | 2 | 0 | 23 | 12 | 11.50 | 0 | 0 | 0 |
| A Lyth | 1 | 2 | 0 | 9 | 9 | 4.50 | 0 | 0 | 3 |
| Y Imtiaz | 2 | 3 | 0 | 5 | 4 | 1.66 | 0 | 0 | 2 |
| J D Warner | 2 | 2 | 0 | 0 | 0 | 0.00 | 0 | 0 | 1 |
| M A Ashraf | 4 | 0 | 0 | 0 | 0 | — | 0 | 0 | 0 |
| N J Firn | 1 | 0 | 0 | 0 | 0 | — | 0 | 0 | 1 |
| J E G Logan | 1 | 0 | 0 | 0 | 0 | — | 0 | 0 | 1 |
| J Read | 3 | 0 | 0 | 0 | 0 | — | 0 | 0 | 11 |
| M A Taylor | 1 | 0 | 0 | 0 | 0 | — | 0 | 0 | 0 |

## BOWLING
*(Qualification 10 wickets)*

| Player | Overs | Mdns | Runs | Wkts | Avge | Best | 5wI | 10wM |
|---|---|---|---|---|---|---|---|---|
| M D Fisher | 104.2 | 23 | 314 | 15 | 20.93 | 4-23 | 0 | 0 |
| B O Coad | 139.2 | 33 | 394 | 17 | 23.17 | 5-38 | 2 | 1 |
| M A Ashraf | 78.4 | 15 | 256 | 10 | 25.60 | 4-36 | 0 | 0 |
| J C Wainman | 98 | 20 | 382 | 12 | 31.83 | 3-86 | 0 | 0 |
| K Carver | 118.5 | 21 | 419 | 12 | 34.91 | 4-85 | 0 | 0 |
| J Shaw | 100.1 | 18 | 399 | 11 | 36.27 | 3-72 | 0 | 0 |

### Also bowled

| Player | Overs | Mdns | Runs | Wkts | Avge | Best | 5wI | 10wM |
|---|---|---|---|---|---|---|---|---|
| G J Maxwell | 22 | 6 | 51 | 4 | 12.75 | 2-14 | 0 | 0 |
| M A Taylor | 11 | 1 | 64 | 4 | 16.00 | 3-48 | 0 | 0 |
| R Gibson | 31 | 10 | 82 | 5 | 16.40 | 3-1 | 0 | 0 |
| R J Sidebottom | 37 | 11 | 87 | 5 | 17.40 | 3-30 | 0 | 0 |
| W M H Rhodes | 55 | 15 | 145 | 8 | 18.12 | 4-18 | 0 | 0 |
| T R Craddock | 45.2 | 5 | 203 | 6 | 33.83 | 4-101 | 0 | 0 |
| J A Thompson | 18 | 3 | 68 | 2 | 34.00 | 1-16 | 0 | 0 |
| Y Imtiaz | 17 | 5 | 73 | 2 | 36.50 | 1-30 | 0 | 0 |
| M J Waite | 76 | 16 | 287 | 7 | 38.14 | 3-22 | 0 | 0 |
| J E G Logan | 20 | 6 | 66 | 1 | 66.00 | 1-53 | 0 | 0 |
| J D Warner | 24 | 3 | 79 | 1 | 79.00 | 1-35 | 0 | 0 |

A J Finch: 2-0-10-0; N J Firn: 5-1-43-0; A Lyth: 3-1-5-0

## Second Eleven Trophy
## Leicestershire v. Yorkshire

Played at Leicester Ivanhoe CC on April 27, 2015
*Leicestershire won by 3 wickets at 6pm*

Toss won by Yorkshire                    Leicestershire 2 points, Yorkshire 0 points

### YORKSHIRE

| | | |
|---|---|---:|
| J A Tattersall, c Ali b Taylor | | 42 |
| R Gibson, b Pearson | | 4 |
| § D M Hodgson, cAli b Naik | | 7 |
| * R M Pyrah, c Ali b Taylor | | 69 |
| B L Ainsley, lbw b Chappell | | 10 |
| M J Waite, b Taylor | | 44 |
| J A Thompson, not out | | 43 |
| T R Craddock, b Taylor | | 2 |
| K Carver, not out | | 1 |
| B O Coad | | |
| M A Ashraf | Did not bat | |
| Extras b 2, lb 4, nb 2, w 12 | | 20 |
| Total (7 wkts, 50 overs) | | 242 |

*FoW:* 1-23 (Gibson), 2-47 (Hodgson), 3-76 (Tattersall), 4-104 (Ainsley), 5-159 (Pyrah), 6-221 (Waite), 7-239 (Craddock)

| | O | M | R | W |
|---|---:|---:|---:|---:|
| Pearson | 10 | 0 | 64 | 1 |
| Wyatt | 8 | 0 | 35 | 0 |
| Taylor | 10 | 0 | 39 | 4 |
| Naik | 9 | 0 | 36 | 1 |
| Sykes | 9 | 0 | 36 | 0 |
| Chappell | 4 | 0 | 26 | 1 |

### LEICESTERSHIRE

| | | |
|---|---|---:|
| M G Pardoe, c Hodgson b Pyrah | | 62 |
| * M A G Boyce, c Tattersall b Ashraf | | 6 |
| § L J Hill, c Hodgson b Ashraf | | 12 |
| A M Ali, c Pyrah b Carver | | 87 |
| M H Cross, not out | | 46 |
| R M L Taylor, c Thompson b Craddock | | 1 |
| J K H Naik, c Carver b Craddock | | 2 |
| J S Sykes, b Craddock | | 13 |
| Z J Chappell, not out | | 4 |
| J C Pearson | | |
| A C F Wyatt | Did not bat | |
| Extras b 5, lb 1, nb 2, w 5 | | 13 |
| Total (7 wkts, 46.2 overs) | | 246 |

*FoW:* 1-15 (Boyce), 2-40 (Hill), 3-144 (Pardoe), 4-201 (Ali), 5-202 (Taylor), 6-204 (Naik), 7-242 (Sykes)

| | O | M | R | W |
|---|---:|---:|---:|---:|
| Ashraf | 7 | 0 | 46 | 2 |
| Coad | 7 | 1 | 37 | 0 |
| Pyrah | 6 | 1 | 33 | 1 |
| Waite | 5 | 0 | 18 | 0 |
| Carver | 9 | 0 | 42 | 1 |
| Craddock | 8.2 | 0 | 51 | 3 |
| Gibson | 4 | 0 | 13 | 0 |

Umpires: P K Baldwin and M Qureshi            Scorers: P M Johnson and J R Virr

# Second Eleven Trophy
## Yorkshire v. Derbyshire

Played at Marske-by-the-Sea CC on June 15, 2015
*Derbyshire won by 4 wickets at 5.29pm*

Toss won by Yorkshire

Yorkshire 0 points, Derbyshire 2 points

### YORKSHIRE

| | | |
|---|---|--:|
| J A Tattersall, c Wainwright b Clare | | 35 |
| R Gibson, c Hemmings b Davis | | 20 |
| § A J Hodd, c Wainwright b Hemmings | | 14 |
| D M Hodgson, b Clare | | 22 |
| * W M H Rhodes, c Wainwright b Critchley | | 26 |
| M Hussain, lbw b Clare | | 0 |
| M J Waite, c Critcheley b Wainwright | | 50 |
| J C Wainman, run out (Hughes) | | 1 |
| K Carver, run out (Wood) | | 11 |
| B O Coad, st H R Hosein b Critchely | | 12 |
| M A Ashraf, not out | | 1 |
| Extras lb 1, w 6 | | 7 |
| Total (45.2 overs) | | 199 |

*FoW:* 1-29 (Gibson), 2-54 (Hodd), 3-86 (Tattersall), 4-95 (Hodgson), 5-95 (Hussain), 6-151 (Rhodes), 7-153 (Wainman), 8-169 (Carver), 9-196 (Waite), 10-199 (Coad)

| | O | M | R | W |
|---|--:|--:|--:|--:|
| Davis | 8 | 0 | 52 | 1 |
| Hemmings | 7 | 0 | 42 | 1 |
| Cork | 7 | 0 | 27 | 0 |
| Clare | 5 | 1 | 14 | 3 |
| Hughes | 3 | 0 | 13 | 0 |
| Wainwright | 8 | 0 | 30 | 1 |
| Critcheley | 7.2 | 0 | 20 | 2 |

### DERBYSHIRE

| | | |
|---|---|--:|
| * J L Clare, lbw b Wainman | | 7 |
| T A Wood, c Tattersall b Wainman | | 10 |
| R Bramwell, c Ashraf b Coad | | 31 |
| A L Hughes, c Gibson b Wainman | | 6 |
| § H R Hosein, b Rhodes | | 41 |
| Rahib Ali, b Ashraf | | 12 |
| G T G Cork, not out | | 44 |
| M J J Critcheley, not out | | 44 |
| D J Wainwright | | |
| R P Hemmings | Did not bat | |
| W S Davis | | |
| Extras lb 3, nb 2, w 3 | | 8 |
| Total (6 wkts, 45.5 overs) | | 203 |

*FoW:* 1-7 (Clare), 2-23 (Wood), 3-39 (Hughes), 4-77 (Bramwell), 5-102 (Rahib Ali), 6-124 (Hosein)

| | O | M | R | W |
|---|--:|--:|--:|--:|
| Ashraf | 10 | 2 | 47 | 1 |
| Wainman | 10 | 2 | 39 | 3 |
| Coad | 10 | 1 | 40 | 1 |
| Carver | 10 | 1 | 37 | 0 |
| Rhodes | 5 | 0 | 24 | 1 |
| Waite | 0.5 | 0 | 13 | 0 |

Umpires: J R Burn and R J Warren          Scorers: H Clayton and Mrs J E M Hough

# Second Eleven Trophy
## Yorkshire v. Lancashire

Played at Pudsey Congs CC on July 9, 2015
*Lancashire won by 9 wickets at 4.02pm*

Toss won by Lancashire                          Yorkshire 0 points, Lancashire 2 points

### YORKSHIRE

| | | |
|---|---|---:|
| § A J Hodd, c Jones b Bailey | .................... | 18 |
| D M Hodgson, c Jones b Bailey | ................. | 1 |
| G J Maxwell, lbw b Parry | ..................... | 39 |
| R Gibson, c Jones b Parry | ..................... | 33 |
| L E Plunkett, b Mahmood | ...................... | 2 |
| M J Waite, lbw b Kerrigan | ..................... | 35 |
| * R M Pyrah, c Jones b Lamb | ................... | 4 |
| J A Thompson, c Lamb b Kerrigan | ............... | 0 |
| T R Craddock, b Kerrigan | ...................... | 6 |
| J C Wainman, c Mellor b Kerrigan | .............. | 1 |
| K Carver, not out | ............................. | 8 |
| Extras lb 2, nb 2, w 10 | ....................... | 14 |
| Total (36.3 overs) | ................... | 161 |

*FoW:* 1-9 (Hodgson), 2-27 (Hodd), 3-83 (Maxwell), 4-88 (Plunkett), 5-120 (Gibson), 6-132 (Pyrah), 7-133 (Thompson), 8-147 (Waite), 9-152 (Craddock), 10-161 (Wainman)

| | O | M | R | W |
|---|---|---|---|---|
| Bailey | 6 | 0 | 17 | 2 |
| Griffiths | 6 | 0 | 34 | 0 |
| Mahmood | 9 | 0 | 48 | 1 |
| Parry | 8 | 0 | 33 | 2 |
| Lamb | 4 | 0 | 19 | 1 |
| Kerrigan | 3.3 | 1 | 8 | 4 |

### LANCASHIRE

| | | |
|---|---|---:|
| § A J Mellor, c Hodd b Gibson | .................. | 17 |
| H Hameed, not out | ............................. | 54 |
| L A Procter, not out | .......................... | 79 |
| L S Livingstone | | |
| R P Jones | | |
| D J Lamb | | |
| * S D Parry | Did not bat | |
| T E Bailey | | |
| S C Kerrigan | | |
| G T Griffiths | | |
| S Mahmood | | |
| Extras b 4, nb 4, w 8 | ..................... | 16 |
| Total (1 wkt, 29.5 overs) | ............... | 166 |

*FoW:* 1-33 (Mellor)

| | O | M | R | W |
|---|---|---|---|---|
| Wainman | 2 | 0 | 11 | 0 |
| Waite | 3 | 0 | 10 | 0 |
| Plunkett | 7 | 0 | 29 | 0 |
| Gibson | 4 | 0 | 15 | 1 |
| Pyrah | 4 | 0 | 18 | 0 |
| Craddock | 3 | 1 | 21 | 0 |
| Carver | 3.5 | 0 | 35 | 0 |
| Maxwell | 3 | 0 | 23 | 0 |

Umpires: A Davies and B J Debenham                    Scorers: H Clayton ands C Rimmer

## Second Eleven Trophy
## Unicorns v. Yorkshire

Played at Marlins, Long Marston, Hertfordshire, on July 15, 2015
*Unicorns won by 7 wickets at 5pm*

Toss won by the Unicorns

Unicorns 2 points, Yorkshire 0 points

### YORKSHIRE

| | |
|---|---|
| E Callis, c Syddall b Ali | 13 |
| J A Tattersall, b Burton | 2 |
| § D M Hodgson, b Ali | 38 |
| M Hussain, c Weston b Ali | 1 |
| M J Waite, c Bulcock b Stephens | 10 |
| * R M Pyrah, b Stephens | 1 |
| J A Thompson, c Thomason b Ali | 0 |
| T R Craddock, b Stephens | 4 |
| J C Wainman, c and b Bulcock | 38 |
| J D Warner, st Thomason b Payne | 12 |
| B O Coad, not out | 8 |
| Extras lb 3, w 4 | 7 |
| Total (44.4 overs) | 134 |

*FoW:* 1-6 (Tattersall), 2-46 (Callis), 3-52 (Hussain), 4-63 (Hodgson), 5-68 (Pyrah), 6-69 (Thompson), 7-85 (Waite), 8-85 (Craddock), 9-120 (Warner), 10-134 (Wainman)

| | O | M | R | W |
|---|---|---|---|---|
| Syddall | 8 | 1 | 20 | 0 |
| Burton | 4 | 0 | 31 | 1 |
| Ali | 10 | 1 | 18 | 4 |
| Stephens | 10 | 4 | 22 | 3 |
| Bulcock | 4.4 | 0 | 23 | 1 |
| Payne | 8 | 0 | 17 | 1 |

### UNICORNS

| | | |
|---|---|---|
| A S T West, lbw b Coad | | 0 |
| L P Weston, c Tattersall b Coad | | 10 |
| § L J Thomason, c Hodgson b Waite | | 55 |
| H C Stephens, not out | | 47 |
| C J Whittock, not out | | 2 |
| A T Thomson | | |
| T R H Burton | | |
| M J Payne | Did not bat | |
| T Bulcock | | |
| S A Ali | | |
| * A J Syddall | | |
| Extras lb 4, nb 6, w 11 | | 21 |
| Total (3 wkts, 29.4 overs) | | 135 |

*FoW:* 1-0 (West), 2-21 (Weston), 3-119 (Thomason)

| | O | M | R | W |
|---|---|---|---|---|
| Coad | 5 | 0 | 15 | 2 |
| Warner | 4.4 | 0 | 28 | 0 |
| Pyrah | 4 | 0 | 20 | 0 |
| Craddock | 6 | 0 | 34 | 0 |
| Wainman | 4 | 1 | 11 | 0 |
| Thompson | 2 | 0 | 6 | 0 |
| Waite | 4 | 0 | 17 | 1 |

Umpires: I D Blackwell and N J Hall          Scorers: K B O'Connell and H Clayton

# Second Eleven Trophy
## Yorkshire v. Warwickshire

Played at York CC on July 20, 2015
*Yorkshire won by 48 runs at 5.43pm*

Toss won by Warwickshire                    Yorkshire 2 points, Warwickshire 0 points

### YORKSHIRE

| | | |
|---|---|--:|
| § A J Hodd, c McKay b Thomason | ............... | 28 |
| R Gibson, c Poysden b Adair | .................. | 15 |
| G J Maxwell, c Gordon b Poysden | .............. | 77 |
| D M Hodgson, c Umeed b Poysden | ............. | 18 |
| M J Waite, b Poysden | ....................... | 7 |
| * R M Pyrah, c McKay b Javid | ................. | 4 |
| T R Craddock, lbw b Javid | .................... | 1 |
| M D Fisher, c Umeed b Poysden | ............... | 2 |
| K Carver, c McKay b Gordon | .................. | 39 |
| J D Warner, c and b Javid | .................... | 5 |
| B O Coad, not out | .......................... | 12 |
| Extras lb 2, nb 2, w 2 | | 6 |
| Total (48.4 overs) | ............ | 214 |

*FoW:* 1-31 (Gibson), 2-72 (Hodd), 3-141 (Maxwell), 4-144 (Hodgson), 5-150 (Pyrah), 6-154 (Waite), 7-154 (Craddock), 8-156 (Fisher), 9-186 (Warner), 10-214 (Carver)

| | O | M | R | W |
|---|--:|--:|--:|--:|
| Adair ................ | 7 | 0 | 39 | 1 |
| Milnes ............... | 10 | 1 | 56 | 0 |
| Gordon .............. | 7.4 | 0 | 37 | 1 |
| Thomason ............ | 4 | 0 | 20 | 1 |
| Poysden ............. | 10 | 2 | 39 | 4 |
| Javid ................ | 10 | 3 | 21 | 3 |

### WARWICKSHIRE

| | | |
|---|---|--:|
| A R I Umeed, c Hodd b Coad | ................... | 7 |
| * F R J Coleman, lbw b Fisher | .................. | 16 |
| T P Lewis, c Waite b Fisher | .................... | 1 |
| J P Webb, c Hodd b Coad | ...................... | 6 |
| A Javid, lbw b Pyrah | ......................... | 14 |
| A D Thomason, c Craddock b Fisher | ............ | 38 |
| T P Milnes, c and b Waite | ..................... | 21 |
| § P J McKay, not out | ......................... | 49 |
| M R Adair, c Coad b Fisher | .................... | 2 |
| J E Poysden, c Hodd b Pyrah | ................... | 1 |
| R O Gordon, b Fisher | ......................... | 0 |
| Extras lb 7, nb 2, w 2 | | 11 |
| Total (39.5 overs) | .................. | 166 |

*FoW:* 1-22 (Umeed), 2-23 (Lewis), 3-26 (Coleman), 4-32 (Webb), 5-68 (Javid), 6-92 (Milnes), 7-149 (Thomason), 8-157 (Adair), 9-165 (Poysden), 10-166 (Gordon)

| | O | M | R | W |
|---|--:|--:|--:|--:|
| Fisher .................. | 9.5 | 2 | 35 | 5 |
| Coads .................. | 8 | 2 | 16 | 2 |
| Pyrah .................. | 9 | 1 | 30 | 2 |
| Waite .................. | 4 | 0 | 19 | 1 |
| Warner ................. | 4 | 0 | 22 | 0 |
| Carver ................. | 3 | 0 | 17 | 0 |
| Maxwell ............... | 2 | 0 | 20 | 0 |

Umpires: I J Dixon and S A Garrett          Scorers: H Clayton and S Smith

## Second Eleven Trophy
## Durham v. Yorkshire

Played at Durham ICG, Chester-le-Street on August 10, 2015
*Durham won by 123 runs at 5.40pm*

Toss won by the Yorkshire — Durham 2 points, Yorkshire 0 points

### DURHAM

| | | |
|---|---|---|
| * K K Jennings, not out | | 151 |
| § P Mustard, c Callis b Carver | | 63 |
| C S MacLeod, not out | | 104 |
| S W Poynter | | |
| J A Tattersall | | |
| W J Weighell | | |
| J Coughlin | Did not bat | |
| G S Randhawa | | |
| B J McCarthy | | |
| G T Main | | |
| G H I Harding | | |
| Extras b 2, lb 9, w 2 | | 13 |
| Total (1 wkt, 50 overs) | | 331 |

*FoW:* 1-148 (Mustard)

| | O | M | R | W |
|---|---|---|---|---|
| Shaw | 7 | 0 | 51 | 0 |
| Ashraf | 8 | 0 | 65 | 0 |
| Rhodes | 5 | 0 | 36 | 0 |
| Pyrah | 10 | 1 | 30 | 0 |
| Imtiaz | 5 | 0 | 16 | 0 |
| Carver | 9 | 0 | 64 | 1 |
| Gibson | 6 | 0 | 58 | 0 |

### YORKSHIRE

| | |
|---|---|
| E Callis, c Poynter b Randhawa | 46 |
| R Gibson, c Tattersall b Main | 52 |
| * W M H Rhodes, c Harding b Randhawa | 15 |
| § D M Hodgson, c Macleod b Randhawa | 28 |
| M Hussain, lbw b Harding | 18 |
| J A Thompson, b Harding | 0 |
| R M Pyrah, b Randhawa | 0 |
| Y Imtiaz, c Mustard b MacLeod | 15 |
| J Shaw, c Poynter b Coughlin | 10 |
| K Carver, not out | 7 |
| M A Ashraf, c Harding b MacLeod | 4 |
| Extras lb 7, w 6 | 13 |
| Total (45.2 overs) | 208 |

*FoW:* 1-85 (Gibson), 2-119 (Callis), 3-127 (Rhodes), 4-156 (Hussain), 5-156 (Thompson),
6-157 (Pyrah), 7-179 (Hodgson), 8-196 (Shaw), 9-198 (Imtiaz), 10-208 (Ashraf)

| | O | M | R | W |
|---|---|---|---|---|
| Weighell | 4 | 0 | 30 | 0 |
| McCarthy | 5 | 0 | 27 | 0 |
| Jennings | 6 | 0 | 26 | 0 |
| Main | 5 | 1 | 18 | 1 |
| Randhawa | 10 | 1 | 36 | 4 |
| Harding | 10 | 0 | 49 | 2 |
| Coughlin | 3 | 0 | 9 | 1 |
| MacLeod | 2.2 | 0 | 6 | 2 |

Umpires: P R Gardner and M A Gough — Scorers: R V Hilton and H Clayton

# SECOND ELEVEN TROPHY 2015

*The counties played only six games in the group stages against nine previously.*
*The change was made to accommodate more T20 games.*

## NORTHERN GROUP – FINAL TABLE *(2014 in brackets)*

| | | P | W | L | No result | Aban. | Points | Net run rate |
|---|---|---|---|---|---|---|---|---|
| 1 | Derbyshire (9) . . . . . . . . . . . | 6 | 6 | 0 | 0 | 0 | 12 | 1.463 |
| 2 | Durham (8) . . . . . . . . . . . . . | 6 | 5 | 0 | 1 | 0 | 11 | 1.273 |
| 3 | Worcestershire (6) . . . . . . . . | 6 | 3 | 2 | 1 | 0 | 7 | -0.041 |
| 4 | Unicorns (-) . . . . . . . . . . . . | 6 | 3 | 3 | 0 | 0 | 6 | 0.089 |
| 5 | Leicestershire (1) . . . . . . . . | 6 | 3 | 3 | 0 | 0 | 6 | -0.193 |
| 6 | Lancashire (2) . . . . . . . . . . . | 6 | 3 | 3 | 0 | 0 | 6 | -0.358 |
| 7 | Northamptonshire (-) . . . . . . | 6 | 2 | 4 | 0 | 0 | 4 | -0.261 |
| 8 | Nottinghamshire (5) . . . . . . | 6 | 2 | 4 | 0 | 0 | 4 | -0.503 |
| 9 | Warwickshire (4) . . . . . . . . | 6 | 1 | 5 | 0 | 0 | 2 | -0.283 |
| **10** | **Yorkshire (3) . . . . . . . . . . . .** | **6** | **1** | **5** | **0** | **0** | **2** | **-1.095** |

## SOUTHERN GROUP – FINAL TABLE *(2014 in brackets)*

| | | P | W | L | No result | Aban. | Points | Net run rate |
|---|---|---|---|---|---|---|---|---|
| 1 | Somerset (4) . . . . . . . . . . . . | 6 | 4 | 0 | 0 | 2 | 10 | 1.910 |
| 2 | Surrey (5) . . . . . . . . . . . . . . | 6 | 4 | 1 | 1 | 0 | 9 | 1.379 |
| 3 | Essex (3) . . . . . . . . . . . . . . . | 6 | 3 | 2 | 1 | 0 | 7 | 0.988 |
| 4 | Kent (6) . . . . . . . . . . . . . . . | 6 | 3 | 2 | 0 | 1 | 7 | 0.823 |
| 5 | Middlesex (2) . . . . . . . . . . . | 6 | 3 | 3 | 0 | 0 | 7 | -0.147 |
| 6 | Hampshire (9) . . . . . . . . . . . | 6 | 3 | 3 | 0 | 0 | 6 | -0.278 |
| 7 | Sussex (1) . . . . . . . . . . . . . . | 6 | 3 | 3 | 0 | 0 | 6 | -0.617 |
| 8 | Gloucestershire (10) . . . . . . | 6 | 2 | 4 | 0 | 0 | 4 | -0.406 |
| 9 | Glamorgan (-) . . . . . . . . . . . | 6 | 1 | 3 | 0 | 2 | 4 | -0.457 |
| 10 | MCC Young Cricketers (-) . . | 6 | 0 | 5 | 0 | 1 | 1 | -2.560 |

## SEMI-FINALS

Surrey (241) lost to Derbyshire (243-5) by five wickets
Somerset (281) lost to Durham (282-4) by six wickets

## FINAL

Derbyshire (247-8) beat Durham (237) by 10 runs

# SECOND ELEVEN TROPHY

## PREVIOUS WINNERS

1986    **Northamptonshire**, who beat Essex by 14 runs
1987    **Derbyshire**, who beat Hampshire by 7 wickets
1988    **Yorkshire**, who beat Kent by 7 wickets
1989    **Middlesex**, who beat Kent by 6 wickets
1990    **Lancashire**, who beat Somerset by 8 wickets
1991    **Nottinghamshire**, who beat Surrey by 8 wickets
1992    **Surrey**, who beat Northamptonshire by 8 wickets
1993    **Leicestershire**, who beat Sussex by 142 runs
1994    **Yorkshire**, who beat Leicestershire by 6 wickets
1995    **Leicestershire**, who beat Gloucestershire by 3 runs
1996    **Leicestershire**, who beat Durham by 46 runs
1997    **Surrey**, who beat Gloucestershire by 3 wickets
1998    **Northamptonshire**, who beat Derbyshire by 5 wickets
1999    **Kent**, who beat Hampshire by 106 runs.
2000    **Leicestershire,** who beat Hampshire by 25 runs.
2001    **Surrey**, who beat Somerset by 6 wickets
2002    **Kent**, who beat Hampshire by 5 wickets
2003    **Hampshire**, who beat Warwickshire by 8 wickets
2004    **Worcestershire**, who beat Essex by 8 wickets
2005    **Sussex**, who beat Nottinghamshire by 6 wickets
2006    **Warwickshire**, who beat Yorkshire by 93 runs
2007    **Middlesex**, who beat Somerset by 1 run
2008    **Hampshire**, who beat Essex by 7 runs
2009    **Yorkshire,** who beat Lancashire by 2 wickets
2010    **Essex**, who beat Lancashire by 14 runs
2011    **Nottinghamshire**, who beat Lancashire by 4 wickets
2012    **Lancashire**, who beat Durham by 76 runs
2013    **Lancashire**, who beat Nottinghamshire by 76 runs
2014    **Leicestershire**, who beat Lancashire by 168 runs

# SECOND ELEVEN TROPHY
# AVERAGES 2015

Played 6     Won 1     Lost 5

## BATTING AND FIELDING

*(Qualification 3 innings)*

| Player | M. | I. | N.O. | Runs | H.S. | Avge | 100s | 50s | ct/st |
|---|---|---|---|---|---|---|---|---|---|
| K Carver | 5 | 5 | 3 | 66 | 39 | 33.00 | 0 | 0 | 1 |
| B O Coad | 4 | 3 | 2 | 32 | 12* | 32.00 | 0 | 0 | 1 |
| M J Waite | 5 | 5 | 0 | 146 | 50 | 29.20 | 0 | 1 | 2 |
| J A Tattersall | 3 | 3 | 0 | 79 | 42 | 26.33 | 0 | 0 | 3 |
| R Gibson | 5 | 5 | 0 | 124 | 52 | 24.80 | 0 | 1 | 1 |
| A J Hodd | 3 | 3 | 0 | 60 | 28 | 20.00 | 0 | 0 | 4 |
| D M Hodgson | 6 | 6 | 0 | 114 | 38 | 19.00 | 0 | 0 | 3 |
| R M Pyrah | 5 | 5 | 0 | 78 | 69 | 15.60 | 0 | 1 | 1 |
| J A Thompson | 4 | 4 | 1 | 43 | 43* | 14.33 | 0 | 0 | 1 |
| J C Wainman | 3 | 3 | 0 | 40 | 38 | 13.33 | 0 | 0 | 0 |
| M Hussain | 3 | 3 | 0 | 19 | 18 | 6.33 | 0 | 0 | 0 |
| T R Craddock | 4 | 4 | 0 | 13 | 6 | 3.25 | 0 | 0 | 1 |

### Also batted

| Player | M. | I. | N.O. | Runs | H.S. | Avge | 100s | 50s | ct/st |
|---|---|---|---|---|---|---|---|---|---|
| G J Maxwell | 2 | 2 | 0 | 16 | 77 | 58.00 | 0 | 1 | 0 |
| E Callis | 2 | 2 | 0 | 59 | 46 | 29.50 | 0 | 0 | 1 |
| W M H Rhodes | 2 | 2 | 0 | 41 | 26 | 20.50 | 0 | 0 | 0 |
| Y Imtiaz | 1 | 1 | 0 | 15 | 15 | 15.00 | 0 | 0 | 0 |
| B L Ainsley | 1 | 1 | 0 | 10 | 10 | 10.00 | 0 | 0 | 0 |
| J Shaw | 1 | 1 | 0 | 10 | 10 | 10.00 | 0 | 0 | 0 |
| J D Warner | 2 | 2 | 0 | 17 | 12 | 8.50 | 0 | 0 | 0 |
| M A Ashraf | 3 | 2 | 1 | 5 | 4 | 5.00 | 0 | 0 | 1 |
| M D Fisher | 1 | 1 | 0 | 2 | 2 | 2.00 | 0 | 0 | 0 |
| L E Plunkett | 1 | 1 | 0 | 2 | 2 | 2.00 | 0 | 0 | 0 |

## BOWLING

*(Qualification 5 wickets)*

| Player | Overs | Mdns | Runs | Wkts | Avge | Best | 4wI |
|---|---|---|---|---|---|---|---|
| M D Fisher | 9.5 | 2 | 35 | 5 | 7.00 | 5-35 | 1 |
| B O Coad | 30 | 4 | 108 | 5 | 21.60 | 2-15 | 0 |

### Also bowled

| Player | Overs | Mdns | Runs | Wkts | Avge | Best | 4wI |
|---|---|---|---|---|---|---|---|
| J C Wainman | 16 | 3 | 61 | 3 | 20.33 | 3-39 | 0 |
| T R Craddock | 17.2 | 0 | 106 | 3 | 35.33 | 3-51 | 0 |
| M J Waite | 16.5 | 0 | 77 | 2 | 38.50 | 1-17 | 0 |
| R M Pyrah | 33 | 3 | 131 | 3 | 43.66 | 2-30 | 0 |
| M A Ashraf | 25 | 2 | 158 | 3 | 52.66 | 1-23 | 0 |
| W M H Rhodes | 10 | 0 | 60 | 1 | 60.00 | 1-24 | 0 |
| R Gibson | 14 | 0 | 86 | 1 | 86.00 | 1-15 | 0 |
| K Carver | 34.5 | 2 | 195 | 2 | 97.50 | 1-42 | 0 |
| Y Imtiaz | 5 | 0 | 16 | 0 | — | — | 0 |
| G J Maxwell | 5 | 0 | 43 | 0 | — | — | 0 |
| L E Plunkett | 7 | 0 | 29 | 0 | — | — | 0 |
| J Shaw | 7 | 0 | 51 | 0 | — | — | 0 |
| J A Thompson | 2 | 0 | 6 | 0 | — | — | 0 |
| J D Warner | 8.4 | 0 | 50 | 0 | — | — | 0 |

# Second Eleven Twenty20
## Lancashire v. Yorkshire

Played at Northop Hall, Flintshire, on May 8, 2015
*Lancashire won by 9 wickets (D/L method) at 1.04pm*

Toss won by Yorkshire      Lancashire 2 points, Yorkshire 0 points

### YORKSHIRE

| | |
|---|---|
| § A J Hodd, c Parry b Griffiths | 18 |
| R Gibson, c Lilley b Procter | 22 |
| D M Hodgson, c Mahmood b Parry | 7 |
| J A Tattersall, b Parry | 3 |
| W M H Rhodes, c Brown b Parkinson | 19 |
| * R M Pyrah, b Lilley | 5 |
| M J Waite, not out | 48 |
| J A Thompson, st Gowers b Parkinson | 2 |
| T R Craddock, not out | 8 |
| B O Coad | |
| M A Ashraf      Did not bat | |
| Extras lb 3, w 7 | 10 |
| Total (7 wkts, 20 overs) | 142 |

*FoW:* 1-37 (Gibson), 2-45 (Hodd), 3-53 (Tattersall), 4-54 (Hodgson), 5-65 (Pyrah), 6-86 (Rhodes), 7-102 (Thompson)

| | O | M | R | W |
|---|---|---|---|---|
| Lilley | 4 | 0 | 28 | 1 |
| Mahmood | 4 | 0 | 37 | 0 |
| Griffiths | 3 | 0 | 24 | 1 |
| Procter | 2 | 0 | 7 | 1 |
| Parry | 4 | 0 | 24 | 2 |
| Parkinson | 3 | 0 | 19 | 2 |

### LANCASHIRE

*When rain arrived Lancashire, with one wicket down,
needed to have scored 42 runs*

| | |
|---|---|
| H Hameed, c Rhodes b Pyrah | 5 |
| L S Livingstone, not out | 35 |
| K R Brown, not out | 4 |
| * S D Parry | |
| L A Procter | |
| A M Lilley | |
| G T Griffiths      Did not bat | |
| S Mahmood | |
| M W Parkinson | |
| § A M Gowers | |
| R P Jones | |
| Extras w 1 | 1 |
| Total (1 wkt, 7 overs) | 45 |

*FoW:* 1-12 (Hameed)

| | O | M | R | W |
|---|---|---|---|---|
| Ashraf | 2 | 0 | 13 | 0 |
| Coad | 1 | 0 | 11 | 0 |
| Waite | 1 | 0 | 13 | 0 |
| Pyrah | 2 | 0 | 4 | 1 |
| Craddock | 1 | 0 | 4 | 0 |

Umpires: P J Hartley and Naeem Ashraf      Scorers: C Rimmer and H Clayton

# Second Eleven Twenty20
## Lancashire v. Yorkshire

(Second game)

At Northop Hall, Flintshire, on May 8, 2015
*Match abandoned without a ball bowled*

No toss

Lancashire 1 point, Yorkshire 1 point

Umpires: P J Hartley and Naeem Ashraf

Scorers: C Rimmer and H Clayton

## Derbyshire v. Yorkshire

At Glossop CC on May 19, 2015
*Match abandoned without a ball bowled*

No toss

Derbyshire 1 point, Yorkshire 1 point

Umpires: A G Wharf and I P Laurence

Scorers: J Wallis and H Clayton

## Derbyshire v. Yorkshire

(Second game)

At Glossop CC on May 19, 2015
*Match abandoned without a ball bowled*

No toss

Derbyshire 1 point, Yorkshire 1 point

Umpires: A G Wharf and I P Laurence

Scorers: J Wallis and H Clayton

## Second Eleven Twenty20
## Yorkshire v. Nottinghamshire

Played at Harrogate CC on May 21, 2015
*Yorkshire won by 8 runs (D/L method) at 3.15pm*

Toss won by Nottinghamshire      Yorkshire 2 points, Notinghamshire 0 points

### YORKSHIRE

| | | |
|---|---|---:|
| E Callis, c Gidman b Hutton | .................... | 10 |
| R Gibson, lbw b Tillcock | ..................... | 59 |
| § D M Hodgson, lbw b Hutton | .................. | 9 |
| * W M H Rhodes, lbw b Gidman | ................ | 0 |
| J A Tattersall, lbw b Gidman | .................. | 25 |
| M J Waite, b Kitt | ............................ | 0 |
| J A Thompson, b Tillcock | ..................... | 7 |
| S A Patterson, not out | ........................ | 18 |
| K Carver, c Tillcock b Hutton | ................ | 13 |
| B O Coad, not out | ........................... | 0 |
| M A Ashraf | | |
| J C Wainman      Did not bat | | |
| Extras lb 7, w 6 | | 13 |
| Total (8 wkts, 20 overs) | ................. | 154 |

*FoW:* 1-10 (Callis), 2-51 (Hodgson), 3-52 (Rhodes), 4-111 (Tattersall), 5-112 (Waite), 6-119 (Thompson), 7-132 (Gibson), 8-152 (Carver).

| | O | M | R | W |
|---|---|---|---|---|
| Hutton .................. | 4 | 0 | 21 | 3 |
| Kitt ..................... | 3 | 0 | 27 | 1 |
| Gidman .................. | 4 | 0 | 43 | 2 |
| Webster ................. | 1 | 0 | 7 | 0 |
| Tillcock ................. | 4 | 0 | 16 | 2 |
| Wood ................... | 3 | 0 | 27 | 0 |
| Marshall ................ | 1 | 0 | 6 | 0 |

### NOTTINGHAMSHIRE

*When rain arrived Nottinghamshire, with four wickets down, needed to have scored 131 runs*

| | | |
|---|---|---:|
| W T Root, c Hodgsdon b Gibson | ................ | 27 |
| A Dal, c Hodgson b Ashraf | ................... | 4 |
| S K W Wood, c Gibson b Rhodes | ............... | 5 |
| W R S Gidman, b Patterson | ................... | 19 |
| B A Hutton, not out | .......................... | 28 |
| A D Tillcock, not out | ........................ | 32 |
| § T J Moores | | |
| * P J Franks | | |
| C R Marshall      Did not bat | | |
| B M Kitt | | |
| S W Webster | | |
| Extras b 1, lb 4, w 2 | .................... | 7 |
| Total (4 wkts, 16 overs) | ................ | 122 |

*FoW:* 1-15 (Dal), 2-22 (Wood), 3-44 (Root), 4-70 (Gidman).

| | O | M | R | W |
|---|---|---|---|---|
| Coad ..................... | 3 | 0 | 30 | 0 |
| Ashraf .................. | 3 | 0 | 27 | 1 |
| Rhodes .................. | 2 | 0 | 18 | 1 |
| Gibson .................. | 3 | 0 | 15 | 1 |
| Patterson ................ | 3 | 0 | 11 | 1 |
| Carver .................. | 2 | 0 | 16 | 0 |

Umpires: N A Mallender and S J Malone      Scorers: H Clayton and Mrs A Cusworth

# Second Eleven Twenty20
# Yorkshire v. Nottinghamshire

Played at Harrogate CC on May 21, 2015

*Nottinghamshire won by 6 wickets at 5.42pm*

Toss won by Nottinghamshire     Yorkshire 0 points, Nottinghamshire 2 points

## YORKSHIRE

| | | |
|---|---|---:|
| A W Gale, b Hutton | ............................ | 6 |
| R Gibson, c Wood b Tillcock | ................... | 20 |
| § D M Hodgson, lbw b Tillcock | ................ | 44 |
| * W M H Rhodes, not out | ....................... | 61 |
| J A Tattersall, st Moores b Marshall | .............. | 4 |
| M J Waite, not out | ............................ | 23 |
| J A Thompson | | |
| K Carver | | |
| M A Ashraf | Did not bat | |
| M D Fisher | | |
| J C Wainman | | |
| Extras b 1, lb 1, w 3 | ......................... | 5 |
| Total (4 wkts, 20 overs) | ................ | 163 |

*FoW:* 1-12 (Gale), 2-49 (Gibson), 3-80 (Hodgson), 4-90 (Tattersall)

| | O | M | R | W |
|---|---:|---:|---:|---:|
| Wood | 2 | 0 | 11 | 0 |
| Kitt | 4 | 0 | 29 | 0 |
| Hutton | 4 | 0 | 38 | 1 |
| Webster | 2 | 0 | 16 | 0 |
| Gidman | 3 | 0 | 28 | 0 |
| Tillcock | 4 | 0 | 33 | 2 |
| Marshall | 1 | 0 | 6 | 1 |

## NOTTINGHAMSHIRE

| | | |
|---|---|---:|
| W T Root, c Thompson b Wainman | ............... | 1 |
| A Dal, b Waite | ........................... | 30 |
| S K W Wood, b Gibson | ...................... | 44 |
| W R S Gidman, not out | ...................... | 60 |
| * B A Hutton, c Tattersall b Fisher | ................ | 17 |
| A D Tillcock, not out | ........................ | 6 |
| § T J Moores | | |
| C R Marshall | | |
| B M Kitt | Did not bat | |
| S W Webster | | |
| M Carter | | |
| Extras lb 2, nb 2, w 4 | ...................... | 8 |
| Total (4 wkts, 18.1 overs) | ............... | 166 |

*FoW:* 1-2 (Root), 2-41 (Dal), 3-117 (Wood), 4-146 (Hutton)

| | O | M | R | W |
|---|---:|---:|---:|---:|
| Wainman | 3.1 | 0 | 20 | 1 |
| Ashraf | 3 | 0 | 32 | 0 |
| Waite | 1 | 0 | 9 | 1 |
| Fisher | 4 | 0 | 32 | 1 |
| Gibson | 3 | 0 | 27 | 1 |
| Rhodes | 1 | 0 | 11 | 0 |
| Carver | 3 | 0 | 33 | 0 |

Umpires: N A Mallender and S J Malone     Scorers: H Clayton and Mrs A Cusworth

## Second Eleven Twenty20
## Yorkshire v. Durham

Played at York CC on May 26, 2015
*Yorkshire won by 9 runs at 2.16pm*

Toss won by Durham                    Yorkshire 2 points, Durham 0 points

### YORKSHIRE

| | | |
|---|---|---:|
| § A J Hodd, c Poynter b Harrison | ................. | 22 |
| R Gibson, c McCarthy b Carse | ..................... | 11 |
| * D M Hodgson, c Buckley b Hickey | ............. | 23 |
| J A Tattersall, st Poynter b Hickey | ............... | 30 |
| E Callis, c and b Pringle | ......................... | 2 |
| M J Waite, run out (McCarthy) | .................. | 20 |
| J A Thompson, not out | .......................... | 15 |
| M D Fisher, run out (Burnham) | ................. | 4 |
| M A Ashraf | | |
| K Carver | Did not bat | |
| B O Coad | | |
| Extras lb 3, nb 4 | ......................... | 7 |
| Total (7 wkts, 20 overs) | ................ | 134 |

*FoW:* 1-33 (Hodd), 2-33 (Gibson), 3-81 (Hodgson), 4-84 (Callis), 5-100 (Tattersall), 6-119 (Waite), 7-134 (Fisher).

| | O | M | R | W |
|---|---|---|---|---|
| Pringle ................. | 4 | 0 | 25 | 1 |
| Harrison ................. | 4 | 0 | 32 | 1 |
| McCarthy ................. | 2 | 0 | 18 | 0 |
| Carse ................. | 3 | 1 | 12 | 1 |
| Bousfield ................. | 2 | 0 | 14 | 0 |
| Hickey ................. | 4 | 0 | 23 | 2 |
| Buckley ................. | 1 | 0 | 7 | 0 |

### DURHAM

| | | |
|---|---|---:|
| G Clark, c Waite b Ashraf | ....................... | 1 |
| A J Hickey, c Coad b Waite | ..................... | 21 |
| * R D Pringle, c Hodd b Ashraf | ................. | 10 |
| J T A Burnham, c Hodgson b Ashraf | ............. | 6 |
| § S W Poynter, c Fisher b Waite | ................. | 4 |
| D E Budge, c Hodd b Waite | ..................... | 10 |
| J P Bousfield, not out | .......................... | 37 |
| B A Carse, c Coad b Gibson | ..................... | 13 |
| B J McCarthy, b Coad | .......................... | 9 |
| R S Buckley, not out | ............................ | 0 |
| J Harrison | Did not bat | |
| Extras lb 3, nb 2, w 9 | ..................... | 14 |
| Total (8 wkts, 20 overs) | ................ | 125 |

*FoW:* 1-16 (Clark), 2-31 (Pringle), 3-39 (Burnham), 4-44 (Hickey), 5-52 (Poynter), 6-62 (Budge), 7-94 (Carse), 8-125 (McCarthy).

| | O | M | R | W |
|---|---|---|---|---|
| Ashraf ................. | 4 | 0 | 13 | 3 |
| Coad ................. | 2 | 0 | 21 | 1 |
| Fisher ................. | 4 | 0 | 26 | 0 |
| Waite ................. | 4 | 0 | 23 | 3 |
| Gibson ................. | 4 | 0 | 31 | 1 |
| Carver ................. | 2 | 0 | 8 | 0 |

Umpires: I J Dixon and B V Taylor                    Scorers: H Clayton and G Maddison

# Second Eleven Twenty20
## Yorkshire v. Durham

Played at York CC on May 26, 2015
*Durham won by 5 wickets at 5.39pm*

Toss won by Yorkshire                    Yorkshire 0 points, Durham 2 points

### YORKSHIRE

| | | |
|---|---|---|
| A J Hodd, c Poynter b Bousfield | | 41 |
| R Gibson, c Clark b Bousfield | | 30 |
| * § D M Hodgson, c Clark b Carse | | 38 |
| J A Tattersall, c Clark b Carse | | 8 |
| J A Thompson, b Carse | | 11 |
| M J Waite, c Poynter b Harrison | | 10 |
| E Callis, b Carse | | 4 |
| M D Fisher, not out | | 3 |
| K Carver, not out | | 1 |
| B O Coad | | |
| M A Ashraf | Did not bat | |
| Extras lb 4, w 6 | | 10 |
| Total (7 wkts, 20 overs) | | 156 |

*FoW:* 1-49 (Gibson), 2-115 (Hodd), 3-122 (Hodgson), 4-136 (Tattersall), 5-137 (Thompson), 6-143 (Callis), 7-155 (Waite)

| | O | M | R | W |
|---|---|---|---|---|
| Pringle | 2 | 0 | 16 | 0 |
| Harrison | 4 | 0 | 32 | 1 |
| McCarthy | 2 | 0 | 12 | 0 |
| Bousfield | 3 | 0 | 28 | 2 |
| Whitehead | 4 | 0 | 22 | 0 |
| Carse | 4 | 0 | 30 | 4 |
| Hickey | 1 | 0 | 12 | 0 |

### DURHAM

| | | |
|---|---|---|
| G Clark. lbw b Waite | | 50 |
| A J Hickey, c Waite b Carver | | 35 |
| * R D Pringle, b Coad | | 35 |
| § S W Poynter, b Carver, | | 9 |
| D E Budge, c Tattersall b Coad | | 1 |
| J T A Burnham, not out | | 14 |
| J P Bousfield, not out | | 8 |
| B A Carse | | |
| B G Whitehead | Did not bat | |
| B J McCarthy | | |
| J Harrison | | |
| Extras lb 5, w 3 | | 8 |
| Total (5 wkts, 18.5 overs) | | 160 |

*FoW:* 1-81 (Clark), 2-99 (Hickey), 3-136 (Poynter), 4-137 (Budge), 5-137 (Pringle)

| | O | M | R | W |
|---|---|---|---|---|
| Fisher | 4 | 1 | 24 | 0 |
| Ashraf | 4 | 0 | 38 | 0 |
| Waite | 2 | 0 | 24 | 1 |
| Coad | 3.5 | 1 | 30 | 2 |
| Carver | 4 | 0 | 30 | 2 |
| Gibson | 1 | 0 | 9 | 0 |

Umpires: I J Dixon and B V Taylor          Scorers: H Clayton and G Maddison

# Second Eleven Twenty20
## Yorkshire v. Northamptonshire

Played at Barnsley CC on June 11, 2015
*Northamptonshire won by 10 runs at 2.17pm*

Toss won by Northamptonshire          Yorkshire 0 points, Northamptonshire 2 points

### NORTHAMPTONSHIRE

| | | |
|---|---|---:|
| A S T West, not out | .......................... | 91 |
| K J Coetzer, c Wainman b Gibson | ................ | 3 |
| * § D Murphy, c Finch b Rhodes | ................ | 48 |
| S A Zaib, not out | ............................ | 20 |
| A Patel | | |
| M J Plater | | |
| T B Sole | | |
| B W Sanderson | Did not bat | |
| M A Chambers | | |
| D A Buton | | |
| J Jakeman | | |
| Extras b 1, lb 4, nb 3, w 1 | ................ | 9 |
| Total (2 wkts, 20 overs) | ................ | 171 |

*FoW:* 1-21 (Coetzer), 2-131 (Murphy)

| | O | M | R | W |
|---|---|---|---|---|
| Ashraf | 2 | 0 | 31 | 0 |
| Wainman | 3 | 0 | 22 | 0 |
| Gibson | 4 | 0 | 32 | 1 |
| Pyrah | 3 | 0 | 27 | 0 |
| Middlebrook | 4 | 0 | 19 | 0 |
| Carver | 2 | 0 | 23 | 0 |
| Rhodes | 2 | 0 | 12 | 1 |

### YORKSHIRE

| | | |
|---|---|---:|
| A J Finch, b Burton | | 13 |
| A J Hodd, c Patel b Burton | ...................... | 4 |
| R Gibson, c Sanderson b Coetzer | ................ | 36 |
| § D M Hodgson, c Sole b Chambers | .............. | 20 |
| W M H Rhodes, c Zaib b Sole | .............. | 9 |
| * R M Pyrah, not out | ........................ | 40 |
| M J Waite, c Jakeman b Burton | .............. | 1 |
| J D Middlebrook, st Murphy b Coetzer | .............. | 7 |
| J C Wainman, c Sanderson b Chambers | .............. | 11 |
| K Carver, not out | ............................ | 0 |
| M A Ashraf | Did not bat | |
| Extras b 8, lb 3, nb 2, w 7 | ................ | 20 |
| Total (8 wkts, 20 overs) | ................ | 161 |

*FoW:* 1-22 (Finch), 2-25 (Hodd), 3-79 (Gibson), 4-89 (Rhodes), 5-90 (Hodgson), 6-107 (Waite), 7-122 (Middlebrook), 8-149 (Wainman)

| | O | M | R | W |
|---|---|---|---|---|
| Sole | 2 | 0 | 18 | 1 |
| Sanderson | 4 | 0 | 32 | 0 |
| Chambers | 4 | 0 | 26 | 2 |
| Burton | 3 | 0 | 19 | 3 |
| Coetzer | 4 | 0 | 38 | 2 |
| Jakeman | 3 | 0 | 17 | 0 |

Umpires: S J Malone and P R Polland          Scorers: H Clayton and M E Woolley

# Second Eleven Twenty20
# Yorkshire v. Northamptonshire

Played at Barnsley CC on June 11, 2015
*Northamptonshire won by 4 runs at 5.53pm*

Toss won by Northamptonshire          Yorkshire 0 points, Northamptonshire 2 points

## NORTHAMPTONSHIRE

| | | |
|---|---|---:|
| A S T West, c Lees b Ashraf | | 21 |
| K J Coetzer, c Rhodes b Pyrah | | 18 |
| * § D Murphy, not out | | 71 |
| S A Zaib, c Gibson b Carver | | 4 |
| A Patel, c Wainman b Gibson | | 33 |
| M J Plater, c Gibson b Rhodes | | 15 |
| J D Fawcett, run out (Rhodes) | | 5 |
| M A Chambers, not out | | 1 |
| B W Sanderson | | |
| D A Buton | Did not bat | |
| J Jakeman | | |
| Extras b 1, w 9 | | 10 |
| Total (6 wkts, 20 overs) | | 178 |

*FoW:* 1-24 (West), 2-601 (Coetzer), 3-68 (Zaib), 4-131 (Patel), 5-156 (Plater), 6-174 (Fawcett)

| | O | M | R | W |
|---|---|---|---|---|
| Ashraf | 3 | 0 | 31 | 1 |
| Wainman | 1 | 0 | 10 | 0 |
| Gibson | 4 | 0 | 39 | 1 |
| Rhodes | 4 | 0 | 33 | 1 |
| Pyrah | 4 | 0 | 22 | 1 |
| Carver | 2 | 0 | 21 | 1 |
| Finch | 2 | 0 | 21 | 0 |

## YORKSHIRE

| | | |
|---|---|---:|
| A Z Lees, run out (Sanderson) | | 10 |
| A J Finch, c Plater b Sanderson | | 32 |
| R Gibson, b Jakeman | | 34 |
| § D M Hodgson, c Burton b Sanderson | | 47 |
| W M H Rhodes, c Zaib b Chanbers | | 35 |
| * R M Pyrah, c Zaib b Chanbers | | 0 |
| M J Waite, not out | | 10 |
| E Callis, not out | | 2 |
| J C Wainman | | |
| K Carver | Did not bat | |
| M A Ashraf | | |
| Extras lb 2, w 2w | | 4 |
| Total (6 wkts, 20 overs) | | 174 |

*FoW:* 1-24 (Lees), 2-50 (Finch), 3-100 (Gibson), 4-159 (Hodgson), 5-162 (Rhodes), 6-162 (Pyrah)

| | O | M | R | W |
|---|---|---|---|---|
| Sanderson | 4 | 0 | 30 | 2 |
| Chambers | 4 | 0 | 40 | 2 |
| Burton | 4 | 0 | 21 | 0 |
| Coetzer | 2 | 0 | 35 | 0 |
| Jakeman | 3 | 0 | 23 | 1 |
| Zaib | 3 | 0 | 23 | 0 |

Umpires: S J Malone and P R Polland          Scorers: H Clayton and M E Woolley

# Second Eleven Twenty20
## Worcestershire v. Yorkshire

Played at Barnt Green on June 25, 2015
*Yorkshire won by 33 runs at 2.02pm*

Toss won by Yorkshire

Worcestershire 0 points, Yorkshire 2 points

### YORKSHIRE

| | | |
|---|---|--:|
| § A J Hodd, c Fraine b G H Rhodes | | 28 |
| R Gibson, lbw b Barnard | | 11 |
| D M Hodgson, c Clarke b Munro | | 14 |
| * W M H Rhodes, c Williams b Choudhry | | 43 |
| R M Pyrah, c and b Bernard | | 31 |
| J A Thompson, not out | | 31 |
| M J Waite, not out | | 0 |
| M A Ashraf | | |
| K Carver | Did not bat | |
| B O Coad | | |
| J Shaw | | |
| Extras lb 2, w 1 | | 3 |
| Total (5 wkts, 20 overs) | | 161 |

*FoW:* 1-12 (Gibson), 2-47 (Hodgson), 3-66 (Hodd), 4-114 (Rhodes), 5-149 (Pyrah)

| | O | M | R | W |
|---|---|---|---|---|
| Kervezee | 4 | 0 | 32 | 0 |
| Barnard | 4 | 0 | 40 | 2 |
| Brown | 1 | 0 | 11 | 0 |
| Munro | 3 | 0 | 17 | 1 |
| Choudhry | 4 | 0 | 30 | 1 |
| G H Rhodes | 2 | 0 | 14 | 1 |
| Williams | 2 | 0 | 15 | 0 |

### WORCESTERSHIRE

| | | |
|---|---|--:|
| § J M Clarke, c W M H Rhodes b Coad | | 0 |
| G H Rhodes, lbw b Coad | | 0 |
| E G Barnard, c Hodgson b Ashraf | | 5 |
| C Munro, c Shaw b Carver | | 56 |
| A N Kervezee, b Coad | | 45 |
| A Hepburn, b Carver | | 3 |
| * S H Choudhry, c Gibson b Carver | | 6 |
| W A R Fraine, run out (Coad) | | 6 |
| R C J Aucott, c Gibson b Carver | | 0 |
| D R Williams, lbw b Carver | | 0 |
| P R Brown, not out | | 0 |
| Extras lb 4, w 3 | | 7 |
| Total (15 overs) | | 128 |

*FoW:* 1-1 (Clarke), 2-2 (G H Rhodes), 3-9 (Barnard), 4-74 (Munro), 5-87 (Hepburn), 6-101 (Choudhry); 7-109 (Fraine); 8-109 (Aucott); 9-109 (Williams); 10-128 (Kervezee)

| | O | M | R | W |
|---|---|---|---|---|
| Coad | 3 | 0 | 25 | 3 |
| Ashraf | 2 | 0 | 16 | 1 |
| Shaw | 1 | 0 | 19 | 0 |
| W M H Rhodes, | 1 | 0 | 10 | 0 |
| Carver | 4 | 1 | 20 | 5 |
| Pyrah | 4 | 0 | 34 | 0 |

Umpires: M Burns and A C Harris

Scorers: P M Mellish and J R Virr

# Second Eleven Twenty20
## Worcestershire v. Yorkshire

Played at Barnt Green on June 25, 2015
*Worcestershire won by 15 runs at 5.43pm*

Toss won by Worcestershire        Worcestershire 2 points, Yorkshire 0 points

### WORCESTERSHIRE

| | |
|---|---|
| R K Oliver, c Hodgson b Warner | 17 |
| * S H Choudhry, c Waite b Shaw | 2 |
| T C Fell, c Thompson b Warner | 18 |
| A N Kervezee, c Shaw b Rhodes | 34 |
| § J M Clarke, c Shaw b Maxwell | 56 |
| A Hepburn, c Hodgson b Rhodes | 5 |
| G H Rhodes, lbw b Carver | 4 |
| W A R Fraine, c Maxwell b W M H Rhodes | 24 |
| C J Russell, c Maxwell b Shaw | 4 |
| D R Williams, not out | 13 |
| P R Brown, not out | 0 |
| Extras b 4, w 3 | 7 |
| Total (9 wkts, 20 overs) | 184 |

*FoW:* 1-19 (Choudhry), 2-28 (Oliver), 3-39 (Fell), 4-126 (Clarke), 5-137 (Hepburn), 6-142 (W M H Rhodes), 7-144 (Kervezee), 8-171 (Russell), 9-172 (Fraine)

| | O | M | R | W |
|---|---|---|---|---|
| Maxwell | 3 | 0 | 19 | 1 |
| Ashraf | 2 | 0 | 30 | 0 |
| Shaw | 2 | 0 | 18 | 2 |
| Warner | 2 | 0 | 23 | 2 |
| Carver | 4 | 0 | 32 | 1 |
| Gibson | 3 | 0 | 21 | 0 |
| W M H Rhodes | 4 | 0 | 37 | 3 |

### YORKSHIRE

| | |
|---|---|
| G J Maxwell, c Fell b Russell | 14 |
| R Gibson, c Fell b Russell | 7 |
| § D M Hodgson, st Clarke b Williams | 47 |
| * W M H Rhodes, b G H Rhodes | 25 |
| J A Thompson, c G H Rhodes b Williams | 13 |
| M J Waite, c Oliver b Hepburn | 31 |
| R M Pyrah, c Rhodes b Russell | 10 |
| J Shaw, run out (Kervezee) | 0 |
| J D Warner, b Choudhry | 4 |
| K Carver, not out | 10 |
| M A Ashraf, not out | 0 |
| Extras b 1, lb 1, nb 2, w 4 | 8 |
| Total (9 wkts, 20 overs) | 169 |

*FoW:* 1-17 (Maxwell), 2-21 (Gibson), 3-80 (W M H Rhodes), 4-100 (Thompson), 5-140 (Waite), 6-144 (Hodgson), 7-144 (Shaw), 8-149 (Warner), 9-168 (Pyrah)

| | O | M | R | W |
|---|---|---|---|---|
| Kervesee | 4 | 0 | 28 | 0 |
| Russell | 4 | 0 | 36 | 3 |
| Brown | 1 | 0 | 14 | 0 |
| Choudhry | 4 | 0 | 26 | 1 |
| Rhodes | 3 | 0 | 32 | 1 |
| Williams | 3 | 0 | 18 | 2 |
| Hepburn | 1 | 0 | 13 | 1 |

Umpires: M Burns and A C Harris       Scorers: P M Mellish and J R Virr

# SECOND ELEVEN TWENTY20 2015

Two matches played against the same opponents at the same venue on the same day. Previously there were four groups, but these were arranged into two larger groups for 2015 so that more *T20* cricket could be played. Therefore no comparision with finishing positions in 2014 is given.

## NORTHERN GROUP

|    |                   | P  | W | L | Tie | No result | Aban. | Points | Net run rate |
|----|-------------------|----|---|---|-----|-----------|-------|--------|--------------|
| 1  | Lancashire        | 12 | 9 | 2 | 0   | 0         | 1     | 19     | 1.904        |
| 2  | Durham            | 12 | 8 | 1 | 1   | 1         | 1     | 19     | 0.982        |
| 3  | Worcestershire    | 12 | 6 | 4 | 0   | 0         | 2     | 14     | 0.097        |
| 4  | Nottinghamshire   | 12 | 7 | 5 | 0   | 0         | 0     | 14     | -0.415       |
| 5  | Derbyshire        | 12 | 4 | 4 | 0   | 1         | 3     | 12     | -0.243       |
| 6  | Northamptonshire  | 12 | 5 | 7 | 0   | 0         | 0     | 10     | -0.340       |
| 7  | Warwickshire      | 12 | 5 | 7 | 0   | 0         | 0     | 10     | -0.393       |
| **8**  | **Yorkshire**  | **12** | **3** | **6** | **0** | **0** | **3** | **9** | **-0.086** |
| 9  | Unicorns          | 12 | 2 | 7 | 1   | 0         | 2     | 7      | -0.595       |
| 10 | Leicestershire    | 12 | 3 | 9 | 0   | 0         | 0     | 6      | -0.655       |

## SOUTHERN GROUP

|    |                       | P  | W | L | Tie | No result | Aban. | Points | Net run rate |
|----|-----------------------|----|---|---|-----|-----------|-------|--------|--------------|
| 1  | Kent                  | 12 | 8 | 1 | 0   | 1         | 2     | 19     | 1.939        |
| 2  | Middlesex             | 12 | 6 | 2 | 0   | 0         | 4     | 16     | 1.548        |
| 3  | Sussex                | 12 | 6 | 4 | 0   | 0         | 2     | 14     | 0.707        |
| 4  | Hampshire             | 12 | 6 | 4 | 0   | 0         | 2     | 14     | 0.148        |
| 5  | Essex                 | 12 | 5 | 5 | 0   | 0         | 2     | 12     | 0.323        |
| 6  | Somerset              | 12 | 6 | 6 | 0   | 0         | 0     | 12     | 0.008        |
| 7  | Gloucestershire       | 12 | 2 | 4 | 0   | 0         | 6     | 10     | -0.424       |
| 8  | Glamorgan             | 12 | 4 | 8 | 0   | 0         | 0     | 8      | -0.867       |
| 9  | MCC Young Cricketers  | 12 | 4 | 8 | 0   | 0         | 0     | 8      | -1.311       |
| 10 | Surrey                | 12 | 2 | 7 | 0   | 1         | 2     | 7      | -1.426       |

## SEMI-FINALS

| Kent (184-9) | beat Durham (161-8) | by 23 runs |
| Lancashire (148-4) | lost to Middlesex (151-6) | by four wickets |

## FINAL

| Kent (115) | lost to Middlesex (118-6) | by four wickets |

## PREVIOUS WINNERS

| 2011 | **Sussex**, who beat Durham by 24 runs |
| 2012 | **England Under-19s**, who beat Sussex by eight wickets |
| 2013 | **Surrey**, who beat Middlesex by six runs |
| 2014 | **Leicesterhire**, who beat Somerset by 11 runs |

# SECOND ELEVEN TWENTY20
## AVERAGES 2015

Played 12     Won 3     Lost 6     Abandoned 3

## BATTING AND FIELDING

*(Qualification 3 innings)*

| Player | M. | I. | N.O. | Runs | H.S. | Avge | 50s | Strike Rate | Ct/St |
|---|---|---|---|---|---|---|---|---|---|
| W M H Rhodes | 7 | 7 | 1 | 192 | 61* | 32.00 | 1 | 142.22 | 3 |
| M J Waite | 9 | 9 | 4 | 143 | 48* | 28.60 | 0 | 138.83 | 0 |
| D M Hodgson | 9 | 9 | 0 | 249 | 47 | 27.66 | 0 | 111.16 | 6 |
| R Gibson | 9 | 9 | 0 | 230 | 59 | 25.55 | 1 | 149.35 | 5 |
| K Carver | 8 | 4 | 3 | 24 | 13 | 24.00 | 0 | 120.00 | 0 |
| A J Hodd | 5 | 5 | 0 | 113 | 41 | 22.60 | 0 | 120.21 | 2 |
| R M Pyrah | 5 | 5 | 1 | 86 | 40* | 21.50 | 0 | 110.25 | 0 |
| J A Thompson | 7 | 6 | 2 | 79 | 31* | 19.75 | 0 | 123.43 | 2 |
| J A Tattersall | 5 | 5 | 0 | 70 | 30 | 14.00 | 0 | 109.37 | 2 |
| E Callis | 4 | 4 | 1 | 18 | 10 | 6.00 | 0 | 58.06 | 0 |
| **Also batted** | | | | | | | | | |
| A J Finch | 2 | 2 | 0 | 45 | 32 | 22.50 | 0 | 140.62 | 1 |
| G J Maxwell | 1 | 1 | 0 | 14 | 14 | 14.00 | 0 | 200.00 | 2 |
| J C Wainman | 4 | 1 | 0 | 11 | 11 | 11.00 | 0 | 137.50 | 0 |
| A Z Lees | 1 | 1 | 0 | 10 | 10 | 10.00 | 0 | 111.11 | 1 |
| M D Fisher | 3 | 2 | 1 | 7 | 4 | 7.00 | 0 | 100.00 | 1 |
| J D Middlebrook | 1 | 1 | 0 | 7 | 7 | 7.00 | 0 | 77.77 | 0 |
| A W Gale | 1 | 1 | 0 | 6 | 6 | 6.00 | 0 | 66.66 | 0 |
| J D Warner | 1 | 1 | 0 | 4 | 4 | 4.00 | 0 | 66.66 | 0 |
| M A Ashraf | 9 | 1 | 1 | 0 | 0* | — | 0 | — | 0 |
| B O Coad | 5 | 1 | 1 | 0 | 0* | — | 0 | — | 2 |
| J Shaw | 2 | 1 | 0 | 0 | 0 | — | 0 | — | 3 |
| T R Craddock | 1 | 1 | 1 | 8 | 8* | — | 0 | — | 0 |
| S A Patterson | 1 | 1 | 1 | 18 | 18* | — | 0 | — | 0 |

## BOWLING

*(Qualification 5 wickets)*

| Player | Overs | Mdns | Runs | Wkts | Avge | Best | Strike Rate | Econ. | 4wI |
|---|---|---|---|---|---|---|---|---|---|
| M J Waite | 8 | 0 | 69 | 5 | 13.80 | 3-23 | 13.80 | 8.62 | 0 |
| B O Coad | 12.5 | 1 | 117 | 6 | 19.50 | 3-25 | 12.83 | 9.11 | 0 |
| W M H Rhodes | 14 | 0 | 121 | 6 | 20.16 | 3-37 | 14.00 | 8.64 | 0 |
| K Carver | 23 | 1 | 183 | 9 | 20.33 | 5-20 | 15.33 | 7.95 | 1 |
| R Gibson | 22 | 0 | 174 | 5 | 34.80 | 1-15 | 26.40 | 7.90 | 0 |
| M A Ashraf | 25 | 0 | 231 | 6 | 38.50 | 3-13 | 25.00 | 9.24 | 0 |
| **Also bowled** | | | | | | | | | |
| J D Warner | 2 | 0 | 23 | 2 | 11.50 | 2-23 | 6.00 | 11.50 | 0 |
| J Shaw | 3 | 0 | 37 | 2 | 18.50 | 2-18 | 9.00 | 12.33 | 0 |
| R M Pyrah | 13 | 0 | 87 | 2 | 43.50 | 1-4 | 39.00 | 6.69 | 0 |
| S A Patterson | 3 | 0 | 11 | 1 | 11.00 | 1-11 | 18.00 | 3.66 | 0 |
| G J Maxwell | 3 | 0 | 19 | 1 | 19.00 | 1-19 | 18.00 | 6.33 | 0 |
| J C Wainman | 7.1 | 0 | 52 | 1 | 52.00 | 1-20 | 43.00 | 7.25 | 0 |
| M D Fisher | 12 | 1 | 82 | 1 | 82.00 | 1-32 | 72.00 | 6.83 | 0 |
| J D Middlebrook | 4 | 0 | 19 | 0 | — | — | — | 4.75 | 0 |
| A J Finch | 2 | 0 | 21 | 0 | — | — | — | 10.50 | 0 |
| T R Craddock | 1 | 0 | 4 | 0 | — | — | — | 4.00 | 0 |

# Other Second Eleven Match
## Yorkshire v. Glamorgan

Played at Headingley, Leeds, on April 14, 15 and 16, 2015
*Yorkshire won by 7 wickets at 12.01pm on the Third Day*

Toss won by Glamorgan

Close of play: First Day, Yorkshire 194-9 (Shaw 10, Fisher 0, 55 overs); Second Day, Yorkshire (2) 52-2 (Gale 34, Callis 5, 19 overs)

| GLAMORGAN First Innings | | | Second Innings | |
|---|---|---|---|---|
| D M Housego, lbw b Fisher | 8 | | c Tattersall b Coad | 51 |
| U A Qureshi, c Thompson b Shaw | 26 | | c Waite b Wainman | 4 |
| * B J Wright, c Callis b Wainman | 48 | | run out (Thompson) | 15 |
| W G R Vanderspar, c Tattersall b Shaw | 0 | | c Thompson b Wainman | 13 |
| G C Holmes, c Hodgson b Fisher | 7 | | b Fisher | 46 |
| § A G Milton, c Callis b Fisher | 0 | | b Shaw | 16 |
| A G Salter, lbw b Wainman | 8 | | b Wainman | 23 |
| R A J Smith, lbw b Shaw | 16 | | Did not bat | |
| J R Murphy, not out | 33 | | (8) lbw b Tattersall | 25 |
| K A Bull, c Hodgson b Wainman | 0 | | (9) lbw b Shaw | 8 |
| D Penrhyn Jones, c Tattersall b Coad | 5 | | (10) not out | 4 |
| L J Carey | Did not bat | | (11) st Hodgson b Coad | 21 |
| Extras b 1, nb 12, w 1 | 14 | | Extras b 1, lb 5, nb 12 | 18 |
| Total (46.3 overs) | 165 | | Total (62.5 overs) | 244 |

FoW: 1-10 (Housego), 2-70 (Qureshi), 3-70 (Vanderspar), 4-86 (Holmes), 5-90 (Milton),
1st 6-94 (Wright), 7-109 (Salter), 8-130 (Smith), 9-135 (Bull), 10-165 (Penrhyn Jones)

FoW: 1-16 (Qureshi), 2-42 (Wright), 3-87 (Vanderspar), 4-91 (Housego), 5-116 (Milton),
2nd 6-168 (Holmes), 7-205 (Salter), 8-209 (Murphy), 9-217 (Bull), 10-244 (Carey)

| | O | M | R | W | | O | M | R | W |
|---|---|---|---|---|---|---|---|---|---|
| Fisher | 11 | 2 | 34 | 3 | Fisher | 11 | 2 | 47 | 1 |
| Wainman | 3 | 1 | 71 | 3 | Wainman | 12 | 3 | 41 | 3 |
| Shaw | 11 | 1 | 41 | 3 | Shaw | 16 | 3 | 55 | 2 |
| Coad | 9.3 | 2 | 18 | 1 | Coad | 13.5 | 5 | 36 | 2 |
| Gibson | 2 | 2 | 0 | 0 | Gibson | 4 | 0 | 28 | 0 |
| | | | | | Tattersall | 6 | 2 | 31 | 1 |

| YORKSHIRE First Innings | | | Second Innings | |
|---|---|---|---|---|
| E Callis, c Murphy b Penrhyn Jones | 42 | | (4) not out | 30 |
| J A Tattersall, lbw b Penrhyn Jones | 17 | | c Wright b Murphy | 5 |
| * § D M Hodgson, b Carey | 30 | | c Milton b Carey | 8 |
| A W Gale, lbw b Vanderspar | 12 | | (1) c Milton b Penrhyn Jones | 71 |
| R Gibson, lbw b Carey | 7 | | not out | 24 |
| M J Waite, lbw b Salter | 23 | | | |
| J A Thompson, c Housego b Penrhyn Jones | 5 | | | |
| T R Craddock, b Salter | 14 | | | |
| J Shaw, not out | 47 | | | |
| J C Wainman, b Bull | 1 | | | |
| M D Fisher, b Penrhyn Jones | 19 | | | |
| B O Coad | Did not bat | | | |
| Extras b 6, lb 6, nb 33, w 1 | 46 | | Extras lb 8, nb 2 | 10 |
| Total (73 overs) | 263 | | Total (3 wkts, 35.4 overs) | 148 |

FoW: 1-58 (Tattersall), 2-85 (Callis), 3-109 (Gale), 4-125 (Hodgson), 5-130 (Gibson),
1st 6-160 (Thompson), 7-168 (Waite), 8-191 (Craddock), 9-194 (Wainman), 10-263 (Fisher)
2nd: 1-6 (Tattersall), 2-41 (Hodgson), 3-118 (Gale)

| | O | M | R | W | | O | M | R | W |
|---|---|---|---|---|---|---|---|---|---|
| Smith | 5.5 | 2 | 31 | 0 | Penrhyn Jones | 7 | 0 | 37 | 1 |
| Murphy | 7 | 1 | 24 | 0 | Murphy | 11 | 1 | 35 | 1 |
| Penrhyn Jones | 18 | 3 | 63 | 4 | Carey | 11 | 0 | 36 | 1 |
| Carey | 15 | 1 | 62 | 2 | Bull | 6.4 | 1 | 32 | 0 |
| Salter | 14 | 6 | 34 | 2 | | | | | |
| Vanderspar | 8.1 | 2 | 32 | 1 | | | | | |
| Bull | 5 | 2 | 5 | 1 | | | | | |

Umpires: I L Herbert and N A Mallender        Scorers: J A Virr and G Watkins

## Other Second Eleven Match
## Gloucestershire v. Yorkshire

Played at Bristol on April 20, 21 and 22, 2015

*Gloucestershire won by an innings and 63 runs at 12.44pm on the Third Day*

Toss won by Gloucestershire

Close of play: First Day, Gloucestershire 135-2 (Gilmour 12, Cockbain 21, 31 overs);
Second Day, Yorkshire (2) 70-5 (Waite 15, Thompson 17, 27 overs)

### YORKSHIRE

| First Innings | | Second Innings | |
|---|--:|---|--:|
| E Callis, c Howell b M D Taylor | 2 | c Howell b M D Taylor | 8 |
| J A Tattersall, c Herring b Hampton | 6 | b Payne | 6 |
| * § D M Hodgson, not out | 105 | c Herring b Payne | 1 |
| B L Ainsley, c Hammond b Howell | 31 | c Herring b M D Taylor | 10 |
| R Gibson, c Herring b Montgomery | 52 | b Payne | 6 |
| M J Waite, b Montgomery | 0 | c Cockbain b M D Taylor | 42 |
| J A Thompson, c Cockbain b M D Taylor | 15 | c Hammond b Payne | 32 |
| J Shaw, b Howell | 2 | c Gilmour b Payne | 0 |
| J C Wainman, c Smith b Hampton | 6 | lbw b Payne | 6 |
| K Carver, b Smith | 22 | c Herring b Montgomery | 25 |
| B O Coad, run out (Hampton) | 0 | not out | 23 |
| J E G Logan | Did not bat | | |
| Extras b 5, lb 16 | 21 | Extras b 1, lb 6, nb 2 | 9 |
| Total (72.2 overs) | 256 | Total (51.1 overs) | 168 |

*FoW:* 1-2 (Callis), 2-2 (Tattersall), 3-60 (Ainsley), 4-152 (Gibson), 5-152 (Waite),
1st 6-177 (Thompson), 7-188 (Shaw), 8-197 (Wainman), 9-256 (Carver). 10-256 (Coad)
*FoW:* 1-14 (Callis), 2-14 (Tattersall), 3-25 (Ainsley), 4-25 (Hodgson), 5-42 (Gibson),
2nd 6-98 (Thompson), 7-98 (Shaw), 8-118 (Wainman), 9-118 (Waite), 10-168 (Carver)

| | O | M | R | W | | O | M | R | W |
|---|--:|--:|--:|--:|---|--:|--:|--:|--:|
| M D Taylor | 12 | 2 | 30 | 2 | M D Taylor | 13 | 3 | 43 | 3 |
| Hampton | 14 | 2 | 50 | 2 | Hampton | 2 | 0 | 15 | 0 |
| Payne | 13 | 3 | 48 | 0 | Payne | 15 | 3 | 33 | 6 |
| Montgomery | 8 | 1 | 37 | 2 | Howell | 4 | 1 | 20 | 0 |
| Howell | 13 | 5 | 26 | 2 | Montgomery | 9.1 | 4 | 32 | 1 |
| Smith | 5.2 | 0 | 20 | 1 | Hammond | 3 | 1 | 3 | 0 |
| J M R Taylor | 7 | 1 | 24 | 0 | Smith | 5 | 2 | 15 | 0 |

### GLOUCESTERSHIRE

| | |
|---|--:|
| M A H Hammond, lbw b Waite | 44 |
| T M J Smith, lbw b Wainman | 50 |
| B S Gilmour, b Shaw | 54 |
| * I A Cockbain, lbw b Coad | 150 |
| B A C Howell, c Thompson b Carver | 15 |
| § C L Herring, b Logan | 11 |
| J M R Taylor, c Logan b Shaw | 128 |
| J L N Garrett, c Tattersall b Coad | 1 |
| R J Montgomery, c Gibson b Coad | 2 |
| D A Payne, b Shaw | 14 |
| M D Taylor, not out | 0 |
| T R G Hampton | Did not bat |
| Extras b 5, lb 4, nb 8, w 1 | 18 |
| Total (105.2 overs) | 487 |

*FoW:* 1-98 (Smith), 2-98 (Hammond), 3-212 (Gilmour), 4-271 (Howell), 5-288 (Herring), 6-400
(Cockbain), 7-406 (Garrett), 8-408 (Montgomery), 9-478 (Payne), 10-487 (J M R Taylor)

| | O | M | R | W |
|---|--:|--:|--:|--:|
| Coad | 25 | 7 | 79 | 3 |
| Wainman | 19 | 4 | 92 | 1 |
| Shaw | 18.2 | 1 | 74 | 3 |
| Waite | 17 | 2 | 81 | 1 |
| Carver | 19 | 1 | 112 | 1 |
| Logan | 7 | 1 | 40 | 1 |

Umpires: I D Blackwell and R C Hampshire          Scorers: S Cashmore and J R Virr

# Other Second Eleven Match
## Kent v. Yorkshire

Played at Polo Farm, Canterbury, on May 12, 13, 14 and 15, 2015
*Match drawn at 6.24pm on the Fourth Day*

Toss won by Yorkshire

Close of play: First Day, Yorkshire 455-8 (Waite 64, Coad 0, 96 overs); Second Day, Kent 336-6 (Meddings 7, Claydon 20, 83 overs); Third Day. no play

| First Innings | YORKSHIRE | | Second innings | |
|---|---|---|---|---|
| J A Tattersall, c Riley b Claydon | 12 | | E Callis, c Sehmi b Hunn | 5 |
| A J Hodd, c Ball b Bernard | 179 | | J A Tattersall, c Sehmi b Smith | 16 |
| * § D M Hodgson, c Blake b Hunn | 14 | | not out | 73 |
| R M Pyrah, c Sehmi b Claydon | 16 | | M Hussain, c Dickson b Hunn | 4 |
| L E Plunkett, c Blake b Claydon | 101 | | R Gibson, c Hunn b Imran Qayyum | 72 |
| R Gibson, c and b Ball | 34 | | M J Waite, not out | 1 |
| M J Waite, not out | 85 | | K Carver | |
| J C Wainman, c Blake b Ball | 3 | | M A Ashraf | |
| K Carver, b Hunn | 7 | | J Shutt | Did not bat |
| B O Coad, c Sehmi b Hunn | 19 | | J D Warner | |
| M A Ashraf, lbw b Hunn | 0 | | J C Wainman | |
| J Shutt | Did not bat | | B O Coad | |
| Extras b 10, lb 8, nb 4, w 6 | 28 | | Extras b 4, nb 2 | 6 |
| Total (106.3 overs) | 498 | | Total (4 wkts dec, 29 overs) | 177 |

*FoW:* 1-28 (Tattersall), 2-99 (Hodgson), 3-159 (Pyrah), 4-278 (Hodd), 5-325 (Gibson),
1st 6-412 (Plunkett), 7-435 (Carver), 8-454 (Carver), 9-498 (Coad), 10-498 (Ashraf)
2nd 1-6 (Callis), 2-40 (Tattersall), 3-49 (Hussain), 4-162 (Gibson)

| | O | M | R | W | | | O | M | R | W |
|---|---|---|---|---|---|---|---|---|---|---|
| Claydon | 29 | 6 | 98 | 3 | | Hunn | 8 | 0 | 17 | 2 |
| Hunn | 21.3 | 1 | 71 | 4 | | Smith | 9 | 0 | 65 | 1 |
| Bernard | 11 | 0 | 93 | 1 | | Bernard | 5 | 0 | 29 | 0 |
| Ball | 27 | 0 | 122 | 2 | | Imran Qayyum | 4 | 0 | 25 | 1 |
| Riley | 10 | 1 | 43 | 0 | | Riley | 3 | 0 | 37 | 0 |
| Imran Qayyum | 3 | 0 | 23 | 0 | | | | | | |
| Dickson | 5 | 0 | 30 | 0 | | | | | | |

| First Innings | KENT | | Second innings | |
|---|---|---|---|---|
| N J Selman, c Hodd b Wainman | 0 | | c Waite b Coad | 82 |
| S R Dickson, c Pyrah b Plunkett | 139 | | c Wainman b Waite | 65 |
| A J Ball, c Plunkett b Ashraf | 92 | | Z Crawley, st Hodgson b Shutt | 58 |
| * A J Blake, c Tattersall b Plunkett | 7 | | B Dial, b Coad | 2 |
| B Dial, c Hodd b Wainman | 44 | | § R T Sehmi, c Hodgson b Shutt | 1 |
| § R T Sehmi, c Hodd b Ashraf | 7 | | J Meddings, run out (Wainman) | 20 |
| J Meddings, not out | 7 | | C F Hartley, c Hussain b Ashraf | 37 |
| M E Claydon, not out | 20 | | D C E Smith, b Ashraf | 17 |
| A E N Riley | | | b Ashraf, | 0 |
| M D Hunn | Did not bat | | not out | 3 |
| Imran Qayyum | | | not out | 0 |
| H R Bernard | | | Did not bat | |
| Extras b 12, lb 8, nb 4, w 1 | 25 | | Extras b 8, lb 1, nb 2 | 11 |
| Total (6 wkts dec, 83 overs) | 336 | | Total (9 wkts, 67 overs) | 296 |

*FoW:* 1-0 (Selman), 2-228 (Dickson), 3-240 (Blake), 4-273 (Ball), 5-291 (Sehmi),
1st 6-314 (Dial)
*FoW:* 1-93 (Dickson), 2-206 (Selman), 3-209 (Dial), 4-217 (Crawley), 5-222 (Sehmi),
2nd 6-269 (Hartley), 7-290 (Meddings), 8-291 (Riley), 9-296 (Smith)

| | O | M | R | W | | | O | M | R | W |
|---|---|---|---|---|---|---|---|---|---|---|
| Wainman | 11 | 3 | 55 | 2 | | Wainman | 9 | 0 | 47 | 0 |
| Ashraf | 17 | 6 | 37 | 2 | | Ashraf | 13 | 1 | 49 | 3 |
| Pyrah | 9 | 4 | 25 | 0 | | Coad | 14 | 5 | 40 | 2 |
| Plunkett | 15 | 4 | 39 | 2 | | Warner | 10 | 2 | 37 | 0 |
| Coad | 10 | 2 | 47 | 0 | | Waite | 4 | 0 | 19 | 1 |
| Carver | 7 | 0 | 35 | 0 | | Shutt | 17 | 2 | 95 | 2 |
| Shutt | 14 | 0 | 78 | 0 | | | | | | |

Full substitutes: Yorkshire — E Callis for L E Plunkett, M Hussain for A J Hodd and J D Warner for R M Pyrah; Kent — C F Hartley for A J Ball, Z Crawley for A J Blake and D C E Smith for M E Claydon.

Umpires: R C Ellis and R J Warren

Scorers: A L Bateup and J R Virr

Played at Hove on August 4, 5, 6 and 7, 2015
*Sussex won by 9 wickets at 12.23pm on the Fourth Day*

Toss won by Yorkshire

Close of play: First Day, Yorkshire 285-8 (Firn 75, Ashraf 11, 97 overs); Second Day, Sussex 394-6 (Cammish 58, Burgoyne 41, 88 overs); Third Day, Yorkshire 234-9 (Ashraf 47, Shutt 6, 93 overs)

| First Innings | YORKSHIRE | Second Innings | |
|---|---|---|---|
| E Callis, lbw b Anyon | 21 | run out (van Buuren) | 20 |
| B L Ainsley, c Jackson b Sakande | 29 | c Garton b Anyon | 15 |
| M Hussain, c Hudson-Prentice b Hobden | 24 | c Moses b Burgoyne | 24 |
| * § D M Hodgson, c Jackson b Sakande | 25 | lbw b Hudson-Prentice | 14 |
| Y Imtiaz, c Jackson b Sakande | 1 | b van Buuren | 2 |
| J A Thompson, lbw b Sakande | 0 | lbw b Burgoyne | 6 |
| J Shaw, lbw b van Buuren | 57 | lbw b van Buuren | 11 |
| N J Firn, b Whittingham | 75 | b Burgoyne | 16 |
| J C Wainman, c Jackson b Sakande | 21 | c Jackson b Anyon | 27 |
| M A Ashraf, not out | 12 | not out | 49 |
| J Shutt, b Whittingham | 0 | c Burgoyne b Whittinham | 8 |
| Extras b 2, lb 3, nb 16 | 21 | Extras b 22, lb 23, nb 6 | 51 |
| Total (102.2 overs) | 286 | Total (96.1 overs) | 243 |

*FoW:* 1-48 (Ainsley), 2-71 (Callis), 3-101 (Hussain), 4-106 (Imtiaz), 5-110 (Thompson), 1st 6-117 (Hodgson), 7-209 (Shaw), 8-248 (Wainman), 9-286 (Firn), 10-286 (Shutt)

*FoW:* 1-42 (Ainsley), 2-53 (Callis), 3-89 (Hodgson), 4-95 (Hussain), 5-101 (Imtiaz), 2nd 6-107 (Thompson), 7-127 (Shaw), 8-153 (Firn), 9-183 (Wainman), 10-243 (Shutt)

| | O | M | R | W | | O | M | R | W |
|---|---|---|---|---|---|---|---|---|---|
| Hobden | 12 | 3 | 41 | 1 | Whittingham | 8.1 | 3 | 23 | 1 |
| Sakande | 21 | 8 | 49 | 5 | Sakande | 5 | 1 | 14 | 0 |
| Whittingham | 15.2 | 2 | 70 | 2 | Burgoyne | 35 | 14 | 59 | 3 |
| Anyon | 10 | 2 | 23 | 1 | Anyon | 12 | 6 | 36 | 2 |
| Burgoyne | 22 | 6 | 64 | 0 | Garton | 10 | 4 | 16 | 0 |
| Hudson-Prentice | 10 | 4 | 13 | 0 | Moses | 4 | 0 | 18 | 0 |
| van Buuren | 12 | 1 | 21 | 1 | Hudson-Prentice | 5 | 1 | 11 | 1 |
| | | | | | van Buuren | 17 | 8 | 21 | 2 |

| First Innings | SUSSEX | Second Innings | |
|---|---|---|---|
| * § C F Jackson, c Callis b Thompson | 105 | not out | 30 |
| T J Haines, c Hussain b Wainman | 13 | c Firn b Ashraf | 14 |
| H Z Finch, b Thompson | 38 | not out | 31 |
| G L van Buuren, c Shaw b Shutt | 18 | | |
| F J Hudson-Prentice, c Hodgson b Ashraf | 27 | | |
| P D Salt, b Ashraf | 56 | | |
| L G Cammish, c Ainsley b Ashraf | 69 | | |
| P I Burgoyne, run out (Thompson) | 69 | | |
| G H S Garton, c Callis (Callis) | 11 | | |
| A Sakande, c Hodgson b Ashraf | 0 | | |
| S G Whittingham, not out | 8 | | |
| Extras b 6, lb 32 | 38 | Extras lb 1, nb 2 | 3 |
| Total (103.3 overs) | 452 | Total (1 wkt, 14.2 overs) | 78 |

J E Anyon, M E Hobden and T H Moses bowled but did not bat

*FoW:* 1-27 (Haines), 2-166 (Finch), 3-185 (Jackson), 4-193 (van Buuren), 5-275 (Hudson-Prentice), 1st 6-298 (Salt), 7-422 (Burgoyne), 8-435 (Garton), 9-441 (Sakande), 10-452 (Cammish

2nd: 1-24 (Haines)

| | O | M | R | W | | O | M | R | W |
|---|---|---|---|---|---|---|---|---|---|
| Wainman | 17 | 3 | 86 | 1 | Wainman | 5 | 2 | 23 | 0 |
| Ashraf | 28.3 | 9 | 73 | 4 | Ashraf | 5 | 2 | 10 | 1 |
| Firn | 4 | 0 | 47 | 0 | Shaw | 2.2 | 0 | 18 | 0 |
| Shaw | 16 | 5 | 81 | 0 | Shutt | 2 | 0 | 26 | 0 |
| Thompson | 15 | 4 | 64 | 2 | | | | | |
| Shutt | 18 | 5 | 65 | 1 | | | | | |
| Imtiaz | 5 | 0 | 30 | 0 | | | | | |

Umpires: T Burstow and R J Warren     Scorers: G J Irwin and Sarah R Smith

## Somerset v. Yorkshire

Played at Taunton Vale on September 2, 3 and 4, 2015
*Match drawn at 4.32pm on the Third Day*
Toss won by Yorkshire
Close of play, First Day, Yorkshire 31-2 (Rhodes 17, Brook 10, 15 overs); Second Day, Somerset 64-2 (Byrom 27, Rouse 21, 17 overs)

| First Innings | SOMERSET | | Second innings | |
|---|---|---|---|---|
| A J Hose, c Wainman b Shaw | 83 | | b Fisher | 0 |
| E J Byrom, c Thompson b Carver | 48 | | c Hodd b Warner | 27 |
| A W R Barrow, c Fisher b Leaning | 123 | | c Thompson b Shaw | 15 |
| T D Rouse, st Hodd b Leaning | 25 | | c Brook b Carver | 76 |
| J H Davey, b Warner | 8 | | c Gibson b Wainman | 19 |
| G A Bartlett, lbw b Leaning | 0 | | c Hodd b Waite | 84 |
| § M D Bates, lbw b Waite | 19 | | | |
| M T C Waller, c Fisher b Shaw | 29 | | (7) not out | 10 |
| * G H Dockrell, c Leaning b Shaw | 18 | | (8) not out | 24 |
| A C Thomas, not out | 0 | | | |
| D Klein, c Rhodes b Shaw | 0 | | | |
| L T Redrup | Did not bat | | | |
| Extras b 12, lb 10, nb 12, w 1 | 35 | | Extras b 5, lb 2, nb 4, w 5 | 16 |
| Total (86.5 overs) | 388 | | Total (6 wkts dec, 54 overs) | 271 |

*FoW*: 1-120 (Byrom), 2-167 (Hose), 3-275 (Rouse), 4-298 (Davey), 5-299 (Bartlett),
1st  6-334 (Bates), 7-346 (Barrow), 8-388 (Waller), 9-388 (Dockrell), 10-388 (Klein)
*FoW*: 1-0 (Hose), 2-30 (Barrow), 3-64 (Byrom), 4-93 (Davey), 5-231 (Bartlett),
2nd  6-239 (Rouse)

| | O | M | R | W | | | O | M | R | W |
|---|---|---|---|---|---|---|---|---|---|---|
| Fisher | 15 | 2 | 57 | 0 | | Fisher | 4 | 2 | 8 | 1 |
| Shaw | 9.5 | 4 | 25 | 4 | | Waite | 9 | 1 | 67 | 1 |
| Wainman | 12 | 1 | 65 | 0 | | Shaw | 5 | 1 | 15 | 1 |
| Warner | 9 | 2 | 37 | 1 | | Warner | 7 | 2 | 26 | 1 |
| Waite | 9 | 1 | 40 | 1 | | Rhodes | 4 | 1 | 7 | 0 |
| Carver | 14 | 1 | 61 | 1 | | Carver | 12 | 0 | 64 | 1 |
| Leaning | 18 | 0 | 81 | 3 | | Wainman | 4 | 0 | 14 | 1 |
| | | | | | | Leaning | 6 | 0 | 46 | 0 |
| | | | | | | Thompson | 3 | 0 | 17 | 0 |

| First Innings | YORKSHIRE | | Second innings | |
|---|---|---|---|---|
| * W M H Rhodes, c Bates b Redrup | 65 | | b Thomas | 17 |
| § A J Hodd, c Klein b Davey | 0 | | not out | 99 |
| J A Leaning, lbw b Thomas | 0 | | lbw b Klein | 12 |
| H C Brook, c Waller b Klein | 22 | | c Waller b Klein | 17 |
| R Gibson, lbw b Dockrell | 7 | | c Davey b Dockrell | 25 |
| M J Waite, c Bates b Davey | 59 | | not out | 0 |
| J A Thompson, lbw b Klein | 40 | | | |
| J Shaw, lbw b Dockrell | 18 | | | |
| M D Fisher, c and b Redrup | 33 | | | |
| J C Wainman, not out | 14 | | | |
| K Carver | | | | |
| J D Warner | Did not bat | | | |
| Extras b 9, lb 5, nb 30, w 1 | 45 | | Extras b 4, nb 2 | 6 |
| Total (9 wkts dec, 99.3 overs) | 303 | | Total (4 wkts, 36 overs) | 176 |

*FoW*: 1-8 (Hodd), 2-9 (Leaning), 3-92 (Brook), 4-104 (Rhodes), 5-108 (Gibson),
1st  6-158 (Thompson), 7-210 (Shaw), 8-266 (Waite), 9-303 (Fisher)
2nd  1-48 (Rhodes), 2-70 (Leaning), 3-122 (Brook), 4-169 (Gibson)

| | O | M | R | W | | | O | M | R | W |
|---|---|---|---|---|---|---|---|---|---|---|
| Thomas | 19 | 6 | 41 | 0 | | Thomas | 7 | 1 | 22 | 1 |
| Davey | 19 | 5 | 51 | 2 | | Davey | 4.5 | 1 | 26 | 0 |
| Klein | 19 | 2 | 95 | 2 | | Redrup | 8.1 | 0 | 56 | 0 |
| Redrup | 12.3 | 1 | 48 | 2 | | Klein | 9 | 1 | 29 | 2 |
| Dockrell | 20 | 3 | 33 | 2 | | Dockrell | 5 | 0 | 36 | 1 |
| Waller | 9 | 2 | 19 | 0 | | Rouse | 2 | 1 | 9 | 0 |
| Bartlett | 1 | 0 | 2 | 0 | | | | | | |

Umpires: S E Lavis and R J Warren          Scorers: Mrs L M Rhodes and J R Virr

# Other Second Eleven Match
# Yorkshire v. Lancashire

Played at Scarborough on September 15, 16 and 17, 2015
*Yorkshire won by 164 runs at 2.47pm on the Third Day*

Toss won by Lancashire

Close of play: First Day, no play; Second Day, Yorkshire 352-9 (Read 29, Warner 4, 86 overs)

| First Innings | YORKSHIRE | Second innings | |
|---|---|---|---|
| E Callis, b Sandham | 57 | | |
| M Hussain, c Livingstone b Mahmood | 16 | | |
| H C Brook, c Livingstone b Mahmood | 16 | c Gowers b Livingstone | 4 |
| R Gibson, lbw b Parkinson | 55 | | |
| M J Waite, c Sandham b Edwards | 143 | | |
| J A Thompson, st Gowers b Parkinson | 11 | | |
| Y Imtiaz, c Jones b Parkinson | 3 | | |
| * J Shaw, b Reece | 0 | | |
| J C Wainman, b Reece | 0 | | |
| § J Read, not out | 35 | (2) not out | 9 |
| J D Warner, run out (Bohannon) | 7 | (1) c Gowers b Bohannon | 0 |
| J E G Logan | Did Not Bat | | |
| Extras b 3, lb 5, nb 10 | 18 | Extras | 0 |
| Total (87.4 overs) | 361 | Total (2 wkts dec, 3.5 overs) | 13 |

*FoW:* 1-25 (Hussain), 2-47 (Brook), 3-136 (Gibson), 4-160 (Callis), 5-206 (Thompson),
1st 6-221 (Imtiaz), 7-230 (Shaw), 8-248 (Wainman), 9-338 ((Waite), 10-361 (Warner)
2nd 1-0 (Warner), 2-13 (Brook)

| | O | M | R | W | | O | M | R | W |
|---|---|---|---|---|---|---|---|---|---|
| Mahmood | 18 | 3 | 44 | 2 | Bohannon | 2 | 0 | 10 | 1 |
| Edwards | 14 | 4 | 52 | 1 | Livingstone | 1.5 | 0 | 3 | 1 |
| Lamb | 7 | 0 | 35 | 0 | | | | | |
| Sandham | 11 | 1 | 48 | 1 | | | | | |
| Reece | 13 | 1 | 73 | 2 | | | | | |
| Parkinson | 23 | 5 | 92 | 3 | | | | | |
| Bohannon | 1 | 0 | 6 | 0 | | | | | |
| Jones | 0.4 | 0 | 3 | 0 | | | | | |

## LANCASHIRE

*(First Innings forfeited)*

| | | |
|---|---|---|
| L M Reece, c Wainman b Warner | | 16 |
| H E Dearden, c Read b Waite | | 19 |
| * L A Procter, c Gibson b Logan | | 9 |
| L S Livingstone, c Thompson b Logan | | 47 |
| R P Jones, c Shaw b Logan | | 43 |
| J J Bohannon, st Read b Logan | | 21 |
| J Sandham, c Read b Logan | | 0 |
| D J Lamb, st Read b Logan | | 8 |
| § A M Gowers, c Callis b Logan | | 0 |
| M W Parkinson, c Waite b Logan | | 23 |
| G A Edwards, not out | | 0 |
| S Mahmood | Did not bat | |
| Extras b 4, lb 2, nb 18 | | 24 |
| Total (42.4 overs) | | 210 |

*FoW:* 1-44 (Dearden), 2-46 (Reece), 3-102 (Procter), 4-102 (Livingstone), 5-137 (Bohannon),
6-139 (Sandham), 7-157 (Lamb), 8-157 (Gowers), 9-210 (Jones), 10-210 (Parkinson)

| | O | M | R | W |
|---|---|---|---|---|
| Shaw | 7 | 0 | 41 | 0 |
| Wainman | 11 | 3 | 35 | 0 |
| Warner | 6 | 1 | 17 | 1 |
| Waite | 4 | 1 | 35 | 1 |
| Logan | 14.4 | 0 | 76 | 8 |

Umpires: K Fergusson and T Lungley          Scorers: J Emmerson and J R Virr

# RECORDS SECTION

All records in this section relate to First-Class Yorkshire matches except where stated

## HONOURS

### County Champions (34)
1867, 1870, 1893, 1896, 1898, 1900, 1901, 1902, 1905, 1908, 1912, 1919,
1922, 1923, 1924, 1925, 1931, 1932, 1933, 1935, 1937, 1938, 1939,
1946, 1959, 1960, 1962, 1963, 1966, 1967, 1968, 2001, 2014, 2015

### Joint Champions (2)
1869, 1949

### Promoted to Division 1
2005, 2012

### Gillette Cup Winners (2)
1965, 1969

### Cheltenham & Gloucester Trophy (1)
2002

### Benson & Hedges Cup Winners (1)
1987

### John Player Special League Winners (1)
1983

### Fenner Trophy Winners (3)
1972, 1974, 1981

### Asda Challenge Winners (1)
1987

### Ward Knockout Cup (1)
1989

### Joshua Tetley Festival Trophy (7)
1991, 1992 (Joint), 1993, 1994, 1996, 1997 and 1998

### Tilcon Trophy Winners (2)
1978 and 1988

### Pro-Arch Trophy (1)
2007-08

### Emirates Airlines T20 (1)
2015

### Second Eleven Champions (4)
1977, 1984, 1991, 2003

### Joint Champions (1)
1987

### Minor Counties Champions (5)
1947, 1957, 1958, 1968, 1971

### Under-25 Competition Winners (3)
1976, 1978, 1987

### Bain Clarkson Trophy Winners (2)
1988 and 1994

### Second Eleven Trophy (1)
2009

# YORKSHIRE'S CHAMPIONSHIP CAPTAINS

## 1867 to 2015

| | |
|---|---|
| * R Iddison (2) | 1867, 1870 |
| Lord Hawke (8) | 1893, 1896, 1898, 1900, 1901, 1902, 1905, 1908 |
| Sir Archibald White (1) | 1912 |
| D C F Burton (1) | 1919 |
| G Wilson (3) | 1922, 1923, 1924 |
| A W Lupton (1) | 1925 |
| F E Greenwood (2) | 1931, 1932 |
| A B Sellers (6) | 1933, 1935, 1937, 1938, 1939, 1946 |
| J R Burnet (1) | 1959 |
| J V Wilson (2) | 1960, 1962 |
| D B Close (4) | 1963, 1966, 1967, 1968 |
| D Byas (1) | 2001 |
| A W Gale (2) | 2014, 2015 |

## Joint Champions

| | |
|---|---|
| * R Iddison (1) | 1869 |
| N W D Yardley (1) | 1949 |

*\* R Iddison was captain when Yorkshire were Champion county, the County Championship starting in 1890.*

# RECORDS SECTION INDEX

**The County Championship**

The County Championship was officially constituted in 1890, and before that Yorkshire were generally considered Champions by the Press in 1867 and 1870, and equal top in 1869. From 1873 the list was generally accepted in the form as it is today.

|  |  | *Yorkshire's Position* |  |  | *Yorkshire's Position* |
|---|---|---|---|---|---|
| 1873 | Gloucestershire / Nottinghamshire | 7th | 1909 | Kent | 3rd |
| 1874 | Gloucestershire | 4th | 1910 | Kent | 8th |
| 1875 | Nottinghamshire | 4th | 1911 | Warwickshire | 7th |
| 1876 | Gloucestershire | 3rd | **1912** | **Yorkshire** | **1st** |
| 1877 | Gloucestershire | 7th | 1913 | Kent | 2nd |
| 1878 | Middlesex | 6th | 1914 | Surrey | 4th |
| 1879 | Nottinghamshire/Lancashire | 6th | **1919** | **Yorkshire** | **1st** |
| 1880 | Nottinghamshire | 5th | 1920 | Middlesex | 4th |
| 1881 | Lancashire | 3rd | 1921 | Middlesex | 3rd |
| 1882 | Nottinghamshire/Lancashire | 3rd | **1922** | **Yorkshire** | **1st** |
| 1883 | Nottinghamshire | 2nd | **1923** | **Yorkshire** | **1st** |
| 1884 | Nottinghamshire | 3rd | **1924** | **Yorkshire** | **1st** |
| 1885 | Nottinghamshire | 2nd | **1925** | **Yorkshire** | **1st** |
| 1886 | Nottinghamshire | 4th | 1926 | Lancashire | 2nd |
| 1887 | Surrey | 3rd | 1927 | Lancashire | 3rd |
| 1888 | Surrey | 2nd | 1928 | Lancashire | 4th |
| 1889 | Surrey/Lancashire / Nottinghamshire | 7th | 1929 | Nottinghamshire | 2nd |
| 1890 | Surrey | 3rd | 1930 | Lancashire | 3rd |
| 1891 | Surrey | 8th | **1931** | **Yorkshire** | **1st** |
| 1892 | Surrey | 6th | **1932** | **Yorkshire** | **1st** |
| **1893** | **Yorkshire** | **1st** | **1933** | **Yorkshire** | **1st** |
| 1894 | Surrey | 2nd | 1934 | Lancashire | 5th |
| 1895 | Surrey | 3rd | **1935** | **Yorkshire** | **1st** |
| **1896** | **Yorkshire** | **1st** | 1936 | Derbyshire | 3rd |
| 1897 | Lancashire | 4th | **1937** | **Yorkshire** | **1st** |
| **1898** | **Yorkshire** | **1st** | **1938** | **Yorkshire** | **1st** |
| 1899 | Surrey | 3rd | **1939** | **Yorkshire** | **1st** |
| **1900** | **Yorkshire** | **1st** | **1946** | **Yorkshire** | **1st** |
| **1901** | **Yorkshire** | **1st** | 1947 | Middlesex | 7th |
| **1902** | **Yorkshire** | **1st** | 1948 | Glamorgan | 4th |
| 1903 | Middlesex | 3rd | **1949** | **Yorkshire**/Middlesex | **1st** |
| 1904 | Lancashire | 2nd | 1950 | Lancashire/Surrey | 3rd |
| **1905** | **Yorkshire** | **1st** | 1951 | Warwickshire | 2nd |
| 1906 | Kent | 2nd | 1952 | Surrey | 2nd |
| 1907 | Nottinghamshire | 2nd | 1953 | Surrey | 12th |
| **1908** | **Yorkshire** | **1st** | 1954 | Surrey | 2nd |
|  |  |  | 1955 | Surrey | 2nd |
|  |  |  | 1956 | Surrey | 7th |
|  |  |  | 1957 | Surrey | 3rd |

|  |  | *Yorkshire's Position* |  |  | *Yorkshire's Position* |
|---|---|---|---|---|---|
| 1958 | Surrey | 11th | 1987 | Nottinghamshire | 8th |
| **1959** | **Yorkshire** | **1st** | 1988 | Worcestershire | 13th |
| **1960** | **Yorkshire** | **1st** | 1989 | Worcestershire | 16th |
| 1961 | Hampshire | 2nd | 1990 | Middlesex | 10th |
| **1962** | **Yorkshire** | **1st** | 1991 | Essex | 14th |
| **1963** | **Yorkshire** | **1st** | 1992 | Essex | 16th |
| 1964 | Worcestershire | 5th | 1993 | Middlesex | 12th |
| 1965 | Worcestershire | 4th | 1994 | Warwickshire | 13th |
| **1966** | **Yorkshire** | **1st** | 1995 | Warwickshire | 8th |
| **1967** | **Yorkshire** | **1st** | 1996 | Leicestershire | 6th |
| **1968** | **Yorkshire** | **1st** | 1997 | Glamorgan | 6th |
| 1969 | Glamorgan | 13th | 1998 | Leicestershire | 3rd |
| 1970 | Kent | 4th | 1999 | Surrey | 6th |
| 1971 | Surrey | 13th | 2000 | Surrey | 3rd |
| 1972 | Warwickshire | 10th | **2001** | **Yorkshire** | **1st** |
| 1973 | Hampshire | 14th | 2002 | Surrey | 9th |
| 1974 | Worcestershire | 11th | 2003 | Sussex | Div 2, 4th |
| 1975 | Leicestershire | 2nd | 2004 | Warwickshire | Div 2, 7th |
| 1976 | Middlesex | 8th | 2005 | Nottinghamshire | Div 2, 3rd |
| 1977 | Kent/Middlesex | 12th | 2006 | Sussex | Div 1, 6th |
| 1978 | Kent | 4th | 2007 | Sussex | Div 1, 6th |
| 1979 | Essex | 7th | 2008 | Durham | Div 1, 7th |
| 1980 | Middlesex | 6th | 2009 | Durham | Div 1, 7th |
| 1981 | Nottinghamshire | 10th | 2010 | Nottinghamshire | Div 1, 3rd |
| 1982 | Middlesex | 10th | 2011 | Lancashire | Div 1, 8th |
| 1983 | Essex | 17th | 2012 | Warwickshire | Div 2, 2nd |
| 1984 | Essex | 14th | 2013 | Durham | Div 1, 2nd |
| 1985 | Middlesex | 11th | **2014** | **Yorkshire** | **Div 1, 1st** |
| 1986 | Essex | 10th | **2015** | **Yorkshire** | **Div 1, 1st** |

## SEASON-BY-SEASON RECORD OF ALL FIRST-CLASS MATCHES PLAYED BY YORKSHIRE 1863-2015

| Season | Played | Won | Lost | Drawn | Abd§ | Season | Played | Won | Lost | Drawn | Abd§ |
|---|---|---|---|---|---|---|---|---|---|---|---|
| 1863 | 4 | 2 | 1 | 1 | 0 | 1921 | 30 | 17 | 5 | 8 | 0 |
| 1864 | 7 | 2 | 4 | 1 | 0 | 1922 | 33 | 20 | 2 | 11 | 0 |
| 1865 | 9 | 0 | 7 | 2 | 0 | 1923 | 35 | 26 | 1 | 8 | 0 |
| 1866 | 3 | 0 | 2 | 1 | 0 | 1924 | 35 | 18 | 4 | 13 | 0 |
| 1867 | 7 | 7 | 0 | 0 | 0 | 1925 | 36 | 22 | 0 | 14 | 0 |
| 1868 | 7 | 4 | 3 | 0 | 0 | 1926 | 35 | 14 | 0 | 21 | 1 |
| 1869 | 5 | 4 | 1 | 0 | 0 | 1927 | 34 | 11 | 3 | 20 | 1 |
| 1870 | 7 | 6 | 0 | 1 | 0 | 1928 | 32 | 9 | 0 | 23 | 0 |
| 1871 | 7 | 3 | 3 | 1 | 0 | 1929 | 35 | 11 | 2 | 22 | 0 |
| 1872 | 10 | 2 | 7 | 1 | 0 | 1930 | 34 | 13 | 3 | 18 | 2 |
| 1873 | 13 | 7 | 5 | 1 | 0 | 1931 | 33 | 17 | 1 | 15 | 1 |
| 1874 | 14 | 10 | 3 | 1 | 0 | 1932 | 32 | 21 | 2 | 9 | 2 |
| 1875 | 12 | 6 | 4 | 2 | 0 | 1933 | 36 | 21 | 5 | 10 | 0 |
| 1876 | 12 | 5 | 3 | 4 | 0 | 1934 | 35 | 14 | 7 | 14 | 0 |
| 1877 | 14 | 2 | 7 | 5 | 0 | 1935 | 36 | 24 | 2 | 10 | 0 |
| 1878 | 20 | 10 | 7 | 3 | 0 | 1935-6 | 3 | 1 | 0 | 2 | 0 |
| 1879 | 17 | 7 | 5 | 5 | 0 | 1936 | 35 | 14 | 2 | 19 | 0 |
| 1880 | 20 | 6 | 8 | 6 | 0 | 1937 | 34 | 22 | 3 | 9 | 1 |
| 1881 | 20 | 11 | 6 | 3 | 0 | 1938 | 36 | 22 | 2 | 12 | 0 |
| 1882 | 24 | 11 | 9 | 4 | 0 | 1939 | 34 | 23 | 4 | 7 | 1 |
| 1883 | 19 | 10 | 2 | 7 | 0 | 1945 | 2 | 0 | 0 | 2 | 0 |
| 1884 | 20 | 10 | 6 | 4 | 0 | 1946 | 31 | 20 | 1 | 10 | 0 |
| 1885 | 21 | 8 | 3 | 10 | 0 | 1947 | 32 | 10 | 9 | 13 | 0 |
| 1886 | 21 | 5 | 8 | 8 | 0 | 1948 | 31 | 11 | 6 | 14 | 0 |
| 1887 | 20 | 6 | 5 | 9 | 0 | 1949 | 33 | 16 | 3 | 14 | 0 |
| 1888 | 20 | 7 | 7 | 6 | 0 | 1950 | 34 | 16 | 6 | 12 | 1 |
| 1889 | 16 | 3 | 11 | 2 | 1 | 1951 | 35 | 14 | 3 | 18 | 0 |
| 1890 | 20 | 10 | 4 | 6 | 0 | 1952 | 34 | 17 | 3 | 14 | 0 |
| 1891 | 17 | 5 | 11 | 1 | 2 | 1953 | 35 | 7 | 7 | 21 | 0 |
| 1892 | 19 | 6 | 6 | 7 | 0 | 1954 | 35 | 16 | 3 | 16* | 0 |
| 1893 | 23 | 15 | 5 | 3 | 0 | 1955 | 33 | 23 | 6 | 4 | 0 |
| 1894 | 28 | 18 | 6 | 4 | 1 | 1956 | 35 | 11 | 7 | 17 | 0 |
| 1895 | 31 | 15 | 10 | 6 | 0 | 1957 | 34 | 16 | 5 | 13 | 1 |
| 1896 | 32 | 17 | 6 | 9 | 0 | 1958 | 33 | 10 | 8 | 15 | 2 |
| 1897 | 30 | 14 | 7 | 9 | 0 | 1959 | 35 | 18 | 8 | 9 | 0 |
| 1898 | 30 | 18 | 3 | 9 | 0 | 1960 | 38 | 19 | 7 | 12 | 0 |
| 1899 | 34 | 17 | 4 | 13 | 0 | 1961 | 39 | 19 | 5 | 15 | 0 |
| 1900 | 32 | 19 | 1 | 12 | 0 | 1962 | 37 | 16 | 5 | 16 | 0 |
| 1901 | 35 | 23 | 2 | 10 | 0 | 1963 | 33 | 14 | 4 | 15 | 0 |
| 1902 | 31 | 15 | 3 | 13 | 1 | 1964 | 33 | 12 | 4 | 17 | 0 |
| 1903 | 31 | 16 | 5 | 10 | 0 | 1965 | 33 | 12 | 4 | 17 | 0 |
| 1904 | 32 | 10 | 2 | 20 | 1 | 1966 | 32 | 16 | 6 | 10 | 1 |
| 1905 | 33 | 21 | 4 | 8 | 0 | 1967 | 31 | 16 | 5 | 10 | 2 |
| 1906 | 33 | 19 | 6 | 8 | 0 | 1968 | 32 | 13 | 4 | 15 | 0 |
| 1907 | 31 | 14 | 5 | 12 | 2 | 1969 | 29 | 4 | 7 | 18 | 0 |
| 1908 | 33 | 19 | 0 | 14 | 0 | 1970 | 26 | 10 | 5 | 11 | 0 |
| 1909 | 30 | 12 | 5 | 13 | 0 | 1971 | 27 | 5 | 8 | 14 | 0 |
| 1910 | 31 | 11 | 8 | 12 | 0 | 1972 | 21 | 4 | 5 | 12 | 1 |
| 1911 | 32 | 16 | 9 | 7 | 1 | 1973 | 22 | 3 | 5 | 14* | 0 |
| 1912 | 35 | 14 | 3 | 18 | 1 | 1974 | 22 | 6 | 7 | 9 | 1 |
| 1913 | 32 | 16 | 5 | 11 | 0 | 1975 | 21 | 11 | 1 | 9 | 0 |
| 1914 | 31 | 16 | 4 | 11 | 2 | 1976 | 22 | 7 | 7 | 8 | 0 |
| 1919 | 31 | 12 | 5 | 14 | 0 | 1977 | 23 | 7 | 5 | 11 | 1 |
| 1920 | 30 | 17 | 6 | 7 | 0 | 1978 | 24 | 10 | 3 | 11 | 1 |

| Season | Played | Won | Lost | Drawn | Abd§ | Season | Played | Won | Lost | Drawn | Abd§ |
|--------|--------|-----|------|-------|------|--------|--------|-----|------|-------|------|
| 1979 | 22 | 6 | 3 | 13 | 1 | 1997 | 20 | 7 | 4 | 9 | 0 |
| 1980 | 24 | 5 | 4 | 15 | 0 | 1998 | 19 | 9 | 3 | 7 | 0 |
| 1981 | 24 | 5 | 9 | 10 | 0 | 1999 | 17 | 8 | 6 | 3 | 0 |
| 1982 | 22 | 5 | 1 | 16 | 1 | 2000 | 18 | 7 | 4 | 7 | 0 |
| 1983 | 23 | 1 | 5 | 17 | 1 | 2001 | 16 | 9 | 3 | 4 | 0 |
| 1984 | 24 | 5 | 4 | 15 | 0 | 2002 | 16 | 2 | 8 | 6 | 0 |
| 1985 | 25 | 3 | 4 | 18 | 1 | 2003 | 17 | 4 | 5 | 8 | 0 |
| 1986 | 25 | 4 | 6 | 15 | 0 | 2004 | 16 | 3 | 4 | 9 | 0 |
| 1986-7 | 1 | 0 | 0 | 1 | 0 | 2005 | 17 | 6 | 1 | 10 | 0 |
| 1987 | 24 | 7 | 4 | 13 | 1 | 2006 | 16 | 3 | 6 | 7 | 0 |
| 1988 | 24 | 5 | 6 | 13 | 0 | 2007 | 17 | 5 | 4 | 8 | 0 |
| 1989 | 22 | 3 | 9 | 10 | 0 | 2008 | 16 | 2 | 5 | 9 | 0 |
| 1990 | 24 | 5 | 9 | 10 | 0 | 2009 | 17 | 2 | 2 | 13 | 0 |
| 1991 | 24 | 4 | 6 | 14 | 0 | 2010 | 18 | 6 | 2 | 10 | 0 |
| 1991-2 | 1 | 0 | 1 | 0 | 0 | 2011 | 17 | 4 | 6 | 7 | 0 |
| 1992 | 22 | 4 | 6 | 12 | 1 | 2012 | 17 | 5 | 0 | 12 | 0 |
| 1992-3 | 1 | 0 | 0 | 1 | 0 | 2013 | 17 | 8 | 2 | 7 | 0 |
| 1993 | 19 | 6 | 4 | 9 | 0 | 2014 | 17 | 8 | 1 | 8 | 0 |
| 1994 | 20 | 7 | 6 | 7 | 0 | 2015 | 18 | 12 | 1 | 5 | 0 |
| 1995 | 20 | 8 | 8 | 4 | 0 | | | | | | |
| 1995-6 | 2 | 2 | 0 | 0 | 0 | | 3584 | 1511 | 649 | 1424 | 38 |
| 1996 | 19 | 8 | 5 | 6 | 0 | | | | | | |

*Includes one tie in each season.

§ All these matches were abandoned without a ball being bowled, except Yorkshire v Kent at Harrogate, 1904, which was abandoned under Law 9. The two in 1914 and the one in 1939 were abandoned because of war. All these matches are excluded from the total played.

Of the 1,511 matches won, 518 have been by an innings margin, 86 by 200 runs or more, and 133 by 10 wickets. Of the 649 matches lost, 109 have been by an innings margin, 13 by 200 runs or more and 34 by 10 wickets.

## ANALYSIS OF RESULTS VERSUS ALL FIRST-CLASS
## TEAMS 1863-2015

### COUNTY CHAMPIONSHIP

| Opponents | Played | Won | Lost | Drawn | Tied |
|-----------|--------|-----|------|-------|------|
| Derbyshire | 205 | 103 | 19 | 83 | 0 |
| Durham | 34 | 15 | 8 | 11 | 0 |
| Essex | 160 | 84 | 25 | 51 | 0 |
| Glamorgan | 111 | 53 | 13 | 45 | 0 |
| Gloucestershire | 200 | 102 | 43 | 55 | 0 |
| Hampshire | 167 | 74 | 19 | 74 | 0 |
| Kent | 200 | 84 | 39 | 77 | 0 |
| Lancashire | 255 | 75 | 52 | 128 | 0 |
| Leicestershire | 166 | 84 | 15 | 66 | 1 |
| Middlesex | 231 | 82 | 56 | 92 | 1 |
| Northamptonshire | 142 | 67 | 26 | 49 | 0 |
| Nottinghamshire | 252 | 90 | 47 | 115 | 0 |
| Somerset | 171 | 90 | 22 | 59 | 0 |
| Surrey | 240 | 85 | 67 | 88 | 0 |
| Sussex | 199 | 85 | 33 | 81 | 0 |
| Warwickshire | 188 | 84 | 31 | 73 | 0 |
| Worcestershire | 140 | 70 | 21 | 49 | 0 |
| Cambridgeshire | 8 | 3 | 4 | 1 | 0 |
| **Total** | 3069 | 1330 | 540 | 1197 | 2 |

# ANALYSIS OF RESULTS VERSUS ALL FIRST-CLASS
# TEAMS 1863-2015 *(continued.)*

### OTHER FIRST-CLASS MATCHES

| Opponents | Played | Won | Lost | Drawn | Tied |
|---|---|---|---|---|---|
| Derbyshire | 2 | 1 | 1 | 0 | 0 |
| Essex | 2 | 2 | 0 | 0 | 0 |
| Hampshire | 1 | 0 | 0 | 1 | 0 |
| Lancashire | 12 | 5 | 3 | 4 | 0 |
| Leicestershire | 2 | 1 | 1 | 0 | 0 |
| Middlesex | 1 | 1 | 0 | 0 | 0 |
| Nottinghamshire | 2 | 1 | 1 | 0 | 0 |
| Surrey | 1 | 0 | 0 | 1 | 0 |
| Sussex | 2 | 0 | 0 | 2 | 0 |
| Warwickshire | 2 | 0 | 0 | 2 | 0 |
| **Totals** | **27** | **11** | **6** | **10** | **0** |
| Australians | 55 | 6 | 19 | 30 | 0 |
| Indians | 14 | 5 | 1 | 8 | 0 |
| New Zealanders | 10 | 2 | 0 | 8 | 0 |
| Pakistanis | 4 | 1 | 0 | 3 | 0 |
| South Africans | 17 | 1 | 3 | 13 | 0 |
| Sri Lankans | 3 | 0 | 0 | 3 | 0 |
| West Indians | 17 | 3 | 7 | 7 | 0 |
| Zimbabweans | 2 | 0 | 1 | 1 | 0 |
| Bangladesh A | 1 | 1 | 0 | 0 | 0 |
| India A | 2 | 0 | 0 | 2 | 0 |
| Pakistan A | 1 | 1 | 0 | 0 | 0 |
| South Africa A | 1 | 0 | 0 | 1 | 0 |
| **Totals** | **127** | **20** | **31** | **76** | **0** |
| Cambridge University/U C C E | 88 | 42 | 17 | 29 | 0 |
| Canadians | 1 | 1 | 0 | 0 | 0 |
| Combined Services | 1 | 0 | 0 | 1 | 0 |
| Durham MCCU | 1 | 1 | 0 | 0 | 0 |
| England XI's | 6 | 1 | 2 | 3 | 0 |
| Hon. M.B. Hawke's XI | 1 | 0 | 1 | 0 | 0 |
| International XI | 1 | 1 | 0 | 0 | 0 |
| Ireland | 3 | 3 | 0 | 0 | 0 |
| Jamaica | 3 | 1 | 0 | 2 | 0 |
| Leeds/Bradford MCCU | 4 | 1 | 0 | 3 | 0 |
| Liverpool and District* | 3 | 2 | 1 | 0 | 0 |
| Loughborough UCCE | 2 | 1 | 0 | 1 | 0 |
| MCC | 154 | 55 | 39 | 60 | 0 |
| Mashonaland | 1 | 1 | 0 | 0 | 0 |
| Matebeleland | 1 | 1 | 0 | 0 | 0 |
| Minor Counties | 1 | 1 | 0 | 0 | 0 |
| Oxford University | 44 | 21 | 3 | 20 | 0 |
| Philadelphians | 1 | 0 | 0 | 1 | 0 |
| Rest of England | 16 | 4 | 5 | 7 | 0 |
| Royal Air Force | 1 | 0 | 0 | 1 | 0 |
| Scotland** | 11 | 7 | 0 | 4 | 0 |
| South of England | 2 | 1 | 0 | 1 | 0 |
| C. I. Thornton's XI | 5 | 2 | 0 | 3 | 0 |
| United South of England | 1 | 1 | 0 | 0 | 0 |
| Western Province | 2 | 0 | 1 | 1 | 0 |
| Windward Islands | 1 | 0 | 0 | 1 | 0 |
| I Zingari | 6 | 2 | 3 | 1 | 0 |
| **Totals** | **361** | **150** | **72** | **139** | **0** |
| **Grand Totals** | **3584** | **1511** | **649** | **1422** | **2** |

*Matches played in 1889, 1891, 1892 and 1893 are excluded. **Match played in 1878 is included

# HIGHEST MATCH AGGREGATES – OVER 1350 RUNS

| Runs | Wkts | |
|------|------|---|
| 1665 | 33 | Yorkshire (351 and 481) lost to Warwickshire (601:9 dec and 232:4) by 6 wkts at Birmingham, 2002 |
| 1606 | 31 | Yorkshire (438 and 363:5 dec) lost to Somerset (326 and 479:6) by 4 wkts at Taunton, 2009 |
| 1479 | 28 | Yorkshire (405 and 333:4 dec) lost to Somerset (377 and 364:4) by 6 wkts at Taunton , 2010 |
| 1473 | 17 | Yorkshire (600:4 dec. and 231:3 dec.) drew with Worcestershire (453:5 dec. and 189:5) at Scarborough, 1995. |
| 1442 | 29 | Yorkshire (501:6 dec. and 244:6 dec.) beat Lancashire (403:7 dec. and 294) by 48 runs at Scarborough, 1991. |
| 1439 | 32 | Yorkshire (536:8 dec. and 205:7 dec.) beat Glamorgan (482: 7 dec. and 216) by 43 runs at Cardiff, 1996. |
| 1431 | 32 | Yorkshire (388 and 312:6) drew with Sussex (398 and 333:6 dec) at Scarborough, 2011 |
| 1417 | 33 | Yorkshire (422 and 193:7) drew with Glamorgan (466 and 336:6 dec) at Colwyn Bay, 2003 |
| 1406 | 37 | Yorkshire (354 and 341:8) drew with Derbyshire (406 and 305:9 dec) at Derby, 2004 |
| 1400 | 32 | Yorkshire (299 and 439: 4 dec.) drew with Hampshire (296 and 366:8) at Southampton, 2007 |
| 1393 | 35 | Yorkshire (331 and 278) lost to Kent (377 and 407:5 dec) by 175 runs at Maidstone, 1994. |
| 1390 | 34 | Yorkshire (431:8 dec and 265:7) beat Hampshire (429 and 265) by 3 wkts at Southampton, 1995. |
| 1390 | 33 | Durham (573 and 124:3) beat Yorkahire (274 and 419) by 7 wkts at Scarborough, 2013. |
| 1376 | 33 | Yorkshire (531 and 158:3) beat Lancashire (373 and 314) by 7 wkts at Leeds, 2001 |
| 1376 | 20 | Yorkshire (677: 7 dec.) drew with Durham (518 and 181:3 dec.) at Leeds, 2006 |
| 1374 | 36 | Yorkshire (594: 9 dec. and 266:7 dec.) beat Surrey (344 and 170) by 346 runs at The Oval, 2007 |
| 1373 | 36 | Yorkshire (520 and 114:6) drew with Derbyshire (216 and 523) at Derby, 2005 |
| 1364 | 35 | Yorkshire (216 and 433) lost to Warwickshire (316 and 399:5 dec.) by 66 runs at Birmingham, 2006 |
| 1359 | 25 | Yorkshire (561 and 138:3 dec.) drew with Derbyshire (412:4 dec. and 248:8) at Sheffield, 1996. |
| 1359 | 30 | Yorkshire (358 and 321) lost to Somerset (452 and 228:0) by 10 wkts at Taunton, 2011 |
| 1353 | 18 | Yorkshire (377:2 dec. and 300:6) beat Derbyshire (475:7 dec. and 201:3 dec.) by 4 wkts at Scarborough, 1990. |

# LOWEST MATCH AGGREGATES – UNDER 225 RUNS IN A COMPLETED MATCH

| Runs | Wkts | |
|------|------|---|
| 165 | 30 | Yorkshire (46 and 37:0) beat Nottinghamshire (24 and 58 by 10 wkts at Sheffield, 1888. |
| 175 | 29 | Yorkshire (104) beat Essex (30 and 41) by an innings and 33 runs at Leyton, 1901. |
| 182 | 15 | Yorkshire (4:0 dec. and 88.5) beat Northamptonshire (4:0 dec. and 86) by 5 wkts at Bradford, 1931. |
| 193 | 29 | Yorkshire (99) beat Worcestershire (43 and 51) by an innings and 5 runs at Bradford, 1900. |
| 219 | 30 | Yorkshire (113) beat Nottinghamshire (71 and 35) by an innings and 7 runs at Nottingham, 1881. |
| 222 | 32 | Yorkshire (98 and 14:2) beat Gloucestershire (68 and 42) by 8 wkts at Gloucester, 1924. |
| 223 | 40 | Yorkshire (58 and 51) lost to Lancashire (64 and 50) |

**SPECIAL ANNIVERSARIES:** It is 50 years ago this year that Katharine The Duchess of Kent, seen with the Duke, above, accepted Yorkshire County Cricket Club's invitation to become their distinguished Patroness.

Her father, Sir William Worsley, captained Yorkshire in 1928-1929.

June 23 will be 100th anniversary of the birth of Leonard Hutton, one of Yorkshire and England's greatest ever batsmen.

On his birthday, the 364 Club, founded by former Yorkshire CCC chairman, Keith Moss MBE, will be holding their annual lunch at Headingley when the speakers will be former England captain, Mike Brearley, and author and cricket watcher, Lord Jeffrey Archer.

*(Photos: Getty Images)*

**ANDERSON'S HEADINGLEY OVATION!** *Red Rose* paceman Jimmy Anderson had the Headingley Test crowd whooping with delight as he dismissed New Zealand batsman Martin Guptill to become the only England bowler to capture 400 Test wickets. BELOW: Rain on that first day scarcely marred the celebrations.

# THE MASTER OF ALL TRADES

**A YORKSHIREMAN ABROAD:** It has been a hard winter for the England Vice-Captain, Yorkshire's Joe Root. ABOVE: Joe on the way to 88 in the Second Test against Pakistan in Dubai. His dismissal signalled an England collapse. BELOW: Joe continues his fine form with 71 in the fourth One-Day International against Pakistan. *(Photos: Mark Green).* Joe's autobiography, *Bringing Home The Ashes,* is reviewed on Page 94

# YORKSHIRE SALUTES A GREAT LEGEND

**MOURNING BRIAN CLOSE:** Vivien Close arrives at St Chad's Church, Far Headingley, for the Service of Thanksgiving for the life of her husband, former Yorkshire and England captain Brian Close. She is accompanied by their son, Lance, left, and Vivien's brother, Graham Lance. Sir Ian Botham, captained by Brian at Somerset, is pictured below delivering a eulogy.

**BIRD'S EYE VIEW:** Yorkshire President Harold "Dickie" Bird cuts the ribbon to declare the Players' Balcony at Headingley officially open. The former Yorkshire batsman and world-famous umpire shelled out £125,000 to pay for the balcony, which gives players a superb view of the action rather than having to peer through the dressing-room window. Dickie is flanked by, left to right, Alex Lees, Yorkshire Chairman Steve Denison, Director of Cricket Martyn Moxon and Coach Jason Gillespie.

**LOYAL SERVICE:** Operations Director David Ryder, left, receives a voucher for golf equipment, a pair of cricket cufflinks and a bottle of champagne at the YCCC Gala dinner from Chief Executive Mark Arthur in recognition of his service since joining the staff as assistant secretary in 1975. David has retired from full-time employment (see article) but he will continue on a part-time basis until the end of the 2019 season.

# THE SHAPE OF THINGS TO COME

**NEW STAND PLANS:** A series of public exhibitions were held in February to reveal plans for the further redevelopment of Headingley Stadium, including a new cricket and rugby stand. A combination of public and private funding will include financial imput from Yorkshire CCC and Leeds Rhinos. The above impression shows how the stand will look from the cricket side of the stadium, while below can be seen the view for rugby fans.

# YORKSHIRE ACADEMY AT THE DOUBLE

**LEAGUE CUP WINNERS:** Yorkshire Academy, champions of the ECB Yorkshire County Premier League in 2014, came third in 2015 but won the League Cup for the second successive year, above. Back row, left to right: Jonathan Read, Jared Warner, Jordan Thompson, Nathan Firn, Harry Brook, Ben Ainsley and Eliot Callis. Sarah Smith, scorer. Front row: Eddie Barnes, James Logan, Matthew Waite, captain, Yaasar Imtiaz and Mosun Hussain. *(Photo: Richard Damms)*

**GREAT KNOCK:** Academy captain Matthew Waite, batting for Yorkshire in the Royal London One-Day Cup.

Matthew won the Howard Clayton (scorer) Second Team Performance of the Year Award for his late-season innings of 143 from 156 deliveries with 12 fours and seven sixes against the Red Rose county at Scarborough.

# YORKSHIRE ACADEMY AT THE DOUBLE

**BLACK SHEEP TRIUMPH:** It was as Yorkshire League champions the previous year that Yorkshire Academy qualified for the all-Yorkshire Black Sheep Trophy which they also won, above, with some thrilling cricket. Back row, left to right: Karl Carver, Jared Warner, Ryan Gibson, Jordan Thompson, James Logan, Jonathan Read and Harry Brook. Front row: Nathan Firn, Eliot Callis, Matthew Waite, captain, Yaasar Imtiaz and Mosun Hussain. *(Photo: Richard Damms)*

**ENGINE ROOM:** The team behind the Academy's success, left to right: Blaine Clancy, Strength and Conditioning Coach; Richard Robinson, Weetwood groundsman; Matthew Waite, captain; Richard Damms, Academy Head Coach; Sarah Smith, scorer, and Ian Dews, Director of Cricket Development and Second Eleven Coach.

## LOWEST MATCH AGGREGATES – UNDER 325 RUNS
## IN A MATCH IN WHICH ALL 40 WICKETS FELL

| Runs | Wkts | |
|---|---|---|
| 223 | 40 | Yorkshire (58 and 51) lost to Lancashire (64 and 50) by 5 runs at Manchester, 1893. |
| 288 | 40 | Yorkshire (55 and 68) lost to Lancashire (89 and 76) by 42 runs at Sheffield, 1872. |
| 295 | 40 | Yorkshire (71 and 63) lost to Surrey (56 and 105) by 27 runs at The Oval, 1886. |
| 303 | 40 | Yorkshire (109 and 77) beat Middlesex (63 and 54) by 69 runs at Lord's, 1891. |
| 318 | 40 | Yorkshire (96 and 96) beat Lancashire (39 and 87) by 66 runs at Manchester, 1874. |
| 318 | 40 | Yorkshire (94 and 104) beat Northamptonshire (61 and 59) by 78 runs at Bradford, 1955. |
| 319 | 40 | Yorkshire (84 and 72) lost to Derbyshire (106 and 57) by 7 runs at Derby, 1878. |
| 320 | 40 | Yorkshire (98 and 91) beat Surrey (72 and 59) by 58 runs at Sheffield, 1893. |
| 321 | 40 | Yorkshire (88 and 37) lost to I Zingari (103 and 93) by 71 runs at Scarborough, 1877. |
| 321 | 40 | Yorkshire (80 and 67) lost to Derbyshire (129 and 45) by 27 runs at Sheffield, 1879. |

## LARGE MARGINS OF VICTORY – BY AN INNINGS
## AND OVER 250 RUNS

| | |
|---|---|
| Inns and 397 runs | Yorkshire (548:4 dec.) beat Northamptonshire (58 and 93) at Harrogate, 1921 |
| Inns and 387 runs | Yorkshire (662) beat Derbyshire (118 and 157) at Chesterfield, 1898. |
| Inns and 343 runs | Yorkshire (673:8 dec) beat Northamptonshire (184 and 146) at Leeds, 2003 |
| Inns and 321 runs | Yorkshire (437) beat Leicestershire (58 and 58) at Leicester, 1908. |
| Inns and 314 runs | Yorkshire (356:8 dec) beat Northamptonshire (27 and 15) at Northampton, 1908. (Yorkshire's first match v. Northamptonshire). |
| Inns and 313 runs | Yorkshire (555:1 dec.) beat Essex (78 and 164) at Leyton, 1932. |
| Inns and 307 runs | Yorkshire (681:5 dec.) beat Sussex (164 and 210) at Sheffield, 1897. |
| Inns and 302 runs | Yorkshire (660) beat Leicestershire (165 and 193) at Leicester, 1896. |
| Inns and 301 runs | Yorkshire (499) beat Somerset (125 and 73) at Bath, 1899. |
| Inns and 294 runs | Yorkshire (425:7 dec.) beat Gloucestershire (47 and 84) at Bristol, 1964. |

| | |
|---|---|
| Inns and 284 runs | Yorkshire (467:7 dec) beat Leicestershire (111 and 72) at Bradford, 1932. |
| Inns and 282 runs | Yorkshire (481:8 dec) beat Derbyshire (106 and 93) at Huddersfield, 1901. |
| Inns and 280 runs | Yorkshire (562) beat Leicestershire (164 and 118) at Dewsbury, 1903. |
| Inns and 271 runs | Yorkshire (460) beat Hampshire (128 and 61) at Hull, 1900. |
| Inns and 271 runs | Yorkshire (495:5 dec) beat Warwickshire (99 and 125) at Huddersfield, 1922. |
| Inns and 266 runs | Yorkshire (352) beat Cambridgeshire (40 and 46) at Hunslet, 1869. |
| Inns and 260 runs | Yorkshire (521: 7dec.) beat Worcestershire (129 and 132) at Leeds, 2007. |
| Inns and 258 runs | Yorkshire (404:2 dec) beat Glamorgan (78 and 68) at Cardiff, 1922. (Yorkshire's first match v. Glamorgan). |
| Inns and 256 runs | Yorkshire (486) beat Leicestershire (137 and 93) at Sheffield, 1895. |
| Inns and 251 runs | Yorkshire (550) beat Leicestershire (154 and 145) at Leicester, 1933. |

# LARGE MARGINS OF VICTORY – BY OVER 300 RUNS

| | |
|---|---|
| 389 runs | Yorkshire (368 and 280:1 dec) beat Somerset (125 and 134) at Bath, 1906. |
| 370 runs | Yorkshire (194 and 274) beat Hampshire (62 and 36) at Leeds, 1904. |
| 351 runs | Yorkshire (280 and 331) beat Northamptonshire (146 and 114) at Northampton, 1947. |
| 346 runs | Yorkshire (594: 9 dec. and 266: 7 dec.) beat Surrey (344 and 179) at The Oval, 2007. |
| 328 runs | Yorkshire (186 and 318:1 dec) beat Somerset (43 and 133) at Bradford, 1930. |
| 328 runs | Yorkshire (280 and 277:7 dec) beat Glamorgan (104 and 105) at Swansea, 2001 |
| 320 runs | Yorkshire (331 and 353:9 dec) beat Durham (150 and 214) at Chester-le-Street, 2004 |
| 308 runs | Yorkshire (89 and 420) beat Warwickshire (72 and 129) at Birmingham, 1921 |
| 308 runs | Yorkshire (89 and 420) beat Warwickshire (72 and 129) |
| 305 runs | Yorkshire (370 and 305:4 dec) beat Hampshire (227 and 143) at Leeds, 2015 |

# LARGE MARGINS OF VICTORY – BY 10 WICKETS
## (WITH OVER 100 RUNS SCORED IN THE 4th INNINGS)

*4th Innings*

| | |
|---|---|
| 167:0 wkt | Yorkshire (247 and 167:0) beat Northamptonshire 233 and 180) at Huddersfield, 1948. |
| 147:0 wkt | Yorkshire (381 and 147:0) beat Middlesex (384 and 142) at Lord's, 1896. |
| 142:0 wkt | Yorkshire (304 and 142:0) beat Sussex (254 and 188) at Bradford, 1887. |
| 139:0 wkt | Yorkshire (163:9 dec and 139:0) beat Nottinghamshire (234 and 67) at Leeds, 1932. |
| 138:0 wkt | Yorkshire (293 and 138:0) beat Hampshire (251 and 179) at Southampton, 1897. |
| 132:0 wkt | Yorkshire (328 and 132:0) beat Northamptonshire (281 and 175) at Leeds, 2005 |
| 129:0 wkt | Yorkshire (355 and 129:0) beat Durham MCCU (196 and 287) at Durham, 2011 |
| 127:0 wkt | Yorkshire (258 and 127:0) beat Cambridge University (127 and 257) at Cambridge, 1930. |
| 119:0 wkt | Yorkshire (109 and 119:0) beat Essex (108 and 119) at Leeds, 1931. |
| 118:0 wkt | Yorkshire (121 and 118:0) beat MCC (125 and 113) at Lord's, 1883. |
| 116:0 wkt | Yorkshire (147 and 116:0) beat Hampshire (141 and 120) at Bournemouth, 1930. |
| 114:0 wkt | Yorkshire (135 and 114:0) beat Hampshire (71 and 176) at Bournemouth, 1948. |
| 114:0 wkt | Yorkshire (135 and 114:0) beat Hampshire (71 and 176) |
| 105:0 wkt | Yorkshire (307 and 105:0) beat Worcestershire (311 and 100) at Worcester, 2015 |

# HEAVY DEFEATS – BY AN INNINGS
## AND OVER 250 RUNS

| | |
|---|---|
| Inns and 272 runs | Yorkshire (78 and 186) lost to Surrey (536) at The Oval, 1898. |
| Inns and 261 runs | Yorkshire (247 and 89) lost to Sussex (597: 8 dec.) at Hove, 2007. |
| Inns and 255 runs | Yorkshire (125 and 144) lost to All England XI (524) at Sheffield, 1865. |

# HEAVY DEFEATS – BY OVER 300 RUNS

| | |
|---|---|
| 324 runs | Yorkshire (247 and 204) lost to Gloucestershire (291 and 484) at Cheltenham, 1994. |
| 305 runs | Yorkshire (119 and 51) lost to Cambridge University (312 and 163) at Cambridge, 1906. |

# HEAVY DEFEATS – BY 10 WICKETS
# (WITH OVER 100 RUNS SCORED IN THE 4th INNINGS)

*4th Innings*

| | |
|---|---|
| 228:0 wkt | Yorkshire (358 and 321) lost to Somerset (452 and 228:0) at Taunton, 2011 |
| 148:0 wkt | Yorkshire (83 and 216) lost to Lancashire (154 and 148:0) at Manchester, 1875. |
| 119:0 wkt | Yorkshire (92 and 109) lost to Nottinghamshire (86 and 119:0 wkt) at Leeds, 1989. |
| 108:0 wkt | Yorkshire (236 and 107) lost to Hampshire (236 and 108:0 wkt) at Southampton, 2008 |
| 100:0 wkt | Yorkshire (95 and 91) lost to Gloucestershire (88 and 100:0) at Bristol, 1956. |

## NARROW VICTORIES – BY 1 WICKET

Yorkshire (70 and 91:9) beat Cambridgeshire (86 and 74) at Wisbech, 1867.
Yorkshire (91 and 145:9) beat MCC (73 and 161) at Lord's, 1870.
Yorkshire (265 and 154:9) beat Derbyshire (234 and 184) at Derby, 1897.
Yorkshire (177 and 197:9) beat MCC (188 and 185) at Lord's, 1899.
Yorkshire (391 and 241:9) beat Somerset (349 and 281) at Taunton, 1901.
Yorkshire (239 and 168:9) beat MCC (179 and 226) at Scarborough, 1935.
Yorkshire (152 and 90:9) beat Worcestershire (119 and 121) at Leeds, 1946.
Yorkshire (229 and 175:9) beat Glamorgan (194 and 207) at Bradford, 1960.
Yorkshire (265.9 dec and 191:9) beat Worcestershire (227 and 227) at Worcester, 1961.
Yorkshire (329:6 dec and 167:9) beat Essex (339.9 dec and 154) at Scarborough, 1979.
Yorkshire (Innings forfeited and 251:9 beat Sussex (195 and 55.1 dec) at Leeds, 1986.
Yorkshire (314 and 150:9) beat Essex (200 and 261) at Scarborough, 1998.

## NARROW VICTORIES – BY 5 RUNS OR LESS

| | |
|---|---|
| By 1 run | Yorkshire (228 and 214) beat Middlesex (206 and 235) at Bradford, 1976. |
| By 1 run | Yorkshire (383 and inns forfeited) beat Loughborough UCCE (93: 3 dec. and 289) at Leeds, 2007. |
| By 2 runs | Yorkshire (108 and 122) beat Nottinghamshire (56 and 172) at Nottingham, 1870. |
| By 2 runs | Yorkshire (304:9 dec and 135) beat Middlesex (225:2 dec and 212) at Leeds, 1985. |
| By 3 runs | Yorkshire (446:9 dec and 172:4 dec) beat Essex (300:3 dec and 315) at Colchester, 1991. |
| By 5 runs | Yorkshire (271 and 147:6 dec) beat Surrey (198 and 215) at Sheffield, 1950. |
| By 5 runs | Yorkshire (151 and 176) beat Hampshire (165 and 157) at Bradford, 1962. |
| By 5 runs | Yorkshire (376:4 and 106) beat Middlesex (325:8 and 152) at Lord's, 1975 |
| By 5 runs | Yorkshire (323:5 dec and inns forfeited) beat Somerset (inns forfeited and 318) at Taunton, 1986. |

## NARROW DEFEATS – BY 1 WICKET

Yorkshire (224 and 210) lost to Australian Imperial Forces XI (265 and 170:9) at Leeds, 1985.
Yorkshire (101 and 159) lost to Warwickshire (45 and 216:9) at Scarborough, 1934.
Yorkshire (239 and 184:9 dec.) lost to Warwickshire (125 and 302:9) at Birmingham, 1983.
Yorkshire (289 and 153) lost to Surrey (250:2 dec and 193:9) at Guildford, 1991.
Yorkshire (341 and Inns forfeited) lost to Surrey (39:1 dec and 306:9) at Bradford, 1992.

## NARROW DEFEATS – BY 5 RUNS OR LESS

By 1 run     Yorkshire (135 and 297) lost to Essex (139 and 294) at Huddersfield, 1897.
By 1 run     Yorkshire (159 and 232) lost to Gloucestershire (164 and 228) at Bristol, 1906.
By 1 run     Yorkshire (126 and 137) lost to Worcestershire (101 and 163)
                at Worcester, 1968.
By 1 run     Yorkshire (366 and 217) lost to Surrey (409 and 175) at The Oval, 1995.
By 2 runs    Yorkshire (172 and 107) lost to Gloucestershire (157 and 124)
                at Sheffield, 1913.
By 2 runs    Yorkshire (179:9 dec and 144) lost to MCC (109 and 216) at Lord's, 1957.
By 3 runs    Yorkshire (126 and 181) lost to Sussex (182 and 128) at Sheffield, 1883.
By 3 runs    Yorkshire (160 and 71) lost to Lancashire (81 and 153) at Huddersfield, 1889.
By 3 runs    Yorkshire (134 and 158) lost to Nottinghamshire (200 and 95) at Leeds, 1923.
By 4 runs    Yorkshire (169 and 193) lost to Middlesex (105 and 261) at Bradford, 1920.
By 5 runs    Yorkshire (58 and 51) lost to Lancashire (64 and 50) at Manchester, 1893.
By 5 runs    Yorkshire (119 and 115) lost to Warwickshire (167 and 72) at Bradford, 1969.

## HIGH FOURTH INNINGS SCORES – 300 AND OVER

*By Yorkshire*

| | | |
|---|---|---|
| To Win: | 406:4 | beat Leicestershire by 6 wkts at Leicester, 2005 |
| | 402:6 | beat Gloucestershire by 4 wkts at Bristol, 2012 |
| | 400:4 | beat Leicestershire by 6 wkts at Scarborough, 2005 |
| | 339:6 | beat Durham by 4 wkts at Chester-le-Street, 2013 |
| | 331:8 | beat Middlesex by 2 wkts at Lord's, 1910. |
| | 327:6 | beat Nottinghamshire by 4 wkts at Nottingham, 1990.* |
| | 323:5 | beat Nottinghamshire by 5 wkts at Nottingham, 1977. |
| | 318:3 | beat Glamorgan by 7 wkts at Middlesbrough, 1976. |
| | 316:8 | beat Gloucestershire by 2 wkts at Scarborough, 2012 |
| | 309:7 | beat Somerset by 3 wkts at Taunton, 1984. |
| | 305:8 | beat Nottinghamshire by 2 wkts at Worksop, 1982. |
| | 305:5 | beat Hampshire by 5 wkts at West End, Southampton, 2015 |
| | 305:3 | beat Lancashire by 7 wkts at Manchester, 1994. |
| | 304:4 | beat Derbyshire by 6 wkts at Chesterfield, 1959. |
| | 300:4 | beat Derbyshire by 6 wkts at Chesterfield, 1981. |
| | 300:6 | beat Derbyshire by 4 wkts at Scarborough, 1990.* |
| To Draw: | 341:8 | (set 358) drew with Derbyshire at Derby, 2004. |
| | 333:7 | (set 369) drew with Essex at Chelmsford, 2010 |
| | 316:6 | (set 326) drew with Oxford University at Oxford, 1948. |
| | 312:6 | (set 344) drew with Sussex at Scarborough 2011 |
| | 316:7 | (set 320) drew with Somerset at Scarborough, 1990. |
| | 305:5 | (set 392) drew with Kent at Canterbury, 2010 |
| To Lose: | 433 | (set 500) lost to Warwickshire by 66 runs at Birmingham, 2006 |
| | 380 | (set 406) lost to MCC. by 25 runs at Lord's, 1937. |
| | 343 | (set 490) lost to Durham by 146 runs at Leeds 2011 |
| | 324 | (set 485) lost to Northamptonshire by 160 runs at Luton, 1994. |
| | 322 | (set 344) lost to Middlesex by 21 runs at Lord's, 1996. |
| | 309 | (set 400) lost to Middlesex by 90 runs at Lord's 1878. |

*Consecutive matches

*By Opponents:*

| | | |
|---|---|---|
| To Win: | 479:6 | Somerset won by 4 wkts at Taunton, 2009 |
| | 472:3 | Middlesex won by 7 wkts at Lord's, 2014 |
| | 404:5 | Hampshire won by 5 wkts at Leeds, 2006 |
| | 392:4 | Gloucestershire won by 6 wkts at Bristol, 1948. |
| | 364:4 | Somerset won by 6 wkts at Taunton, 2010 |
| | 354:5 | Nottinghamshire won by 5 wkts at Scarborough, 1990. |
| | 337:4 | Worcestershire won by 6 wkts at Kidderminster, 2007. |
| | 334:6 | Glamorgan won by 4 wkts at Harrogate, 1955. |
| | 329:5 | Worcestershire won by 5 wkts at Worcester, 1979. |
| | 306:9 | Surrey won by 1 wkt at Bradford, 1992. |
| | 305:7 | Lancashire won by 3 wkts at Manchester, 1980. |
| | 302:9 | Warwickshire won by 1 wkt at Birmingham, 1983. |

## HIGH FOURTH INNINGS SCORES – 300 AND OVER *(Continued)*

*By Opponents:*

| | | |
|---|---|---|
| *To Draw:* | 366:8 | (set 443) Hampshire drew at Southampton, 2007. |
| | 334:7 | (set 339) MCC. drew at Scarborough, 1911. |
| | 322:9 | (set 334) Middlesex drew at Leeds, 1988. |
| | 317:6 | (set 355) Nottinghamshire drew at Nottingham, 1910. |
| | 300:9 | (set 314) Northamptonshire drew at Northampton, 1990. |
| *To Lose:* | 370 | (set 539) Leicestershire lost by 168 runs at Leicester, 2001 |
| | 319 | (set 364) Gloucestershire lost by 44 runs at Leeds, 1987. |
| | 318 | (set 324) Somerset lost by 5 runs at Taunton, 1986. |
| | 315 | (set 319) Essex lost by 3 runs at Colchester, 1991. |
| | 314 | (set 334) Lancashire lost by 19 runs at Manchester, 1993. |
| | 310 | (set 417) Warwickshire lost by 106 runs at Scarborough, 1939. |
| | 306 | (set 413) Kent lost by 106 runs at Leeds, 1952. |
| | 300 | (set 330) Middlesex lost by 29 runs at Sheffield, 1930. |

## TIE MATCHES

Yorkshire (351:4 dec and 113) tied with Leicestershire (328 and 136) at Huddersfield, 1954.
Yorkshire (106:9 dec and 207) tied with Middlesex (102 and 211) at Bradford, 1973.

## HIGHEST SCORES BY AND AGAINST YORKSHIRE

**Yorkshire versus: —**

| | **By Yorkshire:** | **Against Yorkshire:** |
|---|---|---|
| **Derbyshire:** | | |
| In Yorkshire: | 677:7 dec at Leeds 2013 | 491 at Bradford, 1949 |
| Away: | 662 at Chesterfield, 1898 | 523 at Derby, 2005 |
| **Durham:** | | |
| In Yorkshire: | 677:7 dec. at Leeds, 2006 | 573 at Scarborough, 2013 |
| Away | 589-8 dec at Chester-le-Street, 2014 | 481 at Chester-le-Street, 2007 |
| **Essex:** | | |
| In Yorkshire: | 516 at Scarborough, 2010 | 622:8 dec. at Leeds, 2005 |
| Away: | 555:1 dec. at Leyton, 1932 | 521 at Leyton, 1905 |
| **Glamorgan:** | | |
| In Yorkshire: | 580:9 dec  at Scarborough, 2001 | 498 at Leeds, 1999 |
| Away: | 536:8 dec at Cardiff, 1996 | 482:7 dec. at Cardiff, 1996 |
| **Gloucestershire:** | | |
| In Yorkshire: | 504:7 dec. at Bradford, 1905 | 411 at Leeds, 1992 |
| Away: | 494 at Bristol, 1897 | 574 at Cheltenham, 1990 |
| **Hampshire:** | | |
| In Yorkshire: | 493:1 dec. at Sheffield, 1939 | 498:6 dec at Scarborough, 2010 |
| Away | 585:3 dec at Portsmouth 1920 | 599:3 at Southampton, 2011 |
| **Kent:** | | |
| In Yorkshire | 550:9 at Scarborough, 1995 | 537:9 dec at Leeds, 2012 |
| Away: | 559 at Canterbury, 1887 | 580: 9 dec. at Maidstone, 1998 |
| **Lancashire:** | | |
| In Yorkshire: | 590 at Bradford, 1887 | 517 at Leeds, 2007. |
| Away | 616:6 dec at Manchester, 2014 | 537 at Manchester, 2005 |
| **Leicestershire:** | | |
| In Yorkshire | 562 { at Scarborough, 1901<br>       at Dewsbury, 1903 | 681:7 dec. at Bradford, 1996 |
| Away: | 660  at Leicester, 1896 | 425 at Leicester, 1906 |

# HIGHEST SCORES BY AND AGAINST YORKSHIRE *(Continued)*

Yorkshire versus: —

| **Middlesex:** | **By Yorkshire:** | **Against Yorkshire:** |
|---|---|---|
| In Yorkshire: | 575:7 dec. at Bradford, 1899 | 527 at Huddersfield, 1887 |
| Away | 538:6 dec at Lord's, 1925 | 573:8 dec at Lord's, 2015 |

**Northamptonshire:**

| | | |
|---|---|---|
| In Yorkshire: | 673:8 dec. at Leeds, 2003 | 517:7 dec. at Scarborough, 1999 |
| Away | 546:3 dec at Northampton, 2014 | 531:4 dec at Northampton, 1996 |

**Nottinghamshire:**

| | | |
|---|---|---|
| In Yorkshire: | 572:8 dec at Scarborough, 2013 | 545:7 dec at Leeds, 2010 |
| Away | 534:9 dec at Nottingham, 2011 | 490 at Nottingham, 1897 |

**Somerset:**

| | | |
|---|---|---|
| In Yorkshire: | 525:4 dec. at Leeds, 1953 | 630 at Leeds, 1901 |
| Away: | 589:5 dec at Bath, 2001 | 592 at Taunton, 1892 |

**Surrey:**

| | | |
|---|---|---|
| In Yorkshire: | 582:7 dec. at Sheffield, 1935 | 510 at Leeds, 2002 |
| Away: | 704 at The Oval, 1899 | 634:5 dec at The Oval, 2013 |

**Sussex:**

| | | |
|---|---|---|
| In Yorkshire: | 681:5 dec. at Sheffield, 1897 | 566 at Sheffield, 1937 |
| Away: | 522:7 dec. at Hastings, 1911 | 597:8 dec. at Hove, 2007 |

**Warwickshire:**

| | | |
|---|---|---|
| In Yorkshire | 561:7 dec at Scarborough 2007 | 482 at Leeds, 2011 |
| Away: | 887 at Birmingham, 1896 | 601:9 dec. at Birmingham, 2002 |
| | (Highest score by a First-Class county) | |

**Worcestershire:**

| | | |
|---|---|---|
| In Yorkshire: | 600: 4 dec. at Scarborough, 1995 | 453:5 dec. at Scarborough, 1995 |
| Away: | 560:6 dec. at Worcester, 1928 | 456:8 at Worcester, 1904 |

**Australians:**

| | | |
|---|---|---|
| In Yorkshire: | 377 at Sheffield, 1953 | 470 at Bradford, 1893 |

**Indians:**

| | | |
|---|---|---|
| In Yorkshire: | 385 at Hull, 1911 | 490:5 dec. at Sheffield, 1946 |

**New Zealanders:**

| | | |
|---|---|---|
| In Yorkshire: | 419 at Bradford, 1965 | 370:7 dec. at Bradford, 1949 |

**Pakistanis:**

| | | |
|---|---|---|
| In Yorkshire: | 433:9 dec. at Sheffield, 1954 | 356 at Sheffield, 1954 |

**South Africans:**

| | | |
|---|---|---|
| In Yorkshire: | 579 at Sheffield, 1951 | 454:8 dec at Sheffield, 1951 |

**Sri Lankans:**

| | | |
|---|---|---|
| In Yorkshire: | 314:8 dec. at Leeds, 1991 | 422:8 dec. at Leeds, 1991 |

**West Indians:**

| | | |
|---|---|---|
| In Yorkshire: | 312:5 dec. at Scarborough, 1973 | 426 at Scarborough, 1995 |

**Zimbabweans:**

| | | |
|---|---|---|
| In Yorkshire: | 298:9 dec at Leeds, 1990 | 235 at Leeds, 2000 |

**Cambridge University:**

| | | |
|---|---|---|
| In Yorkshire: | 359 at Scarborough, 1967 | 366 at Leeds, 1998 |
| Away: | 540 at Cambridge, 1938 | 425:7 at Cambridge, 1929 |

**Durham MCCU:**

| | | |
|---|---|---|
| Away: | 355 at Durham, 2011 | 287 at Durham, 2011 |

**Leeds/Bradford MCCU:**

| | | |
|---|---|---|
| In Yorkshire | 454 at Leeds, 2014 | 211 at Leeds, 2012 |

**Loughborough MCCU:**

| | | |
|---|---|---|
| In Yorkshire: | 383:6 dec at Leeds, 2007 | 289 at Leeds, 2007 |

## HIGHEST SCORES BY AND AGAINST YORKSHIRE *(Continued)*

**Yorkshire versus: —**

**MCC:**

|  | **By Yorkshire:** | **Against Yorkshire:** |
|---|---|---|
| In Yorkshire: | 557:8 dec. at Scarborough, 1933 | 478:8 at Scarborough, 1904 |
| Away: | 528:8 dec. at Lord's, 1919 | 488 at Lord's, 1919 |

**Oxford University:**

|  | | |
|---|---|---|
| In Yorkshire: | 173 at Harrogate, 1972 | 190:6 dec at Harrogate, 1972 |
| Away: | 468:6 dec. at Oxford, 1978 | 422:9 dec. at Oxford, 1953 |

# LOWEST SCORES BY AND AGAINST YORKSHIRE

**Yorkshire versus:**

**Derbyshire:**

|  | **By Yorkshire:** | **Against Yorkshire:** |
|---|---|---|
| In Yorkshire: | 50 at Sheffield, 1894 | 20 at Sheffield, 1939 |
| Away: | 44 at Chesterfield, 1948 | 26 at Derby, 1880 |

**Durham:**

|  | | |
|---|---|---|
| In Yorkshire: | 93 at Leeds, 2003 | 125 at Harrogate, 1995 |
| Away: | 108 at Durham, 1992 | 74 at Chester-le-Street, 1998 |

**Essex:**

|  | | |
|---|---|---|
| In Yorkshire: | 31 at Huddersfield, 1935 | 52 at Harrogate, 1900 |
| Away: | 98 at Leyton, 1905 | 30 at Leyton, 1901 |

**Glamorgan:**

|  | | |
|---|---|---|
| In Yorkshire: | 83 at Sheffield, 1946 | 52 at Hull, 1926 |
| Away: | 92 at Swansea, 1956 | 48 at Cardiff, 1924 |

**Gloucestershire:**

|  | | |
|---|---|---|
| In Yorkshire: | 61 at Leeds, 1894 | 36 at Sheffield, 1903 |
| Away: | 35 at Bristol, 1959 | 42 at Gloucester, 1924 |

**Hampshire:**

|  | | |
|---|---|---|
| In Yorkshire: | 23 at Middlesbrough, 1965 | 36 at Leeds, 1904 |
| | Away: | 96 at Bournemouth, 1971    36 at |

**Kent:**

|  | | |
|---|---|---|
| | Southampton, 1898 | |
| In Yorkshire: | 30 at Sheffield, 1865 | 39 { at Sheffield, 1882<br>{ at Sheffield, 1936 |
| Away: | 62 at Maidstone, 1889 | 63 at Canterbury, 1901 |

**Lancashire:**

|  | | |
|---|---|---|
| In Yorkshire: | 33 at Leeds, 1924 | 30 at Holbeck, 1868 |
| Away: | 51 { at Manchester, 1888<br>{ at Manchester, 1893 | 39 at Manchester, 1874 |

**Leicestershire:**

|  | **By Yorkshire:** | **Against Yorkshire:** |
|---|---|---|
| In Yorkshire: | 93 at Leeds, 1935 | 34 at Leeds, 1906 |
| Away: | 47 at Leicester, 1911 | 57 at Leicester, 1898 |

**Middlesex:**

|  | | |
|---|---|---|
| In Yorkshire: | 45 at Leeds, 1898 | 45 at Huddersfield, 1879 |
| Away: | 43 at Lord's, 1888 | 49 at Lord's in 1890 |

**Northamptonshire:**

|  | | |
|---|---|---|
| In Yorkshire: | 85 at Sheffield, 1919 | 51 at Bradford, 1920 |
| Away | 64 at Northampton, 1959 | 15 at Northampton, 1908<br>(and 27 in first innings) |

**Nottinghamshire:**

|  | | |
|---|---|---|
| In Yorkshire: | 32 at Sheffield, 1876 | 24 at Sheffield, 1888 |
| Away: | 43 at Nottingham, 1869 | 13 at Nottingham, 1901<br>(second smallest total<br>by a First-Class county) |

**Yorkshire versus:**

| Somerset: | By Yorkshire: | Against Yorkshire: |
|---|---|---|
| In Yorkshire: | 73 at Leeds, 1895 | 43 at Bradford, 1930 |
| Away: | 83 at Wells, 1949 | 35 at Bath, 1898 |

**Surrey:**

| | | |
|---|---|---|
| In Yorkshire: | 54 at Sheffield, 1873 | 31 at Holbeck, 1883 |
| Away: | 26 at The Oval, 1909 | 44 at The Oval, 1935 |

**Sussex:**

| | | |
|---|---|---|
| In Yorkshire: | 61 at Dewsbury, 1891 | 20 at Hull, 1922 |
| Away: | 42 at Hove, 1922 | 24 at Hove, 1878 |

**Warwickshire:**

| | | |
|---|---|---|
| In Yorkshire: | 49 at Huddersfield, 1951 | 35 at Sheffield, 1979 |
| Away: | 54 at Birmingham, 1964 | 35 at Birmingham, 1963 |

**Worcestershire:**

| | | |
|---|---|---|
| In Yorkshire: | 62 at Bradford, 1907 | 24 at Huddersfield, 1903 |
| Away: | 72 at Worcester, 1977 | 65 at Worcester, 1925 |

**Australians:**

| | | |
|---|---|---|
| In Yorkshire: | 48 at Leeds, 1893 | 23 at Leeds, 1902 |

**Indians:**

| | | |
|---|---|---|
| In Yorkshire: | 146 at Bradford, 1959 | 66 at Harrogate, 1932 |

**New Zealanders:**

| | | |
|---|---|---|
| In Yorkshire: | 189 at Harrogate, 1931 | 134 at Bradford, 1965 |

**Pakistanis:**

| | | |
|---|---|---|
| In Yorkshire: | 137 at Bradford, 1962 | 150 at Leeds, 1967 |

**South Africans:**

| | | |
|---|---|---|
| In Yorkshire: | 113 at Bradford, 1907 | 76 at Bradford, 1951 |

**Sri Lankans:**

| | | |
|---|---|---|
| In Yorkshire: | Have not been dismissed. Lowest is 184:1 dec at Leeds, 1991 | 287:5 dec at Leeds, 1988 |

**West Indians:**

| | | |
|---|---|---|
| In Yorkshire: | 50 at Harrogate, 1906 | 58 at Leeds, 1928 |

**Zimbabweans:**

| | | |
|---|---|---|
| In Yorkshire: | 124 at Leeds, 2000 | 68 at Leeds, 2000 |

**Cambridge University:**

| | | |
|---|---|---|
| In Yorkshire: | 110 at Sheffield, 1903 | 39 at Sheffield, 1903 |
| Away: | 51 at Cambridge, 1906 | 30 at Cambridge, 1928 |

**Durham MCCU:**

| | | |
|---|---|---|
| Away | 355 at Durham, 2011 | 196 at Durham, 2011 |

**Leeds/Bradford MCCU:**

| | | |
|---|---|---|
| In Yorkshire | 135 at Leeds, 2012 | 118 at Leeds, 2013 |

**Loughborough MCCU:**

| | | |
|---|---|---|
| In Yorkshire | 348:5 dec at Leeds, 2010 | 289 at Leeds, 2007 |

**MCC:**

| | | |
|---|---|---|
| In Yorkshire: | 46 { at Scarborough, 1876 / at Scarborough, 1877 | 31 at Scarborough, 1877 |
| Away: | 44 at Lord's, 1880 | 27 at Lord's, 1902 |

**Oxford University:**

| | | |
|---|---|---|
| In Yorkshire: | Have not been dismissed. Lowest is 115:8 at Harrogate, 1972 | 133 at Harrogate, 1972 |
| Away: | 141 at Oxford, 1949 | 46 at Oxford, 1956 |

# INDIVIDUAL INNINGS OF 150 AND OVER

**A complete list of all First-class Centuries up to and including 2007
is to be found in the 2008 edition**

### J M BAIRSTOW (5)

| 205 | v. Nottinghamshire | Nottingham | 2011 |
|-----|-------------------|------------|------|
| 182 | v. Leicestershire | Scarborough | 2012 |
| 186 | v. Derbyshire | Leeds | 2013 |
| 161* | v. Sussex | Arundel | 2014 |
| 219* | v. Durham | Chester-le-Street | 2015 |

### G S BALLANCE (2)

| 174 | v. Northamptonshire | Leeds | 2014 |
|-----|---------------------|-------|------|
| 165 | v. Sussex | Hove | 2015 |

### W BARBER (7)

| 162 | v. Middlesex | Sheffield | 1932 |
|-----|--------------|-----------|------|
| 168 | v. MCC | Lord's | 1934 |
| 248 | v. Kent | Leeds | 1934 |
| 191 | v. Sussex | Leeds | 1935 |
| 255 | v. Surrey | Sheffield | 1935 |
| 158 | v. Kent | Sheffield | 1936 |
| 157 | v. Surrey | Sheffield | 1938 |

### M G BEVAN (2)

| 153* | v. Surrey | The Oval | 1995 |
|------|-----------|----------|------|
| 160* | v. Surrey | Middlesbrough | 1996 |

### H D BIRD (1)

| 181* | v. Glamorgan | Bradford | 1959 |
|------|--------------|----------|------|

### R J BLAKEY (3)

| 204* | v. Gloucestershire | Leeds | 1987 |
|------|--------------------|-------|------|
| 196 | v. Oxford University | Oxford | 1991 |
| 223* | v. Northamptonshire | Leeds | 2003 |

### G BLEWETT (1)

| 190 | v. Northamptonshire | Scarborough | 1999 |
|-----|---------------------|-------------|------|

### M W BOOTH (1)

| 210 | v. Worcestershire | Worcester | 1911 |
|-----|-------------------|-----------|------|

### G BOYCOTT (32)

| 165* | v. Leicestershire | Scarborough | 1963 |
|------|-------------------|-------------|------|
| 151 | v. Middlesex | Leeds | 1964 |
| 151* | v. Leicestershire | Leicester | 1964 |
| 177 | v. Gloucestershire | Bristol | 1964 |
| 164 | v. Sussex | Hove | 1966 |
| 220* | v. Northamptonshire | Sheffield | 1967 |
| 180* | v. Warwickshire | Middlesbrough | 1968 |
| 260* | v. Essex | Colchester (Garrison Ground) | 1970 |
| 169 | v. Nottinghamshire | Leeds | 1971 |
| 233 | v. Essex | Colchester (Garrison Ground) | 1971 |
| 182* | v. Middlesex | Lord's | 1971 |
| 169 | v. Lancashire | Sheffield | 1971 |
| 151 | v. Leicestershire | Bradford | 1971 |
| 204* | v. Leicestershire | Leicester | 1972 |
| 152* | v. Worcestershire | Worcester | 1975 |
| 175* | v. Middlesex | Scarborough | 1975 |
| 201* | v. Middlesex | Lord's | 1975 |

# INDIVIDUAL INNINGS OF 150 AND OVER *(Continued)*

## G BOYCOTT *(Continued)*

| | | | |
|---|---|---|---|
| 161* | v. Gloucestershire | Leeds | 1976 |
| 207* | v. Cambridge University | Cambridge | 1976 |
| 156* | v. Glamorgan | Middlesbrough | 1976 |
| 154 | v Nottinghamshire | Nottingham | 1977 |
| 151* | v Derbyshire | Leeds | 1979 |
| 167 | v Derbyshire | Chesterfield | 1979 |
| 175* | v Nottinghamshire | Worksop | 1979 |
| 154* | v Derbyshire | Scarborough | 1980 |
| 159 | v Worcestershire | Sheffield (Abbeydale Park) | 1982 |
| 152* | v Warwickshire | Leeds | 1982 |
| 214* | v Nottinghamshire | Worksop | 1983 |
| 163 | v Nottinghamshire | Bradford | 1983 |
| 169* | v Derbyshire | Chesterfield | 1983 |
| 153* | v Derbyshire | Harrogate | 1984 |
| 184 | v Worcestershire | Worcester | 1985 |

## T T BRESNAN *(1)*

| | | | |
|---|---|---|---|
| 169* | v. Durham | Chester-le-Street | 2015 |

## G L BROPHY *(1)*

| | | | |
|---|---|---|---|
| 177* | v Worcestershire | Worcester | 2011 |

## J T BROWN *(8)*

| | | | |
|---|---|---|---|
| 168* | v Sussex | Huddersfield | 1895 |
| 203 | v Middlesex | Lord's | 1896 |
| 311 | v Sussex | Sheffield | 1897 |
| 300 | v Derbyshire | Chesterfield | 1898 |
| 150 | v Sussex | Hove | 1898 |
| 168 | v Cambridge University | Cambridge | 1899 |
| 167 | v Australians | Bradford | 1899 |
| 192 | v Derbyshire | Derby | 1899 |

## D BYAS *(5)*

| | | | |
|---|---|---|---|
| 153 | v Nottinghamshire | Worksop | 1991 |
| 156 | v Essex | Chelmsford | 1993 |
| 181 | v Cambridge University | Cambridge | 1995 |
| 193 | v Lancashire | Leeds | 1995 |
| 213 | v Worcestershire | Scarborough | 1995 |

## D B CLOSE *(5)*

| | | | |
|---|---|---|---|
| 164 | v Combined Services | Harrogate | 1954 |
| 154 | v Nottinghamshire | Nottingham | 1959 |
| 198 | v Surrey | The Oval | 1960 |
| 184 | v Nottinghamshire | Scarborough | 1960 |
| 161 | v Northamptonshire | Northampton | 1963 |

## D DENTON *(11)*

| | | | |
|---|---|---|---|
| 153* | v Australians | Bradford | 1905 |
| 165 | v Hampshire | Bournemouth | 1905 |
| 172 | v Gloucestershire | Bradford | 1905 |
| 184 | v Nottinghamshire | Nottingham | 1909 |
| 182 | v Derbyshire | Chesterfield | 1910 |
| 200* | v Warwickshire | Birmingham | 1912 |
| 182 | v Gloucestershire | Bristol | 1912 |
| 221 | v Kent | Tunbridge Wells | 1912 |
| 191 | v Hampshire | Southampton | 1912 |
| 168* | v Hampshire | Southampton | 1914 |
| 209* | v Worcestershire | Worcester | 1920 |

### A W GALE (4)

| | | | |
|---|---|---|---|
| 150 | v. Surrey | The Oval | 2008 |
| 151* | v. Nottinghamshire | Nottingham | 2010 |
| 272 | v. Nottinghamshire | Scarborough | 2013 |
| 164 | v. Worcestershire | Scarborough | 2015 |

### P A GIBB (1)

| | | | |
|---|---|---|---|
| 157* | v. Nottinghamshire | Sheffield | 1935 |

### S HAIGH (1)

| | | | |
|---|---|---|---|
| 159 | v. Nottinghamshire | Sheffield | 1901 |

### L HALL (1)

| | | | |
|---|---|---|---|
| 160 | v. Lancashire | Bradford | 1887 |

### J H HAMPSHIRE (5)

| | | | |
|---|---|---|---|
| 150 | v. Leicestershire | Bradford | 1964 |
| 183* | v. Sussex | Hove | 1971 |
| 157* | v. Nottinghamshire | Worksop | 1974 |
| 158 | v. Gloucestershire | Harrogate | 1974 |
| 155* | v. Gloucestershire | Leeds | 1976 |

### I J HARVEY (1)

| | | | |
|---|---|---|---|
| 209* | v. Somerset | Leeds | 2005 |

### LORD HAWKE (1)

| | | | |
|---|---|---|---|
| 166 | v. Warwickshire | Birmingham | 1896 |

### G H HIRST (15)

| | | | |
|---|---|---|---|
| 186 | v. Surrey | The Oval | 1899 |
| 155 | v. Nottinghamshire | Scarborough | 1900 |
| 214 | v. Worcestershire | Worcester | 1901 |
| 153 | v. Leicestershire | Dewsbury | 1903 |
| 153 | v. Oxford University | Oxford | 1904 |
| 152 | v. Hampshire | Portsmouth | 1904 |
| 157 | v. Kent | Tunbridge Wells | 1904 |
| 341 | v. Leicestershire | Leicester (Aylestone Road) | 1905 |
| 232* | v. Surrey | The Oval | 1905 |
| 169 | v. Oxford University | Oxford | 1906 |
| 158 | v. Cambridge University | Cambridge | 1910 |
| 156 | v. Lancashire | Manchester | 1911 |
| 218 | v. Sussex | Hastings | 1911 |
| 166* | v. Sussex | Hastings | 1913 |
| 180* | v. MCC | Lord's | 1919 |

### P HOLMES (16)

| | | | |
|---|---|---|---|
| 302* | v. Hampshire | Portsmouth | 1920 |
| 150 | v. Derbyshire | Chesterfield | 1921 |
| 277* | v. Northamptonshire | Harrogate | 1921 |
| 209 | v. Warwickshire | Birmingham | 1922 |
| 220* | v. Warwickshire | Huddersfield | 1922 |
| 199 | v. Somerset | Hull | 1923 |
| 315* | v. Middlesex | Lord's | 1925 |
| 194 | v. Leicestershire | Hull | 1925 |
| 159 | v. Hampshire | Southampton | 1925 |
| 180 | v. Gloucestershire | Gloucester | 1927 |
| 175* | v. New Zealanders | Bradford | 1927 |
| 179* | v. Middlesex | Leeds | 1928 |

### P HOLMES *(Continued)*

| | | | |
|---|---|---|---|
| 275 | v. Warwickshire | Bradford | 1928 |
| 285 | v. Nottinghamshire | Nottingham | 1929 |
| 250 | v. Warwickshire | Birmingham | 1931 |
| 224* | v. Essex | Leyton | 1932 |

### L HUTTON (31)

| | | | |
|---|---|---|---|
| 196 | v. Worcestershire | Worcester | 1934 |
| 163 | v. Surrey | Leeds | 1936 |
| 161 | v. MCC | Lord's | 1937 |
| 271* | v. Derbyshire | Sheffield | 1937 |
| 153 | v. Leicestershire | Hull | 1937 |
| 180 | v. Cambridge University | Cambridge | 1938 |
| 158 | v. Warwickshire | Birmingham | 1939 |
| 280* | v. Hampshire | Sheffield | 1939 |
| 151 | v. Surrey | Leeds | 1939 |
| 177 | v. Sussex | Scarborough | 1939 |
| 183* | v. Indians | Bradford | 1946 |
| 171* | v. Northamptonshire | Hull | 1946 |
| 197 | v. Glamorgan | Swansea | 1947 |
| 197 | v. Essex | Southend-on-Sea | 1947 |
| 270* | v. Hampshire | Bournemouth | 1947 |
| 176* | v. Sussex | Sheffield | 1948 |
| 155 | v. Sussex | Hove | 1948 |
| 167 | v. New Zealanders | Bradford | 1949 |
| 201 | v. Lancashire | Manchester | 1949 |
| 165 | v. Sussex | Hove | 1949 |
| 269* | v. Northamptonshire | Wellingborough | 1949 |
| 156 | v. Essex | Colchester (Castle Park) | 1950 |
| 153 | v. Nottinghamshire | Nottingham | 1950 |
| 156 | v. South Africans | Sheffield | 1951 |
| 151 | v. Surrey | The Oval | 1951 |
| 194* | v. Nottinghamshire | Nottingham | 1951 |
| 152 | v. Lancashire | Leeds | 1952 |
| 189 | v. Kent | Leeds | 1952 |
| 178 | v. Somerset | Leeds | 1953 |
| 163 | v. Combined Services | Harrogate | 1954 |
| 194 | v. Nottinghamshire | Nottingham | 1955 |

### R A HUTTON (1)

| | | | |
|---|---|---|---|
| 189 | v. Pakistanis | Bradford | 1971 |

### R ILLINGWORTH (2)

| | | | |
|---|---|---|---|
| 150 | v. Essex | Colchester (Castle Park) | 1959 |
| 162 | v. Indians | Sheffield | 1959 |

### Hon F S JACKSON (3)

| | | | |
|---|---|---|---|
| 160 | v. Gloucestershire | Sheffield | 1898 |
| 155 | v. Middlesex | Bradford | 1899 |
| 158 | v. Surrey | Bradford | 1904 |

### P A JAQUES (7)

| | | | |
|---|---|---|---|
| 243 | v. Hampshire | Southampton (Rose Bowl) | 2004 |
| 173 | v. Glamorgan | Leeds | 2004 |
| 176 | v. Northamptonshire | Leeds | 2005 |
| 219 | v. Derbyshire | Leeds | 2005 |
| 172 | v. Durham | Scarborough | 2005 |
| 160 | v. Gloucestershire | Bristol | 2012 |
| 152 | v. Durham | Scarborough | 2013 |

# INDIVIDUAL INNINGS OF 150 AND OVER *(Continued)*

### R KILNER (5)

| | | | |
|---|---|---|---|
| 169 | v. Gloucestershire | Bristol | 1914 |
| 206* | v. Derbyshire | Sheffield | 1920 |
| 166 | v. Northamptonshire | Northampton | 1921 |
| 150 | v. Northamptonshire | Harrogate | 1921 |
| 150 | v. Middlesex | Lord's | 1926 |

### F LEE (1)

| | | | |
|---|---|---|---|
| 165 | v. Lancashire | Bradford | 1887 |

### A Z LEES (1)

| | | | |
|---|---|---|---|
| 275* | v. Derbyshire | Chesterfield | 2013 |

### D S LEHMANN (13)

| | | | |
|---|---|---|---|
| 177 | v. Somerset | Taunton | 1997 |
| 163* | v. Leicestershire | Leicester | 1997 |
| 182 | v. Hampshire | Portsmouth | 1997 |
| 200 | v. Worcestershire | Worcester | 1998 |
| 187* | v. Somerset | Bath | 2001 |
| 252 | v. Lancashire | Leeds | 2001 |
| 193 | v. Leicestershire | Leicester | 2001 |
| 216 | v. Sussex | Arundel | 2002 |
| 187 | v. Lancashire | Leeds | 2002 |
| 150 | v. Warwickshire | Birmingham | 2006 |
| 193 | v. Kent | Canterbury | 2006 |
| 172 | v. Kent | Leeds | 2006 |
| 339 | v. Durham | Leeds | 2006 |

### E I LESTER (5)

| | | | |
|---|---|---|---|
| 186 | v. Warwickshire | Scarborough | 1949 |
| 178 | v. Nottinghamshire | Nottingham | 1952 |
| 157 | v. Cambridge University | Hull | 1953 |
| 150 | v. Oxford University | Oxford | 1954 |
| 163 | v. Essex | Romford | 1954 |

### M LEYLAND (17)

| | | | |
|---|---|---|---|
| 191 | v. Glamorgan | Swansea | 1926 |
| 204* | v. Middlesex | Sheffield | 1927 |
| 247 | v. Worcestershire | Worcester | 1928 |
| 189* | v. Glamorgan | Huddersfield | 1928 |
| 211* | v. Lancashire | Leeds | 1930 |
| 172 | v. Middlesex | Sheffield | 1930 |
| 186 | v. Derbyshire | Leeds | 1930 |
| 189 | v. Middlesex | Sheffield | 1932 |
| 153 | v. Leicestershire | Leicester (Aylestone Road) | 1932 |
| 166 | v. Leicestershire | Bradford | 1932 |
| 153* | v. Hampshire | Bournemouth | 1932 |
| 192 | v. Northamptonshire | Leeds | 1933 |
| 210* | v. Kent | Dover | 1933 |
| 263 | v. Essex | Hull | 1936 |
| 163* | v. Surrey | Leeds | 1936 |
| 167 | v. Worcestershire | Stourbridge | 1937 |
| 180* | v. Middlesex | Lord's | 1939 |

### E LOCKWOOD (1)

| | | | |
|---|---|---|---|
| 208 | v. Kent | Gravesend | 1883 |

# INDIVIDUAL INNINGS OF 150 AND OVER *(Continued)*

### J D LOVE (4)

| | | | |
|---|---|---|---|
| 163 | v. Nottinghamshire | Bradford | 1976 |
| 170* | v. Worcestershire | Worcester | 1979 |
| 161 | v. Warwickshire | Birmingham | 1981 |
| 154 | v. Lancashire | Manchester | 1981 |

### F A LOWSON (10)

| | | | |
|---|---|---|---|
| 155 | v. Kent | Maidstone | 1951 |
| 155 | v. Worcestershire | Bradford | 1952 |
| 166 | v. Scotland | Glasgow | 1953 |
| 259* | v. Worcestershire | Worcester | 1953 |
| 165 | v. Sussex | Hove | 1954 |
| 164 | v. Essex | Scarborough | 1954 |
| 150* | v. Kent | Dover | 1954 |
| 183* | v. Oxford University | Oxford | 1956 |
| 154 | v. Somerset | Taunton | 1956 |
| 154 | v. Cambridge University | Cambridge | 1957 |

### R G LUMB (2)

| | | | |
|---|---|---|---|
| 159 | v. Somerset | Harrogate | 1979 |
| 165* | v. Gloucestershire | Bradford | 1984 |

### A LYTH (3)

| | | | |
|---|---|---|---|
| 248 * | v. Leicestershire | Leicester | 2012 |
| 230 | v. Northamptonshire | Northampton | 2014 |
| 251 | v. Lancashire | Manchester | 2014 |

### A McGRATH (7)

| | | | |
|---|---|---|---|
| 165 | v. Lancashire | Leeds | 2002 |
| 174 | v. Derbyshire | Derby | 2004 |
| 165* | v. Leicestershire | Leicester | 2005 |
| 173* | v. Worcestershire | Leeds | 2005 |
| 158 | v. Derbyshire | Derby | 2005 |
| 188* | v. Warwickshire | Birmingham | 2007 |
| 211 | v. Warwickshire | Birmingham | 2009 |

### D R MARTYN (1)

| | | | |
|---|---|---|---|
| 238 | v. Gloucestershire | Leeds | 2003 |

### A A METCALFE (7)

| | | | |
|---|---|---|---|
| 151 | v. Northamptonshire | Luton | 1986 |
| 151 | v. Lancashire | Manchester | 1986 |
| 152 | v. MCC | Scarborough | 1987 |
| 216* | v. Middlesex | Leeds | 1988 |
| 162 | v. Gloucestershire | Cheltenham | 1990 |
| 150* | v. Derbyshire | Scarborough | 1990 |
| 194* | v. Nottinghamshire | Nottingham | 1990 |

### A MITCHELL (7)

| | | | |
|---|---|---|---|
| 189 | v. Northamptonshire | Northampton | 1926 |
| 176 | v. Nottinghamshire | Bradford | 1930 |
| 177* | v. Gloucestershire | Bradford | 1932 |
| 150* | v. Worcestershire | Worcester | 1933 |
| 158 | v. MCC | Scarborough | 1933 |
| 152 | v. Hampshire | Bradford | 1934 |
| 181 | v. Surrey | Bradford | 1934 |

### F MITCHELL (2)

| | | | |
|---|---|---|---|
| 194 | v. Leicestershire | Leicester | 1899 |
| 162* | v. Warwickshire | Birmingham | 1901 |

### M D MOXON (14)

| | | | |
|---|---|---|---|
| 153 | v. Lancashire | Leeds | 1983 |
| 153 | v. Somerset | Leeds | 1985 |
| 168 | v. Worcestershire | Worcester | 1985 |
| 191 | v. Northamptonshire | Scarborough | 1989 |
| 162* | v. Surrey | The Oval | 1989 |
| 218* | v. Sussex | Eastbourne | 1990 |
| 200 | v. Essex | Colchester (Castle Park) | 1991 |
| 183 | v. Gloucestershire | Cheltenham | 1992 |
| 171* | v. Kent | Leeds | 1993 |
| 161* | v. Lancashire | Manchester | 1994 |
| 274* | v. Worcestershire | Worcester | 1994 |
| 203* | v. Kent | Leeds | 1995 |
| 213 | v. Glamorgan | Cardiff (Sophia Gardens) | 1996 |
| 155 | v. Pakistan 'A' | Leeds | 1997 |

### E OLDROYD (5)

| | | | |
|---|---|---|---|
| 151* | v. Glamorgan | Cardiff | 1922 |
| 194 | v. Worcestershire | Worcester | 1923 |
| 162* | v. Glamorgan | Swansea | 1928 |
| 168 | v. Glamorgan | Hull | 1929 |
| 164* | v. Somerset | Bath | 1930 |

### D E V PADGETT (1)

| | | | |
|---|---|---|---|
| 161* | v. Oxford University | Oxford | 1959 |

### R PEEL (2)

| | | | |
|---|---|---|---|
| 158 | v. Middlesex | Lord's | 1889 |
| 210* | v. Warwickshire | Birmingham | 1896 |

### A U RASHID (3)

| | | | |
|---|---|---|---|
| 157* | v. Lancashire | Leeds | 2009 |
| 180 | v. Somerset | Leeds | 2013 |
| 159* | v. Lancashire | Manchester | 2014 |

### W RHODES (8)

| | | | |
|---|---|---|---|
| 196 | v. Worcestershire | Worcester | 1904 |
| 201 | v. Somerset | Taunton | 1905 |
| 199 | v. Sussex | Hove | 1909 |
| 176 | v. Nottinghamshire | Harrogate | 1912 |
| 152 | v. Leicestershire | Leicester (Aylestone Road) | 1913 |
| 167* | v. Nottinghamshire | Leeds | 1920 |
| 267* | v. Leicestershire | Leeds | 1921 |
| 157 | v. Derbyshire | Leeds | 1925 |

### P E ROBINSON (2)

| | | | |
|---|---|---|---|
| 150* | v. Derbyshire | Scarborough | 1990 |
| 189 | v. Lancashire | Scarborough | 1991 |

### J E ROOT (4)

| | | | |
|---|---|---|---|
| 160 | v. Sussex | Scarborough | 2011 |
| 222 * | v. Hampshire | Southampton (West End) | 2012 |
| 182 | v. Durham | Chester-le-Street | 2013 |
| 236 | v. Derbyshire | Leeds | 2013 |

2013 innings consecutive

# INDIVIDUAL INNINGS OF 150 AND OVER *(Continued)*

### J W ROTHERY (1)

| 161 | v. Kent | Dover | 1908 |
|---|---|---|---|

### J A RUDOLPH (5)

| 220 | v. Warwickshire | Scarborough | 2007 |
|---|---|---|---|
| 155 | v. Somerset | Taunton | 2008 |
| 198 | v. Worcestershire | Leeds | 2009 |
| 191 | v. Somerset | Taunton | 2009 |
| 228* | v. Durham | Leeds | 2010 |

### H RUDSTON (1)

| 164 | v. Leicestershire | Leicester (Aylestone Rd) | 1904 |
|---|---|---|---|

### J J SAYERS (3)

| 187 | v. Kent | Tunbridge Wells | 2007 |
|---|---|---|---|
| 173 | v. Warwickshire | Birmingham | 2009 |
| 152 | v. Somerset | Taunton | 2009 |

### A B SELLERS (1)

| 204 | v. Cambridge University | Cambridge | 1936 |
|---|---|---|---|

### K SHARP (2)

| 173 | v. Derbyshire | Chesterfield | 1984 |
|---|---|---|---|
| 181 | v. Gloucestershire | Harrogate | 1986 |

### P J SHARPE (4)

| 203* | v. Cambridge University | Cambridge | 1960 |
|---|---|---|---|
| 152 | v. Kent | Sheffield | 1960 |
| 197 | v. Pakistanis | Leeds | 1967 |
| 172* | v. Glamorgan | Swansea | 1971 |

### G A SMITHSON (1)

| 169 | v. Leicestershire | Leicester | 1947 |
|---|---|---|---|

### W B STOTT (2)

| 181 | v. Essex | Sheffield | 1957 |
|---|---|---|---|
| 186 | v. Warwickshire | Birmingham | 1960 |

### H SUTCLIFFE (39)

| 174 | v. Kent | Dover | 1919 |
|---|---|---|---|
| 232 | v. Surrey | The Oval | 1922 |
| 213 | v. Somerset | Dewsbury | 1924 |
| 160 | v. Sussex | Sheffield | 1924 |
| 255* | v. Essex | Southend-on-Sea | 1924 |
| 235 | v. Middlesex | Leeds | 1925 |
| 206 | v. Warwickshire | Dewsbury | 1925 |
| 171 | v. MCC | Scarborough | 1925 |
| 200 | v. Leicestershire | Leicester (Aylestone Road) | 1926 |
| 176 | v. Surrey | Leeds | 1927 |
| 169 | v. Nottinghamshire | Bradford | 1927 |
| 228 | v. Sussex | Eastbourne | 1928 |
| 150 | v. Northamptonshire | Northampton | 1929 |
| 150* | v. Essex | Dewsbury | 1930 |
| 173 | v. Sussex | Hove | 1930 |
| 173* | v. Cambridge University | Cambridge | 1931 |
| 230 | v. Kent | Folkestone | 1931 |
| 183 | v. Somerset | Dewsbury | 1931 |
| 195 | v. Lancashire | Sheffield | 1931 |

### H SUTCLIFFE *(Continued)*

| | | | |
|---|---|---|---|
| 187 | v. Leicestershire | Leicester (Aylestone Road) | 1931 |
| 153* | v. Warwickshire | Hull | 1932 |
| 313 | v. Essex | Leyton | 1932 |
| 270 | v. Sussex | Leeds | 1932 |
| 182 | v. Derbyshire | Leeds | 1932 |
| 194 | v. Essex | Scarborough | 1932 |
| 205 | v. Warwickshire | Birmingham | 1933 |
| 177 | v. Middlesex | Bradford | 1933 |
| 174 | v. Leicestershire | Leicester (Aylestone Road) | 1933 |
| 152 | v. Cambridge University | Cambridge | 1934 |
| 166 | v. Essex | Hull | 1934 |
| 203 | v. Surrey | The Oval | 1934 |
| 187* | v. Worcestershire | Bradford | 1934 |
| 200* | v. Worcestershire | Sheffield | 1935 |
| 212 | v. Leicestershire | Leicester (Aylestone Road) | 1935 |
| 202 | v. Middlesex | Scarborough | 1936 |
| 189 | v. Leicestershire | Hull | 1937 |
| 165 | v. Lancashire | Manchester | 1939 |
| 234* | v. Leicestershire | Hull | 1939 |
| 175 | v. Middlesex | Lord's | 1939 |

### W H H SUTCLIFFE (3)

| | | | |
|---|---|---|---|
| 171* | v. Worcestershire | Worcester | 1952 |
| 181 | v. Kent | Canterbury | 1952 |
| 161* | v. Glamorgan | Harrogate | 1955 |

### K TAYLOR (8)

| | | | |
|---|---|---|---|
| 168* | v. Nottinghamshire | Nottingham | 1956 |
| 159 | v. Leicestershire | Sheffield | 1961 |
| 203* | v. Warwickshire | Birmingham | 1961 |
| 178* | v. Oxford University | Oxford | 1962 |
| 163 | v. Nottinghamshire | Leeds | 1962 |
| 153 | v. Lancashire | Manchester | 1964 |
| 160 | v. Australians | Sheffield | 1964 |
| 162 | v. Worcestershire | Kidderminster | 1967 |

### T L TAYLOR (1)

| | | | |
|---|---|---|---|
| 156 | v. Hampshire | Harrogate | 1901 |

### J TUNNICLIFFE (2)

| | | | |
|---|---|---|---|
| 243 | v. Derbyshire | Chesterfield | 1898 |
| 158 | v. Worcestershire | Worcester | 1900 |

### G ULYETT (1)

| | | | |
|---|---|---|---|
| 199* | v. Derbyshire | Sheffield | 1887 |

### M P VAUGHAN (7)

| | | | |
|---|---|---|---|
| 183 | v. Glamorgan | Cardiff (Sophia Gardens) | 1996 |
| 183 | v. Northamptonshire | Northampton | 1996 |
| 161 | v. Essex | Ilford | 1997 |
| 177 | v. Durham | Chester-le-Street | 1998 |
| 151 | v. Essex | Chelmsford | 1999 |
| 153 | v. Kent | Scarborough | 1999 |
| 155* | v. Derbyshire | Leeds | 2000 |

### E WAINWRIGHT (3)

| | | | |
|---|---|---|---|
| 171 | v. Middlesex | Lord's | 1897 |
| 153 | v. Leicestershire | Leicester | 1899 |
| 228 | v. Surrey | The Oval | 1899 |

### W WATSON (7)

| | | | |
|---|---|---|---|
| 153* | v. Surrey | The Oval | 1947 |
| 172 | v. Derbyshire | Scarborough | 1948 |
| 162* | v. Somerset | Leeds | 1953 |
| 163 | v. Sussex | Sheffield | 1955 |
| 174 | v. Lancashire | Sheffield | 1955 |
| 214* | v. Worcestershire | Worcester | 1955 |
| 162 | v. Northamptonshire | Harrogate | 1957 |

### C WHITE (6)

| | | | |
|---|---|---|---|
| 181 | v. Lancashire | Leeds | 1996 |
| 172* | v. Worcestershire | Leeds | 1997 |
| 186 | v. Lancashire | Manchester | 2001 |
| 183 | v. Glamorgan | Scarborough | 2001 |
| 161 | v. Leicestershire | Scarborough | 2002 |
| 173* | v. Derbyshire | Derby | 2003 |

### K S WILLIAMSON (1)

| | | | |
|---|---|---|---|
| 189 | v. Sussex | Scarborough | 2014 |

### B B WILSON (2)

| | | | |
|---|---|---|---|
| 150 | v. Warwickshire | Birmingham | 1912 |
| 208 | v. Sussex | Bradford | 1914 |

### J V WILSON (7)

| | | | |
|---|---|---|---|
| 157* | v. Sussex | Leeds | 1949 |
| 157 | v. Essex | Sheffield | 1950 |
| 166* | v. Sussex | Hull | 1951 |
| 223* | v. Scotland | Scarborough | 1951 |
| 154 | v. Oxford University | Oxford | 1952 |
| 230 | v. Derbyshire | Sheffield | 1952 |
| 165 | v. Oxford University | Oxford | 1956 |

### M J WOOD (5)

| | | | |
|---|---|---|---|
| 200* | v. Warwickshire | Leeds | 1998 |
| 157 | v. Northamptonshire | Leeds | 2003 |
| 207 | v. Somerset | Taunton | 2003 |
| 155 | v. Hampshire | Scarborough | 2003 |
| 202* | v. Bangladesh 'A' | Leeds | 2005 |

### N W D YARDLEY (2)

| | | | |
|---|---|---|---|
| 177 | v. Derbyshire | Scarborough | 1947 |
| 183* | v. Hampshire | Leeds | 1951 |

### YOUNUS KHAN (2)

| | | | |
|---|---|---|---|
| 202* | v. Hampshire | Southampton (Rose Bowl) | 2007 |
| 217* | v. Kent | Scarborough | 2007 |

# CENTURIES BY CURRENT PLAYERS

### A complete list of all First-class Centuries up to and including 2007 is to be found in the 2008 edition

#### *J M BAIRSTOW (13)*

| | | | |
|---|---|---|---|
| 205 | v. Nottinghamshire | Nottingham | 2011 |
| 136 | v. Somerset | Taunton | 2011 |
| 182 | v. Leicestershire | Scarborough | 2012 |
| 118 | v. Leicestershire | Leicester | 2012 |
| 107 | v. Kent | Leeds | 2012 |
| 186 | v. Derbyshire | Leeds | 2013 |
| 123 | v. Leeds/Bradford | Leeds | 2014 |
| 161* | v. Sussex | Arundel | 2014 |
| 102 | v. Hampshire | Leeds | 2015 |
| 125* | v. Middlesex | Leeds | 2015 |
| 219* | v. Durham | Chester-le-Street ** | 2015 |
| 108 | v. Warwickshire | Birmingham ** | 2015 |

(** consecutive innings)

| | | | |
|---|---|---|---|
| 139 | v. Worcestershire | Scarborough | 2015 |

#### *G S BALLANCE (12)*

| | | | |
|---|---|---|---|
| 111 | v. Warwickshire | Birmingham | 2011 |
| 121* | v. Gloucestershire | Bristol | 2012 |
| 112 | v. Leeds/Bradford MCCU | Leeds | 2013 |
| 107 | v. Somerset | Leeds | 2013 |
| 141 | v. Nottinghamshire | Scarborough | 2013 |
| 112 | v. Warwickshire | Leeds | 2013 |
| 148 | v. Surrey 1st inns | The Oval ** | 2013 |
| 108* | v. Surrey 2nd inns | The Oval ** | 2013 |
| 101 | v. Leeds/Bradford MCCU | Leeds ** | 2014 |

(** consecutive innings)

| | | | |
|---|---|---|---|
| 174 | v. Northamptonshire | Leeds | 2014 |
| 130 | v. Middlesex | Lord's | 2014 |
| 165 | v. Sussex | Hove | 2015 |

#### *T T BRESNAN (4)*

| | | | |
|---|---|---|---|
| 116 | v. Surrey | The Oval | 2007 |
| 101* | v. Warwickshire | Scarborough | 2007 |
| 100* | v. Somerset | Taunton | 2015 |
| 169* | v. Durham | Chester-le-Street | 2015 |

#### *A J FINCH (1)*

| | | | |
|---|---|---|---|
| 110 | v. Warwickshire | Birmingham | 2014 |

#### *A W GALE (19)*

| | | | |
|---|---|---|---|
| 149 | v. Warwickshire | Scarborough | 2006 |
| 138 | v. Hampshire | Leeds | 2008 |
| 150 | v. Surrey | The Oval | 2008 |
| 136 | v. Lancashire | Manchester | 2008 |
| 101 | v. Worcestershire | Worcester | 2009 |
| 121 | v. Lancashire | Manchester | 2009 |
| 101 | v. Somerset | Leeds | 2010 |
| 135 | v. Essex | Scarborough | 2010 |
| 151* | v. Nottinghamshire | Nottingham | 2010 |
| 145* | v. Nottinghamshire | Leeds | 2011 |

## A W GALE *(Continued)*

| | | | |
|---|---|---|---|
| 101* | v. Durham | Chester-le-Street | 2011 |
| 272 | v. Nottinghamshire | Scarborough | 2013 |
| 103 | v. Middlesex | Lord's | 2013 |
| 148 | v. Surrey | Leeds | 2013 |

*(2013 consecutive innings)*

| | | | |
|---|---|---|---|
| 124 | v. Durham | Chester-le-Street | 2014 |
| 126* | v. Middlesex | Scarborough | 2014 |
| 148 | v. Nottinghamshire | Leeds | 2015 |
| 164 | v. Worcestershire | Scarborough | 2015 |
| 125 | v. Hampshire | West End, Southampton | 2015 |

## J A LEANING *(3)*

| | | | |
|---|---|---|---|
| 116 | v. Nottinghamshire | Nottingham | 2015 |
| 123 | v. Somerset | Taunton | 2015 |
| 110 | v. Nottinghamshire | Leeds | 2015 |

## A Z LEES *(6)*

| | | | |
|---|---|---|---|
| 121 | v. Leeds/Bradford MCCU | Leeds | 2013 |
| 100 | v. Middlesex | Lord's | 2013 |
| 275* | v. Derbyshire | Chesterfield | 2013 |
| 138 | v. Northamptonshire | Northampton | 2014 |
| 108 | v. Durham | Leeds | 2014 |
| 100 | v. Nottinghamshire | Nottingham | 2015 |

## A LYTH *(15)*

| | | | |
|---|---|---|---|
| 132 | v. Nottinghamshire | Nottingham | 2008 |
| 142 | v. Somerset | Taunton | 2010 |
| 133 | v. Hampshire | Southampton | 2010 |
| 100 | v. Lancashire | Manchester | 2010 |
| 248* | v. Leicestershire | Leicester | 2012 |
| 111 | v. Leeds/Bradford | Leeds | 2013 |
| 105 | v. Somerset | Taunton | 2013 |
| 130 | v. Leeds/Bradford MCCU | Leeds | 2014 |
| 104 | v. Durham | Chester-le-Street | 2014 |
| 230 | v. Northamptonshire | Northampton | 2014 |
| 143 | v. Durham | Leeds | 2014 |
| 117 | v. Middlesex | Scarborough | 2014 |
| 251 | v. Lancashire | Manchester | 2014 |
| 122 | v. Nottinghamshire | Nottingham | 2014 |
| 113 | v. MCC | Abu Dhabi | 2015 |

## G J MAXWELL *(1)*

| | | | |
|---|---|---|---|
| 140 | v. Durham | Scarborough | 2015 |

## C A PUJARA *(1)*

| | | | |
|---|---|---|---|
| 133* | v. Hampshire | Leeds | 2015 |

## A U RASHID *(10)*

| | | | |
|---|---|---|---|
| 108 | v. Worcestershire | Kidderminster | 2007 |
| 111 | v. Sussex | Hove | 2008 |
| 117* | v. Hampshire | Basingstoke | 2009 |
| 157* | v. Lancashire | Leeds | 2009 |
| 180 | v. Somerset | Leeds | 2013 |
| 110* | v. Warwickshire | Birmingham | 2013 |
| 103 | v. Somerset | Taunton | 2013 |

*(2013 consecutive innings)*

*A U RASHID (Continued)*

| 108 | v. Somerset | Taunton | 2014 |
| 159* | v. Lancashire | Manchester | 2014 |
| 127 | v. Durham | Scarborough | 2015 |

*J E ROOT (5)*

| 160 | v. Sussex | Scarborough | 2011 |
| 222 * | v. Hampshire | Southampton (West End) | 2012 |
| 125 | v. Northamptonshire | Leeds | 2012 |
| 182 | v. Durham | Chester-le-Street | 2013 |
| 236 | v. Derbyshire | Leeds | 2013 |

*K S WILLIAMSON (1)*

| 189 | v. Sussex | Scarborough | 2014 |

# CENTURIES

**(Including highest score)**

| 112 | H Sutcliffe | 313 | v Essex | at Leyton | 1932 |
|-----|-------------|-----|---------|-----------|------|
| 103 | G Boycott | 260* | v Essex | at Colchester (Garrison Gd) | 1970 |
| 85 | L Hutton | 280* | v Hampshire | at Sheffield | 1939 |
| 62 | M Leyland | 263 | v Essex | at Hull | 1936 |
| 61 | D Denton | 221 | v Kent | at Tunbridge Wells | 1912 |
| 60 | P Holmes | 315* | v Middlesex | at Lord's | 1925 |
| 56 | G H Hirst | 341 | v Leicestershire | at Leicester (Aylestone Rd) | 1905 |
| 46 | W Rhodes | 267* | v Leicestershire | at Leeds | 1921 |
| 41 | M D Moxon | 274* | v Worcestershire | at Worcester | 1994 |
| 39 | A Mitchell | 189 | v Northamptonshire | at Northampton | 1926 |
| 37 | E Oldroyd | 194 | v Worcestershire | at Worcester | 1923 |
| 34 | J H Hampshire | 183* | v Sussex | at Hove | 1971 |
| 34 | A McGrath | 211 | v Warwickshire | at Birmingham | 2009 |
| 33 | D B Close | 198 | v Surrey | at The Oval | 1960 |
| 30 | F A Lowson | 259* | v Worcestershire | at Worcester | 1953 |
| 29 | D E V Padgett | 161* | v Oxford University | at Oxford | 1959 |
| 29 | J V Wilson | 230 | v Derbyshire | at Sheffield | 1952 |
| 28 | D Byas | 213 | v Worcestershire | at Scarborough | 1995 |
| 27 | W Barber | 255 | v Surrey | at Sheffield | 1935 |
| 26 | D S Lehmann | 339 | v Durham | at Leeds | 2006 |
| 26 | W Watson | 214* | v Worcestershire | at Worcester | 1955 |
| 25 | A A Metcalfe | 216* | v Middlesex | at Leeds | 1988 |
| 24 | E I Lester | 186 | v Warwickshire | at Scarborough | 1949 |
| 23 | J T Brown | 311 | v Sussex | at Sheffield | 1897 |
| 23 | P J Sharpe | 203* | v Cambridge University | at Cambridge | 1960 |
| 22 | R G Lumb | 165* | v Gloucestershire | at Bradford | 1984 |
| 22 | J Tunnicliffe | 243 | v Derbyshire | at Chesterfield | 1898 |
| 21 | Hon F S Jackson | 160 | v Gloucestershire | at Sheffield | 1898 |
| 20 | M P Vaughan | 183 | v Glamorgan | at Cardiff (Sophia Gardens) | 1996 |
| | *and* | 183 | v Northamptonshire | at Northampton | 1996 |
| 19 | A W Gale | 272 | v. Nottinghamshire | at Scarborough | 2013 |
| 19 | C White | 186 | v Lancashire | at Manchester | 2001 |
| 18 | J A Rudolph | 228* | v Durham | at Leeds | 2010 |
| 18 | E Wainwright | 228 | v Surrey | at The Oval | 1899 |
| 17 | W B Stott | 186 | v Warwickshire | at Birmingham | 1960 |
| 17 | N W D Yardley | 183* | v Hampshire | at Leeds | 1951 |

| 16 | K Taylor | 203* | v Warwickshire | at Birmingham | 1961 |
|----|----------|------|----------------|---------------|------|
| 16 | M J Wood | 207 | v Somerset | at Taunton | 2003 |
| 15 | R Kilner | 206* | v Derbyshire | at Sheffield | 1920 |
| 15 | A Lyth | 251 | v. Lancashire | at Manchester | 2014 |
| 15 | G Ulyett | 199* | v Derbyshire | at Sheffield | 1887 |
| 15 | B B Wilson | 208 | v Sussex | at Bradford | 1914 |
| 14 | R Illingworth | 162 | v Indians | at Sheffield | 1959 |
| 13 | J M Bairstow | 219* | v. Durham | at Chester-le-Street | 2015 |
| 13 | J D Love | 170* | v Worcestershire | at Worcester | 1979 |
| 12 | G S Ballance | 174 | v. Northamptonshire | at Leeds | 2014 |
| 12 | R J Blakey | 223* | v Northamptonshire | at Leeds | 2003 |
| 12 | H Halliday | 144 | v Derbyshire | at Chesterfield | 1950 |
| 11 | P A Jaques | 243 | v. Hampshire | at Southampton (Rose Bowl) | 2004 |
| 11 | K Sharp | 181 | v Gloucestershire | at Harrogate | 1986 |
| 10 | C W J Athey | 134 | v Derbyshire | at Derby | 1982 |
| 10 | Lord Hawke | 166 | v Warwickshire | at Birmingham | 1896 |
| 10 | F Mitchell | 194 | v Leicestershire | at Leicester | 1899 |
| 10 | A U Rashid | 180 | v. Somerset | at Leeds | 2013 |
| 9 | D L Bairstow | 145 | v Middlesex | at Scarborough | 1980 |
| 9 | M G Bevan | 160* | v Surrey | at Middlesbrough | 1996 |
| 9 | L Hall | 160 | v Lancashire | at Bradford | 1887 |
| 9 | J J Sayers | 187 | v Kent | at Tunbridge Wells | 2007 |
| 8 | W Bates | 136 | v Sussex | at Hove | 1886 |
| 8 | M J Lumb | 144 | v Middlesex | at Southgate | 2006 |
| 8 | T L Taylor | 156 | v Hampshire | at Harrogate | 1901 |
| 7 | J B Bolus | 146* | v Hampshire | at Portsmouth | 1960 |
| 7 | E Robinson | 135* | v Leicestershire | at Leicester (Aylestone Rd) | 1921 |
| 7 | P E Robinson | 189 | v Leicestershire | at Scarborough | 1991 |
| 6 | A Z Lees | 275* | v. Derbyshire | at Chesterfield | 2013 |
| 6 | E Lockwood | 208 | v Kent | at Gravesend | 1883 |
| 6 | R Peel | 210* | v Warwickshire | at Birmingham | 1896 |
| 6 | W H H Sutcliffe | 181 | v Kent | at Canterbury | 1952 |
| 5 | C M Old | 116 | v Indians | at Bradford | 1974 |
| 5 | J E Root | 236 | v. Derbyshire | at Leeds | 2013 |
| 4 | T T Bresnan | 169* | v. Durham | at Chester-le-Street | 2015 |
| 4 | I Grimshaw | 129* | v Cambridge University | at Sheffield | 1885 |
| 4 | S Haigh | 159 | v Nottinghamshire | at Sheffield | 1901 |
| 4 | S N Hartley | 114 | v Gloucestershire | at Bradford | 1982 |
| 4 | R A Hutton | 189 | v Pakistanis | at Bradford | 1971 |
| 4 | A B Sellers | 204 | v Cambridge University | at Cambridge | 1936 |
| 3 | G L Brophy | 177* | v Worcestershire | at Worcester | 2011 |
| 3 | P Carrick | 131* | v Northamptonshire | at Northampton | 1980 |
| 3 | A J Dalton | 128 | v Middlesex | at Leeds | 1972 |
| 3 | A Drake | 147* | v Derbyshire | at Chesterfield | 1911 |
| 3 | J A Leaning | 123 | v. Somerset | at Taunton | 2015 |
| 3 | F Lee | 165 | v Lancashire | at Bradford | 1887 |
| 3 | G G Macaulay | 125* | v Nottinghamshire | at Nottingham | 1921 |
| 3 | R Moorhouse | 113 | v Somerset | at Taunton | 1896 |
| 3 | R M Pyrah | 134* | v Loughborough MCCU | at Leeds | 2010 |
| 3 | J W Rothery | 161 | v Kent | at Dover | 1908 |
| 3 | J Rowbotham | 113 | v Surrey | at The Oval | 1873 |
| 3 | T F Smailes | 117 | v Glamorgan | at Cardiff | 1938 |
| 3 | Younus Khan | 217* | v Kent | at Scarborough | 2007 |
| 2 | M W Booth | 210 | v Worcestershire | at Worcester | 1911 |
| 2 | D C F Burton | 142* | v Hampshire | at Dewsbury | 1919 |
| 2 | K R Davidson | 128 | v Kent | at Maidstone | 1934 |

| 2 | P A Gibb | 157* | v Nottinghamshire | at Sheffield | 1935 |
|---|---|---|---|---|---|
| 2 | P J Hartley | 127* | v Lancashire | at Manchester | 1988 |
| 2 | I J Harvey | 209* | v Somerset | at Leeds | 2005 |
| 2 | C Johnson | 107 | v Somerset | at Sheffield | 1973 |
| 2 | S A Kellett | 125* | v Derbyshire | at Chesterfield | 1991 |
| 2 | N Kilner | 112 | v Leicestershire | at Leeds | 1921 |
| 2 | B Parker | 138* | v Oxford University | at Oxford | 1997 |
| 2 | A Sellers | 105 | v Middlesex | at Lord's | 1893 |
| 2 | E Smith (Morley) | 129 | v Hampshire | at Bradford | 1899 |
| 2 | G A Smithson | 169 | v Leicestershire | at Leicester | 1947 |
| 2 | G B Stevenson | 115* | v Warwickshire | at Birmingham | 1982 |
| 2 | F S Trueman | 104 | v Northamptonshire | at Northampton | 1963 |
| 2 | C Turner | 130 | v Somerset | at Sheffield | 1936 |
| 2 | D J Wainwright | 104* | v Sussex | at Hove | 2008 |
| 2 | T A Wardall | 106 | v Gloucestershire | at Gloucester (Spa Ground) | 1892 |
| 1 | Azeem Rafiq | 100 | v Worcestershire | at Worcester | 2009 |
| 1 | A T Barber | 100 | v England XI | at Sheffield | 1929 |
| 1 | H D Bird | 181* | v Glamorgan | at Bradford | 1959 |
| 1 | T J D Birtles | 104 | v Lancashire | at Sheffield | 1914 |
| 1 | G S Blewett | 190 | v Northamptonshire | at Scarborough | 1999 |
| 1 | M T G Elliott | 127 | v Warwickshire | at Birmingham | 2002 |
| 1 | T Emmett | 104 | v Gloucestershire | at Clifton | 1873 |
| 1 | G M Fellows | 109 | v Lancashire | at Manchester | 2002 |
| 1 | A J Finch | 110 | v Warwickshire | at Birmingham | 2014 |
| 1 | J N Gillespie | 123* | v Surrey | at The Oval | 2007 |
| 1 | D Gough | 121 | v Warwickshire | at Leeds | 1996 |
| 1 | A K D Gray | 104 | v Somerset | at Taunton | 2003 |
| 1 | A P Grayson | 100 | v Worcestershire | at Worcester | 1994 |
| 1 | F E Greenwood | 104* | v Glamorgan | at Hull | 1929 |
| 1 | G M Hamilton | 125 | v Hampshire | at Leeds | 2000 |
| 1 | W E Harbord | 109 | v Oxford University | at Oxford | 1930 |
| 1 | R Iddison | 112 | v Cambridgeshire | at Hunslet | 1869 |
| 1 | W G Keighley | 110 | v Surrey | at Leeds | 1951 |
| 1 | R A Kettleborough | | | | |
| | | 108 | v Essex | at Leeds | 1996 |
| 1 | B Leadbeater | 140* | v Hampshire | at Portsmouth | 1976 |
| 1 | D R Martyn | 238 | v Gloucestershire | at Leeds | 2003 |
| 1 | G J Maxwell | 140 | v. Durham | at Scarborough | 2015 |
| 1 | J T Newstead | 100* | v Nottinghamshire | at Nottingham | 1908 |
| 1 | C A Pujara | 133* | v. Hampshire | at Leeds | 2015 |
| 1 | R B Richardson | 112 | v Warwickshire | at Birmingham | 1993 |
| 1 | H Rudston | 164 | v Leicestershire | at Leicester (Aylestone Road) | 1904 |
| 1 | A Sidebottom | 124 | v Glamorgan | at Cardiff (Sophia Gardens) | 1977 |
| 1 | I G Swallow | 114 | v MCC | at Scarborough | 1987 |
| 1 | S R Tendulkar | 100 | v Durham | at Durham | 1992 |
| 1 | J Thewlis | 108 | v Surrey | at The Oval | 1868 |
| 1 | C T Tyson | 100* | v Hampshire | at Southampton | 1921 |
| 1 | H Verity | 101 | v Jamaica | at Kingston (Sabina Park) | 1935/36 |
| 1 | A Waddington | 114 | v Worcestershire | at Leeds | 1927 |
| 1 | W A I Washington | | | | |
| | | 100* | v Surrey | at Leeds | 1902 |
| 1 | H Wilkinson | 113 | v MCC | at Scarborough | 1904 |
| 1 | W H Wilkinson | 103 | v Sussex | at Sheffield | 1909 |
| 1 | K S Williamson | 189 | v. Sussex | at Scarborough | 2014 |
| 1 | E R Wilson | 104* | v Essex | at Bradford | 1913 |
| 1 | A Wood | 123* | v Worcestershire | at Sheffield | 1935 |
| 1 | J D Woodford | 101 | v Warwickshire | at Middlesbrough | 1971 |

## SUMMARY OF CENTURIES
## FOR AND AGAINST YORKSHIRE 1863-2015

| FOR YORKSHIRE | | | | AGAINST YORKSHIRE | | |
|---|---|---|---|---|---|---|
| Total | In Yorkshire | Away | | Total | In Yorkshire | Away |
| 110 | 65 | 45 | Derbyshire | 57 | 27 | 30 |
| 30 | 14 | 16 | Durham | 23 | 13 | 10 |
| 75 | 34 | 41 | Essex | 46 | 21 | 25 |
| 68 | 38 | 30 | Glamorgan | 23 | 13 | 10 |
| 87 | 41 | 46 | Gloucestershire | 53 | 27 | 26 |
| 91 | 38 | 53 | Hampshire | 57 | 25 | 32 |
| 81 | 37 | 44 | Kent | 60 | 29 | 31 |
| 111 | 56 | 55 | Lancashire | 113 | 58 | 55 |
| 97 | 52 | 45 | Leicestershire | 46 | 23 | 23 |
| 95 | 48 | 47 | Middlesex | 88 | 37 | 51 |
| 81 | 35 | 46 | Northamptonshire | 53 | 25 | 28 |
| 125 | 59 | 66 | Nottinghamshire | 83 | 33 | 50 |
| 100 | 49 | 51 | Somerset | 58 | 21 | 37 |
| 114 | 48 | 66 | Surrey | 107 | 38 | 69 |
| 90 | 42 | 48 | Sussex | 77 | 33 | 44 |
| 105 | 36 | 69 | Warwickshire | 73 | 28 | 45 |
| 74 | 32 | 42 | Worcestershire | 42 | 15 | 27 |
| 1 | 1 | 0 | Cambridgeshire | 0 | 0 | 0 |
| **1535** | **725** | **810** | **Totals** | **1059** | **466** | **593** |
| 9 | 9 | 0 | Australians | 16 | 16 | 0 |
| 9 | 9 | 0 | Indians | 7 | 7 | 0 |
| 8 | 8 | 0 | New Zealanders | 3 | 3 | 0 |
| 5 | 5 | 0 | Pakistanis | 1 | 1 | 0 |
| 9 | 9 | 0 | South Africans | 7 | 7 | 0 |
| 5 | 5 | 0 | Sri Lankans | 1 | 1 | 0 |
| 5 | 5 | 0 | West Indians | 6 | 6 | 0 |
| 1 | 1 | 0 | Zimbabweans | 0 | 0 | 0 |
| 3 | 3 | 0 | Bangladesh 'A' | 1 | 1 | 0 |
| 0 | 0 | 0 | India 'A' | 1 | 1 | 0 |
| 1 | 1 | 0 | Pakistan 'A' | 1 | 1 | 0 |
| 45 | 1 | 44 | Cambridge University | 20 | 2 | 18 |
| 2 | 2 | 0 | Combined Services | 0 | 0 | 0 |
| 1 | 0 | 1 | Durham MCCU | 1 | 0 | 1 |
| 4 | 3 | 1 | England XI's | 3 | 2 | 1 |
| 0 | 0 | 0 | International XI | 1 | 1 | 0 |
| 1 | 0 | 1 | Ireland | 0 | 0 | 0 |
| 3 | 0 | 3 | Jamaica | 3 | 0 | 3 |
| 6 | 6 | 0 | Leeds/Bradford MCCU | 0 | 0 | 0 |
| 1 | 0 | 1 | Liverpool & District | 0 | 0 | 0 |
| 2 | 2 | 0 | Loughborough MCCU | 1 | 1 | 0 |
| 1 | 0 | 1 | Mashonaland | 0 | 0 | 0 |
| 2 | 0 | 2 | Matabeleland | 1 | 0 | 1 |
| 53 | 38 | 15 | MCC | 52 | 34 | 18 |
| 39 | 0 | 39 | Oxford University | 11 | 0 | 11 |
| 6 | 0 | 6 | Rest of England | 15 | 0 | 15 |
| 9 | 5 | 4 | Scotland | 1 | 0 | 1 |
| 3 | 3 | 0 | C I Thornton's XI | 4 | 4 | 0 |
| 0 | 0 | 0 | Western Province | 1 | 0 | 1 |
| 1 | 1 | 0 | I Zingari | 1 | 1 | 0 |
| **234** | **116** | **118** | **Totals** | **161** | **91** | **70** |
| **1769** | **841** | **928** | **Grand Totals** | **1220** | **557** | **663** |

# FOUR CENTURIES IN ONE INNINGS

|  |  |  | F S Jackson | ................ | 117 |
|  |  |  | E Wainwright | ................ | 126 |
| 1896 | v. | Warwickshire | Lord Hawke | ................ | 166 |
|  |  | at Birmingham | R Peel | ................ | *210 |

(First instance in First-Class cricket)

# THREE CENTURIES IN ONE INNINGS

|  |  |  | L Hall | ................ | 116 |
| 1884 | v. | Cambridge University | W Bates | ................ | 133 |
|  |  | at Cambridge | I Grimshaw | ................ | 115 |
|  |  |  | G Ulyett | ................ | 124 |
| 1887 | v. | Kent | L Hall | ................ | 110 |
|  |  | at Canterbury | F Lee | ................ | 119 |
|  |  |  | J T Brown | ................ | 311 |
| 1897 | v. | Sussex | J Tunnicliffe | ................ | 147 |
|  |  | at Sheffield | E Wainwright | ................ | *104 |
|  |  |  | F S Jackson | ................ | 155 |
| 1899 | v. | Middlesex | D Denton | ................ | 113 |
|  |  | at Bradford | F Mitchell | ................ | 121 |
|  |  |  | D Denton | ................ | 105 |
| 1904 | v. | Surrey | G H Hirst | ................ | 104 |
|  |  | at The Oval | J Tunnicliffe | ................ | *139 |
|  |  |  | H Sutcliffe | ................ | 118 |
| 1919 | v. | Gloucestershire | D Denton | ................ | 122 |
|  |  | at Leeds | R Kilner | ................ | 115 |
|  |  |  | P Holmes | ................ | 130 |
| 1925 | v. | Glamorgan | H Sutcliffe | ................ | 121 |
|  |  | at Huddersfield | E Robinson | ................ | *108 |
|  |  |  | P Holmes | ................ | 105 |
| 1928 | v. | Middlesex | E Oldroyd | ................ | 108 |
|  |  | at Lord's | A Mitchell | ................ | 105 |
|  |  |  | H Sutcliffe | ................ | 129 |
| 1928 | v. | Essex | P Holmes | ................ | 136 |
|  |  | at Leyton | M Leyland | ................ | *133 |
|  |  |  | E Oldroyd | ................ | 168 |
| 1929 | v. | Glamorgan | W Barber | ................ | 114 |
|  |  | at Hull | F E Greenwood | ................ | *104 |
|  |  |  | H Sutcliffe | ................ | 107 |
| 1933 | v. | MCC | A Mitchell | ................ | 158 |
|  |  | at Scarborough | M Leyland | ................ | 133 |
|  |  |  | H Sutcliffe | ................ | 129 |
| 1936 | v. | Surrey | L Hutton | ................ | 163 |
|  |  | at Leeds | M Leyland | ................ | *163 |
|  |  |  | H Sutcliffe | ................ | 189 |
| 1937 | v. | Leicestershire | L Hutton | ................ | 153 |
|  |  | at Hull | M Leyland | ................ | *118 |
|  |  |  | L Hutton | ................ | 137 |
| 1947 | v. | Leicestershire | N W D Yardley | ................ | 100 |
|  |  | at Leicester | G.A Smithson | ................ | 169 |
|  |  |  | J H Hampshire | ................ | *116 |
| 1971 | v. | Oxford University | R A Hutton | ................ | 101 |
|  |  | at Oxford | A J Dalton | ................ | 111 |

# THREE CENTURIES IN ONE INNINGS *(Continued)*

|  |  |  |  |
|---|---|---|---|
|  |  | G Boycott | 141 |
| 1975 | v. Gloucestershire<br>at Bristol | R G Lumb | 101 |
|  |  | J H Hampshire | *106 |
|  |  | M D Moxon | 130 |
| 1995 | v. Cambridge University<br>at Cambridge | D Byas | 181 |
|  |  | M G Bevan | *113 |
|  |  | M J Wood | 102 |
| 2001 | v. Leicestershire<br>at Leeds | M J Lumb | 122 |
|  |  | D S Lehmann | 104 |
|  |  | C White | 183 |
| 2001 | v. Glamorgan<br>at Scarborough | M J Wood | 124 |
|  |  | D Byas | 104 |
|  |  | J A Rudolph | 122 |
| 2007 | v. Surrey<br>at The Oval | T T Bresnan | 116 |
|  |  | J N Gillespie | *123 |
|  |  | A Lyth | 130 |
| 2014 | v. Leeds/Bradford MCCU<br>At Leeds | G S Ballance | 101 |
|  |  | J M Bairstow | 123 |

## CENTURY IN EACH INNINGS

| D Denton | 107 and 109* | v. Nottinghamshire at Nottingham, 1906 |
|---|---|---|
| G H Hirst | 111 and 117* | v. Somerset at Bath, 1906 |
| D Denton | 133 and 121 | v. MCC at Scarborough, 1908 |
| W Rhodes | 128 and 115 | v. MCC at Scarborough, 1911 |
| P Holmes | 126 and 111* | v. Lancashire at Manchester, 1920 |
| H Sutcliffe | 107 and 109* | v. MCC at Scarborough, 1926 |
| H Sutcliffe | 111 and 100* | v. Nottinghamshire at Nottingham, 1928 |
| E I Lester | 126 and 142 | v. Northamptonshire at Northampton, 1947 |
| L Hutton | 197 and 104 | v. Essex at Southend, 1947 |
| E I Lester | 125* and 132 | v. Lancashire at Manchester, 1948 |
| L Hutton | 165 and 100 | v. Sussex at Hove, 1949 |
| L Hutton | 103 and 137 | v. MCC at Scarborough, 1952 |
| G Boycott | 103 and 105 | v. Nottinghamshire at Sheffield, 1966 |
| G Boycott | 163 and 141* | v. Nottinghamshire at Bradford, 1983 |
| M D Moxon | 123 and 112* | v. Indians at Scarborough, 1986 |
| A A Metcalfe | 194* and 107 | v. Nottinghamshire at Nottingham, 1990 |
| M P Vaughan | 100 and 151 | v. Essex at Chelmsford, 1999 |
| Younus Khan | 106 and 202* | v. Hampshire at Southampton, 2007 |
| G S Ballance | 148 and 108* | v. Surrey at The Oval, 2013 |

## HIGHEST INDIVIDUAL SCORES
## FOR AND AGAINST YORKSHIRE

**Highest For Yorkshire:**
341  G H Hirst v. Leicestershire at Leicester, 1905
**Highest Against Yorkshire:**
318*  W G Grace for Gloucestershire at Cheltenham, 1876

Yorkshire versus:

| **Derbyshire** | *For Yorkshire:* | 300 — J T Brown at Chesterfield, 1898 |
|---|---|---|
|  | *Against:* | 270* — C F Hughes at Leeds, 2013 |
| *Most Centuries* | *For Yorkshire:* | G Boycott 9 |
|  | *Against:* | K J Barnett and W Storer 4 each |
| **Durham** | *For Yorkshire:* | 339 — D S Lehmann at Leeds, 2006 |
|  | *Against:* | 184 — M J di Venuto at Chester-le-Street, 2008 |
| *Most Centuries* | *For Yorkshire:* | A McGrath 5 |
|  | *Against:* | M J Di Venuto 4 |

Yorkshire versus

**Essex** | *For Yorkshire:* | 313 — H Sutcliffe at Leyton, 1932
| *Against:* | 219* — D J Insole at Colchester, 1949
*Most Centuries* | *For Yorkshire:* | H Sutcliffe 9
| *Against:* | F L Fane, K W R Fletcher, G A Gooch and D J Insole 3 each

**Glamorgan** | *For Yorkshire:* | 213 — M D Moxon at Cardiff, 1996
| *Against:* | 202* — H Morris at Cardiff, 1996
*Most Centuries* | *For Yorkshire:* | G Boycott, P Holmes and H Sutcliffe 5 each
| *Against:* | H Morris 5

**Gloucestershire** | *For Yorkshire:* | 238 — D R Martyn at Leeds, 2003
| *Against:* | 318* — W G Grace at Cheltenham, 1876
*Most Centuries* | *For Yorkshire:* | G Boycott 6
| *Against:* | W G Grace 9

**Hampshire** | *For Yorkshire:* | 302* — P Holmes at Portsmouth, 1920
| *Against:* | 300* — M A Carberry at Southampton, 2011
*Most Centuries* | *For Yorkshire:* | H Sutcliffe 6
| *Against:* | C P Mead 10

**Kent** | *For Yorkshire:* | 248 — W Barber at Leeds, 1934.
| *Against:* | 207 — D P Fulton at Maidstone, 1998
*Most Centuries* | *For Yorkshire:* | A McGrath 6
| *Against:* | F E Woolley 5

**Lancashire** | *For Yorkshire:* | 252 — D S Lehmann at Leeds, 2001
| *Against:* | 225 — G D Lloyd at Leeds, 1997 (Non-Championship)
| | 206 — S G Law at Leeds, 2007
*Most Centuries* | *For Yorkshire:* | G Boycott and H Sutcliffe 9 each
| *Against:* | M A Atherton and C H Lloyd 6 each.

**Leicestershire** | *For Yorkshire:* | 341— G H Hirst at Leicester, 1905
| *Against:* | 218— J J Whitaker at Bradford, 1996
*Most Centuries* | *For Yorkshire:* | H Sutcliffe 10
| *Against:* | J J Whitaker and C J B Wood 5 each

**Middlesex** | *For Yorkshire:* | 315* — P Holmes at Lord's, 1925
| *Against:* | 243* — A J Webbe at Huddersfield, 1887
*Most Centuries* | *For Yorkshire:* | P Holmes and H Sutcliffe 7 each
| *Against:* | M W Gatting 8

**Northamptonshire** | *For Yorkshire:* | 277* — P Holmes at Harrogate, 1921
| *Against:* | 235 — A J Lamb at Leeds, 1990
*Most Centuries* | *For Yorkshire:* | H Sutcliffe 5
| *Against:* | W Larkins 5

**Nottinghamshire** | *For Yorkshire:* | 285 — P Holmes at Nottingham, 1929
| *Against:* | 251* — D J Hussey at Leeds, 2010
*Most Centuries* | *For Yorkshire:* | G Boycott 15
| *Against:* | R T Robinson 6

**Somerset** | *For Yorkshire:* | 213 — H Sutcliffe at Dewsbury, 1924
| *Against:* | 297 — M J Wood at Taunton, 2005
*Most Centuries* | *For Yorkshire:* | G Boycott 6
| *Against:* | L C H Palairet, IVA. Richards, M E Trescothick 5 each

**Surrey** | *For Yorkshire:* | 255 — W Barber at Sheffield, 1935
| *Against:* | 273 — T W Hayward at The Oval, 1899
*Most Centuries* | *For Yorkshire:* | H Sutcliffe 9
| *Against:* | J B Hobbs 8

Yorkshire versus

| | | |
|---|---|---|
| **Sussex** | *For Yorkshire:* | 311 — J T Brown at Sheffield, 1897 |
| | *Against:* | 274* — M W Goodwin at Hove, 2011 |
| *Most Centuries* | *For Yorkshire:* | L Hutton 8 |
| | *Against:* | C B Fry 7 |
| **Warwickshire** | *For Yorkshire:* | 275 — P Holmes at Bradford, 1928 |
| | *Against:* | 225 — D P Ostler at Birmingham, 2002 |
| *Most Centuries* | *For Yorkshire:* | G Boycott and H Sutcliffe 8 each |
| | *Against:* | D L Amiss, H E Dollery, R B Khanhai and W G Quaife 4 each. |
| **Worcestershire** | *For Yorkshire:* | 274* — M D Moxon at Worcester, 1994 |
| | *Against:* | 259 — D Kenyon at Kidderminster, 1956 |
| *Most Centuries* | *For Yorkshire:* | M Leyland 6 |
| | *Against:* | D Kenyon and G M Turner 5 each |
| **Australians** | *For Yorkshire:* | 167 — J T Brown at Bradford, 1899 |
| | *Against:* | 193* — B C Booth at Bradford, 1964 |
| *Most Centuries* | *For Yorkshire:* | G Boycott and D Denton 2 each |
| | *Against:* | N C O'Neill 2 |
| **Indians** | *For Yorkshire:* | 183* — L Hutton at Bradford, 1946 |
| | *Against:* | 244* — V S Hazare at Sheffield, 1946 |
| *Most Centuries* | *For Yorkshire:* | M D Moxon 2 |
| | *Against:* | V S Hazare, VMankad, PR Umrigar D K Gaekwad, G A Parkar and R Lamba 1 each |
| **New Zealanders** | *For Yorkshire:* | 175 — P Holmes at Bradford, 1927 |
| | *Against:* | 126 — W M Wallace at Bradford, 1949 |
| *Most Centuries* | *For Yorkshire:* | L Hutton and DB Close 2 each |
| | *Against:* | H G Vivian, WM Wallace and J G Wright 1 each |
| **Pakistanis** | *For Yorkshire:* | 197 — P J Sharpe at Leeds, 1967 |
| | *Against:* | 139 — A H Kardar at Sheffield, 1954 |
| *Most Centuries* | *For Yorkshire:* | P J Sharpe 2 |
| | *Against:* | A H Kardar 1 |
| **South Africans** | *For Yorkshire:* | 156 — L Hutton at Sheffield, 1951 |
| | *Against:* | 168 — I J Seidle at Sheffield, 1929 |
| *Most Centuries* | *For Yorkshire:* | L Hutton 2 |
| | *Against:* | H B Cameron, J D Lindsay, B Mitchell, D P B Morkel, I J Seidle, L J Tancred, C B van Ryneveld 1 each |
| **Sri Lankans** | *For Yorkshire:* | 132 — M D Moxon at Leeds, 1988 |
| | *Against:* | 112 — S A R Silva at Leeds, 1988 |
| *Most Centuries* | *For Yorkshire:* | K Sharp 2 |
| | *Against:* | S A R Silva 1 |
| **West Indians** | *For Yorkshire:* | 112* — D Denton at Harrogate, 1906 |
| | *Against:* | 164 — S F A Bacchus at Leeds, 1980 |
| *Most Centuries* | *For Yorkshire:* | M G Bevan, D Denton, L Hutton, R G Lumb and A A Metcalfe 1 each |
| | *Against:* | S F A Bacchus, C O Browne, S Chanderpaul P A Goodman, C L Hooper and G St A Sobers 1 each |

# HIGHEST INDIVIDUAL SCORES FOR AND AGAINST
## YORKSHIRE *(continued)*

Yorkshire versus

| | | |
|---|---|---|
| **Zimbabweans** | *For Yorkshire:* | 113 — M D Moxon at Leeds, 1990 |
| | *Against:* | 89 — G J Whittall at Leeds, 2000 |
| *Most Centuries* | *For Yorkshire:* | M D Moxon 1 |
| | *Against:* | None |
| **Cambridge** | *For Yorkshire:* | 207* — G Boycott at Cambridge, 1976 |
| **University** | *Against:* | 171* — G L Jessop at Cambridge, 1899 |
| | | 171 — P B H May at Cambridge, 1952 |
| *Most Centuries* | *For Yorkshire:* | H Sutcliffe 4 |
| | *Against:* | G M Kemp 2 |
| **Durham MCCU** | *For Yorkshire:* | 139 — J J Sayers at Durham, 2011 |
| | *Against:* | 127 — T Westley at Durham, 2011 |
| *Most Centuries* | *For Yorkshire:* | J J Sayers 1 |
| | *Against:* | T Westley 1 |
| **Leeds Bradford MCCU** | *For Yorkshire:* | 130 — A Lyth at Leeds, 2014 |
| | *Against:* | 69 — A MacQueen at Leeds, 2012 |
| *Most Centuries* | *For Yorkshire:* | J M Bairstow and A Lyth, 2 each |
| **Loughborough MCCU** | *For Yorkshire:* | 134* — R M Pyrah at Leeds, 2010 |
| | *Against:* | 107 — C P Murtagh at Leeds, 2007 |
| *Most Centuries* | *For Yorkshire:* | R M Pyrah 2 |
| | *Against:* | C P Murtagh 1 |
| **MCC** | *For Yorkshire:* | 180* — G H Hirst at Lord's, 1919 |
| | *Against:* | 214 — E H Hendren at Lord's, 1919 |
| *Most Centuries* | *For Yorkshire:* | L Hutton 8 |
| | *Against:* | R E S Wyatt 5 |
| **Oxford University** | *For Yorkshire:* | 196 — R J Blakey at Oxford, 1991 |
| | *Against:* | 201 — J E Raphael at Oxford, 1904 |
| *Most Centuries* | *For Yorkshire:* | M Leyland 4 |
| | *Against:* | A A Baig and Nawab of Pataudi (Jun.) 2 each |

J B Hobbs scored 11 centuries against Yorkshire – the highest by any individual (8 for Surrey and 3 for the Rest of England).

Three players have scored 10 centuries against Yorkshire – W G Grace (9 for Gloucestershire and 1 for MCC). E H Hendren (6 for Middlesex, 3 for MCC and 1 for the Rest of England) and C P Mead (all 10 for Hampshire).

# CARRYING BAT THROUGH A COMPLETED INNINGS

| Batsman | Score | Total | Against | Season |
|---|---|---|---|---|
| G R Atkinson | 30* | 73 | Nottinghamshire at Bradford | 1865 |
| L Hall | 31* | 94 | Sussex at Hove | 1878 |
| L Hall | 124* | 331 | Sussex at Hove | 1883 |
| L Hall | 128* | 285 | Sussex at Huddersfield | 1884 |
| L Hall | 32* | 81 | Kent at Sheffield | 1885 |
| L Hall | 79* | 285 | Surrey at Sheffield | 1885 |
| L Hall | 37* | 96 | Derbyshire at Derby | 1885 |
| L Hall | 50* | 173 | Sussex at Huddersfield | 1886 |
| L Hall | 74* | 172 | Kent at Canterbury | 1886 |
| G Ulyett | 199* | 399 | Derbyshire at Sheffield | 1887 |
| L Hall | 119* | 334 | Gloucestershire at Dewsbury | 1887 |
| L Hall | 82* | 218 | Sussex at Hove | 1887 |
| L Hall | 34* | 104 | Surrey at The Oval | 1888 |
| L Hall | 129* | 461 | Gloucestershire at Clifton | 1888 |
| L Hall | 85* | 259 | Middlesex at Lord's | 1889 |
| L Hall | 41* | 106 | Nottinghamshire at Sheffield | 1891 |
| W Rhodes | 98* | 184 | MCC at Lord's | 1903 |
| W Rhodes | 85* | 152 | Essex at Leyton | 1910 |
| P Holmes | 145* | 270 | Northamptonshire at Northampton | 1920 |
| H Sutcliffe | 125* | 307 | Essex at Southend | 1920 |
| P Holmes | 175* | 377 | New Zealanders at Bradford | 1927 |
| P Holmes | 110* | 219 | Northamptonshire at Bradford | 1929 |
| H Sutcliffe | 104* | 170 | Hampshire at Leeds | 1932 |
| H Sutcliffe | 114* | 202 | Rest of England at The Oval | 1933 |
| H Sutcliffe | 187* | 401 | Worcestershire at Bradford | 1934 |
| H Sutcliffe | 135* | 262 | Glamorgan at Neath | 1935 |
| H Sutcliffe | 125* | 322 | Oxford University at Oxford | 1939 |
| L Hutton | 99* | 200 | Leicestershire at Sheffield | 1948 |
| L Hutton | 78* | 153 | Worcestershire at Sheffield | 1949 |
| F A Lowson | 76* | 218 | MCC at Lord's | 1951 |
| W B Stott | 144* | 262 | Worcestershire at Worcester | 1959 |
| D E V Padgett | 115* | 230 | Gloucestershire at Bristol | 1962 |
| G Boycott | 114* | 297 | Leicestershire at Sheffield | 1968 |
| G Boycott | 53* | 119 | Warwickshire at Bradford | 1969 |
| G Boycott | 182* | 320 | Middlesex at Lord's | 1971 |
| G Boycott | 138* | 232 | Warwickshire at Birmingham | 1971 |
| G Boycott | 175* | 360 | Nottinghamshire at Worksop | 1979 |
| G Boycott | 112* | 233 | Derbyshire at Sheffield | 1983 |
| G Boycott | 55* | 183 | Warwickshire at Leeds | 1984 |
| G Boycott | 55* | 131 | Surrey at Sheffield | 1985 |
| M J Wood | 60* | 160 | Somerset at Scarborough | 2004 |
| J J Sayers | 122* | 326 | Middlesex at Scarborough | 2006 |
| J J Sayers | 149* | 414 | Durham at Leeds | 2007 |
| A Lyth | 248* | 486 | Leicestershire at Leicester | 2012 |

44 instances, of which L Hall (14 times), G Boycott (8) and H Sutcliffe (6) account for 28 between them.

The highest percentage of an innings total is 61.17 by H. Sutcliffe (104* v. Hampshire at Leeds in 1932) but P Holmes was absent ill, so only nine wickets fell.

Other contributions exceeding 55% are:

        59.48% G Boycott   (138*   v. Warwickshire at Birmingham, 1971)
        56.87% G Boycott   (182*   v. Middlesex at Lord's, 1971)
        56.43% H Sutcliffe  (114*   v. Rest of England at The Oval, 1933)
        55.92% W Rhodes   (85*   v. Essex at Leyton, 1910)

## 2,000 RUNS IN A SEASON

| Batsman | Season | M | I | NO | Runs | HS | Avge | 100s |
|---|---|---|---|---|---|---|---|---|
| G H Hirst | 1904 | 32 | 44 | 3 | 2257 | 157 | 55.04 | 8 |
| D Denton | 1905 | 33 | 52 | 2 | 2258 | 172 | 45.16 | 8 |
| G H Hirst | 1906 | 32 | 53 | 6 | 2164 | 169 | 46.04 | 6 |
| D Denton | 1911 | 32 | 55 | 4 | 2161 | 137* | 42.37 | 6 |
| D Denton | 1912 | 36 | 51 | 4 | 2088 | 221 | 44.23 | 6 |
| P Holmes | 1920 | 30 | 45 | 6 | 2144 | 302* | 54.97 | 7 |
| P Holmes | 1925 | 35 | 49 | 9 | 2351 | 315* | 58.77 | 6 |
| H Sutcliffe | 1925 | 34 | 48 | 8 | 2236 | 235 | 55.90 | 7 |
| H Sutcliffe | 1928 | 27 | 35 | 5 | 2418 | 228 | 80.60 | 11 |
| P Holmes | 1928 | 31 | 40 | 4 | 2093 | 275 | 58.13 | 6 |
| H Sutcliffe | 1931 | 28 | 33 | 8 | 2351 | 230 | 94.04 | 9 |
| H Sutcliffe | 1932 | 29 | 41 | 5 | 2883 | 313 | 80.08 | 12 |
| M Leyland | 1933 | 31 | 44 | 4 | 2196 | 210* | 54.90 | 7 |
| A Mitchell | 1933 | 34 | 49 | 10 | 2100 | 158 | 53.84 | 6 |
| H Sutcliffe | 1935 | 32 | 47 | 3 | 2183 | 212 | 49.61 | 8 |
| L Hutton | 1937 | 28 | 45 | 6 | 2448 | 271* | 62.76 | 8 |
| H Sutcliffe | 1937 | 32 | 52 | 5 | 2054 | 189 | 43.70 | 4 |
| L Hutton | 1939 | 29 | 44 | 5 | 2316 | 280* | 59.38 | 10 |
| L Hutton | 1947 | 19 | 31 | 2 | 2068 | 270* | 71.31 | 10 |
| L Hutton | 1949 | 26 | 44 | 6 | 2640 | 269* | 69.47 | 9 |
| F A Lowson | 1950 | 31 | 54 | 5 | 2067 | 141* | 42.18 | 5 |
| D E V Padgett | 1959 | 35 | 60 | 8 | 2158 | 161* | 41.50 | 4 |
| W B Stott | 1959 | 32 | 56 | 2 | 2034 | 144* | 37.66 | 3 |
| P J Sharpe | 1962 | 36 | 62 | 8 | 2201 | 138 | 40.75 | 7 |
| G Boycott | 1971 | 18 | 25 | 4 | 2221 | 233 | 105.76 | 11 |
| A A Metcalfe | 1990 | 23 | 44 | 4 | 2047 | 194* | 51.17 | 6 |

## 1,000 RUNS IN A SEASON

| Batsman | | Runs scored | Runs scored | Runs scored |
|---|---|---|---|---|
| C W J Athey | (2) | 1113 in 1980 | 1339 in 1982 | — |
| D L Bairstow | (3) | 1083 in 1981 | 1102 in 1983 | 1163 in 1985 |
| J M Bairstow | (2) | 1015 in 2011 | 1108 in 2015 | — |
| G S Ballance | (1) | 1363 in 2013 | — | — |
| W Barber | (8) | 1000 in 1932 | 1595 in 1933 | 1930 in 1934 |
| | | 1958 in 1935 | 1466 in 1937 | 1455 in 1938 |
| | | 1501 in 1939 | 1170 in 1946 | — |
| M G Bevan | (2) | 1598 in 1995 | 1225 in 1996 | — |
| R J Blakey | (5) | 1361 in 1987 | 1159 in 1989 | 1065 in 1992 |
| | | 1236 in 1994 | 1041 in 2002 | — |
| J B Bolus | (2) | 1245 in 1960 | 1970 in 1961 | — |
| M W Booth | (2) | 1189 in 1911 | 1076 in 1913 | — |
| G Boycott | (19) | 1628 in 1963 | 1639 in 1964 | 1215 in 1965 |
| | | 1388 in 1966 | 1530 in 1967 | 1004 in 1968 |
| | | 1558 in 1970 | 2221 in 1971 | 1156 in 1972 |
| | | 1478 in 1974 | 1915 in 1975 | 1288 in 1976 |
| | | 1259 in 1977 | 1074 in 1978 | 1160 in 1979 |
| | | 1913 in 1982 | 1941 in 1983 | 1567 in 1984 |
| | | 1657 in 1985 | — | — |
| J T Brown | (9) | 1196 in 1894 | 1260 in 1895 | 1755 in 1896 |
| | | 1634 in 1897 | 1641 in 1898 | 1375 in 1899 |
| | | 1181 in 1900 | 1627 in 1901 | 1291 in 1903 |
| D Byas | (5) | 1557 in 1991 | 1073 in 1993 | 1297 in 1994 |
| | | 1913 in 1995 | 1319 in 1997 | — |

288

# 1,000 RUNS IN A SEASON *(Continued)*

| Batsman | | Runs scored | Runs scored | Runs scored |
|---|---|---|---|---|
| D B Close | (13) | 1192 in 1952 | 1287 in 1954 | 1131 in 1955 |
| | | 1315 in 1957 | 1335 in 1958 | 1740 in 1959 |
| | | 1699 in 1960 | 1821 in 1961 | 1438 in 1962 |
| | | 1145 in 1963 | 1281 in 1964 | 1127 in 1965 |
| | | 1259 in 1966 | — | — |
| K R Davidson | (1) | 1241 in 1934 | — | — |
| D Denton | (20) | 1028 in 1896 | 1357 in 1897 | 1595 in 1899 |
| | | 1378 in 1900 | 1400 in 1901 | 1191 in 1902 |
| | | 1562 in 1903 | 1919 in 1904 | 2258 in 1905 |
| | | 1905 in 1906 | 1128 in 1907 | 1852 in 1908 |
| | | 1765 in 1909 | 1106 in 1910 | 2161 in 1911 |
| | | 2088 in 1912 | 1364 in 1913 | 1799 in 1914 |
| | | 1213 in 1919 | 1324 in 1920 | — |
| A Drake | (2) | 1487 in 1911 | 1029 in 1913 | — |
| A W Gale | (2) | 1076 in 2013 | 1045 in 2015 | — |
| A P Grayson | (1) | 1046 in 1994 | — | — |
| S Haigh | (1) | 1031 in 1904 | — | — |
| L Hall | (1) | 1120 in 1887 | — | — |
| H Halliday | (4) | 1357 in 1948 | 1484 in 1950 | 1351 in 1952 |
| | | 1461 in 1953 | — | — |
| J H Hampshire | (12) | 1236 in 1963 | 1280 in 1964 | 1424 in 1965 |
| | | 1105 in 1966 | 1244 in 1967 | 1133 in 1968 |
| | | 1079 in 1970 | 1259 in 1971 | 1124 in 1975 |
| | | 1303 in 1976 | 1596 in 1978 | 1425 in 1981 |
| Lord Hawke | (1) | 1005 in 1895 | — | — |
| G H Hirst | (19) | 1110 in 1896 | 1248 in 1897 | 1546 in 1899 |
| | | 1752 in 1900 | 1669 in 1901 | 1113 in 1902 |
| | | 1535 in 1903 | 2257 in 1904 | 1972 in 1905 |
| | | 2164 in 1906 | 1167 in 1907 | 1513 in 1908 |
| | | 1151 in 1909 | 1679 in 1910 | 1639 in 1911 |
| | | 1119 in 1912 | 1431 in 1913 | 1655 in 1914 |
| | | 1312 in 1919 | — | — |
| P Holmes | (14) | 1876 in 1919 | 2144 in 1920 | 1458 in 1921 |
| | | 1614 in 1922 | 1884 in 1923 | 1610 in 1924 |
| | | 2351 in 1925 | 1792 in 1926 | 1774 in 1927 |
| | | 2093 in 1928 | 1724 in 1929 | 1957 in 1930 |
| | | 1431 in 1931 | 1191 in 1932 | — |
| L Hutton | (12) | 1282 in 1936 | 2448 in 1937 | 1171 in 1938 |
| | | 2316 in 1939 | 1322 in 1946 | 2068 in 1947 |
| | | 1792 in 1948 | 2640 in 1949 | 1581 in 1950 |
| | | 1554 in 1951 | 1956 in 1952 | 1532 in 1953 |
| R Illingworth | (5) | 1193 in 1957 | 1490 in 1959 | 1029 in 1961 |
| | | 1610 in 1962 | 1301 in 1964 | — |
| F S Jackson | (4) | 1211 in 1896 | 1300 in 1897 | 1442 in 1898 |
| | | 1468 in 1899 | — | — |
| P A Jaques | (2) | 1118 in 2004 | 1359 in 2005 | — |
| S A Kellett | (2) | 1266 in 1991 | 1326 in 1992 | — |
| R Kilner | (10) | 1586 in 1913 | 1329 in 1914 | 1135 in 1919 |
| | | 1240 in 1920 | 1137 in 1921 | 1132 in 1922 |
| | | 1265 in 1923 | 1002 in 1925 | 1021 in 1926 |
| | | 1004 in 1927 | — | — |
| A Z Lees | (1) | 1018 in 2014 | — | — |
| D S Lehmann | (5) | 1575 in 1997 | 1477 in 2000 | 1416 in 2001 |
| | | 1136 in 2002 | 1706 in 2006 | — |

| Batsman | Runs scored | Runs scored | Runs scored |
|---|---|---|---|
| E I Lester .............. | (6) 1256 in 1948 | 1774 in 1949 | 1015 in 1950 |
| | 1786 in 1952 | 1380 in 1953 | 1330 in 1954 |
| M Leyland .............. | (17) 1088 in 1923 | 1203 in 1924 | 1560 in 1925 |
| | 1561 in 1926 | 1478 in 1927 | 1554 in 1928 |
| | 1407 in 1929 | 1814 in 1930 | 1127 in 1931 |
| | 1821 in 1932 | 2196 in 1933 | 1228 in 1934 |
| | 1366 in 1935 | 1621 in 1936 | 1120 in 1937 |
| | 1640 in 1938 | 1238 in 1939 | — |
| J D Love | (2) 1161 in 1981 | 1020 in 1983 | |
| F A Lowson .............. | (8) 1678 in 1949 | 2067 in 1950 | 1607 in 1951 |
| | 1562 in 1952 | 1586 in 1953 | 1719 in 1954 |
| | 1082 in 1955 | 1428 in 1956 | — |
| M J Lumb ............... | (1) 1038 in 2003 | — | — |
| R G Lumb ............. | (5) 1002 in 1973 | 1437 in 1975 | 1070 in 1978 |
| | 1465 in 1979 | 1223 in 1980 | — |
| A Lyth ................. | (2) 1509 in 2010 | 1619 in 2014 | — |
| A McGrath | (3) 1425 in 2005 | 1293 in 2006 | 1219 in 2010 |
| A A Metcalfe ............ | (6) 1674 in 1986 | 1162 in 1987 | 1320 in 1988 |
| | 1230 in 1989 | 2047 in 1990 | 1210 in 1991 |
| A Mitchell ............. | (10) 1320 in 1928 | 1633 in 1930 | 1351 in 1932 |
| | 2100 in 1933 | 1854 in 1934 | 1530 in 1935 |
| | 1095 in 1936 | 1602 in 1937 | 1305 in 1938 |
| | 1219 in 1939 | — | — |
| F Mitchell ............... | (2) 1678 in 1899 | 1801 in 1901 | — |
| R Moorhouse ............ | (1) 1096 in 1895 | — | — |
| M D Moxon ............ | (11) 1016 in 1984 | 1256 in 1985 | 1298 in 1987 |
| | 1430 in 1988 | 1156 in 1989 | 1621 in 1990 |
| | 1669 in 1991 | 1314 in 1992 | 1251 in 1993 |
| | 1458 in 1994 | 1145 in 1995 | — |
| E Oldroyd ............... | (10) 1473 in 1921 | 1690 in 1922 | 1349 in 1923 |
| | 1607 in 1924 | 1262 in 1925 | 1197 in 1926 |
| | 1390 in 1927 | 1304 in 1928 | 1474 in 1929 |
| | 1285 in 1930 | — | — |
| D E V Padgett ........... | (12) 1046 in 1956 | 2158 in 1959 | 1574 in 1960 |
| | 1856 in 1961 | 1750 in 1962 | 1380 in 1964 |
| | 1220 in 1965 | 1194 in 1966 | 1284 in 1967 |
| | 1163 in 1968 | 1078 in 1969 | 1042 in 1970 |
| R Peel .................. | (1) 1193 in 1896 | — | — |
| W Rhodes ............... | (17) 1251 in 1904 | 1353 in 1905 | 1618 in 1906 |
| | 1574 in 1908 | 1663 in 1909 | 1355 in 1910 |
| | 1961 in 1911 | 1030 in 1912 | 1805 in 1913 |
| | 1325 in 1914 | 1138 in 1919 | 1329 in 1921 |
| | 1368 in 1922 | 1168 in 1923 | 1030 in 1924 |
| | 1256 in 1925 | 1071 in 1926 | — |
| E Robinson .............. | (2) 1104 in 1921 | 1097 in 1929 | — |
| P E Robinson ............ | (3) 1173 in 1988 | 1402 in 1990 | 1293 in 1991 |
| J A Rudolph ............. | (4) 1078 in 2007 | 1292 in 2008 | 1366 in 2009 |
| | 1375 in 2010 | — | — |
| J J Sayers ............... | (1) 1150 in 2009 | — | — |
| A B Sellers .............. | (1) 1109 in 1938 | — | — |
| K Sharp ................. | (1) 1445 in 1984 | — | — |

| Batsman | | Runs scored | Runs scored | Runs scored |
|---|---|---|---|---|
| P J Sharpe | (10) | 1039 in 1960 | 1240 in 1961 | 2201 in 1962 |
| | | 1273 in 1964 | 1091 in 1965 | 1352 in 1967 |
| | | 1256 in 1968 | 1012 in 1969 | 1149 in 1970 |
| | | 1320 in 1973 | — | — |
| W B Stott | (5) | 1362 in 1957 | 1036 in 1958 | 2034 in 1959 |
| | | 1790 in 1960 | 1409 in 1961 | — |
| H Sutcliffe | (21) | †1839 in 1919 | 1393 in 1920 | 1235 in 1921 |
| | | 1909 in 1922 | 1773 in 1923 | 1720 in 1924 |
| | | 2236 in 1925 | 1672 in 1926 | 1814 in 1927 |
| | | 2418 in 1928 | 1485 in 1929 | 1636 in 1930 |
| | | 2351 in 1931 | 2883 in 1932 | 1986 in 1933 |
| | | 1511 in 1934 | 2183 in 1935 | 1295 in 1936 |
| | | 2054 in 1937 | 1660 in 1938 | 1416 in 1939 |

† First season in First-Class cricket – The record for a debut season.

| Batsman | | Runs scored | Runs scored | Runs scored |
|---|---|---|---|---|
| W H H Sutcliffe | (1) | 1193 in 1955 | — | — |
| K Taylor | (6) | 1306 in 1959 | 1107 in 1960 | 1494 in 1961 |
| | | 1372 in 1962 | 1149 in 1964 | 1044 in 1966 |
| T L Taylor | (2) | 1236 in 1901 | 1373 in 1902 | — |
| S R Tendulkar | (1) | 1070 in 1992 | — | — |
| J Tunnicliffe | (12) | 1333 in 1895 | 1368 in 1896 | 1208 in 1897 |
| | | 1713 in 1898 | 1434 in 1899 | 1496 in 1900 |
| | | 1295 in 1901 | 1274 in 1902 | 1650 in 1904 |
| | | 1096 in 1905 | 1232 in 1906 | 1195 in 1907 |
| C Turner | (1) | 1153 in 1934 | — | — |
| G Ulyett | (4) | 1083 in 1878 | 1158 in 1882 | 1024 in 1885 |
| | | 1285 in 1887 | — | — |
| M P Vaughan | (4) | 1066 in 1994 | 1235 in 1995 | 1161 in 1996 |
| | | 1161 in 1998 | — | — |
| E Wainwright | (3) | 1492 in 1897 | 1479 in 1899 | 1044 in 1901 |
| W A I Washington | (1) | 1022 in 1902 | — | — |
| W Watson | (8) | 1331 in 1947 | 1352 in 1948 | 1586 in 1952 |
| | | 1350 in 1953 | 1347 in 1954 | 1564 in 1955 |
| | | 1378 in 1956 | 1455 in 1957 | — |
| W H Wilkinson | (1) | 1282 in 1908 | — | — |
| B B Wilson | (5) | 1054 in 1909 | 1455 in 1911 | 1453 in 1912 |
| | | 1533 in 1913 | 1632 in 1914 | — |
| J V Wilson | (12) | 1460 in 1949 | 1548 in 1950 | 1985 in 1951 |
| | | 1349 in 1952 | 1531 in 1953 | 1713 in 1954 |
| | | 1799 in 1955 | 1602 in 1956 | 1287 in 1957 |
| | | 1064 in 1960 | 1018 in 1961 | 1226 in 1962 |
| A Wood | (1) | 1237 in 1935 | — | — |
| M J Wood | (4) | 1080 in 1998 | 1060 in 2001 | 1432 in 2003 |
| | | 1005 in 2005 | — | — |
| N W D Yardley | (4) | 1028 in 1939 | 1299 in 1947 | 1413 in 1949 |
| | | 1031 in 1950 | — | — |

# PLAYERS WHO HAVE SCORED CENTURIES
# FOR AND AGAINST YORKSHIRE

| Player | | For | Venue | Season |
|---|---|---|---|---|
| **C W J Athey (5)** | 114* | Gloucestershire | Bradford | 1984 |
| (10 for Yorkshire) | 101 | Gloucestershire | Gloucester | 1985 |
| | 101* | Gloucestershire | Leeds | 1987 |
| | 112 | Sussex | Scarborough | 1993 |
| | 100 | Sussex | Eastbourne | 1996 |
| **M G Bevan (1)** | 142 | Leicestershire | Leicester | 2002 |
| (9 for Yorkshire) | | | | |
| **J B Bolus (2)** | 114 | Nottinghamshire | Bradford | 1963 |
| (7 for Yorkshire) | 138 | Derbyshire | Sheffield | 1973 |
| **D B Close (1)** | 102 | Somerset | Taunton | 1971 |
| (33 for Yorkshire) | | | | |
| **M T G Elliott (1)** | 125 | Glamorgan | Leeds | 2004 |
| (1 for Yorkshire) | | | | |
| **P A Gibb (1)** | 107 | Essex | Brentwood | 1951 |
| (2 for Yorkshire) | | | | |
| **P A Jaques (1)** | 222 | Northamptonshire | Northampton | 2003 |
| (7 for Yorkshire) | | | | |
| **N Kilner (2)** | 119 | Warwickshire | Hull | 1932 |
| (2 for Yorkshire) | 197 | Warwickshire | Birmingham | 1933 |
| **M J Lumb (1)** | 135 | Nottinghamshire | Scarborough | 2013 |
| (8 for Yorkshire) | | | | |
| **P J Sharpe (1)** | 126 | Derbyshire | Chesterfield | 1976 |
| (23 for Yorkshire) | | | | |

# BATSMEN WHO HAVE SCORED OVER 10,000 RUNS

| Player | M | I | NO | Runs | HS | Av'ge | 100s |
|---|---|---|---|---|---|---|---|
| H Sutcliffe | 602 | 864 | 96 | 38558 | 313 | 50.20 | 112 |
| D Denton | 676 | 1058 | 61 | 33282 | 221 | 33.38 | 61 |
| G Boycott | 414 | 674 | 111 | 32570 | 260* | 57.85 | 103 |
| G H Hirst | 717 | 1050 | 128 | 32024 | 341 | 34.73 | 56 |
| W Rhodes | 883 | 1195 | 162 | 31075 | 267* | 30.08 | 46 |
| P Holmes | 485 | 699 | 74 | 26220 | 315* | 41.95 | 60 |
| M Leyland | 548 | 720 | 82 | 26180 | 263 | 41.03 | 62 |
| L Hutton | 341 | 527 | 62 | 24807 | 280* | 53.34 | 85 |
| D B Close | 536 | 811 | 102 | 22650 | 198 | 31.94 | 33 |
| J H Hampshire | 456 | 724 | 89 | 21979 | 183* | 34.61 | 34 |
| J V Wilson | 477 | 724 | 75 | 20548 | 230 | 31.66 | 29 |
| D E V Padgett | 487 | 774 | 63 | 20306 | 161* | 28.55 | 29 |
| J Tunnicliffe | 472 | 768 | 57 | 19435 | 243 | 27.33 | 22 |
| M D Moxon | 277 | 476 | 42 | 18973 | 274* | 43.71 | 41 |
| A Mitchell | 401 | 550 | 69 | 18189 | 189 | 37.81 | 39 |
| P J Sharpe | 411 | 666 | 71 | 17685 | 203* | 29.72 | 23 |
| E Oldroyd | 383 | 509 | 58 | 15891 | 194 | 35.23 | 37 |
| J T Brown | 345 | 567 | 41 | 15694 | 311 | 29.83 | 23 |
| W Barber | 354 | 495 | 48 | 15315 | 255 | 34.26 | 27 |
| R Illingworth | 496 | 668 | 131 | 14986 | 162 | 27.90 | 14 |
| D Byas | 268 | 449 | 42 | 14398 | 213 | 35.37 | 28 |
| G Ulyett | 355 | 618 | 31 | 14157 | 199* | 24.11 | 15 |
| R J Blakey | 339 | 541 | 84 | 14150 | 223* | 30.96 | 12 |
| A McGrath | 242 | 405 | 29 | 14091 | 211 | 37.47 | 34 |
| W Watson | 283 | 430 | 65 | 13953 | 214* | 38.22 | 26 |
| F A Lowson | 252 | 404 | 31 | 13897 | 259* | 37.25 | 30 |
| Lord Hawke | 510 | 739 | 91 | 13133 | 166 | 20.26 | 10 |
| R Kilner | 365 | 478 | 46 | 13018 | 206* | 30.13 | 15 |
| D L Bairstow | 429 | 601 | 113 | 12985 | 145 | 26.60 | 9 |
| K Taylor | 303 | 505 | 35 | 12864 | 203* | 27.37 | 16 |
| N W D Yardley | 302 | 420 | 56 | 11632 | 183* | 31.95 | 17 |
| R G Lumb | 239 | 395 | 30 | 11525 | 165* | 31.57 | 22 |
| E Wainwright | 352 | 545 | 30 | 11092 | 228 | 21.53 | 18 |
| S Haigh | 513 | 687 | 110 | 10993 | 159 | 19.05 | 4 |
| E I Lester | 228 | 339 | 27 | 10616 | 186 | 34.02 | 24 |
| A A Metcalfe | 184 | 317 | 19 | 10465 | 216* | 35.11 | 25 |
| C White | 221 | 350 | 45 | 10376 | 186 | 34.01 | 19 |
| Hon F S Jackson | 207 | 328 | 22 | 10371 | 160 | 33.89 | 21 |
| J D Love | 247 | 388 | 58 | 10263 | 170* | 31.10 | 13 |

# RECORD PARTNERSHIPS FOR YORKSHIRE

| | | | | | |
|---|---|---|---|---|---|
| 1st wkt | 555 | P Holmes (224*) | and H Sutcliffe (313) | v. Essex at Leyton | 1932 |
| 2nd wkt | 346 | W Barber (162) | and M Leyland (189) | v. Middlesex at Sheffield | 1932 |
| 3rd wkt | 346 | J J Sayers (173) | and A McGrath (211) | v. Warwickshire at Birmingham | 2009 |
| 4th wkt | 358 | D S Lehmann (339) | and M J Lumb (98) | v. Durham at Leeds | 2006 |
| 5th wkt | 340 | E Wainwright (228) | and G H Hirst (186) | v. Surrey at The Oval | 1899 |
| 6th wkt | 276 | M Leyland (191) | and E Robinson (146*) | v. Glamorgan at Swansea | 1926 |
| 7th wkt | 366* | J M Bairstow (219*) | and T T Bresnan (169*) | v, Durham at Chester-le-Street | 2015 |
| 8th wkt | 292 | R Peel (210*) | and Lord Hawke (166) | v. Warwickshire at Birmingham | 1896 |
| 9th wkt | 246 | T T Bresnan (116) | and J N Gillespie (123*) | v. Surrey at The Oval | 2007 |
| 10th wkt | 149 | G Boycott (79) | and G B Stevenson (115*) | v. Warwickshire at Birmingham | 1982 |

# RECORD PARTNERSHIPS AGAINST YORKSHIRE

| | | | | | |
|---|---|---|---|---|---|
| 1st wkt | 372 | R R Montgomerie (127) | and M B Loye (205) | for Northamptonshire at Northampton | 1996 |
| 2nd wkt | 417 | K J Barnett (210*) | and TA Tweats (189) | for Derbyshire at Derby | 1997 |
| 3rd wkt | 523 | M A Carberry (300*) | and N D McKenzie (237) | for Hampshire at Southampton | 2011 |
| 4th wkt | 447 | R Abel (193) | and T Hayward (273) | for Surrey at The Oval | 1899 |
| 5th wkt | 261 | W G Grace (318*) | and W O Moberley (103) | for Gloucestershire at Cheltenham | 1876 |
| 6th wkt | 294 | D R Jardine (157) | and P G H Fender (177) | for Surrey at Bradford | 1928 |
| 7th wkt | 315 | D M Benkenstein (151) | and O D Gibson (155) | for Durham at Leeds | 2006 |
| 8th wkt | 178 | A P Wells (253*) | and B T P Donelan (59) | for Sussex at Middlesbrough | 1991 |
| 9th wkt | 233 | I J L Trott (161*) | and J S Patel (120) | for Warwickshire at Birmingham | 2009 |
| 10th wkt | 132 | A Hill (172*) | and M Jean-Jacques (73) | for Derbyshire at Sheffield | 1986 |

# CENTURY PARTNERSHIPS FOR THE FIRST WICKET IN BOTH INNINGS

| | | | | | |
|---|---|---|---|---|---|
| 128 | 108 | G Ulyett (82 and 91) | and L Hall (87 and 37) | v. Sussex at Hove | 1885 |

*(First instance in First-Class cricket)*

| | | | | | |
|---|---|---|---|---|---|
| 138 | 147* | J T Brown (203 and 81*) | and J Tunnicliffe (62 and 63*) | v. Middlesex at Lord's | 1896 |

*(Second instance in First-Class cricket)*

| | | | | | |
|---|---|---|---|---|---|
| 105 | 265* | P Holmes (51 and 127*) | and H Sutcliffe (71 and 131*) | v. Surrey at The Oval | 1926 |
| 184 | 210* | P Holmes (83 and 101*) | and H Sutcliffe (111 and 100*) | v. Nottinghamshire at Nottingham | 1928 |
| 110 | 117 | L Hutton (95 and 86) | and W Watson (34 and 57) | v. Lancashire at Manchester | 1947 |
| 122 | 230 | W B Stott (50 and 114) | and K Taylor (79 and 140) | v. Nottinghamshire at Nottingham | 1957 |
| 136 | 138 | J B Bolus (108 and 71) | and K Taylor (89 and 75) | v. Cambridge University at Cambridge | 1962 |
| 105 | 105 | G Boycott (38 and 64) | and K Taylor (85 and 49) | v. Leicestershire at Leicester | 1963 |
| 116 | 112* | K Taylor (45 and 68) | and J H Hampshire (68 and 67*) | v. Oxford University at Oxford | 1964 |
| 104 | 104 | G Boycott (117 and 49*) | and R G Lumb (47 and 57) | v. Sussex at Leeds | 1974 |
| 134 | 185* | M D Moxon (57 and 89*) | and A A Metcalfe (216* and 78*) | v. Middlesex at Leeds | 1988 |
| 118 | 129* | G S Ballance (72 and 73*) | and J J Sayers (139 and 53*) | v. Durham MCCU at Durham | 2011 |

# CENTURY PARTNERSHIPS FOR THE FIRST WICKET
## IN BOTH INNINGS BUT WITH CHANGE OF PARTNER

| 109 | | W H H Sutcliffe (82) and F A Lowson (46) |
| | 143 | W H H Sutcliffe (88) and W Watson (52) v. Canadians at Scarborough, 1954 |
| 109 | | G Boycott (70) and R G Lumb (44) |
| | 135 | G Boycott (74) and JH Hampshire (58) v. Northamptonshire at Bradford, 1977 |

## CENTURY PARTNERSHIPS

FIRST WICKET (Qualification 200 runs)

| | |
|---|---|
| 555 | P Holmes (224*) and H Sutcliffe (313) v. Essex at Leyton, 1932 |
| 554 | J T Brown (300) and J Tunnicliffe (243) v. Derbyshire at Chesterfield, 1898 |
| 378 | J T Brown (311) and J Tunnicliffe (147) v. Sussex at Sheffield, 1897 |
| 375 | A Lyth (230) and (A Z Lees (138) v. Northamptonshire at Northampton, 2014 |
| 362 | M D Moxon (213) and M P Vaughan (183) v. Glamorgan at Cardiff, 1996 |
| 351 | G Boycott (184) and M D Moxon (168) v. Worcestershire at Worcester, 1985 |
| 347 | P Holmes (302*) and H Sutcliffe (131) v. Hampshire at Portsmouth, 1920 |
| 323 | P Holmes (125) and H Sutcliffe (195) v. Lancashire at Sheffield, 1931 |
| 315 | H Sutcliffe (189) and L Hutton (153) v. Leicestershire at Hull, 1937 |
| 315 | H Sutcliffe (116) and L Hutton (280*) v. Hampshire at Sheffield, 1939 |
| 309 | P Holmes (250) and H Sutcliffe (129) v. Warwickshire at Birmingham, 1931 |
| 309 | C White (186) and M J Wood (115) v. Lancashire at Manchester, 2001 |
| 290 | P Holmes (179*) and H Sutcliffe (104) v. Middlesex at Leeds, 1928 |
| 288 | G Boycott (130*) and R G Lumb (159) v. Somerset at Harrogate, 1979 |
| 286 | L Hutton (156) and F A Lowson (115) v. South Africans at Sheffield, 1951 |
| 282 | M D Moxon (147) and A A Metcalfe (151) v. Lancashire at Manchester, 1986 |
| 281* | W B Stott (138*) and K Taylor (130*) v. Sussex at Hove, 1960 |
| 279 | P Holmes (133) and H Sutcliffe (145) v. Northamptonshire at Northampton, 1919 |
| 274 | P.Holmes (199) and H Sutcliffe (139) v. Somerset at Hull, 1923 |
| 274 | P Holmes (180) and H Sutcliffe (134) v. Gloucestershire at Gloucester, 1927 |
| 272 | P Holmes (194) and H Sutcliffe (129) v. Leicestershire at Hull, 1925 |
| 272 | M J Wood (202*) and J J Sayers (115) v. Bangladesh 'A' at Leeds, 2005 |
| 270 | A Lyth (143) and A Z Lees (108) v. Durham at Leeds, 2014 |
| 268 | P Holmes (136) and H Sutcliffe (129) v. Essex at Leyton, 1928 |
| 267 | W Barber (248) and L Hutton (70) v. Kent at Leeds, 1934 |
| 265* | P Holmes (127*) and H Sutcliffe (131*) v. Surrey at The Oval, 1926 |
| 264 | G Boycott (161*) and R G Lumb (132) v. Gloucestershire at Leeds, 1976 |
| 253 | P Holmes (123) and H Sutcliffe (132) v. Lancashire at Sheffield, 1919 |
| 248 | G Boycott (163) and A A Metcalfe (122) v. Nottinghamshire at Bradford, 1983 |
| 245 | L Hutton (152) and F A Lowson (120) v. Lancashire at Leeds, 1952 |
| 244 | J A Rudolph (149) and J J Sayers (86) v Nottinghamshire at Nottingham, 2009 |
| 241 | P Holmes (142) and H Sutcliffe (123*) v. Surrey at The Oval, 1929 |
| 240 | G Boycott (233) and P J Sharpe (92) v. Essex at Colchester, 1971 |
| 238* | P Holmes (126*) and H Sutcliffe (105*) v. Cambridge University at Cambridge, 1923 |
| 236 | G Boycott (131) and K Taylor (153) v. Lancashire at Manchester, 1964 |
| 235 | P Holmes (130) and H Sutcliffe (132*) v. Glamorgan at Sheffield, 1930 |
| 233 | G Boycott (141*) and R G Lumb (90) v. Cambridge University at Cambridge, 1973 |
| 233 | H Halliday (116) and W Watson (108) v. Northamptonshire at Northampton, 1948 |
| 231 | M P Vaughan (151) and D Byas (90) v. Essex at Chelmsford, 1999 |
| 230 | H Sutcliffe (118) and L Hutton (163) v. Surrey at Leeds, 1936 |
| 230 | W B Stott (114) and K Taylor (140*) v. Nottinghamshire at Nottingham, 1957 |
| 228 | H Halliday (90) and J V Wilson (223*) v. Scotland at Scarborough, 1951 |
| 228 | G Boycott (141) and R G Lumb (101) v. Gloucestershire at Bristol, 1975 |
| 227 | P Holmes (110) and H Sutcliffe (119) v. Leicestershire at Leicester, 1928 |
| 225 | R G Lumb (101) and C W J Athey (125*) v. Gloucestershire at Sheffield, 1980 |
| 224 | C W J Athey (114) and J D Love (104) v. Warwickshire at Birmingham, 1980 |

| | |
|---|---|
| 222 | W B Stott (141) and K Taylor (90) v. Sussex at Bradford, 1958 |
| 221 | P Holmes (130) and H Sutcliffe (121) v. Glamorgan at Huddersfield, 1925 |
| 221 | M D Moxon (141) and A A Metcalfe (73) v. Surrey at The Oval, 1992 |
| 221 | A Lyth (111) and A Z Lees (121) v. Leeds/Bradford MCCU at Leeds, 2013 |
| 219 | P Holmes (102) and A Mitchell (130*) v. Somerset at Bradford, 1930 |
| 218 | M Leyland (110) and H Sutcliffe (235) v. Middlesex at Leeds, 1925 |
| 218 | R G Lumb (145) and M D Moxon (111) v. Derbyshire at Sheffield, 1981 |
| 210* | P Holmes (101*) and H Sutcliffe (100*) v. Nottinghamshire at Nottingham, 1928 |
| 210 | G Boycott (128) and P J Sharpe (197) v. Pakistanis at Leeds, 1967 |
| 209 | F A Lowson (115) and D E V Padgett (107) v. Scotland at Hull, 1956 |
| 208 | A Mitchell (85) and E Oldroyd (111) v. Cambridge University at Cambridge, 1929 |
| 207 | A Mitchell (90) and W Barber (107) v. Middlesex at Lord's, 1935 |
| 206 | G Boycott (118) and R G Lumb (87) v. Glamorgan at Sheffield, 1978 |
| 204 | M D Moxon (66) and A A Metcalfe (162) v. Gloucestershire at Cheltenham, 1990 |
| 203 | L Hutton (119) and F A Lowson (83) v. Somerset at Huddersfield, 1952 |
| 203 | M D Moxon (117) and S A Kellett (87) v. Somerset at Middlesbrough, 1992 |
| 203 | M D Moxon (134) and M P Vaughan (106) v. Matebeleland at Bulawayo, 1996 |
| 200* | P Holmes (107*) and H Sutcliffe (80*) v. Oxford University at Oxford, 1930 |

Note: P Holmes and H Sutcliffe shared 69 century opening partnerships for Yorkshire; G Boycott and R G Lumb 29; L Hutton and F A Lowson 22; M D Moxon and A A Metcalfe 21; J T Brown and J Tunnicliffe 19; H Sutcliffe and L Hutton 15, and L Hall and G Ulyett 12.

SECOND WICKET (Qualification 200 runs)

| | |
|---|---|
| 346 | W Barber (162) and M Leyland (189) v. Middlesex at Sheffield, 1932 |
| 343 | F A Lowson (183*) and J V Wilson (165) v. Oxford University at Oxford, 1956 |
| 333 | P Holmes (209) and E Oldroyd (138*) v. Warwickshire at Birmingham, 1922 |
| 314 | H Sutcliffe (255*) and E Oldroyd (138) v. Essex at Southend-on-Sea, 1924 |
| 311 | A Z Lees (275*) and P A Jaques (139) v. Derbyshire at Chesterfield, 2013 |
| 305 | J W.Rothery (134) and D Denton (182) v. Derbyshire at Chesterfield, 1910 |
| 302 | W Watson (172) and J V Wilson (140) v. Derbyshire at Scarborough, 1948 |
| 301 | P J Sharpe (172*) and D E V Padgett (133) v. Glamorgan at Swansea, 1971 |
| 288 | H Sutcliffe (165) and A Mitchell (136) v. Lancashire at Manchester, 1939 |
| 280 | L Hall (160) and F Lee (165) v. Lancashire at Bradford, 1887 |
| 266* | K Taylor (178*) and D E V Padgett (107*) v. Oxford University at Oxford, 1962 |
| 261* | P A Jaques (152) and K S Williamson (97) v. Durham at Scarborough, 2013 |
| 261* | L Hutton (146*) and J V Wilson (110*) v. Scotland at Hull, 1949 |
| 260 | R G Lumb (144) and K Sharp (132) v. Glamorgan at Cardiff, 1984 |
| 258 | H Sutcliffe (230) and E Oldroyd (93) v. Kent at Folkestone, 1931 |
| 253 | B B Wilson (150) and D Denton (200*) v. Warwickshire at Birmingham, 1912 |
| 248 | H Sutcliffe (200) and M. Leyland (116) v. Leicestershire at Leicester, 1926 |
| 244 | P. Holmes (138) and E Oldroyd (151*) v. Glamorgan at Cardiff, 1922 |
| 243 | G Boycott (141) and J D Love (163) v. Nottinghamshire at Bradford, 1976 |
| 243 | C White (183) and M J Wood (124) v. Glamorgan at Scarborough, 2001 |
| 237 | H Sutcliffe (118) and D Denton (122) v. Gloucestershire at Leeds, 1919 |
| 237 | M D Moxon (132) and K Sharp (128) v. Sri Lankans at Leeds, 1988 |
| 236 | F A Lowson (112) and J V Wilson (157) v. Essex at Leeds, 1950 |
| 235 | M D Moxon (130) and D Byas (181) v. Cambridge University at Cambridge, 1995 |
| 230 | L Hutton (180) and A Mitchell (100) v. Cambridge University at Cambridge, 1938 |
| 230 | M P Vaughan (109) and B Parker (138*) v. Oxford University at Oxford, 1997. |
| 227 | M J Wood (102) and M J Lumb (122) v. Leicestershire at Leeds, 2001 |
| 225 | H Sutcliffe (138) and E Oldroyd (97) v. Derbyshire at Dewsbury, 1928 |
| 223 | M D Moxon (153) and R J Blakey (90) v. Somerset at Leeds, 1985 |
| 222 | H Sutcliffe (174) and D Denton (114) v. Kent at Dover, 1919 |
| 219 | F S Jackson (155) and D Denton (113) v. Middlesex at Bradford, 1899 |
| 217 | R G Lumb (107) and J D Love (107) v. Oxford University at Oxford, 1978 |
| 216 | M P Vaughan (105) and D Byas (102) v. Somerset at Bradford, 1994 |

# CENTURY PARTNERSHIPS *(Continued)*

THIRD WICKET (Qualification 200 runs) *(Continued)*

| | |
|---|---|
| 201 | H Sutcliffe (87) and W Barber (130) v. Leicestershire at Leicester, 1938 |
| 200 | M D Moxon (274*) and A P Grayson (100) v. Worcestershire at Worcester, 1994 |

FOURTH WICKET (Qualification 175 runs)

| | |
|---|---|
| 358 | D S Lehmann (339) and M J Lumb (98) v. Durham at Leeds, 2006 |
| 330 | M J Wood (116) and D R Martyn (238) v. Gloucestershire at Leeds, 2003 |
| 312 | D Denton (168*) and G H Hirst (146) v. Hampshire at Southampton, 1914 |
| 299 | P Holmes (277*) and R Kilner (150) v. Northamptonshire at Harrogate, 1921 |
| 272 | D Byas (138) and A McGrath (137) v. Hampshire at Harrogate, 1996 |
| 271 | B B Wilson (208) and W Rhodes (113) v. Sussex at Bradford, 1914 |
| 259 | A Drake (115) and G H Hirst (218) v. Sussex at Hastings, 1911 |
| 258 | J Tunnicliffe (128) and G H Hirst (152) v. Hampshire at Portsmouth, 1904 |
| 258 | P E Robinson (147) and D Byas (117) v. Kent at Scarborough, 1989 |
| 249 | W B Stott (143) and G Boycott (145) v. Lancashire at Sheffield, 1963 |
| 247* | R G Lumb (165*) and S N Hartley (104*) v. Gloucestershire at Bradford, 1984 |
| 247 | M Leyland (263) and L Hutton (83) v. Essex at Hull, 1936 |
| 238 | D S Lehmann (216) and M J Lumb (92) v. Susex at Arundel, 2002 |
| 233 | D Byas (120) and P E Robinson (189) v. Lancashire at Scarborough, 1991 |
| 231 | J E Root (236) and J M Bairstow (186) v. Derbyshire at Leeds, 2013 |
| 226 | W H Wilkinson (89) and G H Hirst (140) v. Northamptonshire at Hull, 1909 |
| 225 | C H Grimshaw (85) and G H Hirst (169) v. Oxford University at Oxford, 1906 |
| 212 | B B Wilson (108) and G H Hirst (166*) v. Sussex at Hastings, 1913 |
| 212 | G Boycott (260*) and J H Hampshire (80) v. Essex at Colchester, 1970 |
| 211 | J V Wilson (120) and W Watson (108) v. Derbyshire at Harrogate, 1951 |
| 210* | A Mitchell (150*) and M Leyland (117*) v. Worcestershire at Worcester, 1933 |
| 210 | E I. Lester (178) and W Watson (97) v. Nottinghamshire at Nottingham, 1952 |
| 207 | D Byas (213) and C White (107*) v. Worcestershire at Scarborough, 1995 |
| 206 | J A Rudolph (121) and A W Gale (150) v. Surrey at The Oval, 2008 |
| 205* | G Boycott (151*) and P J Sharpe (79*) v. Leicestershire at Leicester, 1964 |
| 205 | E Oldroyd (121) and R Kilner (117) v. Worcestershire at Dudley, 1922 |
| 205 | W Watson (162*) and E I Lester (98) v. Somerset at Leeds, 1953 |
| 204 | A W Gale (148) and G S Ballance (90) v. Surrey at Leeds, 2013 |
| 201* | J H Hampshire (105*) and D B Close (101*) v. Surrey at Bradford, 1965 |
| 203 | P A Jaques (160) and G S Ballance (121*) v. Gloucestershire at Bristol, 2012 |
| 201 | W H H Sutcliffe (181) and L Hutton (120) v. Kent at Canterbury, 1952 |
| 200 | J V Wilson (92) and W Watson (122) v. Somerset at Taunton, 1950 |
| 198 | A A Metcalfe (138) and D Byas (95) v. Warwickshire at Leeds, 1989 |
| 198 | A W Gale (124) and J M Bairstow (95) v. Durham at Chester-le-Street, 2014 |
| 197 | N W D Yardley (177) and A Coxon (58) v. Derbyshire at Scarborough, 1947 |
| 197 | A Lyth (248*) and J M Bairstow (118) v. Leicestershire at Leicester, 2012 |
| 196 | M D Moxon (130) and D L Bairstow (104) v. Derbyshire at Harrogate, 1987 |
| 193 | A Drake (85) and G H Hirst (156) v. Lancashire at Manchester, 1911 |
| 192 | J V Wilson (132) and W Watson (105) v. Essex at Bradford, 1955 |
| 191 | M Leyland (114) and C Turner (63) v. Essex at Ilford, 1938 |
| 188 | H Myers (60) and G H Hirst (158) v. Cambridge University at Cambridge, 1910 |
| 187 | E Oldroyd (168) and F E Greenwood (104*) v. Glamorgan at Hull, 1929 |
| 187 | K Taylor (203*) and W B Stott (57) v. Warwickshire at Birmingham, 1961 |
| 186 | D S Lehmann (193) and D Byas (100) v. Leicestershire at Leicester, 2001 |
| 184 | J H Hampshire (96) and R Illingworth (100*) v. Leicestershire at Sheffield, 1968 |
| 182* | E I Lester (101*) and W Watson (103*) v. Nottinghamshire at Bradford, 1952 |
| 180* | G Boycott (207*) and B Leadbeater (50*) v. Cambridge University |
| | at Cambridge, 1976 |
| 180 | J Tunnicliffe (139*) and G H Hirst (108) v. Surrey at The Oval, 1904 |
| 179 | J H Hampshire (179) and S N Hartley (63) v. Surrey at Harrogate, 1981 |
| 179 | M D Moxon (171*) and R J Blakey (71) v. Kent at Leeds, 1993 |
| 178 | E I Lester (186) and J V Wilson (71) v. Warwickshire at Scarborough, 1949 |
| 177 | J D Love (105*) and J H Hampshire (89) v. Lancashire at Manchester, 1980 |
| 175 | L Hutton (177) and W Barber (84) v. Sussex at Scarborough, 1939 |
| 175 | A McGrath (188*) and J A Rudolph (82) v. Warwickshire at Birmingham, 2007 |

# CENTURY PARTNERSHIPS *(Continued)*

FIFTH WICKET (Qualification 150 runs)

| | |
|---|---|
| 340 | E Wainwright (228) and G H Hirst (186) v. Surrey at The Oval, 1899 |
| 329 | F Mitchell (194) and E Wainwright (153) v. Leicestershire at Leicester, 1899 |
| 297 | A W Gale (272) and G S Ballance (141) v. Nottinghamshire at Scarborough, 2013 |
| 276 | W Rhodes (104*) and R Kilner (166) v. Northamptonshire at Northampton, 1921 |
| 273 | L Hutton (270*) and N W D Yardley (136) v. Hampshire at Bournemouth, 1947 |
| 245* | H Sutcliffe (107*) and W Barber (128*) v. Northamptonshire at Northampton, 1939 |
| 229 | D S Lehmann (193) and C White (79) v. Kent at Canterbury, 2006 |
| 217 | D B Close (140*) and R Illingworth (107) v. Warwickshire at Sheffield, 1962 |
| 207 | G S Ballance (107) and A U Rashid (180) v. Somerset at Leeds, 2013 |
| 198 | E Wainwright (145) and R Peel (111) v. Sussex at Bradford, 1896 |
| 198 | W Barber (168) and K R Davidson (101*) v. MCC at Lord's, 1934 |
| 196* | R Kilner (115*) and G H Hirst (82*) v. Gloucestershire at Leeds, 1919 |
| 195 | M J Lumb (93) and C White (173*) v. Derbyshire at Derby, 2003 |
| 194* | Younus Khan (202*) and G L Brophy (100*) v. Hampshire at Southampton, 2007 |
| 193 | A Mitchell (189) and W Rhodes (88) v. Northamptonshire at Northampton, 1926 |
| 193 | J D Love (106) and S N Hartley (108) v. Oxford University at Oxford, 1985 |
| 192 | C W J Athey (114*) and J D Love (123) v. Surrey at The Oval, 1982 |
| 191* | L Hutton (271*) and C Turner (81*) v. Derbyshire at Sheffield, 1937 |
| 191 | M G Bevan (105) and A A Metcalfe (100) v. West Indians at Scarborough, 1995 |
| 190* | R J Blakey (204*) and J D Love (79*) v. Gloucestershire at Leeds, 1987 |
| 189 | J E Root (160) and G S Ballance (87) v. Sussex at Scarborough 2011 |
| 188 | D E V Padgett (146) and J V Wilson (72) v. Sussex at Middlesbrough, 1960 |
| 187 | J V Wilson (230) and H Halliday (74) v. Derbyshire at Sheffield, 1952 |
| 185 | G Boycott (104*) and K Sharp (99) v. Kent at Tunbridge Wells, 1984 |
| 182 | E Lockwood (208) and E Lumb (40) v. Kent at Gravesend, 1882 |
| 182 | B B Wilson (109) and W Rhodes (111) v. Sussex at Hove, 1910 |
| 182 | D B Close (164) and J V Wilson (55) v. Combined Services at Harrogate, 1954 |
| 182 | A W Gale (126*) and J A Leaning (76) v. Middlesex at Scarborough, 2014 |
| 181 | A A Metcalfe (149) and J D Love (88) v. Glamorgan at Leeds, 1986 |
| 177 | Hon F S Jackson (87) and G H Hirst (232*) v. Surrey at The Oval, 1905 |
| 176 | L Hutton (176*) and A Coxon (72) v. Sussex at Sheffield, 1948 |
| 175 | A Drake (108) and R Kilner (77) v. Cambridge University at Cambridge, 1913 |
| 173 | H Sutcliffe (206) and R Kilner (124) v. Warwickshire at Dewsbury, 1925 |
| 170 | W Rhodes (157) and R Kilner (87) v. Derbyshire at Leeds, 1925 |
| 170 | J V Wilson (130*) and N W D Yardley (67) v. Lancashire at Manchester, 1954 |
| 169 | W Watson (147) and A B Sellers (92) v. Worcestershire at Worcester, 1947 |
| 168 | A T Barber (63) and A Mitchell (122*) v. Worcestershire at Worcester, 1929 |
| 167 | J M Bairstow (136) and G S Ballance (61) v. Somerset at Taunton 2011 |
| 165 | E Oldroyd (143) and W Rhodes (110) v. Glamorgan at Leeds, 1922 |
| 165 | K Sharp (100*) and P Carrick (73) v. Middlesex at Lord's, 1980 |
| 164 | A A Metcalfe (151) and D L Bairstow (88) v. Northamptonshire at Luton, 1986 |
| 159* | J D Love (170*) and D L Bairstow (52*) v. Worcestershire at Worcester, 1979 |
| 159 | D B Close (128) and R Illingworth (74) v. Lancashire at Sheffield, 1959 |
| 159 | J H Hampshire (183*) and C Johnson (53) v. Sussex at Hove, 1971 |
| 158* | G Boycott (153*) and P E Robinson (74) v. Derbyshire at Harrogate, 1984 |
| 157 | T L Taylor (135*) and G H Hirst (72) v. An England XI at Hastings, 1901 |
| 157 | G H Hirst (142) and F Smith (51) v. Somerset at Bradford, 1903 |
| 157 | W Barber (87) and N W D Yardley (101) v. Surrey at The Oval, 1937 |
| 156 | A McGrath (158) and I J Harvey (103) v. Derbyshire at Derby, 2005 |
| 153 | S N Hartley (87) and M D Moxon (112*) v. Indians at Scarborough, 1986 |
| 152 | J H Hampshire (83) and S N Hartley (106) v. Nottinghamshire at Nottingham, 1981 |
| 151* | G H Hirst (102*) and R Kilner (50*) v. Kent at Bradford, 1913 |
| 151 | G H Hirst (120) and F Smith (55) v. Kent at Leeds, 1903 |
| 151 | W Rhodes (57) and R Kilner (90) v. Nottinghamshire at Nottingham, 1925 |

# CENTURY PARTNERSHIPS *(Continued)*

SIXTH WICKET (Qualification 150 runs)

| | |
|---|---|
| 296 | A Lyth (251) and A U Rashid (159*) v. Lancashire at Manchester, 2014 |
| 276 | M Leyland (191) and E Robinson (124*) v. Glamorgan at Swansea, 1926 |
| 252 | C White (181) and R J Blakey (109*) v. Lancashire at Leeds, 1996 |
| 233 | M W Booth (210) and G H Hirst (100) v. Worcestershire at Worcester, 1911 |
| 229 | W Rhodes (267*) and N Kilner (112) v. Leicestershire at Leeds, 1921 |
| 225 | E Wainwright (91) and Lord Hawke (127) v. Hampshire at Southampton, 1899 |
| 217* | H Sutcliffe (200*) and A Wood (123*) v. Worcestershire at Sheffield, 1935 |
| 214 | W Watson (214*) and N W D Yardley (76) v. Worcestershire at Worcester, 1955 |
| 205 | G H Hirst (125) and S Haigh (159) v. Nottinghamshire at Sheffield, 1901 |
| 200 | D Denton (127) and G H Hirst (134) v. Essex at Bradford, 1902 |
| 198 | M Leyland (247) and W Rhodes (100*) v. Worcestershire at Worcester, 1928 |
| 190 | W Rhodes (126) and M Leyland (79) v. Middlesex at Bradford, 1923 |
| 190 | J A Rudolph (122) and A U Rashid (86) v. Surrey at The Oval, 2007 |
| 188 | W Watson (174) and R Illingworth (53) v. Lancashire at Sheffield, 1955 |
| 188 | M P Vaughan (161) and R J Blakey (92) v. Essex at Ilford, 1997. |
| 188 | G S Ballance (111) and A U Rashid (82) v. Warwickshire at Birmingham 2011 |
| 184 | R Kilner (104) and M W Booth (79) v. Leicestershire at Leeds, 1913 |
| 183 | G H Hirst (131) and E Smith (129) v. Hampshire at Bradford, 1899 |
| 183 | W Watson (139*) and R Illingworth (78) v. Somerset at Harrogate, 1956 |
| 178* | D Denton (108*) and G H Hirst (112*) v. Lancashire at Manchester, 1902 |
| 178* | N W D Yardley (100*) and R Illingworth (71*) v. Gloucestershire at Bristol, 1955 |
| 178 | E Robinson (100) and D C F Burton (83) v. Derbyshire at Hull, 1921 |
| 178 | H Sutcliffe (135) and P A Gibb (157*) v. Nottinghamshire at Sheffield, 1935 |
| 175 | G M Fellows (88) and R J Blakey (103) v. Warwickshire at Birmingham, 2002 |
| 174 | D S Lehmann (136) and G M Hamilton (73) v. Kent at Maidstone, 1998 |
| 172 | A J Dalton (119*) and D L Bairstow (62) v. Worcestershire at Dudley, 1971 |
| 170* | A U Rashid 103*) and A J Hodd (68*) v. Somerset at Taunton, 2013 |
| 170 | A W Gale (101) and T T Bresnan (97) v. Worcestershire at Worcester, 2009 |
| 169 | W Barber (124) and H Verity (78*) v. Warwickshire at Birmingham, 1933 |
| 169 | R Illingworth (162) and J Birkenshaw (37) v. Indians at Sheffield, 1959 |
| 166 | E Wainwright (116) and E Smith (61) v. Kent at Catford, 1900 |
| 166 | D B Close (161) and F S Trueman (104) v. Northamptonshire at Northampton, 1963 |
| 162* | G Boycott (220*) and J G Binks (70*) v. Northamptonshire at Sheffield, 1967 |
| 161* | D L Bairstow (100*) and P Carrick (59*) v. Middlesex at Leeds, 1983 |
| 159* | D S Lehmann (187*) and R J Blakey (78*) v. Somerset at Bath, 2001 |
| 159 | J M Bairstow (182) and A McGrath (90) v. Leicestershire at Scarborough, 2012 |
| 156 | W Rhodes (82*) and E Robinson (94) v. Derbyshire at Chesterfield, 1919 |
| 154 | C Turner (84) and A Wood (79) v. Glamorgan at Swansea, 1936 |
| 153* | J A Rudolph (92*) and A U Rashid (73*) v. Worcestershire at Kidderminster, 2007 |
| 153 | J A Rudolph (69*) and J M Bairstow (81) v. Warwickshire at Birmingham, 2010 |
| 151 | D Denton (91) and W Rhodes (76) v. Middlesex at Sheffield, 1904 |
| 151 | G Boycott (152*) and P Carrick (75) v. Warwickshire at Leeds, 1982 |
| 150 | G Ulyett (199*) and J M Preston (93) v. Derbyshire at Sheffield, 1887 |

SEVENTH WICKET (Qualification 125 runs)

| | |
|---|---|
| 254 | W Rhodes (135) and D C F Burton (142*) v. Hampshire at Dewsbury, 1919 |
| 247 | P Holmes (285) and W Rhodes (79) v. Nottinghamshire at Nottingham, 1929 |
| 215 | E Robinson (135*) and D C F Burton (110) v. Leicestershire at Leicester, 1921 |
| 185 | E Wainwright (100) and G H Hirst (134) v. Gloucestershire at Bristol, 1897 |
| 183 | G H Hirst (341) and H Myers (57) v. Leicestershire at Leicester, 1905 |
| 183 | J A Rudolph (220) and T T Bresnan (104*) v. Warwickshire at Scarborough, 2007 |
| 180 | C Turner (130) and A Wood (97) v. Somerset at Sheffield, 1936 |
| 168 | G L Brophy (99) and A U Rashid (157*) v. Lancashire at Leeds, 2009 |
| 170 | G S Blewett (190) and G M Hamilton (84*) v. Northamptonshire at Scarborough, 1999 |
| 166 | R Peel (55) and I Grimshaw (122*) v. Derbyshire at Holbeck, 1886 |
| 162 | E Wainwright (109) and S Haigh (73) v. Somerset at Taunton, 1900 |
| 162 | R J Blakey (90) and R K J Dawson (87) v. Kent at Canterbury, 2002 |
| 162 | A W Gale (149) and G L Brophy (97) v. Warwickshire at Scarborough, 2006 |

| 161 | R G Lumb (118) and C M Old (89) v. Worcestershire at Bradford, 1980 |
|---|---|
| 160 | J Tunnicliffe (158) and D Hunter (58*) v. Worcestershire at Worcester, 1900 |
| 157* | F A Lowson (259*) and R Booth (53*) v. Worcestershire at Worcester, 1953 |
| 157 | K S Wiiliamson (189) and T T Bresnan (61) v. Sussex at Scarborough, 2014 |
| 155 | D Byas (122*) and P Carrick (61) v. Leicestershire at Leicester.1991. |
| 154* | G H Hirst (76*) and J T Newstead (100*) v. Nottinghamshire at Nottingham, 1908 |
| 148 | J Rowbotham (113) and J Thewlis (50) v. Surrey at The Oval, 1873 |
| 147 | E Wainwright (78) and G Ulyett (73) v. Somerset at Taunton, 1893 |
| 147 | M P Vaughan (153) and R J Harden (64) v. Kent at Scarborough, 1999 |
| 143 | C White (135*) and A K D Gray (60) v. Durham at Chester-le-Street, 2003 |
| 141 | G H Hirst (108*) and S Haigh (48) v. Worcestershire at Worcester, 1905 |
| 141 | J H Hampshire (149*) and J G Binks (72) v. MCC at Scarborough, 1965 |
| 140 | E Wainwright (117) and S Haigh (54) v. CI Thornton's XI at Scarborough, 1900 |
| 140 | D Byas (67) and P J Hartley (75) v. Derbyshire at Chesterfield, 1990 |
| 138 | D Denton (78) and G H Hirst (103*) v. Sussex at Leeds, 1905 |
| 136 | GH Hirst (93) and S Haigh (138) v. Warwickshire at Birmingham, 1904 |
| 136 | E Robinson (77*) and A Wood (65) v. Glamorgan at Scarborough, 1931 |
| 133* | W Rhodes (267*) and M Leyland (52*) v. Leicestershire at Leeds, 1921 |
| 133* | E I Lester (86*) and A B Sellers (73*) v. Northamptonshire at Northampton, 1948 |
| 133 | D Byas (100) and P W Jarvis (80) v. Northamptonshire at Scarborough, 1992 |
| 133 | W Rhodes (196) and S Haigh (59*) v. Worcestershire at Worcester, 1904 |
| 131* | D L Bairstow (79*) and A Sidebottom (52*) v. Oxford University at Oxford, 1981 |
| 130 | P J Sharpe (64) and J V Wilson (134) v. Warwickshire at Birmingham, 1962 |
| 128 | W Barber (66) and T F Smailes (86) v. Cambridge University at Cambridge, 1938 |
| 128 | D B Close (88*) and A Coxon (59) v. Essex at Leeds, 1949 |
| 126 | E Wainwright (171) and R Peel (46) v. Middlesex at Lord's, 1897 |
| 126 | W Rhodes (91) and G G Macaulay (63) v. Hampshire at Hull, 1925 |
| 126 | J C Balderstone (58) and J G Binks (59) v. Middlesex at Lord's, 1964 |
| 126 | J M Bairstow (70) and A U Rashid (59) v. Kent at Canterbury, 2010 |
| 125 | A B Sellers (109) and T F Smailes (65) v. Kent at Bradford, 1937 |

EIGHTH WICKET (Qualification 125 runs)

| 292 | R Peel (210*) and Lord Hawke (166) v. Warwickshire at Birmingham, 1896 |
|---|---|
| 238 | I J Harvey (209*) and T T Bresnan (74) v. Somerset at Leeds, 2005 |
| 192* | W Rhodes (108*) and G G Macaulay (101*) v. Essex at Harrogate, 1922 |
| 192 | A U Rashid (117*) and A Shahzad (78) v. Hampshire at Basingstoke, 2009 |
| 180 | W Barber (191) and T F Smailes (89) v. Sussex at Leeds, 1935 |
| 165 | S Haigh (62) and Lord Hawke (126) v. Surrey at The Oval, 1902 |
| 163 | G G Macaulay (67) and A Waddington (114) v. Worcestershire at Leeds, 1927 |
| 159 | E Smith (95) and W Rhodes (105) v. MCC at Scarborough, 1901 |
| 157 | A Shahzad (88) and D J Wainwright (85*) v. Sussex at Hove, 2009 |
| 156 | G S Ballance (112) and R J Sidebottom (40) v. Leeds/Bradford MCCU at Leeds, 2013 |
| 152 | W Rhodes (98) and J W Rothery (70) v. Hampshire at Portsmouth, 1904 |
| 151 | W Rhodes (201) and Lord Hawke (51) v. Somerset at Taunton, 1905 |
| 151 | R J Blakey (80*) and P J Hartley (89) v. Sussex at Eastbourne, 1996 |
| 149 | G L Brophy (177*) and R J Sidebottom (61) v. Worcestershire at Worcester 2011 |
| 147 | J P G Chadwick (59) and F S Trueman (101) v. Middlesex at Scarborough, 1965 |
| 146 | S Haigh (159) and Lord Hawke (89) v. Nottinghamshire at Sheffield, 1901 |
| 144 | G L Brophy (85) and D J Wainwright (102*) v. Warwickshire at Scarborough, 2009 |
| 138 | E Wainwright (100) and Lord Hawke (81) v. Kent at Tonbridge, 1899 |
| 137 | E Wainwright (147) and Lord Hawke (75) v. Middlesex at Lord's, 1897 |
| 135 | P W Jarvis (55) and P J Hartley (69) v. Nottinghamshire at Nottingham, 1992 |
| 133 | R Illingworth (61) and F S Trueman (74) v. Leicestershire at Leicester, 1955 |
| 132 | G H Hirst (103) and E Smith (59) v. Middlesex at Sheffield, 1904 |
| 132 | W Watson (119) and J H Wardle (65) v. Leicestershire at Leicester, 1949 |
| 131 | P E Robinson (85) and P Carrick (64) v. Surrey at Harrogate, 1990 |
| 130 | E Smith (98) and Lord Hawke (54) v. Lancashire at Leeds, 1904 |
| 128 | H Verity (96*) and T F Smailes (77) v. Indians at Bradford, 1936 |
| 128 | D L Bairstow (145) and G B Stevenson (11) v. Middlesex at Scarborough, 1980 |

# CENTURY PARTNERSHIPS *(Continued)*

| | |
|---|---|
| 127 | E Robinson (70*) and A Wood (62) v. Middlesex at Leeds, 1928 |
| 126 | R Peel (74) and E Peate (61) v. Gloucestershire at Bradford, 1883 |
| 126 | M W Booth (56) and E R Wilson (104*) v. Essex at Bradford, 1913 |
| 126 | J D Middlebrook (84) and C E W Silverwood (70) v. Essex at Chelmsford, 2001 |
| 126 | M J Lumb (115*) and D Gough (72) v. Hampshire at Southampton, 2003 |

## NINTH WICKET (Qualification 100 runs)

| | |
|---|---|
| 246 | T T Bresnan (116) and J N Gillespie (123*) v. Surrey at The Oval, 2007 |
| 192 | G H Hirst (130*) and S Haigh (85) v. Surrey at Bradford, 1898 |
| 179 | R A Hutton (189) and G A Cope (30*) v. Pakistanis at Bradford, 1971 |
| 176* | R Moorhouse (59*) and G H Hirst (115*) v. Gloucestershire at Bristol, 1894 |
| 173 | S Haigh (85) and W Rhodes (92*) v. Sussex at Hove, 1902 |
| 167 | H Verity (89) and T F Smailes (80) v. Somerset at Bath, 1936 |
| 162 | W Rhodes (94*) and S Haigh (84) v. Lancashire at Manchester, 1904 |
| 161 | E Smith (116*) and W Rhodes (79) v. Sussex at Sheffield, 1900 |
| 154 | R M Pyrah (117) and R J Sidebottom (52) v.Lancashire at Leeds 2011 |
| 150 | J M Bairstow (205) and R J Sidebottom (45*) v. Nottinghamshire at Nottingham 2011 |
| 150 | Azeem Rafiq (100) and M J Hoggard (56*) v. Worcestershire at Worcester, 2009 |
| 149* | R J Blakey (63*) and A K D Gray (74*) v. Leicestershire at Scarborough, 2002 |
| 149 | G H Hirst (232*) and D Hunter (40) v. Surrey at The Oval, 1905 |
| 146 | G H Hirst (214) and W Rhodes (53) v. Worcestershire at Worcester, 1901 |
| 144 | T T Bresnan (91) and J N Gillespie (44) v. Hampshire at Leeds, 2006 |
| 140 | A U Rashid (111) and D J Wainwright (104) v. Sussex at Hove, 2008 |
| 136 | R Peel (210*) and G H Hirst (85) v. Warwickshire at Birmingham, 1896 |
| 125* | L Hutton (269*) and A Coxon (65*) v. Northamptonshire at Wellingborough, 1949 |
| 124 | P J Hartley (87*) and P W Jarvis (47) v. Essex at Chelmsford, 1986 |
| 120 | G H Hirst (138) and W Rhodes (38) v. Nottinghamshire at Nottingham, 1899 |
| 119 | A B Sellers (80*) and E P Robinson (66) v. Warwickshire at Birmingham, 1938 |
| 118 | S Haigh (96) and W Rhodes (44) v. Somerset at Leeds, 1901 |
| 114 | E Oldroyd (194) and A Dolphin (47) v. Worcestershire at Worcester, 1923 |
| 114 | N Kilner (102*) and G G Macaulay (60) v. Gloucestershire at Bristol, 1923 |
| 113 | G G Macaulay (125*) and A Waddington (44) v. Nottinghamshire at Nottingham, 1921 |
| 113 | A Wood (69) and H.Verity (45*) v. MCC at Lord's, 1938 |
| 112 | G H Hirst (78) and Lord Hawke (61*) v. Essex at Leyton, 1907 |
| 109 | Lees Whitehead (60) and W Rhodes (81*) v. Sussex at Harrogate, 1899 |
| 108 | A McGrath (133*) and C E W Silverwood (80) v. Durham at Chester-le-Street, 2005 |
| 106 | L E Plunkett (86) and S A Patterson (43) v. Warwickshire at Leeds, 2014 |
| 105 | J V Wilson (134) and A G Nicholson (20*) v. Nottinghamshire at Leeds, 1962 |
| 105 | C M Old (100*) and H P Cooper (30) v. Lancashire at Manchester, 1978 |
| 105 | C White (74*) and J D Batty (50) v. Gloucestershire at Sheffield, 1993 |
| 104 | L Hall (129*) and R Moorhouse (86) v. Gloucestershire at Clifton, 1888 |
| 100 | G Pollitt (51) and Lees Whitehead (54) v. Hampshire at Bradford, 1899 |

## TENTH WICKET (Qualification 100 runs)

| | |
|---|---|
| 149 | G Boycott (79) and G B Stevenson (115*) v. Warwickshire at Birmingham, 1982 |
| 148 | Lord Hawke (107*) and D Hunter (47) v. Kent at Sheffield, 1898 |
| 144 | A Sidebottom (124) and A L Robinson (30*) v. Glamorgan at Cardiff, 1977 |
| 121 | J T Brown (141) and D Hunter (25*) v. Liverpool & District at Liverpool, 1894 |
| 118 | Lord Hawke (110*) and D Hunter (41) v. Kent at Leeds, 1896 |
| 113 | P J Hartley (88*) and R D Stemp (22) v. Middlesex at Lord's, 1996 |
| 110 | C E W Silverwood (45*) and R D Stemp (65) v. Durham at Chester-le-Street, 1996 |
| 109 | A Shahzad (70) and R J Sidebottom (28*) v. Worcestershire at Scarborough, 2011 |
| 108 | Lord Hawke (79) and Lees Whitehead (45*) v. Lancashire at Manchester, 1903 |
| 108 | G Boycott (129) and M K Bore (37*) v. Nottinghamshire at Bradford, 1973 |
| 106 | A B Sellers (79) and D V Brennan (30) v. Worcestershire at Worcester, 1948 |
| 103 | A Dolphin (62*) and E Smith (49) v. Essex at Leyton, 1919 |
| 102 | D Denton (77*) and D Hunter (45) v. Cambridge University at Cambridge, 1895 |

# FIFTEEN WICKETS OR MORE IN A MATCH

### A complete list of 12, 13 and 14 wickets in a match up to and including 2007 is to be found in the 2008 edition

*W E BOWES (1)*

16 for 35 (8 for 18 and 8 for 17) v. Northamptonshire at Kettering, 1935

*A DRAKE (1)*

15 for 51 (5 for 16 and 10 for 35) v. Somerset at Weston-super-Mare, 1914

*T EMMETT (1)*

16 for 38 (7 for 15 and 9 for 23) v. Cambridgeshire at Hunslet, 1869

*G H HIRST (1)*

15 for 63 (8 for 25 and 7 for 38) v. Leicestershire at Hull, 1907

*R ILLINGWORTH (1)*

15 for 123 (8 for 70 and 7 for 53) v. Glamorgan at Swansea, 1960

*R PEEL (1)*

15 for 50 (9 for 22 and 6 for 28) v. Somerset at Leeds, 1895

*W RHODES (1)*

15 for 56 (9 for 28 and 6 for 28) v. Essex at Leyton, 1899

*H VERITY (4)*

17 for 91 (8 for 47 and 9 for 44) v. Essex at Leyton, 1933
15 for 129 (8 for 56 and 7 for 73) v. Oxford University at Oxford, 1936
15 for 38 (6 for 26 and 9 for 12) v. Kent at Sheffield, 1936
15 for 100 (6 for 52 and 9 for 48) v. Essex at Westcliffe-on-Sea, 1936

*J H WARDLE (1)*

16 for 112 (9 for 48 and 7 for 64) v. Sussex at Hull, 1954

# TEN WICKETS IN A MATCH
### (including best analysis)

| | | | | | | |
|---|---|---|---|---|---|---|
| 61 | W Rhodes | 15 for | 56 | v Essex | at Leyton | 1899 |
| 48 | H Verity | 17 for | 91 | v Essex | at Leyton | 1933 |
| 40 | G H Hirst | 15 for | 63 | v Leicestershire | at Hull | 1907 |
| 31 | G G Macaulay | 14 for | 92 | v Gloucestershire | at Bristol | 1926 |
| 28 | S Haigh | 14 for | 43 | v Hampshire | at Southampton | 1898 |
| 27 | R Peel | 14 for | 33 | v Nottinghamshire | at Sheffield | 1888 |
| 25 | W E Bowes | 16 for | 35 | v Northamptonshire | at Kettering | 1935 |
| 25 | J H Wardle | 16 for | 112 | v Sussex | at Hull | 1954 |
| 22 | E Peate | 14 for | 77 | v Surrey | at Huddersfield | 1881 |
| 20 | F S Trueman | 14 for | 123 | v Surrey | at The Oval | 1960 |
| 19 | T Emmett | 16 for | 38 | v Cambridgeshire | at Hunslet | 1869 |
| 17 | R Appleyard | 12 for | 43 | v Essex | at Bradford | 1951 |
| 15 | E Wainwright | 14 for | 77 | v Essex | at Bradford | 1896 |
| 11 | R Illingworth | 15 for | 123 | v Glamorgan | at Swansea | 1960 |
| 10 | A Waddington | 13 for | 48 | v Northamptonshire | at Northampton | 1920 |
| 9 | M W Booth | 14 for | 160 | v Essex | at Leyton | 1914 |
| 9 | R Kilner | 12 for | 55 | v Sussex | at Hove | 1924 |
| 8 | W Bates | 11 for | 47 | v Nottinghamshire | at Nottingham | 1881 |
| 8 | G Freeman | 13 for | 60 | v Surrey | at Sheffield | 1869 |
| 7 | E P Robinson | 13 for | 115 | v Lancashire | at Leeds | 1939 |
| 7 | D Wilson | 13 for | 52 | v Warwickshire | at Middlesbrough | 1967 |

| | | | | |
|---|---|---|---|---|
| 6 G A Cope | 12 for 116 | v Glamorgan | at Cardiff (Sophia Gardens) | 1968 |
| 6 A Hill | 12 for 59 | v Surrey | at The Oval | 1871 |
| 6 T F Smailes | 14 for 58 | v Derbyshire | at Sheffield | 1939 |
| 5 P Carrick | 12 for 89 | v Derbyshire | at Sheffield (Abbeydale Pk) | 1983 |
| 5 J M Preston | 13 for 63 | v MCC | at Scarborough | 1888 |
| 5 E Robinson | 12 for 95 | v Northamptonshire | at Huddersfield | 1927 |
| 4 J T Newstead | 11 for 72 | v Worcestershire | at Bradford | 1907 |
| 3 T W Foster | 11 for 93 | v Liverpool & District | at Liverpool | 1894 |
| 3 G P Harrison | 11 for 76 | v Kent | at Dewsbury | 1883 |
| 3 F S Jackson | 12 for 80 | v Hampshire | at Southampton | 1897 |
| 3 P W Jarvis | 11 for 92 | v Middlesex | at Lord's | 1986 |
| 3 S P Kirby | 13 for 154 | v Somerset | at Taunton | 2003 |
| 3 A G Nicholson | 12 for 73 | v Glamorgan | at Leeds | 1964 |
| 3 R K Platt | 10 for 87 | v Surrey | at The Oval | 1959 |
| 3 A Sidebottom | 11 for 64 | v Kent | at Sheffield (Abbeydale Pk) | 1980 |
| 3 R J Sidebottom | 11 for 43 | v Kent | at Leeds | 2000 |
| 3 G Ulyett | 12 for 102 | v Lancashire | at Huddersfield | 1889 |
| 2 T Armitage | 13 for 46 | v Surrey | at Sheffield | 1876 |
| 2 R Aspinall | 14 for 65 | v Northamptonshire | at Northampton | 1947 |
| 2 J T Brown (Darfield) | 12 for 109 | v Gloucestershire | at Huddersfield | 1899 |
| 2 R O Clayton | 12 for 104 | v Lancashire | at Manchester | 1877 |
| 2 D B Close | 11 for 116 | v Kent | at Gillingham | 1965 |
| 2 M J Cowan | 12 for 87 | v Warwickshire | at Birmingham | 1960 |
| 2 A Coxon | 10 for 57 | v Derbyshire | at Chesterfield | 1949 |
| 2 D Gough | 10 for 80 | v Lancashire | at Leeds | 1995 |
| 2 G M Hamilton | 11 for 72 | v Surrey | at Leeds | 1998 |
| 2 P J Hartley | 11 for 68 | v Derbyshire | at Chesterfield | 1995 |
| 2 R A Hutton | 11 for 62 | v Lancashire | at Manchester | 1971 |
| 2 E Leadbeater | 11 for 162 | v Nottinghamshire | at Nottingham | 1950 |
| 2 M A Robinson | 12 for 124 | v Northamptonshire | at Harrogate | 1993 |
| 2 M Ryan | 10 for 77 | v Leicestershire | at Bradford | 1962 |
| 2 E Smith (Morley) | 10 for 97 | v MCC | at Scarborough | 1893 |
| 2 G B Stevenson | 11 for 74 | v Nottinghamshire | at Nottingham | 1980 |
| 2 S Wade | 11 for 56 | v Gloucestershire | at Cheltenham | 1886 |
| 2 E R Wilson | 11 for 109 | v Sussex | at Hove | 1921 |
| 1 A B Bainbridge | 12 for 111 | v Essex | at Harrogate | 1961 |
| 1 J Birkenshaw | 11 for 134 | v Middlesex | at Leeds | 1960 |
| 1 A Booth | 10 for 91 | v Indians | at Bradford | 1946 |
| 1 H P Cooper | 11 for 96 | v Northamptonshire | at Northampton | 1976 |
| 1 A Drake | 15 for 51 | v Somerset | at Weston-Super-Mare | 1914 |
| 1 L Greenwood | 11 for 71 | v Surrey | at The Oval | 1867 |
| 1 P M Hutchison | 11 for 102 | v Pakistan 'A' | at Leeds | 1997 |
| 1 L Hutton | 10 for 101 | v Leicestershire | at Leicester (Aylestone Rd) | 1937 |
| 1 R Iddison | 10 for 68 | v Surrey | at Sheffield | 1864 |
| 1 M Leyland | 10 for 94 | v Leicestershire | at Leicester (Aylestone Rd) | 1933 |
| 1 J D Middlebrook | 10 for 170 | v Hampshire | at Southampton | 2000 |
| 1 F W Milligan | 12 for 110 | v Sussex | at Sheffield | 1897 |
| 1 H Myers | 12 for 192 | v Gloucestershire | at Dewsbury | 1904 |
| 1 C M Old | 11 for 46 | v Gloucestershire | at Middlesbrough | 1969 |
| 1 D Pickles | 12 for 133 | v Somerset | at Taunton | 1957 |
| 1 A U Rashid | 11 for 114 | v Worcestershire | at Worcester | 2011 |
| 1 W Ringrose | 11 for 135 | v Australians | at Bradford | 1905 |
| 1 C E W Silverwood | 12 for 148 | v Kent | at Leeds | 1997 |
| 1 W Slinn | 12 for 53 | v Nottinghamshire | at Nottingham | 1864 |
| 1 J Waring | 10 for 63 | v Lancashire | at Leeds | 1966 |
| 1 F Wilkinson | 10 for 129 | v Hampshire | at Bournemouth | 1938 |
| 1 A C Williams | 10 for 66 | v Hampshire | at Dewsbury | 1919 |

# TEN WICKETS IN AN INNINGS

| Bowler | | | | Year |
|---|---|---|---|---|
| A Drake | 10 for 35 | v. | Somerset at Weston-super-Mare | 1914 |
| H Verity | 10 for 36 | v. | Warwickshire at Leeds | 1931 |
| *H Verity | 10 for 10 | v. | Nottinghamshire at Leeds | 1932 |
| T F Smailes | 10 for 47 | v. | Derbyshire at Sheffield | 1939 |

*Includes the hat trick.

# EIGHT WICKETS OR MORE IN AN INNINGS

**(Ten wickets in an innings also listed above)**

**A complete list of seven wickets in an innings up to and including 2007 is to be found in the 2008 edition**

### R APPLEYARD (1)

8 for 76 v. MCC at Scarborough, 1951

### R ASPINALL (1)

8 for 42 v. Northamptonshire at Northampton, 1947

### W BATES (2)

8 for 45 v. Lancashire at Huddersfield, 1878
8 for 21 v. Surrey at The Oval, 1879

### M W BOOTH (4)

8 for 52 v. Leicestershire at Sheffield, 1912
8 for 47 v. Middlesex at Leeds, 1912
8 for 86 v. Middlesex at Sheffield, 1913
8 for 64 v. Essex at Leyton, 1914

### W E BOWES (9)

8 for 77 v. Leicestershire at Dewsbury, 1929
8 for 69 v. Middlesex at Bradford, 1930
9 for 121 v. Essex at Scarborough, 1932
8 for 62 v. Sussex at Hove, 1932
8 for 69 v. Gloucestershire at Gloucester, 1933
8 for 40 v. Worcestershire at Sheffield, 1935
8 for 18 v. Northamptonshire at Kettering, 1935
8 for 17 v. Northamptonshire at Kettering, 1935
8 for 56 v. Leicestershire at Scarborough, 1936

### J T BROWN (Darfield) (1)

8 for 40 v. Gloucestershire at Huddersfield, 1899

### P CARRICK (2)

8 for 33 v. Cambridge University at Cambridge, 1973
8 for 72 v. Derbyshire at Scarborough, 1975

### R O CLAYTON (1)

8 for 66 v. Lancashire at Manchester, 1877

### D B CLOSE (2)

8 for 41 v. Kent at Leeds, 1959
8 for 43 v. Essex at Leeds, 1960

### H P COOPER (1)

8 for 62 v. Glamorgan at Cardiff, 1975

# EIGHT WICKETS OR MORE IN AN INNINGS *(Continued)*

### *G A COPE (1)*

8 for 73 v. Gloucestershire at Bristol, 1975

### *M J COWAN (1)*

9 for 43 v. Warwickshire at Birmingham, 1960

### *A COXON (1)*

8 for 31 v. Worcestershire at Leeds, 1946

### *A DRAKE (2)*

8 for 59 v. Gloucestershire at Sheffield, 1913
10 for 35 v. Somerset at Weston-super-Mare, 1914

### *T EMMETT (8)*

9 for 34 v. Nottinghamshire at Dewsbury, 1868
9 for 23 v. Cambridgeshire at Hunslet, 1869
8 for 31 v. Nottinghamshire at Sheffield, 1871
8 for 46 v. Gloucestershire at Clifton, 1877
8 for 16 v. MCC at Scarborough, 1877
8 for 22 v. Surrey at The Oval, 1881
8 for 52 v. MCC at Scarborough, 1882
8 for 32 v. Sussex at Huddersfield, 1884

### *S D FLETCHER (1)*

8 for 58 v. Essex at Sheffield, 1988

### *T W FOSTER (1)*

9 for 59 v. MCC at Lord's, 1894

### *G FREEMAN (2)*

8 for 11 v. Lancashire at Holbeck, 1868
8 for 29 v. Surrey at Sheffield, 1869

### *L GREENWOOD (1)*

8 for 35 v. Cambridgeshire at Dewsbury, 1867

### *S HAIGH (5)*

8 for 78 v. Australians at Bradford, 1896
8 for 35 v. Hampshire at Harrogate, 1896
8 for 21 v. Hampshire at Southampton, 1898
8 for 33 v. Warwickshire at Scarborough, 1899
9 for 25 v. Gloucestershire at Leeds, 1912

### *P J HARTLEY (2)*

8 for 111 v. Sussex at Hove, 1992
9 for 41 v. Derbyshire at Chesterfield, 1995

### *G H HIRST (8)*

8 for 59 v. Warwickshire at Birmingham, 1896
8 for 48 v. Australians at Bradford, 1899
8 for 25 v. Leicestershire at Hull, 1907
9 for 45 v. Middlesex at Sheffield, 1907
9 for 23 v. Lancashire at Leeds, 1910
8 for 80 v. Somerset at Sheffield, 1910
9 for 41 v. Worcestershire at Worcester, 1911
9 for 69 v. MCC at Lord's, 1912

### *R ILLINGWORTH (5)*

8 for 69 v. Surrey at The Oval, 1954
9 for 42 v. Worcestershire at Worcester, 1957
8 for 70 v. Glamorgan at Swansea, 1960
8 for 50 v. Lancashire at Manchester, 1961
8 for 20 v. Worcestershire at Leeds, 1965

### *R KILNER (2)*

8 for 26 v. Glamorgan at Cardiff, 1923
8 for 40 v. Middlesex at Bradford, 1926

### *S P KIRBY (1)*

8 for 80 v. Somerset at Taunton, 2003

### *E LEADBEATER (1)*

8 for 83 v. Worcestershire at Worcester, 1950

### *M LEYLAND (1)*

8 for 63 v. Hampshire at Huddersfield, 1938

### *G G MACAULAY (3)*

8 for 43 v. Gloucestershire at Bristol, 1926
8 for 37 v. Derbyshire at Hull, 1927
8 for 21 v. Indians at Harrogate, 1932

### *H MYERS (1)*

8 for 81 v. Gloucestershire at Dewsbury, 1904

### *A G NICHOLSON (2)*

9 for 62 v. Sussex at Eastbourne, 1967
8 for 22 v. Kent at Canterbury, 1968

### *E PEATE (6)*

8 for 24 v. Lancashire at Manchester, 1880
8 for 30 v. Surrey at Huddersfield, 1881
8 for 69 v. Sussex at Hove, 1881
8 for 32 v. Middlesex at Sheffield, 1882
8 for 5 v. Surrey at Holbeck, 1883
8 for 63 v. Kent at Gravesend, 1884

### *R PEEL (6)*

8 for 12 v. Nottinghamshire at Sheffield, 1888
8 for 60 v. Surrey at Sheffield, 1890
8 for 54 v. Cambridge University at Cambridge, 1893
9 for 22 v. Somerset at Leeds, 1895
8 for 27 v. South of England XI at Scarborough, 1896
8 for 53 v. Kent at Halifax, 1897

### *J M PRESTON (2)*

8 for 27 v. Sussex at Hove, 1888
9 for 28 v. MCC at Scarborough, 1888

# EIGHT WICKETS OR MORE IN AN INNINGS *(Continued)*

### *W RHODES (18)*

9 for 28 v. Essex at Leyton, 1899
8 for 38 v. Nottinghamshire at Nottingham, 1899
8 for 68 v. Cambridge University at Cambridge, 1900
8 for 43 v. Lancashire at Bradford, 1900
8 for 23 v. Hampshire at Hull, 1900
8 for 72 v. Gloucestershire at Bradford, 1900
8 for 28 v. Essex at Harrogate, 1900
8 for 53 v. Middlesex at Lord's, 1901
8 for 55 v. Kent at Canterbury, 1901
8 for 26 v. Kent at Catford, 1902
8 for 87 v. Worcestershire at Worcester, 1903
8 for 61 v. Lancashire at Bradford, 1903
8 for 90 v. Warwickshire at Birmingham, 1905
8 for 92 v. Northamptonshire at Northampton, 1911
8 for 44 v. Warwickshire at Bradford, 1919
8 for 39 v. Sussex at Leeds, 1920
8 for 48 v. Somerset at Huddersfield, 1926
9 for 39 v. Essex at Leyton, 1929

### *W RINGROSE (1)*

9 for 76 v. Australians at Bradford, 1905

### *E ROBINSON (3)*

9 for 36 v. Lancashire at Bradford, 1920
8 for 32 v. Northamptonshire at Huddersfield, 1927
8 for 13 v. Cambridge University at Cambridge, 1928

### *E P ROBINSON (2)*

8 for 35 v. Lancashire at Leeds, 1939
8 for 76 v. Surrey at The Oval, 1946

### *M A ROBINSON (1)*

9 for 37 v. Northamptonshire at Harrogate, 1993

### *A SIDEBOTTOM (1)*

8 for 72 v. Leicestershire at Middlesbrough, 1986

### *T F SMAILES (2)*

8 for 68 v. Glamorgan at Hull, 1938
10 for 47 v. Derbyshire at Sheffield, 1939

### *G B STEVENSON (2)*

8 for 65 v. Lancashire at Leeds, 1978
8 for 57 v. Northamptonshire at Leeds, 1980

### *F S TRUEMAN (8)*

8 for 70 v. Minor Counties at Lord's, 1949
8 for 68 v. Nottinghamshire at Sheffield, 1951
8 for 53 v. Nottinghamshire at Nottingham, 1951
8 for 28 v. Kent at Dover, 1954
8 for 84 v. Nottinghamshire at Worksop, 1962
8 for 45 v. Gloucestershire at Bradford, 1963
8 for 36 v. Sussex at Hove, 1965
8 for 37 v. Essex at Bradford, 1966

# EIGHT WICKETS OR MORE IN AN INNINGS *(Continued)*

### H VERITY (20)

9 for 60 v. Glamorgan at Swansea, 1930
10 for 36 v. Warwickshire at Leeds, 1931
8 for 33 v. Glamorgan at Swansea, 1931
8 for 107 v. Lancashire at Bradford, 1932
8 for 39 v. Northamptonshire at Northampton, 1932
10 for 10 v. Nottinghamshire at Leeds, 1932
8 for 47 v. Essex at Leyton, 1933
9 for 44 v. Essex at Leyton, 1933
9 for 59 v. Kent at Dover, 1933
8 for 28 v. Leicestershire at Leeds, 1935
8 for 56 v. Oxford University at Oxford, 1936
8 for 40 v. Worcestershire at Stourbridge, 1936
9 for 12 v. Kent at Sheffield, 1936
9 for 48 v. Essex at Westcliff-on-Sea, 1936
8 for 42 v. Nottinghamshire at Bradford, 1936
9 for 43 v. Warwickshire at Leeds, 1937
8 for 80 v. Sussex at Eastbourne, 1937
8 for 43 v. Middlesex at The Oval, 1937
9 for 62 v. MCC at Lord's, 1939
8 for 38 v. Leicestershire at Hull, 1939

### A WADDINGTON (3)

8 for 34 v. Northamptonshire at Leeds, 1922
8 for 39 v. Kent at Leeds, 1922
8 for 35 v. Hampshire at Bradford, 1922

### E WAINWRIGHT (3)

8 for 49 v. Middlesex at Sheffield, 1891
9 for 66 v. Middlesex at Sheffield, 1894
8 for 34 v. Essex at Bradford, 1896

### J H WARDLE (4)

8 for 87 v. Derbyshire at Chesterfield, 1948
8 for 26 v. Middlesex at Lord's, 1950
9 for 48 v. Sussex at Hull, 1954
9 for 25 v. Lancashire at Manchester, 1954

### C WHITE (1)

8 for 55 v. Gloucestershire at Gloucester, 1998

### A C WILLIAMS (1)

9 for 29 v. Hampshire at Dewsbury, 1919

### R WOOD (1)

8 for 45 v. Scotland at Glasgow, 1952

# SIX WICKETS IN AN INNINGS AT LESS THAN FOUR RUNS EACH

**A complete list of 5 wickets at less than 4 runs each up to and including 2007 is to be found in the 2008 edition**

*R APPLEYARD (2)*

6 for 17 v. Essex at Bradford, 1951
6 for 12 v. Hampshire at Bournemouth, 1954

*T ARMITAGE (1)*

6 for 20 v. Surrey at Sheffield, 1876

*R ASPINALL (1)*

6 for 23 v. Northamptonshire at Northampton, 1947

*W BATES (5)*

6 for 11 v. Middlesex at Huddersfield, 1879
6 for 22 v. Kent at Bradford, 1881
6 for 17 v. Nottinghamshire at Nottingham, 1881
6 for 12 v. Kent at Sheffield, 1882
6 for 19 v. Lancashire at Dewsbury, 1886

*A BOOTH (1)*

6 for 21 v. Warwickshire at Birmingham, 1946

*W E BOWES (4)*

6 for 17 v. Middlesex at Lord's, 1934
6 for 16 v. Lancashire at Bradford, 1935
6 for 20 v. Gloucestershire at Sheffield, 1936
6 for 23 v. Warwickshire at Birmingham, 1947

*J T BROWN (Darfield) (1)*

6 for 19 v. Worcestershire at Worcester, 1899

*R.O CLAYTON (1)*

6 for 20 v. Nottinghamshire at Sheffield, 1876

*A COXON (1)*

6 for 17 v. Surrey at Sheffield, 1948

*T EMMETT (6)*

6 for 7 v. Surrey at Sheffield, 1867
6 for 13 v. Lancashire at Holbeck, 1868
6 for 21 v. Middlesex at Scarborough, 1874
6 for 12 v. Derbyshire at Sheffield, 1878
6 for 19 v. Derbyshire at Bradford, 1881
6 for 22 v. Australians at Bradford, 1882

*H FISHER (1)*

6 for 11 v. Leicestershire at Bradford, 1932

# SIX WICKETS IN AN INNINGS AT LESS THAN FOUR
## RUNS EACH *(Continued)*

### *S HAIGH (10)*

6 for 18 v. Derbyshire at Bradford, 1897
6 for 22 v. Hampshire at Southampton, 1898
6 for 21 v. Surrey at The Oval, 1900
6 for 23 v. Cambridge University at Cambridge, 1902
6 for 19 v. Somerset at Sheffield, 1902
6 for 22 v. Cambridge University at Sheffield, 1903
6 for 21 v. Hampshire at Leeds, 1904
6 for 21 v. Nottinghamshire at Sheffield, 1905
6 for 13 v. Surrey at Leeds, 1908
6 for 14 v. Australians at Bradford, 1912

### *A HILL (2)*

6 for 9 v. United South of England XI at Bradford, 1874
6 for 18 v. MCC at Lord's, 1881

### *G H HIRST (7)*

6 for 23 v. MCC at Lord's, 1893
6 for 20 v. Lancashire at Bradford, 1906
6 for 12 v. Northamptonshire at Northampton, 1908
6 for 7 v. Northamptonshire at Northampton, 1908
6 for 23 v. Surrey at Leeds, 1908
6 for 23 v. Lancashire at Manchester, 1909
6 for 20 v. Surrey at Sheffield, 1909

### *R ILLINGWORTH (2)*

6 for 15 v. Scotland at Hull, 1956
6 for 13 v. Leicestershire at Leicester, 1963

### *F S JACKSON (1)*

6 for 19 v. Hampshire at Southampton, 1897

### *R KILNER (5)*

6 for 22 v. Essex at Harrogate, 1922
6 for 13 v. Hampshire at Bournemouth, 1922
6 for 14 v. Middlesex at Bradford, 1923
6 for 22 v. Surrey at Sheffield, 1923
6 for 15 v. Hampshire at Portsmouth, 1924

### *G G MACAULAY (10)*

6 for 10 v. Warwickshire at Birmingham, 1921
6 for 3 v. Derbyshire at Hull, 1921
6 for 8 v. Northamptonshire at Northampton, 1922
6 for 12 v. Glamorgan at Cardiff, 1922
6 for 18 v. Northamptonshire at Bradford, 1923
6 for 19 v. Northamptonshire at Northampton, 1925
6 for 22 v. Leicestershire at Leeds, 1926
6 for 11 v. Leicestershire at Hull, 1930
6 for 22 v. Leicestershire at Bradford, 1933
6 for 22 v. Middlesex at Leeds, 1934

# SIX WICKETS IN AN INNINGS AT LESS THAN FOUR
## RUNS EACH *(Continued)*

### *E PEATE (5)*

6 for 14 v. Middlesex at Huddersfield, 1879
6 for 12 v. Derbyshire at Derby, 1882
6 for 13 v. Gloucestershire at Moreton-in-Marsh, 1884
6 for 16 v. Sussex at Huddersfield, 1886
6 for 16 v. Cambridge University at Sheffield, 1886

### *R PEEL (4)*

6 for 21 v. Nottinghamshire at Sheffield, 1888
6 for 19 v. Australians at Huddersfield, 1888
6 for 22 v. Gloucestershire at Bristol, 1891
6 for 19 v. Leicestershire at Scarborough, 1896

### *A C RHODES (1)*

6 for 19 v. Cambridge University at Cambridge, 1932

### *W RHODES (12)*

6 for 21 v. Somerset at Bath, 1898
6 for 16 v. Gloucestershire at Bristol, 1899
6 for 4 v. Nottinghamshire at Nottingham, 1901
6 for 15 v. MCC at Lord's, 1902
6 for 16 v. Cambridge University at Cambridge, 1905
6 for 9 v. Essex at Huddersfield, 1905
6 for 22 v. Derbyshire at Glossop, 1907
6 for 17 v. Leicestershire at Leicester, 1908
6 for 13 v. Sussex at Hove, 1922
6 for 23 v. Nottinghamshire at Leeds, 1923
6 for 22 v. Cambridge University at Cambridge, 1924
6 for 20 v. Gloucestershire at Dewsbury, 1927

### *W RINGROSE (1)*

6 for 20 v. Leicestershire at Dewsbury, 1903

### *R J SIDEBOTTOM (1)*

6 for 16 v. Kent at Leeds, 2000

### *W SLINN (1)*

6 for 19 v. Nottinghamshire at Nottingham, 1864

### *G B STEVENSON(1)*

6 for 14 v. Warwickshire at Sheffield, 1979

### *F S TRUEMAN (4)*

6 for 23 v. Oxford University at Oxford, 1955
6 for 23 v. Oxford University at Oxford, 1958
6 for 18 v. Warwickshire at Birmingham, 1963
6 for 20 v. Leicestershire at Sheffield, 1968

### *H VERITY (5)*

6 for 11 v. Surrey at Bradford, 1931
6 for 21 v. Glamorgan at Swansea, 1931
6 for 12 v. Derbyshire at Hull, 1933
6 for 10 v. Essex at Ilford, 1937
6 for 22 v. Hampshire at Bournemouth, 1939

## SIX WICKETS IN AN INNINGS AT LESS THAN FOUR
## RUNS EACH *(Continued)*

### *A WADDINGTON (2)*

6 for 21 v. Northamptonshire at Harrogate, 1921
6 for 21 v. Northamptonshire at Northampton, 1923

### *S WADE (1)*

6 for 18 v. Gloucestershire at Dewsbury, 1887

### *E WAINWRIGHT (4)*

6 for 16 v. Sussex at Leeds, 1893
6 for 23 v. Sussex at Hove, 1893
6 for 18 v. Sussex at Dewsbury, 1894
6 for 22 v. MCC at Scarborough, 1894

### *J H WARDLE (8)*

6 for 17 v. Sussex at Sheffield, 1948
6 for 10 v. Scotland at Edinburgh, 1950
6 for 12 v. Gloucestershire at Hull, 1950
6 for 20 v. Kent at Scarborough, 1950
6 for 23 v. Somerset at Sheffield, 1951
6 for 21 v. Glamorgan at Leeds, 1951
6 for 18 v. Gloucestershire at Bristol, 1951
6 for 6 v. Gloucestershire at Bristol, 1955

### *D WILSON (3)*

6 for 22 v. Sussex at Bradford, 1963
6 for 15 v. Gloucestershire at Middlesbrough, 1966
6 for 22 v. Middlesex at Sheffield, 1966

## FOUR WICKETS IN FOUR BALLS

A Drake v. Derbyshire at Chesterfield, 1914

## FOUR WICKETS IN FIVE BALLS

F S Jackson v. Australians at Leeds, 1902
A Waddington v. Northamptonshire at Northampton, 1920
G G Macaulay v. Lancashire at Manchester, 1933
P J Hartley v. Derbyshire at Chesterfield, 1995
D Gough v. Kent at Leeds, 1995
J D Middlebrook v. Hampshire at Southampton, 2000

# BEST BOWLING ANALYSES IN A MATCH
# FOR AND AGAINST YORKSHIRE

**Best For Yorkshire:**
17 for 91 (8 for 47 and 9 for 44) H Verity v Essex at Leyton, 1933

**Against Yorkshire:**
17 for 91 (9 for 62 and 8 for 29) H Dean for Lancashire at Liverpool, 1913
(non-championship)

County Championship
16 for 114 (8 for 48 and 8 for 66) G Burton for Middlesex at Sheffield, 1888

Yorkshire versus:

| | | |
|---|---|---|
| **Derbyshire** | *For Yorkshire:* | 14 for 58 (4 for 11 and 10 for 47) T F Smailes at Sheffield, 1939 |
| | *Against:* | 13 for 65 (7 for 33 and 6 for 32) W Mycroft at Sheffield, 1879 |
| *Most 10 wickets in a match* | *For Yorkshire:* | P Carrick and E Peate 4 each |
| | *Against:* | W Mycroft 3 |
| **Durham** | *For Yorkshire:* | 10 for 101 (6 for 57 and 4 for 44) M A Robinson at Durham, 1992 |
| | *Against:* | 10 for 144 (7 for 81 and 3 for 63) O D Gibson at Chester-le-Street, 2007 |
| *Most 10 wickets in a match* | *For Yorkshire:* | M A Robinson 1 |
| | *Against:* | G R Breese and O D Gibson 1 each |
| **Essex** | *For Yorkshire:* | 17 for 91 (8 for 47 and 9 for 44) H Verity at Leyton, 1933 |
| | *Against:* | 14 for 127 (7 for 37 and 7 for 90) W Mead at Leyton, 1899 |
| *Most 10 wickets in a match* | *For Yorkshire:* | W Rhodes 7 |
| | *Against:* | J K Lever, W Mead 2 each |
| **Glamorgan** | *For Yorkshire:* | 15 for 123 (8 for 70 and 7 for 53) R Illingworth at Swansea. 1960 |
| | *Against:* | 12 for 76 (7 for 30 and 5 for 46) D J Shepherd at Cardiff, 1957 |
| *Most 10 wickets in a match* | *For Yorkshire:* | H Verity 5 |
| | *Against:* | D J Shepherd, J S Pressdee 1 each |
| **Gloucestershire** | *For Yorkshire:* | 14 for 64 (7 for 58 and 7 for 6) R Illingworth at Harrogate, 1967 |
| | *Against:* | 15 for 79 (8 for 33 and 7 for 46) W G Grace at Sheffield, 1872 |
| *Most 10 wickets in a match* | *For Yorkshire:* | W Rhodes 8 |
| | *Against:* | E G Dennett 5 |
| **Hampshire** | *For Yorkshire:* | 14 for 43 (8 for 21 and 6 for 22) S Haigh at Southampton, 1898 |
| | *Against:* | 12 for 145 (7 for 78 and 5 for 67) D Shackleton at Bradford, 1962 |
| *Most 10 wickets in a match* | *For Yorkshire:* | W Rhodes, E Robinson, H Verity 3 each |
| | *Against:* | A S Kennedy 3 |

Yorkshire versus

| | | |
|---|---|---|
| **Kent** | *For Yorkshire:* | 15 for 38 (6 for 26 and 9 for 12) |
| | | H Verity at Sheffield, 1936 |
| | *Against:* | 13 for 48 (5 for 13 and 8 for 35) |
| | | A Hearne at Sheffield, 1885 |
| *Most 10 wickets* | *For Yorkshire:* | E Peate and J H Wardle 4 each |
| *in a match* | *Against:* | C Blythe 6 |
| **Lancashire** | *For Yorkshire:* | 14 for 80 (6 for 56 and 8 for 24) |
| | | E Peate at Manchester, 1880 |
| | *Against:* | 17 for 91 (9 for 62 and 8 for 29) |
| | | H Dean at Liverpool, 1913 (non-championship) |
| | | 14 for 90 (6 for 47 and 8 for 43) |
| | | R Tattersall at Leeds, 1956 (championship) |
| *Most 10 wickets* | *For Yorkshire:* | T Emmett 5 |
| *in a match* | *Against:* | J Briggs 8 |
| **Leicestershire** | *For Yorkshire:* | 15 for 63 (8 for 25 and 7 for 38) |
| | | G H Hirst at Hull, 1907 |
| | *Against:* | 12 for 139 (8 for 85 and 4 for 54) |
| | | A D Pougher at Leicester, 1895 |
| *Most 10 wickets* | *For Yorkshire:* | G H Hirst 5 |
| *in a match* | *Against:* | A D Pougher 2 |
| **Middlesex** | *For Yorkshire:* | 13 for 94 (6 for 61 and 7 for 33) |
| | | S Haigh at Leeds, 1900 |
| | *Against:* | 16 for 114 (8 for 48 and 8 for 66) |
| | | G Burton at Sheffield, 1888 |
| *Most 10 wickets* | *For Yorkshire:* | W Rhodes 5 |
| *in a match* | *Against:* | J T Hearne 7 |
| **Northamptonshire** | *For Yorkshire:* | 16 for 35 (8 for 18 and 8 for 17) |
| | | W E Bowes at Kettering, 1935 |
| | *Against:* | 15 for 31 (7 for 22 and 8 for 9) |
| | | G E Tribe at Northampton, 1958 |
| *Most 10 wickets* | *For Yorkshire:* | W E Bowes, G G Macaulay, H Verity, |
| *in a match* | | A Waddington 3 each |
| | *Against:* | G E Tribe 3 |
| **Nottinghamshire** | *For Yorkshire:* | 14 for 33 (8 for 12 and 6 for 21) |
| | | R Peel at Sheffield, 1888 |
| | *Against:* | 14 for 94 (8 for 38 and 6 for 56) |
| | | F Morley at Nottingham, 1878 |
| *Most 10 wickets* | *For Yorkshire:* | G H Hirst 5 |
| *in a match* | *Against:* | F Morley, J C Shaw 4 each |
| **Somerset** | *For Yorkshire:* | 15 for 50 (9 for 22 and 6 for 28) |
| | | R Peel at Leeds, 1895 |
| | *Against:* | 15 for 71 (6 for 30 and 9 for 41) |
| | | L C Braund at Sheffield, 1902 |
| *Most 10 wickets* | *For Yorkshire:* | G H Hirst 7 |
| *in a match* | *Against:* | L C Braund 3 |

# BEST BOWLING ANALYSES IN A MATCH
## FOR AND AGAINST YORKSHIRE *(continued)*

Yorkshire versus

| | | |
|---|---|---|
| **Surrey** | *For Yorkshire:* | 14 for 77 (6 for 47 and 8 for 30) |
| | | E Peate at Huddersfield, 1881 |
| | *Against:* | 15 for 154 (7 for 55 and 8 for 99) |
| | | T Richardson at Leeds, 1897 |
| *Most 10 wickets* | *For Yorkshire:* | W Rhodes 7 |
| *in a match* | *Against:* | G A Lohmann, T Richardson 6 each |
| **Sussex** | *For Yorkshire:* | 16 for 112 (9 for 48 and 7 for 64) |
| | | J H Wardle at Hull, 1954 |
| | *Against:* | 12 for 110 (6 for 71 and 6 for 39) |
| | | G R Cox at Sheffield, 1907 |
| *Most 10 wickets* | *For Yorkshire:* | R Peel, E Wainwright 3 each |
| *in a match* | *Against:* | Twelve players 1 each |
| **Warwickshire** | *For Yorkshire:* | 14 for 92 (9 for 43 and 5 for 49) |
| | | H Verity at Leeds, 1937 |
| | *Against:* | 12 for 55 (5 for 21 and 7 for 34) |
| | | T W Cartwright at Bradford, 1969 |
| *Most 10 wickets* | *For Yorkshire:* | S Haigh 4 |
| *in a match* | *Against:* | E F Field 4 |
| **Worcestershire** | *For Yorkshire:* | 14 for 211 (8 for 87 and 6 for 124) |
| | | W Rhodes at Worcester, 1903 |
| | *Against:* | 13 for 76 (4 for 38 and 9 for 38) |
| | | J A Cuffe at Bradford, 1907 |
| *Most 10 wickets* | *For Yorkshire:* | S Haigh, G G Macaulay 4 each |
| *in a match* | *Against:* | N Gifford 2 |
| **Australians** | *For Yorkshire:* | 13 for 149 (8 for 48 and 5 for 101) |
| | | G H Hirst at Bradford, 1899 |
| | *Against:* | 13 for 170 (6 for 91 and 7 for 79) |
| | | J M Gregory at Sheffield, 1919 |
| *Most 10 wickets* | *For Yorkshire:* | S Haigh 2 |
| *in a match* | *Against:* | C V Grimmett, F R Spofforth, C T B Turner, H Trumble 2 each |

# BEST BOWLING ANALYSES IN AN INNINGS
## FOR AND AGAINST YORKSHIRE

**Best For Yorkshire:**
10 for 10 H Verity v Nottinghamshire at Leeds, 1932

**Against Yorkshire:**
10 for 37 C V Grimmett for Australians at Sheffield, 1930
(non-championship)

County Championship
10 for 51 H Howell for Warwickshire at Birmingham, 1923

Yorkshire versus:

| | | | |
|---|---|---|---|
| **Derbyshire** | *For Yorkshire:* | 10 for 47 | T F Smailes at Sheffield, 1939 |
| | *Against:* | 9 for 27 | J J Hulme at Sheffield, 1894 |
| *Most 5 wickets* | *For Yorkshire:* | S Haigh, E Peat, W Rhodes 11 each | |
| *in an innings* | *Against:* | W Mycroft 10 | |

## BEST BOWLING ANALYSES IN AN INNINGS
## FOR AND AGAINST YORKSHIRE *(continued)*

Yorkshire versus

| | | | |
|---|---|---|---|
| **Durham** | *For Yorkshire:* | 6 for 37 | R D Stemp at Durham, 1994 |
| | | 6 for 37 | J N Gillespie at Chester-le-Street, 2006 |
| | *Against:* | 7 for 58 | J Wood at Leeds, 1999 |
| *Most 5 wickets* | *For Yorkshire:* | D Gough and M J Hoggard 2 each | |
| *in an innings* | *Against:* | G R Breese, S J E Brown, S J Harmison | |
| | | and G Onions 2 each | |
| **Essex** | *For Yorkshire:* | 9 for 28 | W Rhodes at Leyton, 1899 |
| | *Against:* | 8 for 44 | F G Bull at Bradford, 1896 |
| *Most 5 wickets* | *For Yorkshire:* | W Rhodes 18 | |
| *in an innings* | *Against:* | W Mead 14 | |
| **Glamorgan** | *For Yorkshire:* | 9 for 60 | H Verity at Swansea, 1930 |
| | *Against:* | 9 for 43 | J S Pressdee at Swansea, 1965 |
| *Most 5 wickets* | *For Yorkshire:* | H Verity 12 | |
| *in an innings* | *Against:* | D J Shepherd 6 | |
| **Gloucestershire** | *For Yorkshire:* | 9 for 25 | S Haigh at Leeds, 1912 |
| | *Against:* | 9 for 36 | C W L Parker at Bristol, 1922 |
| *Most 5 wickets* | *For Yorkshire:* | W Rhodes 22 | |
| *in an innings* | *Against:* | T W J Goddard 17 | |
| **Hampshire** | *For Yorkshire:* | 9 for 29 | A C Williams at Dewsbury, 1919 |
| | *Against:* | 8 for 49 | O W Herman at Bournemouth, 1930 |
| *Most 5 wickets* | *For Yorkshire:* | G H Hirst 10 | |
| *in an innings* | *Against:* | A S Kennedy 10 | |
| **Kent** | *For Yorkshire:* | 9 for 12 | H Verity at Sheffield, 1936 |
| | *Against:* | 8 for 35 | A Hearne at Sheffield, 1885 |
| *Most 5 wickets* | *For Yorkshire:* | W Rhodes 12 | |
| *in an innings* | *Against:* | A P Freeman 14 | |
| **Lancashire** | *For Yorkshire:* | 9 for 23 | G H Hirst at Leeds, 1910 |
| | *Against:* | 9 for 41 | A Mold at Huddersfield, 1890 |
| *Most 5 wickets* | *For Yorkshire:* | T Emmett 16 | |
| *in an innings* | *Against:* | J Briggs 19 | |
| **Leicestershire** | *For Yorkshire:* | 8 for 25 | G H Hirst at Hull, 1907 |
| | *Against:* | 9 for 63 | C T Spencer at Huddersfield, 1954 |
| *Most 5 wickets* | *For Yorkshire:* | G H Hirst 15 | |
| *in an innings* | *Against:* | H A Smith 7 | |
| **Middlesex** | *For Yorkshire:* | 9 for 45 | G H Hirst at Sheffield 1907 |
| | *Against:* | 9 for 57 | F A Tarrant at Leeds, 1906 |
| *Most 5 wickets* | *For Yorkshire:* | W Rhodes 18 | |
| *in an innings* | *Against:* | J T Hearne 21 | |
| **Northamptonshire** | *For Yorkshire:* | 9 for 37 | M A Robinson at Harrogate, 1993 |
| | *Against:* | 9 for 30 | A E Thomas at Bradford, 1920 |
| *Most 5 wickets* | *For Yorkshire:* | G G Macaulay 14 | |
| *in an innings* | *Against:* | G E Tribe, W Wells 7 each | |
| **Nottinghamshire** | *For Yorkshire:* | 10 for 10 | H Verity at Leeds, 1932 |
| | *Against:* | 8 for 32 | J C Shaw at Nottingham, 1865 |
| *Most 5 wickets* | *For Yorkshire:* | W Rhodes 17 | |
| *in an innings* | *Against:* | F Morley 17 | |

# BEST BOWLING ANALYSES IN AN INNINGS
## FOR AND AGAINST YORKSHIRE *(continued)*

Yorkshire versus

| | | | |
|---|---|---|---|
| **Somerset** | *For Yorkshire:* | 10 for 35 | A Drake at Weston-super-Mare, 1914 |
| | *Against:* | 9 for 41 | L C Braund at Sheffield, 1902 |
| *Most 5 wickets* | *For Yorkshire:* | G H Hirst 16 | |
| *in an innings* | *Against:* | E J Tyler 8 | |
| **Surrey** | *For Yorkshire:* | 8 for 5 | E Peate at Holbeck, 1883 |
| | *Against:* | 9 for 47 | T Richardson at Sheffield, 1893 |
| *Most 5 wickets* | *For Yorkshire:* | W Rhodes 17 | |
| *in an innings* | *Against:* | W Southerton 19 | |
| **Sussex** | *For Yorkshire:* | 9 for 48 | J H Wardle at Hull, 1954 |
| | *Against:* | 9 for 34 | James Langridge at Sheffield, 1934 |
| *Most 5 wickets* | *For Yorkshire:* | W Rhodes 14 | |
| *in an innings* | *Against:* | G R Cox, J A Snow 6 each | |
| **Warwickshire** | *For Yorkshire:* | 10 for 36 | H Verity at Leeds, 1930 |
| | *Against:* | 10 for 51 | H Howell at Birmingham, 1923 |
| *Most 5 wickets* | *For Yorkshire:* | W Rhodes 18 | |
| *in an innings* | *Against:* | E F Field, W E Hollies 7 each | |
| **Worcestershire** | *For Yorkshire:* | 9 for 41 | G H Hirst at Worcester, 1911 |
| | *Against:* | 9 for 38 | J A Cuffe at Bradford, 1907 |
| *Most 5 wickets* | *For Yorkshire:* | S Haigh, W Rhodes 11 each | |
| *in an innings* | *Against:* | R T D Perks 7 | |
| **Australians** | *For Yorkshire:* | 9 for 76 | W Ringrose at Bradford, 1905 |
| | *Against:* | 10 for 37 | C V Grimmett at Sheffield, 1930 |
| *Most 5 wickets* | *For Yorkshire:* | R Peel 7 | |
| *in an innings* | *Against:* | F R Spofforth 7 | |

## HAT-TRICKS

G Freeman v. Lancashire at Holbeck, 1868
G Freeman v. Middlesex at Sheffield, 1868
A Hill v. United South of England XI at Bradford, 1874
A Hill v. Surrey at The Oval, 1880
E Peate v. Kent at Sheffield, 1882
G Ulyett v. Lancashire at Sheffield, 1883
E Peate v. Gloucestershire at Moreton-in-Marsh, 1884
W Fletcher v. MCC at Lord's, 1892
E Wainwright v. Sussex at Dewsbury, 1894
G H Hirst v. Leicestershire at Leicester, 1895
J T Brown v. Derbyshire at Derby, 1896
R Peel v. Kent at Halifax, 1897
S Haigh v. Derbyshire at Bradford, 1897
W Rhodes v. Kent at Canterbury, 1901
S Haigh v. Somerset at Sheffield, 1902
H A Sedgwick v. Worcestershire at Hull, 1906
G Deyes v. Gentlemen of Ireland at Bray, 1907
G H Hirst v. Leicestershire at Hull, 1907
J T Newstead v. Worcestershire at Bradford, 1907
S Haigh v. Lancashire at Manchester, 1909
M W Booth v. Worcestershire at Bradford, 1911
A Drake v. Essex at Huddersfield, 1912

## HAT-TRICKS *(Continued)*

M W Booth v. Essex at Leyton, 1912
A Drake v. Derbyshire at Chesterfield, 1914 (4 in 4)
W Rhodes v. Derbyshire at Derby, 1920
A Waddington v. Northamptonshire at Northampton, 1920 (4 in 5)
G G Macaulay v. Warwickshire at Birmingham, 1923
E Robinson v. Sussex at Hull, 1928
G G Macaulay v. Leicestershire at Hull, 1930
E Robinson v. Kent at Gravesend, 1930
H Verity v. Nottinghamshire at Leeds, 1932
H Fisher v. Somerset at Sheffield, 1932 (all lbw)
G G Macaulay v. Glamorgan at Cardiff, 1933
G G Macaulay v. Lancashire at Manchester, 1933 (4 in 5)
M.Leyland v. Surrey at Sheffield, 1935
E Robinson v. Kent at Leeds, 1939
A Coxon v. Worcestershire at Leeds, 1946
F S Trueman v. Nottinghamshire at Nottingham, 1951
F S Trueman v. Nottinghamshire at Scarborough, 1955
R Appleyard v. Gloucestershire at Sheffield, 1956
F S.Trueman v. MCC at Lord's, 1958
D Wilson v. Nottinghamshire at Middlesbrough, 1959
F S Trueman v. Nottinghamshire at Bradford, 1963
D Wilson v. Nottinghamshire at Worksop, 1966
D Wilson v. Kent at Harrogate, 1966
G A Cope v. Essex at Colchester, 1970
A L Robinson v. Nottinghamshire at Worksop, 1974
P W Jarvis v. Derbyshire at Chesterfield, 1985
P J Hartley v. Derbyshire at Chesterfield, 1995 (4 in 5)
D Gough v. Kent at Leeds, 1995 (4 in 5)
C White v. Gloucestershire at Gloucester, 1998
M J Hoggard v. Sussex at Hove, 2009

52 Hat-Tricks: G G Macaulay and F S Trueman took four each, S Haigh and D Wilson three each. There have been seven hat-tricks versus Kent and Nottinghamshire, and six versus Derbyshire.

## 200 WICKETS IN A SEASON

| Bowler | Season | Overs | Maidens | Runs | Wickets | Average |
|--------|--------|-------|---------|------|---------|---------|
| W Rhodes | 1900 | 1366.4 | 411 | 3054 | 240 | 12.72 |
| W Rhodes | 1901 | 1455.3 | 474 | 3497 | 233 | 15.00 |
| G H Hirst | 1906 | 1111.1 | 262 | 3089 | 201 | 15.36 |
| G G Macaulay | 1925 | 1241.2 | 291 | 2986 | 200 | 14.93 |
| R Appleyard† | 1951 | 1323.2 | 394 | 2829 | 200 | 14.14 |

† First full season in First-Class cricket.

## 100 WICKETS IN A SEASON

| Bowler | | Wickets taken | Wickets taken | Wickets taken |
|--------|--|---------------|---------------|---------------|
| R Appleyard | (3) | 200 in 1951 | 141 in 1954 | 110 in 1956 |
| A Booth | (1) | 111 in 1946 | — | — |
| M W Booth | (3) | 104 in 1912 | 167 in 1913 | 155 in 1914 |
| W E Bowes | (8) | 117 in 1931 | 168 in 1932 | 130 in 1933 |
| | | 109 in 1934 | 154 in 1935 | 113 in 1936 |
| | | 106 in 1938 | 107 in 1939 | — |

# 100 WICKETS IN A SEASON *(Continued)*

| Bowler | | Wickets taken | Wickets taken | Wickets taken |
|---|---|---|---|---|
| D B Close | (2) | 105 in 1949 | 114 in 1952 | — |
| A Coxon | (2) | 101 in 1949 | 129 in 1950 | — |
| A Drake | (2) | 115 in 1913 | 158 in 1914 | — |
| T Emmett | (1) | 112 in 1886 | — | — |
| S Haigh | (10) | 100 in 1898 | 160 in 1900 | 154 in 1902 |
| | | 102 in 1903 | 118 in 1904 | 118 in 1905 |
| | | 161 in 1906 | 120 in 1909 | 100 in 1911 |
| | | 125 in 1912 | — | — |
| G H Hirst | (12) | 150 in 1895 | 171 in 1901 | 121 in 1903 |
| | | 114 in 1904 | 100 in 1905 | 201 in 1906 |
| | | 169 in 1907 | 164 in 1908 | 138 in 1910 |
| | | 130 in 1911 | 113 in 1912 | 100 in 1913 |
| R Illingworth | (5) | 103 in 1956 | 120 in 1961 | 116 in 1962 |
| | | 122 in 1964 | 105 in 1968 | — |
| R Kilner | (4) | 107 in 1922 | 143 in 1923 | 134 in 1924 |
| | | 123 in 1925 | — | — |
| G G Macaulay | (10) | 101 in 1921 | 130 in 1922 | 163 in 1923 |
| | | 184 in 1924 | 200 in 1925 | 133 in 1926 |
| | | 130 in 1927 | 117 in 1928 | 102 in 1929 |
| | | 141 in 1933 | — | — |
| J T Newstead | (1) | 131 in 1908 | — | — |
| A G Nicholson | (2) | 113 in 1966 | 101 in 1967 | — |
| E Peate | (3) | 131 in 1880 | 133 in 1881 | 165 in 1882 |
| R Peel | (6) | 118 in 1888 | 132 in 1890 | 106 in 1892 |
| | | 134 in 1894 | 155 in 1895 | 108 in 1896 |
| W Rhodes | (22) | 141 in 1898 | 153 in 1899 | 240 in 1900 |
| | | 233 in 1901 | 174 in 1902 | 169 in 1903 |
| | | 118 in 1904 | 158 in 1905 | 113 in 1906 |
| | | 164 in 1907 | 100 in 1908 | 115 in 1909 |
| | | 105 in 1911 | 117 in 1914 | 155 in 1919 |
| | | 156 in 1920 | 128 in 1921 | 100 in 1922 |
| | | 127 in 1923 | 102 in 1926 | 111 in 1928 |
| | | 100 in 1929 | — | — |
| E Robinson | (1) | 111 in 1928 | — | — |
| E P Robinson | (4) | 104 in 1938 | 120 in 1939 | 149 in 1946 |
| | | 108 in 1947 | — | — |
| T F Smailes | (4) | 105 in 1934 | 125 in 1936 | 120 in 1937 |
| | | 104 in 1938 | — | — |
| F S Trueman | (8) | 129 in 1954 | 140 in 1955 | 104 in 1959 |
| | | 150 in 1960 | 124 in 1961 | 122 in 1962 |
| | | 121 in 1965 | 107 in 1966 | — |
| H Verity | (9) | 169 in 1931 | 146 in 1932 | 168 in 1933 |
| | | 100 in 1934 | 199 in 1935 | 185 in 1936 |
| | | 185 in 1937 | 137 in 1938 | 189 in 1939 |
| A Waddington | (5) | 100 in 1919 | 140 in 1920 | 105 in 1921 |
| | | 132 in 1922 | 105 in 1925 | — |
| E Wainwright | (3) | 114 in 1893 | 157 in 1894 | 102 in 1896 |
| J H Wardle | (10) | 148 in 1948 | 100 in 1949 | 172 in 1950 |
| | | 122 in 1951 | 169 in 1952 | 126 in 1953 |
| | | 122 in 1954 | 159 in 1955 | 146 in 1956 |
| | | 106 in 1957 | — | — |
| D Wilson | (3) | 100 in 1966 | 107 in 1968 | 101 in 1969 |

# BOWLERS WHO HAVE TAKEN OVER 500 WICKETS

| Player | M | Runs | Wkts | Av'ge | Best |
|---|---|---|---|---|---|
| W Rhodes | 883 | 57634 | 3598 | 16.01 | 9 for 28 |
| G H Hirst | 717 | 44716 | 2481 | 18.02 | 9 for 23 |
| S Haigh | 513 | 29289 | 1876 | 15.61 | 9 for 25 |
| G G Macaulay | 445 | 30554 | 1774 | 17.22 | 8 for 21 |
| F S Trueman | 459 | 29890 | 1745 | 17.12 | 8 for 28 |
| H Verity | 278 | 21353 | 1558 | 13.70 | 10 for 10 |
| J H Wardle | 330 | 27917 | 1539 | 18.13 | 9 for 25 |
| R Illingworth | 496 | 26806 | 1431 | 18.73 | 9 for 42 |
| W E Bowes | 301 | 21227 | 1351 | 15.71 | 9 for 121 |
| R Peel | 318 | 20638 | 1311 | 15.74 | 9 for 22 |
| T Emmett | 299 | 15465 | 1216 | 12.71 | 9 for 23 |
| D Wilson | 392 | 22626 | 1104 | 20.49 | 7 for 19 |
| P Carrick | 425 | 30530 | 1018 | 29.99 | 8 for 33 |
| E Wainwright | 352 | 17744 | 998 | 17.77 | 9 for 66 |
| D B Close | 536 | 23489 | 967 | 24.29 | 8 for 41 |
| Emmott Robinson | 413 | 19645 | 893 | 21.99 | 9 for 36 |
| A G Nicholson | .282 | 17296 | 876 | 19.74 | 9 for 62 |
| R Kilner | 365 | 14855 | 857 | 17.33 | 8 for 26 |
| A Waddington | 255 | 16203 | 835 | 19.40 | 8 for 34 |
| T F Smailes | 262 | 16593 | 802 | 20.68 | 10 for 47 |
| E Peate | 154 | 9986 | 794 | 12.57 | 8 for 5 |
| Ellis P Robinson | 208 | 15141 | 735 | 20.60 | 8 for 35 |
| C M Old | 222 | 13409 | 647 | 20.72 | 7 for 20 |
| R Appleyard | 133 | 9903 | 642 | 15.42 | 8 for 76 |
| W Bates | 202 | 10692 | 637 | 16.78 | 8 for 21 |
| G A Cope | 230 | 15627 | 630 | 24.80 | 8 for 73 |
| P J Hartley | 195 | 17438 | 579 | 30.11 | 9 for 41 |
| A Sidebottom | 216 | 13852 | 558 | 24.82 | 8 for 72 |
| M W Booth | 144 | 11017 | 557 | 19.17 | 8 for 47 |
| A Hill | 140 | 7002 | 542 | 12.91 | 7 for 14 |
| Hon F S Jackson | 207 | 9690 | 506 | 19.15 | 7 for 42 |

## BOWLERS UNCHANGED IN A MATCH

### (IN WHICH THE OPPONENTS WERE DISMISSED TWICE)

There have been 31 instances. The first and most recent are listed below.
A complete list is to be found in the 2008 edition.

**First:** L Greenwood (11 for 71) and G Freeman (8 for 73) v. Surrey
at The Oval, 1867
*Yorkshire won by an innings and 111 runs*

**Most Recent:** E Robinson (8 for 65) and G G Macaulay (12 for 50) v. Worcestershire
at Leeds, 1927
*Yorkshire won by an innings and 106 runs*

# FIELDERS (IN MATCHES FOR YORKSHIRE)

## MOST CATCHES IN AN INNINGS

| | | | |
|---|---|---|---|
| 6 | E P Robinson | v. Leicestershire | at Bradford, 1938 |
| 5 | J Tunnicliffe | v. Leicestershire | at Leeds, 1897 |
| 5 | J Tunnicliffe | v. Leicestershire | at Leicester, 1900 |
| 5 | J Tunnicliffe | v. Leicestershire | at Scarborough, 1901 |
| 5 | A B Sellers | v. Essex | at Leyton, 1933 |
| 5 | D Wilson | v. Surrey | at The Oval, 1969 |
| 5 | R G Lumb | v. Gloucestershire | at Middlesbrough, 1972 |

## MOST CATCHES IN A MATCH

| | | | |
|---|---|---|---|
| 7 | J Tunnicliffe | v. Leicestershire | at Leeds, 1897 |
| 7 | J Tunnicliffe | v. Leicestershire | at Leicester, 1900 |
| 7 | A B Sellers | v Essex | at Leyton, 1933 |
| 7 | E P Robinson | v. Leicestershire | at Bradford, 1938 |
| 7 | A Lyth | v. Middlesex | at Scarborough, 2014 |

## MOST CATCHES IN A SEASON

| | | |
|---|---|---|
| 70 | J Tunnicliffe | in 1901 |
| 70 | P J Sharpe | in 1962 |
| 61 | J Tunnicliffe | in 1895 |
| 60 | J Tunnicliffe | in 1904 |
| 59 | J Tunnicliffe | in 1896 |
| 57 | J V Wilson | in 1955 |
| 54 | J V Wilson | in 1961 |
| 53 | J V Wilson | in 1957 |
| 51 | J V Wilson | in 1951 |

## MOST CATCHES IN A CAREER

| | | |
|---|---|---|
| 665 | J Tunnicliffe | (1.40 per match) |
| 586 | W Rhodes | (0.66 per match) |
| 564 | D B Close | (1.05 per match) |
| 525 | P J Sharpe | (1.27 per match) |
| 520 | J V Wilson | (1.09 per match) |
| 518 | G H Hirst | (0.72 per match) |

# WICKET-KEEPERS IN MATCHES FOR YORKSHIRE

## MOST DISMISSALS IN AN INNINGS

| 7 | (7ct) | D L Bairstow | v. Derbyshire | at Scarborough | 1982 |
|---|---|---|---|---|---|
| 6 | (6ct) | J Hunter | v. Gloucestershire | at Gloucester | 1887 |
| 6 | (5ct,1st) | D Hunter | v. Surrey | at Sheffield | 1891 |
| 6 | (6ct) | D Hunter | v. Middlesex | at Leeds | 1909 |
| 6 | (2ct,4st) | W R Allen | v. Sussex | at Hove | 1921 |
| 6 | (5ct,1st) | J G Binks | v. Lancashire | at Leeds | 1962 |
| 6 | (6ct) | D L Bairstow | v. Lancashire | at Manchester | 1971 |
| 6 | (6ct) | D L Bairstow | v. Warwickshire | at Bradford | 1978 |
| 6 | (5ct,1st) | D L Bairstow | v. Lancashire | at Leeds | 1980 |
| 6 | (6ct) | D L Bairstow | v. Derbyshire | at Chesterfield | 1984 |
| 6 | (6ct) | R J Blakey | v. Sussex | at Eastbourne | 1990 |
| 6 | (5ct,1st) | R J Blakey | v. Gloucestershire | at Cheltenham | 1992 |
| 6 | (5ct,1st) | R J Blakey | v. Glamorgan | at Cardiff | 1994 |
| 6 | (6ct) | R J Blakey | v. Glamorgan | at Leeds | 2003 |
| 6 | (6ct) | G L Brophy | v. Durham | at Chester-le-Street | 2009 |
| 6 | (6ct) | J M Bairstow | v. Middlesex | at Leeds | 2013 |
| 6 | (6ct) | J M Bairstow | v. Sussex | at Arundel | 2014 |

## MOST DISMISSALS IN A MATCH

| 11 | (11ct) | D L Bairstow | v. Derbyshire | at Scarborough | 1982 |
|---|---|---|---|---|---|
| | | (Equalled World Record) | | | |
| 9 | (9ct) | J.Hunter | v. Gloucestershire | at Gloucester | 1887 |
| 9 | (8ct,1st) | A Dolphin | v. Derbyshire | at Bradford | 1919 |
| 9 | (9ct) | D L Bairstow | v. Lancashire | at Manchester | 1971 |
| 9 | (9ct) | R J Blakey | v. Sussex | at Eastbourne | 1990 |
| 8 | (2ct,6st) | G Pinder | v. Lancashire | at Sheffield | 1872 |
| 8 | (2ct,6st) | D Hunter | v. Surrey | at Bradford | 1898 |
| 8 | (7ct,1st) | A Bairstow | v. Cambridge University | at Cambridge | 1899 |
| 8 | (8ct) | A Wood | v. Northamptonshire | at Huddersfield | 1932 |
| 8 | (8ct) | D L Bairstow | v. Lancashire | at Leeds | 1978 |
| 8 | (7ct,1st) | D L Bairstow | v. Derbyshire | at Chesterfield | 1984 |
| 8 | (6ct,2st) | D L Bairstow | v. Derbyshire | at Chesterfield | 1985 |
| 8 | (8ct) | R J Blakey | v. Hampshire | at Southampton | 1989 |
| 8 | (8ct) | R J Blakey | v. Northamptonshire | at Harrogate | 1993 |
| 8 | (8ct) | A J Hodd | v. Glamorgan | at Leeds | 2012 |
| 8 | (8ct) | J M Bairstow | v. Middlesex | at Leed | 2013 |

## MOST DISMISSALS IN A SEASON    MOST DISMISSALS IN A CAREER

| 107 | (96ct,11st) | J G Binks, 1960 | 1186 | (863ct,323st) | D Hunter (2.29 per match) |
|---|---|---|---|---|---|
| 94 | (81ct,13st) | JG Binks, 1961 | 1044 | (872ct,172st) | J G Binks (2.12 per match) |
| 89 | (75ct,14st) | A Wood, 1934 | 1038 | (907ct,131st) | D L Bairstow (2.41 per match) |
| 88 | (80ct,8st) | J G Binks, 1963 | 855 | (612ct,243st) | A Wood (2.09 per match) |
| 86 | (70ct,16st) | J G Binks, 1962 | 829 | (569ct,260st) | A Dolphin (1.94 per match) |
| 82 | (52ct,30st) | A Dolphin, 1919 | 824 | (768ct, 56st) | R J Blakey (2.43 per match) |
| 80 | (57ct,23st) | A. Wood, 1935 | | | |

# YORKSHIRE PLAYERS WHO HAVE
# COMPLETED THE "DOUBLE"

## (all First-Class matches)

| Player | Year | Runs | Average | Wickets | Average |
|---|---|---|---|---|---|
| M W Booth (1) ............. | 1913 | 1,228 | 27.28 | 181 | 18.46 |
| D B Close (2) ............. | †1949 | 1,098 | 27.45 | 113 | 27.87 |
| | 1952 | 1,192 | 33.11 | 114 | 24.08 |
| A Drake (1) ............... | 1913 | 1,056 | 23.46 | 116 | 16.93 |
| S Haigh (1) ............... | 1904 | 1,055 | 26.37 | 121 | 19.85 |
| G H Hirst (14) ............ | 1896 | 1,122 | 28.20 | 104 | 21.64 |
| | 1897 | 1,535 | 35.69 | 101 | 23.22 |
| | 1901 | 1,950 | 42.39 | 183 | 16.38 |
| | 1903 | 1,844 | 47.28 | 128 | 14.94 |
| | 1904 | 2,501 | 54.36 | 132 | 21.09 |
| | 1905 | 2,266 | 53.95 | 110 | 19.94 |
| | ††1906 | 2,385 | 45.86 | 208 | 16.50 |
| | 1907 | 1,344 | 28.38 | 188 | 15.20 |
| | 1908 | 1,598 | 38.97 | 114 | 14.05 |
| | 1909 | 1,256 | 27.30 | 115 | 20.05 |
| | 1910 | 1,840 | 32.85 | 164 | 14.79 |
| | 1911 | 1,789 | 33.12 | 137 | 20.40 |
| | 1912 | 1,133 | 25.75 | 118 | 17.37 |
| | 1913 | 1,540 | 35.81 | 101 | 20.13 |
| R Illingworth (6) ........... | 1957 | 1,213 | 28.20 | 106 | 18.40 |
| | 1959 | 1,726 | 46.64 | 110 | 21.46 |
| | 1960 | 1,006 | 25.79 | 109 | 17.55 |
| | 1961 | 1,153 | 24.53 | 128 | 17.90 |
| | 1962 | 1,612 | 34.29 | 117 | 19.45 |
| | 1964 | 1,301 | 37.17 | 122 | 17.45 |
| F S Jackson (1) ............. | 1898 | 1,566 | 41.21 | 104 | 15.67 |
| R Kilner (4) ............... | 1922 | 1,198 | 27.22 | 122 | 14.73 |
| | 1923 | 1,404 | 32.24 | 158 | 12.91 |
| | 1925 | 1,068 | 30.51 | 131 | 17.92 |
| | 1926 | 1,187 | 37.09 | 107 | 22.52 |
| R Peel (1) ................. | 1896 | 1,206 | 30.15 | 128 | 17.50 |
| W Rhodes (16) ............. | 1903 | 1,137 | 27.07 | 193 | 14.57 |
| | 1904 | 1,537 | 35.74 | 131 | 21.59 |
| | 1905 | 1,581 | 35.93 | 182 | 16.95 |
| | 1906 | 1,721 | 29.16 | 128 | 23.57 |
| | 1907 | 1,055 | 22.93 | 177 | 15.57 |
| | 1908 | 1,673 | 31.56 | 115 | 16.13 |
| | 1909 | 2,094 | 40.26 | 141 | 15.89 |
| | 1911 | 2,261 | 38.32 | 117 | 24.07 |
| | 1914 | 1,377 | 29.29 | 118 | 18.27 |
| | 1919 | 1,237 | 34.36 | 164 | 14.42 |
| | 1920 | 1,123 | 28.07 | 161 | 13.18 |
| | 1921 | 1,474 | 39.83 | 141 | 13.27 |
| | 1922 | 1,511 | 39.76 | 119 | 12.19 |
| | 1923 | 1,321 | 33.02 | 134 | 11.54 |
| | 1924 | 1,126 | 26.18 | 109 | 14.46 |
| | 1926 | 1,132 | 34.30 | 115 | 14.86 |
| T F Smailes (1) ............. | 1938 | 1,002 | 25.05 | 113 | 20.84 |
| E Wainwright (1) ............ | 1897 | 1,612 | 35.82 | 101 | 23.06 |

† First season in First-Class cricket.

†† The only instance in First-Class cricket of 2,000 runs and 200 wickets in a season.

H Sutcliffe (194) and M Leyland (45) hit 102 off six consecutive overs for Yorkshire v. Essex at Scarborough in 1932.

From 1898 to 1930 inclusive, Wilfred Rhodes took no less than 4,187 wickets, and scored 39,969 runs in First-Class cricket at home and abroad, a remarkable record. He also took 100 wickets and scored 1,000 in a season 16 times, and G H Hirst 14 times.

Of players with a qualification of not less than 50 wickets, Wilfred Rhodes was first in bowling in First-Class cricket in 1900, 1901, 1919, 1920, 1922, 1923 and 1926; Schofield Haigh in 1902, 1905, 1908 and 1909; Mr E R Wilson in 1921; G G Macaulay in 1924; H Verity in 1930, 1933, 1935, 1937 and 1939; W E Bowes in 1938; A Booth in 1946; R Appleyard in 1951 and 1955, and F S Trueman in 1952 and 1963.

The highest aggregate of runs made in one season in First-Class cricket by a Yorkshire player is 3,429 by L Hutton in 1949. This total has been exceeded three times, viz: D C S Compton 3,816 and W J Edrich 3,539 in 1947, and 3,518 by T Hayward in 1906. H Sutcliffe scored 3,336 in 1932.

Three players have taken all 10 Yorkshire wickets in an innings. G Wootton, playing for All England XI at Sheffield in 1865, took all 10 wickets for 54 runs. H Howell performed the feat for Warwickshire at Edgbaston in 1923 at a cost of 51 runs; and C V Grimmett, Australia, took all 10 wickets for 37 runs at Sheffield in 1930.

The match against Sussex at Dewsbury on June 7th and 8th, 1894, was brought to a summary conclusion by a remarkable bowling performance on the part of Edward Wainwright. In the second innings of Sussex, he took the last five wickets in seven balls, including the "hat trick". In the whole match he obtained 13 wickets for only 38 runs.

M D Moxon has the unique distinction of scoring a century in each of his first two First-Class matches in Yorkshire — 116 (2nd inns.) v. Essex at Leeds and 111 (1st inns.) v. Derbyshire at Sheffield, June 1981).

In the Yorkshire v. Norfolk match — played on the Hyde Park Ground, Sheffield, on July 14th to 18th, 1834 — 851 runs were scored in the four innings, of which no fewer than 128 were extras: 75 byes and 53 wides. At that time wides were not run out, so that every wide included in the above total represents a wide actually bowled. This particular achievement has never been surpassed in the annals of county cricket.

L Hutton reached his 1,000 runs in First-Class cricket in 1949 as early as June 9th.

W Barber reached his 1,000 runs in 1934 on June 13th. P Holmes reached his 1,000 in 1925 on June 16th, as also did H Sutcliffe in 1932. J T Brown reached his 1,000 in 1899 on June 22nd. In 1905, D Denton reached his 1,000 runs on June 26th; and in 1906 G H Hirst gained the same total on June 27th.

In 1912, D Denton scored over 1,000 runs during July, while M Leyland and H Sutcliffe both scored over 1,000 runs in August 1932.

L Hutton scored over 1,000 in June and over 1,000 runs in August 1949.

H Verity took his 100th wicket in First-Class cricket as early as June 19th in 1936 and on June 27th in 1935. In 1900, W Rhodes obtained his 100th wicket on June 21st, and again on the same date in 1901, while G H Hirst obtained his 100th wicket on June 28th, 1906.

In 1930, Yorkshiremen (H Sutcliffe and H Verity) occupied the first places by English players in the batting and the bowling averages of First-Class cricket, which is a record without precedent. H Sutcliffe was also first in the batting averages in 1931 and 1932.

G Boycott was the first player to have achieved an average of over 100 in each of two English seasons. In 1971, he scored 2,503 runs for an average of 100.12, and in 1979 he scored 1,538 runs for an average of 102.53.


FIRST-CLASS MATCHES BEGUN AND FINISHED IN ONE DAY

Yorkshire v. Somerset, at Huddersfield, July 9th, 1894.

Yorkshire v. Hampshire, at Southampton, May 27th, 1898

Yorkshire v. Worcestershire, at Bradford, May 7th, 1900

**YORKSHIRE TEST CRICKETERS 1877-2016** (Correct to January 27, 2016)

For England

| Player | M. | I | NO | Runs | HS. | Av'ge. | 100s | 50s | Balls | R | W | Av'ge | Best | 5wI | 10wM | c/st |
|---|---|---|---|---|---|---|---|---|---|---|---|---|---|---|---|---|
| APPLEYARD, R ..1954-56 | 9 | 9 | 6 | 51 | 19* | 17.00 | — | — | 1,596 | 554 | 31 | 17.87 | 5-51 | 1 | — | 4 |
| ARMITAGE, T ......1877 | 2 | 3 | 0 | 33 | 21 | 11.00 | — | — | 12 | 15 | 0 | — | — | — | — | 0 |
| ATHEY, C W J ..1980-88 | 23 | 41 | 1 | 919 | 123 | 22.97 | 1 | 4 | — | — | — | — | — | — | — | 13 |
| BAIRSTOW, D L ..1979-81 | 4 | 7 | 1 | 125 | 59 | 20.83 | — | 1 | — | — | — | — | — | — | — | 12/1 |
| BAIRSTOW, J M .2012-15/16 | 24 | 41 | 4 | 1,204 | 150* | 32.54 | 1 | 6 | — | — | — | — | — | — | — | 42/1 |
| BALLANCE, G S 2013/14-15 | 15 | 27 | 2 | 1,194 | 156 | 47.76 | 4 | 6 | — | — | — | — | — | — | — | 14 |
| BARBER, W ........1935 | 2 | 4 | 0 | 83 | 44 | 20.75 | — | — | 12 | 5 | 0 | — | — | — | — | 1 |
| BATES, W .....1881-87 | 15 | 26 | 2 | 656 | 64 | 27.33 | — | 5 | 2,364 | 821 | 50 | 16.42 | 7-28 | 4 | 1 | 9 |
| BINKS, J G .......1964 | 2 | 4 | 0 | 91 | 55 | 22.75 | — | 1 | — | — | — | — | — | — | — | 8/0 |
| BLAKEY, R J .....1993 | 2 | 2 | 0 | 7 | 6 | 1.75 | — | — | — | — | — | — | — | — | — | 2/0 |
| BOOTH, M W ..1913-14 | 2 | 2 | 0 | 46 | 32 | 23.00 | — | — | 312 | 130 | 7 | 18.57 | 4-49 | — | — | 0 |
| BOWES, W E ..1932-46 | 15 | 11 | 5 | 28 | 10* | 4.66 | — | — | 3,655 | 1,519 | 68 | 22.33 | 6-33 | 6 | — | 2 |
| †BOYCOTT, G ..1964-82 | 108 | 193 | 23 | 8,114 | 246* | 47.72 | 22 | 42 | 944 | 382 | 7 | 54.57 | 3-47 | — | — | 33 |
| BRENNAN, D V .....1951 | 2 | 2 | 0 | 16 | 16 | 8.00 | — | — | — | — | — | — | — | — | — | 0/1 |
| BRESNAN, T T ..2009-13/14 | 23 | 26 | 4 | 575 | 91 | 26.13 | — | 3 | 4,674 | 2,357 | 72 | 32.73 | 5-48 | 1 | — | 8 |
| BROWN, J T ...1894-99 | 8 | 16 | 3 | 470 | 140 | 36.15 | 1 | 1 | 35 | 22 | 0 | — | — | — | — | 7 |
| †CLOSE, D B ..1949-76 | 22 | 37 | 2 | 887 | 70 | 25.34 | — | 4 | 1,212 | 532 | 18 | 29.55 | 4-35 | — | — | 24 |
| COPE, G A ....1977-78 | 3 | 3 | 0 | 40 | 22 | 13.33 | — | — | 864 | 277 | 8 | 34.62 | 3-102 | 1 | — | 1 |
| COXON, A ......1948 | 1 | 2 | 0 | 19 | 19 | 9.50 | — | — | 378 | 172 | 3 | 57.33 | 2-90 | — | — | 0 |
| DAWSON, R K J ..2002-03 | 7 | 13 | 3 | 114 | 19* | 11.40 | — | — | 1,116 | 677 | 11 | 61.54 | 4-134 | — | — | 3 |
| DENTON, D ..1905-10 | 11 | 22 | 1 | 424 | 104 | 20.19 | 1 | 1 | — | — | — | — | — | — | — | 8 |
| DOLPHIN, A ......1921 | 1 | 2 | 0 | 1 | 1 | 0.50 | — | — | — | — | — | — | — | — | — | 1/0 |
| EMMETT, T ..1877-82 | 7 | 13 | 1 | 160 | 48 | 13.33 | — | — | 728 | 284 | 9 | 31.55 | 7-68 | 1 | — | 9 |
| GIBB, PA ...1938-46 | 8 | 13 | 0 | 581 | 120 | 44.69 | 2 | 3 | — | — | — | — | — | — | — | 3/1 |
| GOUGH, D ..1994-2003 | 58 | 86 | 18 | 855 | 65 | 12.57 | — | 2 | 11,821 | 6,503 | 229 | 28.39 | 6-42 | 9 | — | 13 |

**For England**

## YORKSHIRE TEST CRICKETERS 1877-2016 (Continued)

| Player | M. | I | NO | Runs | HS. | Av'ge. | 100s | 50s | Balls | R | W | Av'ge | Best | 5wI | 10wM | c/st |
|---|---|---|---|---|---|---|---|---|---|---|---|---|---|---|---|---|
| GREENWOOD, A ....1877 | 2 | 4 | 0 | 77 | 49 | 19.25 | — | — | — | — | — | — | — | — | — | 2 |
| HAIGH, S ....1899-1912 | 11 | 18 | 3 | 113 | 25 | 7.53 | — | — | 1,294 | 622 | 24 | 25.91 | 6-11 | 1 | — | 8 |
| HAMILTON, G.M. ....1999 | 1 | 2 | 0 | 0 | 0 | 0.00 | — | — | 90 | 63 | 0 | — | — | — | — | 0 |
| HAMPSHIRE, J H ..1969-75 | 8 | 16 | 1 | 403 | 107 | 26.86 | 1 | 2 | — | — | — | — | — | — | — | 9 |
| †HAWKE, LORD ...1896-99 | 5 | 8 | 1 | 55 | 30 | 7.85 | — | — | — | — | — | — | — | — | — | 3 |
| HILL, A ....1877 | 2 | 4 | 2 | 101 | 49 | 50.50 | — | — | 340 | 130 | 7 | 18.57 | 4-27 | — | — | 1 |
| HIRST, G H ...1897-1909 | 24 | 38 | 3 | 790 | 85 | 22.57 | — | 5 | 3,967 | 1,770 | 59 | 30.00 | 5-48 | 3 | — | 18 |
| HOGGARD, M J ..2000-2008 | 67 | 92 | 27 | 473 | 38 | 7.27 | — | — | 13,909 | 7,564 | 248 | 30.50 | 7-61 | 7 | 1 | 24 |
| HOLMES, P ....1921-32 | 7 | 14 | 1 | 357 | 88 | 27.46 | — | 4 | — | — | — | — | — | — | — | 3 |
| HUNTER, J ....1884-85 | 5 | 7 | 2 | 93 | 39* | 18.60 | — | — | — | — | — | — | — | — | — | 8/3 |
| †HUTTON, L ...1937-55 | 79 | 138 | 15 | 6,971 | 364 | 56.67 | 19 | 33 | 260 | 232 | 3 | 77.33 | 1-2 | — | — | 57 |
| HUTTON, R A ....1971 | 5 | 8 | 2 | 219 | 81 | 36.50 | — | 2 | 738 | 257 | 9 | 28.55 | 3-72 | — | — | 9 |
| †ILLINGWORTH, R .1958-73 | 61 | 90 | 11 | 1,836 | 113 | 23.24 | 2 | 5 | 11,934 | 3,807 | 122 | 31.20 | 6-29 | 3 | — | 45 |
| †JACKSON, Hon F S 1893-1905 | 20 | 33 | 4 | 1,415 | 144* | 48.79 | 5 | 6 | 1,587 | 799 | 24 | 33.29 | 5-52 | 1 | — | 10 |
| JARVIS, P W ...1988-93 | 9 | 15 | 2 | 132 | 29* | 10.15 | — | — | 1,912 | 965 | 21 | 45.95 | 4-107 | — | — | 2 |
| KILNER, R ....1924-26 | 9 | 8 | 1 | 233 | 74 | 33.28 | — | 2 | 2,368 | 734 | 24 | 30.58 | 4-51 | — | — | 6 |
| LEADBEATER, E ..1951-52 | 2 | 2 | 0 | 40 | 38 | 20.00 | — | — | 289 | 218 | 2 | 109.00 | 1-38 | — | — | 3 |
| LEYLAND, M ...1928-38 | 41 | 65 | 5 | 2,764 | 187 | 46.06 | 9 | 10 | 1,103 | 585 | 6 | 97.50 | 3-91 | — | — | 13 |
| LOWSON, F A ..1951-55 | 7 | 13 | 0 | 245 | 68 | 18.84 | — | 2 | — | — | — | — | — | — | — | 5 |
| LYTH A ....2015 | 7 | 13 | 0 | 265 | 107 | 20.38 | 1 | — | 6 | 0 | 0 | — | — | — | — | 8 |
| McGRATH, A ...2003 | 4 | 5 | 0 | 201 | 81 | 40.20 | — | 2 | 102 | 56 | 4 | 14.00 | 3-16 | — | — | 3 |
| MACAULAY, G G .1923-33 | 8 | 10 | 4 | 112 | 76 | 18.66 | — | 1 | 1,701 | 662 | 24 | 27.58 | 5-64 | 1 | — | 5 |
| MILLIGAN, F W ...1899 | 2 | 4 | 0 | 58 | 38 | 14.50 | — | — | 45 | 29 | 0 | — | — | — | — | 1 |
| MITCHELL, A ..1933-36 | 6 | 10 | 0 | 298 | 72 | 29.80 | — | 2 | 6 | 4 | 0 | — | — | — | — | 9 |
| *MITCHELL, F ....1899 | 2 | 4 | 0 | 88 | 41 | 22.00 | — | — | — | — | — | — | — | — | — | 2 |

For England

## YORKSHIRE TEST CRICKETERS 1877-2016 (Continued)

| Player | M. | I | NO | Runs | HS. | Av'ge | 100s | 50s | Balls | R | W | Av'ge | Best | 5wI | 10wM | c/st |
|---|---|---|---|---|---|---|---|---|---|---|---|---|---|---|---|---|
| MOXON, M D ......1986-89 | 10 | 17 | 1 | 455 | 99 | 28.43 | — | 3 | 48 | 30 | 0 | — | — | — | — | 10 |
| OLD, C M ......1972-81 | 46 | 66 | 9 | 845 | 65 | 14.82 | — | 2 | 8,858 | 4,020 | 143 | 28.11 | 7-50 | 4 | — | 22 |
| PADGETT, D E V ......1960 | 2 | 4 | 0 | 51 | 31 | 12.75 | — | — | 12 | 8 | 0 | — | — | — | — | 0 |
| PEATE, E ......1881-86 | 9 | 14 | 8 | 70 | 13 | 11.66 | — | — | 2,096 | 682 | 31 | 22.00 | 6-85 | 2 | — | 2 |
| PEEL, R ......1884-96 | 20 | 33 | 4 | 427 | 83 | 14.72 | — | 3 | 5,216 | 1,715 | 101 | 16.98 | 7-31 | 5 | 1 | 17 |
| PLUNKET, L E ..2005/6-2014 | 13 | 20 | 5 | 238 | 55* | 15.86 | — | 1 | 2659 | 1536 | 41 | 37.46 | 5-64 | 1 | — | 3 |
| RASHID A U ......2015/16 | 3 | 5 | 0 | 103 | 61 | 20.60 | — | 1 | 821 | 556 | 8 | 69.50 | 5-64 | 1 | — | 0 |
| RHODES, W ......1899-1930 | 58 | 98 | 21 | 2,325 | 179 | 30.19 | 2 | 11 | 8,231 | 3,425 | 127 | 26.96 | 8-68 | 6 | 1 | 60 |
| ROOT, J E ...2012-15/16 | 39 | 72 | 10 | 3,406 | 200* | 54.93 | 9 | 19 | 1239 | 613 | 12 | 51.08 | 2- 9 | — | — | 41 |
| SHARPE, P J ......1963-69 | 12 | 21 | 4 | 786 | 111 | 46.23 | 1 | 4 | — | — | — | — | — | — | — | 17 |
| SHAHZAD, A ......2010 | 1 | 1 | 0 | 5 | 5 | 5.00 | — | — | 102 | 63 | 4 | 15.75 | 3-45 | — | — | 2 |
| SIDEBOTTOM, A ......1985 | 1 | 1 | 0 | 2 | 2 | 2.00 | — | — | 112 | 65 | 1 | 65.00 | 1-65 | — | — | 0 |
| SIDEBOTTOM, R J ..2001-10 | 22 | 31 | 11 | 313 | 31 | 15.65 | — | — | 4,812 | 2,231 | 79 | 28.24 | 7-47 | 5 | — | 5 |
| SILVERWOOD, CEW1997-2003 | 6 | 7 | 3 | 29 | 10 | 7.25 | — | — | 828 | 444 | 11 | 40.36 | 5-91 | 1 | — | 2 |
| SMAILES, T F ......1946 | 1 | 1 | 0 | 25 | 25 | 25.00 | — | — | 120 | 62 | 3 | 20.66 | 3-44 | — | — | 0 |
| SMITHSON, G A ......1948 | 2 | 3 | 0 | 70 | 35 | 23.33 | — | — | — | — | — | — | — | — | — | 0 |
| †STANYFORTH, R T 1927-28 | 4 | 6 | 1 | 13 | 6* | 2.60 | — | — | — | — | — | — | — | — | — | 7/2 |
| STEVENSON, G B ..1980-81 | 2 | 2 | 1 | 28 | 27* | 28.00 | — | — | 312 | 183 | 5 | 36.60 | 3-111 | — | — | 0 |
| SUTCLIFFE, H ......1924-35 | 54 | 84 | 9 | 4,555 | 194 | 60.73 | 16 | 23 | — | — | — | — | — | — | — | 23 |
| TAYLOR, K ......1959-64 | 3 | 5 | 0 | 57 | 24 | 11.40 | — | — | 12 | 6 | 0 | — | — | — | — | 1 |
| TRUEMAN, F S ...1952-65 | 67 | 85 | 14 | 981 | 39* | 13.81 | — | — | 15,178 | 6,625 | 307 | 21.57 | 8-31 | 17 | 3 | 64 |
| ULYETT, G ......1877-90 | 25 | 39 | 0 | 949 | 149 | 24.33 | 1 | 7 | 2,627 | 1,020 | 50 | 20.40 | 7-36 | 1 | — | 19 |
| †VAUGHAN M P ..1999-2008 | 82 | 147 | 9 | 5,719 | 197 | 41.44 | 18 | 18 | 978 | 561 | 6 | 93.50 | 2-71 | — | — | 44 |
| VERITY, H ......1931-39 | 40 | 44 | 12 | 669 | 66* | 20.90 | — | 3 | 11,173 | 3,510 | 144 | 24.37 | 8-43 | 5 | 2 | 30 |
| WADDINGTON, A ..1920-21 | 2 | 4 | 0 | 16 | 7 | 4.00 | — | — | 276 | 119 | 1 | 119.00 | 1-35 | — | — | 1 |
| WAINWRIGHT, E ..1893-98 | 5 | 9 | 0 | 132 | 49 | 14.66 | — | — | 127 | 73 | 0 | — | — | — | — | 2 |

**For England**

## YORKSHIRE TEST CRICKETERS 1877-2016 (Continued)

| Player | M. | I | NO | Runs | HS. | Av'ge. | 100s | 50s | Balls | R | W | Av'ge | Best | 5wI | 10wM | c/st |
|---|---|---|---|---|---|---|---|---|---|---|---|---|---|---|---|---|
| WARDLE, J H ......1948-57 | 28 | 41 | 8 | 653 | 66 | 19.78 | — | 2 | 6,597 | 2,080 | 102 | 20.39 | 7-36 | 5 | 1 | 12 |
| WATSON, W ......1951-59 | 23 | 37 | 3 | 879 | 116 | 25.85 | 2 | 3 | — | — | — | — | — | — | — | 8 |
| WHITE, C ......1994-2002 | 30 | 50 | 7 | 1,052 | 121 | 24.46 | 1 | 5 | 3,959 | 2,220 | 59 | 37.62 | 5-32 | 3 | — | 14 |
| WILSON, C E M ......1899 | 2 | 4 | 1 | 42 | 18 | 14.00 | — | — | — | — | — | — | — | — | — | 0 |
| WILSON, D ......1964-71 | 6 | 7 | 1 | 75 | 42 | 12.50 | — | — | 1,472 | 466 | 11 | 42.36 | 2-17 | — | — | 1 |
| WILSON, E R ......1921 | 1 | 2 | 0 | 10 | 5 | 5.00 | — | — | 123 | 36 | 3 | 12.00 | 2-28 | — | — | 0 |
| WOOD, A ......1938-39 | 4 | 5 | 1 | 80 | 53 | 20.00 | — | 1 | — | — | — | — | — | — | — | 10/1 |
| †YARDLEY, N W D ...1938-50 | 20 | 34 | 2 | 812 | 99 | 25.37 | — | 4 | 1,662 | 707 | 21 | 33.66 | 3-67 | — | — | 14 |

†Captained England
*Also represented and captained South Africa

**For South Africa**

| Player | M. | I | NO | Runs | HS. | Av'ge. | 100s | 50s | Balls | R | W | Av'ge | Best | 5wI | 10wM | c/st |
|---|---|---|---|---|---|---|---|---|---|---|---|---|---|---|---|---|
| †MITCHELL, F ......1912 | 3 | 6 | 0 | 28 | 12 | 4.66 | — | — | — | — | — | — | — | — | — | 0 |

†Captained South Africa

**Overseas Players**

(Qualification: 20 first-class matches for Yorkshire)

**For Australia**

| Player | M. | I | NO | Runs | HS. | Av'ge. | 100s | 50s | Balls | R | W | Av'ge | Best | 5wI | 10wM | c/st |
|---|---|---|---|---|---|---|---|---|---|---|---|---|---|---|---|---|
| BEVAN, M G ......1994-98 | 18 | 30 | 3 | 785 | 91 | 29.07 | — | 6 | 1,285 | 703 | 29 | 24.24 | 6-82 | 1 | 1 | 8 |
| GILLESPIE, J N ...1996-2006 | 71 | 93 | 28 | 1,218 | 201* | 18.73 | 1 | 2 | 14,234 | 6,770 | 259 | 26.13 | 7-37 | 8 | 1 | 27 |
| JAQUES, P A ...2005-2008 | 11 | 19 | 0 | 902 | 150 | 47.47 | 3 | 6 | — | — | — | — | — | — | — | 7 |
| LEHMANN, D S ...1999-2004 | 27 | 42 | 2 | 1,798 | 177 | 44.95 | 5 | 10 | 974 | 412 | 15 | 27.46 | 3-42 | — | — | 11 |

**For South Africa**

| Player | M. | I | NO | Runs | HS. | Av'ge. | 100s | 50s | Balls | R | W | Av'ge | Best | 5wI | 10wM | c/st |
|---|---|---|---|---|---|---|---|---|---|---|---|---|---|---|---|---|
| RUDOLPH, J A ...2003-12/13 | 48 | 83 | 9 | 2,622 | 222* | 35.43 | 6 | 11 | 664 | 432 | 4 | 108.00 | 1-1 | — | — | 29 |

**For West Indies**

| Player | M. | I | NO | Runs | HS. | Av'ge. | 100s | 50s | Balls | R | W | Av'ge | Best | 5wI | 10wM | c/st |
|---|---|---|---|---|---|---|---|---|---|---|---|---|---|---|---|---|
| RICHARDSON, R B 1983-84/95 | 86 | 146 | 12 | 5,949 | 194 | 44.39 | 16 | 27 | 66 | 18 | 0 | — | — | — | — | 90 |

# CENTURIES FOR ENGLAND

### C W J ATHEY (1)
123 v Pakistan at Lord's, 1987

### J M BAIRSTOW (1)
150* v. South Africa at Cape Town, 2016

### G S BALLANCE (4)
104* v. Sri Lanka at Lord's, 2014
256 v. India at Southampton, 2014
110 v. India at Lord's, 2014
122 v. West Indies at North Sound, 2015

### G BOYCOTT (22)
113 v. Australia at The Oval, 1964
117 v. South Africa at Port Elizabeth, 1965
246* v. India at Leeds, 1967
116 v. West Indies at Georgetown, 1968
128 v. West Indies at Manchester, 1969
106 v. West Indies at Lord's, 1969
142* v. Australia at Sydney, 1971
119* v. Australia at Adelaide, 1971
121* v. Pakistan at Lord's, 1971
112 v. Pakistan at Leeds, 1971
115 v. New Zealand at Leeds, 1973
112 v West Indies at Port-of-Spain, 1974
107 v. Australia at Nottingham, 1977
191 v. Australia at Leeds, 1977
100* v. Pakistan at Hyderabad, 1978
131 v. New Zealand at Nottingham, 1978
155 v. India at Birmingham, 1979
125 v. India at The Oval, 1979
128* v. Australia at Lord's, 1980
104* v. West Indies at St John's, 1981
137 v. Australia at The Oval, 1981
105 v. India at Delhi, 1981

### J T BROWN (1)
140 v. Australia at Melbourne, 1895

### D DENTON (1)
104 v. South Africa at Old Wanderers, Johannesburg, 1910

### P A GIBB (2)
106 v. South Africa at Old Wanderers, Johannesburg, 1938
120 v. South Africa at Kingsmead, Durban, 1939

### J H HAMPSHIRE (1)
107 v. West Indies at Lord's, 1969

### L HUTTON (19)
100 v. New Zealand at Manchester, 1937
100 v. Australia at Nottingham, 1938
364 v. Australia at The Oval, 1938
196 v. West Indies at Lord's, 1939
165* v. West Indies at The Oval, 1939
122* v. Australia at Sydney, 1947
100 v. South Africa at Leeds, 1947
158 v. South Africa at Ellis Park, J'b'rg, 1948
123 v. South Africa at Ellis Park, J'b'rg, 1949
101 v. New Zealand at Leeds, 1949
206 v. New Zealand at The Oval, 1949
202* v. West Indies at The Oval, 1950
156* v. Australia at Adelaide, 1951
100 v. South Africa at Leeds, 1951
150 v. India at Lord's, 1952
104 v. India at Manchester, 1952
145 v. Australia at Lord's, 1953
169 v. West Indies at Georgetown, 1954
205 v. West Indies at Kingston, 1954

### R ILLINGWORTH (2)
113 v. West Indies at Lord's, 1969
107 v. India at Manchester, 1971

### Hon. F S JACKSON (5)
103 v. Australia at The Oval, 1893
118 v. Australia at The Oval, 1899
128 v. Australia at Manchester, 1902
144* v. Australia at Leeds, 1905
113 v. Australia at Manchester, 1905

# CENTURIES FOR ENGLAND

## M LEYLAND (9)

137 v. Australia at Melbourne, 1929
102 v. South Africa at Lord's, 1929
109 v. Australia at Lord's, 1934
153 v. Australia at Manchester, 1934
110 v. Australia at The Oval, 1934

161 v. South Africa at The Oval, 1935
126 v. Australia at Woolloongabba, Brisbane, 1936
111* v. Australia at Melbourne, 1937
187 v. Australia at The Oval, 1938

## A LYTH (1)

107 v. New Zealand at Leeds 2015

## W RHODES (2)

179 v. Australia at Melbourne, 1912
152 v. South Africa at Old Wanderers, Johannesburg, 1913

## J E ROOT (9)

104 v. New Zealand at Leeds, 2013
200* v. Sri Lanka at Lord's, 2014
149* v. India at The Oval, 2014
134 v. Australia at Cardiff 2015
110 v. South Africa at Johannesburgh 2016

180 v. Australia at Lord's, 2013
154* v. India at Nottingham, 2014
182* v. West Indies at St George's, 2015
130 v. Australia at Nottingham, 2015

## P J SHARPE (1)

111 v. New Zealand at Nottingham, 1969

## H SUTCLIFFE (16)

122 v. South Africa at Lord's, 1924
115 v. Australia at Sydney, 1924
176 v. Australia at Melbourne, 1925 (1st Inns)
127 v. Australia at Melbourne, 1925 (2nd Inns)
143 v. Australia at Melbourne, 1925
161 v. Australia at The Oval, 1926
102 v. South Africa at Old Wanderers, Jbg.1927
135 v. Australia at Melbourne, 1929

114 v. South Africa at Birmingham, 1929
100 v. South Africa at Lord's, 1929
104 v. South Africa at The Oval, 1929 (1st inns)
109* v. South Africa at The Oval, 1929 (2nd inns)
161 v. Australia at The Oval, 1930
117 v. New Zealand at The Oval, 1931
109* v. New Zealand at Manchester, 1931
194 v. Australia at Sydney, 1932

## G ULYETT (1)

149 v. Australia at Melbourne, 1882

## M P VAUGHAN (18)

120 v. Pakistan at Manchester, 2001
115 v. Sri Lanka at Lord's, 2002
100 v. India at Lord's, 2002
197 v. India at Nottingham, 2002
195 v. India at The Oval, 2002
177 v. Australia at Adelaide, 2002
145 v. Australia at Melbourne, 2002
183 v. Australia at Sydney, 2003
156 v. South Africa at Birmingham, 2003

105 v. Sri Lanka at Kandy, 2003
140 v. West Indies at Antigua, 2004
103 v. West Indies at Lord's (1st inns) 2004
101* v. West Indies at Lord's (2nd inns) 2004
120 v. Bangladesh at Lord's, 2005
166 v. Australia at Manchester,2005
103 v. West Indies at Leeds, 2007
124 v. India at Nottingham, 2007
106 v. New Zealand at Lord's, 2008

## W WATSON (2)

109 v. Australia at Lord's, 1953

116 v. West Indies at Kingston, 1954

## C WHITE (1)

121 v. India at Ahmedabad, 2001

## Summary of the Centuries

| versus | Total | In England | Away |
|---|---|---|---|
| Australia | 43 | 24 | 19 |
| Bangladesh | 1 | 1 | 0 |
| India | 16 | 14 | 2 |
| New Zealand | 11 | 11 | 0 |
| Pakistan | 5 | 4 | 1 |
| South Africa | 20 | 10 | 10 |
| Sri Lanka | 4 | 3 | 1 |
| West Indies | 19 | 10 | 9 |
| Totals | 119 | 77 | 42 |

**For Australia**

### J N GILLESPIE (1)

201* v. Bangladesh at Chittagong, 2006

### P A JAQUES (3)

100 v. Sri Lanka at Brisbane, 2007  108 v. West Indies at Bridgetown, 2008
150 v. Sri Lanka at Hobart, 2007

### D S LEHMANN (5)

160 v. West Indies at Port of Spain, 2003  129 v. Sri Lanka at Galle, 2004
110 v. Bangladesh at Darwin, 2003  153 v. Sri Lanka at Columbo, 2004
177 v. Bangladesh at Cairns, 2003

# 10 WICKETS IN A MATCH FOR ENGLAND

### W BATES (1)
14 for 102 (7 for 28 and 7 for 74) v. Australia at Melbourne, 1882

### M J HOGGARD (1)
12 for 205 (5 for 144 and 7 for 61) v. South Africa at Johannesburg, 2005

### R PEEL (1)
11 for 68 (7 for 31 and 4 for 37) v. Australia at Mancester, 1888

**Note:** The scorebook for the Australia v. England Test match at Sydney in February 1888
shows that the final wicket to fall was taken by W Attewell, and not by Peel

Peel therefore took 9, and not 10 wickets, in the match

His career totals have been amended to take account of this alteration

### W RHODES (1)
15 for 124 (7 for 56 and 8 for 68) v. Australia at Melbourne, 1904

### R J SIDEBOTTOM (1)
10 for 139 (4 for 90 and 6 for 49) v. New Zealand at Hamilton, 2008

### F S TRUEMAN (3)
11 for 88 (5 for 58 and 6 for 30) v. Australia at Leeds, 1961
11 for 152 (6 for 100 and 5 for 52) v. West Indies at Lord's, 1963*
12 for 119 (5 for 75 and 7 for 44) v. West Indies at Birmingham, 1963*
*consecutive Tests*

### H VERITY (2)
11 for 153 (7 for 49 and 4 for 104) v. India at Chepauk, Madras, 1934
15 for 104 (7 for 61 and 8 for 43) v. Australia at Lord's, 1934

### J H WARDLE (1)
12 for 89 (5 for 53 and 7 for 36) v. South Africa at Cape Town, 1957

## Summary of Ten Wickets in a Match

| versus | Total | In England | Away |
|---|---|---|---|
| Australia | 5 | 3 | 2 |
| India | 1 | — | 1 |
| New Zealand | 1 | — | 1 |
| Pakistan | — | — | — |
| South Africa | 2 | — | 2 |
| Sri Lanka | — | — | — |
| West Indies | 2 | 2 | — |
| Totals | 11 | 5 | 6 |

**For Australia**

### M G BEVAN (1)
10 for 113 (4 for 31and 6 for 82) v. West Indies at Adelaide, 1997

# 5 WICKETS IN AN INNINGS FOR ENGLAND

### R APPLEYARD (1)
5 for 51 v. Pakistan at Nottingham, 1954

### W BATES (4)
7 for 28 v. Australia at Melbourne, 1882    5 for 31 v. Australia at Adelaide, 1884
7 for 74 v. Australia at Melbourne, 1882    5 for 24 v. Australia at Sydney, 1885

# 5 WICKETS IN AN INNINGS FOR ENGLAND *(Continued)*

## W E BOWES (6)

| | | | | | | | |
|---|---|---|---|---|---|---|---|
| 6-34 | v. New Zealand | at Auckland | 1933 | 5-100 | v. South Africa | at Manchester | 1935 |
| 6-142 | v. Australia | at Leeds | 1934* | 5-49 | v. Australia | at The Oval | 1938 |
| 5-55 | v. Australia | at The Oval | 1934* | 6-33 | v. West Indies | at Manchester | 1939 |

*consecutive Test matches*

## T T BRESNAN (1)

5-48   v. India          at Nottingham   2011

## T EMMETT (1)

7-68   v. Australia      at Melbourne   1879

## D GOUGH (9)

| | | | | | | | |
|---|---|---|---|---|---|---|---|
| 6-49 | v. Australia | at Sydney | 1995 | 5-70 | v. South Africa | at Johannesburg | 1999 |
| 5-40 | v.New Zealand | at Wellington | 1997 | 5-109 | v. West Indies | at Birmingham | 2000 |
| 5-149 | v. Australia | at Leeds | 1997 | 5-61 | v. Pakistan | at Lord's | 2001 |
| 6-42 | v.South Africa | at Leeds | 1998 | 5-103 | v. Australia | at Leeds | 2001 |
| 5-96 | v. Australia | at Melbourne | 1998 | | | | |

## S HAIGH (1)

6-11   v. South Africa   at Cape Town   1909

## G H HIRST (3)

| | | | | | | | |
|---|---|---|---|---|---|---|---|
| 5-77 | v. Australia | at The Oval | 1902 | 5-58 | v. Australia | at Birmingham | 1909 |
| 5-48 | v. Australia | at Melbourne | 1904 | | | | |

## M J HOGGARD (7)

| | | | | | |
|---|---|---|---|---|---|
| 7-63 | v. New Zealand | at Christchurch | 2002 | 5-73 | v. Bangladesh at Chester-le-Street |
| 5-92 | v. Sri Lanka | at Birmingham | 2002 | | 2005 |
| 5-144 | v. South Africa | at Johannesburg | 2005* | 6-57 v. India | at Nagpur 2006 |
| 7-61 | v. South Africa | at Johannesburg | 2005* | 7-109 v. Australia | at Adelaide 2006 |

*Consecutive Test innings*

## R ILLINGWORTH (3)

| | | | | | | | |
|---|---|---|---|---|---|---|---|
| 6-29 | v. India | at Lord's | 1967 | 5-70 | v. India | at The Oval | 1971 |
| 6-87 | v. Australia | at Leeds | 1968 | | | | |

## Hon F S JACKSON (1)

5-52   v. Australia      at Nottingham   1905

## G G MACAULAY (1)

5-64   v. South Africa   at Cape Town   1923

## C M OLD (4)

| | | | | | | | |
|---|---|---|---|---|---|---|---|
| 5-113 | v. New Zealand | at Lord's | 1973 | 6-54 | v. New Zealand | at Wellington | 1978 |
| 5-21 | v. India | at Lord's | 1974 | 7-50 | v. Pakistan | at Birmingham | 1978 |

## E PEATE (2)

5-43   v. Australia      at Sydney 1882   6-85   v. Australia      at Lord's      1884

## R PEEL (5)

| | | | | | | | |
|---|---|---|---|---|---|---|---|
| 5-51 | v. Australia | at Adelaide | 1884 | 6-67 | v. Australia | at Sydney | 1894 |
| 5-18 | v. Australia | at Sydney | 1888 | 6-23 | v. Australia | at The Oval | 1896 |
| 7-31 | v. Australia | at Manchester | 1888 | | | | |

## L E PLUNKETT (1)

5-64   v. Sri Lanka      at Leeds      2014

## A U RASHID (1)

5-64   v. Pakistan      at Abu Dhabi   2015

# 5 WICKETS IN AN INNINGS FOR ENGLAND *(Continued)*

## W RHODES (6)

| | | | | | | | |
|---|---|---|---|---|---|---|---|
| 7-17 | v. Australia | at Birmingham | 1902 | 7-56 | v. Australia | at Melbourne | 1904* |
| 5-63 | v. Australia | at Sheffield | 1902 | 8-68 | v. Australia | at Melbourne | 1904* |
| 5-94 | v. Australia | at Sydney | 1903* | 5-83 | v. Australia | at Manchester | 1909 |

*\*consecutive Test innings*

## C E W SILVERWOOD (1)

5-91   v. South Africa   at Cape Town   2000

## R J SIDEBOTTOM (5)

| | | | | | | | |
|---|---|---|---|---|---|---|---|
| 5-88 | v. West Indies | at Chester-le-Street | | 5-105 | v. New Zealand | at Wellington | 2008 |
| | | | 2007 | 7-47 | v. New Zealand | at Napier | 2008 |
| 6-49 | v. New Zealand | at Hamilton | 2008 | 6-47 | v. New Zealand | at Nottingham | 2008 |

## F S TRUEMAN (17)

| | | | | | | | |
|---|---|---|---|---|---|---|---|
| 8-31 | v. India | at Manchester | 1952 | 6-31 | v. Pakistan | at Lord's | 1962 |
| 5-48 | v. India | at The Oval | 1952 | 5-62 | v. Australia | at Melbourne | 1963 |
| 5-90 | v. Australia | at Lord's | 1956 | 7-75 | v. New Zealand | at Christchurch | 1963 |
| 5-63 | v. West Indies | at Nottingham | 1957 | 6-100 | v. West Indies | at Lord's | 1963* |
| 5-31 | v. New Zealand | at Birmingham | 1958 | 5-52 | v. West Indies | at Lord's | 1963* |
| 5-35 | v. West Indies | at Port-of-Spain | 1960 | 5-75 | v. West Indies | at Birmingham | 1963* |
| 5-27 | v. South Africa | at Nottingham | 1960 | 7-44 | v. West Indies | at Birmingham | 1963* |
| 5-58 | v. Australia | at Leeds | 1961* | 5-48 | v. Australia | at Lord's | 1964 |
| 6-30 | v. Australia | at Leeds | 1961* | | | | |

## G ULYETT (1)

7-36   v. Australia   at Lord's   1884

## H VERITY (5)

| | | | | | | | |
|---|---|---|---|---|---|---|---|
| 5-33 | v. Australia | at Sydney | 1933 | 8-43 | v. Australia | at Lord's | 1934* |
| 7-49 | v. India | at Chepauk, Madras | 1934 | 5-70 | v. South Africa | at Cape Town | 1939 |
| 7-61 | v. Australia | at Lord's | 1934* | | | | |

## J H WARDLE (5)

| | | | | | | | |
|---|---|---|---|---|---|---|---|
| 7-56 | v. Pakistan | at The Oval | 1954 | 7-36 | v. South Africa | at Cape Town | 1957* |
| 5-79 | v. Australia | at Sydney | 1955 | 5-61 | v. South Africa | at Kingsmead Durban | 1957* |
| 5-53 | v. South Africa | at Cape Town | 1957* | | | | |

## C WHITE (3)

| | | | | | | | |
|---|---|---|---|---|---|---|---|
| 5-57 | v. West Indies | at Leeds | 2000 | 5-32 | v. West Indies | at The Oval | 2000 |
| | 5-127 | v. Australia | at Perth | 2002 | | | |

*\*consecutive Test innings*

## Summary of Five Wickets in an Innings

| versus | Total | In England | Away |
|---|---|---|---|
| Australia | 42 | 22 | 20 |
| Bangladesh | 1 | 1 | 0 |
| India | 8 | 6 | 2 |
| New Zealand | 11 | 3 | 8 |
| Pakistan | 6 | 5 | 1 |
| South Africa | 13 | 3 | 10 |
| Sri Lanka | 2 | 2 | 0 |
| West Indies | 11 | 10 | 1 |
| Totals | 94 | 52 | 42 |

# 5 WICKETS IN AN INNINGS

### M G BEVAN (1)

| | | | |
|---|---|---|---|
| 6-82 | v. West Indies | at Adelaide | 1997 |

### J N GILLESPIE (8)

| | | | |
|---|---|---|---|
| 5-54 | v. South Africa | at Port Elizabeth | 1997 |
| 7-37 | v. England | at Leeds | 1997 |
| 5-88 | v. England | at Perth | 1998 |
| 5-89 | v. West Indies | at Adelaide | 2000 |
| 6-40 | v. West Indies | at Melbourne | 2000 |
| 5-53 | v. England | at Lord's | 2001 |
| 5-39 | v. West Indies | at Georgetown | 2003 |
| 5-56 | v. India | at Nagpur | 2004 |

## HAT-TRICKS

| | | | |
|---|---|---|---|
| W Bates | v. Australia | at Melbourne | 1882 |
| D Gough | v. Australia | at Sydney | 1998 |
| M J Hoggard | v. West Indies | at Bridgetown | 2004 |
| R J Sidebottom | v. New Zealand | at Hamilton | 2008 |

## FOUR WICKETS IN FIVE BALLS

| | | | |
|---|---|---|---|
| C M Old | v. Pakistan | at Birmingham | 1978 |

## THREE WICKETS IN FOUR BALLS

| | | | |
|---|---|---|---|
| R Appleyard | v. New Zealand | at Auckland | 1955 |
| D Gough | v. Pakistan | at Lord's | 2001 |

# YORKSHIRE PLAYERS WHO PLAYED ALL THEIR TEST CRICKET AFTER LEAVING YORKSHIRE

## For England

| Player | M. | I | NO | Runs | HS. | Av'ge | 100s | 50s | Balls | R | W | Av'ge | Best | 5wI | 10wM | c/st |
|---|---|---|---|---|---|---|---|---|---|---|---|---|---|---|---|---|
| BALDERSTONE, J C ...1976 | 2 | 4 | 0 | 39 | 35 | 9.75 | — | — | 96 | 80 | 1 | 80.00 | 1:80 | — | — | 1 |
| BATTY, G J ...2003 | 4 | 7 | 1 | 136 | 38 | 22.66 | — | — | 992 | 504 | 8 | 63.00 | 3:55 | — | — | 0 |
| BIRKENSHAW, J ...1973-74 | 5 | 7 | 0 | 148 | 64 | 21.14 | — | 1 | 1,017 | 469 | 13 | 36.07 | 5:57 | 1 | — | 3 |
| BOLUS, J B ...1963-64 | 7 | 12 | 0 | 496 | 88 | 41.33 | — | 4 | 18 | 16 | 0 | — | — | — | — | 2 |
| †PARKIN, C H ...1920-24 | 10 | 16 | 3 | 160 | 36 | 12.30 | — | — | 2,095 | 1,128 | 32 | 35.25 | 5:38 | 2 | — | 3 |
| RHODES, S J ...1994-95 | 11 | 17 | 5 | 294 | 65* | 24.50 | — | 1 | — | — | — | — | — | — | — | 46/3 |
| †SUGG, F H ...1888 | 2 | 2 | 0 | 55 | 31 | 27.50 | — | — | — | — | — | — | — | — | — | 0 |
| WARD, A ...1893-95 | 7 | 13 | 0 | 487 | 117 | 37.46 | 1 | 3 | — | — | — | — | — | — | — | 1 |
| WOOD, B ...1972-78 | 12 | 21 | 0 | 454 | 90 | 21.61 | — | 2 | 98 | 50 | 0 | — | — | — | — | 6 |

## For South Africa

| Player | M. | I | NO | Runs | HS. | Av'ge | 100s | 50s | Balls | R | W | Av'ge | Best | 5wI | 10wM | c/st |
|---|---|---|---|---|---|---|---|---|---|---|---|---|---|---|---|---|
| THORNTON, P G ...1902 | 1 | 1 | 1 | 1 | 1* | — | — | — | 24 | 20 | 1 | 20.00 | 1:20 | — | — | 1 |

†Born outside Yorkshire

## CENTURIES
## FOR ENGLAND

A WARD (1)
117 v. Australia at Sydney, 1894

## 5 WICKETS IN AN INNINGS
## FOR ENGLAND

J BIRKENSHAW (1)
5 : 57 v. Pakistan at Karachi, 1973

C H PARKIN (2)
5 : 60 v. Australia at Adelaide, 1921
5 : 38 v. Australia at Manchester, 1921

# YORKSHIRE'S TEST CRICKET RECORDS

## R APPLEYARD

Auckland 1954-55: took 3 wickets in 4 balls as New Zealand were dismissed for the lowest total in Test history (26).

## C W J ATHEY

Perth 1986-87: shared an opening stand of 223 with B C Broad – England's highest for any wicket at the WACA Ground.

## W BATES

Melbourne 1882-83 (Second Test): achieved the first hat-trick for England when he dismissed P S McDonnell, G Giffen and G J Bonnor in Australia's first innings. Later in the match, he became the first player to score a fifty (55) and take 10 or more wickets (14 for 102) in the same Test.

## W E BOWES

Melbourne 1932-33: enjoyed the unique satisfaction of bowling D G Bradman first ball in a Test match (his first ball to him in Test cricket).

## G BOYCOTT

Leeds 1967: scored 246 not out off 555 balls in 573 minutes to establish the record England score against India. His first 100 took 341 minutes (316 balls) and he was excluded from the next Test as a disciplinary measure; shared in hundred partnerships for three successive wickets.

Adelaide 1970-71: with J H Edrich, became the third opening pair to share hundred partnerships in both innings of a Test against Australia.

Port-of-Spain 1973-74: first to score 99 and a hundred in the same Test.

Nottingham 1977: with A P E Knott, equalled England v. Australia sixth-wicket partnership record of 215 – the only England v. Australia stand to be equalled or broken since 1938. Batted on each day of the five-day Test (second after M L Jaisimha to achieve this feat).

Leeds 1977: first to score his 100th First Class hundred in a Test; became the fourth England player to be on the field for an entire Test.

Perth: 1978-79: eighth to score 2,000 runs for England against Australia.

Birmingham 1979: emulated K F Barrington by scoring hundreds on each of England's six current home grounds.

Perth: 1979-80: fourth to carry his bat through a completed England innings (third v. Australia) and the first to do so without scoring 100; first to score 99 not out in a Test.

Lord's 1981: 100th Test for England – second after M C Cowdrey (1968).

The Oval, 1981: second after Hon F S Jackson to score five hundreds v. Australia in England.

Gained three Test records from M C Cowdrey: exceeded England aggregate of 7,624 runs in 11 fewer Tests (Manchester 1981); 61st fifty – world record (The Oval 1981); 189th innings – world record (Bangalore 1981-82).

Delhi, 4.23p.m. on 23 December 1981: passed G St.A Sobers's world Test record of 8,032 runs, having played 30 more innings and batted over 451 hours (cf. 15 complete five-day Tests); his 22nd hundred equalled the England record.

## J T BROWN

Melbourne 1894-95: his 28-minute fifty remains the fastest in Test cricket, and his 95-minute hundred was a record until 1897-98; his third-wicket stand of 210 with A Ward set a Test record for any wicket.

337

# YORKSHIRE'S TEST CRICKET RECORDS (*Continued*)

## D B CLOSE

Manchester 1949: at 18 years 149 days he became – and remains – the youngest to represent England.

Melbourne 1950-51: became the youngest (19 years 301 days) to represent England against Australia.

## T EMMETT

Melbourne 1878-79: first England bowler to take seven wickets in a Test innings.

## P A GIBB

Johannesburg 1938-39: enjoyed a record England debut, scoring 93 and 106 as well as sharing second-wicket stands of 184 and 168 with E Paynter.

Durban 1938-39: shared record England v. South Africa second-wicket stand of 280 with W J Edrich, his 120 in 451 minutes including only two boundaries.

## D GOUGH

Sydney 1998-99: achieved the 23rd hat-trick in Test cricket (ninth for England and first for England v. Australia since 1899).

Lord's 2001: took 3 wickets in 4 balls v. Pakistan.

## S HAIGH

Cape Town 1898-99: bowled unchanged through the second innings with A E Trott, taking 6 for 11 as South Africa were dismissed for 35 in the space of 114 balls.

## J H HAMPSHIRE

Lord's 1969: became the first England player to score 100 at Lord's on his debut in Tests.

## A HILL

Melbourne 1876-77: took the first wicket to fall in Test cricket when he bowled N Thompson, and held the first catch when he dismissed T P Horan.

## G H HIRST

The Oval: 1902: helped to score the last 15 runs in a match-winning tenth-wicket partnership with W Rhodes.

Birmingham 1909: shared all 20 Australian wickets with fellow left-arm spinner C Blythe (11 for 102).

## M J HOGGARD

Bridgetown 2004: became the third Yorkshire player to take a hat-trick in Test cricket (see W Bates and D Gough). It was the 10th hat-trick for England and the third for England versus West Indies.

## L HUTTON

Nottingham 1938: scored 100 in his first Test against Australia.

The Oval 1938: his score (364) and batting time (13 hours 17 minutes – the longest innings in English First-Class cricket) remain England records, and were world Test records until 1958. It remains the highest Test score at The Oval. His stand of 382 with M Leyland is the England second-wicket record in all Tests and the highest for any wicket against Australia. He also shared a record England v. Australia sixth-wicket stand of 216 with J Hardstaff Jr. – the first instance of a batsman sharing in two stands of 200 in the same Test innings. 770 runs were scored during his innings (Test record) which was England's 100th century against Australia, and contained 35 fours. England's total of 903 for 7 declared remains the Ashes Test record.

Lord's 1939: added 248 for the fourth wicket with D C S Compton in 140 minutes.

## L HUTTON *(Continued)*

The Oval 1939: shared (then) world-record third-wicket stand of 264 with W R Hammond, which remains the record for England v. West Indies. Hutton's last eight Tests had brought him 1,109 runs.

The Oval 1948: last out in the first innings, he was on the field for all but the final 57 minutes of the match.

Johannesburg 1948-49: shared (then) world-record first-wicket stand of 359 in 310 minutes with C Washbrook on the opening day of Test cricket at Ellis Park; it remains England's highest opening stand in all Tests.

The Oval 1950: scored England's first 200 in a home Test v. West Indies, and remains alone in carrying his bat for England against them; his 202 not out (in 470 minutes) is the highest score by an England batsman achieving this feat.

Adelaide 1950-51: only England batsman to carry his bat throughout a complete Test innings twice, and second after R Abel (1891-92) to do so for any country against Australia.

Manchester 1951: scored 98 not out, just failing to become the first to score his 100th First Class hundred in a Test match.

The Oval 1951: became the only batsman to be out 'obstructing the field' in Test cricket.

1952: first professional to be appointed captain of England in the 20th Century.

The Oval 1953: first captain to win a rubber after losing the toss in all five Tests.

Kingston 1953-54: scored the first 200 by an England captain in a Test overseas.

## R ILLINGWORTH

Manchester 1971: shared record England v. India eighth-wicket stand of 168 with P. Lever.

## Hon. F S JACKSON

The Oval 1893: his 100 took 135 minutes, and was the first in a Test in England to be completed with a hit over the boundary (then worth only four runs).

The Oval 1899: his stand of 185 with T W Hayward was then England's highest for any wicket in England, and the record opening partnership by either side in England v. Australia Tests.

Nottingham 1905: dismissed M A Noble, C Hill and J Darling in one over (W01W0W).

Leeds 1905: batted 268 minutes for 144 not out – the first hundred in a Headingley Test.

Manchester 1905: first to score five Test hundreds in England.

The Oval 1905: first captain to win every toss in a five-match rubber.

## M LEYLAND

Melbourne 1928-29: scored 137 in his first innings against Australia.

1934: first to score three hundreds in a rubber against Australia in England.

Brisbane 1936-37: scored England's only 100 at 'The Gabba' before 1974-75.

The Oval 1938: contributed 187 in 381 minutes to the record Test total of 903 for 7 declared, sharing in England's highest stand against Australia (all wickets) and record second-wicket stand in all Tests: 382 with L Hutton. First to score hundreds in his first and last innings against Australia.

## G G MACAULAY

Cape Town 1922-23: fourth bowler (third for England) to take a wicket (G A L Hearne) with his first ball in Test cricket. Made the winning hit in the fourth of only six Tests to be decided by a one-wicket margin.

Leeds 1926: shared a match-saving ninth-wicket stand of 108 with G Geary.

# YORKSHIRE'S TEST CRICKET RECORDS *(Continued)*

## C M OLD

Birmingham 1978: took 4 wickets in 5 balls in his 19th over (0WW no-ball WW1) to emulate the feat of M J C Allom.

## R PEEL

Took his 50th wicket in his ninth Test and his 100th in his 20th Test – all against Australia.

## W RHODES

Birmingham 1902: his first-innings analysis of 7 for 17 remains the record for all Tests at Edgbaston.

The Oval 1902: helped to score the last 15 runs in a match-winning tenth-wicket partnership with G H Hirst.

Sydney 1903-04: shared record England v. Australia tenth-wicket stand of 130 in 66 minutes with R E Foster.

Melbourne 1903-04: first to take 15 wickets in England v. Australia Tests; his match analysis of 15 for 124 remains the record for all Tests at Melbourne.

Melbourne 1911-12: shared record England v. Australia first-wicket stand of 323 in 268 minutes with J B Hobbs.

Johannesburg 1913-14: took his 100th wicket and completed the first 'double' for England (in 44 matches).

Sydney 1920-21: first to score 2,000 runs and take 100 wickets in Test cricket.

Adelaide 1920-21: third bowler to take 100 wickets against Australia.

The Oval 1926: set (then) record of 109 wickets against Australia.

Kingston 1929-30: ended the world's longest Test career (30 years 315 days) as the oldest Test cricketer (52 years 165 days).

## H SUTCLIFFE

Birmingham 1924: shared the first of 15 three-figure partnerships with J B Hobbs at the first attempt.

Lord's 1924: shared stand of 268 with J B Hobbs, which remains the first-wicket record for all Lord's Tests, and was then the England v. South Africa record.

Sydney 1924-25: his first opening stands against Australia with J B Hobbs realised 157 and 110.

Melbourne 1924-25 (Second Test): with J B Hobbs achieved the first instance of a batting partnership enduring throughout a full day's Test match play; they remain the only England pair to achieve this feat, and their stand of 283 in 289 minutes remains the longest for the first wicket in this series. Became the first to score 100 in each innings of a Test against Australia, and the first Englishman to score three successive hundreds in Test cricket.

Melbourne 1924-25 (Fourth Test): first to score four hundreds in one rubber of Test matches; it was his third 100 in successive Test innings at Melbourne. Completed 1,000 runs in fewest Test innings (12) – since equalled.

Sydney 1924-25: his aggregate of 734 runs was the record for any rubber until 1928-29.

The Oval 1926: shared first-wicket stand of 172 with J B Hobbs on a rain-affected pitch.

The Oval 1929: first to score hundreds in each innings of a Test twice; only England batsman to score four hundreds in a rubber twice.

Sydney 1932-33: his highest England innings of 194 overtook J B Hobbs's world record of 15 Test hundreds.

## F S TRUEMAN

Leeds 1952: reduced India to 0 for 4 in their second innings by taking 3 wickets in 8 balls on his debut.

Manchester 1952: achieved record England v. India innings analysis of 8 for 31.

The Oval 1952: set England v. India series record with 29 wickets.

## F S TRUEMAN *(Continued)*

Leeds 1961: took 5 for 0 with 24 off-cutters at a reduced pace v. Australia.

Lord's 1962: shared record England v. Pakistan ninth-wicket stand of 76 with T W Graveney.

Christchurch 1962-63: passed J B Statham's world Test record of 242 wickets; his analysis of 7 for 75 remains the record for Lancaster Park Tests and for England in New Zealand.

Birmingham 1963: returned record match analysis (12 for 119) against West Indies in England and for any Birmingham Test, ending with a 6 for 4 spell from 24 balls.

The Oval 1963: set England v. West Indies series record with 34 wickets.

The Oval 1964: first to take 300 wickets in Tests.

## G ULYETT

Sydney 1881-82: with R G Barlow shared the first century opening partnership in Test cricket (122).

Melbourne 1881-82: his 149 was the first Test hundred for England in Australia, and the highest score for England on the first day of a Test in Australia until 1965-66.

## M P VAUGHAN

Scored 1481 runs in 2002 – more than any other England player in a calendar year, surpassing the 1379 scored by D L Amiss in 1979. It was the fourth highest in a calendar year.

Scored 633 runs in the 2002-3 series versus Australia – surpassed for England in a five Test series versus Australia only by W R Hammond, who scored 905 runs in 1928-29, H Sutcliffe (734 in 1924-25), J B Hobbs (662 in 1911-12) and G Boycott (657 in 1970-71), when he played in five of the six Tests.

Scored six Test Match centuries in 2002 to equal the record set for England by D C S Compton in 1947.

Lord's 2004: scored a century in each innings (103 and 101*) versus West Indies and so became the third player (after G A Headley and G A Gooch) to score a century in each innings of a Test match at Lord's.

Lord's 2005: only the second player (J B Hobbs is the other) to have scored centuries in three consecutive Test match innings at Lord's. Scored the 100th century for England by a Yorkshire player.

## H VERITY

Lord's 1934: took 14 for 80 on the third day (six of them in the final hour) to secure England's first win against Australia at Lord's since 1896. It remains the most wickets to fall to one bowler in a day of Test cricket in England. His match analysis of 15 for 104 was then the England v. Australia record, and has been surpassed only by J C Laker.

## W WATSON

Lord's 1953: scored 109 in 346 minutes in his first Test against Australia.

## N W D YARDLEY

Melbourne 1946-47: dismissed D G Bradman for the third consecutive innings without assistance from the field. Became the first to score a fifty in each innings for England and take five wickets in the same match.

Nottingham 1947: shared record England v. South Africa fifth-wicket stand of 237 with D C S Compton.

\* \* \*

Facts adapted by Bill Frindall from his *England Test Cricketers – The Complete Record from 1877* (Collins Willow, 1989). With later additions.

# TEST MATCHES AT HEADINGLEY, LEEDS 1899-2015

1899 **Australia 172** (J Worrall 76) and **224** (H Trumble 56, J T Hearne hat-trick). **England 220** (A F A Lilley 55, H Trumble 5 for 60) and **19 for 0 wkt.**
**Match drawn**
Toss: Australia

1905 **England 301** (Hon F S Jackson 144*) and **295 for 5 wkts dec** (J T Tyldesley 100, T W Hayward 60, W. W. Armstrong 5 for 122). **Australia 195** (W W Armstrong 66, A R Warren 5 for 57) and **224 for 7 wkts** (M A Noble 62).
**Match drawn**
Toss: England

1907 **England 76** (G A Faulkner 6 for 17) and **162** (C B Fry 54). **South Africa 110** (C Blythe 8 for 59) and **75** (C Blythe 7 for 40).
**England won by 53 runs**
Toss: England

1909 **Australia 188** and **207** (S F Barnes 6 for 63). **England 182** (J Sharp 61, J T Tyldesley 55, C G Macartney 7 for 58) and **87** (A Cotter 5 for 38).
**Australia won by 126 runs**
Toss: Australia

1912 **England 242** (F E Woolley 57) and **238** (R H Spooner 82, J B Hobbs 55). **South Africa 147** (S F Barnes 6 for 52) and **159.**
**England won by 174 runs**
Toss: England

1921 **Australia 407** (C G Macartney 115, W W Armstrong 77, C E Pellew 52, J M Taylor 50) and **273 for 7 wkts dec** (T J E Andrew 92). **England 259** (J W H T Douglas 75, Hon L H Tennyson 63, G Brown 57) and **202.**
**Australia won by 219 runs**
Toss: Australia

1924 **England 396** (E H Hendren 132, H Sutcliffe 83) and **60 for 1 wkt.** **South Africa 132** (H W Taylor 59*, M W Tate 6 for 42) and **323** (H W Taylor 56, R H Catterall 56).
**England won by 9 wickets**
Toss: England

1926 **Australia 494** (C G Macartney 151, W M Woodfull 141, A J Richardson 100). **England 294** (G G Macaulay 76, C V Grimmett 5 for 88) and **254 for 3 wkts** (H Sutcliffe 94, J B Hobbs 88).
**Match drawn**
Toss: England

1929 **South Africa 236** (R H Catterall 74, C L Vincent 60, A P Freeman 7 for 115) and **275** (H G Owen-Smith 129). **England 328** (F E Woolley 83, W R Hammond 65, N A Quinn 6 for 92) and **186 for 5 wkts** (F E Woolley 95*).
**England won by 5 wickets**
Toss: South Africa

1930 **Australia 566** (D G Bradman 334, A F Kippax 77, W M Woodfull 50, M W Tate 5 for 124). **England 391** (W R Hammond 113, C V Grimmett 5 for 135) and **95 for 3 wkts.**
**Match drawn**
Toss: Australia

1934 **England 200** and **229 for 6 wkts.** **Australia 584** (D G Bradman 304, W H Ponsford 181, W E Bowes 6 for 142).
**Match drawn**
Toss: England

1935 **England 216** (W R Hammond 63, A Mitchell 58) and **294 for 7 wkts dec** (W R Hammond 87*, A Mitchell 72, D Smith 57). **South Africa 171** (E A B Rowan 62) and **194 for 5 wkts** (B Mitchell 58).
**Match drawn**
Toss: England

1938 **England 223** (W R Hammond 76, W .J O'Reilly 5 for 66) and **123** (.W J O'Reilly 5 for 56). **Australia 242** (D G Bradman 103, B A Barnett 57) and **107 for 5 wkts.**
**Australia won by 5 wickets**
Toss: England

1947 **South Africa 175** (B Mitchell 53, A Nourse 51) and **184** (A D Nourse 57). **England 317 for 7 wkts dec** (L Hutton 100, C Washbrook 75) and **47 for 0 wkt.**
**England won by 10 wickets**
Toss: South Africa

1948 **England 496** (C Washbrook 143, W .J Edrich 111, L Hutton 81, A V Bedser 79) and **365 for 8 wkts dec** (D C S. Compton 66, C Washbrook 65, L Hutton 57, W J Edrich 54). **Australia 458** (R N Harvey 112, S J E Loxton 93, R R Lindwall 77, K R Miller 58) and **404 for 3 wkts** (A R Morris 182, D G Bradman 173*).
**Australia won by 7 wickets**
Toss: England

1949 **England 372** (D C S Compton 114, L Hutton 101, T B Burtt 5 for 97, J Cowie 5 for 127) and **267 for 4 wkts dec** (C Washbrook 103*, W J Edrich 70). **New Zealand 341** (F B Smith 96, M P Donnelly 64, T E Bailey 6 for 118) and **195 for 2 wkts** (B Sutcliffe 82, F Smith 54*).
**Match drawn**                                           Toss: England

1951 **South Africa 538** (E A B Rowan 236, P N F Mansell 90, C B. van Ryneveld 83, R A McLean 67) and **87 for 0 wkt** (E A B Rowan 60*). **England 505** (P B H May 138, L Hutton 100, T E Bailey 95, F A Lowson 58, A M B Rowan 5 for 174).
**Match drawn**                                           Toss: South Africa

1952 **India 293** (V L Manjrekar 133, V S Hazare 89) and 165 (D G Phadkar 64, V S Hazare 56). **England 334** (T W Graveney 71, T G Evans 66, Ghulam Ahmed 5 for 100) and **128 for 3 wkts** (R T Simpson 51).
**England won by 7 wickets**                              Toss: India

1953 **England 167** (T W Graveney 55, R R Lindwall 5 for 54) and **275** (W J Edrich 64, D C S Compton 61). **Australia 266** (R N Harvey 71, G B Hole 53, A V Bedser 5 for 95) and **147 for 4 wkts**.
**Match drawn**                                           Toss: Australia

1955 **South Africa 171** and **500** (D J McGlew 133, W R Endean 116*, T L Goddard 74, H J Keith 73). **England 191** (D C S Compton 61) and **256** (P B H May 97, T L Goddard 5 for 69, H J Tayfield 5 for 94).
**South Africa won by 224 runs**                          Toss: South Africa

1956 **England 325** (P B H May 101, C Washbrook 98). **Australia 143** (J C Laker 5 for 58) and **140** (R N Harvey 69, J C Laker 6 for 55).
**England won by an innings and 42 runs**                 Toss: England

1957 **West Indies 142** (P J Loader 6 for 36, including hat-trick) and **132**. **England 279** (P B H May 69, M C Cowdrey 68, Rev D S Sheppard 68, F M M Worrell 7 for 70).
**England won by an innings and 5 runs**                  Toss: West Indies

1958 **New Zealand 67** (J C Laker 5 for 17) and **129** (G A R Lock 7 for 51). **England 267 for 2 wkts dec** (P B H May 113*, C A Milton 104*).
**England won by an innings and 71 runs**                 Toss: New Zealand

1959 **India 161** and **149**. **England 483 for 8 wkts dec** (M C Cowdrey 160, K F Barrington 80, W G A Parkhouse 78, G Pullar 75).
**England won by an innings and 173 runs**                Toss: India

1961 **Australia 237** (R N Harvey 73, C C McDonald 54, F S Trueman 5 for 58) and **120** (R N Harvey 53, F S Trueman 6 for 30); **England 299** (M C Cowdrey 93, G Pullar 53, A K Davidson 5 for 63) and **62 for 2 wkts**.
**England won by 8 wickets**                              Toss: Australia

1962 **England 428** (P H Parfitt 119, M J Stewart 86, D A Allen 62, Munir Malik 5 for 128). **Pakistan 131** (Alimuddin 50) and **180** (Alimuddin 60, Saeed Ahmed 54).
**England won by an innings and 117 runs**                Toss: Pakistan

1963 **West Indies 397** (G St A Sobers 102, R B Kanhai 92, J S Solomon 62) and **229** (B F Butcher 78, G St.A Sobers 52). **England 174** (G A R Lock 53, C C Griffith 6 for 36) and **231** (J M Parks 57, D B Close 56).
**West Indies won by 221 runs**                           Toss: West Indies

1964 **England 268** (J M Parks 68, E R Dexter 66, N J N Hawke 5 for 75) and 229 (K F Barrington 85). **Australia 389** (P J P Burge 160, W M Lawry 78) and **111 for 3 wkts** (I R Redpath 58*).
**Australia won by 7 wickets**                            Toss: England

1965 **England 546 for 4 wkts dec** (J H Edrich 310*, K F Barrington 163). **New Zealand 193** (J R Reid 54) and **166** (V Pollard 53, F J Titmus 5 for 19).
**England won by an innings and 187 runs**                Toss: England

1966 **West Indies 500 for 9 wkts dec** (G.St.A Sobers 174, S M Nurse 137). **England 240** (B L D'Oliveira 88, G.St.A Sobers 5 for 41) and **205** (R W Barber 55, L R Gibbs 6 for 39).
**West Indies won by an innings and 55 runs**             Toss: West Indies

1967 **England 550 for 4 wkts dec** (G Boycott 246*, B L D'Oliveira 109, K F Barrington 93, T W Graveney 59) and **126 for 4 wkts**. **India 164** (Nawab of Pataudi jnr 64) and **510** (Nawab of Pataudi jnr 148, A L Wadekar 91, F M Engineer 87, Hanumant Singh 73). **England won by 6 wickets**      Toss: England

1968 **Australia 315** (I R Redpath 92, I M Chappell 65) and **312** (I M Chappell 81, K D Walters 56, R Illingworth 6 for 87). **England 302** (R M Prideaux 64, J H Edrich 62, A N Connolly 5 for 72) and **230 for 4 wkts** (J H Edrich 65). **Match drawn**      Toss: Australia

1969 **England 223** (J H Edrich 79) and **240** (G.St A Sobers 5 for 42). **West Indies 161** and **272** (B F Butcher 91, G S Camacho 71). **England won by 30 runs**      Toss: England

1971 **England 316** (G Boycott 112, B L D'Oliveira 74) and **264** (B L D'Oliveira 72, D L Amiss 56) **Pakistan 350** (Zaheer Abbas 72, Wasim Bari 63, Mushtaq Mohammad 57) and **205** (Sadiq Mohammad 91). **England won by 25 runs**      Toss: England

1972 **Australia 146** (K R Stackpole 52) and **136** (D L Underwood 6 for 45). **England 263** (R Illingworth 57, A A Mallett 5 for 114) and **21 for 1 wkt**. **England won by 9 wickets**      Toss: Australia

1973 **New Zealand 276** (M G Burgess 87, V Pollard 62) and **142** (G M Turner 81, G G Arnold 5 for 27). **England 419** (G Boycott 115, K W R Fletcher 81, R Illingworth 65, R O Collinge 5 for 74). **England won by an innings and 1 run**      Toss: New Zealand

1974 **Pakistan 285** (Majid Khan 75, Safraz Nawaz 53) and **179**. **England 183** and **238 for 6 wkts** (J H Edrich 70, K W R Fletcher 67*). **Match drawn**      Toss: Pakistan

1975 **England 288** (D S Steele 73, J H Edrich 62, A W Greig 51, G J Gilmour 6 for 85) and **291** (D S Steele 92). **Australia 135** (P H Edmonds 5 for 28) and **220 for 3 wkts** (R B McCosker 95*, I M Chappell 62). **Match drawn**      Toss: England

1976 **West Indies 450** (C G Greenidge 115, R C Fredericks 109, I V A Richards 66, L G Rowe 50) and **196** (C L King 58, R G D Willis 5 for 42). **England 387** (A W Greig 116, A P E Knott 116) and **204** (A W Greig 76*). **West Indies won by 55 runs**      Toss: West Indies

1977 **England 436** (G Boycott 191, A P E Knott 57). **Australia 103** (I T Botham 5 for 21) and **248** (R W Marsh 63). **England won by an innings and 85 runs**      Toss: England

1978 **Pakistan 201** (Sadiq Mohammad 97). **England 119 for 7 wkts** (Safraz Nawaz 5 for 39). **Match drawn**      Toss: Pakistan

1979 **England 270** (I T Botham 137). **India 223 for 6 wkts** (S M Gavaskar 78, D B Vengsarkar 65*). **Match drawn**      Toss: England

1980 **England 143 and 227 for 6 wkts dec** (G A Gooch 55). **West Indies 245**. **Match drawn**      Toss: West Indies

1981 **Australia 401 for 9 wkts dec** (J Dyson 102, K J Hughes 89, G N Yallop 58, I T Botham 6 for 95) and **111** (R G D Willis 8 for 43). **England 174** (I T Botham 50) and **356** (I T Botham 149*, G R Dilley 56, T M Alderman 6 for 135). **England won by 18 runs**      Toss: Australia

1982 **Pakistan 275** (Imran Khan 67*, Mudassar Nazar 65, Javed Miandad 54) and **199** (Javed Miandad 52, I T Botham 5 for 74). **England 256** (D I Gower 74, I T Botham 57, Imran Khan 5 for 49) and **219 for 7 wkts** (G Fowler 86). **England won by 3 wickets**      Toss: Pakistan

1983 **England 225** (C J Tavaré 69, A J Lamb 58, B L Cairns 7 for 74) and **252** (D I Gower 112*, E J Chatfield 5 for 95). **New Zealand 377** (J G Wright 93, B A Edgar 84, R J Hadlee 75) and **103 for 5 wkts** (R G D Willis 5 for 35). **New Zealand won by 5 wickets**      Toss: New Zealand

1984 **England 270** (A J Lamb 100) and **159** (G Fowler 50, M D Marshall 7 for 53). **West Indies 302** (H A Gomes 104*, M A Holding 59, P J W Allott 6 for 61) and **131 for 2 wkts.**
**West Indies won by 8 wickets**                                                    Toss: England

1985 **Australia 331** (A M J Hilditch 119) and **324** (W B Phillips 91, A M J Hilditch 80, K C Wessels 64, J E Emburey 5 for 82). **England 533** (R T Robinson 175, I T Botham 60, P R Downton 54, M W Gatting 53) and **123 for 5 wkts.**
**England won by 5 wickets**                                                        Toss: Australia

1986 **India 272** (D B Vengsarkar 61) and **237** (D B Vengsarkar 102*). **England 102** (R M H Binny 5 for 40) and **128.**
**India won by 279 runs**                                                            Toss: India

1987 **England 136** (D J Capel 53) and **199** (D I Gower 55, Imran Khan 7 for 40). **Pakistan 353** (Salim Malik 99, Ijaz Ahmed 50, N A Foster 8 for 107).
**Pakistan won by an innings and 18 runs**                                          Toss: England

1988 **England 201** (A J Lamb 64*) and **138** (G A Gooch 50). **West Indies 275** (R A Harper 56, D L Haynes 54, D R Pringle 5 for 95) and **67 for 0 wkt.**
**West Indies won by 10 wickets**                                                   Toss: West Indies

1989 **Australia 601 for 7 wkts dec** (S R Waugh 177*, M A Taylor 136, D M Jones 79, M G Hughes 71, A R Border 66) and **230 for 3 wkts dec** (M A Taylor 60, A R Border 60*). **England 430** (A J Lamb 125, K J Barnett 80, R A Smith 66, T M Alderman 5 for 107) and **191.** (G A Gooch 68, T M Alderman 5 for 44).
**Australia won by 210 runs**                                                        Toss: England

1991 **England 198** (R A Smith 54) and **252** (G A Gooch 154*, C E L Ambrose 6 for 52). **West Indies 173** (I V A Richards 73) and **162** (R B Richardson 68).
**England won by 115 runs**                                                          Toss: West Indies

1992 **Pakistan 197** (Salim Malik 82*) and **221** (Salim Malik 84*, Ramiz Raja 63, N A Mallinder 5 for 50). **England 320** (G A Gooch 135, M A Atherton 76, Waqar Younis 5 for 117) and **99 for 4 wkts.**
**England won by 6 wickets**                                                         Toss: Pakistan

1993 **Australia 653 for 4 wkts dec** (A R Border 200*, S R Waugh 157*, D C Boon 107, M J Slater 67, M E Waugh 52). **England 200** (G A Gooch 59, M A Atherton 55, P R Reiffel 5 for 65) and **305** (A J Stewart 78, M A Atherton 63).
**Australia won by an innings and 148 runs**                                        Toss: Australia

1994 **England 477 for 9 wkts dec** (M A Atherton 99, A J Stewart 89, G P Thorpe 72, S J Rhodes 65*) and **267 for 5 wkts dec** (G A Hick 110, G P Thorpe 73). **South Africa 447** (P N Kirsten 104, B M McMillan 78, C R Matthews 62*) and **116 for 3 wkts** (G Kirsten 65).
**Match drawn**                                                                      Toss: England

1995 **England 199** (M A Atherton 81, I R Bishop 5 for 32) and **208** (G P Thorpe 61). **West Indies 282** (S L Campbell 69, J C Adams 58, B C Lara 53) and **129 for 1 wkt** (C L Hooper 73*).
**West Indies won by 9 wickets**                                                    Toss: West Indies

1996 **Pakistan 448** (Ijaz Ahmed 141, Mohin Khan 105, Salim Malik 55, Asif Mujtaba 51, D G Cork 5 for 113) and **242 for 7 wkts dec** (Inzamam-ul-Haq 65, Ijaz Ahmed sen 52) **England 501** (A J Stewart 170, N V Knight 113, J P Crawley 53).
**Match drawn**                                                                      Toss: England

1997 **England 172** (J N. Gillespie 7 for 37) and **268** (N Hussain 105, J P Crawley 72, P R Reiffel 5 for 49). **Australia 501 for 9 wkts dec** (M T G Elliott 199, R T Ponting 127, P R Reiffel 54*, D Gough 5 for 149).
**Australia won by an innings and 61 runs**                                         Toss: Australia

1998 **England 230** (M A Butcher 116) and **240** (N Hussain 94, S M Pollock 5 for 53, A A Donald 5 for 71). **South Africa 252** (W J. Cronje 57, A R C Fraser 5 for 42) and **195** (J N Rhodes 85, B M McMillan 54, D Gough 6 for 42).
**England won by 23 runs**                                                           Toss: England

2000 **West Indies 172** (R R Sarwan 59*, C White 5 for 57) and **61** (A R Caddick 5 for 14). **England 272** (M P Vaughan 76, G A Hick 59).
**England won by an innings and 39 runs**                                           Toss: West Indies

2001 **Australia 447** (R T Ponting 144, D R Martyn 118, M E Waugh 72, D Gough 5 for 103) and **176 for 4 wkts dec** (R T Ponting 72). **England 309** (A J Stewart 76*, G D McGrath 7 for 76) and **315 for 4 wkts** (M A Butcher 173*, N Hussain 55).
**England won by 6 wickets** Toss: Australia

2002 **India 628 for 8 wkts dec** (S R Tendulkar 193, R S Dravid 148, S C Ganguly 128, S B Bangar 68). **England 273** (A J Stewart 78*, M P Vaughan 61) and **309** (N Hussain 110.)
**India won by an innings and 46 runs** Toss: India

2003 **South Africa 342** (G Kirsten 130, M Zondeki 59, J A Rudolph 55) and **365** (A J Hall 99*, G Kirsten 60). **England 307** (M A Butcher 77, M E Trescothick 59, A Flintoff 55) and **209** (M A Butcher 61, A Flintoff 50, J H Kallis 6 for 54.)
**South Africa won by 191 runs** Toss: South Africa

2004 **New Zealand 409** (S P Fleming 97, M H W Papps 86, B B McCullum 54) and **161.** **England 526** (M E Trescothick 132, G O Jones 100, A Flintoff 94, A J Strauss 62) and **45 for 1 wkt**
**England won by 9 wickets** Toss: England

2006 **England 515** (K P Pietersen 135, I R Bell 119, Umar Gul 5 for 123) and **345** (A J Strauss 116, M E Trescothick 58, C M W Reid 55). **Pakistan 538** (Mohammad Yousuf 192, Younis Khan 173) and **155.**
**England won by 167 runs** Toss: England

2007 **England 570 for 7 wkts dec** (K P Pietersen 226, M P Vaughan 103, M J Prior 75). **West Indies 146** and **141** (D J Bravo 52).
**England won by an innings and 283 runs** Toss: England

2008 **England 203** and **327** (S C J Broad 67*, A Cook 60). **South Africa 522** (A B de Villiers 174, A G Prince 149) and **9 for 0 wkt.**
**South Africa won by 10 wickets** Toss: South Africa

2009 **England 102** (P M Siddle 5 for 21) and **263** (G P Swann 62, S C J Broad 61, M G Johnson 5 for 69). **Australia 445** (M J North 110, M J Clarke 93, R T Ponting 78, S R Watson 51, S C J Broad 6 for 91).
**Australia won by an innings and 80 runs** Toss: England

2010 **Australia 88** and **349** (R T Ponting 66, M J Clarke 77, S P D Smith 77). **Pakistan 258** (S R Watson 6-33) and **180-7** (Imran Farhat 67, Azhar Ali 51).
**Pakistan won by 3 wickets** Toss: Australia
*(This was a Home Test Match for Pakistan)*

2012 **South Africa 419** (A N Petersen 182, G C Smith 52) and **258-9 dec** (J A Rudolph 69, GC Smith 52, S C J Broad 5-69). **England 425** (K P Pietersen 149, M J Prior 68) and **130-4.**
**Match drawn** Toss: England

2013 **England 354** (J E Root 104, J M Bairstow 64, T A Boult 5-57) and **287-5 dec** (A N Cook 130, I J L Trott 76). **New Zealand 174** and **220** (L R P L Taylor 70, G P Swann 6-90)
**England won by 247 runs** Toss: England

2014 **Sri Lanka 257** (K C Sangakkara 79, L E Plunkett 5-64) and **457** (K C Sangakkara 55, DPMD Jayawardene 79, A D Mathews 160). **England 365** (S D Robson 127, G S Ballance 74, I R Bell 64) and **249** (M M Ali 108*, K T G D Prasad 5-50)
**Sri Lanka won by 100 runs** Toss: England

2015 **New Zealand 350** (T W M Latham 84, L Ronchi 88, S C J Broad 5-109) and **454-8 dec** (M J Guptill 70, B B McCullum 55, B J Watling 120, M D Craig 58*). **England 350** (A Lyth 107, A N Cook 75) and **255** (A N Cook 56, J C Buttler 73)
**New Zealand won by 199 runs** Toss: England

## SUMMARY OF RESULTS

| ENGLAND | First played | Last played | Played | Won | Lost | Drawn |
|---|---|---|---|---|---|---|
| v. Australia | 1899 | 2009 | 24 | 7 | 9 | 8 |
| v. India | 1952 | 2002 | 6 | 3 | 2 | 1 |
| v. New Zealand | 1949 | 2015 | 8 | 5 | 2 | 1 |
| v. Pakistan | 1962 | 2006 | 9 | 5 | 1 | 3 |
| v. South Africa | 1907 | 2012 | 13 | 6 | 3 | 4 |
| v. Sri Lanka | 2014 | 2014 | 1 | 0 | 1 | 0 |
| v. West Indies | 1957 | 2007 | 12 | 5 | 6 | 1 |
| Totals | 1899 | 2015 | 73 | 31 | 24 | 18 |

# SIX HIGHEST AGGREGATES

| *Runs* | *Wkts* | |
|------|------|---|
| 1723 | 31 | in 1948 (England 496 and 365 for 8 wkts dec; Australia 458 and 404 for 3 wkts) |
| 1553 | 40 | in 2006 (England 515 and 345; Pakistan 538 and 155) |
| 1452 | 30 | in 1989 (Australia 601 for 7 wkts dec and 230 for 3 wkts dec; England 430 and 191) |
| 1409 | 40 | in 2015 (New Zealand 350 and 454 for 8 wkts dec; England 350 and 255) |
| 1350 | 28 | in 1967 (England 550 for 4 wkts dec and 126 for 4 wkts; India 164 and 510) |
| 1311 | 35 | in 1985 (Australia 331 and 324; England 533 and 123 for 5 wkts) |

**Note:** The highest aggregate prior to the Second World War

| 1141 | 37 | in 1921 (Australia 407 and 272 for 7 wkts dec; England 259 and 202) |
|------|------|---|

# SIX LOWEST AGGREGATES

| *Runs* | *Wkts* | |
|------|------|---|
| 423 | 40 | in 1907 (England 76 and 162; South Africa 110 and 75) |
| 463 | 22 | in 1958 (New Zealand 67 and 129; England 267 for 2 wkts) |
| 505 | 30 | in 2000 (West Indies 172 and 61; England 272) |
| 553 | 30 | in 1957 (West Indies 142 and 132; England 279) |
| 566 | 31 | in 1972 (Australia 146 and 136; England 263 and 21 for 1 wkt) |
| 608 | 30 | in 1956 (England 325; Australia 143 and 140) |

# SIX HIGHEST TOTALS

| | |
|---|---|
| 653 for 4 wkts dec | Australia v. England, 1993 |
| 608 for 8 wkts dec | India v. England, 2002 |
| 601 for 7 wkts dec | Australia v. England, 1989 |
| 584 | Australia v. England, 1934 |
| 570 for 7 wkts dec | England v. West Indies, 2007 |
| 566 | Australia v. England, 1930 |

# SIX LOWEST TOTALS

| | |
|---|---|
| 61 | West Indies v. England, 2000 |
| 67 | New Zealand v. England, 1958 |
| 75 | South Africa v. England, 1907 |
| 76 | England v. South Africa, 1907 |
| 87 | England v Australia, 1909 |
| 88 | Australia v. Pakistan, 2010 |

# SIX HIGHEST INDIVIDUAL SCORES

## For England

| | |
|---|---|
| 310* | J H Edrich versus New Zealand, 1965 |
| 246* | G Boycott versus India, 1967 |
| 226 | K P Pietersen versusWest Indies, 2007 |
| 191 | G Boycott versus Australia, 1977 |
| 175 | R T Robinson versus Australia, 1985 |
| 173* | M A Butcher versus Australia, 2001 |

| For Australia | | For Pakistan | |
|---|---|---|---|
| 334 | D G Bradman, 1930 | 192 | Mohammad Yousuf, 2006 |
| 304 | D G Bradman, 1934 | 173 | Younis Khan, 2006 |
| 200* | A R Border, 1993 | 141 | Ijaz Ahmed, 1996 |
| 199 | M T G Elliott, 1997 | 105 | Moin Khan, 1996 |
| 182 | A R Morris, 1948 | 99 | Salim Malik, 1987 |
| 181 | W H Ponsford, 1934 | 97 | Sadiq Mohammad, 1978 |

## SIX HIGHEST INDIVIDUAL SCORES *(Continued)*

| | For India | | For South Africa |
|---|---|---|---|
| 193 | S R Tendulkar, 2002 | 236 | E A B Rowan, 1951 |
| 148 | Nawab of Pataudi jnr, 1967 | 182 | A N Petersen, 2012 |
| 148 | R S Dravid, 2002 | 174 | A B de Villiers, 2008 |
| 133 | V L Manjrekar, 1952 | 149 | A G Prince, 2008 |
| 128 | S C Ganguly, 2002 | 133 | D J McGlew, 1955 |
| 102* | D B Vengsarkar, 1986 | 130 | G Kirsten, 2003 |

| | For New Zealand | | For West Indies |
|---|---|---|---|
| 120 | B J Watling , 2015 | 174 | G St.A Sobers, 1966 |
| 97 | S P Fleming, 2004 | 137 | S M Nurse, 1966 |
| 96 | F B Smith, 1949 | 115 | C G. Greenidge, 1976 |
| 93 | J G Wright, 1983 | 109 | R C Fredericks, 1976 |
| 88 | L Ronchi, 2015 | 104* | H A Gomes, 1984 |
| 87 | M G Burgess, 1973 | 102 | G St A Sobers, 1963 |

## HUNDRED BEFORE LUNCH

**First day**

| 112* | C G Macartney for Australia, 1926 |
|---|---|
| 105* | D G Bradman for Australia, 1930 |

**Third day**

| 102 | (from 27* to 129) H G Owen-Smith for South Africa, 1929 |
|---|---|

## CARRYING BAT THROUGH A COMPLETED INNINGS

154* out of 252  G A Gooch, England v. West Indies, 1991

## MOST CENTURIES IN AN INNINGS

| 3 | 1926 | C G Macartney (151), W M Woodfull (141) and A J Richardson for Australia |
|---|---|---|
| 3 | 1993 | A R Border (200*), S R Waugh (157*) and D C Boon (107) for Australia |
| 3 | 2002 | S R Tendulkar (193), R S Dravid (148) and S C Ganguly (128) for India |

## MOST CENTURIES IN A MATCH

| 5 | 1948 | C Washbrook (143) and W J Edrich (111) for England; R N Harvey (112), A R Morris (182) and D G Bradman (173*) for Australia |
|---|---|---|
| 5 | 2006 | K P Pietersen (135), I R Bell (119) and A J Strauss (116) for England; Younis Khan (173) and Mohammad Yousuf (192) for Pakistan |
| 4 | 1976 | C G Greenidge (115) and R C Fredericks (109) for West Indies; A W Greig (116) and A P E Knott (116) for England |
| 4 | 1996 | Ijaz Ahmed (141) and Moin Khan (105) for Pakistan; A J Stewart (170) and N V Knight (113) for England |
| 4 | 2002 | S R Tendulkar (193), R S Dravid (148) and S C Ganguly (128) for India; N Hussain (110) for England |

# CENTURY PARTNERSHIPS

### For England
### (six highest)
### For the 1st wicket

| | |
|---|---|
| 177 | A Lyth (107) and A N Cook (75) v. New Zealand, 2015 |
| 168 | L Hutton (81) and C Washbrook (143) v. Australia, 1948 (1st inns) |
| 168 | G A Gooch (135) and M A Atherton (76) v. Pakistan, 1992 |
| 158 | M E Trescothick (58) and A J Strauss (116) v. Pakistan, 2006 |
| 156 | J B Hobbs (88) and H Sutcliffe (94) v. Australia, 1926 |
| 153 | M E Trescothick (132) and A J Strauss (62) v. New Zealand, 2004 |

### For all other wickets

| | |
|---|---|
| 369 | (2nd wkt) J H Edrich (310*) and K F Barrington (163) v. New Zealand, 1965 |
| 252 | (4th wkt) G Boycott (246*) and B L D'Oliveira (109) v. India, 1967 |
| 194* | (3rd wkt) C A Milton (104*) and P B H May (113*) v. New Zealand, 1958 |
| 193 | (4th wkt) M C Cowdrey (160) and K F Barrington (80) v. India, 1959 |
| 187 | (4th wkt) P B H May (101) and C Washbrook (98) v. Australia, 1956 |
| 181 | (3rd wkt) M A Butcher (173*) and N Hussain (55) v. Australia, 2001 |

### For Australia
### (six highest)
### For the 1st wkt – none

### For all other wickets

| | |
|---|---|
| 388 | (4th wkt) W H Ponsford (181) and D G Bradman (304), 1934 |
| 332* | (5th wkt) A R Border (200*) and S R Waugh (157*), 1993 |
| 301 | (2nd wkt) A R Morris (182) and D G Bradman (173*), 1948 |
| 268 | (5th wkt) M T G Elliott (199) and R T Ponting (127), 1997 |
| 235 | (2nd wkt) W M Woodfull (141) and C G Macartney (151), 1926 |
| 229 | (3rd wkt) D G Bradman (334) and A F Kippax (77), 1930 |

### For other countries in total
### India

| | |
|---|---|
| 249 | (4th wkt) S R Tendulkar (193) and S C Ganguly (128), 2002 |
| 222 | (4th wkt) V S Hazare (89) and V L Manjrekar (133), 1952 |
| 170 | (2nd wkt) S B Bangar (68) and R S Dravid (148), 2002 |
| 168 | (2nd wkt) F M Engineer (87) and A L Wadekar (91), 1967 |
| 150 | (3rd wkt) R S Dravid (148) and S R Tendulkar (193), 2002 |
| 134 | (5th wkt) Hanumant Singh (73) and Nawab of Pataudi jnr (148), 1967 |
| 105 | (6th wkt) V S Hazare (56) and D G Phadkar (64), 1952 |

### New Zealand

| | |
|---|---|
| 169 | (2nd wkt) M H W Papps (86) and S P Fleming (97), 2004 |
| 121 | (5th wkt) B B McCullum (55) and B J Watling (120), 2015 |
| 120 | (5th wkt) M P Donnelly (64) and F B Smith (96), 1949 |
| 120 | (6th wkt) T W M Latham (84) and L Ronchi (88), 2015 |
| 116 | (2nd wkt) J G Wright (93) and M D Crowe (37), 1983 |
| 112 | (1st wkt) B Sutcliffe (82) and V J Scott (43), 1949 |
| 106 | (5th wkt) M G Burgess (87) and V Pollard (62), 1973 |

### Pakistan

| | |
|---|---|
| 363 | (3rd wkt) Younis Khan (173) and Mohammad Yousuf (192), 2006 |
| 130 | (4th wkt) Ijaz Ahmed (141) and Salim Malik (55), 1996 |
| 129 | (3rd wkt) Zaheer Abbas (72) and Mushtaq Mohammed (57), 1971 |
| 112 | (7th wkt) Asif Mujtaba (51) and Moin Khan (105), 1996 |
| 110 | (2nd wkt) Imran Farhat (67) and Azhar Ali (51), 2010 v. Australia |
| 100 | (3rd wkt) Mudassar Nazar (65) and Javed Miandad (54), 1982 |
| 100 | (4th wkt) Majid Khan (75) and Zaheer Abbas (48), 1974 |

## CENTURY PARTNERSHIPS *(Continued)*

### South Africa

| | | | | |
|---|---|---|---|---|
| 212 | (5th wkt) | A G Prince (149) | and A B de Villiers (174) | 2008 |
| 198 | (2nd wkt) | E A B Rowan (236) | and C B van Ryneveld (83) | 1951 |
| 176 | (1st wkt) | D J McGlew (133) | and T L Goddard (74) | 1955 |
| 150 | (8th wkt) | G Kirsten (130) | and M Zondeki (59) | 2003 |
| 120 | (1st wkt) | A N Petersen (182) | and G C Smith (52) | 2012 |
| 120 | (1st wkt) | J A Rudolph (69) | and G C Smith (52) | 2012 |
| 117 | (6th wkt) | J N Rhodes (85) | and B M McMillan (54) | 1998 |
| 115 | (7th wkt) | P N Kirsten (104) | and B M McMillan (78) | 1994 |
| 108 | (5th wkt) | E A B Rowan (236) | and R A McLean (67) | 1951 |
| 103 | (10th wkt) | H G Owen-Smith (129) | and A J Bell (26*) | 1929 |

### Sri Lanka

| | | | | |
|---|---|---|---|---|
| 149 | (8th wkt) | A D Mathews (160) | and H M R K B Herath (48) | 2014 |

### West Indies

| | | | | |
|---|---|---|---|---|
| 265 | (5th wkt) | S M Nurse (137) | and G St A Sobers (174) | 1966 |
| 192 | (1st wkt) | R C Fredericks (109) | and C G Greenidge (115) | 1976 |
| 118* | (2nd wkt) | C L Hooper (73*) | and B C Lara (48*) | 1995 |
| 143 | (4th wkt) | R B Kanhai (92) | and G St A Sobers (102) | 1963 |
| 108 | (3rd wkt) | G S Camacho (71) | and B F Butcher (91) | 1969 |
| 106 | (1st wkt) | C G Greenidge (49) | and D L Haynes (43) | 1984 |

## 6 BEST INNINGS ANALYSES

### For England

| | | | |
|---|---|---|---|
| 8-43 | R G D Willis | v. Australia | 1981 |
| 8-59 | C Blythe | v. South Africa | 1907 (1st inns) |
| 8-107 | N A Foster | v. Pakistan | 1987 |
| 7-40 | C Blythe | v. South Africa, | 1907 (2nd inns) |
| 7-51 | G A R Lock | v. New Zealand | 1958 |
| 7-115 | A P Freeman | v. South Africa | 1929 |

### For Australia

| | | | |
|---|---|---|---|
| 7-37 | J N Gillespie | 1997 | |
| 7-58 | C G Macartney | 1909 | |
| 7-76 | G D McGrath | 2001 | |
| 6-33 | S R Watson | 2010 | v. Pakistan |
| 6-85 | G J Gilmour | 1975 | |
| 6-135 | T M Alderman | 1981 | |

# 5 WICKETS IN AN INNINGS

### For India (2)

| | | |
|---|---|---|
| 5-40 | R M H Binny | 1986 |
| 5-100 | Ghulam Ahmed | 1952 |

### For New Zealand (6)

| | | |
|---|---|---|
| 7-74 | B L Cairns | 1983 |
| 5-57 | T A Boult | 2013 |
| 5-74 | R O Collinge | 1973 |
| 5-95 | E J Chatfield | 1983 |
| 5-97 | T B Burtt | 1949 |
| 5-127 | J Cowie | 1949 |

### For Pakistan (6)

| | | |
|---|---|---|
| 7-40 | Imran Khan | 1987 |
| 5-39 | Sarfraz Nawaz | 1978 |
| 5-49 | Imran Khan | 1982 |
| 5-117 | Waqar Younis | 1992 |
| 5-123 | Umar Gul | 2006 |
| 5-128 | Munir Malik | 1962 |

### For South Africa (6)

| | | |
|---|---|---|
| 6-17 | G A Faulkner | 1907 |
| 6-92 | N A Quinn | 1929 |
| 6-54 | J H Kallis | 2003 |
| 5-53 | S M Pollock | 1998 |
| 5-69 | T L Goddard | 1955 |
| 5-71 | A A Donald | 1998 |
| 5-94 | H J Tayfield | 1955 |
| 5-174 | A M B Rowan | 1951 |

### For Sri Lanka

| | | |
|---|---|---|
| 5-50 | K T G D Prasad | 2014 |

### For West Indies (8)

| | | |
|---|---|---|
| 7-53 | M D Marshall | 1984 |
| 7-70 | F M Worrell | 1957 |
| 6-36 | C C Griffith | 1963 |
| 6-39 | L R Gibbs | 1996 |
| 6-52 | C E L Ambrose | 1991 |
| 5-32 | I R Bishop | 1995 |
| 5-41 | G.St.A Sobers | 1966 |
| 5-42 | G.St A Sobers | 1969 |

# 10 WICKETS IN A MATCH

### For England (8)

| | | | | |
|---|---|---|---|---|
| 15-99 | (8-59 and 7-40) | C Blythe | v. South Africa | 1907 |
| 11-65 | (4-14 and 7-51) | G A R Lock | v. New Zeland | 1958 |
| 11-88 | (5-58 and 6-30) | F S Trueman | v. Australia | 1961 |
| 11-113 | (5-58 and 6-55) | J C Laker | v. Australia | 1956 |
| 10-82 | (4-37 and 6-45) | D L Underwood | v. Australia | 1972 |
| 10-115 | (6-52 and 4-63) | S F Barnes | v. South Africa | 1912 |
| 10-132 | (4-42 and 6-90) | G P Swann | v. New Zealand | 2013 |
| 10-207 | (7-115 and 3-92) | A P Freeman | v. South Africa | 1929 |

### For Australia (3)

| | | | | |
|---|---|---|---|---|
| 11-85 | (7-58 and 4-27) | C G Macartney | 1909 |
| 10-122 | (5-66 and 5-56) | W J O'Reilly | 1938 |
| 10-151 | (5-107 and 5-44) | T M Alderman | 1989 |

### For New Zealand (1)

| | | | |
|---|---|---|---|
| 10-144 | (7-74 and 3-70) | B L Cairns | 1983 |

### For Pakistan (1)

| | | | |
|---|---|---|---|
| 10-77 | (3-37 and 7-40) | Imran Khan | 1987 |

**Note:** Best bowling in a match for:

| | | | | |
|---|---|---|---|---|
| India | 7-58 | (5-40 and 2-18) | R M H Binney | 1986 |
| Sri Lanka | 6-125 | (1-75 and 5-50) | K T G D Prasad | 2014 |
| South Africa | 9-75 | (6-17 and 3-58) | G A Faulkner | 1907 |
| West Indies | 9-81 | (6 -36 and 3-45) | C C Griffith | 1963 |

# HAT-TRICKS

| | | |
|---|---|---|
| J T Hearne | v. Australia | 1899 |
| P J Loader | v. West Indies | 1957 |

# TEST MATCH AT BRAMALL LANE, SHEFFIELD 1902

1902 **Australia 194** (S F Barnes 6 for 49) and **289** (C Hill 119, V T Trumper 62, W Rhodes 5 for 63) **England 145** (J V Saunders 5 for 50, M A Noble 5 for 51) and **195** (A C MacLaren 63, G L Jessop 55, M A Noble 6 for 52).
**Australia won by 143 runs**                                    Toss: Australia

# YORKSHIRE ONE-DAY INTERNATIONAL CRICKETERS 1971-2015/16 (Correct to December 16, 2015)

| Player | M | I | NO | Runs | HS | Av'ge | 100s | 50s | Balls | Runs | W | Av'ge | Best | 4wI | Ct/St |
|---|---|---|---|---|---|---|---|---|---|---|---|---|---|---|---|
| ATHEY, C W J .....1980-88 | 31 | 30 | 3 | 848 | 142* | 31.40 | 2 | 4 | — | — | — | — | — | — | 16 |
| BAIRSTOW, D L .....1979-84 | 21 | 20 | 6 | 206 | 23* | 14.71 | 0 | 0 | — | — | — | — | — | — | 17/4 |
| BAIRSTOW, J M .2011-15/16 | 12 | 10 | 2 | 260 | 83* | 32.50 | 0 | 1 | — | — | — | — | — | — | 10/1 |
| BALLANCE, G S .2013-14/15 | 16 | 15 | 1 | 297 | 79 | 21.21 | 0 | 2 | — | — | — | — | — | — | 8 |
| BLAKEY, R J .....1992-93 | 3 | 2 | 0 | 25 | 25 | 12.50 | 0 | 0 | — | — | — | — | — | — | 2/1 |
| BOYCOTT, G .....1971-81 | 36 | 34 | 4 | 1,082 | 105 | 36.06 | 1 | 9 | 168 | 105 | 5 | 21.00 | 2-14 | — | 5 |
| BRESNAN, T T .....2006-15 | 85 | 64 | 20 | 871 | 80 | 19.79 | 0 | 1 | 4,221 | 3,813 | 109 | 34.98 | 5-48 | 4 | 20 |
| COPE, G A .....1977-78 | 2 | 1 | 1 | 1 | 1* | — | 0 | 0 | 112 | 35 | 2 | 17.50 | 1-16 | — | 0 |
| GOUGH, D .....1994-2006 | 158 | 87 | 38 | 609 | 46* | 12.42 | 0 | 0 | 8,422 | 6,154 | 234 | 26.29 | 5-44 | 10 | 24 |
| HAMPSHIRE, J H ..1971-72 | 3 | 3 | 1 | 48 | 25* | 24.00 | 0 | 0 | — | — | — | — | — | — | 0 |
| HOGGARD, M J ...2001-06 | 26 | 6 | 2 | 17 | 7 | 4.25 | 0 | 0 | 1,306 | 1,152 | 32 | 36.00 | 5-49 | 1 | 5 |
| JARVIS, P W .....1988-93 | 16 | 8 | 2 | 31 | 16* | 5.16 | 0 | 0 | 879 | 672 | 24 | 28.00 | 5-35 | 2 | 1 |
| LOVE, J D .............1981 | 3 | 3 | 0 | 61 | 43 | 20.33 | 0 | 0 | — | — | — | — | — | — | 1 |
| McGRATH, A .....2003-04 | 14 | 12 | 2 | 166 | 52 | 16.60 | 0 | 1 | 228 | 175 | 4 | 43.75 | 1-13 | — | 4 |
| MOXON, M D .....1985-88 | 8 | 8 | 0 | 174 | 70 | 21.75 | 0 | 1 | — | — | — | — | — | — | 5 |
| OLD, C M .....1973-81 | 32 | 25 | 7 | 338 | 51* | 18.77 | 0 | 1 | 1,755 | 999 | 45 | 22.20 | 4-8 | 2 | 8 |
| PLUNKETT, L E 2005/6-2015 | 34 | 30 | 11 | 414 | 56 | 21.78 | 0 | 1 | 1,603 | 1578 | 45 | 35.06 | 3-24 | 0 | 10 |
| RASHID, A U .2009-15/16 | 20 | 13 | 4 | 231 | 69 | 25.66 | 0 | 0 | 972 | 972 | 22 | 44.18 | 4-55 | 2 | 8 |
| ROOT, J E .2012/13-15/16 | 63 | 59 | 6 | 2,221 | 121 | 41.90 | 6 | 11 | 846 | 814 | 12 | 67.83 | 2-15 | — | 30 |
| SHAHZAD, A .....2010-11 | 11 | 8 | 2 | 39 | 9 | 6.50 | 0 | 0 | 588 | 490 | 12 | 40.83 | 3-41 | — | 4 |
| SIDEBOTTOM, R J .2001-10 | 25 | 18 | 8 | 133 | 24 | 13.30 | 0 | 0 | 1,277 | 1,039 | 29 | 35.82 | 3-19 | — | 6 |
| SILVERWOOD, C E W 1996-2001 | 7 | 4 | 3 | 17 | 12 | 4.25 | 0 | 0 | 306 | 244 | 6 | 40.66 | 3-43 | — | 0 |
| STEVENSON, G B ..1980-81 | 4 | 4 | 0 | 43 | 28* | 43.00 | 0 | 0 | 192 | 125 | 7 | 17.85 | 4-33 | 1 | 2 |
| VAUGHAN, M P ...2001-07 | 86 | 83 | 10 | 1,982 | 90* | 27.15 | 0 | 16 | 796 | 649 | 16 | 40.56 | 4-22 | 1 | 25 |
| WHITE, C .....1994-2003 | 51 | 41 | 5 | 568 | 57* | 15.77 | 0 | 1 | 2,364 | 1,726 | 65 | 26.55 | 5-21 | 2 | 12 |
| **For Scotland** | | | | | | | | | | | | | | | |
| BLAIN, J A R ...1999-2009 | 33 | 25 | 6 | 284 | 41 | 14.94 | 0 | 0 | 1,329 | 1,173 | 41 | 28.60 | 5-22 | 4 | 8 |
| HAMILTON, G M .1999-2010 | 38 | 38 | 3 | 1,231 | 119 | 35.17 | 2 | 7 | 220 | 160 | 3 | 53.33 | 2-36 | — | 6/1 |
| WARDLAW, I .2012/14/15 | 22 | 14 | 8 | 21 | 7* | 3.50 | 0 | 0 | 1,108 | 1036 | 36 | 28.77 | 4-22 | 2 | 1 |

## YORKSHIRE PLAYERS WHO PLAYED ALL THEIR ONE-DAY INTERNATIONAL CRICKET AFTER LEAVING YORKSHIRE

### For England

| Player | M | I | NO | Runs | HS | Av'ge | 100s | 50s | Balls | Runs | W | Av'ge | Best | 4wI | Ct/St |
|---|---|---|---|---|---|---|---|---|---|---|---|---|---|---|---|
| BATTY, G J ........2002-09 | 10 | 8 | 2 | 30 | 17 | 5.00 | 0 | 0 | 440 | 366 | 5 | 73.20 | 2-40 | — | 4 |
| CLOSE, D B ........1972 | 3 | 3 | 0 | 49 | 43 | 16.33 | 0 | 0 | 18 | 21 | 0 | — | — | — | 1 |
| GRAYSON, A P ....2000-01 | 2 | 2 | 0 | 6 | 6 | 3.00 | 0 | 0 | 90 | 60 | 3 | 20.00 | 3-40 | — | 1 |
| ILLINGWORTH, R .1971-72 | 3 | 2 | 0 | 5 | 4 | 2.50 | 0 | 0 | 130 | 84 | 4 | 21.00 | 3-50 | — | 1 |
| LUMB, M J ........2013/14 | 3 | 3 | 0 | 165 | 106 | 55.00 | 1 | 0 | — | — | — | — | — | — | 1 |
| RHODES, S J ......1989-95 | 9 | 8 | 2 | 107 | 56 | 17.83 | 0 | 1 | — | — | — | — | — | — | 9/2 |
| WHARF, A G ......2004-05 | 13 | 5 | 3 | 19 | 9 | 9.50 | 0 | 0 | 584 | 428 | 18 | 23.77 | 4-24 | 1 | 1 |
| WOOD, B ..........1972-82 | 13 | 12 | 2 | 314 | 78* | 31.40 | 0 | 2 | 420 | 224 | 9 | 24.88 | 2-14 | — | 6 |

### Overseas Players
(Qualification: 24 List A matches for Yorkshire)

#### For Australia

| Player | M | I | NO | Runs | HS | Av'ge | 100s | 50s | Balls | Runs | W | Av'ge | Best | 4wI | Ct/St |
|---|---|---|---|---|---|---|---|---|---|---|---|---|---|---|---|
| BEVAN, M G ...1994-2004 | 232 | 196 | 67 | 6,912 | 108* | 53.58 | 6 | 46 | 1,966 | 1,655 | 36 | 45.97 | 3-36 | — | 128 |
| HARVEY, I J ..1997/98-2004 | 73 | 51 | 11 | 715 | 48* | 17.87 | 0 | 0 | 3,279 | 2,577 | 85 | 30.31 | 4-16 | 4 | 17 |
| JAQUES, P A ..2006-2007 | 6 | 6 | 0 | 125 | 94 | 20.83 | 0 | 1 | — | — | — | — | — | — | 3 |
| LEHMANN, D S .1996-2005 | 117 | 101 | 22 | 3,078 | 119 | 38.96 | 4 | 17 | 1,793 | 1,445 | 52 | 27.78 | 4-7 | 1 | 26 |

#### For South Africa

| Player | M | I | NO | Runs | HS | Av'ge | 100s | 50s | Balls | Runs | W | Av'ge | Best | 4wI | Ct/St |
|---|---|---|---|---|---|---|---|---|---|---|---|---|---|---|---|
| RUDOLPH, J A ......2003-06 | 43 | 37 | 6 | 1,157 | 81 | 37.32 | 0 | 7 | 24 | 26 | 0 | — | — | — | 11 |

#### For West Indies

| Player | M | I | NO | Runs | HS | Av'ge | 100s | 50s | Balls | Runs | W | Av'ge | Best | 4wI | Ct/St |
|---|---|---|---|---|---|---|---|---|---|---|---|---|---|---|---|
| RICHARDSON, R B 1983-96 | 224 | 217 | 30 | 6,248 | 122 | 33.41 | 5 | 44 | 58 | 46 | 1 | 46.00 | 1-4 | — | 75 |

# LIMITED-OVERS INTERNATIONAL MATCHES
## AT HEADINGLEY, LEEDS 1973-2015

1973 **West Indies 181** (54 overs) (R B Kanhai 55). **England 182 for 9 wkts** (54.3 overs) (M H Denness 66).
**England won by 1 wicket**            **Award: M H Denness**

1974 **India 265** (53.5 overs) (B P Patel 82, A L Wadekar 67). **England 266 for 6 wkts** (51.1 overs) (J H Edrich 90).
**England won by 4 wickets**            **Award: J H Edrich**

1975 **Australia 278 for 7 wkts** (60 overs) (R Edwards 80*). **Pakistan 205** (53 overs) (Majid Khan 65, Asif Iqbal 53, D K Lillee 5 for 34).
**Australia won by 73 runs**            **Award: D K Lillee**

1975 **East Africa 120** (55.3 overs). **India 123 for 0 wkt** (29.5 overs) (S M Gavaskar 65* F M Engineer 54*).
**India won by 10 wickets**            **Award: F M Engineer**

1975 **England 93** (36.2 overs) (G J Gilmour 6 for 14). **Australia 94 for 6 wkts** (28.4 overs).
**Australia won by 4 wickets**            **Award: G J Gilmour**

1979 **Canada 139 for 9 wkts** (60 overs). **Pakistan 140 for 2 wkts** (40.1 overs) (Sadiq Mohammed 57*).
**Pakistan won by 8 wickets**            **Award: Sadiq Mohammed**

1979 **India 182 (55.5 overs)** (S M Gavaskar 55). **New Zealand 183 for 2 wkts** (57 overs) (B A Edgar 84*).
**New Zealand won by 8 wickets**            **Award: B A Edgar**

1979 **England 165 for 9 wkts** (60 overs). **Pakistan 151** (56 overs) (Asif Iqbal 51, M Hendrick 4 for 15)
**England won by 14 runs**            **Award: M Hendrick**

1980 **West Indies 198** (55 overs) (C G Greenidge 78). **England 174** (51.2 overs) (C J Tavaré 82*).
**West Indies won by 24 runs**            **Award: C J Tavaré**

1981 **Australia 236 for 8 wkts** (55 overs) (G M Wood 108). **England 165** (46.5 overs) (R M Hogg 4 for 29).
**Australia won by 71 runs**            **Award: G M Wood**

1982 **India 193** (55 overs) (Kapil Dev 60, I T Botham 4 for 56). **England 194 for 1 wkt** (50.1 overs) (B Wood 78*, C J Tavaré 66).
**England won by 9 wickets**            **Award: B Wood**

1983 **West Indies 252 for 9 wkts** (60 overs) (H A Gomes 78). **Australia 151** (30.3 overs) (W W Davis 7 for 51).
**West Indies won by 101 runs**            **Award: W W Davis**

1983 **Pakistan 235 for 7 wkts** (60 overs) (Imran Khan 102*, Shahid Mahboob 77, A L F de Mel 5 for 39). **Sri Lanka 224** (58.3 overs) (S Wettimuny 50, Abdul Qadir 5 for 44).
**Pakistan won by 11 runs**            **Award: Abdul Qadir**

1983 **Sri Lanka 136** (50.4 overs). **England 137 for 1 wkt** (24.1 overs) (G Fowler 81*).
**England won by 9 wickets**            **Award: R G D Willis**

1986 **New Zealand 217 for 8 wkts** (55 overs) (J J Crowe 66). **England 170** (48.2 overs).
**New Zealand won by 47 runs**            **Award: J J Crowe**

1988 **England 186 for 8 wkts** (55 overs). **West Indies 139** (46.3 overs).
**England won by 47 runs**            **Award: D R Pringle**

1990 **England 295 for 6 wkts** (55 overs) (R A Smith 128, G A Gooch 55). **New Zealand 298 for 6 wkts** (54.5 overs) (M J Greatbatch 102*, J G Wright 52, A H Jones 51).
**New Zealand won by 4 wickets**            **Award: M J Greatbatch**

1990 **England 229** (54.3 overs) (A J Lamb 56, D I Gower 50). **India 233 for 4 wkts** (53 overs) (S V Manjrekar 82, M Azharuddin 55*)
**India won by 6 wickets**            **Award: A Kumble**

1996 **India 158** (40.2 overs). **England 162 for 4 wkts** (39.3 overs) (G P Thorpe 79*).
**England won by 6 wickets**                                     **Award: G P Thorpe**

1997 **Australia 170 for 8 wkts** (50 overs) (S M Pollock 56). **England 175 for 4 wkts** (40.1 overs) (G P Thorpe 75*, A J Hollioake 66*).
**England won by 6 wickets**                                     **Award: G P Thorpe**

1998 **South Africa 205 for 8 wkts** (50 overs) (S M Pollock 56). **England 206 for 3 wkts** (35 overs) (A D Brown 59, N V Knight 51).
**England won by 7 wickets**                                     **Award: A D Brown**

1999 **Pakistan 275 for 8 wkts** (50 overs) (Inzamam-ul-Haq 81, Abdur Razzaq 60). **Australia 265** (49.5 overs) (M G Bevan 61, Wasim Akram 4-40).
**Pakistan won by 10 runs**                              **Award: Inazmam-ul-Haq**

1999 **Zimbabwe 175** (49.3 overs) (M A Goodwin 57). **New Zealand 70 for 3 wkts** (15 overs).
**No result**                                                        **No Award**

1999 **South Africa 271 for 7 wkts** (50 overs) (H H Gibbs 101, D J Cullinan 50). **Australia 275 for 5 wkts** (49.4 overs) (S R. Waugh 120*, R T Ponting 69).
**Australia won by 5 wickets**                                   **Award: S R Waugh**

2001 **England 156 (45.2 overs)** (B C Hollioake 53, Waqar Younis 7 for 36). **Pakistan 153 for 4 wkts** (39.5 overs) (Abdur Razzaq 75).
**Pakistan won — England conceding the match following a pitch invasion.**
                                                               **Award: Waqar Younis**

2002 **Sri Lanka 240 for 7 wkts** (32 overs) (S T Jayasuriya 112). **England 241 for 7 wkts** (31.2 overs) (M E Trescothick 82).
**England won by 3 wickets**                                 **Award: S T Jayasuriya**

2003 **England 81 for 4 wkts. Zimbabwe** did not bat.
**No result**                                                        **No Award**

2004 **West Indies 159** (40.1 overs). **England 160 for 3 wkts** (22 overs) (M E Trescothick 55).
**England won by 7 wickets**                                   **Award: S J Harmison**

2005 **Bangladesh 208 for 7 wkts** (50 overs) (Belim 81, A Flintoff 4-29). **England 209 for 5 wkts** (38.5 overs) (A J Strauss 98)
**England won by 5 wickets**                                    **Award: A J Strauss**

     **Australia 219 for 7 wkts** (50 overs) (P D Collingwood 4-34). **England 221 for 1 wkt** (46 overs) (M E Trescothick 104*, M P Vaughan 59*).
**England won by 9 wickets**                               **Award: M E Trescothick**

2006 **England 321 for 7 wkts** (50 overs) (M E Trescothick 121, S L Malinga 4-44). **Sri Lanka 324 for 2 wkts** (37.3 overs) (S T Jayasuriya 152, W U Tharanga 109).
**Sri Lanka won by 8 wickets**                               **Award: S T Jayasuriya**

2007 **India 324 for 6 wkts** (50 overs) (Yuvraj Singh 72, S R Tendulkar 71, S C Ganguly 59, G Gambhir 51). **England 242 for 8 wkts** (39 overs) (P D Collingwood 91*)
**India won by 38 runs** *(D/L Method)*                        **Award: S C Ganguly**

2008 **England 275 for 4 wkts** (50 overs) (K P Pietersen 90*, A Flintoff 78). **South Africa 255** (J H Kallis 52).
**England won by 20 runs**                                   **Award: K P Pietersen**

2009 **England v. West Indies**             **Match abandoned without a ball bowled**

2010 **Pakistan 294 for 8 wkts** (50 overs) (Kamran Akmal 74, Asad Shafiq 50, S C J Broad 4-81). **England 295 for 6 wkts** (A J Strauss 126, I J L Trott 53)
**England won by 4 wickets**                                    **Award: A J Strauss**

2011 **Sri Lanka 309 for 5 wkts** (50 overs) (D P M D Jayawardene 144, K C Sangakkara 69) **England** 240 all out (E J G Morgan 52)
**Sri Lanka won by 69 runs**                        **Award: D P M D Jayawardene**

2012 **England v. West Indies**             **Match abandoned without a ball bowled**

2013 **England v. Australia**               **Match abandoned without a ball bowled**

2014 **England 294 for 7 wkts** (50 overs) (J E Root 113). **India** 253 all out (48.4 overs) (R A Jadeja 87)
**England won by 41 runs**                                    **Award: J E Root**

2015 **Australia 299 for 7 wkts** (50 overs) (G J Bailey 75, G J Maxwell 85, M S Wade 50*).
**England 304 for 7 wkts** (48.2 overs) (E J G Morgan 92, P J Cummins 4-49)
**England won by 7 wickets**                                 **Award: E J G Morgan**

## SUMMARY OF RESULTS

| ENGLAND | Played | Won | Lost |
|---|---|---|---|
| v. Australia | 5 | 3 | 2 |
| v. Bangladesh | 1 | 1 | 0 |
| v. India | 6 | 4 | 2 |
| v. New Zealand | 2 | 0 | 2 |
| v. Pakistan | 3 | 2 | 1 |
| v. South Africa | 2 | 2 | 0 |
| v. Sri Lanka | 4 | 2 | 2 |
| v. West Indies | 4 | 3 | 1 |
| v. Zimbabwe | 1* | 0 | 0 |
| Totals | 28 | 17 | 10 |

*No result. In addition to two matches v. West Indies abandoned
and one match v. Australia abandoned

## CENTURIES

| 152 | S J Jayasuriya | for Sri Lanka | v. England | 2006 |
|------|------|------|------|------|
| 144 | D P M D Jayawardene | for Sri Lanka | v. England | 2011 |
| 128 | R A Smith | for England | v. New Zealand | 1990 |
| 126 | A J Strauss | for England | v. Pakistan | 2010 |
| 121 | M E Trescothick | for England | v. Sri Lanka | 2006 |
| 120* | S R Waugh | for Australia | v. South Africa | 1999 |
| 113 | J E Root | for England | v. India | 2014 |
| 112 | S J Jayasuriya | for Sri Lanka | v. England | 2002 |
| 109 | W U Tharanga | for Sri Lanka | v. England | 2006 |
| 108 | G M Wood | for Australia | v. England | 1981 |
| 104* | M E Trescothick | for England | v. Australia | 2005 |
| 102* | Imran Khan | for Pakistan | v. Sri Lanka | 1983 |
| 102* | M J Greatbatch | for New Zealand | v. England | 1990 |
| 101 | H H Gibbs | for South Africa | v. Australia | 1999 |

## 4 WICKETS IN AN INNINGS

| 7-36 | Waqar Younis | for Pakistan | v. England | 2001 |
|------|------|------|------|------|
| 7-51 | W W Davis | for West Indies | v. Australia | 1983 |
| 6-14 | G J Gilmour | for Australia | v. England | 1975 |
| 5-34 | D K Lillee | for Australia | v. Pakistan | 1975 |
| 5-39 | A L F de Mel | for Sri Lanka | v. Pakistan | 1983 |
| 5-44 | Abdul Qadir | for Pakistan | v. Sri Lanka | 1983 |
| 4-15 | M Hendrick | for England | v. Pakistan | 1979 |
| 4-29 | R M Hogg | for Australia | v England | 1981 |
| 4-29 | A Flintoff | for England | v. Bangladesh | 2005 |
| 4-34 | P D Collingwood | for England | v. Australia | 2005 |
| 4-40 | Wasim Akram | for Pakistan | v. Australia | 1999 |
| 4-44 | S L Malinga | for Sri Lanka | v. England | 2006 |
| 4-49 | P J Cummins | Australia | v. England | 2015 |
| 4-56 | I T Botham | for England | v. India | 1982 |
| 4-81 | S J C Broad | for England | v. Pakistan | 2010 |

## LIMITED-OVERS INTERNATIONAL MATCHES
## AT NORTH MARINE ROAD, SCARBOROUGH 1976-1978

1976 **England 202 for 8 wkts** (55 overs) (G D Barlow 80*, A M E Roberts 4 for 32).
**West Indies 207 for 4 wkts** (41 overs) (I V A Richards 119*).
**West Indies won by 6 wickets**                          **Award: I V A Richards**

1978 **England 206 for 8 wkts** (55 overs) (G A Gooch 94, B L Cairns 5 for 28).
**New Zealand 187 for 8 wkts** (55 overs) (B E Congdon 52*).
**England won by 19 runs**                                **Award: G A Gooch**

# LIST OF PLAYERS AND CAREER AVERAGES IN ALL FIRST-CLASS MATCHES FOR YORKSHIRE 1863-2015

Based on research by John T Potter, Roy D Wilkinson and the late Anthony Woodhouse

The Editor and Statistics Editor welcome any information which will help in keeping this list up to date. The present compilers do not believe that we should alter the status of matches from that determined at the time they were played. Therefore, these averages include the matches versus Gentlemen of Scotland in 1878, and exclude the matches versus Liverpool and District played in 1889, 1891, 1892 and 1893 in line with what appear to be the decisions of the Club at the time.

* Played as an amateur    © Awarded County Cap    § Born outside Yorkshire

| Player | Date of Birth | Date of Death (if known) | First Played | Last Played | M | Inns | NO | Runs | HS | Av'ge | 100s | Runs | Wkts | Av'ge | Ct/St |
|---|---|---|---|---|---|---|---|---|---|---|---|---|---|---|---|
| Ackroyd, A * | Aug. 29, 1858 | Oct. 3, 1927 | 1879 | 1879 | 1 | 1 | 0 | 2 | 2* | 2.00 | 0 | 7 | 0 | — | 0 |
| Allen, S * | Dec 20, 1893 | Oct 9, 1978 | 1924 | 1924 | 1 | 2 | 0 | 8 | 6 | 4.00 | 0 | 116 | 2 | 58.00 | 0 |
| Allen, W R | Apr 14, 1893 | Oct 14, 1950 | 1921 | 1925 | 30 | 32 | 10 | 475 | 95* | 21.59 | — | — | — | — | 45/21 |
| Ambler, J | Feb 12, 1860 | Feb 10, 1899 | 1886 | 1886 | 4 | 7 | 0 | 68 | 25 | 9.71 | 0 | 22 | 0 | — | 2 |
| Anderson, G | Jan 20, 1826 | Nov 27, 1902 | 1851 | 1869 | 19 | 31 | 1 | 520 | 99* | 20.80 | 0 | — | — | — | 19 |
| Anderson, P N | Apr. 28, 1966 | | 1988 | 1988 | 1 | 1 | 0 | 0 | 0 | 0.00 | 0 | — | — | — | 1 |
| Anson, C E * | Oct 14, 1889 | Mar 26, 1969 | 1924 | 1924 | 1 | 2 | 0 | 27 | 14 | 13.50 | 0 | 47 | 1 | 47.00 | 1 |
| Appleton, C * | May 15, 1844 | | 1865 | 1865 | 3 | 6 | 1 | 56 | 18 | 11.20 | 0 | — | — | — | 1 |
| Appleyard, R | © June 27, 1924 | Mar 17, 2015 | 1950 | 1958 | 133 | 122 | 43 | 679 | 63 | 8.59 | 0 | 9,903 | 642 | 15.42 | 70 |
| Armitage, C I * | Apr 24, 1849 | Apr 24, 1917 | 1873 | 1878 | 3 | 5 | 0 | 26 | 12 | 5.20 | 0 | 29 | 0 | — | 1 |
| Armitage, T | Apr 25, 1848 | Sept 21, 1922 | 1872 | 1878 | 52 | 85 | 8 | 1,053 | 95 | 13.67 | 0 | 1,614 | 107 | 15.08 | 20 |
| Ash, D L | Feb 18, 1944 | | 1965 | 1965 | 3 | 3 | 0 | 22 | 12 | 7.33 | 0 | 22 | 0 | — | 4 |
| Ashman, J R | May 20, 1926 | | 1951 | 1951 | 1 | 1 | 1 | 0 | 0* | — | 0 | 116 | 4 | 29.00 | 0 |
| Ashraf, Moin A | Jan 5, 1992 | | 2010 | 2013 | 21 | 19 | 5 | 56 | 10 | 4.00 | 0 | 1,268 | 43 | 29.48 | 2 |
| Aspinall, R | © Oct 26, 1918 | Aug 16, 1999 | 1946 | 1950 | 36 | 48 | 8 | 763 | 75* | 19.07 | 0 | 2,670 | 131 | 20.38 | 18 |
| Aspinall, W | Mar 24, 1858 | Jan 27, 1910 | 1880 | 1880 | 2 | 3 | 0 | 16 | 14 | 5.33 | 0 | — | — | — | 1 |
| Asquith, F T | Feb 5, 1870 | Jan 11, 1916 | 1903 | 1903 | 1 | 1 | 0 | 0 | 0 | 0.00 | 0 | — | — | — | — |
| Athey, C W J | © Sept 27, 1957 | | 1976 | 1983 | 151 | 246 | 21 | 6,320 | 134 | 28.08 | 10 | 1,003 | 21 | 47.76 | 144/2 |
| Atkinson, G R | Sept 21, 1830 | May 3, 1906 | 1861 | 1870 | 27 | 38 | 8 | 399 | 44 | 13.30 | 0 | 1,146 | 54 | 21.22 | 14 |
| Atkinson, H | Feb 1, 1881 | Dec 22, 1959 | 1907 | 1907 | 1 | 2 | 0 | 0 | 0 | 0.00 | 0 | 17 | 0 | — | 1 |
| Azeem Rafiq | Feb 27, 1991 | | 2009 | 2014 | 22 | 25 | 2 | 511 | 100 | 22.21 | 1 | 1,717 | 47 | 36.53 | 9 |
| Backhouse, E N | May 13, 1901 | Nov 1, 1936 | 1931 | 1931 | 1 | 1 | 0 | 2 | 2 | 2.00 | 0 | 4 | 0 | — | 1 |
| Badger, H D * | Mar 7, 1900 | Aug 10, 1975 | 1921 | 1922 | 2 | 4 | 2 | 6 | 6* | 3.00 | 0 | 145 | 6 | 24.16 | 1 |

| Player | Date of Birth | Date of Death (if known) | First Played | Last Played | M | Inns | NO | Runs | HS | Av'ge | 100s | Runs | Wkts | Av'ge | Ct/St |
|---|---|---|---|---|---|---|---|---|---|---|---|---|---|---|---|
| Bainbridge, A B | Oct 15, 1932 | | 1961 | 1963 | 5 | 10 | 0 | 93 | 24 | 9.30 | 0 | 358 | 20 | 17.90 | 3 |
| Baines, F E * | June 18, 1864 | Nov 17, 1948 | 1888 | 1888 | 1 | 1 | 0 | 0 | 0 | 0.00 | 0 | — | — | — | 3 |
| Bairstow, A | Aug 4, 1868 | Dec 7, 1945 | 1896 | 1900 | 24 | 24 | 1 | 69 | 12 | 4.92 | 0 | — | — | — | 41/18 |
| Bairstow, D L | © Sept 1, 1951 | Jan 5, 1998 | 1970 | 1990 | 429 | 601 | 113 | 12,985 | 145 | 26.60 | 9 | 192 | 6 | 32.00 | 907/131 |
| **Bairstow, J M** | © Sept 26, 1989 | | 2009 | 2015 | 83 | 132 | 22 | 5,539 | 219* | 50.35 | 13 | 1 | 0 | — | 214/9 |
| Baker, G R | Apr 18, 1862 | Feb 6, 1938 | 1884 | 1884 | 7 | 11 | 1 | 42 | 13 | 4.20 | 0 | 43 | 0 | — | 5 |
| Baker, R * | July 13, 1849 | June 21, 1896 | 1875 | 1875 | 3 | 5 | 1 | 45 | 22 | 11.25 | 0 | 790 | 37 | 21.35 | 3 |
| Balderstone, J C | Nov 16, 1940 | Mar 6, 2000 | 1961 | 1969 | 68 | 81 | 6 | 1,332 | 82 | 17.76 | 0 | 132 | 0 | — | 24 |
| **§Ballance, G S** | © Nov 22, 1989 | | 2008 | 2015 | 63 | 95 | 12 | 4,076 | 174 | 49.10 | 12 | — | — | — | 47 |
| Barber, A T * | © June 17, 1905 | Mar 10, 1985 | 1929 | 1930 | 42 | 54 | 3 | 1,050 | 100 | 20.58 | 0 | 404 | 14 | 28.85 | 40 |
| Barber, W | Apr 18, 1901 | Sept 10, 1968 | 1926 | 1947 | 354 | 495 | 48 | 15,315 | 255 | 34.26 | 27 | 136 | 4 | 34.00 | 163 |
| Barraclough, E S | Mar 30, 1923 | May 21, 1999 | 1949 | 1950 | 5 | 4 | 2 | 43 | 24* | 21.50 | 0 | — | — | — | 2 |
| Bates, W | Nov 19, 1855 | Jan 8, 1900 | 1877 | 1887 | 202 | 331 | 12 | 6,499 | 136 | 20.37 | 8 | 10,692 | 637 | 16.78 | 64 |
| Bates, W E | Mar 5, 1884 | Jan 17, 1957 | 1907 | 1913 | 113 | 167 | 15 | 2,634 | 81 | 17.32 | 0 | 57 | 2 | 28.50 | 14 |
| Batty, G J | Oct 13, 1977 | | 1997 | 1997 | 1 | 2 | 0 | 18 | 18 | 9.00 | 0 | 70 | 2 | 35.00 | 1 |
| Batty, J D | May 15, 1971 | | 1989 | 1994 | 64 | 67 | 20 | 703 | 36 | 14.95 | 0 | 5,286 | 140 | 37.75 | 25 |
| Bayes, G W | Feb 27, 1884 | Dec 6, 1960 | 1910 | 1921 | 18 | 24 | 11 | 165 | 24 | 12.69 | 0 | 1,534 | 48 | 31.95 | 7 |
| Beaumont, H | Oct 14, 1916 | Nov 15, 2003 | 1946 | 1947 | 28 | 46 | 6 | 716 | 60 | 17.90 | 0 | 236 | 9 | 26.22 | 11 |
| Beaumont, J | Sept 16, 1855 | May 1, 1920 | 1877 | 1878 | 5 | 9 | 3 | 60 | 24 | 10.00 | 0 | 50 | 2 | 25.00 | 1 |
| Bedford, H | July 17, 1907 | July 5, 1968 | 1928 | 1939 | 5 | 5 | 1 | 57 | 57 | 14.25 | 0 | 179 | 8 | 22.37 | 1 |
| Bedford, W | Feb 24, 1879 | | 1903 | 1903 | 2 | 2 | 1 | 38 | 30* | 38.00 | 0 | 117 | 2 | 58.50 | 1 |
| Bell, J T | June 16, 1895 | Aug 8, 1974 | 1921 | 1923 | 18 | 8 | 1 | 125 | 78 | 17.85 | 0 | 149 | 8 | 18.62 | 12 |
| Berry, John | Jan 10, 1823 | Feb 26, 1895 | 1849 | 1867 | 3 | 4 | 0 | 68 | 54 | 17.00 | 0 | — | — | — | 1 |
| Berry, Joseph | Nov 29, 1829 | Apr 20, 1894 | 1861 | 1874 | 7 | 7 | 6 | 76 | 31* | 76.00 | 0 | 401 | 7 | 57.28 | 2 |
| Berry, P J | Dec 28, 1966 | | 1986 | 1990 | 9 | 9 | 0 | 86 | 40 | 9.55 | 0 | 793 | 18 | 44.05 | 4 |
| Best T L | Aug 26, 1981 | | 2010 | 2010 | 7 | 4 | 1 | 56 | 44* | 18.66 | 0 | 720 | 10 | 72.00 | 2 |
| Betts, G | Sept 19, 1843 | Sept 26, 1902 | 1873 | 1874 | 9 | 1 | 0 | 2 | 2 | 2.00 | 0 | — | — | — | 1 |
| §Bevan, M G | © May 8, 1970 | | 1995 | 1996 | 32 | 56 | 8 | 2,823 | 160* | 58.81 | 9 | 66 | 0 | — | 24 |
| Binks, J G | Oct 5, 1935 | | 1955 | 1969 | 491 | 587 | 128 | 6,745 | 95 | 14.69 | 0 | — | — | — | 872/172 |
| Binns, J | Mar 31, 1870 | Dec 8, 1934 | 1898 | 1898 | 1 | 1 | 0 | 4 | 4 | 4.00 | 0 | — | — | — | 0/3 |
| Bird, H D | Apr 19, 1933 | | 1956 | 1959 | 14 | 25 | 2 | 613 | 181* | 26.65 | 1 | — | — | — | 3 |

# LIST OF PLAYERS AND CAREER AVERAGES IN ALL FIRST-CLASS MATCHES FOR YORKSHIRE (Continued)

| Player | Date of Birth | Date of Death (if known) | First Played | Last Played | M | Inns | NO | Runs | HS | Av'ge | 100s | Runs | Wkts | Av'ge | Ct/St |
|---|---|---|---|---|---|---|---|---|---|---|---|---|---|---|---|
| Birkenshaw, J ......... | Nov 13, 1940 | | 1958 | 1960 | 30 | 42 | 7 | 588 | 42 | 16.80 | 0 | 1,819 | 69 | 26.36 | 21 |
| Birtles, T J D ...... | Oct 26, 1886 | Jan 13, 1971 | 1913 | 1924 | 37 | 57 | 1 | 876 | 104 | 19.04 | 1 | 20 | 0 | — | 19 |
| Blackburn, J D H * .. | Oct 27, 1924 | Feb 19, 1987 | 1956 | 1956 | 1 | 2 | 1 | 18 | 15 | 9.00 | 0 | — | — | — | 1 |
| Blackburn, J S ... | Sept 24, 1852 | July 8, 1922 | 1876 | 1877 | 6 | 11 | 2 | 102 | 28 | 10.20 | 0 | 173 | 7 | 24.71 | 4 |
| § Blackburn, W E * .. | Nov 24, 1888 | June 3, 1941 | 1919 | 1920 | 10 | 13 | 6 | 26 | 6* | 3.71 | 0 | 1,113 | 45 | 24.73 | 9 |
| § Blain J A R ..... | Jan 4, 1979 | | 2004 | 2010 | 15 | 17 | 7 | 137 | 28 | 13.70 | 0 | 1,312 | 38 | 34.52 | 4 |
| Blake, W ........ | Nov 29, 1854* | Dec 2, 1931 | 1880 | 1880 | 2 | 3 | 0 | 44 | 21 | 14.66 | 0 | 17 | 1 | 17.00 | 4 |
| Blakey, R J ...... | © Jan 15, 1967 | | 1985 | 2003 | 339 | 541 | 84 | 14,150 | 223* | 30.96 | 12 | 68 | 1 | 68.00 | 768/56 |
| Blamires, E ...... | July 31, 1850 | Mar 22, 1886 | 1877 | 1877 | 1 | 2 | 0 | 23 | 17 | 11.50 | 0 | 82 | 5 | 16.40 | 0 |
| § Blewett, G S .... | © Oct 29, 1971 | | 1999 | 1999 | 12 | 23 | 2 | 655 | 190 | 31.19 | 1 | 212 | 5 | 42.40 | 5 |
| Bloom, G R ..... | Sept 13, 1941 | | 1964 | 1964 | 2 | 2 | 0 | 14 | 11 | 7.00 | 0 | — | — | — | 2 |
| Bocking, H ...... | Dec 10, 1835 | Feb 22, 1907 | 1865 | 1865 | 1 | 2 | 0 | 2 | 2 | 2.00 | 0 | — | — | — | 1 |
| Boden, J G * ..... | Dec 27, 1848 | Jan 3, 1928 | 1878 | 1878 | 1 | 1 | 0 | 6 | 6 | 6.00 | 0 | — | — | — | 0 |
| Bolton, B C * .... | Sept 23, 1862 | Nov 18, 1910 | 1890 | 1891 | 4 | 6 | 0 | 25 | 11 | 4.16 | 0 | 252 | 13 | 19.38 | 2 |
| Bolus, J B ...... | Jan 31, 1934 | | 1956 | 1962 | 107 | 179 | 16 | 4,712 | 146* | 29.26 | 7 | 407 | 13 | 31.30 | 45 |
| Booth, A ........ | © Nov 3, 1902 | Aug 17, 1974 | 1931 | 1947 | 36 | 36 | 18 | 114 | 29 | 5.70 | 0 | 1,684 | 122 | 13.80 | 10 |
| Booth, M W ..... | © Dec 10, 1886 | July 1, 1916 | 1908 | 1914 | 144 | 218 | 31 | 4,244 | 210 | 22.69 | 2 | 11,017 | 557 | 19.17 | 114 |
| Booth, P A ...... | Sept 5, 1965 | | 1982 | 1989 | 23 | 29 | 9 | 193 | 33* | 9.65 | 0 | 1,517 | 35 | 43.34 | 7 |
| Booth, R ........ | Oct 1, 1926 | | 1951 | 1955 | 65 | 76 | 28 | 730 | 53* | 15.20 | 0 | — | — | — | 79/29 |
| Bore, M K ...... | June 2, 1947 | | 1969 | 1977 | 74 | 78 | 21 | 481 | 37* | 8.43 | 0 | 4,866 | 162 | 30.03 | 27 |
| Borrill, P D ..... | July 4, 1951 | | 1971 | 1971 | 2 | — | | — | | — | 0 | 61 | 5 | 12.20 | 0 |
| Bosomworth W E | Mar 8, 1847 | June 7, 1891 | 1872 | 1880 | 4 | 7 | 1 | 20 | 7 | 3.33 | 0 | 140 | 9 | 15.55 | 2 |
| Bottomley, I H * | Apr 9, 1855 | Apr 23, 1922 | 1878 | 1880 | 9 | 12 | 0 | 166 | 32 | 13.83 | 0 | 75 | 1 | 75.00 | 5 |
| Bottomley, T .... | Dec 26, 1910 | Feb 19, 1977 | 1934 | 1935 | 6 | 7 | 0 | 142 | 51 | 20.28 | 0 | 188 | 1 | 188.00 | 5 |
| Bower, W H .... | Oct 17, 1857 | Jan 31, 1943 | 1883 | 1883 | 1 | 2 | 0 | 10 | 5 | 5.00 | 0 | — | — | — | 0 |
| Bowes, W E .... | July 25, 1908 | Sept 4, 1987 | 1929 | 1947 | 301 | 257 | 117 | 1,251 | 43* | 8.93 | 0 | 21,227 | 1,351 | 15.71 | 118 |
| Boycott, G ..... | © Oct 21, 1940 | | 1962 | 1986 | 414 | 674 | 111 | 32,570 | 260* | 57.85 | 103 | 665 | 28 | 23.75 | 200 |
| Brackin, T ...... | Jan 5, 1859 | Oct 7, 1924 | 1882 | 1882 | 3 | 6 | 0 | 12 | 9 | 2.00 | 0 | — | — | — | 0 |
| Brayshay, P B * | Oct 14, 1916 | July 6, 2004 | 1952 | 1952 | 1 | 2 | 0 | 20 | 13 | 6.66 | 0 | 104 | 3 | 34.66 | 0 |
| Brearley, H * .... | June 26, 1913 | Aug 14, 2007 | 1937 | 1937 | 1 | 2 | 0 | 17 | 9 | 8.50 | 0 | — | — | — | 0 |
| Brennan, D V * | © Feb 10, 1920 | Jan 9, 1985 | 1947 | 1953 | 204 | 221 | 66 | 1,653 | 47 | 10.66 | 0 | — | — | — | 280/100 |

# LIST OF PLAYERS AND CAREER AVERAGES IN ALL FIRST-CLASS MATCHES FOR YORKSHIRE (Continued)

| Player | Date of Birth | Date of Death (if known) | First Played | Last Played | M | Inns | NO | Runs | HS | Av'ge | 100s | Runs | Wkts | Av'ge | Ct/St |
|---|---|---|---|---|---|---|---|---|---|---|---|---|---|---|---|
| **Bresnan, T T** ...© | **Feb 28, 1985** | | 2003 | 2015 | 123 | 165 | 28 | 4,005 | 169* | 29.23 | 4 | 10,501 | 339 | 30.97 | 58 |
| Britton, G | Feb 7, 1843 | Jan 3, 1910 | 1867 | 1867 | 3 | 5 | 1 | 3 | 3 | 1.50 | 0 | | | | 1 |
| Broadbent, A | June 7, 1879 | July 19, 1958 | 1909 | 1910 | 3 | 5 | 0 | 66 | 29 | 13.20 | 0 | 252 | 5 | 50.40 | 1 |
| Broadhead, W B | May 31, 1903 | Apr 2, 1986 | 1929 | 1929 | 2 | 2 | 0 | 5 | 5 | 2.50 | 0 | | | | 0 |
| Broadhurst, M | June 20, 1974 | | 1991 | 1994 | 5 | 3 | 0 | 7 | 6 | 2.33 | 0 | 231 | 7 | 33.00 | 1 |
| § Brophy, G L ...© | Nov 26, 1975 | | 2006 | 2012 | 73 | 112 | 12 | 3,012 | 177* | 30.12 | 3 | 6 | 0 | — | 176/15 |
| Brook, J W | Feb 1, 1897 | | 1923 | 1923 | 1 | 1 | 0 | 0 | 0 | 0.00 | 0 | | | | 0 |
| Brooke, B | Mar 3, 1930 | Mar.3 1989 | 1950 | 1950 | 2 | 4 | 0 | 16 | 14 | 4.00 | 0 | 191 | 2 | 95.50 | 0 |
| § Brooks, J A ...© | **June 4, 1984** | | 2013 | 2015 | 45 | 47 | 16 | 473 | 50* | 15.25 | 0 | 4,463 | 182 | 24.52 | 14 |
| Broughton, P N | Oct 22, 1935 | | 1956 | 1956 | 6 | 5 | 0 | 19 | 12 | 6.33 | 0 | 365 | 16 | 22.81 | 1 |
| Brown, A | June 10, 1854 | Nov 2, 1900 | 1872 | 1872 | 3 | 3 | 0 | 5 | 5 | 3.00 | 0 | 47 | 3 | 15.66 | 4 |
| Brown, J T (Driffield) © | Aug 20, 1869 | Nov 4, 1904 | 1889 | 1904 | 345 | 567 | 41 | 15,694 | 311 | 29.83 | 23 | 5,183 | 177 | 29.28 | 188 |
| Brown, J T (Darfield) | Nov 24, 1874 | Apr 12, 1950 | 1897 | 1903 | 30 | 32 | 3 | 333 | 37* | 11.48 | 0 | 2,071 | 97 | 21.35 | 18 |
| Brown, W | Nov 19, 1876 | July 27, 1945 | 1902 | 1908 | 2 | 2 | 1 | 2 | 2 | 2.00 | 0 | 84 | 4 | 21.00 | 0 |
| Brownhill, T | Oct 10, 1838 | Jan 6, 1915 | 1861 | 1871 | 14 | 20 | 3 | 185 | 25 | 10.88 | 0 | | | | 7 |
| Brumfitt, J * | Feb. 18, 1917 | Mar 16, 1987 | 1938 | 1938 | 1 | 1 | 0 | 9 | 9 | 9.00 | 0 | | | | 0 |
| Buller, J S | Aug 23, 1909 | Aug 7, 1970 | 1930 | 1930 | 2 | 2 | 0 | 5 | 5 | 2.50 | 0 | | | | 2 |
| Bulmer, J R L | Dec 28, 1867 | Jan 20, 1917 | 1891 | 1891 | 1 | 2 | 0 | 0 | 0 | 0.00 | 0 | | | | 0 |
| Burgess, T | Oct 1, 1859 | Feb 22, 1922 | 1895 | 1895 | 1 | 2 | 1 | 0 | 0* | 0.00 | 0 | | | | 0 |
| Burgin, E | Jan 4, 1924 | Nov 11, 2012 | 1952 | 1953 | 12 | 10 | 3 | 92 | 32 | 13.14 | 0 | 795 | 31 | 25.64 | 2 |
| Burman, J | Oct 5, 1838 | May 14, 1900 | 1867 | 1867 | 1 | 2 | 1 | 1 | 1* | 1.00 | 0 | | | | 0 |
| Burnet, J R * | Oct 11, 1918 | Mar 7, 1999 | 1958 | 1959 | 54 | 75 | 6 | 889 | 54 | 12.88 | 0 | 26 | 1 | 26.00 | 7 |
| § Burrows, M | Aug 18, 1855 | May 29, 1893 | 1880 | 1880 | 6 | 10 | 1 | 82 | 23 | 8.20 | 0 | | | | 2 |
| Burton, D C F * | Sept 13, 1887 | Sept 24, 1971 | 1907 | 1921 | 104 | 130 | 15 | 2,273 | 142* | 19.76 | 0 | 47 | 1 | | 44 |
| Burton, R C * | Apr 11, 1891 | Apr 30, 1971 | 1914 | 1914 | 1 | 2 | 0 | 47 | 47 | 23.50 | 0 | 73 | 6 | 12.16 | 2 |
| Butterfield, E B * | Oct 22, 1848 | May 6, 1899 | 1870 | 1870 | 1 | 2 | 0 | 18 | 10 | 9.00 | 0 | | | | 0 |
| Byas, D ...© | Aug 26, 1963 | | 1986 | 2001 | 268 | 449 | 42 | 14,398 | 213 | 35.37 | 28 | 727 | 12 | 60.58 | 351 |
| Byrom, J L * | July, 20, 1851 | Aug 24, 1931 | 1874 | 1874 | 2 | 4 | 0 | 19 | 11 | 4.75 | 0 | | | | 1 |
| Cammish, J W | May 21, 1921 | July 16, 1974 | 1954 | 1954 | 2 | 1 | 0 | 0 | 0 | 0.00 | 0 | | | | 0 |
| Carrick, P ...© | July, 16 1952 | Jan 11, 2000 | 1970 | 1993 | 425 | 543 | 102 | 9,994 | 131* | 22.66 | 3 | 30,530 | 1,018 | 29.99 | 183 |

# LIST OF PLAYERS AND CAREER AVERAGES IN ALL FIRST-CLASS MATCHES FOR YORKSHIRE (Continued)

| Player | Date of Birth | Date of Death (if known) | First Played | Last Played | M | Inns | NO | Runs | HS | Av'ge | 100s | Runs | Wkts | Av'ge | Ct/St |
|---|---|---|---|---|---|---|---|---|---|---|---|---|---|---|---|
| Carter, Rev E S * | Feb 3, 1845 | May 23, 1923 | 1876 | 1881 | 14 | 21 | 2 | 210 | 39* | 11.05 | 0 | 104 | 8 | 13.00 | 4 |
| Cartman, W H | June 20, 1861 | Jan 16, 1935 | 1891 | 1891 | 3 | 6 | 0 | 57 | 49 | 9.50 | 0 | — | — | — | 0 |
| **Carver, K** | **Mar 26, 1996** | | **2014** | **2015** | **3** | **4** | **2** | **30** | **16** | **15.00** | **0** | **140** | **7** | **20.00** | **1** |
| Cawthray, G | Sept 28, 1913 | Jan 5, 2000 | 1939 | 1952 | 4 | 6 | 0 | 114 | 30 | 19.00 | 0 | 304 | 4 | 76.00 | 1 |
| Chadwick, J P G | Nov 8, 1934 | | 1960 | 1965 | 6 | 9 | 3 | 106 | 59 | 17.66 | 0 | 67 | 2 | 33.50 | 7 |
| Champion, A | Dec 27, 1851 | June 26, 1909 | 1876 | 1879 | 14 | 23 | 4 | 148 | 29 | 7.78 | 0 | 17 | 1 | 17.00 | 7 |
| Chapman, C A | June 8, 1871 | | 1890 | 1898 | 8 | 13 | 2 | 238 | 80 | 21.63 | 0 | — | — | — | 13/3 |
| Charlesworth, A P | Feb 19, 1865 | May 11, 1926 | 1894 | 1895 | 7 | 12 | 1 | 241 | 63 | 21.90 | 0 | — | — | — | 7 |
| § Chichester-Constable, R C J * | Dec 21, 1890 | May 26, 1963 | 1919 | 1919 | 1 | 1 | 0 | 0 | 0 | 0.00 | 0 | — | — | — | 0 |
| Clarkson, A | Sept 5, 1939 | | 1963 | 1963 | 6 | 8 | 1 | 80 | 30 | 11.42 | 0 | 92 | 5 | 18.40 | 5 |
| Claughton, H M | Dec 24, 1891 | Oct 17, 1980 | 1914 | 1919 | 4 | 8 | 2 | 39 | 15 | 6.50 | 0 | 176 | 3 | 58.66 | 1 |
| § Claydon, M E | Nov 25, 1982 | | 2005 | 2006 | 1 | 2 | 0 | 38 | 38 | 19.00 | 0 | 263 | 3 | 87.66 | 0 |
| § Clayton, R O | Jan 1, 1844 | Nov 26, 1901 | 1870 | 1879 | 70 | 115 | 23 | 992 | 62 | 10.78 | 0 | 2,478 | 153 | 16.19 | 26 |
| § Cleary, M F | July 19, 1980 | | 2005 | 2005 | 1 | 2 | 0 | 23 | 12 | 11.50 | 0 | 250 | 8 | 31.25 | 2 |
| Clegg, H | Dec 8, 1850 | Dec 30, 1920 | 1881 | 1881 | 6 | 8 | 1 | 63 | 25* | 9.00 | 0 | — | — | — | 2 |
| Clifford, C C | © July, 5, 1942 | | 1972 | 1972 | 11 | 12 | 4 | 39 | 12* | 4.87 | 0 | 666 | 26 | 25.61 | 5 |
| Close, D B | Feb 24, 1931 | Sept 14, 2015 | 1949 | 1970 | 536 | 811 | 102 | 22,650 | 198 | 31.94 | 33 | 23,489 | 967 | 24.29 | 564 |
| Clough, G D | May 23, 1978 | | 1998 | 1998 | 2 | 2 | 0 | 34 | 33 | 17.00 | 0 | 11 | 0 | — | 0 |
| Collinson, R W * | Nov 6, 1875 | Dec 26, 1963 | 1897 | 1897 | 2 | 3 | 0 | 58 | 34 | 19.33 | 0 | — | — | — | 2 |
| Cooper, H P | Apr 17, 1949 | | 1971 | 1980 | 98 | 107 | 29 | 1,159 | 56 | 14.85 | 0 | 6,327 | 227 | 27.87 | 60 |
| Cooper, P E * | Feb 19, 1885 | May 21, 1950 | 1910 | 1910 | 1 | 2 | 2 | 0 | 0 | 0.00 | 0 | — | — | — | 0 |
| Cope, G A * | © Feb 23, 1947 | | 1966 | 1980 | 230 | 249 | 89 | 2,241 | 78 | 14.00 | 0 | 15,627 | 630 | 24.80 | 64 |
| Corbett, A M | Nov 25, 1855 | Oct 7, 1934 | 1881 | 1881 | 2 | 2 | 0 | 2 | 2 | 1.00 | 0 | — | — | — | 1 |
| Coverdale, S P | Nov 20, 1954 | | 1973 | 1980 | 6 | 4 | 0 | 31 | 18 | 7.75 | 0 | — | — | — | 0 |
| Coverdale, W * | July 8, 1862 | Sept 23, 1934 | 1888 | 1888 | 2 | 2 | 0 | 2 | 1 | 1.00 | 0 | — | — | — | 11/4 |
| Cowan, M J | June 10, 1933 | | 1953 | 1962 | 91 | 84 | 48 | 170 | 19* | 4.72 | 0 | 6,389 | 266 | 24.01 | 37 |
| Cownley, J M * | © Feb 24, 1929 | Nov 7, 1998 | 1952 | 1952 | 2 | 2 | 0 | 2 | 1 | 1.00 | 0 | 119 | 1 | 119.00 | 1 |
| Coxon, V J | © Jan 18, 1916 | Jan 22, 2006 | 1945 | 1950 | 142 | 182 | 33 | 2,747 | 83 | 18.43 | 0 | 9,528 | 464 | 20.53 | 124 |
| Craven, V J | July 31, 1980 | | 2000 | 2004 | 33 | 55 | 6 | 1,206 | 81* | 24.61 | 0 | 584 | 18 | 33.93 | 18 |
| Crawford, G H | Dec 15, 1890 | June 28, 1975 | 1914 | 1926 | 9 | 8 | 0 | 46 | 19 | 5.75 | 0 | 541 | 21 | 25.76 | 3 |

# LIST OF PLAYERS AND CAREER AVERAGES IN ALL FIRST-CLASS MATCHES FOR YORKSHIRE (Continued)

| Player | Date of Birth | Date of Death (if known) | First Played | Last Played | M | Inns | NO | Runs | HS | Av'ge | 100s | Runs | Wkts | Av'ge | Ct/St |
|---|---|---|---|---|---|---|---|---|---|---|---|---|---|---|---|
| Crawford, M G * | July 30, 1920 | Dec 2, 2012 | 1951 | 1951 | 4 | 2 | 0 | 22 | 13 | 11.00 | 0 | 181 | 10 | 18.10 | 1 |
| Creighton, E | July 9, 1859 | Feb 17, 1931 | 1888 | 1888 | 8 | 8 | 2 | 33 | 10 | 5.50 | 0 | | | | 0 |
| Crick, H | Jan 29, 1910 | Feb 10, 1960 | 1937 | 1947 | 8 | 10 | 0 | 88 | 20 | 8.80 | 0 | | | | 18/4 |
| Crookes, R | Oct 9, 1846 | Feb 15, 1897 | 1879 | 1879 | 1 | 2 | 1 | 2 | 2* | 2.00 | 0 | 14 | 0 | | 0 |
| Crossland, S M | Aug 16, 1851 | April 11, 1906 | 1883 | 1886 | 4 | 6 | 2 | 32 | 20 | 8.00 | 0 | | | | 3/5 |
| Crowther, A | Aug 1, 1878 | June 4, 1946 | 1905 | 1905 | 2 | 2 | 0 | 0 | 0 | 0.00 | 0 | | | | 1 |
| Cuttell, W | Jan 28, 1835 | June 10, 1896 | 1862 | 1871 | 15 | 27 | 6 | 271 | 56 | 12.90 | 0 | 596 | 36 | 16.55 | 4 |
| Dalton, A J | Mar 14, 1947 | | 1969 | 1972 | 21 | 31 | 2 | 710 | 128 | 24.48 | 3 | | | | 6 |
| § Darnton, T | Feb 12, 1836 | Oct 18, 1874 | 1864 | 1868 | 13 | 22 | 1 | 314 | 81* | 14.95 | 0 | 349 | 12 | 29.08 | 3 |
| Davidson, K R | © Dec 24, 1905 | Dec 25, 1935 | 1933 | 1935 | 30 | 46 | 5 | 1,331 | 128 | 32.46 | 2 | | | | 18 |
| Dawes, J | Feb 14, 1836 | Not known | 1865 | 1865 | 5 | 9 | 2 | 93 | 28* | 13.28 | 0 | 196 | 5 | 39.20 | 3 |
| Dawood, I | July 23, 1976 | | 2004 | 2005 | 20 | 31 | 7 | 636 | 75 | 26.50 | 0 | | | | 46/3 |
| Dawson, E | May 1, 1835 | Dec 1, 1888 | 1863 | 1874 | 16 | 25 | 1 | 224 | 20 | 9.33 | 0 | | | | 5 |
| Dawson, R K J | © Aug 4, 1980 | | 2001 | 2006 | 72 | 106 | 9 | 2,179 | 87 | 22.46 | 0 | 6,444 | 157 | 41.04 | 39 |
| Dawson, W A * | Dec 3, 1850 | Mar 6, 1916 | 1870 | 1870 | 1 | 2 | 0 | 0 | 0 | 0.00 | 0 | | | | 1 |
| Day, A G * | Sept 20, 1865 | Oct 16, 1908 | 1885 | 1888 | 6 | 10 | 0 | 78 | 25 | 7.80 | 0 | | | | 3 |
| Dennis, F | © June 11, 1907 | Nov 21, 2000 | 1928 | 1933 | 89 | 100 | 28 | 1,332 | 67 | 18.50 | 0 | 4,517 | 156 | 28.95 | 58 |
| Dennis, S J | Oct 18, 1960 | | 1980 | 1988 | 67 | 62 | 24 | 338 | 53* | 8.89 | 0 | 5,548 | 173 | 32.06 | 19 |
| Denton, D | © July 4, 1874 | Feb 16, 1950 | 1894 | 1920 | 676 | 1,058 | 61 | 33,282 | 221 | 33.38 | 61 | 957 | 34 | 28.14 | 360/1 |
| Denton, J | Feb 3, 1865 | July 19, 1946 | 1887 | 1888 | 15 | 24 | 1 | 222 | 59 | 9.65 | 0 | | | | 6 |
| Dewse, H | Feb 23, 1836 | July 8, 1910 | 1873 | 1873 | 1 | 2 | 0 | 14 | 12 | 7.00 | 0 | 15 | | | |
| Deyes, G | Feb 11, 1879 | Jan 11, 1963 | 1905 | 1907 | 17 | 24 | 4 | 44 | 12 | 2.20 | 0 | 944 | 41 | 23.02 | 6 |
| Dick, R D * | Apr 16, 1889 | Dec 14, 1983 | 1911 | 1911 | 1 | 2 | 0 | 2 | 1 | 1.00 | 0 | 37 | 2 | 18.50 | 1 |
| Dobson, M J | Feb 22, 1854 | Sept 17, 1932 | 1879 | 1879 | 2 | 3 | 0 | 1 | 1 | 0.33 | 0 | 106 | 1 | | 1 |
| Doidge, M J | July 2, 1970 | | 1990 | 1990 | 1 | 2 | 0 | 1 | 1 | 0.50 | 0 | 28 | | | 0 |
| Dolphin, A | © Dec 24, 1885 | Oct 23, 1942 | 1905 | 1927 | 427 | 446 | 157 | 3,325 | 66 | 11.50 | 0 | 1,310 | 49 | 26.73 | 569/260 |
| Douglas, J S | Apr 4, 1903 | Dec 27, 1971 | 1925 | 1934 | 23 | 26 | 8 | 125 | 19 | 6.94 | 0 | | | | 14 |
| Drake, A | © Apr 16, 1884 | Feb 14, 1919 | 1909 | 1914 | 156 | 244 | 24 | 4,789 | 147* | 21.76 | 3 | 8,623 | 479 | 18.00 | 93 |
| Drake, A | Sept 1, 1893 | May 22, 1967 | 1923 | 1924 | 3 | 4 | 1 | 21 | 21 | 7.00 | 0 | 117 | 1 | 117.00 | 2 |
| Driver, J | May 16, 1861 | Dec 10, 1946 | 1889 | 1889 | 2 | 4 | 1 | 24 | 8 | 8.00 | 0 | | | | 2 |

# LIST OF PLAYERS AND CAREER AVERAGES IN ALL FIRST-CLASS MATCHES FOR YORKSHIRE (Continued)

| Player | Date of Birth | Date of Death (if known) | First Played | Last Played | M | Inns | NO | Runs | HS | Av'ge | 100s | Runs | Wkts | Av'ge | Ct/St |
|---|---|---|---|---|---|---|---|---|---|---|---|---|---|---|---|
| Dury, T S * | June 12, 1854 | Mar 20, 1932 | 1878 | 1881 | 13 | 24 | 1 | 329 | 46 | 14.30 | 0 | 21 | 0 | — | 3 |
| Dyson, W L | Dec 11, 1857 | May 1, 1936 | 1887 | 1887 | 2 | 4 | 0 | 8 | 6 | 2.00 | 0 | — | — | — | 2 |
| Earnshaw, W | Sept 20, 1867 | Nov 25, 1941 | 1893 | 1896 | 6 | 7 | 3 | 44 | 23 | 11.00 | 0 | 349 | 11 | 31.72 | 6/2 |
| Eastwood, D | Mar 30, 1848 | May 17, 1903 | 1870 | 1877 | 29 | 51 | 2 | 591 | 68 | 12.06 | 0 | 62 | 0 | — | 16 |
| Eckersley, R | Sept 4, 1925 | May 30, 2009 | 1945 | 1945 | 1 | 1 | 0 | 9 | 9* | | 0 | | | | 0 |
| Elam, F W * | Sept 13, 1871 | Mar 19, 1943 | 1900 | 1902 | 2 | 3 | 1 | 48 | 28 | 24.00 | 0 | | | | 0 |
| § Elliott, M T G | Sept 28, 1971 | | 2002 | 2002 | 5 | 10 | 1 | 487 | 127 | 54.11 | 1 | 77 | 1 | 77.00 | 7 |
| Ellis, J E | Nov 10, 1864 | Dec 1, 1927 | 1888 | 1892 | 11 | 15 | 6 | 14 | 4* | 1.55 | 0 | | | | 11/10 |
| Ellis, S * | Nov 23, 1851 | Oct 28, 1930 | 1880 | 1880 | 2 | 3 | 0 | 12 | 9 | 4.00 | 0 | | | | 1 |
| Elms, J E | Dec 24, 1874 | Nov 1, 1951 | 1905 | 1905 | 1 | 2 | 0 | 20 | 20 | 10.00 | 0 | 28 | 1 | 28.00 | 2 |
| Elstub, C J | Feb 3, 1981 | | 2000 | 2002 | 2 | 2 | 1 | 28 | 18* | 28.00 | 0 | 356 | 9 | 39.55 | 1 |
| Emmett, T | © Sept 3, 1841 | June 29, 1904 | 1866 | 1888 | 299 | 484 | 65 | 6,315 | 104 | 15.07 | 1 | 15,465 | 1,216 | 12.71 | 179 |
| Farrar, A | Apr 29, 1884 | Dec 25, 1954 | 1906 | 1906 | 1 | 1 | 0 | 2 | 2 | 2.00 | 0 | | | | 0 |
| Fearnley, M C | Aug 21, 1936 | July 7, 1979 | 1962 | 1964 | 3 | 4 | 2 | 19 | 11* | 9.50 | 0 | 133 | 6 | 22.16 | 1 |
| Featherby, W D | Aug 18, 1888 | Nov 20, 1958 | 1920 | 1920 | 2 | | | | | | — | 12 | 0 | — | 0 |
| Fellows, G M | July 30, 1978 | | 1998 | 2003 | 46 | 71 | 6 | 1,526 | 109 | 23.47 | 1 | 1,202 | 32 | 37.56 | 23 |
| Fiddling, K | Oct 13, 1917 | June 19, 1992 | 1938 | 1946 | 18 | 24 | 6 | 182 | 25 | 10.11 | 0 | | | | 24/13 |
| § **Finch, A J** | © **Nov 27, 1986** | | **2014** | **2015** | **8** | **10** | **1** | **415** | **110** | **46.11** | **1** | **40** | **1** | **40.00** | **11** |
| Firth, A * | Sept 3, 1847 | Jan 16, 1927 | 1869 | 1869 | 1 | 1 | 0 | 4 | 4 | 4.00 | 0 | | | | 0 |
| Firth, Rev E B * | Apr 11, 1863 | July 25, 1905 | 1894 | 1894 | 1 | 1 | 0 | 1 | 1 | 1.00 | 0 | | | | 0 |
| Firth, J | June 27, 1918 | Sept 7, 1981 | 1949 | 1950 | 8 | 8 | 5 | 134 | 67* | 44.66 | 0 | | | | 14/2 |
| Fisher, H | Aug 3, 1903 | Apr 16, 1974 | 1928 | 1936 | 52 | 58 | 14 | 681 | 76* | 15.47 | 0 | 2,621 | 93 | 28.18 | 22 |
| Fisher, I D | Mar 31, 1976 | | 1996 | 2001 | 24 | 32 | 9 | 545 | 68* | 23.69 | 0 | 1,382 | 43 | 32.13 | 1 |
| **Fisher, M D** | © **Nov 9, 1997** | | **2015** | **2015** | **3** | **2** | **1** | **0** | **0*** | **0.00** | **0** | **243** | **5** | **48.60** | **1** |
| Flaxington, S | Oct 14, 1860 | Mar 10, 1895 | 1882 | 1882 | 4 | 8 | 1 | 121 | 57 | 15.12 | 0 | | | | 1 |
| § Fleming, S P | Apr 1, 1973 | | 2003 | 2003 | 7 | 14 | 2 | 469 | 98 | 39.08 | 0 | | | | 13 |
| Fletcher, S D | © June 8, 1964 | | 1983 | 1991 | 107 | 91 | 31 | 414 | 28* | 6.90 | 0 | 7,966 | 234 | 34.04 | 25 |
| Fletcher, W | Feb 16, 1866 | June 1, 1935 | 1892 | 1892 | 5 | 8 | 1 | 80 | 31* | 11.42 | 0 | 157 | 7 | 22.42 | 4 |
| Foord, C W | June 11, 1924 | July 8, 2015 | 1947 | 1953 | 51 | 34 | 16 | 114 | 35 | 6.33 | 0 | 3,412 | 126 | 27.07 | 19 |
| Foster, E | Nov 23, 1873 | April 16, 1956 | 1901 | 1901 | 1 | 1 | 0 | 2 | 2 | 2.00 | 0 | 27 | 0 | — | 0 |

# LIST OF PLAYERS AND CAREER AVERAGES IN ALL FIRST-CLASS MATCHES FOR YORKSHIRE (Continued)

| Player | Date of Birth | Date of Death (if known) | First Played | Last Played | M | Inns | NO | Runs | HS | Av'ge | 100s | Runs | Wkts | Av'ge | Ct/St |
|---|---|---|---|---|---|---|---|---|---|---|---|---|---|---|---|
| Foster, M J | Sept 17, 1972 | | 1993 | 1994 | 5 | 7 | 1 | 165 | 63* | 27.50 | 0 | 156 | 6 | 25.00 | 6 |
| § Foster, T W | Nov 12, 1871 | Jan 31, 1947 | 1894 | 1895 | 14 | 20 | 5 | 138 | 25 | 9.20 | 0 | 952 | 58 | 16.41 | 6 |
| Frank, J * | Dec 17, 1857 | Oct 22, 1940 | 1881 | 1881 | 1 | 2 | 0 | 10 | 7 | 5.00 | 0 | 17 | 1 | 17.00 | 3 |
| Frank, R W * | ©May 29, 1864 | Sept 9, 1950 | 1889 | 1903 | 18 | 28 | 4 | 298 | 58 | 12.41 | 0 | 9 | 0 | — | 8 |
| Freeman, J R | July 27, 1843 | Nov 18, 1895 | 1865 | 1880 | 32 | 54 | 2 | 752 | 53 | 14.46 | 0 | 2,079 | 209 | 9.94 | 16 |
| **Gale, A W** | ©**Nov 28, 1983** | | 2004 | 2015 | 133 | 207 | 16 | 7,155 | 272 | 37.46 | 19 | 238 | 1 | 238.00 | 44 |
| Geldart, C J | Dec 17, 1991 | | 2010 | 2011 | 2 | 2 | 0 | 51 | 34 | 25.50 | 0 | — | — | — | 1 |
| Gibb, P A * | July 11, 1913 | Dec 7, 1977 | 1935 | 1946 | 36 | 54 | 7 | 1,545 | 157* | 32.87 | 3 | 82 | 3 | 27.33 | 25/8 |
| Gibson, B P ** | Mar 31, 1996 | | 2011 | 2011 | 1 | 1 | 0 | 1 | 1* | 1.00 | 0 | — | — | — | 6/0 |
| § Gifkins, C J * | Feb 19, 1856 | Jan 31, 1897 | 1880 | 1880 | 2 | 3 | 1 | 30 | 23 | 15.00 | 0 | — | — | — | 1 |
| Gilbert, C R | Apr 16, 1984 | | 2007 | 2007 | 1 | 1 | 0 | 11 | 11* | 11.00 | 0 | 11 | 0 | — | 1 |
| Gill, F | Sept 3, 1883 | Nov 1, 1917 | 1906 | 1906 | 2 | 4 | 0 | 18 | 11 | 4.50 | 0 | — | — | — | 0 |
| § Gillespie, J N | ©April 19, 1975 | | 2006 | 2007 | 26 | 34 | 11 | 640 | 123* | 27.82 | 1 | 2,013 | 59 | 34.11 | 4 |
| Gillhouley, K | Aug 8, 1934 | | 1961 | 1961 | 24 | 31 | 7 | 323 | 56* | 13.45 | 0 | 1,702 | 77 | 22.10 | 16 |
| Gough, D | Sept 18, 1970 | | 1989 | 2008 | 146 | 188 | 29 | 2,922 | 121 | 18.37 | 1 | 12,487 | 453 | 27.56 | 30 |
| Goulder, A | Aug 16, 1907 | June 11, 1986 | 1929 | 1929 | 2 | 1 | 0 | 3 | 3 | 3.00 | 0 | 90 | 3 | 30.00 | 0 |
| § Gray, A K D | May 19, 1974 | | 2001 | 2004 | 18 | 26 | 3 | 649 | 104 | 28.21 | 1 | 1,357 | 30 | 45.23 | 16 |
| Grayson, A P | Mar 31, 1971 | | 1990 | 1995 | 52 | 80 | 10 | 1,958 | 100 | 27.97 | 1 | 846 | 13 | 65.07 | 36 |
| Greenwood, A | Aug 20, 1847 | Feb 12, 1889 | 1869 | 1880 | 95 | 166 | 12 | 2,762 | 91 | 17.93 | 0 | 9 | 0 | — | 33 |
| Greenwood, F E * | ©Sept 28, 1905 | July 30, 1963 | 1929 | 1932 | 57 | 66 | 8 | 1,458 | 104* | 25.13 | 1 | 36 | 0 | — | 37 |
| Greenwood, L | July 13, 1834 | Nov 1, 1909 | 1861 | 1874 | 50 | 84 | 7 | 885 | 83 | 12.29 | 0 | 1,615 | 85 | 19.00 | 24 |
| Grimshaw, C H | May 12, 1880 | Sept 25, 1947 | 1904 | 1908 | 54 | 75 | 7 | 1,219 | 85 | 17.92 | 0 | 221 | 7 | 31.57 | 42 |
| Grimshaw, I | May 4, 1857 | Jan 18, 1911 | 1880 | 1887 | 125 | 194 | 14 | 3,354 | 129* | 18.63 | 4 | 8 | 0 | — | 76/3 |
| Guy, S M | Nov 17, 1978 | | 2000 | 2011 | 37 | 52 | 6 | 742 | 52* | 16.13 | 0 | — | — | — | 98/12 |
| Haggas, S | Apr 18, 1856 | Mar 14, 1926 | 1878 | 1882 | 31 | 47 | 3 | 478 | 43 | 10.86 | 0 | — | — | — | 10 |
| Haigh, S | ©Mar 19, 1871 | Feb 27, 1921 | 1895 | 1913 | 513 | 687 | 110 | 10,993 | 159 | 19.05 | 4 | 29,289 | 1,876 | 15.61 | 276 |
| Hall, B | Sept 16, 1929 | Feb 27, 1989 | 1952 | 1952 | 1 | 2 | 0 | 14 | 10 | 7.00 | 0 | 55 | 1 | 55.00 | 1 |
| Hall, C H | Apr 5, 1906 | Dec 11, 1976 | 1928 | 1934 | 23 | 22 | 9 | 67 | 15* | 5.15 | 0 | 1,226 | 45 | 27.24 | 11 |

** At 15 years and 27 days on April 27, 2011, First Day of Yorkshire's match v. Durham MCCU, he became the youngest ever English First Class cricketer.

| Player | Date of Birth | Date of Death (if known) | First Played | Last Played | M | Inns | NO | Runs | HS | Av'ge | 100s | Runs | Wkts | Av'ge | Ct/St |
|---|---|---|---|---|---|---|---|---|---|---|---|---|---|---|---|
| § Hall, J | Nov 11, 1815 | Apr 17, 1888 | 1844 | 1863 | 1 | 2 | 0 | 4 | 3 | 2.00 | 0 | — | — | — | 2 |
| Hall, L | Nov 1, 1852 © | Nov 19, 1915 | 1873 | 1894 | 275 | 477 | 58 | 9,757 | 160 | 23.28 | 9 | 781 | 15 | 52.06 | 173 |
| Halliday, H | Feb 9, 1920 © | Aug 27, 1967 | 1938 | 1953 | 182 | 279 | 18 | 8,361 | 144 | 32.03 | 12 | 3,119 | 101 | 30.88 | 140 |
| Halliday, C | Dec 5, 1852 | Mar 23, 1929 | 1872 | 1872 | 3 | 5 | 0 | 27 | 17 | 5.40 | 0 | — | — | — | 2 |
| Hamer, A | Dec 8, 1916 | Nov 3, 1993 | 1938 | 1938 | 2 | 2 | 0 | 3 | 3 | 1.50 | 0 | 64 | 1 | 64.00 | 2 |
| § Hamilton, G M | Sept 16, 1974 © | | 1994 | 2003 | 73 | 108 | 18 | 2,228 | 125 | 24.75 | 1 | 5,479 | 222 | 24.68 | 25 |
| Hampshire, A W | Oct 18, 1950 | | 1975 | 1975 | 1 | 2 | 0 | 18 | 17 | 9.00 | 0 | — | — | — | 1 |
| Hampshire, J | Oct 5, 1913 | May 23, 1997 | 1937 | 1937 | 3 | 2 | 0 | 5 | 5 | 2.50 | 0 | 109 | 5 | 21.80 | 1 |
| Hampshire, J H © | Feb 10, 1941 | | 1961 | 1981 | 456 | 724 | 89 | 21,979 | 183* | 34.61 | 34 | 1,108 | 24 | 46.16 | 368 |
| Hannon-Dalby, O J | Jun 20, 1989 | | 2008 | 2012 | 24 | 25 | 10 | 45 | 11* | 3.00 | 0 | 1,938 | 43 | 45.06 | 2 |
| § Harbord, W E * | Dec 15, 1908 | July 28, 1992 | 1929 | 1935 | 16 | 21 | 1 | 411 | 69 | 20.55 | 0 | — | — | — | 7 |
| § Harden, R J | Aug 16, 1965 | | 1999 | 2000 | 12 | 22 | 3 | 439 | 69 | 23.10 | 0 | — | — | — | 2 |
| Hardisty, C H © | Dec 10, 1885 | | 1906 | 1909 | 38 | 55 | 5 | 991 | 84 | 19.82 | 0 | — | — | — | 18 |
| Hargreaves, H S | Mar 22, 1913 | Sept 29, 1990 | 1934 | 1938 | 18 | 20 | 6 | 51 | 9 | 3.64 | 0 | 1,145 | 55 | 20.81 | 7 |
| § Harmison, S J | Oct 23, 1978 | | 2012 | 2012 | 3 | 3 | 0 | 25 | 23 | 8.33 | 0 | 195 | 8 | 24.37 | 1 |
| Harris, W | Nov 21, 1861 | May 23, 1923 | 1884 | 1887 | 4 | 8 | 2 | 45 | 25 | 7.50 | 0 | 18 | 0 | — | 2 |
| Harrison, G P © | Feb 11, 1862 | Sept 14, 1940 | 1883 | 1892 | 59 | 87 | 26 | 407 | 28 | 6.67 | 0 | 3,276 | 226 | 14.49 | 36 |
| Harrison, H | Jan 26, 1885 | Feb 11, 1962 | 1907 | 1907 | 2 | 1 | 1 | 4 | 4* | — | 0 | 39 | 1 | 19.50 | 1 |
| Harrison, W H | May 27, 1863 | July 15, 1939 | 1888 | 1888 | 3 | 6 | 1 | 12 | 7 | 2.40 | 0 | — | — | — | 0 |
| Hart, H W * | Sept 21, 1859 | Nov 2, 1895 | 1888 | 1888 | 1 | 2 | 0 | 6 | 6 | 3.00 | 0 | 32 | 2 | 16.00 | 1 |
| Hart, P R | Jan 12, 1947 | | 1981 | 1981 | 3 | 5 | 0 | 23 | 11 | 4.60 | 0 | 140 | 2 | 70.00 | 2 |
| Hartington, H E | Sept 18, 1881 | Feb 16, 1950 | 1910 | 1911 | 10 | 10 | 4 | 51 | 16 | 8.50 | 0 | 764 | 23 | 33.21 | 2 |
| Hartley, P J © | Apr 18, 1960 | | 1985 | 1997 | 195 | 237 | 51 | 3,844 | 127* | 20.66 | 2 | 17,438 | 579 | 30.11 | 60 |
| Hartley, S N | Mar 18, 1956 | | 1978 | 1988 | 133 | 199 | 27 | 4,193 | 114 | 24.37 | 4 | 2,052 | 42 | 48.85 | 47 |
| § Harvey, I J | Apr 10, 1972 | | 2004 | 2005 | 20 | 31 | 2 | 1,045 | 209* | 36.03 | 2 | 831 | 37 | 22.45 | 12 |
| Hatton, A G | Mar 25, 1937 | | 1960 | 1961 | 3 | 1 | 1 | 4 | 4* | — | 0 | 202 | 6 | 33.66 | 1 |
| § Hawke, Lord * © | Aug 16, 1860 | Oct 10, 1938 | 1881 | 1911 | 510 | 739 | 91 | 13,133 | 166 | 20.26 | 10 | 16 | 0 | — | 159 |
| Hayley, H | Feb 22, 1860 | June 3, 1922 | 1884 | 1898 | 7 | 12 | 0 | 122 | 24 | 11.09 | 0 | 48 | 1 | — | 3 |
| Haywood, W J | Feb 25, 1841 | Jan 7, 1912 | 1878 | 1878 | 1 | 2 | 0 | 7 | 7 | 3.50 | 0 | 14 | 1 | 14.00 | 1 |
| Hicks, J | Dec 10, 1850 | June 10, 1912 | 1872 | 1876 | 15 | 25 | 3 | 313 | 66 | 14.22 | 0 | 17 | 0 | — | 12 |

| Player | Date of Birth | Date of Death (if known) | First Played | Last Played | M | Inns | NO | Runs | HS | Av'ge | 100s | Runs | Wkts | Av'ge | Ct/St |
|---|---|---|---|---|---|---|---|---|---|---|---|---|---|---|---|
| Higgins, J | Mar 13, 1877 | July 19, 1954 | 1901 | 1905 | 9 | 14 | 5 | 93 | 28* | 10.33 | 0 | — | — | — | 10/3 |
| Hill, A | Nov 14, 1843 | Aug 29, 1910 | 1871 | 1882 | 140 | 223 | 25 | 1,705 | 49 | 8.61 | 0 | 7,002 | 542 | 12.91 | 91 |
| Hill, H* | Nov 29, 1858 | Aug 14, 1935 | 1888 | 1891 | 14 | 27 | 2 | 337 | 34 | 13.48 | 0 | — | — | — | 10 |
| Hill, L.G* | Nov 2, 1860 | Aug 27, 1940 | 1882 | 1882 | 2 | 2 | 0 | 13 | 8 | 6.50 | 0 | — | — | — | 1 |
| Hirst, E T* | May 6, 1857 | Oct 26, 1914 | 1877 | 1888 | 21 | 33 | 2 | 328 | 87* | 10.58 | 0 | — | — | — | 7 |
| Hirst, E W* | Feb 27, 1855 | Oct 24, 1933 | 1881 | 1881 | 2 | 3 | 0 | 33 | 28 | 11.00 | 0 | 3 | 0 | — | 0 |
| Hirst, G H | Sept 7, 1871 | May 10, 1954 | 1891 | 1921* | 717 | 1,050 | 128 | 32,024 | 341 | 34.73 | 56 | 44,716 | 2,481 | 18.02 | 518 |
| Hirst, T H | May 21, 1865 | Apr 3, 1927 | 1899 | 1899 | 1 | 1 | 1 | — | 5* | — | 0 | 27 | 0 | — | 0 |
| § Hodd A J | **Jan 12, 1984** | | 2012 | 2015 | 28 | 33 | 5 | 748 | 68* | 26.71 | 0 | — | — | — | 77/4 |
| Hodgson, D M | Feb 26, 1990 | | 2014 | 2015 | 2 | 3 | 0 | 72 | 35 | 24.00 | 0 | — | — | — | 0 |
| Hodgson, G | July 24, 1938 | | 1964 | 1964 | 1 | 1 | 0 | 4 | 4 | 4.00 | 0 | — | — | — | 0/2 |
| Hodgson, L J | Nov 15, 1828 | Nov 24, 1867 | 1855 | 1866 | 21 | 35 | 14 | 164 | 21* | 7.80 | 0 | 1,537 | 88 | 17.46 | 11 |
| Hodgson, L J | Jun 29, 1986 | | 2009 | 2010 | 3 | 3 | 0 | 99 | 34 | 33.00 | 0 | 158 | 2 | 79.00 | 1 |
| Hodgson, P | Sept 21, 1935 | Mar 30, 2015 | 1954 | 1956 | 13 | 6 | 2 | 33 | 8* | 8.25 | 0 | 648 | 22 | 29.45 | 6 |
| Hoggard, M J ...© | Dec 31, 1976 | | 1996 | 2009 | 102 | 120 | 34 | 956 | 89* | 11.11 | 0 | 8,956 | 331 | 27.05 | 23 |
| Holdsworth, W E N | Sept 17, 1928 | | 1952 | 1953 | 27 | 26 | 12 | 111 | 22* | 7.92 | 0 | 1,598 | 53 | 30.15 | 7 |
| Holgate, G | June 23, 1839 | July 11, 1895 | 1865 | 1867 | 12 | 19 | 0 | 174 | 38 | 9.15 | 0 | — | — | — | 17/1 |
| Holmes, P | Nov 25, 1886 | Sept 3, 1971 | 1913 | 1933 | 485 | 699 | 74 | 26,220 | 315* | 41.95 | 60 | 124 | 1 | 124.00 | 319 |
| Horner, N F | May 10, 1926 | Dec 24, 2003 | 1950 | 1950 | 2 | 4 | 0 | 14 | 8 | 28.50 | 0 | — | — | — | 0 |
| Houseman I J | Oct 12, 1969 | | 1989 | 1991 | 5 | 2 | 1 | 18 | 18 | 18.00 | 0 | 311 | 3 | 103.66 | 0/1 |
| Hoyle, T H | Mar 19, 1884 | June 2, 1953 | 1919 | 1919 | 1 | 2 | 0 | 7 | 7 | 3.50 | 0 | — | — | — | 0 |
| Hudson, B | June 29, 1852 | Nov 11, 1901 | 1880 | 1880 | 3 | 4 | 0 | 13 | 5 | 3.25 | 0 | — | — | — | 2 |
| Hunter, D ...© | Feb 23, 1860 | Jan 11, 1927 | 1888 | 1909 | 517 | 681 | 323 | 4,177 | 58* | 11.66 | 0 | 43 | 0 | — | 863/323 |
| Hunter, J | Aug 3, 1855 | Jan 4, 1891 | 1878 | 1888 | 143 | 213 | 61 | 1,183 | 60* | 7.78 | 0 | — | — | — | 207/102 |
| Hutchison, P M | June 9, 1977 | | 1996 | 2001 | 39 | 39 | 23 | 187 | 30 | 11.68 | 0 | 3,244 | 143 | 22.68 | 8 |
| Hutton, L ...© | June 23, 1916 | Sept 6, 1990 | 1934 | 1955 | 341 | 527 | 62 | 24,807 | 280* | 53.34 | 85 | 4,221 | 154 | 27.40 | 278 |
| Hutton, R A ...© | Sept 6, 1942 | | 1962 | 1974 | 208 | 292 | 45 | 4,986 | 189 | 20.18 | 4 | 10,254 | 468 | 21.91 | 160 |
| Iddison, R | Sept 15, 1834 | Mar 19, 1890 | 1855 | 1876 | 72 | 108 | 15 | 1,916 | 112 | 20.60 | 1 | 1,540 | 102 | 15.09 | 70 |
| Illingworth, R ...© | June 8, 1932 | | 1951 | 1983 | 496 | 668 | 131 | 14,986 | 162 | 27.90 | 14 | 26,806 | 1,431 | 18.73 | 286 |
| § Imran Tahir | Mar 27, 1979 | | 2007 | 2007 | 1 | 1 | 0 | 5 | 5 | 2.50 | 0 | 141 | 0 | — | — |

# LIST OF PLAYERS AND CAREER AVERAGES IN ALL FIRST-CLASS MATCHES FOR YORKSHIRE (Continued)

| Player | Date of Birth | Date of Death (if known) | First Played | Last Played | M | Inns | NO | Runs | HS | Av'ge | 100s | Runs | Wkts | Av'ge | Ct/St |
|---|---|---|---|---|---|---|---|---|---|---|---|---|---|---|---|
| Ingham, P G | Sept 28, 1956 | | 1979 | 1981 | 8 | 14 | 0 | 290 | 64 | 20.71 | 0 | — | — | — | 0 |
| Inglis, J W | Oct 19, 1979 | | 2000 | 2000 | 1 | 2 | 0 | 4 | 2 | 2.00 | 0 | — | — | — | 0 |
| § Inzamam-ul-Haq | Mar 3, 1970 | | 2007 | 2007 | 3 | 4 | 0 | 89 | 51 | 22.25 | 0 | — | — | — | 5 |
| Jackson, Hon F S * | Nov 21, 1870 | Mar 9, 1947 | 1890 | 1907 | 207 | 328 | 22 | 10,371 | 160 | 33.89 | 21 | 9,690 | 506 | 19.15 | 129 |
| Jackson, S R * | July 15, 1859 | July 19, 1941 | 1891 | 1891 | 1 | 2 | 0 | 9 | 9 | 4.50 | 0 | — | — | — | 0 |
| Jacques, T A | Feb 19, 1905 | Feb 23, 1995 | 1927 | 1936 | 28 | 20 | 7 | 162 | 35* | 12.46 | 0 | 1,786 | 57 | 31.33 | 12 |
| Jakeman, F | Jan 10, 1920 | May 18, 1986 | 1946 | 1947 | 10 | 16 | 2 | 262 | 51 | 18.71 | 0 | — | — | — | 3 |
| James, B | Apr 23, 1934 | May 1999 | 1954 | 1954 | 4 | 5 | 3 | 22 | 11* | 11.00 | 0 | 228 | 8 | 28.50 | 0 |
| § Jaques, P A | © May 3, 1979 | | 2004 | 2013 | 53 | 82 | 3 | 4,039 | 243 | 51.12 | 11 | 112 | 1 | 112.00 | 46 |
| Jarvis, P W | © June 29, 1965 | | 1981 | 1993 | 138 | 160 | 46 | 1,898 | 80 | 16.64 | 0 | 11,990 | 449 | 26.70 | 36 |
| Johnson, C | Sept 5, 1947 | | 1969 | 1979 | 100 | 152 | 14 | 2,960 | 107 | 21.44 | 2 | 265 | 4 | 66.25 | 50 |
| Johnson, J | May 16, 1916 | Jan 16, 2011 | 1936 | 1939 | 3 | 3 | 2 | 5 | 4* | 5.00 | 0 | 27 | 5 | 5.40 | 1 |
| Johnson, M | Apr 23, 1958 | | 1981 | 1981 | 4 | 4 | 2 | 2 | 2 | 1.00 | 0 | 301 | 7 | 43.00 | 1 |
| Joy, J | Sept 29, 1826 | Sept 27, 1889 | 1849 | 1867 | 3 | 5 | 0 | 107 | 74 | 21.40 | 0 | 5 | — | — | 3 |
| Judson, A | July 10, 1885 | Apr 8, 1975 | 1920 | 1920 | 1 | — | — | — | — | — | — | 5 | — | — | 0 |
| § Katich, S M | Aug 21, 1975 | | 2002 | 2002 | 1 | 2 | 0 | 37 | 21 | 18.50 | 0 | 25 | 0 | — | 0 |
| Kaye, Harold S * | May 9, 1882 | Nov 6, 1953 | 1907 | 1908 | 18 | 25 | 1 | 243 | 37 | 10.12 | 0 | — | — | — | 9 |
| Kaye, Haven | June 11, 1846 | Jan 24, 1892 | 1872 | 1873 | 8 | 14 | 0 | 117 | 33 | 8.35 | 0 | — | — | — | 3 |
| Keedy, G | Nov 27, 1974 | | 1994 | 1994 | 1 | 1 | 0 | 1 | 1 | 1.00 | 0 | 18 | 0 | — | 0 |
| Keighley, W G * | Jan 10, 1925 | June 14, 2005 | 1947 | 1951 | 35 | 51 | 5 | 1,227 | 110 | 26.67 | 1 | 7 | 0 | — | 12 |
| Kellett, S A | Oct 16, 1967 | | 1989 | 1995 | 86 | 147 | 10 | 4,204 | 125* | 30.68 | 2 | — | — | — | 74 |
| Kennie, G | May 17, 1904 | Apr 11, 1994 | 1927 | 1927 | 1 | 2 | 0 | 6 | 6 | 3.00 | 0 | — | — | — | 1 |
| Kettleborough, R A | Mar 15, 1973 | | 1994 | 1997 | 13 | 19 | 2 | 446 | 108 | 26.23 | 1 | 153 | 3 | 51.00 | 9 |
| Kilburn, S | Oct 16, 1868 | Sept 25, 1940 | 1896 | 1896 | 1 | 1 | 0 | 8 | 8 | 8.00 | 0 | — | — | — | 0 |
| Kilner, N | July 21, 1895 | Apr 28, 1979 | 1919 | 1923 | 69 | 73 | 7 | 1,253 | 112 | 18.98 | 2 | — | — | — | 34 |
| Kilner, R | © Oct 17, 1890 | Apr 5, 1928 | 1911 | 1927 | 365 | 478 | 46 | 13,018 | 206* | 30.13 | 15 | 14,855 | 857 | 17.33 | 231 |
| King, A M | Oct 8, 1932 | | 1955 | 1955 | 4 | 4 | 3 | 12 | 12 | 12.00 | 0 | — | — | — | 0 |
| Kippax, P J | Oct 15, 1940 | | 1961 | 1962 | 4 | 7 | 2 | 37 | 9 | 7.40 | 0 | 279 | 8 | 34.87 | 0 |
| § Kirby, S P | © Oct 4, 1977 | | 2001 | 2004 | 47 | 61 | 14 | 342 | 57 | 7.27 | 0 | 5,143 | 182 | 28.25 | 11 |

# LIST OF PLAYERS AND CAREER AVERAGES IN ALL FIRST-CLASS MATCHES FOR YORKSHIRE (Continued)

| Player | Date of Birth | Date of Death (if known) | First Played | Last Played | M | Inns | NO | Runs | HS | Av'ge | 100s | Runs | Wkts | Av'ge | Ct/St |
|---|---|---|---|---|---|---|---|---|---|---|---|---|---|---|---|
| § Kruis, G J | © May 9, 1974 | | 2005 | 2009 | 54 | 64 | 31 | 617 | 50* | 18.69 | 0 | 5,431 | 154 | 35.26 | 11 |
| § Lambert, G A | Jan 4, 1980 | | 2000 | 2000 | 2 | 3 | 2 | 6 | 3* | 6.00 | 0 | 133 | 4 | 33.25 | 1 |
| Lancaster, W W | Feb 4, 1873 | Dec 30, 1938 | 1895 | 1895 | 7 | 7 | 2 | 163 | 51 | 16.30 | 0 | 29 | 0 | — | 1 |
| § Landon, C W * | May 30, 1850 | Mar 5, 1903 | 1878 | 1882 | 9 | 13 | 0 | 51 | 18 | 3.92 | 0 | 74 | 0 | — | 7 |
| § Law, W * | Apr 9, 1851 | Dec 20, 1892 | 1871 | 1873 | 4 | 7 | 0 | 51 | 22 | 7.28 | 0 | | | — | 3 |
| Lawson, M A K | Oct 24, 1985 | | 2004 | 2007 | 15 | 21 | 5 | 197 | 44 | 12.31 | 0 | 1,699 | 42 | 40.45 | 7 |
| Leadbeater, B | © Aug 14, 1943 | | 1966 | 1979 | 144 | 236 | 27 | 5,247 | 140* | 25.10 | 1 | 5 | 1 | 5.00 | 80 |
| Leadbeater, E | Aug 15, 1927 | Apr 17, 2011 | 1949 | 1956 | 81 | 94 | 29 | 898 | 91 | 13.81 | 0 | 5,657 | 201 | 28.14 | 49 |
| Leadbeater, H * | Dec 31, 1863 | Oct 9, 1928 | 1884 | 1890 | 6 | 10 | 0 | 141 | 65 | 17.62 | 0 | | | — | 4 |
| **§ Leaning, J A** | **© Oct 18, 1993** | | **2013** | **2015** | **29** | **45** | **5** | **1,466** | **123** | **36.65** | **3** | **187** | **1** | **187.00** | **24** |
| Leatham, G A B * | Apr 30, 1851 | June 19, 1932 | 1874 | 1886 | 12 | 18 | 5 | 61 | 14 | 4.69 | 0 | | | — | 21/7 |
| Leather, R S * | Aug 17, 1880 | Jan 31, 1913 | 1906 | 1906 | 1 | 2 | 0 | 19 | 14 | 9.50 | 0 | | | — | 1 |
| Lee, C | Mar 17, 1924 | Sept 4, 1999 | 1952 | 1952 | 2 | 4 | 0 | 98 | 74 | 24.50 | 0 | | | — | — |
| Lee, G H | © Nov 18, 1856 | Sept 13, 1896 | 1882 | 1890 | 105 | 182 | 10 | 3,622 | 165 | 21.05 | 3 | 34 | 0 | — | 53/1 |
| Lee, Herbert | Aug 24, 1854 | Oct 14, 1919 | 1879 | 1879 | 1 | 2 | 0 | 13 | 9 | 6.50 | 0 | | | — | — |
| Lee, J E * | July 2, 1856 | Feb 4, 1908 | 1885 | 1885 | 5 | 6 | 0 | 20 | 12 | 3.33 | 0 | 149 | 2 | 74.50 | 2 |
| Lee, J E * | Mar 23, 1838 | Apr 2, 1880 | 1867 | 1867 | 2 | 3 | 0 | 9 | 6 | 3.00 | 0 | | | — | 0 |
| Lee, J E | Dec 23, 1988 | | 2006 | 2009 | 2 | 3 | 1 | 24 | 21* | 12.00 | 0 | 26 | 0 | — | — |
| **Lees, A Z©** | **Apr 14, 1993** | | **2010** | **2015** | **45** | **72** | **6** | **2,562** | **275*** | **38.81** | **6** | **26** | **0** | **—** | **32** |
| § Legard, A D * | June 19, 1878 | Aug 15, 1939 | 1910 | 1910 | 4 | 5 | 0 | 50 | 15 | 10.00 | 0 | | | — | 1 |
| § Lehmann, D S | © Feb 5, 1970 | | 1997 | 2006 | 88 | 137 | 8 | 8,871 | 339 | 68.76 | 26 | 1,952 | 61 | 32.00 | 35 |
| § Lester, E I | © Feb 18, 1923 | Mar 23, 2015 | 1945 | 1956 | 228 | 339 | 27 | 10,616 | 186 | 34.02 | 24 | 160 | 3 | 53.33 | 106 |
| Leyland, M | © July 20, 1900 | Jan 1, 1967 | 1920 | 1946 | 548 | 720 | 82 | 26,180 | 263 | 41.03 | 62 | 11,079 | 409 | 27.08 | 204 |
| Lilley, A E | Apr 17, 1992 | | 2011 | 2011 | 1 | 1 | 0 | 0 | 0 | 0.00 | 0 | | | — | — |
| Linaker, L | Apr 8, 1885 | Nov 17, 1961 | 1909 | 1909 | 1 | 2 | 0 | 36 | 28 | 18.00 | 0 | 28 | 1 | 28.00 | 1 |
| Lister, B | Dec 9, 1850 | Dec 3, 1919 | 1874 | 1878 | 2 | 2 | 0 | 13 | 10 | 3.60 | 0 | | | — | 2 |
| § Lister-Kaye, K A * | Mar 27, 1892 | Feb 28, 1955 | 1928 | 1928 | 2 | 2 | 1 | 13 | 7* | 13.00 | 0 | 64 | 1 | 64.00 | 2 |
| Lister, J * | May 14, 1930 | Jan 28, 1991 | 1954 | 1954 | 4 | 4 | 0 | 35 | 16 | 8.75 | 0 | | | — | 2 |
| Lockwood, E | Apr 4, 1845 | Dec 19, 1921 | 1868 | 1884 | 214 | 364 | 29 | 7,789 | 208 | 23.25 | 6 | 2,265 | 141 | 16.06 | 164/2 |
| Lockwood, H | Oct 20, 1855 | Feb 18, 1930 | 1877 | 1882 | 16 | 27 | 2 | 408 | 90 | 16.32 | 0 | 37 | 0 | — | 8 |

# LIST OF PLAYERS AND CAREER AVERAGES IN ALL FIRST-CLASS MATCHES FOR YORKSHIRE (Continued)

| Player | Date of Birth | Date of Death (if known) | First Played | Last Played | M | Inns | NO | Runs | HS | Av'ge | 100s | Runs | Wkts | Av'ge | Ct/St |
|---|---|---|---|---|---|---|---|---|---|---|---|---|---|---|---|
| Lodge, J T | Apr 16, 1921 | July 9, 2002 | 1948 | 1948 | 2 | 3 | 0 | 48 | 30 | 16.00 | 0 | 17 | 0 | — | 0 |
| Love, J D © | Apr 22, 1955 | | 1975 | 1989 | 247 | 388 | 58 | 10,263 | 170* | 31.10 | 13 | 835 | 12 | 69.58 | 123 |
| Lowe, G E | Jan 12, 1878 | Aug 15, 1932 | 1902 | 1902 | 1 | 1 | 0 | 5 | 5* | 5.00 | 0 | — | — | — | 1 |
| Lowe J R | Oct 19,1991 | | 2010 | 2010 | 1 | — | — | — | — | — | — | 15 | 0 | — | 0 |
| § Lowson, F A © | July 1, 1925 | Sept 8, 1984 | 1949 | 1958 | 252 | 404 | 31 | 13,897 | 259* | 37.25 | 30 | 15 | 0 | — | 180 |
| § Loxley-Firth, E * | Mar 7, 1886 | Jan 8, 1949 | 1912 | 1912 | 2 | 4 | 0 | 43 | 37 | 10.75 | 0 | — | — | — | 1 |
| § Lucas, D S | Aug 19, 1978 | | 2005 | 2005 | | | | | | | | 84 | 8 | 10.50 | 0 |
| Lumb, E * | Sept 12, 1852 | Apr 5, 1891 | 1872 | 1886 | 14 | 23 | 4 | 311 | 70* | 16.36 | 0 | 199 | 5 | 39.80 | 5 |
| § Lumb, M J | Feb 12, 1980 | | 2000 | 2006 | 78 | 135 | 12 | 4,194 | 144 | 34.09 | 8 | 5 | 0 | — | 43 |
| Lumb, R G | Feb 27, 1950 | | 1970 | 1984 | 239 | 395 | 30 | 11,525 | 165* | 31.57 | 22 | 88 | 0 | — | 129 |
| Lupton, A W * © | Feb 23, 1879 | Apr 14, 1944 | 1908 | 1927 | 104 | 79 | 15 | 668 | 43* | 10.43 | 0 | — | — | — | 25 |
| Lynas, G G | Sept 7, 1832 | Dec 8, 1896 | 1867 | 1867 | 2 | 3 | 0 | 4 | 4* | 2.00 | 0 | — | — | — | 2 |
| **Lyth, A** © | **Sept 25, 1987** | | **2007** | **2015** | **102** | **164** | **8** | **6,672** | **251** | **42.76** | **14** | **723** | **17** | **42.52** | **129** |
| Macaulay, G G © | Dec 7, 1897 | Dec 13, 1940 | 1920 | 1935 | 445 | 430 | 112 | 5,717 | 125* | 17.97 | 3 | 30,554 | 1,774 | 17.22 | 361 |
| McGrath, A © | Oct 6, 1975 | | 1995 | 2012 | 242 | 405 | 29 | 14,091 | 211 | 37.47 | 34 | 4,652 | 128 | 36.34 | 168 |
| McHugh, F P | Nov 15, 1925 | | 1949 | 1949 | 3 | 1 | 1 | 5 | 5* | — | 0 | 147 | 4 | 36.75 | 1 |
| Marshall, A | July 10, 1849 | Aug 3, 1891 | 1874 | 1874 | 3 | 2 | 0 | 0 | — | 0.00 | 0 | 11 | — | — | 0 |
| § Martyn, D R © | Oct 21, 1971 | | 2003 | 2003 | 3 | 3 | 1 | 342 | 238 | 171.00 | 1 | — | — | — | 2 |
| Mason, A | May 2, 1921 | Mar, 2006 | 1947 | 1950 | 18 | 19 | 3 | 105 | 22 | 6.56 | 0 | 1,473 | 51 | 28.88 | 6 |
| Maude, E * | Dec 31, 1839 | July 2, 1876 | 1866 | 1866 | 2 | 2 | 0 | 17 | | 8.50 | 0 | — | — | — | 1 |
| **§ Maxwell, G J** © | **Oct 14, 1988** | | **2015** | **2015** | **4** | **7** | **1** | **244** | **140** | **40.66** | **1** | **144** | **4** | **36.00** | **3** |
| Metcalfe, A A | Dec 25, 1963 | | 1983 | 1995 | 184 | 317 | 19 | 10,465 | 216* | 35.11 | 25 | 344 | 3 | 114.66 | 72 |
| Micklethwait, W H * | Dec 13, 1885 | Oct 7, 1947 | 1911 | 1911 | 1 | 1 | 0 | 44 | 44 | 44.00 | 0 | — | — | — | 1 |
| **Middlebrook, J D** © | **May 13, 1977** | | **1998** | **2015** | **29** | **38** | **3** | **534** | **84** | **15.25** | **0** | **1,899** | **66** | **28.77** | **17** |
| Middlebrook, W | May 23, 1858 | Apr 26, 1919 | 1888 | 1889 | 17 | 27 | 7 | 88 | 19* | 4.40 | 0 | 895 | 50 | 17.90 | 3 |
| Midgley, C A * | Nov 11, 1877 | June 24, 1942 | 1906 | 1906 | 4 | 6 | 2 | 115 | 59* | 28.75 | 0 | 149 | 8 | 18.62 | 3 |
| Milburn, S M | Mar 29, 1972 | | 1992 | 1995 | 6 | 8 | 2 | 22 | | 3.66 | 0 | 431 | 14 | 30.78 | 8 |
| § Milligan, F W * | Mar 19, 1870 | Mar 31, 1900 | 1894 | 1898 | 81 | 113 | 10 | 1,879 | 74 | 18.24 | 0 | 2,736 | 112 | 24.42 | 40 |
| Mitchell, A © | Sept 13, 1902 | Dec 25, 1976 | 1922 | 1945 | 401 | 550 | 69 | 18,189 | 189 | 37.81 | 39 | 291 | 5 | 58.20 | 406 |
| Mitchell, F * © | Aug 13, 1872 | Oct 11, 1935 | 1894 | 1904 | 83 | 125 | 5 | 4,104 | 194 | 34.20 | 10 | 16 | 1 | 16.00 | 52 |

# LIST OF PLAYERS AND CAREER AVERAGES IN ALL FIRST-CLASS MATCHES FOR YORKSHIRE (Continued)

| Player | Date of Birth | Date of Death (if known) | First Played | Last Played | M | Inns | NO | Runs | HS | Av'ge | 100s | Runs | Wkts | Av'ge | Ct/St |
|---|---|---|---|---|---|---|---|---|---|---|---|---|---|---|---|
| Monks, G D | Sept 3, 1929 | | 1952 | 1952 | 1 | 1 | 0 | 3 | 3 | 3.00 | 0 | | | | |
| Moorhouse, R | Sept 7, 1866 | Jan 7, 1921 | 1888 | 1899 | 206 | 315 | 45 | 5,217 | 113 | 19.32 | 8 | 1,232 | 43 | 28.65 | 92 |
| § Morkel, M | Oct 6, 1984 | | 2008 | 2008 | 1 | 2 | 0 | 8 | 4 | 4.00 | 0 | 33 | 1 | 33.00 | 0 |
| Morris, A C © | Oct 4, 1976 | | 1995 | 1997 | 16 | 23 | 2 | 362 | 60 | 17.23 | 0 | 508 | 9 | 56.44 | 8 |
| Mosley, H | Mar 8, 1852 | Nov 29, 1933 | 1881 | 1881 | 2 | 4 | 0 | 1 | 1 | 0.25 | 0 | 34 | 3 | 11.33 | |
| Motley, A * | Feb 5, 1858 | Sept 28, 1897 | 1879 | 1879 | 2 | 2 | 1 | 10 | 8* | 10.00 | 0 | 135 | 7 | 19.28 | |
| Mounsey, J T © | Aug 30, 1871 | Apr 6, 1949 | 1891 | 1897 | 92 | 145 | 21 | 1,939 | 64 | 15.63 | 0 | 444 | 10 | 44.40 | 45 |
| Moxon, M D © | May 4, 1960 | | 1981 | 1997 | 277 | 476 | 42 | 18,973 | 274* | 43.71 | 41 | 1,213 | 22 | 55.13 | 190 |
| Myers, H © | Jan 2, 1875 | June 12, 1944 | 1901 | 1910 | 201 | 289 | 46 | 4,450 | 91 | 18.31 | 0 | 7,095 | 282 | 25.15 | 106 |
| Myers, M | Apr 12, 1847 | Dec 8, 1919 | 1876 | 1878 | 22 | 40 | 4 | 537 | 49 | 14.91 | 0 | 20 | 0 | | 11 |
| § Naved-ul-Hasan, Rana | Feb 18, 1978 | | 2008 | 2009 | 11 | 16 | 3 | 207 | 32 | 15.92 | 0 | 1,018 | 26 | 39.15 | 3 |
| Naylor, J E © | Dec 11, 1930 | June 26, 1996 | 1953 | 1953 | 1 | | | | | | | 88 | 0 | | |
| Newstead, J T © | Sept 8, 1877 | Mar 25, 1952 | 1903 | 1913 | 96 | 128 | 17 | 1,791 | 100* | 16.13 | 1 | 5,555 | 297 | 18.70 | 75 |
| Nicholson, A G © | June 25, 1938 | Nov 3, 1985 | 1962 | 1975 | 282 | 267 | 125 | 1,667 | 55 | 11.73 | 0 | 17,296 | 876 | 19.74 | 85 |
| Nicholson, N G | Oct 17, 1963 | | 1988 | 1989 | 5 | 8 | 3 | 134 | 56* | 26.80 | 0 | 25 | 0 | | 5 |
| Oates, William | Jan 1, 1852 | Dec 9, 1940 | 1874 | 1875 | 7 | 13 | 7 | 34 | 14* | 5.66 | 0 | | | | 5/1 |
| Oates, W F © | June 11, 1929 | May 15, 2001 | 1956 | 1956 | 3 | 3 | 0 | 20 | 6 | 6.66 | 0 | | | | 0 |
| Old, C M © | Dec 22, 1948 | | 1966 | 1982 | 222 | 262 | 56 | 4,785 | 116 | 23.22 | 5 | 13,409 | 647 | 20.72 | 131 |
| Oldham, S | July 26, 1948 | | 1974 | 1985 | 59 | 39 | 18 | 212 | 50 | 10.09 | 0 | 3,849 | 130 | 29.60 | 18 |
| Oldroyd, E © | Oct 1, 1888 | Dec 29, 1964 | 1910 | 1931 | 383 | 509 | 58 | 15,891 | 194 | 35.23 | 37 | 1,658 | 42 | 39.47 | 203 |
| Oyston, C | May 12, 1869 | July 15, 1942 | 1900 | 1909 | 15 | 21 | 8 | 96 | 22 | 7.38 | 0 | 872 | 31 | 28.12 | 3 |
| Padgett, D E V © | July 20, 1934 | | 1951 | 1971 | 487 | 774 | 63 | 20,306 | 161* | 28.55 | 29 | 208 | 6 | 34.66 | 250 |
| Padgett, G H | Oct 9, 1931 | | 1952 | 1952 | 6 | 7 | 4 | 56 | 32* | 18.66 | 0 | 336 | 4 | 84.00 | 5 |
| Padgett, J | Nov 21, 1860 | Aug 2, 1943 | 1882 | 1889 | 6 | 9 | 0 | 92 | 22 | 10.22 | 0 | | | | 2 |
| Parker, B | June 23, 1970 | | 1992 | 1998 | 44 | 71 | 10 | 1,839 | 138* | 30.14 | 2 | 3 | 0 | | 19 |
| § Parkin, C H | Feb 18, 1886 | June 15, 1943 | 1906 | 1906 | 1 | 1 | 1 | 0 | 0 | 0.00 | 0 | 25 | 2 | 12.50 | 4 |
| § Parratt, J | Mar 24, 1859 | May 6, 1905 | 1888 | 1890 | 1 | 2 | 0 | 11 | 5 | 5.50 | 0 | 75 | 1 | 75.00 | 0 |
| § Parton, J W | Jan 31, 1863 | Jan. 30, 1906 | 1889 | 1889 | 2 | 2 | 0 | 16 | 14 | 8.00 | 0 | 4 | 1 | 4.00 | |
| **Patterson, S A ©** | **Oct 3, 1983** | | **2005** | **2015** | **106** | **117** | **34** | **1,369** | **53** | **16.49** | **0** | **7,752** | **280** | **27.68** | **17** |

# LIST OF PLAYERS AND CAREER AVERAGES IN ALL FIRST-CLASS MATCHES FOR YORKSHIRE (Continued)

| Player | Date of Birth | Date of Death (if known) | First Played | Last Played | M | Inns | NO | Runs | HS | Av'ge | 100s | Runs | Wkts | Av'ge | Ct/St |
|---|---|---|---|---|---|---|---|---|---|---|---|---|---|---|---|
| Pearson, H E | Aug 7, 1851 | July 8, 1903 | 1878 | 1880 | 4 | 7 | 5 | 31 | 10* | 15.50 | 0 | 90 | 5 | 18.00 | 1 |
| Pearson, J H | May 14, 1915 | | 1934 | 1936 | 3 | 3 | 0 | 54 | 44 | 18.00 | 0 | | | | 1 |
| Peate, E | Mar 2, 1855 | Mar 11, 1900 | 1879 | 1887 | 154 | 226 | 61 | 1,793 | 95 | 10.86 | 0 | 9,986 | 794 | 12.57 | 97 |
| Peel, R | ◎ Feb 12, 1857 | Aug 12, 1941 | 1882 | 1897 | 318 | 510 | 42 | 9,322 | 210* | 19.91 | 6 | 20,638 | 1,311 | 15.74 | 141 |
| Penny, J H | Sept 29, 1856 | July 29, 1902 | 1891 | 1891 | 1 | 1 | | 8 | 8 | | 0 | 31 | 2 | 15.50 | |
| Pickles, C S | Jan 30, 1966 | | 1985 | 1992 | 58 | 76 | 21 | 1,336 | 66 | 24.29 | 0 | 3,638 | 83 | 43.83 | 24 |
| Pickles D | Nov 16, 1935 | | 1957 | 1960 | 41 | 40 | 20 | 74 | 12 | 3.70 | 0 | 2,062 | 96 | 21.47 | 10 |
| Pinder, G | July 15, 1841 | Jan 15, 1903 | 1867 | 1880 | 125 | 199 | 44 | 1,639 | 57 | 10.57 | 0 | 325 | 19 | 17.10 | 145/102 |
| Platt, R K | ◎ Dec 26, 1932 | | 1955 | 1963 | 96 | 103 | 47 | 405 | 57* | 7.23 | 0 | 6,389 | 282 | 22.65 | 35 |
| **Plunkett, L E** | ◎ **Apr 6, 1985** | | **2013** | **2015** | **26** | **35** | **4** | **700** | **86** | **22.58** | **0** | **2,187** | **82** | **26.67** | **17** |
| Pollard, D | Aug 7, 1835 | Mar 26, 1909 | 1865 | 1865 | 1 | 2 | | 3 | 3 | 1.50 | 0 | 19 | 0 | | 1 |
| Pollitt, G | June 3, 1874 | May 19, 1942 | 1899 | 1899 | 1 | 2 | 0 | 51 | 51 | 51.00 | 0 | | | | 0 |
| Prest, C H * | Dec 9, 1841 | Mar 4, 1875 | 1864 | 1864 | 2 | 4 | 0 | 57 | 31 | 14.25 | 0 | 1 | 0 | | 3 |
| Preston, J M | ◎ Aug 23, 1864 | Nov 26, 1890 | 1885 | 1889 | 79 | 134 | 11 | 1,935 | 93 | 15.73 | 0 | 3,232 | 178 | 18.15 | 36 |
| Pride, T | July 23, 1864 | | 1887 | 1887 | 1 | 1 | | 1 | 1 | 1.00 | 0 | | | | 4/3 |
| Priestley, I M | Sept 25, 1967 | | 1989 | 1989 | 2 | 4 | 2 | 25 | 23 | 12.50 | 0 | 119 | 4 | 29.75 | 1 |
| Pullan, T | Mar 29, 1857 | | 1884 | 1884 | 1 | 2 | 1 | 14 | 14 | 14.00 | 0 | 5 | 0 | | |
| § Pujara, C A | ◎ Jan 25, 1988 | | 2015 | 2015 | 4 | 6 | 1 | 264 | 133* | 52.80 | 1 | | | | 2 |
| Pyrah, R M | ◎ Nov 1, 1982 | | 2004 | 2015 | 51 | 61 | 8 | 1,621 | 134* | 30.58 | 3 | 2527 | 55 | 45.94 | 22 |
| § Radcliffe, E J R H * | Jan 27, 1884 | Nov 23, 1969 | 1909 | 1911 | 64 | 89 | 13 | 826 | 54 | 10.86 | 0 | 134 | 2 | 67.00 | 21 |
| Ramage, A | Nov 29, 1957 | | 1979 | 1983 | 23 | 22 | 9 | 219 | 52 | 16.84 | 0 | 1,649 | 44 | 37.47 | 4 |
| Ramsden, G | Mar 2, 1983 | | 2000 | 2000 | 1 | 1 | 0 | 0 | 0* | | 0 | 68 | 1 | 68.00 | 0 |
| Randhawa, G S | Jan 25, 1992 | | 2011 | 2011 | 1 | 1 | | 5 | 5 | 5.00 | 0 | 62 | 2 | 31.00 | 0 |
| Raper, J R S * | Aug 9, 1909 | Mar 9, 1997 | 1936 | 1947 | 3 | 4 | 0 | 24 | 15 | 6.00 | 0 | | | | 0 |
| **Rashid, A U** | ◎ **Feb 17, 1988** | | **2006** | **2015** | **123** | **170** | **30** | **5,016** | **180** | **35.82** | **10** | **12,553** | **378** | **33.20** | **63** |
| Rawlin, E R | Oct 4, 1897 | Jan 11, 1943 | 1927 | 1936 | 8 | 10 | 1 | 72 | 35 | 8.00 | 0 | 498 | 21 | 23.71 | 2 |
| Rawlin, J T | Nov 10, 1856 | Jan 19, 1924 | 1880 | 1885 | 27 | 36 | 2 | 274 | 31 | 8.05 | 0 | 258 | 11 | 23.45 | 13 |
| Rawlinson, E B | Apr 10, 1837 | Feb 17, 1892 | 1867 | 1875 | 37 | 68 | 5 | 991 | 55 | 15.73 | 0 | 62 | 5 | 12.40 | 16 |
| Redfearn, J | May 13, 1862 | Jan 14, 1931 | 1890 | 1890 | 1 | 1 | 0 | 5 | 5 | 5.00 | 0 | | | | 0 |
| Render, G W A | Jan 5, 1887 | Sept 17, 1922 | 1919 | 1919 | 1 | 1 | 0 | 5 | 5 | 5.00 | 0 | | | | 0 |

# LIST OF PLAYERS AND CAREER AVERAGES IN ALL FIRST-CLASS MATCHES FOR YORKSHIRE (Continued)

| Player | Date of Birth | Date of Death (if known) | First Played | Last Played | M | Inns | NO | Runs | HS | Av'ge | 100s | Runs | Wkts | Av'ge | Ct/St |
|---|---|---|---|---|---|---|---|---|---|---|---|---|---|---|---|
| Rhodes, A C © | Oct 14, 1906 | May 21, 1957 | 1932 | 1934 | 61 | 70 | 19 | 917 | 64* | 17.98 | 0 | 3,026 | 107 | 28.28 | 45 |
| § Rhodes, H E * | Jan 11, 1852 | Sept 10, 1889 | 1878 | 1883 | 10 | 16 | 1 | 269 | 64 | 17.93 | 0 | — | — | — | 1 |
| Rhodes, S J | June 17, 1964 | | 1981 | 1984 | 3 | 2 | 1 | 41 | 35 | 41.00 | 0 | — | — | — | 1 |
| Rhodes, Wilfred © | Oct 29, 1877 | July 8, 1973 | 1898 | 1930 | 883 | 1,195 | 162 | 31,075 | 267* | 30.08 | 46 | 57,634 | 3,598 | 16.01 | 586 |
| Rhodes, William | Mar 4, 1883 | Aug 5, 1941 | 1911 | 1911 | 1 | 1 | | | 1* | | 0 | 40 | 0 | | 0 |
| § Rhodes W M H | Mar 2, 1995 | | 2015 | 2015 | 11 | 18 | 2 | 469 | 79 | 29.31 | 0 | 311 | 12 | 25.91 | 5 |
| Richardson, J A * | Aug 4, 1908 | Apr 2, 1985 | 1936 | 1947 | 17 | 12 | 2 | 308 | 61 | 30.80 | 0 | 90 | 2 | 45.00 | 3 |
| § Richardson, R B | Jan 12, 1962 | | 1993 | 1994 | 7 | 23 | 1 | 1,310 | 112 | 34.47 | 3 | 23 | 1 | 23.00 | 18 |
| § Richardson, S A | Sept 5, 1977 | | 2000 | 2003 | 13 | 23 | 2 | 377 | 69 | 17.95 | 0 | | | | 11 |
| Riley, H | Aug 17, 1875 | Nov 6, 1922 | 1895 | 1900 | 4 | 5 | 1 | 36 | 25* | 9.00 | 0 | 54 | 1 | 54.00 | 1 |
| Riley, M * | Apr 5, 1851 | June 1, 1899 | 1878 | 1882 | 17 | 28 | 1 | 361 | 92 | 13.37 | 0 | 10 | 0 | | 3 |
| Ringrose, W | Sept 2, 1871 | Sept 14, 1943 | 1901 | 1906 | 57 | 66 | 9 | 353 | 23 | 6.19 | 0 | 3,224 | 155 | 20.80 | 25 |
| Robinson, A L | Aug 17, 1946 | | 1971 | 1977 | 84 | 69 | 31 | 365 | 30* | 9.60 | 0 | 4,927 | 196 | 25.13 | 48 |
| Robinson, Edward * | Dec 27, 1862 | Sept 3, 1942 | 1887 | 1887 | 1 | 2 | 1 | 23 | 23* | 23.00 | 0 | | | | 0 |
| Robinson, Emmott © | Nov 16, 1883 | Nov 17, 1969 | 1919 | 1931 | 413 | 455 | 77 | 9,651 | 135* | 25.53 | 7 | 19,645 | 893 | 21.99 | 318 |
| Robinson, E P © | Aug 10, 1911 | Nov 10, 1998 | 1934 | 1949 | 208 | 253 | 46 | 2,596 | 75* | 12.54 | 0 | 15,141 | 735 | 20.60 | 189 |
| Robinson, H | May 12, 1858 | Dec 14, 1909 | 1879 | 1879 | 1 | 2 | | 5 | 4 | 2.50 | 0 | 20 | 1 | 20.00 | — |
| Robinson, M A | Nov 23, 1966 | | 1991 | 1995 | 90 | 93 | 36 | 240 | 23 | 4.21 | 0 | 6,866 | 218 | 31.49 | 17 |
| Robinson, P E © | Aug 3, 1963 | | 1984 | 1991 | 132 | 217 | 31 | 6,668 | 189 | 35.84 | 7 | 238 | 1 | 238.00 | 96 |
| Robinson, W | Nov 29, 1851 | Aug 14, 1919 | 1876 | 1877 | 7 | 14 | 1 | 151 | 36 | 11.61 | 0 | | | | 1 |
| Roebuck C G | Aug 14, 1991 | | 2010 | 2010 | 1 | 1 | | 23 | 23 | 23.00 | 0 | | | | 0 |
| Root, J E © | Dec 30, 1990 | | 2010 | 2014 | 38 | 63 | 7 | 2,463 | 236 | 43.98 | 5 | 530 | 9 | 58.88 | 19 |
| Roper, E * | Apr 8, 1851 | Apr 27, 1921 | 1878 | 1880 | 5 | 7 | 1 | 85 | 68 | 14.16 | 0 | | | | 2 |
| Rothery, J W | Sept 5, 1877 | June 2, 1919 | 1903 | 1910 | 150 | 236 | 18 | 4,614 | 161 | 21.16 | 3 | 44 | 2 | 22.00 | 45 |
| Rowbotham, J | July 8, 1831 | Dec 22, 1899 | 1861 | 1876 | 94 | 162 | 9 | 2,624 | 113 | 17.15 | 3 | 37 | 3 | 12.33 | 52 |
| § Rudolph J A © | May 4, 1981 | | 2007 | 2011 | 68 | 112 | 8 | 5,429 | 228* | 52.20 | 18 | 311 | 1 | 311.00 | 79 |
| Rudston, H | Nov 22, 1879 | Apr 14, 1962 | 1902 | 1907 | 21 | 30 | 0 | 609 | 164 | 20.30 | 0 | | | | 3 |
| Ryan, M | June 23, 1933 | Nov 16, 2015 | 1954 | 1965 | 150 | 149 | 58 | 682 | 26* | 7.49 | 0 | 9,466 | 413 | 22.92 | 59 |
| Ryder, L | Aug 28, 1901 | Jan 24, 1955 | 1924 | 1924 | 2 | 2 | 1 | 1 | 1 | 1.00 | 0 | 151 | 4 | 37.75 | 2 |
| Sanderson B W | Jan 3, 1989 | | 2008 | 2010 | 3 | 2 | 1 | 6 | 6 | 6.00 | 0 | 190 | 6 | 31.66 | 0 |

**LIST OF PLAYERS AND CAREER AVERAGES IN ALL FIRST-CLASS MATCHES FOR YORKSHIRE** (Continued)

| Player | Date of Birth | Date of Death (if known) | First Played | Last Played | M | Inns | NO | Runs | HS | Av'ge | 100s | Runs | Wkts | Av'ge | Ct/St |
|---|---|---|---|---|---|---|---|---|---|---|---|---|---|---|---|
| Savile, G * | Apr. 26, 1847 | Sept 4, 1904 | 1867 | 1874 | 5 | 7 | 1 | 140 | 65 | 20.00 | 0 | — | — | — | 2 |
| Sayers, J J © | Nov 5, 1983 | | 2004 | 2013 | 97 | 161 | 13 | 4,855 | 187 | 32.80 | 9 | 166 | 6 | 27.66 | 60 |
| Schofield, C J © | Mar 21, 1976 | | 1996 | 1996 | 1 | 1 | 0 | 25 | 25 | 25.00 | 0 | — | — | — | 0 |
| Schofield, D | Oct 9, 1947 | | 1970 | 1974 | 3 | 4 | 4 | 13 | 6* | — | 0 | 112 | 5 | 22.40 | 0 |
| Scott, E | July 6, 1834 | Dec 3, 1898 | 1864 | 1864 | 1 | 1 | 0 | 8 | 8 | 8.00 | 0 | 27 | 2 | 13.50 | 1 |
| Sedgwick, H A | Apr 8, 1883 | Dec 28, 1957 | 1906 | 1906 | 3 | 5 | 2 | 53 | 34 | 17.66 | 0 | 327 | 16 | 20.43 | 2 |
| Sellers, Arthur * | May 31, 1870 | Sept 25, 1941 | 1890 | 1899 | 49 | 88 | 1 | 1,643 | 105 | 18.88 | 2 | 84 | 2 | 42.00 | 40 |
| Sellers, A B * © | Mar 5, 1907 | Feb 20, 1981 | 1932 | 1948 | 334 | 437 | 51 | 8,949 | 204 | 23.18 | 4 | 653 | 8 | 81.62 | 264 |
| Shackleton, W A | Mar 9, 1908 | Nov 16, 1971 | 1928 | 1934 | 5 | 6 | 0 | 49 | 25 | 8.16 | 0 | 130 | 6 | 21.66 | 3 |
| Shahzad, Ajmal © | July 27, 1985 | | 2006 | 2012 | 45 | 58 | 14 | 1,145 | 88 | 26.02 | 0 | 4,196 | 125 | 33.56 | 5 |
| Sharp, K | Apr. 6, 1959 | | 1976 | 1990 | 195 | 320 | 35 | 8,426 | 181 | 29.56 | 11 | 836 | 12 | 69.66 | 95 |
| § Sharpe, C M * | Sept 6, 1851 | June 25, 1935 | 1875 | 1875 | 1 | 1 | 0 | 15 | 15 | 15.00 | 0 | 17 | — | — | — |
| Sharpe, P J © | Dec 27, 1936 | May 19, 2014 | 1958 | 1974 | 411 | 666 | 71 | 17,685 | 203* | 29.72 | 23 | 140 | 2 | 70.00 | 526 |
| Shaw, C | Feb 17, 1964 | | 1984 | 1988 | 61 | 58 | 27 | 340 | 31 | 10.96 | 0 | 4,101 | 123 | 33.34 | 9 |
| Shaw, J | Mar 12, 1865 | Jan 22, 1921 | 1896 | 1897 | 3 | 3 | 0 | 8 | 7 | 2.66 | 0 | 181 | 7 | 25.85 | 2 |
| Sheepshanks, E R * | Mar 22, 1910 | Dec 31, 1937 | 1929 | 1929 | 1 | 1 | 0 | 26 | 26 | 26.00 | 0 | — | — | — | 0 |
| Shepherd, D A * | Mar 10, 1916 | May 29, 1998 | 1938 | 1938 | 1 | 1 | 0 | 0 | 0 | 0.00 | 0 | — | — | — | 0 |
| Shotton, W | Dec 1, 1840 | May 26, 1909 | 1865 | 1874 | 2 | 4 | 0 | 13 | 7 | 3.25 | 0 | — | — | — | 0 |
| Sidebottom, A © | Apr 1, 1954 | | 1973 | 1991 | 216 | 249 | 50 | 4,243 | 124 | 22.33 | 1 | 13,852 | 558 | 24.82 | 60 |
| **Sidebottom, R J** © | **Jan 15, 1978** | | **1997** | **2015** | **120** | **150** | **44** | **1542** | **61** | **14.54** | **0** | **8,953** | **394** | **22.72** | **34** |
| Sidgwick, R * | Aug 7, 1851 | 1934 | 1882 | 1882 | 9 | 13 | 0 | 64 | 17 | 4.92 | 0 | — | — | — | 7 |
| Silverwood, C E W © | Mar 15, 1975 | | 1993 | 2005 | 131 | 179 | 33 | 2,369 | 80 | 16.22 | 0 | 11,413 | 427 | 27.62 | 30 |
| Silvester, S | Mar 12, 1951 | | 1976 | 1977 | 6 | 7 | 0 | 30 | 14 | 10.00 | 0 | 313 | 12 | 26.08 | 2 |
| Simpson, E T B * | Mar 5, 1867 | Mar 20, 1944 | 1889 | 1889 | 1 | 2 | 0 | 1 | 1 | 0.50 | 0 | — | — | — | 0 |
| § Sims, Rev H M * | Mar 15, 1853 | Oct 5, 1885 | 1875 | 1877 | 9 | 10 | 2 | 109 | 35* | 12.11 | 0 | 742 | 48 | 15.45 | 5 |
| Slinn, W | Dec 13, 1826 | June 19, 1888 | 1861 | 1864 | 9 | 14 | 3 | 22 | 11 | 2.00 | 0 | — | — | — | 2 |
| Smailes, T F | Mar 27, 1910 | Dec 1, 1970 | 1932 | 1948 | 262 | 339 | 42 | 5,686 | 117 | 19.14 | 3 | 16,593 | 802 | 20.68 | 153 |
| Smales, K | Sept 15, 1927 | Mar 10, 2015 | 1948 | 1950 | 13 | 19 | 9 | 165 | 45 | 10.31 | 0 | 766 | 22 | 34.81 | 11 |
| Smith, A F * | Mar 7, 1847 | Jan 6, 1915 | 1868 | 1874 | 28 | 49 | 4 | 692 | 89 | 15.37 | 0 | — | — | — | 4 |
| Smith, E (Barnsley) | July 11, 1888 | Jan 2, 1972 | 1914 | 1926 | 16 | 21 | 5 | 169 | 49 | 10.56 | 0 | 1,090 | 46 | 23.69 | 5 |

# LIST OF PLAYERS AND CAREER AVERAGES IN ALL FIRST-CLASS MATCHES FOR YORKSHIRE *(Continued)*

| Player | Date of Birth | Date of Death (if known) | First Played | Last Played | M | Inns | NO | Runs | HS | Av'ge | 100s | Runs | Wkts | Av'ge | Ct/St |
|---|---|---|---|---|---|---|---|---|---|---|---|---|---|---|---|
| Smith, Ernest (Morley)*© | Oct 19, 1869 | Feb 9, 1945 | 1888 | 1907 | 154 | 234 | 18 | 4,453 | 129 | 20.61 | 2 | 6,278 | 248 | 25.31 | 112 |
| Smith, Fred (Idle) | Dec 26, 1885 | Not known | 1911 | 1911 | 2 | 1 | 0 | 11 | 11 | 11.00 | 0 | 45 | 2 | 22.50 | 2 |
| Smith, Fred (Yeadon) | Dec 18, 1879 | Oct 20, 1905 | 1903 | 1903 | 13 | 19 | 1 | 292 | 55 | 16.22 | 0 | 7 | 0 | — | 3 |
| Smith, G | Jan 13, 1876 | Jan 16, 1929 | 1901 | 1906 | 2 | 1 | 0 | 7 | 7 | 7.00 | 0 | 7 | 1 | 7.00 | 3 |
| Smith, J | Mar 23, 1833 | Feb 12, 1909 | 1865 | 1865 | 2 | 3 | 0 | 28 | 16 | 9.33 | 0 | 62 | 0 | — | 3 |
| Smith, N | Apr 1, 1949 | — | 1970 | 1971 | 5 | 11 | 5 | 82 | 20 | 13.66 | 0 | 72 | 6 | 12.00 | 14/3 |
| Smith, R | Apr 6, 1944 | Mar 4, 2003 | 1969 | 1970 | 5 | 8 | 3 | 99 | 37* | 19.80 | 0 | — | — | — | 0 |
| Smith, Walker | Aug 14, 1847 | July 7, 1900 | 1874 | 1874 | 5 | 9 | 0 | 152 | 59 | 16.88 | 0 | — | — | — | 3 |
| § Smith, William | Nov 1, 1839 | Apr 19, 1897 | 1865 | 1874 | 11 | 19 | 3 | 260 | 90 | 16.25 | 0 | — | — | — | 8 |
| Smithson, G A | Nov 1, 1926 | Sept 6, 1970 | 1946 | 1950 | 39 | 60 | 5 | 1,449 | 169 | 26.34 | 2 | 84 | 1 | 84.00 | 21 |
| Smurthwaite, J | Oct 17, 1916 | Oct 20, 1989 | 1938 | 1939 | 7 | 9 | 5 | 29 | 20* | 7.25 | 0 | 237 | 12 | 19.75 | 4 |
| Sowden, D | Dec 1, 1853 | July 5, 1921 | 1878 | 1887 | 8 | 11 | 0 | 137 | 37 | 12.45 | 0 | 22 | 0 | — | 1 |
| Squire, D | Dec 31, 1864 | Apr 28, 1922 | 1893 | 1893 | 1 | 2 | 0 | 0 | 0 | 0.00 | 0 | 25 | 0 | — | 0 |
| Squires, P J | Aug 4, 1951 | — | 1972 | 1976 | 49 | 84 | 8 | 1,271 | 70 | 16.72 | 0 | 32 | 0 | — | 14 |
| Stanley, H C * | Feb 16, 1888 | May 18, 1934 | 1911 | 1913 | 8 | 13 | 0 | 155 | 42 | 11.92 | 0 | — | — | — | 6 |
| § Stanyforth, R T * | May 30, 1892 | Feb 20, 1964 | 1928 | 1928 | 3 | 3 | 0 | 26 | 10 | 8.66 | 0 | — | — | — | 2 |
| § Starc, M A | Jan 13, 1990 | — | 2012 | 2012 | 2 | 3 | 1 | 28 | 28* | — | 0 | 153 | 7 | 21.85 | 0 |
| Stead, B | June 21, 1939 | Apr 15, 1980 | 1959 | 1959 | 2 | 3 | 0 | 8 | 8 | 2.66 | 0 | 115 | 7 | 16.42 | 0 |
| § Stemp, R D | Dec 11, 1967 © | | 1993 | 1998 | 104 | 135 | 36 | 1,267 | 65 | 12.79 | 0 | 8,557 | 241 | 35.50 | 49 |
| Stephenson, E | June 5, 1832 | July 5, 1898 | 1861 | 1873 | 36 | 61 | 16 | 803 | 67 | 14.33 | 0 | — | — | — | 30/27 |
| Stephenson, J S * | Nov 10, 1903 | Oct 7, 1975 | 1923 | 1926 | 16 | 19 | 2 | 182 | 60 | 10.70 | 0 | 65 | 0 | — | 5 |
| Stevenson, G B | Dec 16, 1955 © | | 1973 | 1986 | 177 | 217 | 32 | 3,856 | 115* | 20.84 | 2 | 13,254 | 464 | 28.56 | 73 |
| Stott, W B | July 18, 1934 | — | 1952 | 1963 | 187 | 309 | 19 | 9,168 | 186 | 31.61 | 17 | 112 | 7 | 16.00 | 91 |
| Stringer, P M | Feb 23, 1943 | — | 1967 | 1969 | 19 | 17 | 8 | 101 | 15* | 11.22 | 0 | 696 | 32 | 21.75 | 7 |
| Stuchbury, S | June 22, 1954 | — | 1978 | 1981 | 3 | 3 | 2 | 7 | 4* | 7.00 | 0 | 236 | 8 | 29.50 | 2 |
| § Sugg, F H | Jan 11, 1862 | May 29, 1933 | 1883 | 1883 | 3 | 12 | 4 | 80 | 13* | 10.00 | 0 | — | — | — | 4/1 |
| § Sugg, W | May 21, 1860 | May 21, 1933 | 1881 | 1881 | 1 | 1 | 0 | 9 | 9 | 9.00 | 0 | — | — | — | 0 |
| Sullivan, J H B * | Sept 21, 1890 | Feb 8, 1932 | 1912 | 1912 | 1 | 2 | 0 | 41 | 26 | 20.50 | 0 | 43 | 0 | — | 0 |
| Sutcliffe, H | Nov 24, 1894 | Jan 22, 1978 | 1919 | 1945 | 602 | 864 | 96 | 38,558 | 313 | 50.20 | 112 | 381 | 8 | 47.62 | 402 |
| Sutcliffe, W H H *© | Oct 10, 1926 | Sept 16, 1998 | 1948 | 1957 | 177 | 273 | 34 | 6,247 | 181 | 26.13 | 6 | 152 | 6 | 25.33 | 80 |

# LIST OF PLAYERS AND CAREER AVERAGES IN ALL FIRST-CLASS MATCHES FOR YORKSHIRE (Continued)

| Player | Date of Birth | Date of Death (if known) | First Played | Last Played | M | Inns | NO | Runs | HS | Av'ge | 100s | Runs | Wkts | Av'ge | Ct/St |
|---|---|---|---|---|---|---|---|---|---|---|---|---|---|---|---|
| Swallow, I G | Dec 18, 1962 | | 1983 | 1989 | 61 | 82 | 18 | 1,296 | 114 | 20.25 | 1 | 3,270 | 64 | 51.09 | 28 |
| § Swanepoel, P J | Mar 30, 1977 | | 2003 | 2003 | 2 | 3 | 0 | 20 | 17 | 6.66 | 0 | 129 | 3 | 43.00 | 1 |
| § Tait, T | Oct 1, 1872 | Sept 6, 1954 | 1898 | 1899 | 2 | 3 | 1 | 7 | 3 | 3.50 | 0 | | | | |
| Tasker, J * | Feb 4, 1887 | Aug 24, 1975 | 1912 | 1913 | 31 | 43 | 4 | 586 | 67 | 15.02 | 0 | | | | 14 |
| Tattersall, G * © | Apr 21, 1882 | June 29, 1972 | 1905 | 1905 | 1 | 2 | 0 | 26 | 26 | 13.00 | 0 | | | | 0 |
| Taylor, C R | Feb 21, 1981 | | 2001 | 2005 | 16 | 27 | 3 | 416 | 52* | 17.33 | 0 | | | | 8 |
| Taylor, H | Dec 18, 1900 | Oct 28, 1988 | 1924 | 1925 | 9 | 13 | 0 | 153 | 36 | 11.76 | 0 | | | | 1 |
| Taylor, H S | Dec 11, 1856 | Nov 16, 1896 | 1879 | 1879 | 3 | 5 | 0 | 36 | 22 | 7.20 | 0 | | | | 0 |
| Taylor, J | Apr 2, 1850 | May 27, 1924 | 1880 | 1881 | 9 | 13 | 1 | 107 | 44 | 8.91 | 0 | | | | 4 |
| Taylor, K © | Aug 21, 1935 | | 1953 | 1968 | 303 | 505 | 35 | 12,864 | 203* | 27.37 | 16 | 3,680 | 129 | 28.52 | 146 |
| Taylor, N S | June 2, 1963 | | 1982 | 1983 | 8 | 6 | 1 | 10 | 4 | 2.00 | 0 | 720 | 22 | 32.72 | 2 |
| Taylor, T L * © | May 25, 1878 | Mar. 16, 1960 | 1899 | 1906 | 82 | 122 | 10 | 3,933 | 156 | 35.11 | 8 | | | | 47/2 |
| § Tendulkar, S R © | Apr 24, 1973 | | 1992 | 1992 | 16 | 25 | 2 | 1,070 | 100 | 46.52 | 1 | 195 | 4 | 48.75 | 2 |
| !0Thewlis, H | Aug 31, 1865 | Nov 30, 1920 | 1888 | 1888 | 2 | 4 | 1 | 4 | 2* | 1.33 | 0 | | | | 2 |
| Thewlis, John Jun. | Sept 21, 1850 | Aug 9, 1901 | 1879 | 1879 | 3 | 4 | 0 | 21 | 10 | 5.25 | 0 | | | | 2 |
| Thewlis, John Sen. | Mar 11, 1828 | Dec 29, 1899 | 1861 | 1875 | 44 | 80 | 3 | 1,280 | 108 | 16.62 | 1 | | | | 21/1 |
| Thorncroft, N D | Jan 23, 1985 | | 2002 | 2007 | 7 | 10 | 4 | 50 | 30 | 8.33 | 0 | 545 | 16 | 34.06 | 2 |
| Thornton, A | July 20, 1854 | Apr 18, 1915 | 1881 | 1881 | 3 | 4 | 0 | 21 | 7 | 5.25 | 0 | | | | 2 |
| Thornton, G * | Dec 24, 1867 | Jan 31, 1939 | 1891 | 1891 | 3 | 4 | 0 | 21 | 16 | 5.25 | 0 | 74 | 2 | 37.00 | 2 |
| Thorpe, G | Feb 20, 1834 | Mar 2, 1899 | 1864 | 1864 | 1 | 2 | 1 | 14 | 9* | 14.00 | 0 | | | | 0 |
| Threapleton, J W | July 20, 1857 | July 30, 1918 | 1881 | 1881 | 1 | 1 | 0 | 8 | 8* | | 0 | | | | 2/1 |
| Tinsley, H J | Feb 20, 1865 | Dec 10, 1938 | 1890 | 1891 | 9 | 13 | 0 | 56 | 15 | 4.30 | 0 | 57 | 4 | 14.25 | 1 |
| Townsley, R A J | June 24, 1952 | | 1974 | 1975 | 1 | 2 | 0 | 22 | 12 | 5.50 | 0 | 0 | 0 | | |
| Towse, A D | Apr 22, 1968 | | 1988 | 1988 | 1 | 1 | 0 | 1 | 1 | 1.00 | 0 | 50 | 3 | 16.66 | 1 |
| Trueman, F S © | Feb 6, 1931 | July 1, 2006 | 1949 | 1968 | 459 | 533 | 81 | 6,852 | 104 | 15.15 | 2 | 29,890 | 1,745 | 17.12 | 325 |
| Tunnicliffe, J © | Aug 26, 1866 | July 11, 1948 | 1891 | 1907 | 472 | 768 | 57 | 19,435 | 243 | 27.33 | 22 | 388 | 7 | 55.42 | 665 |
| Turner, A | Sept 2, 1885 | Aug 29, 1951 | 1910 | 1911 | 9 | 16 | 1 | 163 | 37 | 10.86 | 0 | | | | 7 |
| Turner, B | July 25, 1938 | Dec 27, 2015 | 1960 | 1961 | 2 | 4 | 2 | 7 | 3* | 3.50 | 0 | 47 | 4 | 11.75 | 0 |
| Turner, C © | Jan 11, 1902 | Nov 19, 1968 | 1925 | 1946 | 200 | 266 | 32 | 6,132 | 130 | 26.20 | 2 | 5,320 | 173 | 30.75 | 181 |
| Turner, F I | Sept 3, 1894 | Oct 1, 1954 | 1924 | 1924 | 5 | 7 | 0 | 33 | 12 | 4.71 | 0 | | | | 2 |

| Player | Date of Birth | Date of Death (if known) | First Played | Last Played | M | Inns | NO | Runs | HS | Av'ge | 100s | Runs | Wkts | Av'ge | Ct/St |
|---|---|---|---|---|---|---|---|---|---|---|---|---|---|---|---|
| Tyson, C T | Jan 24, 1889 | Apr 3, 1940 | 1921 | 1921 | 3 | 5 | 2 | 232 | 100* | 77.33 | 1 | — | — | — | 1 |
| Ullathorne, C E | Apr 11, 1845 | May 2, 1904 | 1868 | 1875 | 27 | 46 | 8 | 283 | 28 | 7.44 | 0 | — | — | — | 19 |
| Ulyett, G | Oct 21, 1851 | June 18, 1898 | 1873 | 1893 | 355 | 618 | 31 | 14,157 | 199* | 24.11 | 15 | 8,181 | 457 | 17.90 | 235 |
| § Usher, J | Feb 26, 1859 | Aug 9, 1905 | 1888 | 1888 | 1 | 2 | 0 | 7 | 5 | 3.50 | 0 | 31 | 2 | 15.50 | 1 |
| van Geloven, J | Jan 4, 1934 | Aug 21, 2003 | 1955 | 1955 | 3 | 2 | 1 | 17 | 16 | 17.00 | 0 | 224 | 6 | 37.33 | 2 |
| § Vaughan, M P | Oct 29, 1974 | | 1993 | 2009 | 151 | 267 | 14 | 9,160 | 183 | 36.20 | 20 | 4,268 | 92 | 46.39 | 55 |
| § Verelst, H W * | July 2, 1846 | Apr 5, 1918 | 1868 | 1869 | 3 | 4 | 1 | 66 | 33* | 22.00 | 0 | — | — | — | 2 |
| Verity, H | May 18, 1905 | July 31, 1943 | 1930 | 1939 | 278 | 294 | 77 | 3,898 | 101 | 17.96 | 1 | 21,353 | 1,558 | 13.70 | 191 |
| Waddington, A | Feb 4, 1893 | Oct 28, 1959 | 1919 | 1927 | 255 | 250 | 65 | 2,396 | 114 | 12.95 | 1 | 16,203 | 835 | 19.40 | 222 |
| Wade, S | Feb 8, 1858 | Nov 5, 1931 | 1886 | 1890 | 65 | 65 | 20 | 1,438 | 74* | 15.80 | 0 | 2,498 | 133 | 18.78 | 31 |
| Wainwright D J | Mar 21, 1985 | | 2004 | 2011 | 29 | 36 | 11 | 914 | 104 | 36.56 | 2 | 2,480 | 69 | 35.94 | 6 |
| Wainwright, E | Apr 8, 1865 | Oct 28, 1919 | 1888 | 1902 | 352 | 545 | 36 | 11,092 | 228 | 21.53 | 18 | 17,744 | 998 | 17.77 | 327 |
| Wainwright, W | Jan 21, 1882 | Dec 31, 1961 | 1903 | 1905 | 24 | 36 | 3 | 648 | 62 | 19.63 | 0 | 582 | 19 | 30.63 | 21 |
| Wake, W R * | May 21, 1852 | Mar 14, 1896 | 1881 | 1881 | 3 | 3 | 0 | 13 | 11 | 4.33 | 0 | — | — | — | 2 |
| Walker, A * | June 22, 1844 | May 26, 1927 | 1863 | 1870 | 9 | 16 | 1 | 138 | 26 | 9.20 | 0 | 74 | 1 | 74.00 | 3 |
| Walker, C | June 26, 1919 | Dec 3, 1992 | 1947 | 1948 | 5 | 9 | 2 | 268 | 91 | 38.28 | 0 | 71 | 2 | 35.50 | 3 |
| Walker, T | Apr 3, 1854 | Aug 28, 1925 | 1879 | 1880 | 14 | 22 | 2 | 179 | 30 | 8.95 | 0 | 7 | 0 | — | 1 |
| Waller, G | Dec 3, 1864 | Dec 11, 1937 | 1893 | 1894 | 3 | 4 | 0 | 17 | 13 | 4.25 | 0 | 70 | 4 | 17.50 | 3 |
| Wallgate, L * | Nov 12, 1849 | May 9, 1887 | 1875 | 1878 | 3 | 3 | 0 | 9 | 6 | 3.00 | 0 | 17 | 1 | 17.00 | 1 |
| Ward, A | Nov 21, 1865 | Jan 6, 1939 | 1886 | 1886 | 4 | 7 | 1 | 41 | 22 | 6.83 | 0 | — | — | — | 1 |
| Ward, F | Aug 31, 1881 | Feb 8, 1948 | 1903 | 1903 | 1 | 1 | 1 | 0 | 0 | 0.00 | 0 | 16 | 0 | — | 0 |
| Ward, H P * | Jan 20, 1899 | Dec 16, 1946 | 1920 | 1920 | 1 | 1 | 0 | 10 | 10* | | 0 | — | — | — | 0 |
| Wardall, T A | Apr 19, 1862 | Dec 20, 1932 | 1884 | 1894 | 43 | 73 | 2 | 1,003 | 106 | 14.12 | 2 | 489 | 23 | 21.26 | 25 |
| Wardlaw, I | Jun 29, 1985 | | 2011 | 2012 | 4 | 3 | 2 | 31 | 17* | 31.00 | 0 | 368 | 4 | 92.00 | 2 |
| Wardle, J H | Jan 8, 1923 | July 23, 1985 | 1946 | 1958 | 330 | 418 | 57 | 5,765 | 79 | 15.96 | 0 | 27,917 | 1,539 | 18.13 | 210 |
| Waring, J S | Oct 1, 1942 | | 1963 | 1966 | 28 | 27 | 15 | 137 | 26 | 11.41 | 0 | 1,122 | 53 | 21.16 | 17 |
| Waring, S | Nov 4, 1838 | Apr 17, 1919 | 1870 | 1870 | 1 | 1 | 0 | 9 | 9 | 9.00 | 0 | — | — | — | 0 |
| Washington, W A I | Dec 11, 1879 | Oct 20, 1927 | 1900 | 1902 | 44 | 62 | 6 | 1,290 | 100* | 23.03 | 1 | — | — | — | 18 |
| Watson, H | Sept 26, 1880 | Nov 24, 1951 | 1908 | 1914 | 29 | 35 | 11 | 141 | 41 | 5.87 | 0 | — | — | — | 46/10 |

# LIST OF PLAYERS AND CAREER AVERAGES IN ALL FIRST-CLASS MATCHES FOR YORKSHIRE (Continued)

| Player | Date of Birth | Date of Death (if known) | First Played | Last Played | M | Inns | NO | Runs | HS | Av'ge | 100s | Runs | Wkts | Av'ge | Ct/St |
|---|---|---|---|---|---|---|---|---|---|---|---|---|---|---|---|
| Watson, W © | Mar 7, 1920 | Apr 24, 2004 | 1939 | 1957 | 283 | 430 | 65 | 13,965 | 214* | 38.22 | 26 | 75 | 0 | — | 170 |
| Waud, B W * | June 4, 1837 | May 31, 1889 | 1862 | 1864 | 6 | 10 | 1 | 165 | 42 | 18.33 | 0 | — | — | — | 2 |
| Webster, C | June 9, 1838 | Jan 6, 1881 | 1861 | 1868 | 3 | 5 | 1 | 30 | 10 | 7.50 | 0 | — | — | — | 1 |
| Webster, H H | May 8, 1844 | Mar 5, 1915 | 1868 | 1868 | 2 | 3 | 0 | 10 | 10 | 3.33 | 0 | — | — | — | 1 |
| § Weekes, L C | July 19, 1971 | — | 1994 | 2000 | 2 | 2 | 0 | 20 | 10 | 10.00 | 0 | 191 | 10 | 19.10 | — |
| West, J | Oct 16, 1844 | Jan 27, 1890 | 1868 | 1876 | 38 | 64 | 13 | 461 | 41 | 9.03 | 0 | 853 | 53 | 16.09 | 14 |
| Wharf, A G | June 4, 1975 | — | 1994 | 1997 | 7 | 9 | 1 | 186 | 62 | 23.25 | 0 | 454 | 11 | 41.27 | 6 |
| Whatmough, F J | Dec 4, 1856 | June 3, 1904 | 1878 | 1882 | 7 | 11 | 1 | 51 | 20 | 5.10 | 0 | 111 | 5 | 22.20 | 4 |
| Wheater, C H * | Mar 4, 1860 | May 11, 1885 | 1880 | 1880 | 2 | 4 | 1 | 45 | 27 | 15.00 | 0 | — | — | — | 2 |
| White, Sir A W * | Oct 14, 1877 | Dec 16, 1945 | 1908 | 1920 | 97 | 128 | 28 | 1,457 | 55 | 14.57 | 0 | 7 | 0 | — | 50 |
| White, C © | Dec 16, 1969 | — | 1990 | 2007 | 221 | 350 | 45 | 10,376 | 186 | 34.01 | 19 | 7,649 | 276 | 27.71 | 140 |
| Whitehead, J P | Sept 3, 1925 | Aug 15, 2000 | 1946 | 1951 | 37 | 38 | 17 | 387 | 58* | 18.42 | 0 | 2,610 | 96 | 27.47 | 11 |
| Whitehead, Lees | Mar 14, 1864 | Nov 22, 1913 | 1889 | 1904 | 119 | 172 | 38 | 2,073 | 67* | 15.47 | 0 | 2,408 | 99 | 24.32 | 68 |
| Whitehead, Luther | June 25, 1869 | Jan 16, 1931 | 1893 | 1893 | 2 | 4 | 0 | 21 | 13 | 5.25 | 0 | — | — | — | — |
| Whiteley, J P | Feb 28, 1955 | — | 1978 | 1982 | 45 | 38 | 17 | 231 | 26 | 11.00 | 0 | 2,410 | 70 | 34.42 | 21 |
| Whiting, C P * | Apr 18, 1888 | Jan 14, 1959 | 1914 | 1920 | 6 | 10 | 2 | 92 | 26 | 11.50 | 0 | 416 | 15 | 27.73 | 2 |
| Whitwell, J P * | Feb 22, 1869 | Nov 6, 1932 | 1890 | 1890 | 1 | 2 | 0 | 8 | 4 | 4.00 | 0 | 11 | 1 | 11.00 | — |
| § Whitwell, W F * | Dec 12, 1867 | Apr 12, 1942 | 1890 | 1890 | 10 | 14 | 2 | 67 | 26 | 5.58 | 0 | 518 | 25 | 20.72 | 2 |
| Widdup, S | Nov 10, 1977 | — | 2000 | 2001 | 11 | 18 | 1 | 245 | 44 | 14.41 | 0 | 22 | 1 | 22.00 | 5 |
| Wigley, D H | Oct 26, 1981 | — | 2002 | 2002 | 5 | 6 | 5 | 19 | 15 | 19.00 | 0 | 116 | 1 | 116.00 | 1 |
| § Wilkinson, A J A * | May 28, 1835 | Dec 11, 1905 | 1865 | 1868 | 5 | 6 | 0 | 129 | 53 | 21.50 | 0 | 57 | 0 | — | — |
| Wilkinson, F | May 23, 1914 | Mar 26, 1984 | 1937 | 1939 | 14 | 14 | 1 | 73 | 18* | 5.61 | 0 | 590 | 26 | 22.69 | 12 |
| Wilkinson, H * | Dec 11, 1877 | Apr 15, 1967 | 1903 | 1905 | 48 | 75 | 3 | 1,382 | 113 | 19.19 | 1 | 121 | 3 | 40.33 | 19 |
| Wilkinson, R | Nov 11, 1977 | — | 1998 | 1998 | 9 | 9 | 8 | 9 | 9 | 9.00 | 0 | 35 | 1 | 35.00 | 1 |
| Wilkinson, W H © | Mar 12, 1881 | June 4, 1961 | 1903 | 1910 | 126 | 192 | 14 | 3,812 | 103 | 21.41 | 1 | 971 | 31 | 31.32 | 93 |
| Williams, A C | May 1, 1887 | June 1, 1966 | 1911 | 1919 | 12 | 14 | 10 | 95 | 48* | 23.75 | 0 | 678 | 30 | 22.60 | 6 |
| § Williamson, K S | Sept 8, 1990 | — | 2013 | 2014 | 14 | 22 | 3 | 1,032 | 189 | 54.31 | 1 | 407 | 9 | 45.22 | 14 |
| Wilson, B B © | Dec 11, 1879 | Sept 14, 1957 | 1906 | 1914 | 185 | 308 | 15 | 8,055 | 208 | 27.50 | 15 | 278 | 2 | 139.00 | 53 |
| Wilson, C E M * | May 15, 1875 | Feb 8, 1944 | 1896 | 1899 | 8 | 13 | 3 | 256 | 91* | 25.60 | 0 | 257 | 12 | 21.41 | — |
| Wilson, D © | Aug 7, 1937 | July 21, 2012 | 1957 | 1974 | 392 | 502 | 85 | 5,788 | 83 | 13.88 | 0 | 22,626 | 1,104 | 20.49 | 235 |

# LIST OF PLAYERS AND CAREER AVERAGES IN ALL FIRST-CLASS MATCHES FOR YORKSHIRE (Continued)

| Player | Date of Birth | Date of Death (if known) | First Played | Last Played | M | Inns | NO | Runs | HS | Av'ge | 100s | Runs | Wkts | Av'ge | Ct/St |
|---|---|---|---|---|---|---|---|---|---|---|---|---|---|---|---|
| Wilson, E R * ...© | Mar 25, 1879 | July 21, 1957 | 1899 | 1923 | 66 | 72 | 18 | 902 | 104* | 16.70 | 1 | 3,106 | 197 | 15.76 | 30 |
| Wilson, Geoffrey * ...© | Aug 21, 1895 | Nov 29, 1960 | 1919 | 1924 | 92 | 94 | 14 | 983 | 70 | 12.28 | 0 | 11 | 0 | — | 33 |
| Wilson, G A * | Feb 2, 1916 | Sept 24, 2002 | 1936 | 1939 | 15 | 25 | 5 | 352 | 55* | 17.60 | 0 | 138 | 1 | 138.00 | 7 |
| Wilson, John * | June 30, 1857 | Nov 11, 1931 | 1887 | 1888 | 4 | 5 | 1 | 17 | 13* | 4.25 | 0 | 165 | 12 | 13.75 | 3 |
| Wilson, J P * | Apr 3, 1889 | Oct 3, 1959 | 1911 | 1912 | 9 | 14 | 1 | 81 | 36 | 6.23 | 0 | 24 | 1 | 24.00 | 2 |
| Wilson, J V | Jan 17, 1921 | June 5, 2008 | 1946 | 1962 | 477 | 724 | 75 | 20,548 | 230 | 31.66 | 29 | 313 | 3 | 104.33 | 520 |
| Wood, A ...© | Aug 25, 1898 | Apr 1, 1973 | 1927 | 1946 | 408 | 481 | 80 | 8,579 | 123* | 21.39 | 1 | 33 | 1 | 33.00 | 612/243 |
| Wood, B | Dec 26, 1942 | | 1964 | 1964 | 2 | 3 | 1 | 63 | 35 | 12.60 | 0 | | | | 4 |
| Wood, C H | July 26, 1934 | June 28, 2006 | 1959 | 1959 | 4 | 4 | 1 | 22 | 10 | 7.33 | 0 | 319 | 11 | 29.00 | 1 |
| Wood, G W | Nov 18, 1862 | Dec 4, 1948 | 1895 | 1895 | 2 | 2 | 0 | 2 | 1 | 1.00 | 0 | | | | 0/1 |
| Wood, H * | Mar 22, 1855 | July 31, 1941 | 1879 | 1880 | 10 | 16 | 1 | 156 | 36 | 10.40 | 0 | 212 | 10 | 21.20 | 8 |
| Wood, J H * | | | 1881 | 1881 | 2 | 1 | 0 | 14 | 14 | 14.00 | 0 | | | | 0 |
| Wood, M J | Apr 6, 1977 | | 1997 | 2007 | 128 | 222 | 20 | 6,742 | 207 | 33.37 | 16 | 27 | 2 | 13.50 | 113 |
| Wood, R | June 3, 1929 | May 22, 1990 | 1952 | 1956 | 22 | 18 | 4 | 60 | 17 | 4.28 | 0 | 1,346 | 51 | 26.39 | 5 |
| Woodford, J D | Sept 9, 1943 | | 1968 | 1972 | 38 | 61 | 2 | 1,204 | 101 | 20.40 | 1 | 185 | 4 | 46.25 | 12 |
| Woodhouse, F E * | May 29, 1868 | Aug 25, 1943 | 1893 | 1894 | 4 | 8 | 0 | 57 | 18 | 7.12 | 0 | | | | 3 |
| Woodhouse, W H * | Apr 16, 1856 | Mar 4, 1938 | 1884 | 1885 | 9 | 13 | 0 | 218 | 63 | 16.76 | 0 | | | | 6 |
| Wormald, A * | May 10, 1855 | Feb 6, 1940 | 1885 | 1891 | 7 | 11 | 3 | 161 | 80 | 20.12 | 0 | | | | 10/2 |
| Worsley, W A * ...© | Apr 5, 1890 | Dec 4, 1973 | 1928 | 1929 | 60 | 50 | 4 | 722 | 60 | 15.69 | 0 | | | | 32 |
| Wrathmell, L F | Jan 22, 1855 | Sept 16, 1928 | 1886 | 1886 | 1 | 2 | 0 | 18 | 17 | 9.00 | 0 | | | | 0 |
| Wright, R | July 19, 1852 | May 25, 1891 | 1877 | 1877 | 2 | 4 | 1 | 28 | 22 | 9.33 | 0 | | | | 0 |
| Wright, T J * | Mar 5, 1900 | Nov 7, 1962 | 1919 | 1919 | 1 | 2 | 0 | 12 | 12 | 12.00 | 0 | | | | 0 |
| Yardley, N W D * ...© | Mar 19, 1915 | Oct 4, 1989 | 1936 | 1955 | 302 | 420 | 56 | 11,632 | 183* | 31.95 | 17 | 5,818 | 195 | 29.83 | 220 |
| Yeadon, D | Dec 10, 1861 | May 30, 1914 | 1888 | 1888 | 3 | 6 | 2 | 41 | 22 | 10.25 | 0 | | | | 5/3 |
| § Younus Khan | Nov 29, 1977 | | 2007 | 2007 | 13 | 19 | 2 | 824 | 217* | 48.47 | 3 | 342 | 8 | 42.75 | 11 |
| § Yuvraj Singh | Dec 12, 1981 | | 2003 | 2003 | 7 | 12 | 2 | 145 | 56 | 14.50 | 0 | 130 | 3 | 43.33 | 12 |

In the career averages it should be noted that the bowling analysis for the second Cambridgeshire innings at Ashton-under-Lyne in 1865 has not been found. G R Atkinson took 3 wickets, W Cuttell 2, G Freeman 4 and R Iddison 1. The respective bowling averages have been calculated excluding these wickets.

# MOST FIRST-CLASS APPEARANCES FOR YORKSHIRE

| Matches | Player | Matches | Player |
|---|---|---|---|
| 883 | W Rhodes (1898-1930) | 477 | J V Wilson (1946-1962) |
| 717 | G H Hirst (1891-1929) | 472 | J Tunnicliffe (1891-1907) |
| 676 | D Denton (1894-1920) | 459 | F S Trueman (1949-1968) |
| 602 | H Sutcliffe (1919-1945) | 456 | J H Hampshire (1961-1981) |
| 548 | M Leyland (1920-1947) | 445 | G G Macaulay (1920-1935) |
| 536 | D B Close (1949-1970) | 429 | D L Bairstow (1970-1990) |
| 517 | D Hunter (1888-1909) | 427 | A Dolphin (1905-1927) |
| 513 | S Haigh (1895-1913) | 425 | P Carrick (1970-1993) |
| 510 | Lord Hawke (1881-1911) | 414 | G Boycott (1962-1986) |
| 496 | R Illingworth (1951-1983) | 413 | E. Robinson (1919-1931) |
| 491 | † J G Binks (1955-1969) | 411 | P J Sharpe (1958-1974) |
| 487 | D E V Padgett (1951-1971) | 408 | A Wood (1927-1946) |
| 485 | P Holmes (1913-1933) | 401 | A Mitchell (1922-1945) |

† Kept wicket in 412 consecutive Championship matches 1955-1969

# MOST TOTAL APPEARANCES FOR YORKSHIRE
## (First-Class, Domestic List A and t20)

| Matches | Player | Matches | Player |
|---|---|---|---|
| 883 | W Rhodes (1898-1930) | 513 | S Haigh (1895-1913) |
| 832 | D L Bairstow (1970-1990) | 510 | Lord Hawke (1881-1911) |
| 729 | P Carrick (1970-1993) | 502 | P J Sharpe (1958-1974) |
| 719 | R J Blakey (1985-2004) | 485 | P Holmes (1913-1933) |
| 717 | G H Hirst (1891-1929) | 477 | J V Wilson (1946-1962) |
| 690 | J H Hampshire (1961-1981) | 472 | J Tunnicliffe (1891-1907) |
| 678 | G Boycott (1962-1986) | 470 | F S Trueman (1949-1968) |
| 676 | D Denton (1894-1920) | 467 | J D Love (1975-1989) |
| 602 | H Sutcliffe (1919-1945) | 453 | D Wilson (1957-1974) |
| 583 | A McGrath (1995-2012) | 452 | A Sidebottom (1973-1991) |
| 581 | D Byas (1986-2001) | 445 | G G Macaulay(1920-1935) |
| 568 | D B Close (1949-1970) | 443 | C M Old (1966-1982) |
| 548 | M Leyland (1920-1947) | 427 | A Dolphin (1905-1927) |
| 546 | C White (1990-2007) | 414 | P J Hartley (1985-1997) |
| 544 | D E V Padgett (1951-1971) | 413 | E Robinson (1919-1931) |
| 537 | R Illingworth (1951-1983) | 408 | A Wood (1927-1946) |
| 521 | J G Binks (1955-1969) | 402 | A G Nicholson (1962-1975) |
| 517 | D Hunter (1888-1909) | 401 | A Mitchell (1922-1945) |
| 514 | M D Moxon (1980-1997) | | |

# ONE DAY RECORDS SECTION

Yorkshire County Cricket Club thanks Statistician JOHN T. POTTER, who in 2014 has revamped and streamlined Yorkshire's One-Day Records Section. John's symbols in the pages that follow are:

$ = Sunday and National Leagues, Pro 40, Clydesdale Bank 40 and Yorkshire Bank 40

# = Benson & Hedges Cup

+ = Gillette Cup, NatWest Trophy, Cheltenham & Gloucester Trophy, Friends Provident Trophy and Royal London Cup

# LIST A
## WINNERS OF THE GILLETTE CUP, NATWEST TROPHY, CHELTENHAM & GLOUCESTER TROPHY FRIENDS PROVIDENT TROPHY AND ROYAL LONDON ONE-DAY CUP

*Yorkshire's Position*

### GILLETTE CUP

| | | |
|---|---|---|
| 1963 | Sussex | Quarter-Final |
| 1964 | Sussex | Round 2 |
| **1965** | **Yorkshire** | **Winner** |
| 1966 | Warwickshire | Round 2 |
| 1967 | Kent | Quarter-Final |
| 1968 | Warwickshire | Round 2 |
| **1969** | **Yorkshire** | **Winner** |
| 1970 | Lancashire | Round 1 |
| 1971 | Lancashire | Round 2 |
| 1972 | Lancashire | Round 1 |
| 1973 | Gloucestershire | Round 1 |
| 1974 | Kent | Quarter-Final |
| 1975 | Lancashire | Round 2 |
| 1976 | Northamptonshire | Round 1 |
| 1977 | Middlesex | Round 2 |
| 1978 | Sussex | Quarter-Final |
| 1979 | Somerset | Quarter-Final |
| 1980 | Middlesex | Semi-Final |

### NATWEST TROPHY

| | | |
|---|---|---|
| 1981 | Derbyshire | Round 1 |
| 1982 | Surrey | Semi-Final |
| 1983 | Somerset | Round 2 |
| 1984 | Middlesex | Round 1 |
| 1985 | Essex | Round 2 |
| 1986 | Sussex | Quarter-Final |
| 1987 | Nottinghamshire | Quarter-Final |

*Yorkshire's Position*

| | | |
|---|---|---|
| 1988 | Middlesex | Round 2 |
| 1989 | Warwickshire | Round 2 |
| 1990 | Lancashire | Quarter-Final |
| 1991 | Hampshire | Round 1 |
| 1992 | Northamptonshire | Round 2 |
| 1993 | Warwickshire | Quarter-Final |
| 1994 | Worcestershire | Round 2 |
| 1995 | Warwickshire | Semi-Final |
| 1996 | Lancashire | Semi-Final |
| 1997 | Essex | Quarter-Final |
| 1998 | Lancashire | Round 2 |
| 1999 | Gloucestershire | Semi-Final |
| 2000 | Gloucestershire | Round 4 |

### CHELTENHAM & GLOUCESTER TROPHY

| | | |
|---|---|---|
| 2001 | Somerset | Quarter-Final |
| **2002** | **Yorkshire** | **Winner** |
| 2003 | Gloucestershire | Round 4 |
| 2004 | Gloucestershire | Semi-Final |
| 2005 | Hampshire | Semi-Final |
| 2006 | Sussex | North 7 (10) |

### FRIENDS PROVIDENT TROPHY

| | | |
|---|---|---|
| 2007 | Durham | North 5 (10) |
| 2008 | Essex | Semi-Final |
| 2009 | Hampshire | Group C 3 (5) |

### ROYAL LONDON ONE-DAY CUP

| | | |
|---|---|---|
| 2014 | Durham | Quarter-Final |

# WINNERS OF THE NATIONAL AND SUNDAY LEAGUES, PRO 40, CLYDESDALE BANK 40 AND YORKSHIRE BANK 40 1969-2014

|  |  | Yorkshire's Position |  |  | Yorkshire's Position |
|---|---|---|---|---|---|
| **SUNDAY LEAGUE** | | | 1993 | Glamorgan | 9th |
| 1969 | Lancashire | 8th | 1994 | Warwickshire | 5th |
| 1970 | Lancashire | 14th | 1995 | Kent | 12th |
| 1971 | Worcestershire | 15th | 1996 | Surrey | 3rd |
| 1972 | Kent | 4th | 1997 | Warwickshire | 10th |
| 1973 | Kent | 2nd | 1998 | Lancashire | 9th |
| 1974 | Leicestershire | =6th | **NATIONAL LEAGUE** | | |
| 1975 | Hampshire | =5th | 1999 | Lancashire | 5th Div 1 |
| 1976 | Kent | 15th | 2000 | Gloucestershire | 2nd Div 1 |
| 1977 | Leicestershire | =13th | 2001 | Kent | 6th Div 1 |
| 1978 | Hampshire | 7th | 2002 | Glamorgan | 4th Div 1 |
| 1979 | Somerset | =4th | 2003 | Surrey | 8th Div 1 |
| 1980 | Warwickshire | =14th | 2004 | Glamorgan | 4th Div 2 |
| 1981 | Essex | =7th | 2005 | Essex | 8th Div 2 |
| 1982 | Sussex | 16th | 2006 | Essex | 9th Div 2 |
| **1983** | **Yorkshire** | **1st** | 2007 | Worcestershire | 6th Div 2 |
| 1984 | Essex | =14th | 2008 | Sussex | 2nd Div 2 |
| 1985 | Essex | 6th | 2009 | Sussex | 7th Div 1 |
| 1986 | Hampshire | 8th | **CLYDESDALE BANK 40** | | |
| 1987 | Worcestershire | =13th | 2010 | Warwickshire | Group B 1 (7) (Semi-Final) |
| 1988 | Worcestershire | 8th | | | |
| 1989 | Lancashire | 11th | 2011 | Surrey | Group A 6 (7) |
| 1990 | Derbyshire | 6th | 2012 | Hampshire | Group C 5 (7) |
| 1991 | Nottinghamshire | 7th | 2013 | Nottinghamshire | Group C 6 (7) |
| 1992 | Middlesex | 15th | | | |

## BENSON & HEDGES WINNERS 1972-2002

|  |  | Yorkshire's Position |  |  | Yorkshire's Position |
|---|---|---|---|---|---|
| 1972 | Leicestershire | Final | 1988 | Hampshire | Group B 4 (5) |
| 1973 | Kent | Group N 3 (5) | 1989 | Nottinghamshire | Group C 3 (5) |
| 1974 | Surrey | Quarter-Final | 1990 | Lancashire | Group C 3 (5) |
| 1975 | Leicestershire | Quarter-Final | 1991 | Worcestershire | Semi-Final |
| 1976 | Kent | Group D 3 (5) | 1992 | Hampshire | Group C 5 (5) |
| 1977 | Gloucestershire | Group D 3 (5) | 1993 | Derbyshire | Round One |
| 1978 | Kent | Group D 4 (5) | 1994 | Warwickshire | Round One |
| 1979 | Essex | Semi-Final | 1995 | Lancashire | Quarter-Final |
| 1980 | Northamptonshire | Group B 4 (5) | 1996 | Lancashire | Semi-Final |
| 1981 | Somerset | Quarter-Final | 1997 | Surrey | Quarter-Final |
| 1982 | Somerset | Group A 5 (5) | 1998 | Essex | Semi-Final |
| 1983 | Middlesex | Group B 5 (5) | 1999 | Gloucestershire | Final |
| 1984 | Lancashire | Semi-Final | 2000 | Gloucestershire | Quarter-Final |
| 1985 | Leicestershire | Group B 3 (5) | 2001 | Surrey | Semi-Final |
| 1986 | Middlesex | Group B 3 (5) | 2002 | Warwickshire | Quarter-Final |
| **1987** | **Yorkshire** | **Winner** | | | |

# SEASON-BY-SEASON RECORD OF ALL LIST A
# MATCHES PLAYED BY YORKSHIRE 1963-2015

| Season | Played | Won | Lost | Tie | N R | Abd | Season | Played | Won | Lost | Tie | N R | Abd |
|---|---|---|---|---|---|---|---|---|---|---|---|---|---|
| 1963 | 2 | 1 | 1 | 0 | 0 | 0 | 1991 | 24 | 13 | 10 | 0 | 1 | 0 |
| 1964 | 1 | 0 | 1 | 0 | 0 | 0 | 1992 | 21 | 8 | 13 | 0 | 0 | 2 |
| 1965 | 4 | 4 | 0 | 0 | 0 | 1 | 1993 | 21 | 10 | 10 | 0 | 1 | 0 |
| 1966 | 1 | 0 | 1 | 0 | 0 | 0 | 1994 | 19 | 11 | 8 | 0 | 0 | 1 |
| 1967 | 2 | 1 | 1 | 0 | 0 | 0 | 1995 | 27 | 15 | 11 | 0 | 1 | 1 |
| 1968 | 1 | 0 | 1 | 0 | 0 | 0 | 1996 | 27 | 18 | 9 | 0 | 0 | 0 |
| 1969 | 19 | 12 | 7 | 0 | 0 | 2 | 1997 | 25 | 14 | 10 | 1 | 0 | 1 |
| 1970 | 17 | 5 | 10 | 0 | 2 | 0 | 1998 | 25 | 14 | 10 | 0 | 1 | 0 |
| 1971 | 15 | 5 | 10 | 0 | 0 | 2 | 1999 | 23 | 13 | 10 | 0 | 0 | 0 |
| 1972 | 25 | 15 | 8 | 0 | 2 | 1 | 2000 | 24 | 13 | 10 | 0 | 1 | 0 |
| 1973 | 21 | 14 | 7 | 0 | 0 | 0 | 2001 | 26 | 13 | 13 | 0 | 0 | 0 |
| 1974 | 22 | 12 | 9 | 0 | 1 | 1 | 2002 | 27 | 16 | 11 | 0 | 0 | 1 |
| 1975 | 22 | 12 | 10 | 0 | 0 | 0 | 2003 | 18 | 6 | 12 | 0 | 0 | 0 |
| 1976 | 22 | 9 | 13 | 0 | 0 | 0 | 2004 | 23 | 13 | 8 | 0 | 2 | 0 |
| 1977 | 19 | 5 | 10 | 0 | 4 | 2 | 2005 | 22 | 8 | 14 | 0 | 0 | 0 |
| 1978 | 22 | 10 | 11 | 0 | 1 | 2 | 2006 | 15 | 4 | 10 | 0 | 1 | 2 |
| 1979 | 21 | 12 | 6 | 0 | 3 | 3 | 2007 | 17 | 8 | 7 | 0 | 2 | 1 |
| 1980 | 23 | 9 | 14 | 0 | 0 | 0 | 2008 | 18 | 10 | 4 | 1 | 3 | 0 |
| 1981 | 19 | 9 | 8 | 0 | 2 | 3 | 2009 | 16 | 6 | 9 | 0 | 1 | 0 |
| 1982 | 23 | 7 | 14 | 1 | 1 | 1 | 2010 | 13 | 10 | 3 | 0 | 0 | 0 |
| 1983 | 19 | 11 | 7 | 0 | 1 | 3 | 2011 | 12 | 5 | 7 | 0 | 0 | 0 |
| 1984 | 23 | 10 | 13 | 0 | 0 | 0 | 2012 | 11 | 4 | 7 | 0 | 0 | 1 |
| 1985 | 19 | 9 | 9 | 0 | 1 | 3 | 2013 | 13 | 4 | 9 | 0 | 0 | 0 |
| 1986 | 22 | 11 | 9 | 1 | 1 | 1 | 2014 | 10 | 6 | 4 | 0 | 0 | 0 |
| 1987 | 24 | 14 | 9 | 0 | 1 | 2 | 2015 | 10 | 5 | 3 | 0 | 2 | 0 |
| 1988 | 21 | 9 | 9 | 0 | 3 | 1 | | | | | | | |
| 1989 | 23 | 10 | 13 | 0 | 0 | 0 | | 961 | 476 | 442 | 4 | 39 | 39 |
| 1990 | 22 | 13 | 9 | 0 | 0 | 1 | | | | | | | |

*Abandoned matches are not included in the list of matches played.*

## ABANDONED LIST A MATCHES (39)

| | |
|---|---|
| 1965 | v. South Africa at Bradford $ |
| 1969 (2) | v. Warwickshire at Harrogate $ |
| | v. Lancashire at Manchester $ |
| 1971 (2) | v. Gloucestershire at Sheffield $ |
| | v. Somerset at Weston-Super-Mare $ |
| 1972 | v. Sussex at Leeds $ |
| 1974 | v. Warwickshire at Leeds $ |
| 1977 (2) | v. Warwickshire at Birmingham $ |
| | v. Surrey at Leeds $ |
| 1978 (2) | v. Essex at Bradford $ |
| | v. Gloucestershire at Hull $ |
| 1979 (3) | v. Leicestershire at Middlesbrough $ |
| | v. Kent at Huddersfield $ |
| | v. Worcestershire at Worcester $ |
| 1981 (3) | v. Warwickshire at Birmingham $ |
| | v. Lancashire at Leeds # |
| | v. Sussex at Hove $ |
| 1982 | v. Glamorgan at Bradford $ |
| 1983 (3) | v. Derbyshire at Chesterfield # |
| | v. Surrey at Leeds $ |
| | v. Essex at Chelmsford $ |

| | |
|---|---|
| 1985 (3) | v. Derbyshire at Scarborough $ |
| | v. Warwickshire at Birmingham $ |
| | v. Lancashire at Leeds $ |
| 1986 | v. Kent at Canterbury $ |
| 1987 (2) | v. Sussex at Hull $ |
| | v. Hampshire at Leeds $ |
| 1988 | v. Northamptonshire at Northampton $ |
| 1990 | v. Glamorgan at Newport $ |
| 1992 (2) | v. Sussex at Hove $ |
| | v. Durham at Darlington $ |
| 1994 | v. Essex at Leeds $ |
| 1995 | v. Derbyshire at Chesterfield # |
| 1997 | v. Sussex at Scarborough $ |
| 2002 | v. Nottinghamshire at Nottingham $ |
| 2006 (2) | v. Nottinghamshire at Leeds + |
| | v. Derbyshire at Derby $ |
| 2007 | v. Warwickshire at Birmingham + |
| 2012 | v. Northamptonshire at Leeds $ |

# ANALYSIS OF LIST A RESULTS V. ALL TEAMS 1963-2015

## DOMESTIC MATCHES

| Opponents | Played | HOME | | | | AWAY | | | | |
|---|---|---|---|---|---|---|---|---|---|---|
| | | Won | Lost | Tied | N. R | Won | Lost | Tied | N. R | Abd |
| Derbyshire | 61 | 19 | 9 | 0 | 1 | 19 | 9 | 1 | 3 | 4 |
| Durham | 27 | 9 | 5 | 0 | 0 | 6 | 6 | 0 | 1 | 1 |
| Essex | 46 | 12 | 12 | 0 | 0 | 9 | 12 | 0 | 0 | 3 |
| Glamorgan | 39 | 9 | 8 | 0 | 0 | 9 | 13 | 0 | 0 | 2 |
| Gloucestershire | 55 | 12 | 12 | 0 | 2 | 8 | 19 | 0 | 2 | 2 |
| Hampshire | 44 | 11 | 9 | 0 | 1 | 9 | 14 | 0 | 0 | 1 |
| Kent | 54 | 13 | 11 | 0 | 1 | 9 | 20 | 0 | 0 | 2 |
| Lancashire | 60 | 9 | 16 | 0 | 2 | 13 | 18 | 0 | 2 | 3 |
| Leicestershire | 64 | 18 | 16 | 0 | 0 | 11 | 16 | 1 | 2 | 1 |
| Middlesex | 48 | 14 | 4 | 0 | 3 | 9 | 16 | 0 | 2 | 0 |
| Northamptonshire | 56 | 16 | 11 | 0 | 3 | 18 | 7 | 0 | 1 | 2 |
| Nottinghamshire | 57 | 18 | 8 | 1 | 2 | 9 | 16 | 0 | 3 | 2 |
| Somerset | 54 | 13 | 14 | 0 | 1 | 11 | 15 | 0 | 0 | 1 |
| Surrey | 54 | 12 | 13 | 0 | 0 | 11 | 18 | 0 | 0 | 2 |
| Sussex | 46 | 11 | 11 | 0 | 1 | 11 | 12 | 0 | 0 | 5 |
| Warwickshire | 59 | 11 | 16 | 1 | 2 | 13 | 16 | 0 | 0 | 6 |
| Worcestershire | 61 | 13 | 18 | 0 | 2 | 17 | 11 | 0 | 0 | 1 |
| Bedfordshire | 1 | 0 | 0 | 0 | 0 | 1 | 0 | 0 | 0 | 0 |
| Berkshire | 2 | 0 | 0 | 0 | 0 | 2 | 0 | 0 | 0 | 0 |
| Cambridgeshire | 3 | 2 | 0 | 0 | 0 | 1 | 0 | 0 | 0 | 0 |
| Cheshire | 1 | 0 | 0 | 0 | 0 | 1 | 0 | 0 | 0 | 0 |
| Combined Universities | 3 | 0 | 2 | 0 | 0 | 1 | 0 | 0 | 0 | 0 |
| Devon | 4 | 0 | 0 | 0 | 0 | 4 | 0 | 0 | 0 | 0 |
| Dorset | 1 | 0 | 0 | 0 | 0 | 1 | 0 | 0 | 0 | 0 |
| Durham (M C) | 3 | 1 | 1 | 0 | 0 | 1 | 0 | 0 | 0 | 0 |
| Herefordshire | 1 | 0 | 0 | 0 | 0 | 1 | 0 | 0 | 0 | 0 |
| Ireland | 4 | 3 | 0 | 0 | 0 | 1 | 0 | 0 | 0 | 0 |
| Minor Counties | 11 | 6 | 0 | 0 | 0 | 5 | 0 | 0 | 0 | 0 |
| Netherlands | 4 | 1 | 1 | 0 | 0 | 1 | 1 | 0 | 0 | 0 |
| Norfolk | 2 | 1 | 0 | 0 | 0 | 1 | 0 | 0 | 0 | 0 |
| Northumberland | 1 | 1 | 0 | 0 | 0 | 0 | 0 | 0 | 0 | 0 |
| Scotland | 16 | 8 | 0 | 0 | 0 | 8 | 0 | 0 | 0 | 0 |
| Shropshire | 2 | 0 | 0 | 0 | 0 | 1 | 1 | 0 | 0 | 0 |
| Unicorns | 4 | 2 | 0 | 0 | 0 | 2 | 0 | 0 | 0 | 0 |
| Wiltshire | 1 | 0 | 0 | 0 | 0 | 1 | 0 | 0 | 0 | 0 |
| Yorkshire Cricket Board | 1 | 0 | 0 | 0 | 0 | 1 | 0 | 0 | 0 | 0 |
| **Total** | **950** | **245** | **197** | **2** | **21** | **227** | **240** | **2** | **16** | **38** |

## OTHER MATCHES

| | | | | | | | | | | |
|---|---|---|---|---|---|---|---|---|---|---|
| Australia | 3 | 0 | 1 | 0 | 2 | 0 | 0 | 0 | 0 | 0 |
| Bangladesh A | 1 | 1 | 0 | 0 | 0 | 0 | 0 | 0 | 0 | 0 |
| South Africa | 0 | 0 | 0 | 0 | 0 | 0 | 0 | 0 | 0 | 1 |
| Sri Lanka A | 3 | 0 | 3 | 0 | 0 | 0 | 0 | 0 | 0 | 0 |
| West Indies | 1 | 1 | 0 | 0 | 0 | 0 | 0 | 0 | 0 | 0 |
| West Indies A | 1 | 0 | 1 | 0 | 0 | 0 | 0 | 0 | 0 | 0 |
| Young Australia | 1 | 1 | 0 | 0 | 0 | 0 | 0 | 0 | 9 | 0 |
| Zimbabwe | 1 | 1 | 0 | 0 | 0 | 0 | 0 | 0 | 0 | 0 |
| **Total** | **11** | **4** | **5** | **0** | **2** | **0** | **0** | **0** | **0** | **1** |
| **Grand Total** | **961** | **249** | **202** | **2** | **23** | **227** | **240** | **2** | **16** | **39** |

*Abandoned matches are not included in the list of matches played.*

# LIST A HIGHEST AND LOWEST SCORES BY AND AGAINST YORKSHIRE
## PLUS INDIVIDUAL BEST BATTING AND BOWLING

*The lowest score is the lowest all-out total or the lowest score at completion of the allotted overs, 10-over matches not included*

**Yorkshire versus:**

### Derbyshire

| | | By Yorkshire | | Against Yorkshire | |
|---|---|---|---|---|---|
| Highest Score: | In Yorkshire | 241:4 | at Leeds 2010 $ | 251:6 | at Leeds 2006 + |
| | Away | 288:6 | at Derby 2002 # | 268:8 | at Chesterfield 2010 $ |
| Lowest Score: | In Yorkshire | 117 | at Huddersfield 1978 $ | 87 | at Scarborough 1973 $ |
| | Away | 132 | at Chesterfield 1986 $ | 127 | at Chesterfield 1972 # |
| Best Batting: | In Yorkshire | 118* S A Kellett | at Leeds 1992 $ | 101 K J Barnett | at Leeds 1989 # |
| | Away | 115* M J Wood | at Derby 2002 # | 109* C J Adams | at Derby 1997 $ |
| Best Bowling: | In Yorkshire | 6-32 S A Patterson | at Leeds 2010 $ | 4-20 F E Rumsey | at Bradford 1973 # |
| | Away | 5-35 C W J Athey | at Chesterfield 1981 $ | 5-24 C J Tunnicliffe | at Derby 1981 # |

### Durham

| | | By Yorkshire | | Against Yorkshire | |
|---|---|---|---|---|---|
| Highest Score: | In Yorkshire | 269:5 | at Leeds 1998 $ | 266:8 | at Leeds 1998 $ |
| | Away | 271:7 | at Chester-le-Street 2002 # | 256:4 | at Chester-le-Street 1995 $ |
| Lowest Score: | In Yorkshire | 133 | at Leeds 1995 $ | 121 | at Scarborough 1997 $ |
| | Away | 122 | at Chester-le-Street 2007 $ | 136 | at Chester-le-Street 1996 $ |
| Best Batting: | In Yorkshire | 119 D S Lehmann | at Leeds 1998 # | 114 W Larkins | at Leeds 1993 $ |
| | Away | 101* C White | at Chester-le-Street 2006 + | 124* J P Maher | at Chester-le-Street 2006 + |
| Best Bowling: | In Yorkshire | 4-18 C White | at Scarborough 1997 $ | 4-20 S J E Brown | at Leeds 1995 $ |
| | Away | 4-26 C E W Silverwood | at Chester-le-Street 1996 $ | 4-31 P D Collingwood | at Chester-le-Street 2000 # |

### Essex

| | | By Yorkshire | | Against Yorkshire | |
|---|---|---|---|---|---|
| Highest Score: | In Yorkshire | 290:6 | at Scarborough 2014 + | 291:5 | at Scarborough 2014 + |
| | Away | 307:3 | at Chelmsford 1995 + | 285:8 | at Chelmsford 2008 + |
| Lowest Score: | In Yorkshire | 54 | at Leeds 2003 $ | 108 | at Leeds 1996 $ |
| | Away | 119:8 | at Colchester 1987 $ | 123 | at Colchester 1974 $ |
| Best Batting: | In Yorkshire | 111* J A Leaning | at Scarborough 2014 + | 119* R N ten Doeschate | at Scarborough 2014 + |
| | Away | 125* A W Gale | at Chelmsford 2010 $ | 136* N Hussain | at Chelmsford 2002 # |
| Best Bowling: | In Yorkshire | 4-20 G B Stevenson | at Barnsley 1977 # | 6-18 R E East | at Hull 1969 $ |
| | Away | 4-31 A L Robinson | at Leyton 1976 $ | 5-20 R E East | at Colchester 1979 $ |

# LIST A HIGHEST AND LOWEST SCORES BY AND AGAINST YORKSHIRE PLUS INDIVIDUAL BEST BATTING AND BOWLING (Continued)

**Yorkshire versus:**

## Glamorgan

| | | By Yorkshire | | Against Yorkshire | |
|---|---|---|---|---|---|
| Highest Score: | In Yorkshire | 253-4 | at Leeds 1991 $ | 216-6 | at Leeds 2013 $ |
| | Away | 257 | at Colwyn Bay 2013 $ | 285:7 | at Colwyn Bay 2013 $ |
| *Lowest Score:* | In Yorkshire | 139 | at Hull 1981 $ | 83 | at Leeds 1987 + |
| | Away | 93-8 | at Swansea 1985 $ | 90 | at Neath 1969 $ |
| *Best Batting:* | In Yorkshire | 96 A A Metcalfe | at Leeds 1991 $ | 97* G P Ellis | at Leeds 1976 $ |
| | Away | 141* M D Moxon | at Cardiff 1991 # | 127 A R Butcher | at Cardiff 1991 # |
| *Best Bowling:* | In Yorkshire | 5-22 P Carrick | at Leeds 2002 $ | 5-26 D S Harrison | at Leeds 2002 $ |
| | Away | 6-40 R J Sidebottom | at Cardiff 1998 $ | 5-16 G C Holmes | at Swansea 1985 $ |

## Gloucestershire

| | | By Yorkshire | | Against Yorkshire | |
|---|---|---|---|---|---|
| *Highest Score:* | In Yorkshire | 263:9 | at Leeds 2015 + | 269 | at Leeds 2009 + |
| | Away | 262:7 | at Bristol 1996 $ | 294:6 | at Cheltenham 2010 $ |
| *Lowest Score:* | In Yorkshire | 115 | at Leeds 1973 $ | 91 | at Scarborough 2001 $ |
| | Away | 133 | at Cheltenham 1999 $ | 90 | at Tewkesbury 1972 $ |
| *Best Batting:* | In Yorkshire | 118 J A Rudolph | at Leeds 2009 + | 146* S Young | at Leeds 1997 $ |
| | Away | 100* J D Love | at Gloucester in 1985 $ | 143* C M Spearman | at Bristol 2004 $ |
| | | 100* R J Blakey | at Cheltenham 1990 $ | | |
| *Best Bowling:* | In Yorkshire | 5-42 N D Thorncroft | at Leeds 2003 $ | 5-33 M C J Ball | at Leeds 2003 $ |
| | Away | 4-25 R D Stemp | at Bristol 1996 $ | 5-42 M C J Ball | at Cheltenham 1999 $ |

## Hampshire

| | | By Yorkshire | | Against Yorkshire | |
|---|---|---|---|---|---|
| *Highest Score:* | In Yorkshire | 259:4 | at Middlesbrough 1985 $ | 257:6 | at Middlesbrough 1985 $ |
| | Away | 264:2 | at Southampton 1995 $ | 261 | at Bournemouth 1977 + |
| *Lowest Score:* | In Yorkshire | 74:9 | at Hull 1970 $ | 50 | at Leeds 1991 # |
| | Away | 118 | at Southampton 1990 + | 133 | at Bournemouth 1976 $ |
| *Best Batting:* | In Yorkshire | 104* D Byas | at Leeds 1999 # | 155* B A Richards | at Hull 1970 $ |
| | Away | 97* M G Bevan | at Southampton 1995 $ | 125* C G Greenidge | at Bournemouth 1986 $ |
| *Best Bowling:* | In Yorkshire | 5-16 G M Hamilton | at Leeds 1998 $ | 5-33 A J Murtagh | at Huddersfield 1977 $ |
| | Away | 5-33 A U Rashid | at Southampton 2014 + | 5-31 D W White | at Southampton 1969 $ |

# LIST A HIGHEST AND LOWEST SCORES BY AND AGAINST YORKSHIRE PLUS INDIVIDUAL BEST BATTING AND BOWLING (Continued)

**Yorkshire versus:**

| | | By Yorkshire | | Against Yorkshire | |
| --- | --- | --- | --- | --- | --- |
| **Kent** | | | | | |
| Highest Score: | In Yorkshire | 299:3 | at Leeds 2002 $ | 232:8 | at Leeds 2011 $ |
| | Away | 263:3 | at Maidstone 1998 $ | 266:5 | at Maidstone 1998 $ |
| Lowest Score: | In Yorkshire | 75 | at Leeds 1995 $ | 133 | at Leeds 1974 $ |
| | | | | 133 | at Leeds 1979 # |
| Best Batting: | Away | 114 | at Canterbury 1978 # | 105 | at Canterbury 1969 $ |
| | In Yorkshire | 130* R J Blakey | at Scarborough 1991 $ | 118* M H Denness | at Canterbury 1976 $ |
| | Away | 102 A McGrath | at Leeds 1974 $ | 118* C J Tavare | at Canterbury 1981 + |
| Best Bowling: | In Yorkshire | 4-15 A G Nicholson | at Canterbury 1969 $ | 6-32 M T Coles | at Leeds 2012 $ |
| | Away | 6-18 D Wilson | | 5-25 B D Julien | at Canterbury 1971 + |
| **Lancashire** | | | | | |
| Highest Score: | In Yorkshire | 292:4 | at Leeds 2006 + | 287:9 | at Leeds 2006 + |
| | Away | 324:7 | at Manchester 2014 + | 293:9 | at Manchester 1996 + |
| Lowest Score: | In Yorkshire | 81 | at Leeds 1998 $ | 68 | at Leeds 2000 $ |
| | In Yorkshire | 81 | at Leeds 2002 $ | | |
| | Away | 125 | at Manchester 1973 # | 123:8 | at Manchester 1976 $ |
| Best Batting: | In Yorkshire | 111* D Byas | at Leeds 1996 $ | 102* N J Speak | at Leeds 1992 $ |
| | Away | 135* A McGrath | at Manchester 2007 + | 141* B J Hodge | at Manchester 2007 + |
| Best Bowling: | In Yorkshire | 5-25 C White | at Leeds 2000 $ | 6-25 G Chapple | at Leeds 1998 $ |
| | Away | 4-18 G S Blewett | at Manchester 1999 + | 5-49 M Watkinson | at Manchester 1991 # |
| **Leicestershire** | | | | | |
| Highest Score: | In Yorkshire | 303:4 | at Leeds 2008 $ | 302:7 | at Leeds 2008 $ |
| | Away | 318:7 | at Leicester 1993 $ | 298:9 | at Leicester 1997 $ |
| Lowest Score: | In Yorkshire | 93 | at Leeds 1998 $ | 53 | at Hull 1975 $ |
| | Away | 89-9 | at Leicester 1989 $ | | at Leicester 2000 $ |
| Best Batting: | In Yorkshire | 120 J A Rudolph | at Leeds 2008 $ | 108 N E Briers | at Bradford 1984 $ |
| | Away | 148 C White | at Leicester 1997 $ | 108 E J H Eckersley | at Leicester 2013 $ |
| Best Bowling: | In Yorkshire | 4-18 H P Cooper | at Leeds 1975 + | 5-24 C W Henderson | at Leeds 2004 $ |
| | Away | 5-16 S Stuchbury | at Leicester 1982 $ | 4-25 J Ormond | at Leicester 2001 # |

# LIST A HIGHEST AND LOWEST SCORES BY AND AGAINST YORKSHIRE PLUS INDIVIDUAL BEST BATTING AND BOWLING (*Continued*)

**Yorkshire versus:**

## Middlesex

| | | By Yorkshire | | | Against Yorkshire | | |
|---|---|---|---|---|---|---|---|
| Highest Score: | In Yorkshire | 271:7 | | at Scarborough 1990 $ | 245:8 | | at Scarborough 2010 $ |
| | Away | 275:4 | | at Lord's 2011 $ | 273:6 | | at Southgate 2004 $ |
| Lowest Score: | In Yorkshire | 148 | | at Leeds 1974 $ | 23 | | at Leeds 1974 $ |
| | Away | 90 | | at Lord's 1964 + | 107 | | at Lord's 1979 # |
| Best Batting: | In Yorkshire | 124* | J A Rudolph | at Scarborough 2010 $ | 104 | P N Weekes | at Leeds 1996 + |
| | Away | 116 | A A Metcalfe | at Lord's 1991 | 125* | O A Shah | at Southgate 2004 $ |
| Best Bowling: | In Yorkshire | 4-6 | R Illingworth | at Hull 1983 $ | 4-24 | N G Cowans | at Leeds 1986 + |
| | Away | 4-28 | H P Cooper | at Lord's 1979 # | 5-44 | T M Lamb | at Lord's 1975 # |

## Northamptonshire

| | | By Yorkshire | | | Against Yorkshire | | |
|---|---|---|---|---|---|---|---|
| Highest Score: | In Yorkshire | 270 | | at Leeds 2005 + | 314:4 | | at Leeds 2007 + |
| | Away | 341:3 | | at Northampton 2006 + | 339:7 | | at Northampton 2006 + |
| Lowest Score: | In Yorkshire | 129 | | at Leeds 2000 $ | 127 | | at Huddersfield 1974 $ |
| | Away | 112 | | at Northampton 1975 $ | 109 | | at Northampton 2000 $ |
| Best Batting: | In Yorkshire | 114* | J H Hampshire | at Scarborough 1978 $ | 132 | U Afzaal | at Leeds 2007 + |
| | Away | 118* | D S Lehmann | at Northampton 2006 + | 161 | D J G Sales | at Northampton 2006 + |
| Best Bowling: | In Yorkshire | 5-38 | C M Old | at Sheffield 1972 $ | 5-16 | B S Crump | at Bradford 1969 $ |
| | Away | 5-29 | P W Jarvis | at Northampton 1992 $ | 5-15 | Sarfraz Nawaz | at Northampton 1975 # |

## Nottinghamshire

| | | By Yorkshire | | | Against Yorkshire | | |
|---|---|---|---|---|---|---|---|
| Highest Score: | In Yorkshire | 352:6 | | at Scarborough 2001 $ | 251:5 | | at Scarborough 1996 $ |
| | Away | 280:4 | | at Nottingham 2007 + | 291:6 | | at Nottingham 2004 $ |
| Lowest Score: | In Yorkshire | 120:9 | | at Scarborough 1998 + | 66 | | at Bradford 1969 $ |
| | Away | 147 | | at Nottingham 1975 $ | 134:8 | | at Nottingham 1973 $ |
| Best Batting: | In Yorkshire | 191 | D S Lehmann | at Scarborough 2001 $ | 101 | M J Harris | at Hull 1973 + |
| | Away | 103 | R B Richardson | at Nottingham 1993 $ | 123 | D W Randall | at Nottingham 1987 $ |
| Best Bowling: | In Yorkshire | 5-17 | A G Nicholson | at Hull 1972 $ | 5-41 | C L Cairns | at Scarborough 1996 $ |
| | Away | 4-12 | C M Old | at Nottingham 1977 # | 5-30 | F D Stephenson | at Nottingham 1991 # |

# LIST A HIGHEST AND LOWEST SCORES BY AND AGAINST YORKSHIRE PLUS INDIVIDUAL BEST BATTING AND BOWLING (Continued)

**Yorkshire versus:**

## Somerset

| | By Yorkshire | | | Against Yorkshire | | |
|---|---|---|---|---|---|---|
| Highest Score: | 283:9 | | at Scarborough 2002 $ | 338:5 | | at Leeds 2013 $ |
| | 343:9 | | at Taunton 2005 $ | 345:4 | | at Taunton 2005 $ |
| Lowest Score: | 110 | | at Scarborough 1977 $ | 103 | | at Sheffield 1972 $ |
| | 120 | | at Taunton 1992 # | 63 | | at Taunton 1965 + |
| Best Batting: | 127 | J A Rudolph | at Scarborough 2007 $ | 140* | P D Trego | at Leeds 2013 $ |
| | 148 | A McGrath | at Taunton 2006 $ | 131 | D B Close | at Bath 1974 $ |
| Best Bowling: | 6-36 | A G Nicholson | at Sheffield 1972 $ | 4-10 | I T Botham | at Scarborough 1979 $ |
| | 6-15 | F S Trueman | at Taunton 1965 + | 5-27 | J Garner | at Bath 1985 $ |

## Surrey

| | By Yorkshire | | | Against Yorkshire | | |
|---|---|---|---|---|---|---|
| Highest Score: | 263:8 | | at Bradford 1985 $ | 375:4 | | at Scarborough 1994 $ |
| | 334:5 | | at The Oval 2005 $ | 329:8 | | at The Oval 2009 + |
| Lowest Score: | 76 | | at Harrogate 1970 + | 90 | | at Leeds 1996 $ |
| | 128:8 | | at The Oval 1971 $ | 134 | | at The Oval 1969 + |
| Best Batting: | 118* | J D Love | at Leeds 1987 $ | 136 | M A Lynch | at Bradford 1985 $ |
| | 146 | G Boycott | at Lord's 1965 + | 177 | S A Newman | at The Oval 2009 + |
| Best Bowling: | 5-25 | D Gough | at Leeds 1998 $ | 7-33 | R D Jackman | at Harrogate 1970 + |
| | 5-29 | R Illingworth | at Lord's 1965 + | 5-22 | R D Jackman | at The Oval 1978 $ |

## Sussex

| | By Yorkshire | | | Against Yorkshire | | |
|---|---|---|---|---|---|---|
| Highest Score: | 302:4 | | at Scarborough 2011 $ | 267 | | at Scarborough 2011 $ |
| | 270 | | at Hove 1963 + | 292 | | at Hove 1963 + |
| Lowest Score: | 89:7 | | at Huddersfield 1969 $ | 85 | | at Bradford 1972 # |
| | 89 | | at Hove 1998 $ | 108 | | at Hove 1971 $ |
| Best Batting: | 132* | J A Rudolph | at Scarborough 2011 $ | 129 | A W Greig | at Scarborough 1976 $ |
| | 111* | J H Hampshire | at Hastings 1973 $ | 103 | L J Wright | at Hove 2012 $ |
| Best Bowling: | 5-34 | G M Hamilton | at Scarborough 2000 $ | 4-15 | Imran Khan | at Sheffield 1985 $ |
| | 5-13 | D Gough | at Hove 1994 $ | 4-10 | M H Yardy | at Hove 2011 $ |

# LIST A HIGHEST AND LOWEST SCORES BY AND AGAINST YORKSHIRE
## PLUS INDIVIDUAL BEST BATTING AND BOWLING (Continued)

Yorkshire versus:

| | | By Yorkshire | | Against Yorkshire | |
|---|---|---|---|---|---|
| **Warwickshire** | | | | | |
| Highest Score: | In Yorkshire | 274:3 | at Leeds 2003 $ | 276:4 | at Leeds 1984 # |
| | Away | 247:8 | at Birmingham 1984 # | 309-3 | at Birmingham 2005 $ |
| Lowest Score: | In Yorkshire | 158 | at Scarborough 2012 $ | 59 | at Leeds 2001 $ |
| | Away | 56 | at Birmingham 1995 $ | 158:9 | at Birmingham 2003 $ |
| Best Batting: | In Yorkshire | 139* S P Fleming | at Leeds 2003 $ | 105 J D Ratcliffe | at Leeds 1993 + |
| | Away | 100* J H Hampshire | at Birmingham 1975 $ | 137 I R Bell | at Birmingham 2005 $ |
| Best Bowling: | In Yorkshire | 5-31 M D Moxon | at Leeds 1991 # | 4-16 N M Carter | at Scarborough 2012 $ |
| | Away | 4-27 H P Cooper | at Birmingham 1973 $ | 7-32 R G D Willis | at Birmingham 1981 # |
| **Worcestershire** | | | | | |
| Highest Score: | In Yorkshire | 290:7 | at Leeds 1982 + | 286:5 | at Leeds 1982 + |
| | Away | 346:6 | at Worcester 2015 + | 289:3 | at Worcester 1996 # |
| Lowest Score: | In Yorkshire | 88 | at Leeds 1995 $ | 86 | at Leeds 1969 $ |
| | Away | 90 | at Worcester 1987 $ | 122 | at Worcester 1975 $ |
| Best Batting: | In Yorkshire | 101 M G Bevan | at Scarborough 1995 $ | 113* G A Hick | at Scarborough 1995 $ |
| | Away | 142 G Boycott | at Worcester 1980 # | 115 Younis Ahmed | at Worcester 1980 # |
| Best Bowling: | In Yorkshire | 7-15 R A Hutton | at Leeds 1969 $ | 5-36 Kabir Ali | at Leeds 2002 $ |
| | Away | 6-14 H P Cooper | at Worcester 1975 $ | 5-30 R J Chapman | at Worcester 1998 $ |
| **Bedfordshire +** | | | | | |
| Highest Score: | Away | 212:6 | at Luton 2001 | 211:9 | at Luton 2001 |
| Best Batting: | Away | 88 D S Lehmann | at Luton 2001 | 34 O J Clayton | at Luton 2001 |
| Best Bowling: | Away | 4-39 R J Sidebottom | at Luton 2001 | 4-54 S R Rashid | at Luton 2001 |
| **Berkshire +** | | | | | |
| Highest Score: | Away | 131:3 | at Reading 1983 | 128:9 | at Reading 1983 |
| Lowest Score: | Away | | | 105 | at Finchampstead 1988 |
| Best Batting: | Away | 74* A A Metcalfe | at Finchampstead 1988 | 29 G R J Roope | at Reading 1983 |
| Best Bowling: | Away | 5-27 G B Stevenson | at Reading 1983 | 1-15 M Lickley | at Reading 1983 |

# LIST A HIGHEST AND LOWEST SCORES BY AND AGAINST YORKSHIRE PLUS INDIVIDUAL BEST BATTING AND BOWLING (Continued)

## Yorkshire versus:

### Cambridgeshire +

| | | By Yorkshire | | | Against Yorkshire | | |
|---|---|---|---|---|---|---|---|
| Highest Score: | In Yorkshire | 177:1 | | at Leeds 1986 | 176: 8 | | at Leeds 1986 |
| | Away | 299:5 | | at March 2003 | 214:8 | | at March 2003 |
| Lowest Score: | In Yorkshire | | | | 176: 8 | | at Leeds 1986 |
| | Away | 299:5 | | at March 2003 | 214:8 | | at March 2003 |
| Best Batting: | In Yorkshire | 75 | M D Moxon | at Leeds 1986 | 85 | J D R Benson | at Leeds 1986 |
| | Away | 118* | M J Wood | at March 2003 | 53 | N T Gadsby | at March 2003 |
| Best Bowling: | In Yorkshire | 3-11 | A G Nicholson | at Castleford 1967 | 2-8 | D H Fairey | at Castleford 1967 |
| | Away | 3-37 | A K D Gray | at March 2003 | 3-53 | Ajaz Akhtar | at March 2003 |

### Cheshire +

| | | By Yorkshire | | | Against Yorkshire | | |
|---|---|---|---|---|---|---|---|
| Highest Score: | Away | 160:0 | | at Oxton 1985 | 159:7 | | at Oxton 1985 |
| Best Batting: | Away | 82* | M D Moxon | at Oxton 1985 | 46 | K Teasdale | at Oxton 1985 |
| Best Bowling: | Away | 2-17 | G B Stevenson | at Oxton 1985 | | | |

### Combined Universities #

| | | By Yorkshire | | | Against Yorkshire | | |
|---|---|---|---|---|---|---|---|
| Highest Score: | In Yorkshire | 197:8 | | at Leeds 1990 | 200:8 | | at Leeds 1990 |
| | Away | 151:1 | | at Oxford 1980 | 150:7 | | at Oxford 1980 |
| Lowest Score: | In Yorkshire | 197:8 | | at Leeds 1990 | 200:8 | | at Leeds 1990 |
| | Away | 151:1 | | at Oxford 1980 | 150:7 | | at Oxford 1980 |
| Best Batting: | In Yorkshire | 74* | C W J Athey | at Oxford 1980 | 63 | S P James | at Leeds 1990 |
| | Away | | | | 63 | J O D Orders | at Oxford 1980 |
| Best Bowling: | In Yorkshire | 3-34 | P J Hartley | at Leeds 1990 | 3-44 | M E W Brooker | at Barnsley 1976 |
| | Away | 2-43 | H P Cooper | at Oxford 1980 | 1-16 | C J Ross | at Oxford 1980 |

### Devon +

| | | By Yorkshire | | | Against Yorkshire | | |
|---|---|---|---|---|---|---|---|
| Highest Score: | Away | 411:6 | | at Exmouth 2004 | 279-8 | | at Exmouth 2004 |
| Lowest Score: | Away | 259:5 | | at Exmouth 2002 | 80 | | at Exmouth 1998 |
| Best Batting: | Away | 160 | M J Wood | at Exmouth 2004 | 83 | P M Roebuck | at Exmouth 1994 |
| Best Bowling: | Away | 4-26 | D S Lehmann | at Exmouth 2002 | 2-42 | A O F Le Fleming | at Exmouth 1994 |

# LIST A HIGHEST AND LOWEST SCORES BY AND AGAINST YORKSHIRE PLUS INDIVIDUAL BEST BATTING AND BOWLING (Continued)

## Yorkshire versus:

### Dorset +

| | | By Yorkshire | | Against Yorkshire | |
|---|---|---|---|---|---|
| Highest Score: | Away | 101:2 | at Bournemouth 2004 | 97 | at Bournemouth 2004 |
| Best Batting: | Away | 71* M J Wood | at Bournemouth 2004 | 23 C L Park | at Bournemouth 2004 |
| Best Bowling: | Away | 4-18 C E W Silverwood | at Bournemouth 2004 | 2-31 D J Worrad | at Bournemouth 2004 |

### Durham M C +

| | | By Yorkshire | | Against Yorkshire | |
|---|---|---|---|---|---|
| Highest Score: | In Yorkshire | 249:6 | at Middlesbrough 1978 | 138:5 | at Middlesbrough 1978 |
| | Away | 214:6 | at Chester-le-Street 1979 | 213:9 | at Chester-le-Street 1979 |
| Lowest Score: | In Yorkshire | 135 | at Harrogate 1973 | 136:7 | at Harrogate 1973 |
| | Away | | | 213:9 | at Chester-le-Street 1979 |
| Best Batting: | In Yorkshire | 110 J H Hampshire | at Middlesbrough 1978 | 52 N A Riddell | at Middlesbrough 1978 |
| | Away | 92 G Boycott | at Chester-le-Street 1979 | 52 Wasim Raja | at Chester-le-Street 1979 |
| Best Bowling: | In Yorkshire | 4-9 C M Old | at Middlesbrough 1978 | 5-15 B R Lander | at Middlesbrough 1978 |
| | Away | 3-39 H P Cooper | at Chester-le-Street 1979 | 2-35 B L Cairns | at Chester-le-Street 1979 |

### Herefordshire +

| | | By Yorkshire | | Against Yorkshire | |
|---|---|---|---|---|---|
| Highest Score: | Away | 275:8 | at Kington 1999 | 124:5 | at Kington 1999 |
| Best Batting: | Away | 77 G S Blewett | at Kington 1999 | 39 R D Hughes | at Kington 1999 |
| Best Bowling: | Away | 2-22 G M Hamilton | at Kington 1999 | 2-41 C W Boroughs | at Kington 1999 |

### Ireland +

| | | By Yorkshire | | Against Yorkshire | |
|---|---|---|---|---|---|
| Highest Score: | In Yorkshire | 299:6 | at Leeds 1995 | 228:7 | at Leeds 1995 |
| | Away | 202:4 | at Belfast 2005 | 201:7 | at Belfast 2005 |
| Lowest Score: | In Yorkshire | 249 | at Leeds 1997 | 53 | at Leeds 1997 |
| | Away | | | 201:7 | at Belfast 2005 |
| Best Batting: | In Yorkshire | 113 C White | at Leeds 1995 | 82 S J S Warke | at Leeds 1995 |
| | Away | 58 M P Vaughan | at Belfast 2005 | 59 E J G Morgan | at Belfast 2005 |
| Best Bowling: | In Yorkshire | 7-27 D Gough | at Leeds 1997 | 3-26 P McCrum | at Leeds 1997 |
| | Away | 4-43 C White | at Belfast 2005 | 1-29 W K McCallan | at Belfast 2005 |

# LIST A HIGHEST AND LOWEST SCORES BY AND AGAINST YORKSHIRE PLUS INDIVIDUAL BEST BATTING AND BOWLING (Continued)

**Yorkshire versus:**

### Minor Counties #

| | | By Yorkshire | Against Yorkshire |
|---|---|---|---|
| Highest Score: | In Yorkshire | 309:5 at Leeds 1997 | 206:6 at Leeds 1988 |
| | Away | 218:3 at Scunthorpe 1975 | 182 at Scunthorpe 1975 |
| | Away | 218:9 at Jesmond 1979 | |
| Lowest Score: | In Yorkshire | 309:5 at Leeds 1997 | 109 at Leeds 1974 |
| | Away | 218:3 at Scunthorpe 1975 | 85 at Jesmond 1979 |
| | Away | 218:9 at Jesmond 1979 | |
| Best Batting: | In Yorkshire | 109* A McGrath at Leeds 1997 | 80* J D Love at Leeds 1991 |
| | Away | 83* G Boycott at Chester-le-Street 1973 | 61 N A Folland at Jesmond 1989 |
| Best Bowling: | In Yorkshire | 6-27 A G Nicholson at Middlesbrough 1972 | 3-37 S Oakes at Leeds 1997 |
| | Away | 5-32 S Oldham at Scunthorpe 1975 | 3-27 I E Conn at Jesmond 1989 |

### Netherlands $

| | | By Yorkshire | Against Yorkshire |
|---|---|---|---|
| Highest Score: | In Yorkshire | 204:6 at Leeds 2010 | 200:8 at Leeds 2010 |
| | Away | 158:5 at Rotterdam 2010 | 154:9 at Rotterdam 2010 |
| Lowest Score: | In Yorkshire | 188:9 at Leeds 2011 | 190:8 at Leeds 2011 |
| | Away | 123 at Amsterdam 2011 | 154:9 at Rotterdam 2010 |
| Best Batting: | In Yorkshire | 83* J A Rudolph at Leeds 2010 | 62 M G Dighton at Leeds 2010 |
| | Away | 46* J M Bairstow at Rotterdam 2010 | 34 P W Borren at Amsterdam 2011 |
| Best Bowling: | In Yorkshire | 3-34 S A Patterson at Leeds 2010 | 3-26 Mudassar Bukhari at Leeds 2011 |
| | Away | 4-24 R M Pyrah at Rotterdam 2010 | 3-28 Mudassar Bukhari at Amsterdam 2011 |

### Norfolk +

| | | By Yorkshire | Against Yorkshire |
|---|---|---|---|
| Highest Score: | In Yorkshire | 106:0 at Leeds 1990 | 104 at Leeds 1990 |
| | Away | 167 at Lakenham 1969 | 78 at Lakenham 1969 |
| Lowest Score: | In Yorkshire | | 104 at Leeds 1990 |
| | Away | 167 at Lakenham 1969 | 78 at Lakenham 1969 |
| Best Batting: | In Yorkshire | 56* M D Moxon at Leeds 1990 | 25 R J Finney at Leeds 1990 |
| | Away | 55 J H Hampshire at Lakenham 1969 | 21 G J Donaldson at Lakenham 1969 |
| Best Bowling: | In Yorkshire | 3-8 P Carrick at Leeds 1990 | |
| | Away | 3-14 C M Old at Lakenham 1969 | 6-48 T I Moore at Lakenham 1969 |

# LIST A HIGHEST AND LOWEST SCORES BY AND AGAINST YORKSHIRE
## PLUS INDIVIDUAL BEST BATTING AND BOWLING (Continued)

**Yorkshire versus:**

### Northumberland +

| | | By Yorkshire | | | Against Yorkshire | | |
|---|---|---|---|---|---|---|---|
| Highest Score: | In Yorkshire | 138: 2 | | | 137 | | at Leeds 1992 |
| Best Batting: | In Yorkshire | 38 | S A Kellett | at Leeds 1992 | 47 | G R Morris | at Leeds 1992 |
| Best Bowling: | In Yorkshire | 3-18 | M A Robinson | at Leeds 1992 | 2-22 | S Greensword | at Leeds 1992 |

### Scotland

| | | By Yorkshire | | | Against Yorkshire | | |
|---|---|---|---|---|---|---|---|
| Highest Score: | In Yorkshire | 317:5 | | at Leeds 1986 # | 244 | | at Leeds 2008 + |
| | Away | 259:8 | | at Edinburgh 2007 + | 217 | | at Edinburgh 2007 + |
| Lowest Score: | In Yorkshire | 228:6 | | at Bradford 1981 # | 142 | | at Leeds 1996 # |
| | Away | 199:8 | | at Edinburgh 2004 $ | 129 | | at Glasgow 1995 # |
| Best Batting: | In Yorkshire | 118* | J D Love | at Bradford 1981 # | 73 | I L Philip | at Leeds 1989 + |
| | Away | 91 | A A Metcalfe | at Glasgow 1987 # | 78 | J A Beukes | at Edinburgh 2005 $ |
| Best Bowling: | In Yorkshire | 5-28 | C E W Silverwood | at Leeds 1996 # | 2-22 | P J C Hoffman | at Leeds 2006 + |
| | Away | 4-20 | R K J Dawson | at Edinburgh 2004 $ | 3-42 | Asim Butt | at Linlithgow 1998 # |

### Shropshire +

| | | By Yorkshire | | | Against Yorkshire | | |
|---|---|---|---|---|---|---|---|
| Highest Score: | Away | 192 | | at Telford 1984 | 229:5 | | at Telford 1984 |
| Lowest Score: | Away | 192 | | at Telford 1984 | 185 | | at Wellington 1976 |
| Best Batting: | Away | 59 | J H Hampshire | at Wellington 1976 | 80 | Mushtaq Mohammad | at Telford 1984 |
| Best Bowling: | Away | 3-17 | A L Robinson | at Wellington 1976 | 3-26 | Mushtaq Mohammad | at Telford 1984 |

### Unicorns $

| | | By Yorkshire | | | Against Yorkshire | | |
|---|---|---|---|---|---|---|---|
| Highest Score: | In Yorkshire | 266:6 | | at Leeds 2013 | 234 | | at Leeds 2013 |
| | Away | 191:5 | | at Chesterfield 2013 | 189:9 | | at Chesterfield 2013 |
| Lowest Score: | In Yorkshire | | | | 150:6 | | at Leeds 2012 |
| | Away | | | | 184 | | at Scarborough 2012 |
| Best Batting: | In Yorkshire | 139 | G S Ballance | at Leeds 2013 | 107 | M S Lineker | at Leeds 2013 |
| | Away | 103* | G S Ballance | at Scarborough 2012 | 83* | T J New | at Scarborough 2012 |
| Best Bowling: | In Yorkshire | 5-22 | J A Leaning | at Leeds 2013 | 2-25 | R J Woolley | at Leeds 2012 |
| | Away | 3-34 | R M Pyrah | at Chesterfield 2013 | 2-31 | W W Lee | at Chesterfield 2013 |

**Yorkshire versus:**

| | | By Yorkshire | | | Against Yorkshire | | |
|---|---|---|---|---|---|---|---|
| **Wiltshire +** | | | | | | | |
| Highest Score: | Away | 304:7 | | at Trowbridge 1987 | 175 | | at Trowbridge 1987 |
| Best Batting: | Away | 85 | A A Metcalfe | at Trowbridge 1987 | 62 | J J Newman | at Trowbridge 1987 |
| Best Bowling: | Away | 4-40 | K Sharp | at Trowbridge 1987 | 2-38 | R C Cooper | at Trowbridge 1987 |
| **Yorkshire Cricket Board +** | | | | | | | |
| Highest Score: | Away | 240:5 | | at Harrogate 2000 | 110 | | at Harrogate 2000 |
| Best Batting: | Away | 70 | M P Vaughan | at Harrogate 2000 | 31 | R A Kettleborough | at Harrogate 2000 |
| Best Bowling: | Away | 5-30 | D Gough | at Harrogate 2000 | 1-25 | A E McKenna | at Harrogate 2000 |
| **Australians** | | | | | | | |
| Highest Score: | In Yorkshire | 188 | | at Leeds 1989 | 297:3 | | at Leeds 1989 |
| Lowest Score: | In Yorkshire | 140 | | at Bradford 1972 | 297:3 | | at Leeds 1989 |
| Best Batting: | In Yorkshire | 105 | G Boycott | at Bradford 1972 | 172 | D C Boon | at Leeds 1989 |
| Best Bowling: | In Yorkshire | 2-23 | D Wilson | at Bradford 1972 | 3-30 | D J Colley | at Bradford 1972 |
| **Bangladesh A** | | | | | | | |
| Highest Score: | In Yorkshire | 198 | | at Leeds 2013 | 191 | | at Leeds 2013 |
| Best Batting: | In Yorkshire | 47* | L E Plunkett | at Leeds 2013 | 69 | Anamul Haque | at Leeds 2013 |
| Best Bowling: | In Yorkshire | 5-30 | Azeem Rafiq | at Leeds 2013 | 3-25 | Elias Sunny | at Leeds 2013 |
| **Sri Lanka A** | | | | | | | |
| Highest Score: | In Yorkshire | 249 | | at Leeds 2014 | 275:9 | | at Leeds 2014 |
| Lowest Score: | In Yorkshire | 179:7 | | at Leeds 2004 | | | |
| Best Batting: | In Yorkshire | 81 | A W Gale | at Leeds 2007 | 100 | L D Chandimal | at Leeds 2007 |
| Best Bowling: | In Yorkshire | 5-51 | A Shahzad | at Leeds 2007 | 4-42 | S Prasanna | at Leeds 2007 |
| **West Indians** | | | | | | | |
| Highest Score: | In Yorkshire | 253:4 | | at Scarborough 1995 | 242 | | at Scarborough 1995 |
| Best Batting: | In Yorkshire | 106 | A McGrath | at Scarborough 1995 | 54 | R B Richardson | at Scarborough 1995 |
| Best Bowling: | In Yorkshire | 3-42 | G M Hamilton | at Scarborough 1995 | 3-48 | R Dhanraj | at Scarborough 1995 |

395

# LIST A HIGHEST AND LOWEST SCORES BY AND AGAINST YORKSHIRE
## PLUS INDIVIDUAL BEST BATTING AND BOWLING *(Continued)*

**Yorkshire versus:**

### West Indians A

|  | | By Yorkshire | | Against Yorkshire | | |
|---|---|---|---|---|---|---|
| *Highest Score:* | 139 | | at Leeds 2002 | 140:2 | | at Leeds 2002 |
| *Best Batting:* | 48 | M J Wood | at Leeds 2002 | 57 | D Ganga | at Leeds 2002 |
| *Best Bowling:* | 1-31 | C J Elstub | at Leeds 2002 | 4-24 | J J C Lawson | at Leeds 2002 |

### Young Australians

|  | | By Yorkshire | | Against Yorkshire | | |
|---|---|---|---|---|---|---|
| *Highest Score:* | 224:6 | | at Leeds 1995 | 156 | | at Leeds 1995 |
| *Best Batting:* | 76 | M P Vaughan | at Leeds 1995 | 51 | A C Gilchrist | at Leeds 1995 |
| *Best Bowling:* | 5-32 | A C Morris | at Leeds 1995 | 2-21 | S Young | at Leeds 1995 |

### Zimbabwe

|  | | By Yorkshire | | Against Yorkshire | | |
|---|---|---|---|---|---|---|
| *Highest Score:* | 203:7 | | at Sheffield 1982 | 202 | | at Sheffield 1982 |
| *Best Batting:* | 98* | G Boycott | at Sheffield 1982 | 53 | D A G Fletcher | at Sheffield 1982 |
| *Best Bowling:* | 3-47 | P W Jarvis | at Sheffield 1982 | 3-30 | D A G Fletcher | at Sheffield 1982 |

# LIST A HIGHEST TEAM TOTALS

## BY YORKSHIRE

| | | | |
|---|---|---|---|
| 411:6 | v. | Devon at Exmouth | 2004 + |
| 352:6 | v. | Nottinghamshire at Scarborough | 2001 $ |
| 345:5 | v. | Nottinghamshire at Leeds | 1996 + |
| 345:6 | v. | Worcestershire at Worcester | 2015 + |
| 343:9 | v. | Somerset at Taunton | 2005 $ |
| 341:3 | v. | Northamptonshire at Northampton | 2006 + |
| 334:5 | v. | Surrey at The Oval | 2005 $ |
| 330:6 | v. | Surrey at The Oval | 2009 + |
| 324:7 | v. | Lancashire at Manchester | 2014 + |
| 318:7 | v. | Leicestershire at Leicester | 1993 $ |
| 317:4 | v. | Surrey at Lord's | 1965 + |
| 317:5 | v. | Scotland at Leeds | 1986 # |
| 310:5 | v. | Leicestershire at Leicester | 1997 + |
| 309:5 | v. | Minor Counties at Leeds | 1997 # |
| 307:3 | v. | Essex at Chelmsford | 1995 + |
| 307:4 | v. | Somerset at Taunton | 2002 $ |
| 304:7 | v. | Wiltshire at Trowbridge | 1986 + |
| 303:3 | v. | Northamptonshire at Northampton | 2002 + |
| 303:4 | v. | Leicestershire at Leeds | 2008 $ |
| 302:4 | v. | Sussex at Scarborough | 2011 $ |
| 299:6 | v. | Ireland at Leeds | 1995 + |
| 299:3 | v | Kent at Leeds | 2002 $ |
| 299:5 | v. | Cambridgeshire at March | 2003 + |

## AGAINST YORKSHIRE

| | | |
|---|---|---|
| 375:4 | for Surrey at Scarborough | 1994 $ |
| 345:4 | for Somerset at Taunton | 2005 $ |
| 339:7 | fo r Northamptonshire at Northampton | 2006 + |
| 338:5 | for Somerset at Leeds | 2013 $ |
| 329:8 | for Surrey at The Oval | 2009 + |
| 325:7 | for Northamptonshire at Northampton | 1992 $ |
| 314:4 | for Northamptonshire at Leeds | 2007 + |
| 309:3 | for Warwickshire at Birmingham | 2005 |
| 308:6 | for Surrey at The Oval | 1995 $ |
| 306:8 | for Somerset at Taunton | 2002 $ |
| 302:7 | for Leicestershire at Leeds | 2008 $ |
| 298:9 | for Leicestershire at Leicester | 1997 $ |
| 297:3 | for Australians at Leeds | 1989 |
| 294:6 | for Gloucestershire at Cheltenham | 2010 $ |
| 293:9 | for Lancashire at Manchester | 1996 + |
| 292 | for Sussex at Hove | 1963 + |
| 291:5 | for Essex at Scarborough | 2014 + |
| 291:6 | for Nottinghamshire at Nottingham | 2004 $ |
| 291:9 | for Gloucestershire at Lord's | 1999 # |
| 291 | for Surrey at The Oval | 2005 $ |
| 289:3 | for Worcestershire at Worcester | 1996 # |
| 287:9 | for Lancashire at Leeds | 2006 $ |

# LIST A HIGHEST INDIVIDUAL SCORES

## BY YORKSHIRE

| | | | | | |
|---|---|---|---|---|---|
| 191 | D S Lehmann | v. | Nottinghamshire at Scarborough | 2001 | $ |
| 160 | M J Wood | v. | Devon at Exmouth | 2004 | + |
| 148 | C White | v. | Leicestershire at Leicester | 1997 | $ |
| 148 | A McGrath | v. | Somerset at Taunton | 2006 | $ |
| 146 | G Boycott | v. | Surrey at Lord's | 1965 | + |
| 142 | G Boycott | v. | Worcestershire at Worcester | 1980 | # |
| 141* | M D Moxon | v | Glamorgan at Cardiff | 1991 | # |
| 139* | S P Fleming | v. | Warwickshire at Leeds | 2003 | $ |
| 139 | G S Ballance | v. | Unicorns at Leeds | 2013 | $ |
| 137 | M D Moxon | v. | Nottinghamshire at Leeds | 1996 | + |
| 135* | A McGrath | v. | Lancashire at Manchester | 2007 | + |
| 132* | J A Rudolph | v. | Sussex at Scarborough | 2011 | $ |
| 130* | R J Blakey | v. | Kent at Scarborough | 1991 | $ |
| 129* | M D Moxon | v. | Surrey at The Oval | 1991 | $ |
| 128* | M T G Elliott | v. | Somerset at Lord's | 2002 | + |

## AGAINST YORKSHIRE

| | | | | |
|---|---|---|---|---|
| 177 | S A Newman for | Surrey at The Oval | 2009 | + |
| 172 | D C Boon for | Australia at Leeds | 1989 | |
| 161 | D J G Sales for | Northamptonshire at Northampton | 2006 | + |
| 155* | B A Richards for | Hampshire at Hull | 1970 | $ |
| 146* | S Young for | Gloucestershire at Leeds | 1997 | $ |
| 143* | C M Spearman for | Gloucestershire at Bristol | 2004 | $ |
| 141* | B J Hodge for | Lancashire at Manchester | 2007 | + |
| 140* | P D Trego for | Somerset at Leeds | 2013 | $ |
| 137* | M Klinger for | Gloucestershire at Leeds | 2015 | + |
| 137 | I R Bell for | Warwickshire at Birmingham | 2005 | $ |
| 136* | N Hussain for | Essex at Chelmsford | 2002 | # |
| 136 | M A Lynch for | Surrey at Bradford | 1985 | $ |
| 135* | D J Bicknell for | Surrey at The Oval | 1989 | + |
| 133 | A D Brown for | Surrey at Scarborough | 1994 | $ |
| 132 | U Afzaal for | Northamptonshire at Leeds | 2007 | + |

## MOST RUNS IN LIST A MATCHES

| | | | | | | |
|---|---|---|---|---|---|---|
| 690 | v. | Devon at Exmouth | 2004 + | Y 411:6 | D 279:8 | |
| 688 | v. | Somerset at Taunton | 2005 $ | S 345:4 | Y 343:9 | |
| 680 | v. | Northamptonshire at Northampton | 2006 + | Y 342:3 | N 339:7 | |
| 659 | v. | Surrey at The Oval | 2009 + | S 329:8 | Y 330:6 | |
| 625 | v. | Surrey at The Oval | 2005 $ | Y 334:5 | S 291 | |
| 613 | v. | Somerset at Taunton | 2002 $ | Y 307:4 | S 306:8 | |
| 605 | v. | Leicestershire at Leeds | 2008 $ | Y 303:4 | L 302:7 | |
| 604 | v. | Surrey at The Oval | 1995 $ | S 308:6 | Y 296:6 | |
| 601 | v. | Lancashire at Manchester | 2014 + | Y 324:7 | L 277 | |
| 596 | v. | Leicestershire at Leicester | 1997 $ | L 298:9 | Y 298:9 | |
| 581 | v. | Worcestershire at Worcester | 1996 # | W 289:3 | Y 292:3 | |
| 581 | v. | Essex at Scarborough | 2014 + | Y 290:6 | E 291:5 | |

# LIST A BEST BOWLING

## *BY YORKSHIRE*

| | | | | | |
|---|---|---|---|---|---|
| 7-15 | R A Hutton | v. | Worcestershire at Leeds | 1969 | $ |
| 7-27 | D Gough | v. | Ireland at Leeds | 1997 | + |
| 6-14 | H P Cooper | v. | Worcestershire at Worcester | 1975 | $ |
| 6-15 | F S Trueman | v. | Somerset at Taunton | 1965 | + |
| 6-18 | D Wilson | v. | Kent at Canterbury | 1969 | $ |
| 6-27 | A G Nicholson | v. | Minor Counties at Middlesbrough | 1972 | # |
| 6-27 | P W Jarvis | v. | Somerset at Taunton | 1989 | $ |
| 6-32 | S A Patterson | v. | Derbyshire at Leeds | 2010 | $ |
| 6-36 | A G Nicholson | v | Somerset At Sheffield | 1972 | $ |
| 6-40 | R J Sidebottom | v. | Glamorgan at Cardiff | 1998 | $ |
| 5-13 | D Gough | v. | Sussex at Hove | 1994 | $ |
| 5-16 | S Stuchbury | v. | Leicestershire at Leicester | 1982 | $ |
| 5-16 | G M Hamilton | v. | Hampshire at Leeds | 1998 | $ |
| 5-17 | A G Nicholson | v. | Nottinghamshire at Hull | 1972 | $ |
| 5-18 | P W Jarvis | v. | Derbyshire at Leeds | 1990 | $ |

## *AGAINST YORKSHIRE*

| | | | | | |
|---|---|---|---|---|---|
| 7-32 | R G D Willis | for | Warwickshire at Birmingham | 1981 | # |
| 7-33 | R D Jackman | for | Surrey at Harrogate | 1970 | + |
| 6-15 | A A Donald | for | Warwickshire at Birmingham | 1995 | $ |
| 6-18 | R E East | for | Essex at Hull | 1969 | $ |
| 6-25 | G Chapple | for | Lancashire at Leeds | 1998 | $ |
| 6-32 | M T Coles | for | Kent at Leeds | 2012 | $ |
| 6-48 | T I Moore | for | Norfolk at Lakenham | 1969 | + |
| 5-15 | B R Lander | for | Durham M C at Harrogate | 1973 | + |
| 5-15 | Sarfraz Nawaz | for | Northamptonshire at Northampton | 1975 | $ |
| 5-16 | B S Crump | for | Northamptonshire at Bradford | 1969 | $ |
| 5-16 | G C Holmes | for | Glamorgan at Swansea | 1985 | $ |
| 5-20 | R E East | for | Essex at Colchester | 1979 | $ |
| 5-22 | R D Jackman | for | Surrey at The Oval | 1978 | $ |
| 5-24 | C J Tunnicliffe | for | Derbyshire at Derby | 1981 | # |
| 5-24 | C W Henderson | for | Leicestershire at Leeds | 2004 | $ |

# LIST A ECONOMICAL BOWLING

## *BY YORKSHIRE*

| | | | | | |
|---|---|---|---|---|---|
| 11-9-3-1 | C M Old | v. | Middlesex at Lord's | 1979 | # |
| 8-5-3-3 | A L Robinson | v. | Derbyshire at Scarborough | 1973 | $ |

## *AGAINST YORKSHIRE*

| | | | | | |
|---|---|---|---|---|---|
| 8-4-6-2 | P J Sainsbury | for | Hampshire at Hull | 1970 | $ |
| 8-5-6-3 | M J Procter | for | Gloucestershire at Cheltenham | 1979 | $ |

# LIST A MOST EXPENSIVE BOWLING

## *BY YORKSHIRE*

| | | | | | |
|---|---|---|---|---|---|
| 9-0-87-1 | T T Bresnan | v. | Somerset at Taunton | 2005 | $ |

## *AGAINST YORKSHIRE*

| | | | | | |
|---|---|---|---|---|---|
| 12-1-96-0 | M E Waugh | for | Essex at Chelmsford | 1995 | + |

## LIST A HAT-TRICKS FOR YORKSHIRE (4)

| | | | | | | | |
|---|---|---|---|---|---|---|---|
| P W Jarvis | v. | Derbyshire at Derby | 1982 $ | D Gough | v. | Ireland at Leeds | 1997 + |
| D Gough | v. | Lancashire at Leeds | 1998 $ | C White | v. | Kent at Leeds | 2000 $ |

## LIST A MAN-OF-THE-MATCH AWARDS (135)

| | | | | | |
|---|---|---|---|---|---|
| M D Moxon | 12 | M P Vaughan | 5 | M J Wood | 3 |
| G Boycott | 11 | A Sidebottom | 4 | R J Blakey | 2 |
| D L Bairstow | 8 | C E W Silverwood | 4 | G L Brophy | 2 |
| C White | 8 | D Byas | 3 | P Carrick | 2 |
| A A Metcalfe | 7 | D Gough | 3 | R A Hutton | 2 |
| J H Hampshire | 6 | P J Hartley | 3 | P J Sharpe | 2 |
| D S Lehmann | 6 | J D Love | 3 | G B Stevenson | 2 |
| C W J Athey | 5 | A McGrath | 3 | | |
| M G Bevan | 5 | C M Old | 3 | | |

One each: T T Bresnan, D B Close, M T G Elliott, G M Fellows, S D Fletcher, G M Hamilton, S N Hartley, P M Hutchinson, R Illingworth, C Johnson, S A Kellett, B Leadbeater, M J Lumb, A G Nicholson, S Oldham, L E Plunkett, R M Pyrah, P E Robinson, R D Stemp, F S Trueman and D Wilson.

## ALL LIST A CENTURIES 1963-2015 (103)

### C W J ATHEY (2)

| | | | | |
|---|---|---|---|---|
| 118 | v. | Leicestershire | at Leicester | 1978 $ |
| 115 | v. | Kent | at Leeds | 1980 + |

### D L BAIRSTOW (1)

| | | | | |
|---|---|---|---|---|
| 103 * | v | Derbyshire | at Derby | 1981 # |

### J M BAIRSTOW (1)

| | | | | |
|---|---|---|---|---|
| 114 | v | Middlesex | at Lord's | 2011 $ |

### G S BALLANCE (2)

| | | | | |
|---|---|---|---|---|
| 139 | v | Unicorns | at Leeds | 2013 $ |
| 103 * | v | Unicorns | at Scarborough | 2012 $ |

### M G BEVAN (2)

| | | | | |
|---|---|---|---|---|
| 103 * | v | Gloucestershire | at Middlesbrough | 1995 $ |
| 101 | v | Worcestershire | at Scarborough | 1995 $ |

### G BOYCOTT (7)

| | | | | |
|---|---|---|---|---|
| 146 | v | Surrey | at Lord's | 1965 + |
| 142 | v | Worcestershire | at Worcester | 1980 # |
| 108 * | v | Northamptonshire | at Huddersfield | 1974 $ |
| 106 | v | Northamptonshire | at Bradford | 1984 # |
| 105 | v | Australians | at Bradford | 1972 |
| 104 * | v | Glamorgan | at Colwyn Bay | 1973 $ |
| 102 | v | Northamptonshire | at Middlesbrough | 1977 # |

### R J BLAKEY (3)

| | | | | |
|---|---|---|---|---|
| 130 | v | Kent | at Scarborough | 1991 $ |
| 105 * | v | Warwickshire | at Scarborough | 1992 $ |
| 100 * | v | Gloucestershire | at Cheltenham | 1990 $ |

### D BYAS (5)

| 116 * | v | Surrey | at The Oval | 1996 # |
|---|---|---|---|---|
| 111 * | v | Lancashire | at Leeds | 1996 $ |
| 106 * | v | Derbyshire | at Chesterfield | 1993 $ |
| 104 * | v | Hampshire | at Leeds | 1999 # |
| 101 * | v | Nottinghamshire | at Leeds | 1994 $ |

### M T G ELLIOTT (3)

| 128 * | v | Somerset | at Lord's | 2002 + |
|---|---|---|---|---|
| 115 * | v | Kent | at Leeds | 2002 $ |
| 109 | v | Leicestershire | at Leicester | 2002 $ |

### S P FLEMING (1)

| 139 * | v | Warwickshire | at Leeds | 2003 $ |
|---|---|---|---|---|

### M J FOSTER (1)

| 118 | v | Leicestershire | at Leicester | 1993 $ |
|---|---|---|---|---|

### A W GALE (2)

| 125 * | v | Essex | at Chelmsford | 2010 $ |
|---|---|---|---|---|
| 112 | v | Kent | at Canterbury | 2011 $ |

### J H HAMPSHIRE (7)

| 119 | v | Leicestershire | at Hull | 1971 $ |
|---|---|---|---|---|
| 114 * | v | Northamptonshire | at Scarborough | 1978 $ |
| 111 * | v | Sussex | at Hastings | 1973 $ |
| 110 | v | Durham M C | at Middlesbrough | 1978 + |
| 108 | v | Nottinghamshire | at Sheffield | 1970 $ |
| 106 * | v | Lancashire | at Manchester | 1972 $ |
| 100 * | v | Warwickshire | at Birmingham | 1975 $ |

### P A JAQUES (1)

| 105 | v | Sussex | at Leeds | 2004 $ |
|---|---|---|---|---|

### S A KELLETT (2)

| 118 * | v | Derbyshire | at Leeds | 1992 $ |
|---|---|---|---|---|
| 107 | v | Ireland | at Leeds | 1995 + |

### J A LEANING (1)

| 111 * | v | Essex | at Scarborough | 2014 + |
|---|---|---|---|---|

### A Z LEES (1)

| 102 | v | Northamptonshire | at Northampton | 2014 + |
|---|---|---|---|---|

### D S LEHMANN (8)

| 191 | v | Nottinghamshire | at Scarborough | 2001 $ |
|---|---|---|---|---|
| 119 | v | Durham | at Leeds | 1998 # |
| 118 * | v | Northamptonshire | at Northampton | 2006 + |
| 105 | v | Glamorgan | at Cardiff | 1995 + |
| 104 | v | Somerset | at Taunton | 2002 $ |
| 103 | v | Derbyshire | at Leeds | 2001 # |
| 103 | v | Leicestershire | at Scarborough | 2001 $ |
| 102 * | v | Derbyshire | ar Derby | 1998 # |

### J D LOVE (4)

| 118 * | v | Scotland | at Bradford | 1981 # |
|---|---|---|---|---|
| 118 * | v | Surrey | at Leeds | 1987 $ |
| 104 * | v | Nottinghamshire | at Hull | 1986 $ |
| 100 * | v | Gloucestershire | at Gloucester | 1985 $ |

### R G LUMB (1)

| | | | | |
|---|---|---|---|---|
| 101 | v | Nottinghamshire | at Scarborough | 1976 $ |

### A LYTH (1)

| | | | | |
|---|---|---|---|---|
| 109 * | v | Sussex | at Scarborough | 2009 $ |

### A McGRATH (7)

| | | | | |
|---|---|---|---|---|
| 148 | v | Somerset | at Taunton | 2006 + |
| 135 * | v | Lancashire | at Manchester | 2007 + |
| 109 * | v | Minor Counties | at Leeds | 1997 # |
| 106 | v | West Indies | at Scarborough | 1995 |
| 105 * | v | Scotland | at Leeds | 2008 + |
| 102 | v | Kent | at Canterbury | 2001 $ |
| 100 | v | Durham | at Leeds | 2007 + |

### G J MAXWELL (1)

| | | | | |
|---|---|---|---|---|
| 111 | v | Worcestershire | at Worcester | 2015 + |

### A A METCALFE (4)

| | | | | |
|---|---|---|---|---|
| 127 * | v | Warwickshire | at Leeds | 1990 + |
| 116 | v | Middlesex | at Lord's | 1991 $ |
| 115 * | v | Gloucestershire | at Scarborough | 1984 $ |
| 114 | v | Lancashire | at Manchester | 1991 # |

### M D MOXON (7)

| | | | | |
|---|---|---|---|---|
| 141 * | v | Glamorgan | at Cardiff | 1991 # |
| 137 | v | Nottinghamshire | at Leeds | 1996+ |
| 129 * | v | Surrey | at The Oval | 1991 $ |
| 112 | v | Sussex | at Middlesbrough | 1991 $ |
| 107 * | v | Warwickshire | at Leeds | 1990 + |
| 106 * | v | Lancashire | at Manchester | 1986 # |
| 105 | v | Somerset | at Scarborough | 1990 $ |

### R B RICHARDSON (1)

| | | | | |
|---|---|---|---|---|
| 103 | v | Nottinghamshire | at Nottingham | 1993 $ |

### J A RUDOLPH (9)

| | | | | |
|---|---|---|---|---|
| 132 * | v | Sussex | at Scarborough | 2011 $ |
| 127 | v | Somerset | at Scarborough | 2007 $ |
| 124 * | v | Middlesex | at Scarborough | 2010 $ |
| 120 | v | Leicestershire | at Leeds | 2008 $ |
| 118 | v | Gloucestershire | at Leeds | 2009 + |
| 106 | v | Warwickshire | at Scarborough | 2010 $ |
| 105 | v | Derbyshire | at Chesterfield | 2010 $ |
| 101 * | v | Essex | at Chelmsford | 2010 $ |
| 100 | v | Leicestershire | at Leeds | 2007 + |

### K SHARP (3)

| | | | | |
|---|---|---|---|---|
| 114 | v | Essex | at Chelmsford | 1985 $ |
| 112 * | v | Worcestershire | at Worcester | 1985 $ |
| 105 * | v | Scotland | at Leeds | 1984 # |

### S R TENDULKAR (1)

| | | | | |
|---|---|---|---|---|
| 107 | v | Lancashire | at Leeds | 1992 $ |

# ALL LIST A CENTURIES 1963-2015 *(Continued)*

### *M P VAUGHAN (3)*

| | | | | |
|---|---|---|---|---|
| 125 * | v | Somerset | at Taunton | 2001 # |
| 116 * | v | Lancashire | at Manchester | 2004 + |
| 116 * | v | Kent | at Leeds | 2005 $ |

### *C WHITE (5)*

| | | | | |
|---|---|---|---|---|
| 148 | v | Leicestershire | at Leicester | 1997 $ |
| 113 | v | Ireland | at Leeds | 1995 + |
| 112 | v | Northamptonshire | at Northampton | 2006 + |
| 101 * | v | Durham | at Chester-le-Street | 2006 + |
| 100 * | v | Surrey | at Leeds | 2002 + |

### *M J WOOD (5)*

| | | | | |
|---|---|---|---|---|
| 160 | v | Devon | at Exmouth | 2004 + |
| 118 * | v | Cambridgeshire | at March | 2003 + |
| 115 * | v | Derbyshire | at Derby | 2002 # |
| 111 | v | Surrey | at The Oval | 2005 $ |
| 105 * | v | Somerset | at Taunton | 2002$ |

### *YOUNUS KHAN (1)*

| | | | | |
|---|---|---|---|---|
| 100 | v | Nottinghamshire | at Nottingham | 2007 + |

# LIST A PARTNERSHIPS OF 150 AND OVER 1963-2015 (43)

242* 1st wkt  M D Moxon (107*)   and A A Metcalfe (127*)  v. Warwickshire at Leeds      1990 +
233* 1st wkt  A W Gale (125*)    and J A Rudolph (101*)   v. Essex at Chelmsford        2010 $
213  1st wkt  M D Moxon (141*)   and A A Metcalfe (84)    v. Glamorgan at Cardiff       1991 #
211* 1st wkt  M D Moxon (93*)    and A A Metcalfe (94*)   v. Warwickshire at Birmingham
                                                                                        1987 #
207  4th wkt  S A Kellett (107)  and C White (113)        v. Ireland at Leeds           1995 +
202  2nd wkt  G Boycott (87)     and C W J Athey (115)    v. Kent at Leeds              1980 +
201  1st wkt  J H Hampshire (86) and C W J Athey (118)    v. Leicestershire at Leicester
                                                                                        1978 $
198* 4th wkt  M T G Elliott (115*) and A McGrath (85*)    v. Kent at Leeds              2002 $
195  1st wkt  A Lyth (84)        and A Z Lees (102)       v. Northamptonshire
                                                                          at Northampton 2014 +
192  2nd wkt  G Boycott (146)    and D B Close (79)       v. Surrey at Lord's           1965 +
190  1st wkt  G Boycott (89*)    and R G Lumb (101)       v. Nottinghamshire
                                                                          at Scarborough 1976 $
190  5th wkt  R J Blakey (96)    and M J Foster (118)     v. Leicestershire at Leicester
                                                                                        1993 $
186  1st wkt  G Boycott (99)     and J H Hampshire (92*)  v. Gloucestershire
                                                                          at Scarborough 1975 $
186  1st wkt  G S Blewett (71)   and D Byas (104*)        v. Hampshire at Leeds         1999 #
184  3rd wkt  M P Vaughan (70)   and D S Lehmann (119)    v. Durham at Leeds            1998 #
181  5th wkt  M T G Elliott (109) and A McGrath (78)      v. Leicestershire at Leicester
                                                                                        2002 $
176  3rd wkt  R J Blakey (86)    and S R Tendulkar (107)  v. Lancashire at Leeds        1992 $
172  2nd wkt  D Byas (86)        and D S Lehmann (99)     v. Kent at Maidstone          1998 $
172  3rd wkt  A McGrath (38)     and D S Lehmann (191)    v. Nottinghamshire
                                                                          at Scarborough 2001 $
171  1st wkt  M D Moxon (112)    and A A Metcalfe (68)    v. Sussex at Middlesbrough 1991 $
170  4th wkt  M J Wood (105*)    and D S Lehmann (104)    v. Somerset at Taunton        2002 $
170  1st wkt  A W Gale (89)      and J A Rudolph (120)    v. Leicestershire at Leeds    2008 $
167* 6th wkt  M G Bevan (95*)    and R J Blakey ((80*)    v. Lancashire at Manchester
                                                                                        1996 #
167* 1st wkt  C White (100*)     and M J Wood (57*)       v. Surrey at Leeds            2002 +
167  1st wkt  M D Moxon( 64)     and A A Metcalfe (116)   v. Middlesex at Lord's        1991 $
167  1st wkt  M J Wood (65)      and S P Fleming (139*)   v. Warwickshire at Leeds      2003 $
166  1st wkt  M D Moxon (82*)    and A A Metcalfe (70)    v. Northamptonshire at Leeds
                                                                                        1988 #
165  1st wkt  M D Moxon (80)     and D Byas (106*)        v. Derbyshire at Chesterfield
                                                                                        1993 $
165  1st wkt  M D Moxon (70)     and D Byas (88*)         v. Northamptonshire at Leeds
                                                                                        1993 $
164* 2nd wkt  G Boycott (91*)    and C W J Athey (79*)    v. Worcestershire at Worcester
                                                                                        1981 $
164  3rd wkt  A McGrath (105*)   and J A Rudolph (82)     v. Scotland at Leeds          2008 +
164  3rd wkt  J A Rudolph (84)   and A McGrath (73)       v. Glamorgan at Scarborough
                                                                                        2008 $
161  1st wkt  M D Moxon (74)     and A A Metcalfe (85)    v. Wiltshire at Trowbridge    1987 +
160* 1st wkt  G Boycott (70*)    and M D Moxon (82*)      v. Cheshire at Oxton          1985 +
160* 5th wkt  G M Fellows (80*)  and C White (73*)        v. Surrey at Leeds            2001 $
160* 3rd wkt  A Lyth (60*)       and G S Ballance (103*)  v. Unicorns at Scarborough
                                                                                        2012 $
160  1st wkt  G Boycott (67)     and J H Hampshire (84)   v. Warwickshire at Birmingham
                                                                                        1973 $
159  2nd wkt  G Boycott (92)     and D B Close (96)       v. Surrey at The Oval         1969 +

404

## LIST A PARTNERSHIPS OF 150 AND OVER *(Continued)*

| | | | | | |
|---|---|---|---|---|---|
| 157 | 2nd wkt | K Sharp (71) | and R J Blakey (79) | v. Worcestershire at Worcester | 1990 $ |
| 155 | *1st wkt | A Lyth (67) | and A Z Lees (69*) | v. Derbyshire at Scarborough | 2014 + |
| 154* | 2nd wkt | J H Hampshire (111*) | and B Leadbeater (57*) | v. Sussex at Hove | 1973 $ |
| 153 | 4th wkt | Younus Khan (100) | and A W Gale ((69*) | v. Nottinghamshire at Nottingham | 2007 + |
| 150* | 5th wkt | S N Hartley (67*) | and J D Love (82*) | v. Hampshire at Middlesbrough | 1983 $ |

## LIST A HIGHEST PARTNERSHIPS FOR EACH WICKET

| | | | | | |
|---|---|---|---|---|---|
| 1st wkt | 242* | M D Moxon (107*) | and A A Metcalfe (127*) | v Warwickshire at Leeds | 1990 + |
| 2nd wkt | 202 | G Boycott (87) | and C W J Athey (115) | v. Kent at Leeds | 1980 + |
| 3rd wkt | 184 | M P Vaughan (70) | and D S Lehmann (119) | v. Durham at Leeds | 1998 # |
| 4th wkt | 207 | S A Kellett (107) | and C White (113) | v. Ireland at Leeds | 1995 + |
| 5th wkt | 190 | R J Blakey (96) | and M J Foster (118) | v. Leicestershire at Leicester | 1993 $ |
| 6th wkt | 167* | M G Bevan (95*) | and R J Blakey ((80*) | v. Lancashire at Manchester | 1996 # |
| 7th wkt | 149 * | J D Love (118*) | and C M Old (78*) | v. Scotland at Bradford | 1981 # |
| 8th wkt | 89 | R J Blakey (60) | and R K J Dawson (41) | v. Leicestershire at Scarborough | 2002 $ |
| 9th wkt | 88 | S N Hartley (67) | and A Ramage (32*) | v. Middlesex at Lord's | 1982 $ |
| 10th wkt | 80* | D L Bairstow (103*) | and M Johnson (4*) | v. Derbyshire at Derby | 1981 # |

# ALL LIST A 5 WICKETS IN AN INNINGS 1963-2015 (56)

*C W J ATHEY (1)*

| 5-35 | v | Derbyshire | at Chesterfield | 1981 $ |

*AZEEM RAFIQ (1)*

| 5-30 | v | Sri Lanka A | at Leeds | 2013 |

*M G BEVAN (1)*

| 5-29 | v | Sussex | at Eastbourne | 1996 $ |

*P CARRICK (2)*

| 5-22 | v | Glamorgan | at Leeds | 1991 $ |
| 5-40 | v | Sussex | at Middlesbrough | 1991 $ |

*H P COOPER (2)*

| 6-14 | v | Worcestershire | at Worcester | 1975 $ |
| 5-30 | v | Worcestershire | at Middlesbrough | 1978 $ |

*D GOUGH (4)*

| 5-13 | v | Sussex | at Hove | 1994 $ |
| 7-27 | v | Ireland | at Leeds | 1997 + |
| 5-25 | v | Surrey | at Leeds | 1998 $ |
| 5-30 | v | Yorkshire C B | at Harrogate | 2000 + |

*G M HAMILTON (2)*

| 5-16 | v | Hampshire | at Leeds | 1998 $ |
| 5-34 | v | Sussex | at Scarborough | 2000 $ |

*P J HARTLEY (4)*

| 5-36 | v | Sussex | at Scarborough | 1993 $ |
| 5-38 | v | Worcestershire | at Worcester | 1990 $ |
| 5-43 | v | Scotland | at Leeds | 1986 # |
| 5-46 | v | Hampshire | at Southampton | 1990 + |

*M J HOGGARD (3)*

| 5-28 | v | Leicestershire | at Leicester | 2000 $ |
| 5-30 | v | Northamptonshire | at Northampton | 2000 $ |
| 5-65 | v | Somerset | at Lord's | 2002 + |

*R A HUTTON (1)*

| 7-15 | v | Worcestershire | at Leeds | 1969 $ |

*R ILLINGWORTH (1)*

| 5-29 | v | Surrey | at Lord's | 1965 + |

*P W JARVIS (3)*

| 6-27 | v | Somerset | at Taunton | 1989 $ |
| 5-18 | v | Derbyshire | at Leeds | 1990 $ |
| 5-29 | v | Northamptonshire | at Northampton | 1992 $ |

*J A LEANING (1)*

| 5-22 | v | Unicorns | at Leeds | 2013 $ |

*A C MORRIS (1)*

| 5-32 | v | Young Australia | at Leeds | 1995 |

*M D MOXON (1)*

| 5-31 | v | Warwickshire | at Leeds | 1991 # |

### A G NICHOLSON (4)

| | | | | |
|---|---|---|---|---|
| 6-27 | v | Minor Counties | at Middlesbrough | 1972 # |
| 6-36 | v | Somerset | at Sheffield | 1972 $ |
| 5-17 | v | Nottinghamshire | at Hull | 1972 $ |
| 5-24 | v | Derbyshire | at Bradford | 1975 # |

### C M OLD (2)

| | | | | |
|---|---|---|---|---|
| 5-33 | v | Sussex | at Hove | 1971 $ |
| 5-38 | v | Northamptonshire | at Sheffield | 1972 $ |

### S OLDHAM (1)

| | | | | |
|---|---|---|---|---|
| 5-32 | v | Minor Counties | at Scunthorpe | 1975 # |

### S A PATTERSON (2)

| | | | | |
|---|---|---|---|---|
| 6-32 | v | Derbyshire | at Leeds | 2010 $ |
| 5-24 | v | Worcestershire | at Worcester | 2015 + |

### A U RASHID (1)

| | | | | |
|---|---|---|---|---|
| 5-33 | v | Hampshire | at Southampton | 2014 + |

### A SHAHZAD (1)

| | | | | |
|---|---|---|---|---|
| 5-51 | v | Sri Lanka A | at Leeds | 2007 |

### C SHAW (1)

| | | | | |
|---|---|---|---|---|
| 5-41 | v | Hampshire | at Bournemouth | 1984 $ |

### A SIDEBOTTOM (2)

| | | | | |
|---|---|---|---|---|
| 5-27 | v | Worcestershire | at Bradford | 1985 # |
| 5-27 | v | Glamorgan | at Leeds | 1987 + |

### R J SIDEBOTTOM (2)

| | | | | |
|---|---|---|---|---|
| 6-40 | v | Glamorgan | at Cardiff | 2003 $ |
| 5-42 | v | Leicestershire | at Leicester | 2003 $ |

### C E W SILVERWOOD (1)

| | | | | |
|---|---|---|---|---|
| 5-28 | v | Scotland | at Leeds | 1996 # |

### G B STEVENSON (4)

| | | | | |
|---|---|---|---|---|
| 5-27 | v | Berkshire | at Reading | 1983 + |
| 5-28 | v | Kent | at Canterbury | 1978 # |
| 5-41 | v | Leicestershire | at Leicester | 1976 $ |
| 5-50 | v | Worcestershire | at Leeds | 1982 # |

### S STUCHBURY (1)

| | | | | |
|---|---|---|---|---|
| 5-16 | v | Leicestershire | at Leicester | 1982 $ |

### N D THORNICROFT (1)

| | | | | |
|---|---|---|---|---|
| 5-42 | v | Gloucestershire | at Leeds | 2003 $ |

### F S TRUEMAN (1)

| | | | | |
|---|---|---|---|---|
| 6-15 | v | Somerset | at Taunton | 1965 + |

### C WHITE (2)

| | | | | |
|---|---|---|---|---|
| 5-19 | v | Somerset | at Scarborough | 2002 $ |
| 5-25 | v | Lancashire | at Leeds | 2000 # |

### D WILSON (2)

| | | | | |
|---|---|---|---|---|
| 6-18 | v | Kent | at Canterbury | 1969 $ |
| 5-25 | v | Lancashire | at Bradford | 1972 # |

## ALL LIST A PLAYERS WHO HAVE TAKEN 4 WICKETS
## IN AN INNINGS 1963-2015 (158) AND BEST FIGURES

| 11 | C M Old | 4-9 | v | Durham M C | at Middlesbrough | 1978 + |
|----|---------|-----|---|------------|------------------|--------|
| 10 | C White | 4-14 | v | Lancashire | at Leeds | 2000 $ |
| | | 4-14 | v | Surrey | at The Oval | 2005 $ |
| 9 | A Sidebottom | 4-15 | v | Worcestershire | at Leeds | 1987 # |
| 8 | P W Jarvis | 4-13 | v | Worcestershire | at Leeds | 1986 $ |
| 8 | D Gough | 4-17 | v | Nottinghamshire | at Nottingham | 2000 # |
| 8 | G B Stevenson | 4-20 | v | Essex | at Barnsley | 1977 # |
| 7 | S D Fletcher | 4-11 | v | Kent | at Canterbury | 1988 $ |
| 6 | C E W Silverwood | 4-11 | v | Leicestershire | at Leicester | 2000 $ |
| 6 | H P Cooper | 4-18 | v | Leicestershire | at Leeds | 1975 + |
| 5 | S Oldham | 4-13 | v | Nottinghamshire | at Nottingham | 1989 $ |
| 5 | R M Pyrah | 4-24 | v | Netherlands | at Rotterdam | 2010 $ |
| 4 | P Carrick | 4-13 | v | Derbyshire | at Bradford | 1983 $ |
| 4 | R K J Dawson | 4-13 | v | Derbyshire | at Derby | 2002 # |
| 4 | T T Bresnan | 4-25 | v | Somerset | at Leeds | 2005 $ |
| 4 | G M Hamilton | 4-27 | v | Warwickshire | at Birmingham | 1995 $ |
| 3 | R A Hutton | 4-18 | v | Surrey | at The Oval | 1972 $ |
| 3 | A G Nicholson | 4-15 | v | Kent | at Leeds | 1974 $ |
| 3 | P J Hartley | 4-21 | v | Scotland | at Glasgow | 1995 # |
| 3 | A L Robinson | 4-25 | v | Surrey | at The Oval | 1974 $ |
| 3 | R D Stemp | 4-25 | v | Gloucestershire | at Bristol | 1996 $ |
| 3 | M P Vaughan | 4-27 | v | Gloucestershire | at Bristol | 2000 $ |
| 2 | M K Bore | 4-21 | v | Sussex | at Middlesbrough | 1970 $ |
| | | 4-21 | v | Worcestershire | at Worcester | 1970 $ |
| 2 | J D Woodford | 4-23 | v | Northamptonshire | at Northampton | 1970 $ |
| | | 4-23 | v | Warwickshire | at Middlesbrough | 1971 $ |
| 2 | G J Kruis | 4-17 | v | Derbyshire | at Leeds | 2007 $ |
| 2 | D Wilson | 4-22 | v | Nottinghamshire | at Bradford | 1969 $ |
| 2 | V J Craven | 4-22 | v | Kent | at Scarborough | 2003 $ |
| 2 | M A Robinson | 4-23 | v | Northamptonshire | at Leeds | 1993 $ |
| 2 | S N Hartley | 4-32 | v | Derbyshire | at Leeds | 1989 # |
| 2 | A U Rashid | 4-38 | v | Northamptonshire | at Northampton | 2012 $ |
| 2 | A McGrath | 4-41 | v | Surrey | at Leeds | 2003 $ |
| 1 | R Illingworth | 4-6 | v | Middlesex | at Hull | 1983 $ |
| 1 | M Johnson | 4-18 | v | Scotland | at Bradford | 1981 # |
| 1 | G S Blewett | 4-18 | v | Lancashire | at Manchester | 1999 + |
| 1 | G M Fellows | 4-19 | v | Durham | at Leeds | 2002 $ |
| 1 | A P Grayson | 4-25 | v | Glamorgan | at Cardiff | 1994 $ |
| 1 | C J Elstub | 4-25 | v | Surrey | at Leeds | 2001 $ |
| 1 | D S Lehmann | 4-26 | v | Devon | at Exmouth | 2002 + |
| 1 | S A Patterson | 4-28 | v | Worcestershire | at Worcester | 2011 $ |
| 1 | C Shaw | 4-29 | v | Middlesex | at Leeds | 1988 $ |
| 1 | A G Wharf | 4-29 | v | Nottinghamshire | at Leeds | 1996 # |
| 1 | F S Trueman | 4-30 | v | Nottinghamshire | at Middlesbrough | 1963 + |
| 1 | J D Batty | 4-33 | v | Kent | at Scarborough | 1991 $ |
| 1 | P M Hutchinson | 4-34 | v | Gloucestershire | at Gloucester | 1998 $ |
| 1 | A K D Gray | 4-34 | v | Kent | at Leeds | 2002 $ |
| 1 | A Shahzad | 4-34 | v | Middlesex | at Lord's | 2010 $ |
| 1 | P M Stringer | 4-35 | v | Derbyshire | at Sheffield | 1969 $ |
| 1 | C S Pickles | 4-36 | v | Somerset | at Scarborough | 1990 $ |
| 1 | M J Hoggard | 4-39 | v | Surrey | at Leeds | 2000 # |
| 1 | R J Sidebottom | 4-39 | v | Bedfordshire | at Luton | 2001 + |
| 1 | K Sharp | 4-40 | v | Wiltshire | at Trowbridge | 1987 + |
| 1 | T L Best | 4-46 | v | Essex | at Chelmsford | 2010 $ |
| 1 | A C Morris | 4-49 | v | Leicestershire | at Leicester | 1997 $ |
| 1 | D B Close | 4-60 | v | Sussex | at Hove | 1963 + |

# CAREER AVERAGES FOR YORKSHIRE

## ALL LIST A MATCHES OF 40 TO 65 OVERS 1963-2015

| Player | M | Inns | NO | Runs | HS | Av'ge | 100s | 50s | Runs | Wkts | Av'ge | Ct/St |
|---|---|---|---|---|---|---|---|---|---|---|---|---|
| Ashraf, M A . . . | 22 | 6 | 4 | 3 | 3* | 1.50 | 0 | 0 | 895 | 23 | 38.91 | 4 |
| Athey, C W J . . | 140 | 129 | 14 | 3662 | 118 | 31.84 | 2 | 25 | 431 | 19 | 22.68 | 46 |
| Azeem Rafiq . . . | 15 | 11 | 4 | 116 | 34* | 16.57 | 0 | 0 | 483 | 17 | 28.41 | 4 |
| Bairstow, D L . | 403 | 317 | 71 | 5180 | 103* | 21.05 | 1 | 19 | 17 | 0 | — | 390/31 |
| **Bairstow, J M** . | 36 | 32 | 4 | 761 | 114 | 27.17 | 1 | 3 | 0 | 0 | — | 27/1 |
| Baker, T M . . . . | 4 | 1 | 0 | 3 | 3 | 3.00 | 0 | 0 | 89 | 4 | 22.25 | 3 |
| Balderstone, J C | 13 | 11 | 2 | 173 | 46 | 19.22 | 0 | 0 | 38 | 2 | 19.00 | 3 |
| **Ballance, G S** . | 39 | 37 | 7 | 1616 | 139 | 53.86 | 2 | 11 | 0 | 0 | — | 17 |
| Batty, J D . . . . | 38 | 16 | 7 | 50 | 13* | 5.55 | 0 | 0 | 1297 | 42 | 30.88 | 18 |
| Berry, P J . . . . . | 1 | 0 | 0 | 0 | 0 | — | 0 | 0 | 28 | 0 | — | 0 |
| Best, T L . . . . . | 5 | 1 | 1 | 8 | 8* | — | 0 | 0 | 166 | 10 | 16.60 | 1 |
| Bevan, M G . . . | 48 | 45 | 12 | 2110 | 103* | 63.93 | 2 | 19 | 540 | 28 | 19.28 | 11 |
| Binks, J G . . . . | 30 | 21 | 3 | 247 | 34 | 13.72 | 0 | 0 | 0 | 0 | — | 26/8 |
| Blain, J A R . . . | 15 | 8 | 3 | 34 | 11* | 6.80 | 0 | 0 | 462 | 14 | 33.00 | 3 |
| Blakey, R J . . . | 373 | 319 | 84 | 7361 | 130* | 31.32 | 3 | 35 | 0 | 0 | — | 369/59 |
| Blewett, G S . . . | 17 | 17 | 0 | 345 | 77 | 20.29 | 0 | 2 | 196 | 11 | 17.81 | 7 |
| Booth, P A . . . . . | 5 | 2 | 1 | 7 | 6* | 7.00 | 0 | 0 | 147 | 3 | 49.00 | 1 |
| Bore, M K . . . . . | 55 | 24 | 10 | 90 | 15 | 6.42 | 0 | 0 | 1600 | 50 | 32.00 | 15 |
| Boycott, G . . . . | 264 | 255 | 38 | 8699 | 146 | 40.08 | 7 | 63 | 1095 | 25 | 43.80 | 92 |
| **Bresnan, T T** . . | 151 | 104 | 26 | 1368 | 61 | 17.53 | 3 | | 5248 | 164 | 32.00 | 43 |
| Broadhurst, M . . | 1 | 0 | 0 | 0 | 0 | — | 0 | 0 | 27 | 0 | — | 0 |
| **Brooks, J A** . . . | 11 | 3 | 2 | 6 | 2.00 | | 0 | 0 | 419 | 14 | 29.92 | 2 |
| Brophy, G L . . . | 68 | 57 | 12 | 1240 | 93* | 27.55 | 0 | 9 | 0 | 0 | — | 67/14 |
| Byas, D . . . . . . . | 313 | 301 | 35 | 7782 | 116* | 29.25 | 5 | 44 | 659 | 25 | 26.36 | 128 |
| **Callis, E** . . . . . . | 1 | 1 | 0 | 0 | 0 | 0.00 | 0 | 0 | 0 | 0 | — | 0 |
| Carrick, P . . . . | 304 | 206 | 53 | 2159 | 54 | 14.11 | 0 | 2 | 7408 | 236 | 31.38 | 70 |
| **Carver, K** . . . . | 5 | 1 | 1 | 35 | 35* | — | 0 | 0 | 108 | 2 | 54.00 | 1 |
| Chapman, C A . . | 10 | 7 | 4 | 94 | 34* | 31.33 | 0 | 0 | 0 | 0 | — | 7 |
| Claydon, M E . . | 7 | 2 | 0 | 15 | 9 | 7.50 | 0 | 0 | 293 | 8 | 36.62 | 0 |
| Cleary, M F . . . . | 4 | 3 | 1 | 50 | 23* | 25.00 | 0 | 0 | 159 | 2 | 79.50 | 0 |
| Close, D B . . . . | 32 | 31 | 2 | 631 | 96 | 21.75 | 0 | 3 | 475 | 23 | 20.65 | 14 |
| **Coad, B O** . . . . | 7 | 3 | 3 | 3 | 2* | — | 0 | 0 | 282 | 3 | 94.00 | 3 |
| Cooper, H P . . . | 142 | 74 | 34 | 483 | 29* | 12.07 | 0 | 0 | 4184 | 177 | 23.63 | 26 |
| Cope, G A . . . . | 37 | 20 | 13 | 96 | 18* | 13.71 | 0 | 0 | 1020 | 24 | 42.50 | 9 |
| Coverdale, S P . . | 3 | 3 | 2 | 18 | 17* | 18.00 | 0 | 0 | 0 | 0 | — | 3 |
| Craven, V J . . . . | 42 | 39 | 5 | 580 | 59 | 17.05 | 0 | 2 | 353 | 21 | 16.80 | 14 |
| Dalton, A J . . . . | 17 | 16 | 1 | 280 | 55 | 18.66 | 0 | 1 | 0 | 0 | — | 4 |
| Dawood, I . . . . . | 25 | 20 | 4 | 260 | 57 | 16.25 | 0 | 1 | 0 | 0 | — | 18/8 |
| Dawson, R K J . | 92 | 58 | 12 | 431 | 41 | 9.36 | 0 | 0 | 2784 | 91 | 30.59 | 31 |
| Dennis, S J . . . . | 56 | 24 | 11 | 114 | 16* | 8.76 | 0 | 0 | 1736 | 42 | 41.33 | 7 |
| Elliott, M T G . . | 6 | 6 | 3 | 394 | 128* | 131.33 | 3 | 0 | 0 | 0 | — | 0 |
| Elstub, C J . . . . | 10 | 4 | 4 | 6 | 4* | — | 0 | 0 | 290 | 12 | 24.16 | 0 |
| Fellows, G M . . | 95 | 79 | 15 | 1342 | 80* | 20.96 | 0 | 4 | 836 | 22 | 38.00 | 27 |
| Fisher, I D . . . . | 28 | 12 | 3 | 68 | 20 | 7.55 | 0 | 0 | 708 | 29 | 24.41 | 6 |
| **Fisher, M D** . . . | 13 | 5 | 3 | 62 | 34 | 31.00 | 0 | 0 | 431 | 11 | 39.18 | 2 |
| Fleming, S P . . . | 7 | 7 | 1 | 285 | 139* | 47.50 | 1 | 1 | 0 | 0 | — | 3 |
| Fletcher, S D . . | 129 | 32 | 18 | 109 | 16* | 7.78 | 0 | 0 | 4686 | 164 | 28.57 | 34 |
| Foster, M J . . . . | 20 | 14 | 1 | 199 | 118 | 15.30 | 1 | 0 | 370 | 6 | 61.66 | 6 |
| **Gale, A W** . . . . | 125 | 116 | 11 | 3256 | 125* | 31.00 | 2 | 17 | 0 | 0 | — | 24 |
| **Gibson, R** . . . . . | 5 | 4 | 1 | 19 | 9 | 6.33 | 0 | 0 | 158 | 5 | 31.60 | 1 |
| Gilbert, C R . . . . | 5 | 4 | 0 | 55 | 37 | 13.75 | 0 | 0 | 199 | 8 | 24.87 | 2 |
| Gillespie, J N . . | 18 | 4 | 1 | 29 | 15* | 9.66 | 0 | 0 | 601 | 18 | 33.38 | 6 |
| Gough, D . . . . . | 214 | 120 | 33 | 1280 | 72* | 14.71 | 0 | 1 | 6798 | 291 | 23.36 | 43 |
| Gray, A K D . . . | 31 | 19 | 7 | 130 | 30* | 10.83 | 0 | 0 | 843 | 25 | 33.72 | 8 |
| Grayson, A P . . . | 66 | 49 | 8 | 587 | 55 | 14.31 | 0 | 1 | 1441 | 39 | 36.94 | 19 |
| Guy, S M . . . . . | 32 | 23 | 4 | 282 | 40 | 14.84 | 0 | 0 | 0 | 0 | — | 35/11 |
| Hamilton, G M . | 101 | 70 | 18 | 1059 | 57* | 20.36 | 0 | 2 | 2803 | 121 | 23.16 | 15 |
| Hampshire, A W | 4 | 3 | 0 | 3 | 3 | 1.00 | 0 | 0 | 0 | 0 | — | 1 |

| Player | M | Inns | NO | Runs | HS | Av'ge | 100s | 50s | Runs | Wkts | Av'ge | Ct/St |
|---|---|---|---|---|---|---|---|---|---|---|---|---|
| Hampshire, J H . | 234 | 223 | 24 | 6296 | 119 | 31.63 | 7 | 36 | 26 | 1 | 26.00 | 69 |
| Hannon-Dalby, O J | 5 | 1 | 1 | 21 | 21* | 0 | 0 | | 202 | 5 | 40.40 | 3 |
| Harden, R J . . . | 19 | 16 | 2 | 230 | 42 | 16.42 | 0 | 0 | 0 | 0 | — | 4 |
| Hartley, P J . . . | 219 | 145 | 49 | 1609 | 83 | 16.76 | 0 | 4 | 7476 | 283 | 26.41 | 40 |
| Hartley, S N . . . | 171 | 154 | 31 | 2815 | 83* | 22.88 | 0 | 13 | 2153 | 67 | 32.13 | 52 |
| Harvey, J H . . . | 28 | 27 | 2 | 637 | 74 | 25.48 | 0 | 3 | 950 | 30 | 31.66 | 8 |
| **Hodd, A J** . . . . . | 21 | 15 | 2 | 292 | 69* | 22.46 | 0 | 1 | 0 | 0 | — | 28/4 |
| Hodgson, D M . | 12 | 10 | 1 | 272 | 90 | 30.22 | 0 | 3 | 0 | 0 | — | 10/2 |
| Hodgson, L J . . | 6 | 2 | 0 | 9 | 9 | 4.50 | 0 | 0 | 161 | 4 | 40.25 | 1 |
| Hoggard, M J . . | 83 | 28 | 19 | 41 | 7* | 4.55 | 0 | 0 | 2682 | 118 | 22.72 | 7 |
| Hutchison, P M . | 32 | 11 | 8 | 18 | 4* | 6.00 | 0 | 0 | 844 | 43 | 19.62 | 3 |
| Hutton, R A . . . | 107 | 80 | 25 | 1075 | 65 | 19.54 | 0 | 4 | 3000 | 128 | 23.43 | 27 |
| Illingworth, R . . | 41 | 15 | 11 | 171 | 45 | 42.75 | 0 | 0 | 793 | 40 | 19.82 | 14 |
| Ingham, P G . . . | 12 | 10 | 4 | 312 | 87* | 52.00 | 0 | 2 | 0 | 0 | — | 2 |
| Inzamam ul Haq | 3 | 3 | 0 | 69 | 53 | 23.00 | 0 | 1 | 0 | 0 | — | 0 |
| Jaques, P A . . . . | 43 | 42 | 2 | 1588 | 105 | 39.70 | 1 | 13 | 0 | 0 | — | 16 |
| Jarvis, P W . . . . | 144 | 74 | 28 | 529 | 42 | 11.50 | 0 | 0 | 4684 | 213 | 21.99 | 33 |
| Johnson, C . . . . | 129 | 102 | 22 | 1615 | 73* | 20.18 | 0 | 4 | 28 | 2 | 14.00 | 33 |
| Johnson, M . . . . | 14 | 6 | 3 | 34 | 15* | 11.33 | 0 | 0 | 455 | 12 | 37.91 | 2 |
| Katich, S M . . . | 3 | 3 | 2 | 79 | 40* | 79.00 | 0 | 0 | 0 | 0 | — | 2 |
| Kellett, S A . . . | 56 | 51 | 3 | 1207 | 118* | 25.14 | 2 | 4 | 16 | 0 | — | 14 |
| Kettleborough, R A | 10 | 6 | 3 | 71 | 28 | 23.66 | 0 | 0 | 72 | 3 | 24.00 | 4 |
| Kirby, S P . . . . . | 29 | 12 | 3 | 38 | 15 | 4.22 | 0 | 0 | 1061 | 24 | 44.20 | 6 |
| Kruis, G J . . . . | 55 | 22 | 11 | 138 | 31* | 12.54 | 0 | 0 | 1793 | 62 | 28.91 | 9 |
| Lawson, M A K . | 4 | 4 | 0 | 30 | 20 | 7.50 | 0 | 0 | 141 | 3 | 47.00 | 1 |
| Leadbeater, B . . | 105 | 100 | 19 | 2245 | 90 | 27.71 | 0 | 11 | 95 | 5 | 19.00 | 26 |
| **Leaning, J A** . . | **24** | **21** | **5** | **591** | **111*** | **36.93** | **1** | **4** | **141** | **7** | **20.14** | **11** |
| Lee, J E . . . . . . | 4 | 0 | 0 | 0 | 0 | 0.00 | 0 | 0 | 116 | 7 | 16.57 | 0 |
| **Lees, A Z** . . . . | **27** | **26** | **2** | **898** | **102** | **37.41** | **1** | **8** | **0** | **0** | **—** | **7** |
| Lehmann, D S . . | 130 | 126 | 20 | 5229 | 191 | 49.33 | 8 | 38 | 1990 | 79 | 25.18 | 41 |
| Lester, E I . . . . | 1 | 1 | 0 | 0 | 0 | 0.00 | 0 | 0 | 0 | 0 | — | 0 |
| Love, J D . . . . . | 220 | 203 | 33 | 4298 | 118* | 25.28 | 4 | 18 | 129 | 5 | 25.80 | 44 |
| Lucas, D S . . . . | 5 | 2 | 0 | 40 | 32 | 20.00 | 0 | 0 | 187 | 3 | 62.33 | 1 |
| Lumb, M J . . . . | 104 | 98 | 8 | 2606 | 92 | 28.95 | 0 | 18 | 28 | 0 | — | 31 |
| Lumb, R G . . . . | 137 | 123 | 13 | 2784 | 101 | 25.30 | 1 | 16 | 0 | 0 | — | 21 |
| **Lyth, A** . . . . . . | **86** | **80** | **7** | **2377** | **109*** | **32.56** | **1** | **12** | **188** | **2** | **94.00** | **36** |
| McGrath, A . . . | 275 | 253 | 39 | 7220 | 148 | 33.73 | 7 | 44 | 2514 | 79 | 31.82 | 91 |
| **Maxwell, G J** . . | **8** | **7** | **1** | **312** | **111** | **52.00** | **1** | **2** | **144** | **3** | **48.00** | **4** |
| Metcalfe, A Z . . | 194 | 189 | 15 | 5584 | 127* | 32.09 | 4 | 36 | 44 | 2 | 22.00 | 44 |
| Middlebrook, J D | 18 | 11 | 3 | 61 | 15* | 7.62 | 0 | 0 | 530 | 13 | 40.76 | 5 |
| Milburn, S M . . | 4 | 2 | 1 | 14 | 13* | 14.00 | 0 | 0 | 118 | 2 | 59.00 | 1 |
| Miller, D A . . . . | 3 | 3 | 0 | 45 | 44 | 15.00 | 0 | 0 | 0 | 0 | — | 3 |
| Morris, A C . . . . | 27 | 17 | 5 | 212 | 48* | 17.66 | 0 | 0 | 464 | 21 | 22.09 | 5 |
| Moxon, M D . . . | 237 | 229 | 21 | 7380 | 141* | 35.48 | 7 | 49 | 1202 | 34 | 35.35 | 77 |
| Nicholson, A G . | 120 | 46 | 22 | 155 | 15* | 6.45 | 0 | 0 | 2951 | 173 | 17.05 | 16 |
| Nicholson, N G . | 2 | 2 | 1 | 1 | 1* | 1.00 | 0 | 0 | 0 | 0 | — | 0 |
| Old, C M . . . . . | 221 | 169 | 38 | 2572 | 82* | 19.63 | 0 | 10 | 5841 | 308 | 18.96 | 56 |
| Oldham, S . . . . | 106 | 40 | 21 | 192 | 38* | 10.10 | 0 | 0 | 3136 | 142 | 22.08 | 17 |
| Padgett, D E V . | 57 | 54 | 3 | 1069 | 68 | 20.96 | 0 | 2 | 25 | 1 | 25.00 | 13 |
| Parker, B . . . . . | 73 | 61 | 8 | 965 | 69 | 18.20 | 0 | 1 | 18 | 0 | — | 12 |
| **Patterson, S A** . | **66** | **27** | **16** | **183** | **25*** | **16.63** | **0** | **0** | **2333** | **83** | **28.10** | **9** |
| Pickles, C S . . . | 71 | 48 | 20 | 375 | 37* | 13.39 | 0 | 0 | 2403 | 63 | 38.14 | 23 |
| **Plunkett, L E** . . | **12** | **10** | **6** | **218** | **53** | **54.50** | **0** | **1** | **464** | **17** | **27.29** | **7** |
| Pyrah, R M . . . | 114 | 75 | 20 | 978 | 69 | 17.78 | 0 | 2 | 3572 | 133 | 26.85 | 35 |
| Ramage, A . . . . | 34 | 17 | 8 | 134 | 32* | 14.88 | 0 | 0 | 1178 | 30 | 39.26 | 3 |
| Ramsden, G . . . | 1 | 0 | 0 | 0 | — | — | 0 | 0 | 26 | 2 | 13.00 | 0 |
| Rana Naved -ul-Hasan . . . . . . | 17 | 16 | 1 | 375 | 74 | 25.00 | 0 | 3 | 681 | 26 | 26.19 | 5 |
| **Rashid, A U** . . . | **86** | **60** | **18** | **860** | **71** | **20.47** | **0** | **1** | **3014** | **105** | **28.70** | **25** |
| Rhodes, S J . . . . | 2 | 1 | 0 | 6 | 6 | 6.00 | 0 | 0 | 0 | 0 | — | 3 |

| Player | M | Inns | NO | Runs | HS | Av'ge | 100s | 50s | Runs | Wkts | Av'ge | Ct/St |
|---|---|---|---|---|---|---|---|---|---|---|---|---|
| **Rhodes, W M H** | 16 | 13 | 2 | 185 | 46 | 16.81 | 0 | 0 | 288 | 10 | 28.80 | 4 |
| Richardson. R B | 28 | 28 | 6 | 993 | 103 | 45.13 | 1 | 8 | 0 | 0 | — | 5 |
| Richardson, S A | 1 | 1 | 0 | 7 | 7 | 7.00 | 0 | 0 | 0 | 0 | — | 0 |
| Robinson, A L | 92 | 36 | 19 | 127 | 18* | 7.47 | 0 | 0 | 2588 | 105 | 24.64 | 14 |
| Robinson, M A | 89 | 30 | 16 | 41 | 7 | 2.92 | 0 | 0 | 2795 | 91 | 30.71 | 7 |
| Robinson, O E | 3 | 2 | 2 | 16 | 12* | — | 0 | 0 | 66 | 0 | — | 4 |
| Robinson, P E | 135 | 123 | 15 | 2738 | 78* | 25.35 | 0 | 14 | 0 | 0 | — | 47 |
| **Root, J E** | 16 | 15 | 2 | 443 | 63 | 34.07 | 0 | 2 | 222 | 7 | 31.71 | 9 |
| Rudolph, J A | 65 | 62 | 10 | 3090 | 132* | 59.42 | 9 | 19 | 37 | 0 | — | 32 |
| Ryan, M | 3 | 2 | 1 | 7 | 6* | 7.00 | 0 | 0 | 149 | 5 | 29.80 | 3 |
| Sadler, J L | 1 | 1 | 0 | 19 | 19 | 19.00 | 0 | 0 | 0 | 0 | — | 0 |
| Sanderson, B W | 10 | 2 | 1 | 14 | 12* | 14.00 | 0 | 0 | 247 | 8 | 30.87 | 5 |
| Sayers, J J | 31 | 30 | 2 | 594 | 62 | 21.21 | 0 | 5 | 79 | 1 | 79.00 | 2 |
| Scofield, D | 3 | 1 | 0 | 0 | 0 | 0.00 | 0 | 0 | 111 | 2 | 55.50 | 1 |
| Shahzad. A | 30 | 22 | 7 | 243 | 59* | 16.20 | 0 | 1 | 1182 | 34 | 34.76 | 7 |
| Sharp, K | 206 | 191 | 18 | 4776 | 114 | 27.60 | 3 | 28 | 48 | 4 | 12.00 | 68 |
| Sharpe, P J | 91 | 86 | 4 | 1515 | 89* | 18.47 | 0 | 8 | 11 | 0 | — | 53 |
| Shaw, C | 48 | 20 | 10 | 127 | 26 | 12.70 | 0 | 0 | 1396 | 58 | 24.06 | 8 |
| Sidebottom, A | 236 | 131 | 47 | 1279 | 52* | 15.22 | 0 | 1 | 6918 | 260 | 26.60 | 51 |
| **Sidebottom, R J** | 113 | 51 | 22 | 303 | 30* | 10.44 | 0 | 0 | 3631 | 124 | 29.28 | 24 |
| Silverwood, C E W | 166 | 94 | 33 | 892 | 61 | 14.62 | 0 | 4 | 5212 | 224 | 23.26 | 25 |
| Smith, N | 7 | 2 | 1 | 5 | 5 | 5.00 | 0 | 0 | 0 | 0 | — | 2 |
| Smith, R | 3 | 2 | 0 | 17 | 17 | 8.50 | 0 | 0 | 0 | 0 | — | 1 |
| Squires, P J | 56 | 48 | 5 | 708 | 79* | 16.46 | 0 | 3 | 4 | 0 | — | 10 |
| Starc, M A | 4 | 2 | 2 | 5 | 4* | — | 0 | 0 | 181 | 8 | 22.62 | 1 |
| Stemp, R D | 88 | 28 | 10 | 118 | 23* | 6.55 | 0 | 0 | 2996 | 100 | 29.96 | 14 |
| Stevenson, G B | 217 | 158 | 23 | 1710 | 81* | 12.66 | 0 | 2 | 6820 | 290 | 23.51 | 38 |
| Stott, W B | 2 | 2 | 0 | 30 | 30 | 15.00 | 0 | 0 | 0 | 0 | — | 0 |
| Stringer, P M | 11 | 8 | 6 | 29 | 13* | 14.50 | 0 | 0 | 256 | 15 | 17.06 | 3 |
| Stuchbury, S | 22 | 8 | 4 | 21 | 9* | 5.25 | 0 | 0 | 677 | 29 | 23.34 | 2 |
| Swallow, I G | 8 | 5 | 3 | 37 | 17* | 18.50 | 0 | 0 | 198 | 2 | 99.00 | 5 |
| Swanepoel, P J | 3 | 2 | 2 | 9 | 8* | — | 0 | 0 | 100 | 3 | 33.33 | 0 |
| Tattersall, J A | 1 | 1 | 0 | 0 | 0 | 0.00 | 0 | 0 | 0 | 0 | — | 0 |
| Taylor, C R | 6 | 5 | 0 | 102 | 28 | 20.40 | 0 | 0 | 0 | 0 | — | 3 |
| Taylor, K | 10 | 10 | 0 | 135 | 30 | 13.50 | 0 | 0 | 168 | 11 | 15.27 | 3 |
| Taylor, N S | 1 | 0 | 0 | 0 | 0 | — | 0 | 0 | 45 | 1 | 45.00 | 1 |
| Tendulkar, S R | 17 | 17 | 2 | 540 | 107 | 36.00 | 1 | 1 | 167 | 6 | 27.83 | 3 |
| Thornicroft, N D | 14 | 7 | 4 | 52 | 20 | 17.33 | 0 | 0 | 591 | 17 | 34.76 | 3 |
| Townsley, R A J | 5 | 4 | 1 | 81 | 34 | 27.00 | 0 | 0 | 62 | 0 | — | 1 |
| Trueman, F S | 11 | 9 | 1 | 127 | 28 | 15.87 | 0 | 0 | 348 | 21 | 16.57 | 5 |
| Vaughan, M P | 183 | 178 | 13 | 4966 | 125* | 30.09 | 3 | 29 | 1860 | 60 | 31.00 | 56 |
| **Wainman, J C** | 1 | 1 | 0 | 33 | 33 | 33.00 | 0 | 0 | 51 | 3 | 17.00 | 1 |
| Wainwright, D J | 48 | 21 | 13 | 150 | 26 | 18.75 | 0 | 0 | 1427 | 38 | 37.55 | 16 |
| **Waite, M E** | 2 | 2 | 1 | 23 | 12 | 23.00 | 0 | 0 | 69 | 0 | — | 0 |
| Wardlaw, I | 17 | 10 | 4 | 56 | 18 | 9.33 | 0 | 0 | 686 | 24 | 28.58 | 3 |
| Waring, J | 1 | 1 | 1 | 1 | 1* | — | 0 | 0 | 11 | 0 | — | 0 |
| Warren, A C | 1 | 1 | 0 | 3 | 3 | 3.00 | 0 | 0 | 35 | 1 | 35.00 | 0 |
| Wharf, A G | 6 | 1 | 1 | 2 | 2* | — | 0 | 0 | 176 | 8 | 22.00 | 1 |
| White, C | 292 | 266 | 39 | 6384 | 148 | 28.12 | 5 | 28 | 6120 | 248 | 24.67 | 84 |
| Whiteley, J P | 6 | 4 | 0 | 19 | 14 | 4.75 | 0 | 0 | 195 | 2 | 97.50 | 1 |
| Widdup, S | 4 | 4 | 0 | 49 | 38 | 12.25 | 0 | 0 | 0 | 0 | — | 2 |
| Wigley, D H | 1 | 1 | 0 | 0 | 0 | 0.00 | 0 | 0 | 38 | 0 | — | 0 |
| Williamson, K A | 109 | 9 | 0 | 229 | 70 | 25.44 | 0 | 1 | 42 | 1 | 42.00 | 4 |
| Wilson, D | 61 | 47 | 8 | 430 | 46 | 11.02 | 0 | 0 | 1527 | 76 | 20.09 | 22 |
| Wood, G L | 1 | 1 | 0 | 26 | 26 | 26.00 | 0 | 0 | 0 | 0 | — | 0 |
| Wood, M J | 145 | 134 | 14 | 3270 | 160 | 27.25 | 5 | 14 | 76 | 3 | 25.33 | 57 |
| Woodford, J D | 72 | 57 | 14 | 890 | 69* | 20.69 | 0 | 2 | 1627 | 77 | 21.12 | 25 |
| Younus Khan | 11 | 8 | 0 | 248 | 100 | 31.00 | 1 | 0 | 144 | 2 | 72.00 | 5 |
| Yuvraj Singh | 9 | 9 | 0 | 196 | 50 | 21.77 | 0 | 1 | 197 | 3 | 65.66 | 1 |

**For England**  YORKSHIRE T20i CRICKETERS 2003-2015/6 (Correct to December 1, 2015)

| Player | M | I | NO | Runs | HS | Av'ge | 100s | 50s | Balls | Runs | W | Av'ge | Best | 4wI | Ct/St |
|---|---|---|---|---|---|---|---|---|---|---|---|---|---|---|---|
| BAIRSTOW, J M ..2011-15 | 19 | 15 | 4 | 195 | 60* | 17.72 | 0 | 1 | 663 | 887 | 24 | 36.95 | 3-10 | 0 | 23 |
| BRESNAN, T T ..2006-13/14 | 34 | 22 | 9 | 216 | 47* | 16.61 | 0 | 0 | 72 | 91 | 7 | 13.00 | 3-21 | 0 | 10 |
| PLUNKETT, L E .2006-15/16 | 3 | 1 | 0 | 1 | 1 | 1.00 | 0 | 0 | 174 | 232 | 7 | 33.14 | 2-18 | 0 | 2 |
| RASHID, A U ..2009-15/16 | 10 | 4 | 3 | 20 | 9* | 20.00 | 0 | 0 | 54 | 96 | 4 | 24.00 | 1-13 | 0 | 2 |
| ROOT, J E ..2012-15/16 | 12 | 10 | 2 | 303 | 90* | 37.87 | 0 | 2 | 66 | 97 | 3 | 32.33 | 2-38 | 0 | 5 |
| SHAHZAD, A .....2010-11 | 3 | 1 | 1 | 0 | 0* | — | 0 | 0 | — | — | — | — | — | — | 1 |
| VAUGHAN, M P" ...2005-7 | 2 | 2 | 0 | 27 | 27 | 13.50 | 0 | 0 | — | — | — | — | — | — | 0 |
| **For Scotland** | | | | | | | | | | | | | | | |
| BLAIN, J A R .....2007-8 | 6 | 3 | 1 | 4 | 3* | 2.00 | 0 | 0 | 120 | 108 | 6 | 18.00 | 2-23 | 0 | 1 |
| HAMILTON, G M ..2007-10 | 12 | 8 | 0 | 90 | 32 | 11.25 | 0 | 0 | — | — | — | — | — | 0 | 3 |
| WARDLAW, I .2012/13-13/14 | 4 | 1 | 0 | 1 | 1 | 1.00 | 0 | 0 | 96 | 145 | 9 | 16.11 | 4-40 | 0 | 0 |

**YORKSHIRE PLAYERS WHO PLAYED ALL THEIR T20i CRICKET AFTER LEAVING YORKSHIRE**

**For England**

| Player | M | I | NO | Runs | HS | Av'ge | 100s | 50s | Balls | Runs | W | Av'ge | Best | 4wI | Ct/St |
|---|---|---|---|---|---|---|---|---|---|---|---|---|---|---|---|
| BATTY, G J ...........2009 | 1 | 1 | 0 | 4 | 4 | 4.00 | 0 | 0 | 18 | 17 | 0 | — | — | 0 | 0 |
| GOUGH, D .......2005-06 | 2 | 0 | 1 | 0 | — | — | — | 3 | 41 | 49 | 3 | 16.33 | 3-16 | 0 | 0 |
| LUMB, M J ...2010-13/14 | 27 | 27 | 1 | 552 | 63 | 21.23 | 0 | 0 | — | — | — | — | — | — | 8 |
| SIDEBOTTOM, R J .2007-10 | 18 | 1 | 1 | 5 | 5* | — | 0 | 0 | 367 | 437 | 23 | 19.00 | 3-16 | 0 | 5 |

**Overseas Players**
(Qualification: 20 t20 matches for Yorkshire)

**For South Africa**

| Player | M | I | NO | Runs | HS | Av'ge | 100s | 50s | Balls | Runs | W | Av'ge | Best | 4wI | Ct/St |
|---|---|---|---|---|---|---|---|---|---|---|---|---|---|---|---|
| RUDOLPH, J A.......2006 | 1 | 1 | 1 | 6 | 6* | — | 0 | 0 | — | — | — | — | — | 0 | 0 |

# T20 RECORDS SECTION
## TROPHY WINNERS 2003-2015

|      |                |                    |      |               |                    |
|------|----------------|--------------------|------|---------------|--------------------|
|      |                | *Yorkshire's Position* |      |               | *Yorkshire's Position* |
| 2003 | Surrey ............. | Group N 2 (6) | 2010 | Hampshire ......... | Group N 6 (9) |
| 2004 | Leicestershire ..... | Group N 5 (6) | 2011 | Leicestershire ..... | Group N 6 (9) |
| 2005 | Somerset ......... | Group N 4 (6) | 2012 | Hampshire ......... | Final |
| 2006 | Leicestershire ..... | Quarter-Final | 2013 | Hampshire ......... | Group N 6 (6) |
| 2007 | Kent ............. | Quarter-Final | 2014 | Warwickshire ..... | Group N 5 (9) |
| 2008 | Middlesex ........ | Group N 3 (6) | 2015 | Lancashire ........ | Group N 8 (9) |
| 2009 | Sussex ........... | Group N 5 (6) |      |               |                    |

## SEASON-BY-SEASON RECORD OF ALL T20 MATCHES
## PLAYED BY YORKSHIRE 2003-2015

| Season | Played | Won | Lost | Tie | N R | Abd | Season | Played | Won | Lost | Tie | N R | Abd |
|--------|--------|-----|------|-----|-----|-----|--------|--------|-----|------|-----|-----|-----|
| 2003 | 5 | 3 | 2 | 0 | 0 | 0 | 2011 | 15 | 6 | 7 | 0 | 2 | 1 |
| 2004 | 5 | 2 | 3 | 0 | 0 | 0 | 2012 | 12 | 9 | 2 | 0 | 1 | 1 |
| 2005 | 8 | 3 | 5 | 0 | 0 | 0 | 2012/13 | 6 | 2 | 3 | 0 | 1 | 0 |
| 2006 | 9 | 4 | 4 | 0 | 1 | 0 | 2013 | 10 | 2 | 7 | 1 | 0 | 0 |
| 2007 | 8 | 4 | 4 | 0 | 0 | 1 | 2014 | 11 | 6 | 5 | 0 | 0 | 3 |
| 2008 | 9 | 5 | 3 | 1 | 0 | 1 | 2015 | 14 | 5 | 8 | 1 | 0 | 0 |
| 2009 | 10 | 4 | 6 | 0 | 0 | 0 |        |        |     |      |     |     |     |
| 2010 | 16 | 6 | 9 | 1 | 0 | 0 |        | 138 | 61 | 68 | 4 | 5 | 7 |

*Abandoned matches are not included in the list of matches played.*

## ANALYSIS OF T20 RESULTS V. ALL TEAMS 2003-2015
## DOMESTIC MATCHES

| | HOME | | | | | AWAY | | | | |
|--|--|--|--|--|--|--|--|--|--|--|
| *Opponents* | Played | Won | Lost | Tied | N. R | Won | Lost | Tied | N. R | Abd |
| Derbyshire | 21 | 7 | 5 | 0 | 0 | 7 | 1 | 0 | 1 | 0 |
| Durham | 24 | 7 | 4 | 1 | 0 | 5 | 6 | 0 | 1 | 0 |
| Essex | 1 | 0 | 0 | 0 | 0 | 0 | 1 | 0 | 0 | 0 |
| Hampshire | 1 | 0 | 0 | 0 | 0 | 0 | 1 | 0 | 0 | 0 |
| Lancashire | 21 | 6 | 3 | 1 | 0 | 4 | 7 | 0 | 0 | 3 |
| Leicestershire | 18 | 4 | 4 | 0 | 0 | 3 | 6 | 1 | 0 | 1 |
| Northamptonshire | 7 | 0 | 3 | 0 | 0 | 2 | 1 | 1 | 0 | 1 |
| Nottinghamshire | 24 | 5 | 6 | 0 | 1 | 4 | 8 | 0 | 0 | 0 |
| Sussex | 2 | 0 | 0 | 0 | 0 | 1 | 1 | 0 | 0 | 0 |
| Warwickshire | 7 | 1 | 3 | 0 | 0 | 0 | 2 | 0 | 1 | 1 |
| Worcestershire | 6 | 3 | 1 | 0 | 0 | 0 | 2 | 0 | 0 | 1 |
| **Total** | **132** | **33** | **29** | **2** | **1** | **26** | **36** | **2** | **3** | **7** |

### OTHER MATCHES

| | | | | | | | | | | |
|--|--|--|--|--|--|--|--|--|--|--|
| Uva | 1 | 0 | 0 | 0 | 0 | 1 | 0 | 0 | 0 | 0 |
| Trinidad and Tobago | 1 | 0 | 0 | 0 | 0 | 1 | 0 | 0 | 0 | 0 |
| Sydney Sixers | 1 | 0 | 0 | 0 | 0 | 0 | 1 | 0 | 0 | 0 |
| Mumbai | 1 | 0 | 0 | 0 | 0 | 0 | 0 | 0 | 1 | 0 |
| Highveld | 1 | 0 | 0 | 0 | 0 | 0 | 1 | 0 | 0 | 0 |
| Chennai | 1 | 0 | 0 | 0 | 0 | 0 | 1 | 0 | 0 | 0 |
| **Total** | **6** | **0** | **0** | **0** | **0** | **2** | **3** | **0** | **1** | **0** |
| **Grand Total** | **138** | **33** | **29** | **2** | **1** | **28** | **39** | **2** | **4** | **7** |

# ABANDONED T20 MATCHES (7)

| 2007 | v. Lancashire at Leeds | 2014 | v. Warwickshire at Birmingham |
|------|------------------------|------|-------------------------------|
| 2008 | v. Leicestershire at Leeds | | v. Lancashire at Leeds |
| 2011 | v. Northamptonshire at Leeds | | v. Worcestershire at Worcester |
| 2012 | v. Lancashire at Manchester | | |

## T20 HIGHEST TEAM TOTALS

### BY YORKSHIRE

| 213:7 | v. | Worcestershire at Leeds | 2010 |
|-------|-----|-------------------------|------|
| 212:5 | v. | Worcestershire at Leeds | 2012 |
| 211:6 | v. | Leicestershire at Leeds | 2004 |
| 210:3 | v. | Derbyshire at Derby | 2006 |
| 209:4 | v. | Nottinghamshire at Leeds | 2015 |
| 207:7 | v. | Nottinghamshire at Nottingham | 2004 |
| 202:8 | v. | Lancashire at Manchester | 2015 |
| 200:5 | v. | Nottinghamshire at Leeds | 2014 |
| 198:4 | v. | Durham at Leeds | 2003 |
| 198:4 | v. | Derbyshire at Leeds | 2005 |
| 196:5 | v. | Nottinghamshire at Leeds | 2003 |
| 194:5 | v. | Durham at Leeds | 2015 |
| 187:7 | v. | Worcestershire at Worcester | 2010 |
| 186:5 | v. | Derbyshire at Leeds | 2003 |
| 186:8 | v. | Durham at Chester-le-Street | 2014 |

### AGAINST YORKSHIRE

| 231:6 | for Lancashire at Manchester | 2015 |
|-------|------------------------------|------|
| 222:6 | for Derbyshire at Leeds | 2010 |
| 221:3 | for Leicestershire at Leeds | 2004 |
| 215:6 | for Nottinghamshire at Nottingham | 2011 |
| 215:6 | for Durham at Chester-le-Street | 2013 |
| 210:7 | for Nottinghamshire at Nottingham | 2004 |
| 208:7 | for Worcestershire at Worcester | 2010 |
| 207:6 | for Lancashire at Manchester | 2005 |
| 201:5 | for Nottinghamshire at Leeds | 2014 |
| 195:4 | for Nottinghamshire at Nottingham | 2006 |
| 195:8 | for Derbyshire at Leeds | 2005 |
| 193:5 | for Sussex at Hove | 2007 |
| 191:4 | for Leicestershire at Leeds | 2011 |
| 191:6 | for Durham at Leeds | 2015 |
| 191:6 | for Worcestershire at Leeds | 2015 |

# T20 HIGHEST INDIVIDUAL SCORES

## *BY YORKSHIRE*

| | | | | |
|---|---|---|---|---|
| 109 | I J Harvey | v. | Derbyshire at Leeds | 2005 |
| 108* | I J Harvey | v. | Lancashire at Leeds | 2004 |
| 102* | J M Bairstow | v. | Durham at Chester-le-Street | 2014 |
| 101* | H H Gibbs | v | Northamptonshire at Northampton | 2010 |
| 96* | M J Wood | v. | Nottinghamshire at Nottingham | 2004 |
| 92* | G J Maxwell | v. | Nottinghamshire at Leeds | 2015 |
| 92 | P A Jaques | v. | Leicestershire at Leeds | 2004 |
| 92 | J M Bairstow | v. | Durham at Leeds | 2015 |
| 91 | A W Gale | v. | Nottinghamshire at Leeds | 2009 |
| 89 | A J Finch | v. | Nottinghamshire at Leeds | 2014 |
| 88 | A J Finch | v. | Lancashire at Manchester | 2014 |
| 84* | M J Lumb | v. | Lancashire at Leeds | 2006 |
| 79* | A W Gale | v. | Derbyshire at Chesterfield | 2009 |

## *AGAINST YORKSHIRE*

| | | | | |
|---|---|---|---|---|
| 111 | D L Maddy | for | Leicestershire at Leeds | 2004 |
| 101 | S G Law | for | Lancashire at Manchester | 2005 |
| 100* | G M Smith | for | Derbyshire at Leeds | 2008 |
| 97 | B J Hodge | for | Leicestershire at Leicester | 2003 |
| 96* | A M McDonald | for | Leicestershire at Leeds | 2011 |
| 94 | L E Bosman | for | Derbyshire at Leeds | 2010 |
| 91* | G Clark | for | Durham at Leeds | 2015 |
| 91* | R A Whiteley | for | Worcestershire at Leeds | 2015 |
| 91 | M A Ealham | for | Nottinghamshire at Nottingham | 2004 |
| 91 | P Mustard | for | Durham at Chester-le-Street | 2013 |
| 90* | S R Patel | for | Nottinghamshire at Leeds | 2015 |
| 85 | A Flintoff | for | Lancashire at Leeds | 2004 |
| 83 | J Moss | for | Derbyshire at Leeds | 2005 |
| 82* | A C Voges | for | Nottinghamshire at Leeds | 2009 |

# T20 BEST BOWLING

## BY YORKSHIRE

| | | | | |
|---|---|---|---|---|
| 5-16 | R M Pyrah | v. | Durham at Scarborough | 2011 |
| 5-21 | J A Brooks | v. | Leicestershire at Leeds | 2013 |
| 5-22 | M D Fisher | v. | Derbyshire at Leeds | 2015 |
| 4-18 | M A Ashraf | v. | Derbyshire at Derby | 2012 |
| 4-20 | R M Pyrah | v. | Durham at Leeds | 2008 |
| 4-20 | A U Rashid | v. | Leicestershire at Leeds | 2010 |
| 4-21 | R M Pyrah | v. | Worcestershire at Leeds | 2011 |
| 4-21 | B W Sanderson | v. | Derbyshire at Derby | 2011 |
| 4-21 | J A Brooks | v. | Derbyshire at Leeds | 2013 |
| 4-23 | Rana Naved | v. | Nottinghamshire at Leeds | 2009 |
| 4-24 | A U Rashid | v. | Nottinghamshire at Nottingham | 2008 |
| 4-25 | R J Sidebottom | v. | Durham at Chester-le-Street | 2012 |
| 4-26 | A U Rashid | v. | Lancashire at Leeds | 2011 |
| 4-30 | S A Patterson | v. | Lancashire at Leeds | 2010 |
| 4-33 | C J McKay | v. | Derbyshire at Leeds | 2010 |

## AGAINST YORKSHIRE

| | | | | |
|---|---|---|---|---|
| 4-9 | C K Langeveldt | for | Derbyshire at Leeds | 2008 |
| 4-19 | K H D Barker | for | Warwickshire at Birmingham | 2010 |
| 4-19 | J S Patel | for | Warwickshire at Leeds | 2014 |
| 4-21 | J Needham | for | Derbyshire at Leeds | 2009 |
| 4-23 | A J Hall | for | Northamptonshire at Northampton | 2011 |
| 4-25 | J A Morkel | for | Derbyshire at Chesterfield | 2013 |
| 4-25 | I G Butler | for | Northamptonshire at Leeds | 2014 |
| 4-31 | Shakib al Hasan | for | Worcestershire at Worcester | 2011 |
| 4-37 | K K Jennings | for | Durham at Chester-le-Street | 2015 |
| 4-38 | S J Harmison | for | Durham at Leeds | 2008 |
| 3-3 | J K H Naik | for | Leicestershire at Leeds | 2011 |
| 3-6 | B J Hodge | for | Leicestershire at Leicester | 2003 |
| 3-6 | J N Snape | for | Leicestershire at Leicester | 2007 |
| 3-9 | J J Cobb | for | Leicestershire at Leicester | 2013 |
| 3-10 | D M Benkenstein | for | Durham at Leeds | 2005 |
| 3-10 | D G Cork | for | Lancashire at Manchester | 2005 |
| 3-10 | D L Maddy | for | Warwickshire at Leeds | 2011 |

# T20 ECONOMICAL BOWLING

## BY YORKSHIRE

| | | | | |
|---|---|---|---|---|
| 4-0-12-2 | T T Bresnan | v. | Lancashire at Manchester | 2008 |

## AGAINST YORKSHIRE

| | | | | |
|---|---|---|---|---|
| 4-0-9-4 | C K Langeveldt | for | Derbyshire at Leeds | 2008 |

# T20 MOST EXPENSIVE BOWLING

## BY YORKSHIRE

| | | | | |
|---|---|---|---|---|
| 4-0-65-2 | M J Hoggard | v. | Lancashire at Leeds | 2005 |

## AGAINST YORKSHIRE

| | | | | |
|---|---|---|---|---|
| 4-0-58-0 | G Welsh | for | Derbyshire at Leeds | 2003 |

# T20 HIGHEST AND LOWEST SCORES BY AND AGAINST YORKSHIRE
## PLUS INDIVIDUAL BEST BATTING AND BOWLING

*The lowest score is the lowest all-out score or the lowest score at completion of the allotted overs, five-over matches not included.*

**Yorkshire versus:**

### Derbyshire

| | | By Yorkshire | | Against Yorkshire | |
|---|---|---|---|---|---|
| Highest Score: | In Yorkshire | 198:4 | at Leeds 2005 | 222:5 | at Leeds 2010 |
| | Away | 210:3 | at Derby 2006 | 158:6 | at Chesterfield 2008 |
| Lowest Score: | In Yorkshire | 119:8 | at Leeds 2013 | 124 | at Chesterfield 2014 |
| | Away | 109 | at Derby 2012 | 119:7 | at Leeds 2007 |
| Best Batting: | In Yorkshire | 109 | I J Harvey | at Leeds 2005 | 100* G M Smith at Leeds 2008 |
| | Away | 79* | A W Gale | at Chesterfield 2009 | 68 G M Smith at Chesterfield 2008 |
| Best Bowling: | In Yorkshire | 5-22 | M D Fisher | at Leeds 2015 | 4-9 C K Langeveldt at Leeds 2008 |
| | Away | 4-18 | M A Ashraf | at Derby 2012 | 4-25 J A Morkel at Chesterfield 2013 |

### Durham

| | | By Yorkshire | | Against Yorkshire | |
|---|---|---|---|---|---|
| Highest Score: | In Yorkshire | 198:4 | at Leeds 2003 | 191:6 | at Leeds 2015 |
| | Away | 186:8 | at Chester-le-Street 2014 | 215:6 | at Chester-le-Street 2013 |
| Lowest Score: | In Yorkshire | 95 | at Leeds 2014 | 116:8 | at Leeds 2009 |
| | Away | 90:9 | at Chester-le-Street 2009 | 98 | at Chester-le-Street 2006 |
| Best Batting: | In Yorkshire | 92 | J M Bairstow | at Leeds 2015 | 91* G Clark at Leeds 2015 |
| | Away | 102* | J M Bairstow | at Chester-le-Street 2014 | 91 P Mustard at Chester-le-Street 2013 |
| Best Bowling: | In Yorkshire | 5-16 | R M Pyrah | at Scarborough 2011 | 4-38 S J Harmison at Leeds 2008 |
| | Away | 4-25 | R J Sidebottom | at Chester-le-Street 2012 | 4-37 K K Jennings at Chester-le-Street 2015 |

### Essex

| | | By Yorkshire | | Against Yorkshire | |
|---|---|---|---|---|---|
| Highest Score: | Away | 143:7 | at Chelmsford 2006 | 149:5 | at Chelmsford 2006 |
| Best Batting: | Away | 43 | G L Brophy | at Chelmsford 2006 | 48* J S Foster at Chelmsford 2006 |
| Best Bowling: | Away | 2-22 | A Shahzad | at Chelmsford 2006 | 2-11 T J Phillips at Chelmsford 2006 |

### Hampshire

| | | By Yorkshire | | Against Yorkshire | |
|---|---|---|---|---|---|
| Highest Score: | Away | 140:6 | at Cardiff 2012 | 150:6 | at Cardiff 2012 |
| Best Batting: | Away | 72* | D A Miller | at Cardiff 2012 | 43 J H K Adams at Cardiff 2012 |
| Best Bowling: | Away | 2-20 | R J Sidebottom | at Cardiff 2012 | 3-26 C P Wood at Cardiff 201241 |

# T20 HIGHEST AND LOWEST SCORES BY AND AGAINST YORKSHIRE PLUS INDIVIDUAL BEST BATTING AND BOWLING (Continued)

*The lowest score is the lowest all-out score or the lowest score at completion of the allotted overs, five-over matches not included.*

## Yorkshire versus:

| | | By Yorkshire | | Against Yorkshire | |
|---|---|---|---|---|---|
| **Lancashire** | | | | | |
| Highest Score: | In Yorkshire | 185:8 | at Leeds 2015 | 186:6 | at Leeds 2015 |
| | Away | 202:8 | at Manchester 2015 | 231:4 | at Manchester 2015 |
| Lowest Score: | In Yorkshire | 111:8 | at Leeds 2009 | 131:9 | at Leeds 2004 |
| | Away | 97 | at Manchester 2005 | 104:3 | at Manchester 2003 |
| Best Batting: | In Yorkshire | 108* | I J Harvey at Leeds 2004 | 85 | A Flintoff at Leeds 2004 |
| | Away | 88 | A J Finch at Manchester 2014 | 101 | S G Law at Manchester 2005 |
| Best Bowling: | In Yorkshire | 4-26 | A U Rashid at Leeds 2011 | 3-27 | J P Faulkner at Leeds 2015 |
| | Away | 3-15 | Azeem Rafiq at Manchester 2011 | 3-10 | D G Cork at Manchester 2005 |
| **Leicestershire** | | | | | |
| Highest Score: | In Yorkshire | 211:6 | at Leeds 2004 | 221:3 | at Leeds 2004 |
| | Away | 177:5 | at Leicester 2005 | 175:4 | at Leicester 2010 |
| Lowest Score: | In Yorkshire | 134 | at Leeds 2006 | 113:9 | at Leeds 2013 |
| | Away | 105 | at Leicester 2013 | 147:9 | at Leicester 2012 |
| Best Batting: | In Yorkshire | 92 | P A Jaques at Leeds 2004 | 111 | D L Maddy at Leeds 2004 |
| | Away | 77 | I J Harvey at Leicester 2005 | 97 | B J Hodge at Leicester 2003 |
| Best Bowling: | In Yorkshire | 5-21 | J A Brooks at Leeds 2013 | 3-3 | J K H Naik at Leeds 2011 |
| | Away | 2-19 | R M Pyrah at Leicester 2010 | 3-6 | B J Hodge at Leicester 2003 |
| | Away | 2-19 | M A Starc at Leicester 2012 | | |
| **Northamptonshire** | | | | | |
| Highest Score: | In Yorkshire | 162:7 | at Leeds 2014 | 165:7 | at Leeds 2014 |
| | Away | 181:3 | at Northampton 2014 | 180:5 | at Northampton 2010 |
| Lowest Score: | In Yorkshire | | | 151:7 | at Leeds 2010 |
| | Away | 144 | at Northampton 2011 | 132:7 | at Northampton 2011 |
| Best Batting: | In Yorkshire | 36 | L E Plunkett at Leeds 2014 | 43 | D J Willey at Leeds 2014 |
| | Away | 101* | H H Gibbs at Northampton 2010 | 76 | R E Levi at Northampton 2014 |
| Best Bowling: | In Yorkshire | 3-23 | A U Rashid at Leeds 2010 | 4-25 | I G Butler at Leeds |
| | Away | 2-18 | R J Sidebottom at Northampton 2011 | 4-23 | A J Hall at Northampton 2011 |

# T20 HIGHEST AND LOWEST SCORES BY AND AGAINST YORKSHIRE PLUS INDIVIDUAL BEST BATTING AND BOWLING (Continued)

*The lowest score is the lowest all-out score or the lowest score at completion of the allotted overs, five-over matches not included.*

**Yorkshire versus:**

| | | By Yorkshire | | Against Yorkshire | |
|---|---|---|---|---|---|
| **Nottinghamshire** | | | | | |
| Highest Score: | In Yorkshire | 209:4 | at Leeds 2015 | 201:4 | at Leeds 2014 |
| | Away | 207:7 | at Nottingham 2004 | 215:6 | at Nottingham 2011 |
| Lowest Score: | In Yorkshire | 141:8 | at Leeds 2008 | 155:6 | at Leeds 2009 |
| | Away | 112:7 | at Nottingham 2010 | 136:6 | at Nottingham 2008 |
| Best Batting: | In Yorkshire | 92* G J Maxwell | at Leeds 2015 | 90* S R Patel | at Leeds 2015 |
| | Away | 96* M J Wood | at Nottingham 2004 | 91 M A Ealham | at Nottingham 2004 |
| Best Bowling: | In Yorkshire | 4-23 Rana Naved-ul-Hasan | at Leeds 2009 | 3-38 J T Ball | at Leeds 2014 |
| | Away | 4-24 A U Rashid | at Nottingham 2008 | 3-17 S R Patel | at Nottingham 2013 |
| **Sussex** | | | | | |
| Highest Score: | Away | 172:6 | at Cardiff 2012 | 193:5 | at Hove 2007 |
| Lowest Score: | Away | 155 | at Hove 2007 | 136:8 | at Cardiff 2012 |
| Best Batting: | Away | 68* J M Bairstow | at Cardiff 2012 | 80* C D Nash | at Cardiff 2012 |
| Best Bowling: | Away | 2-22 T T Bresnan | at Cardiff 2012 | 3-22 S B Styris | at Cardiff 2012 |
| **Warwickshire** | | | | | |
| Highest Score: | In Yorkshire | 161:8 | at Leeds 2011 | 164:5 | at Leeds 2011 |
| | Away | 132:7 | at Birmingham 2015 | 145:8 | at Birmingham 2010 |
| Lowest Score: | In Yorkshire | 121:9 | at Leeds 2010 | 145 | at Leeds 2015 |
| | Away | 131 | at Birmingham 2010 | | |
| Best Batting: | In Yorkshire | 63 A Z Lees | at Leeds 2015 | 64 W T S Porterfield | at Leeds 2011 |
| | Away | 45 J A Leaning | at Birmingham 2015 | 49* J O Troughton | at Birmingham 2010 |
| Best Bowling: | In Yorkshire | 3-22 R M Pyrah | at Leeds 2010 | 4-19 J S Patel | at Leeds 2014 |
| | Away | 3-25 S A Patterson | at Birmingham 2010 | 4-19 K H D Barker | at Birmingham 2010 |

**Yorkshire versus:**

| | | By Yorkshire | Against Yorkshire |
|---|---|---|---|
| **Worcestershire** | | | |
| Highest Score: | In Yorkshire | 213:7 at Leeds 2010 | 191:6 at Leeds 2015 |
| | Away | 187:7 at Worcester 2010 | 208:7 at Worcester 2010 |
| Lowest Score: | In Yorkshire | 117 at Leeds 2015 | 109 at Leeds 2010 |
| | Away | 142 at Worcester 2011 | 183:7 at Worcester 2011 |
| Best Batting: | In Yorkshire | 65 J E Root at Leeds 2012 | 91* R A Whiteley at Leeds 2015 |
| | Away | 39 A McGrath at Worcester 2010 | 56 A N Kervezee at Worcester 2011 |
| Best Bowling: | In Yorkshire | 4-21 R M Pyrah at Leeds 2011 | 3-29 B L d'Oliveira at Leeds 2015 |
| | Away | 3-30 A Shahzad at Worcester 2011 | 4-31 Shakib al Hasan at Worcester 2011 |
| **Chennai** | | | |
| Highest Score: | Away | 140:6 at Durban 2012 | 141:6 at Durban 2012 |
| Best Batting: | Away | 58 G S Ballance at Durban 2012 | 47 S Badrinath at Durban 2012 |
| Best Bowling: | Away | 3-23 I Wardlaw at Durban 2012 | 2-12 J A Morkel at Durban 2012 |
| **Highveld** | | | |
| Highest Score: | Away | 131:7 at Johannesburg 2012 | 134:5 at Johannesburg 2012 |
| Best Batting: | Away | 31 P A Jaques at Johannesburg 2012 | 32 Q de Kock at Johannesburg 2012 |
| Best Bowling: | Away | 2-21 S A Patterson at Johannesburg 2012 | 2-23 A M Phangiso at Johannesburg 2012 |
| **Mumbai** | | | |
| Highest Score: | Away | | 156:6 at Cape Town 2012 |
| Best Batting: | Away | | 37 D R Smith at Cape Town |
| Best Bowling: | Away | 2-36 Azeem Rafiq at Cape Town 2012 | |
| **Sydney Sixers** | | | |
| Highest Score: | Away | 96:9 at Cape Town 2012 | 98:2 at Cape Town 2012 |
| Best Batting: | Away | 25 J E Root | 43* M J Lumb at Cape Town 2012 |
| Best Bowling: | Away | 1-21 Azeem Rafiq | 3-22 M A Starc at Cape Town 2012 |
| **Trinidad and Tobago** | | | |
| Highest Score: | Away | 154:4 at Centurion 2012 | 148:9 at Centurion 2012 |
| Best Batting: | Away | 64* G S Ballance at Centurion 2012 | 59 D Ramdin at Centurion 2012 |
| Best Bowling: | Away | 3-13 R J Sidebottom at Centurion 2012 | 1-16 K Y G Ottley at Centurion 2012 |
| **Uva** | | | |
| Highest Score: | Away | 151:5 at Johannesburg 2012 | 150:7 at Johannesburg 2012 |
| Best Batting: | Away | 39* D A Miller at Johannesburg 2012 | 29 S H T Kandamby at Johannesburg 2012 |
| Best Bowling: | Away | 2-29 M A Ashraf at Johannesburg 2012 | 3-32 E M D Y Munaweera at Johannesburg 2012 |

# T20 MAN OF THE MATCH AWARDS (62)

| | | | | | |
|---|---|---|---|---|---|
| A W Gale | 8 | D A Miller | 3 | H H Gibbs | 2 |
| A McGrath | 6 | Azeem Rafiq | 2 | P A Jaques | 2 |
| R M Pyrah | 5 | J M Bairstow | 3 | J A Leaning | 2 |
| I J Harvey | 3 | T T Bresnan | 2 | A Z Lees | 2 |
| A Lyth | 3 | A J Finch | 2 | M J Lumb | 2 |

One each: G S Ballance, J A Brooks, M E Claydon, M D Fisher, S P Fleming, D S Lehmann, G J Maxwell, A U Rashid, J E Root, J A Rudolph, B W Sanderson, J J Sayers, A Shahzad, D J Wainwright and C White

# T20 PARTNERSHIPS OF 100 AND OVER 2003-2015 (14)

| | | | | | | |
|---|---|---|---|---|---|---|
| 137* | 2nd wkt | A W Gale | (60*) | and H H Gibbs (76*) | v. Durham at Leeds | 2010 |
| 131 | 1st wkt | A Lyth | (78) | and P A Jaques (64) | v. Derbyshire at Leeds | 2012 |
| 129 | 2nd wkt | A W Gale | (91) | and M P Vaughan (41*) | v. Nottinghamshire at Leeds | 2009 |
| 124 | 2nd wkt | I J Harvey | (109) | and P A Jaques (37) | v. Derbyshire at Leeds | 2005 |
| 121 | 3rd wkt | J A Rudolph | (56) | and A McGrath (59) | v. Leicestershire at Leicester | 2008 |
| 116 | 1st wkt | A W Gale | (70) | and P A Jaques (48) | v. Leicestershire at Leeds | 2012 |
| 108 | 2nd wkt | I J Harvey | (108*) | and P A Jaques (48) | v. Lancashire at Leeds | 2004 |
| 108 | 2nd wkt | A Lyth | (59) | and H H Gibbs (40) | v. Worcestershire at Leeds | 2010 |
| 104 | 1st wkt | A W Gale | (43) | and J A Rudolph (61) | v. Leicestershire at Leicester | 2009 |
| 104 | 2nd wkt | A Z Lees | (63) | and J A Leaning (60*) | v. Warwickshire at Leeds | 2015 |
| 103* | 5th wkt | G S Ballance | (64*) | and A U Rashid (33*) | v. Trinidad & Tobago at Centurion | 2012/13 |
| 103 | 1st wkt | A W Gale | (65*) | and J A Rudolp (53) | v. Leicestershire at Leicester | 2010 |
| 101 | 2nd wkt | M J Wood | (57) | and M J Lumb (55) | v. Nottinghamshire at Leeds | 2003 |
| 101 | 3rd wkt | A J Hodd | (70) | and G J Maxwell (92*) | v. Nottinghamshire at Leeds | 2015 |

# T20 HIGHEST PARTNERSHIPS FOR EACH WICKET

| | | | | | | |
|---|---|---|---|---|---|---|
| 1st wkt | 131 | A Lyth | (78) | and P A Jaques (64) | v. Derbyshire at Leeds | 2012 |
| 2nd wkt | 137* | A W Gale | (60*) | and H H Gibbs (76*) | v. Durham at Leeds | 2010 |
| 3rd wkt | 121 | J A Rudolph | (56) | and A McGrath (59) | v. Leicestershire at Leicester | 2008 |
| 4th wkt | 93 | P A Jaques | (92) | and T T Bresnan (42) | v. Leicestershire at Leeds | 2004 |
| 5th wkt | 103* | G S Ballance | (64*) | and A U Rashid (33*) | v. Trinidad & Tobago at Centurion | 2012/13 |
| 6th wkt | 65 | A McGrath | (39) | and A U Rashid (34) | v. Worcestershire at Worcester | 2010 |
| 7th wkt | 68* | T T Bresnan | (45*) | and A U Rashid (29*) | v. Warwickshire at Leeds | 2014 |
| 8th wkt | 54 | T T Bresnan | (51) | and J D Middlebrook (29*) | v. Lancashire at Manchester | 2015 |
| 9th wkt | 33* | A U Rashid | (5*) | and D Gough (20*) | v. Lancashire at Leeds | 2008 |
| 10th wkt | 28* | A U Rashid | (28*) | and G J Kruis (12*) | v. Durham at Chester-le-Street | 2009 |

421

# ALL WHO HAVE TAKEN 4 WICKETS IN AN INNINGS (15)

### R M PYRAH (3)

| 5-16 | v. Durham | at Scarborough | 2011 |
|------|-----------|----------------|------|
| 4-20 | v. Durham | at Leeds | 2006 |
| 4-21 | v. Worcestershire | at Leeds | 2011 |

### A U RASHID (3)

| 4-20 | v. Leicestershire | at Leeds | 2011 |
|------|-------------------|----------|------|
| 4-24 | v. Nottingham | at Nottingham | 2008 |
| 4-26 | v. Lancashire | at Leeds | 2011 |

### J A BROOKS (2)

| 5-21 | v. Leicestershire | at Leeds | 2013 |
|------|-------------------|----------|------|
| 4-21 | v. Derbyshire | at Leeds | 2013 |

### M D FISHER (1)

| 5-22 | v. Derbyshire | at Leeds | 2015 |
|------|---------------|----------|------|

### M A ASHRAF (1)

| 4-18 | v. Derbyshire | at Derby | 2012 |
|------|---------------|----------|------|

### B W SANDERSON (1)

| 4-21 | v. Derbyshire | at Derby | 2011 |
|------|---------------|----------|------|

### RANA NAVED-UL-HASAN (1)

| 4-23 | v. Nottinghamshire | at Leeds | 2009 |
|------|--------------------|----------|------|

### R J SIDEBOTTOM (1)

| 4-25 | v. Durham | at Chester-le-Street | 2012 |
|------|-----------|----------------------|------|

### S A PATTERSON (1)

| 4-30 | v. Lancashire | at Leeds | 2010 |
|------|---------------|----------|------|

### C J MCKAY (1)

| 4-33 | v. Derbyshire | at Leeds | 2010 |
|------|---------------|----------|------|

# CAREER AVERAGES FOR YORKSHIRE

## ALL t20 MATCHES 2003-2015

| Player | M | Inns | NO | Runs | HS | Av'ge | 100s | 50s | Runs | Wkts | Av'ge | Ct/St |
|---|---|---|---|---|---|---|---|---|---|---|---|---|
| Ashraf, M A … | 17 | 1 | 0 | 4 | 4 | 4.00 | 0 | 0 | 462 | 17 | 27.17 | 1 |
| Azeem Rafiq … | 60 | 27 | 17 | 131 | 21* | 13.10 | 0 | 0 | 1,510 | 62 | 24.35 | 27 |
| **Bairstow, J M** . | 60 | 55 | 10 | 1207 | 102* | 26.82 | 1 | 4 | **0** | **0** | — | 23/7 |
| **Ballance, G S** .. | 48 | 43 | 7 | 968 | 68 | 26.88 | 0 | 3 | **0** | **0** | — | 29 |
| Best, T L …… | 8 | 3 | 2 | 10 | 10* | 10.00 | 0 | 0 | 243 | 7 | 34.71 | 4 |
| Blakey, R J …. | 7 | 5 | 1 | 119 | 32 | 29.75 | 0 | 0 | 0 | 0 | — | 5/1 |
| **Bresnan, T T** .. | 71 | 52 | 20 | 742 | 51 | 23.18 | 0 | 1 | 1753 | 65 | 26.96 | 25 |
| **Brooks, J A** … | 13 | 0 | 0 | **0** | | | **0** | **0** | 314 | 13 | 24.15 | 4 |
| Brophy, G L … | 54 | 46 | 9 | 717 | 57* | 19.37 | 0 | 2 | 0 | 0 | — | 25/7 |
| **Carver, K** …… | 3 | 1 | 0 | 2 | 2 | 2.00 | 0 | 0 | 30 | 0 | — | 1 |
| Claydon, M E .. | 7 | 2 | 2 | 14 | 12* | — | 0 | 0 | 188 | 5 | 37.60 | 2 |
| **Coad, B O** …. | 2 | 1 | 1 | 2 | 2* | — | 0 | 0 | 54 | 4 | 13.50 | 0 |
| Craven, V J …. | 6 | 6 | 4 | 76 | 44* | 38.00 | 0 | 0 | 67 | 0 | — | 3 |
| Dawood, I …… | 11 | 8 | 3 | 44 | 15 | 8.80 | 0 | 0 | 0 | 0 | — | 5/2 |
| Dawson, R K J . | 22 | 8 | 3 | 71 | 22 | 14.20 | 0 | 0 | 558 | 24 | 23.25 | 7 |
| **Finch, A J** ….. | 16 | 16 | 0 | 332 | 89 | 20.75 | 0 | 2 | 24 | 1 | 24.00 | 16 |
| **Fisher, M D** … | 13 | 1 | 1 | 0 | 0* | — | **0** | **0** | 362 | 16 | 22.62 | 5 |
| Fleming, S P .. | 4 | 4 | 0 | 62 | 58 | 15.50 | 0 | 1 | 0 | 0 | — | 1 |
| **Gale, A W** ….. | 104 | 97 | 8 | 2260 | 91 | 25.39 | 0 | 16 | **0** | **0** | — | 30 |
| Gibbs, H H …. | 15 | 15 | 3 | 443 | 101* | 36.91 | 1 | 2 | 0 | 0 | — | 8 |
| **Gibson, R** …… | 3 | 2 | 0 | 32 | 18 | 16.00 | 0 | 0 | 30 | 0 | — | 1 |
| Gilbert, C R …. | 13 | 9 | 2 | 107 | 38* | 15.28 | 0 | 0 | 0 | 0 | — | 7 |
| Gillespie, J N .. | 17 | 4 | 2 | 14 | 8* | 7.00 | 0 | 0 | 422 | 17 | 24.82 | 5 |
| Gough, D …… | 17 | 7 | 3 | 42 | 20* | 10.50 | 0 | 0 | 416 | 16 | 26.00 | 2 |
| Gray, A K D … | 8 | 3 | 0 | 17 | 13 | 5.66 | 0 | 0 | 211 | 9 | 23.44 | 4 |
| Guy, S M …… | 10 | 6 | 1 | 44 | 13 | 8.80 | 0 | 0 | 0 | 0 | — | 2 |
| Hamilton, G M . | 3 | 3 | 1 | 41 | 41* | 20.50 | 0 | 0 | 0 | 0 | — | 1 |
| Hannon-Dalby, O J | 2 | 0 | 0 | 0 | — | | 0 | 0- | 58 | 3 | 19.33 | 0 |
| Harvey, I …… | 10 | 10 | 1 | 438 | 109* | 48.66 | 2 | 2 | 258 | 10 | 25.80 | 4 |
| **Hodd, A J** ….. | 14 | 13 | 3 | 142 | 70 | 14.20 | 0 | 1 | **0** | **0** | — | 6/1 |
| Hodgson, D M . | 16 | 14 | 2 | 213 | 52* | 17.75 | 0 | 1 | 0 | 0 | — | 9/1 |
| Hodgson, L J .. | 2 | 1 | 1 | 39 | 39* | — | 0 | 0 | 59 | 2 | 29.50 | 1 |
| Hoggard, M J .. | 15 | 2 | 1 | 19 | 18 | 19.00 | 0 | 0 | 472 | 13 | 36.30 | 4 |
| Jaques, P A …. | 34 | 32 | 3 | 907 | 92 | 31.27 | 0 | 6 | 15 | 0 | — | 5 |
| Kirby, S P …… | 3 | 0 | 0 | 0 | — | | 0 | 0 | 119 | 4 | 29.75 | 1 |
| Kruis, G J …… | 20 | 5 | 3 | 41 | 22 | 20.50 | 0 | 0 | 486 | 19 | 25.57 | 6 |
| Lawson, M A K . | 2 | 1 | 1 | 4 | 4* | — | 0 | 0 | 87 | 3 | 29.00 | 1 |
| **Leaning, J A** … | 18 | 17 | 6 | 352 | 60* | 32.00 | 0 | 1 | 30 | 0 | — | 6 |
| **Lees, A Z** …. | 21 | 21 | 2 | 523 | 67* | 27.52 | 0 | 3 | **0** | **0** | — | 8 |
| Lehmann, D S .. | 9 | 9 | 3 | 252 | 48 | 42.00 | 0 | 0 | 180 | 8 | 22.50 | 4 |
| Lumb, M J …. | 26 | 26 | 3 | 442 | 84* | 19.21 | 0 | 4 | 65 | 3 | 21.66 | 8 |
| **Lyth, A** …….. | 61 | 52 | 2 | 939 | 78 | 18.78 | 0 | 2 | 56 | 3 | 18.66 | 25 |
| McGrath, A …. | 66 | 61 | 12 | 1403 | 73* | 28.63 | 0 | 8 | 698 | 23 | 30.34 | 26 |
| McKay, C J …. | 8 | 6 | 3 | 54 | 21* | 18.00 | 0 | 0 | 258 | 10 | 25.80 | 1 |
| **Maxwell, G J** .. | 12 | 12 | 1 | 229 | 92* | 20.81 | 0 | 1 | 264 | 12 | 22.00 | 6 |
| **Middlebrook, J D** | 4 | 2 | 2 | 33 | 29* | — | 0 | 0 | 101 | 4 | 25.25 | 1 |
| Miller, A …… | 14 | 13 | 4 | 457 | 74* | 50.77 | 0 | 4 | 0 | 0 | — | 7 |
| **Patterson, S A** .. | 32 | 6 | 4 | 6 | 3* | 3.00 | 0 | 0 | 945 | 28 | 33.75 | 4 |
| **Plunkett, L E** .. | 20 | 15 | 2 | 212 | 36 | 16.30 | 0 | 0 | 564 | 23 | 24.52 | 5 |
| Pyrah, R M …. | 105 | 71 | 21 | 593 | 42 | 11.86 | 0 | 0 | 2,315 | 108 | 21.43 | 40 |

| Player | M | Inns | NO | Runs | HS | Av'ge | 100s | 50s | Runs | Wkts | Av'ge | Ct/St |
|---|---|---|---|---|---|---|---|---|---|---|---|---|
| Rana | | | | | | | | | | | | |
| Naved-ul-Hasan | 8 | 8 | 2 | 63 | 20* | 10.50 | 0 | 0 | 159 | 11 | 14.45 | 2 |
| **Rashid, A U** ... | **77** | **50** | **12** | **516** | **36*** | **13.57** | **0** | **0** | **1959** | **77** | **25.44** | **25** |
| **Rhodes, W M H** | **8** | **7** | **0** | **39** | **13** | **5.57** | **0** | **0** | **140** | **7** | **20.00** | **0** |
| Robinson, O E .. | 7 | 3 | 0 | 5 | 3 | 1.66 | 0 | 0 | 162 | 6 | 27.00 | 3 |
| **Root, J E** ..... | **29** | **25** | **4** | **478** | **65** | **22.76** | **0** | **2** | **224** | **4** | **56.00** | **9** |
| Rudolph, J A ... | 39 | 35 | 5 | 710 | 61 | 23.66 | 0 | 3 | 145 | 6 | 24.16 | 7 |
| Sanderson, B W | 4 | 0 | 0 | 0 | 0 | — | 0 | 0 | 74 | 6 | 12.33 | 0 |
| Sayers, J J ..... | 17 | 14 | 0 | 253 | 44 | 18.07 | 0 | 0 | 0 | 0 | — | 5 |
| Shahzad, A .... | 22 | 16 | 4 | 129 | 20 | 10.75 | 0 | 0 | 576 | 17 | 33.88 | 5 |
| **Shaw, J** ....... | **2** | **1** | **1** | **0** | **0*** | **—** | **0** | **0** | **61** | **0** | **—** | **0** |
| **Sidebottom, R J** | **40** | **16** | **10** | **87** | **16*** | **14.50** | **0** | **0** | **1,069** | **42** | **25.45** | **9** |
| Silverwood, C E W | 9 | 5 | 2 | 32 | 13* | 10.66 | 0 | 0 | 264 | 7 | 37.71 | 0 |
| Starc, M A ..... | 10 | 2 | 1 | 0 | 0* | 0.00 | 0 | 0 | 218 | 21 | 10.38 | 1 |
| Swanepoel, P J . | 2 | 1 | 1 | 2 | 2* | — | 0 | 0 | 60 | 3 | 20.00 | 1 |
| Taylor, C R .... | 2 | 2 | 1 | 10 | 10* | 10.00 | 0 | 0 | 0 | 0 | — | 0 |
| Vaughan, M P .. | 16 | 16 | 1 | 292 | 41* | 19.46 | 0 | 0 | 81 | 1 | 81.00 | 2 |
| Wainwright, D J | 26 | 9 | 6 | 23 | 6* | 7.66 | 0 | 0 | 551 | 21 | 26.23 | 9 |
| **Waite, M J** .... | **2** | **1** | **1** | **14** | **14*** | **—** | **0** | **0** | **45** | **0** | **—** | **1** |
| Wardlaw, I ..... | 10 | 1 | 1 | 1 | 1 | — | 0 | 0 | 179 | 5 | 35.80 | 0 |
| Warren, A C ... | 2 | 0 | 0 | 0 | — | — | 0 | 0 | 70 | 4 | 17.50 | 0 |
| White, C ...... | 33 | 31 | 0 | 570 | 55 | 18.38 | 0 | 2 | 132 | 2 | 66.00 | 8 |
| Williamson, K S | 5 | 5 | 0 | 93 | 41 | 18.60 | 0 | 0 | 37 | 3 | 12.33 | 1 |
| Wood, M J ..... | 15 | 15 | 3 | 328 | 96* | 27.33 | 0 | 2 | 32 | 2 | 16.00 | 11 |
| Younus Khan ... | 2 | 2 | 0 | 55 | 40 | 27.50 | 0 | 0 | 32 | 2 | 16.00 | 0 |
| Yuvraj Singh ... | 5 | 5 | 0 | 154 | 71 | 30.80 | 0 | 1 | 51 | 5 | 10.20 | 0 |

# SECOND ELEVEN RECORDS
## in the
## SECOND ELEVEN CHAMPIONSHIP 1959-1961 AND 1975-2015

### SUMMARY OF RESULTS BY SEASON

| Season | Played | Won | Lost | Drawn | Tied | Abandoned | Position in Championship |
|---|---|---|---|---|---|---|---|
| 1959 | 10 | 4 | 1 | 5 | 0 | 0 | 7 |
| 1960 | 10 | 1 | 3 | 6 | 0 | 0 | 14 |
| 1961 | 9 | 2 | 2 | 5 | 0 | 1 | 11 |
| 1975 | 14 | 4 | 0 | 10 | 0 | 0 | 4 |
| 1976 | 14 | 5 | 5 | 4 | 0 | 0 | 5 |
| **1977** | **16** | **9** | **0** | **7** | **0** | **1** | **1** |
| 1978 | 15 | 5 | 2 | 8 | 0 | 1 | 4 |
| 1979 | 16 | 5 | 0 | 11 | 0 | 0 | 3 |
| 1980 | 14 | 5 | 2 | 7 | 0 | 1 | 5 |
| 1981 | 16 | 2 | 3 | 11 | 0 | 0 | 11 |
| 1982 | 16 | 2 | 3 | 11 | 0 | 0 | 14 = |
| 1983 | 11 | 5 | 1 | 5 | 0 | 3 | 2 |
| **1984** | **15** | **9** | **3** | **3** | **0** | **0** | **1** |
| 1985 | 14 | 3 | 3 | 8 | 0 | 1 | 12 |
| 1986 | 16 | 5 | 1 | 10 | 0 | 0 | 5 |
| **1987** | **15** | **5** | **2** | **8** | **0** | **1** | **1 =** |
| 1988 | 16 | 4 | 1 | 11 | 0 | 0 | 9 |
| 1989 | 17 | 2 | 3 | 12 | 0 | 0 | 9 = |
| 1990 | 16 | 1 | 6 | 9 | 0 | 0 | 17 |
| **1991** | **16** | **8** | **1** | **7** | **0** | **0** | **1** |
| 1992 | 17 | 5 | 2 | 10 | 0 | 0 | 5 |
| 1993 | 17 | 6 | 1 | 10 | 0 | 0 | 3 |
| 1994 | 17 | 6 | 2 | 9 | 0 | 0 | 2 |
| 1995 | 17 | 7 | 1 | 9 | 0 | 0 | 5 |
| 1996 | 17 | 6 | 3 | 8 | 0 | 0 | 4 |
| 1997 | 16 | 8 | 5 | 3 | 0 | 1 | 2 |
| 1998 | 15 | 4 | 2 | 9 | 0 | 0 | 9 |
| 1999 | 16 | 3 | 8 | 5 | 0 | 1 | 14 |
| 2000 | 14 | 5 | 2 | 7 | 0 | 1 | 5 |
| 2001 | 12 | 8 | 2 | 2 | 0 | 1 | 2 |
| 2002 | 12 | 5 | 1 | 6 | 0 | 0 | 3 |
| **2003** | **10** | **7** | **1** | **2** | **0** | **0** | **1** |
| 2004 | 7 | 2 | 0 | 5 | 0 | 1 | 8 |
| 2005 | 12 | 2 | 4 | 6 | 0 | 0 | 10 |
| 2006 | 14 | 6 | 4 | 4 | 0 | 0 | 3 |
| 2007 | 12 | 4 | 5 | 3 | 0 | 0 | 10 |
| 2008 | 12 | 4 | 4 | 4 | 0 | 2 | 5 |
| 2009 | 9 | 5 | 0 | 4 | 0 | 0 | (Group A) 2 |
| 2010 | 9 | 2 | 4 | 3 | 0 | 0 | (Group A) 8 |
| 2011 | 9 | 0 | 4 | 4 | 1 | 0 | (Group A) 10 |
| 2012 | 7 | 1 | 2 | 4 | 0 | 2 | (North) 9 |
| 2013 | 9 | 3 | 4 | 2 | 0 | 0 | (North) 4 |
| 2014 | 9 | 2 | 1 | 6 | 0 | 0 | (North) 4 |
| 2015 | 9 | 2 | 0 | 4 | 3 | 0 | (North) 7 |
| Totals | 584 | 189 | 1 | 108 | 286 | 18 | |

*Matches abandoned without a ball being bowled are not counted as a match played.*
*The Championship was divided into two groups from 2009, each team playng each other*
*once. The two group winners play for the Championship*

# ANALYSIS OF RESULTS AGAINST EACH OPPONENT

| County | Played | Won | Lost | Drawn | Tied | Abandoned | First Played |
|---|---|---|---|---|---|---|---|
| Derbyshire | 55 | 13 | 8 | 34 | 0 | 3 | 1959 |
| Durham | 30 | 11 | 6 | 13 | 0 | 2 | 1992 |
| Essex | 13 | 9 | 2 | 2 | 0 | 0 | 1990 |
| Glamorgan | 40 | 11 | 3 | 26 | 0 | 2 | 1975 |
| Gloucestershire | 10 | 3 | 3 | 4 | 0 | 0 | 1990 |
| Hampshire | 12 | 4 | 1 | 7 | 0 | 0 | 1990 |
| Kent | 26 | 5 | 4 | 17 | 0 | 1 | 1981 |
| Lancashire | 67 | 14 | 18 | 35 | 0 | 3 | 1959 |
| Leicestershire | 29 | 11 | 7 | 10 | 1 | 1 | 1975 |
| MCC Young Cricketers | 5 | 3 | 1 | 1 | 0 | 0 | 2005 |
| MCC Universities | 3 | 1 | 0 | 2 | 0 | 0 | 2011 |
| Middlesex | 18 | 7 | 2 | 9 | 0 | 0 | 1977 |
| Northamptonshire | 47 | 14 | 6 | 27 | 0 | 2 | 1959 |
| Nottinghamshire | 58 | 17 | 11 | 30 | 0 | 2 | 1959 |
| Scotland | 2 | 1 | 0 | 1 | 0 | 0 | 2007 |
| Somerset | 18 | 9 | 3 | 6 | 0 | 0 | 1988 |
| Surrey | 36 | 9 | 9 | 18 | 0 | 2 | 1976 |
| Sussex | 16 | 6 | 5 | 5 | 0 | 0 | 1990 |
| Warwickshire | 60 | 21 | 13 | 26 | 0 | 0 | 1959 |
| Worcestershire | 39 | 20 | 6 | 13 | 0 | 0 | 1961 |
| Totals | 584 | 189 | 108 | 286 | 1 | 18 | |

Note: Matches abandoned are not included in the total played.

### Highest Total

*By Yorkshire:*     538 for 9 wkts dec v. Worcestershire at Stamford Bridge, 2007
*Against Yorkshire:*     567 for 7 wkts dec by Middlesex at RAF Vine Lane, Uxbridge, 2000

### Lowest Total

*By Yorkshire:*     67 v. Worcestershire at Barnt Green, 2013
*Against Yorkshire:*     36 by Lancashire at Elland, 1979

### Highest Individual Score

*For Yorkshire:*     273* by R J Blakey v. Northamptonshire at Northampton, 1986
*Against Yorkshire:*     235 by O A Shah for Middlesex at Leeds, 1999

### Century in Each Innings

| | | | |
|---|---|---|---|
| *For Yorkshire:* | C White | 209* and 115* | v. Worcestershire at Worcester, 1990 |
| | K Sharp | 150* and 127 | v. Essex at Elland, 1991 |
| | A A Metcalfe | 109 and 136* | v. Somerset at North Perrott, 1994 |
| | R A Kettleborough | 123 and 192* | v. Nottinghamshire at Todmorden, 1996 |
| | C R Taylor | 201* and 129 | v. Sussex at Hove, 2005 |
| | A W Gale | 131 and 123 | v. Somerset at Taunton, 2006 |
| | J J Sayers | 157 and 105 | v. Lancashire at Leeds, 2007 |
| *Against Yorkshire:* | N Nannan | 100 and 102* | for Nottinghamshire at Harrogate, 1979 |
| | G D Lloyd | 134 and 103 | for Lancashire at Scarborough, 1989 |
| | A J Swann | 131 and 100 | for Northamptonshire at York, 1998 |
| | G J Kennis | 114 and 114 | for Somerset at Taunton, 1999 |

### Best Bowling in an Innings

*For Yorkshire:*     9 for 27 by G A Cope v. Northamptonshire at Northampton, 1979
*Against Yorkshire:*     8 for 15 by I Folley for Lancashire at Heywood, 1983

### Best Bowling in a Match

*For Yorkshire:*     13 for 92 (6 for 48 and 7 for 44) by M K Bore v. Lancashire at Harrogate, 1976
*Against Yorkshire:*     13 for 100 (7 for 45 and 6 for 55) by N J Perry for Glamorgan at Cardiff, 1978

# Totals of 450 and over

## By Yorkshire (27)

| Score | Versus | Ground | Season |
|---|---|---|---|
| 538 for 9 wkts dec | Worcestershire | Stamford Bridge | 2007 |
| 534 for 5 wkts dec | Lancashire | Stamford Bridge | 2003 |
| 530 for 8 wkts dec | Nottinghamshire | Middlesbrough | 2000 |
| 514 for 3 wkts dec | Somerset | Taunton | 1988 |
| 509 for 4 wkts dec | Northamptonshire | Northampton | 1986 |
| 502 | Derbyshire | Chesterfield | 2003 |
| 501 for 5 wkts dec | MCC Young Cricketers | Stamford Bridge | 2009 |
| 497 | Derbyshire | Chesterfield | 2005 |
| 495 for 5 wkts dec | Somerset | Taunton | 2006 |
| 488 for 8 wkts dec | Warwickshire | Harrogate | 1984 |
| 486 for 6 wkts dec | Glamorgan | Leeds | 1986 |
| 480 | Leicestershire | Market Harborough | 2013 |
| 476 for 3 wkts dec | Glamorgan | Gorseinon | 1984 |
| 475 for 9 wkts dec | Nottinghamshire | Nottingham | 1995 |
| 474 for 3 wkts dec | Glamorgan | Todmorden | 2003 |
| 474 | Durham | Stamford Bridge | 2003 |
| 470 | Lancashire | Leeds | 2006 |
| 469 | Warwickshire | Castleford | 1999 |
| 462 | Scotland | Stamford Bridge | 2007 |
| 461 for 8 wkts dec | Essex | Stamford Bridge | 2006 |
| 459 for 3 wkts dec | Leicestershire | Oakham | 1997 |
| 459 for 6 wkts dec | Glamorgan | Bradford | 1992 |
| 457 for 9 wkts dec | Kent | Canterbury | 1983 |
| 456 for 5 wkts dec | Gloucestershire | Todmorden | 1990 |
| 456 for 6 wkts dec | Nottinghamshire | York | 1986 |
| 454 for 9 wkts dec | Derbyshire | Chesterfield | 1959 |
| 452 for 9 wkts dec | Glamorgan | Cardiff | 2005 |

## Against Yorkshire (13)

| Score | For | Ground | Season |
|---|---|---|---|
| 567 for 7 wkts dec | Middlesex | RAF Vine Lane, Uxbridge | 2000 |
| 555 for 7 wkts dec | Derbyshire | Stamford Bridge | 2002 |
| 530 for 9 wkts dec | Leicestershire | Hinckley | 2015 |
| 525 for 7 wkts dec | Sussex | Hove | 2005 |
| 493 for 8 wkts dec | Nottinghamshire | Lady Bay, Nottingham | 2002 |
| 488 for 8 wkts dec | Warwickshire | Castleford | 1999 |
| 486 | Essex | Chelmsford | 2000 |
| 485 | Gloucestershire | North Park, Cheltenham | 2001 |
| 477 | Lancashire | Headingley | 2006 |
| 471 | Warwickshire | Clifton Park, York | 2010 |
| 458 | Lancashire | Bradford | 1997 |
| 454 for 7 wkts dec | Lancashire | Todmorden | 1993 |
| 450 for 7 wkts (inns closed) | Derbyshire | Bradford | 1980 |

# Completed Innings under 75

By Yorkshire (5)

| Score | Versus | Ground | Season |
|---|---|---|---|
| 67 | Worcestershire | Barnt Green (1st inns) | 2013 |
| 68 | Worcestershire | Barnt Green (2nd inns) | 2013 |
| 69 | Lancashire | Heywood | 1983 |
| 74 | Derbyshire | Chesterfield | 1960 |
| 74 | Nottinghamshire | Bradford | 1998 |

Against Yorkshire (10)

| Score | By | Ground | Season |
|---|---|---|---|
| 36 | Lancashire | Elland | 1979 |
| 49 | Leicestershire | Leicester | 2008 |
| 50 | Lancashire | Liverpool | 1984 |
| 60 | Derbyshire | Bradford | 1977 |
| 60 | Surrey | Sunbury-on-Thames | 1977 |
| 62 | MCC YC | High Wycombe | 2005 |
| 64 | Nottinghamshire | Brodsworth | 1959 |
| 66 | Leicestershire | Lutterworth | 1977 |
| 72 | Sussex | Horsham | 2003 |
| 74 | Worcestershire | Barnsley | 1978 |

# Individual Scores of 150 and over (63)

| Score | Player | Versus | Ground | Season |
|---|---|---|---|---|
| 273* | R J Blakey | Northamptonshire | Northampton | 1986 |
| 238* | K Sharp | Somerset | Taunton | 1988 |
| 233 | P E Robinson | Kent | Canterbury | 1983 |
| 221* | K Sharp | Gloucestershire | Todmorden | 1990 |
| 219 | G M Hamilton | Derbyshire | Chesterfield | 2003 |
| 218* | A McGrath | Surrey | Elland | 1994 |
| 212 | G S Ballance | MCC Young Cricketers | Stamford Bridge | 2009 |
| 209* | C White | Worcestershire | Worcester | 1990 |
| 205 | C R Taylor | Glamorgan | Todmorden | 2003 |
| 204 | B Parker | Gloucestershire | Bristol | 1993 |
| 203 | A McGrath | Durham | Headingley | 2005 |
| 202* | J M Bairstow | Leicestershire | Oakham | 2009 |
| 202 | M J Wood | Essex | Stamford Bridge | 2006 |
| 201* | C R Taylor | Sussex | Hove | 2005 |
| 200* | D Byas | Worcestershire | Worcester | 1992 |
| 200* | A McGrath | Northamptonshire | Northampton | 2012 |
| 192* | R A Kettleborough | Nottinghamshire | Todmorden | 1996 |
| 191 | P E Robinson | Warwickshire | Harrogate | 1984 |
| 191 | M J Wood | Derbyshire | Rotherham | 2000 |
| 191 | M J Lumb | Nottinghamshire | Middlesbrough | 2000 |
| 189* | C S Pickles | Gloucestershire | Bristol | 1991 |
| 186 | A McGrath | MCC Universities | York | 2011 |
| 184 | J D Love | Worcestershire | Headingley | 1976 |
| 183 | A W Gale | Durham | Stamford Bridge | 2006 |
| 174 | G L Brophy | Worcestershire | Stamford Bridge | 2007 |
| 173 | S N Hartley | Warwickshire | Edgbaston | 1980 |
| 173 | A A Metcalfe | Glamorgan | Gorseinon | 1984 |
| 173 | B Parker | Sussex | Hove | 1996 |
| 173 | R A Kettleborough | Leicestershire | Oakham School | 1997 |

428

## Individual Scores of 150 and over *(Continued)*

| Score | Player | Versus | Ground | Season |
|-------|--------|--------|--------|--------|
| 172 | A C Morris | Lancashire | York | 1995 |
| 170* | R A J Townsley | Glamorgan | Harrogate | 1975 |
| 169 | J E Root | Warwickshire | York | 2010 |
| 168 | M J Wood | Leicestershire | Oakham School | 1997 |
| 166 | A A Metcalfe | Lancashire | York | 1984 |
| 166 | C A Chapman | Northamptonshire | York | 1998 |
| 165* | A Lyth | Durham | Stamford Bridge | 2006 |
| 165 | J J Sayers | Sussex | Hove | 2006 |
| 164* | A W Gale | Leicestershire | Harrogate | 2002 |
| 164 | J C Balderstone | Nottinghamshire | Harrogate | 1960 |
| 163* | J E Root | Leicestershire | Oakham | 2009 |
| 163 | A A Metcalfe | Derbyshire | Chesterfield | 1992 |
| 162* | D Byas | Surrey | Scarborough | 1987 |
| 160 | A A Metcalfe | Somerset | Bradford | 1993 |
| 157 | J J Sayers | Lancashire | Headingley | 2007 |
| 155 | S M Guy | Derbyshire | Chesterfield | 2005 |
| 154* | C R Taylor | Surrey | Whitgift School | 2005 |
| 153* | A A Metcalfe | Warwickshire | Bingley | 1995 |
| 153 | C White | Worcestershire | Marske-by-the-Sea | 1991 |
| 153 | R A Stead | Surrey | Todmorden | 2002 |
| 152 | A A Metcalfe | Gloucestershire | Bristol | 1993 |
| 151* | P E Robinson | Nottinghamshire | York | 1986 |
| 151* | S J Foster | Kent | Elland | 1992 |
| 151* | J J Sayers | Durham | Stamford Bridge | 2004 |
| 151 | P J Hartley | Somerset | Clevedon | 1989 |
| 151 | A McGrath | Somerset | Elland | 1995 |
| 151 | V J Craven | Glamorgan | Todmorden | 2003 |
| 150* | K Sharp | Essex | Elland | 1991 |
| 150* | G M Fellows | Hampshire | Todmorden | 1998 |
| 150* | S M Guy | Nottinghamshire | Headingley | 2005 |
| 150* | J A Leaning | Worcestershire | Worcester | 2011 |
| 150 | K Sharp | Glamorgan | Ebbw Vale | 1983 |
| 150 | S N Hartley | Nottinghamshire | Worksop | 1988 |
| 150 | C R Taylor | Derbyshire | Chesterfield | 2003 |

## 7 Wickets in an Innings (30)

| Analysis | Player | Versus | Ground | Season |
|----------|--------|--------|--------|--------|
| 9 for 27 | G A Cope | Northamptonshire | Northampton | 1977 |
| 9 for 62 | M K Bore | Warwicshire | Scarborough | 1976 |
| 8 for 53 | S J Dennis | Nottinghamshire | Nottingham | 1983 |
| 8 for 57 | M K Bore | Lancashire | Manchester | 1977 |
| 8 for 79 | P J Berry | Derbyshire | Harrogate | 1991 |
| 7 for 13 | P Carrick | Northamptonshire | Marske-by-the-Sea | 1977 |
| 7 for 21 | S Silvester | Surrey | Sunbury-on-Thames | 1977 |
| 7 for 22 | J A R Blain | Surrey | Purley | 2004 |
| 7 for 32 | P W Jarvis | Surrey | The Oval | 1984 |
| 7 for 34 | P Carrick | Glamorgan | Leeds | 1986 |
| 7 for 37 | P M Hutchison | Warwickshire | Coventry | 2001 |

# 7 Wickets in an Innings *(Continued)*

| Analysis | Player | Versus | Ground | Season |
|----------|--------|--------|--------|--------|
| 7 for 39 | G M Hamilton | Sussex | Leeds | 1995 |
| 7 for 40 | M K Bore | Worcestershire | Old Hill | 1976 |
| 7 for 44 | M K Bore | Lancashire | Harrogate | 1976 |
| 7 for 44 | J P Whiteley | Worcestershire | Leeds | 1979 |
| 7 for 51 | J D Middlebrook | Derbyshire | Rotherham | 2000 |
| 7 for 53 | J P Whiteley | Warwickshire | Birmingham | 1980 |
| 7 for 55 | C White | Leicestershire | Bradford | 1990 |
| 7 for 58 | K Gillhouley | Derbyshire | Chesterfield | 1960 |
| 7 for 58 | P J Hartley | Lancashire | Leeds | 1985 |
| 7 for 63 | M J Hoggard | Worcestershire | Harrogate | 1998 |
| 7 for 65 | M K Bore | Nottinghamshire | Steetley | 1976 |
| 7 for 70 | J D Batty | Leicestershire | Bradford | 1992 |
| 7 for 71 | J D Batty | Hampshire | Harrogate | 1994 |
| 7 for 81 | K Gillhouley | Lancashire | Scarborough | 1960 |
| 7 for 84 | I J Houseman | Kent | Canterbury | 1989 |
| 7 for 88 | I G Swallow | Nottinghamshire | Nottingham | 1983 |
| 7 for 90 | A P Grayson | Kent | Folkestone | 1991 |
| 7 for 93 | D Pickles | Nottinghamshire | Nottingham | 1960 |
| 7 for 94 | K Gillhouley | Northamptonshire | Redcar | 1960 |

## 12 Wickets in a Match (6)

| Analysis | | Player | Versus | Ground | Season |
|----------|---|--------|--------|--------|--------|
| 13 for 92 | (6-48 and 7-44) | M K Bore | Lancashire | Harrogate | 1976 |
| 13 for 110 | (7-70 and 6-40) | J D Batty | Leicestershire | Bradford | 1992 |
| 13 for 111 | (4-49 and 9-62) | M K Bore | Warwickshire | Scarborough | 1976 |
| 12 for 69 | (5-32 and 7-37) | P M Hutchison | Warwickshire | Coventry | 2001 |
| 12 for 120 | (5-39 and 7-81) | K Gillhouley | Lancashire | Scarborough | 1960 |
| 12 for 162 | (5-78 and 7-84) | I J Houseman | Kent | Canterbury | 1989 |

## Hat-tricks (4)

| Player | Versus | Ground | Season |
|--------|--------|--------|--------|
| I G Swallow | Warwickshire | Harrogate | 1984 |
| S D Fletcher | Nottinghamshire | Marske-by-the-Sea | 1987 |
| I G Swallow | Derbyshire | Chesterfield | 1988 |
| M Broadhurst | Essex | Southend-on-Sea | 1992 |

# ANNUAL REPORT
## and
## Statement of Account
## for the year ended
## December 31, 2015

# CHAIRMAN'S STATEMENT

### *An incredible year*

2015 turned out to be quite a year to assume the Chairmanship of Yorkshire County Cricket Club! Brilliantly led by Andrew Gale, our team won the County Championship for the 34th time and back-to-back titles for the first time in nearly 50 years. It was no ordinary win.

In total 21 players were used over the season, with seven of the squad being called up to repre-

**STEVE DENISON**

sent England at different times, adding to the disruption caused by injuries and Gale's early-season absence. The ability of our coaching team, superbly led by Martyn Moxon and Jason Gillespie, to manage the constant disruption throughout the season is testimony to their skill and the winning mindset they have instilled in the team. The stats will go down in history: most wins (11 out of 16), highest points (286) and the greatest winning margin (68 points). Incredible!

### *White-ball ambitions*

But there is no complacency in the dressing-room. The desire of our players to win the treble is as strong as ever, and there is clear acknowledgement that we have to do better with the white ball. The disappointment of not reaching the Royal London One-Day Cup final at Lord's was incredibly painful, and we have yet to fulfil our potential in the NatWest T20 Blast. The YCCC contribution to Adelaide Strikers' success in the Big Bash and the signing of David Willey are evidence of our intention to compete for trophies across all formats in 2016.

### *Sustained success*

Members often say to me that YCCC is too much about business and not enough about cricket. My answer is always the same: it's not true, but the reality is that without a sustainable business model for the Club there will be no cricket. Without the repeated injection of loans from Colin Graves, YCCC would have been bust years ago. But continually borrowing more is no way to run a business, and there is no Fairy Godmother waiting in the wings to bail us out. We have therefore successfully completed a financial restructuring of the Club during the year with Colin's loan repaid.

So, we are two years into a seven-year plan through to the end of our international staging agreement and the World Cup in 2019. I'll provide more details to members at the AGM, but the reality is that clearing our debts over the next 10-15 years has to be a key priority. We successfully refinanced at the end of 2015, reducing the annual interest bill by nearly £300,000 per annum, and virtually all aspects of the commercial side of the Club made significant progress last year. Achieving a small profit in 2015 was an important milestone, and the positive trends in revenues across all categories have continued into the New Year. We have clear plans to drive revenues and profit forward over the next few years.

But we still face substantial headwinds. Headingley's status as an international ground is not guaranteed beyond 2019, compounded by considerable uncertainty over the format and quantity of international cricket after that date. We are determined to make Headingley one of the best sporting venues in the country, and plans are being formulated for the joint redevelopment of the Football Stand with our Leeds Rugby neighbours, a complicated and expensive process. Each party will have to inject around £15 million, and we are working hard to raise at least £8 million of our share by way of grants. Our target is to have the new stand open in time for the *Ashes* Test and Pakistan ODI which will take place in 2019, together with four World Cup matches that are contingent on its completion. This will, of course, provide significantly enhanced facilities which will be available for use by the members as we develop operating and commercial plans. Achievement of our vision and plans will be far from easy, and will require resolve and unity in equal measure.

### *Influencing the future of English cricket*

Success on and off the pitch is also important in the context of shaping domestic cricket. The new regime at the ECB is considering a wide range of options for both red and white-ball cricket, and I am determined that Yorkshire will play a key part in influencing their strategy by being at the heart of any decision-making. Your Board is unanimous in the belief that there is nothing more important than four-day cricket, and we will do our utmost to preserve the integrity and importance of the County Championship while supporting changes to white-ball cricket to make the game accessible to the widest possible audience.

### Strong unit

If you follow Jason Gillespie on Twitter you'll know that he regularly uses "strong unit" to describe our players. Thanks to his outstanding leadership with Martyn Moxon and Andrew Gale that's exactly what they are, with a unity of purpose and spirit that's largely founded on growing our own talent. Our young players all gained valuable experience last season, and Alex Lees has been confirmed as one day skipper for 2016. But "strong unit" also applies to YCCC in its entirety, because we are stronger together, and unity ensures that we are best placed to secure the long-term future of Yorkshire cricket and remain the envy of all other counties.

### Bright future

I would like to say a few personal thank-yous, beginning with Colin Graves for his unstinting commitment and financial support to the Club over many years. I wish Colin well with the challenges he faces with the national game. Thanks also to Dickie Bird for a superb second year as President, attending every match and being the perfect ambassador for the Club.

Finally, thanks to my fellow board members, Mark Arthur and every member of his staff who have worked tirelessly for the benefit of the Club and you as members. So here we are at the start of the new season. Yorkshire is again the county all others are trying to emulate, with the realistic prospect of a Championship treble and nearly half of our first team firmly established or pressing hard for a place in the England squad. *Strong Yorkshire, Strong England* is once more the mantra, with Joe Root one of the top batsman in the world, Jonny Bairstow the Cricket Writers' Player of the Year and Jack Leaning the Young Player of the Year.

Thank you for your continued support, which is hugely appreciated by everyone at the Club. By all pulling together in the same direction, both on and off the pitch, your board, staff and players have delivered an exceptional result. I hope you are as proud as I am of what YCCC has achieved over the past two years.

I wish you all a healthy, exciting and successful season in 2016.

STEVE DENISON
Executive Chairman
The Yorkshire
County Cricket Club

# CHIEF EXECUTIVE'S REPORT

**MARK ARTHUR**

The 2015 season will once again be hailed as one of success for Yorkshire County Cricket Club. We won the County Championship for the 34th time, breaking modern-day records in the process. However, success was not limited to the men's first team. Yorkshire Women won their County Championship, while there was also success for the Men's Over 50s, the Girls' Under 13s and Under 15s, and the Academy won both the Yorkshire League Cup and the Black Sheep Trophy. Woodhouse Grange CC won the National Village Cup Final at Lord's for the fourth and last time, as they also won promotion to the new Yorkshire Premier League North, making themselves ineligible for the village competition in the future.

Off the field it was another year of excellent progress. New state-of-the-art floodlights were installed at Headingley, and thanks to the generosity of our President, Dickie Bird, we now have a splendid viewing balcony for the players. The floodlights are a game changer for us commercially, allowing a later start to the evening NatWest T20 Blast matches. Consequently, domestic ticket sales increased by 58 per cent. Test Match ticket sales were up by 24 per cent, and income from our retail operation has grown by 106 per cent in the last two years. Overall, income is up by 14 per cent on the previous year and 23 per cent on 2013, confirming that the Club is moving in the right direction.

In 2016 we welcome Sri Lanka for the first Test Match of the summer and, at the time of writing, ticket sales are up by 6,000 on last year. In September we host Pakistan for the first ever Day/Night One-Day International at Headingley under permanent floodlights, which we expect to be a sellout. On the domestic front the men will be looking to be competitive in all three competitions as they seek to emulate the great teams of the Sixties by winning three Championships in a row. Two is excellent in the modern era, particularly with so many Yorkshire players representing England, but three would be spectacular. We also see the start of the Women's Cricket Super League in 2016, and Yorkshire will be one of six teams to play in the inaugural *T20* competition. And Yorkshire finally has a pyramid structure at the highest level of club cricket. Four ECB premier leagues will battle it out during the season, with the finalists competing in Abu Dhabi for the right to call themselves the best club team in Yorkshire.

Steady and measured progress is being made with regard to the devel-

434

opment of the North/South Stand at Headingley. We are busy fundraising, planning and agreeing the future operational joint venture with Leeds Rugby. Details will be released at the appropriate time, and an EGM will be called to get approval from the membership. In the meantime you will see greater activity on the rugby side as they have to redevelop their South Stand before we embark upon the joint venture.

Park Avenue Cricket Ground in Bradford will complete phase one by mid-summer 2016. A non-turf pitch was laid last summer to allow more cricket to be played at the famous old ground. Eight non-turf nets are being constructed on the old football pitch, along with complementary changing facilities. The cost of this project is £570,000, which has been fully funded by the ECB and Bradford MDC. We are progressing with the fundraising for phase two, which includes the refurbishment of the cricket ground and construction of a pavilion capable of hosting disability cricket, England Women's cricket, Women's Super League cricket, schools and community cricket, club and potentially first-class cricket. Essentially, we are very excited that Park Avenue will once again be a first-class ground for the wider cricketing community.

Scarborough again proved to be the most popular ground on the county circuit, drawing crowds of 5,000 per day and affirming the popularity of festival cricket. Thanks to Bill Mustoe and his team for being outstanding hosts and preparing one of the best pitches in the country.

On a sadder note, over 20 of our clubs were flooded during the Christmas period, causing unprecedented damage. The Yorkshire cricket family has come together to support these clubs, along with tremendous financial support from the ECB and Sport England. Having visited all the affected clubs with players and colleagues, I am amazed by the positivity and resilience of the volunteers at each and every club. The majority should enjoy a full season at their home ground, and the fundraising continues to help those worst affected.

Since I have been at Yorkshire I have tried to bring the components and stakeholders of Yorkshire Cricket closer together for the betterment of the game, and I would like to thank all who have worked with me in that process. There are too many to mention individually, but you know who you are. We have a long way to go to achieve our ambitions, but we will get there, and cricket in Yorkshire will be stronger than ever.

Thanks to all the players for a memorable 2015. Now for 2016!

Enjoy the season.


MARK ARTHUR
Chief Executive
Yorkshire County Cricket Club

# FINANCE DIRECTOR'S REPORT

**PAUL HUDSON**

This was a year of significant progress in the finances of Yorkshire County Cricket Club.

In terms of trading results, revenues and EBITDA both continued to improve, and we achieved a retained profit for the first time since 2009, which was an *Ashes* Test year. Overall revenues at £8.4m were 14 per cent up on last year and £1.6m higher than in 2013. We have successfully driven growth across all activities, including ticket sales, commercial and hospitality income, and membership. Revenue from the ECB also increased, as we are rewarded for growing talent for both our own first team and the England team.

We retained out strong focus on costs, and most increases were in line with sales. The success of our international players adversely affected our annual players' wage bill, which rose by £358,000, including the cost of maintaining a larger squad to cover for our players representing England.

Overheads increased year on year by £299,000 due to a combination of factors. We stopped charging ticket booking fees, which had previously offset overheads, and there were increases in marketing and retail spend to drive revenues.

Notwithstanding these cost pressures, our gross margin increased by £1m compared to 2013, and we achieved year-on-year growth of 23 per cent in EBITDA. Both very creditable results.

Our new floodlights were installed during the year at a total cost of £1.5m. This was financed in part by a grant from the ECB of £0.7m, with the balance funded by a finance-lease agreement that will largely be repaid by further ECB monies due in 2018.

Turning to the financing of the Club, Colin Graves's appointment as ECB Chairman meant that we had to refinance his loans so that YCCC would be financially independent from him.

To put things in context, a bar chart shows the change in our debt from 2002 to the start of 2015. Our debt increased substantially over the period to £23.9m, largely as a result of purchasing Headingley, other ground-development projects and the payment of interest on loans.

Against this background it was becoming harder for the Club to pay interest and make capital repayments under the various loan agreements, and we decided to review the relationships with all of our debt providers: the Graves family trusts, Leeds City Council, HSBC and Leeds Beckett University. As a result, we have refinanced the Club.

The Graves family trusts, which are entirely independent from him in his personal capacity, have provided loans of £18.9m, which has allowed the previous loans from Colin, the Graves family trusts and Leeds City Council to be repaid. As part of the refinancing we are grateful to Leeds City Council, who after reviewing the actual cost of interest that the council had incurred in servicing the debt which demonstrated that the cost to the council of the loan has been fully met by the Club, accepted £6.5m in settlement of the £7.4m capital outstanding on the loan.

As part of the final settlement the club was not charged a sum of £326,000 during the year in respect of interest on the loan.

We are also grateful to both HSBC and Leeds Beckett University for reducing the rates of interest charged on their loans. HSBC have also granted the Club a capital repayment holiday until 2018.

The impact of the refinancing is a reduction in our annual interest charge of almost £300,000 per year, and there are no scheduled capital repayments until 2019.

Cash from perimeter advertising will begin to be received again after 2019; catering rights will revert to the Club after 2020, and the *Ashes* and World Cup in 2019 should generate significant cash inflows. The Club is in a stronger financial position than it has been at any time in recent years.

PAUL HUDSON
Director of Finance
Yorkshire County Cricket Club

# DIRECTOR OF PROFESSIONAL CRICKET'S REPORT

You may recall that in my report last year I said there could be a challenge around the corner with the possibility that up to six players may be selected for the England tour to the West Indies in April-May 2015.

This became a reality, and it is very pleasing for our support staff that the work and planning we did during last winter enabled us to cope with the international selections and still manage to regain the County Championship title. In fact, we had to use 21 players last season in the LVCC.

Despite the disruption the players were able to put their names into the record books. They achieved the record number of points and wins since the Championship was split into two divisions. The winning margin of 68 points is the largest since 1979, and it was Yorkshire's most convincing victory since 1931. Our unbeaten run in the County Championship of 26 consecutive games was the Club's best sequence since 1947.

**MARTYN MOXON**

In all of the season's seven Test matches England had three Yorkshire players in the top five of the batting order. This is the first time any county has been represented in such a way. The fact that we had six players on the Test tour of the West Indies is also a record.

All in all some outstanding statistics – the players should be very proud of their achievements.

Having said all that, I think everyone will probably agree that we did not bat as well as a team last year as in 2014. We very much relied on a couple of individuals getting us out of trouble in most matches, and there were some outstanding partnerships that turned the game our way. In my opinion the two most notable were the Bairstow and Bresnan unbeaten partnership of 366 at Durham and the 248 of Maxwell and Rashid at Scarborough, again against Durham. There were, of course, important contributions over the season from other players, but I believe these two in particular were huge in the context of the season.

As inconsistent as our batting may have been, the same cannot be said of our bowling. Once again there were tremendous individual performances, but as a group our bowlers were outstanding. The seamers never let the opposition settle, and our spinners also played a big part and took 46 wickets between them. I would like to make special mention of James

Middlebrook, who joined us at very short notice early in the season and played with great pride and passion. His experience was invaluable, and I would like to thank him for his contribution to our success.

Our challenge is to keep winning, and make it three in a row. It will be no easy task, but if the players play to their potential it is achievable.

As far as one-day cricket is concerned, reaching the semi-final of the Royal London competition was pleasing and an improvement on last year, but it was disappointing to lose when we had such a good start to the game. Unfortunately, our innings fell away in the final 15 overs, and then we had no answer to some excellent batting from Michael Klinger.

The biggest disappointment of the summer was our *T20* campaign. Given the recruitment of Aaron Finch and Glen Maxwell along with our own talent, we would have expected to at least reach the quarter-finals. Our results in *T20* cricket over the last three years have been extremely frustrating. I can assure you that we have done a lot of talking and worked hard to try and improve. However, we haven't seen any kind of consistency in this form of the game in recent years.

There are two main areas that we are looking to address. Firstly, we have to try and have a settled team who know their roles. Secondly, the batsmen need to formulate a method and trust it, and the bowlers need to be able to execute their skills better under pressure.

With regard to the first point, we set out last season with that intention. However, through injuries, England selections and poor form we never achieved that settled team, and we found ourselves scrambling around for solutions. Discussions between Alex Lees, Jason Gillespie and myself are ongoing on how we can achieve continuity given the playing schedule that we face and our desire to be successful in all three formats of the game. The second issue is something that, once again, the players have discussed at length and are working on this winter.

In four-day cricket we have a tried-and-tested process for winning that the players trust. We are yet to achieve this in *T20* cricket, but there is a real determination within the squad to develop the successful formula. The signing of David Willey will strengthen our team, and we are very much looking forward to welcoming him to Headingley. We will also have Kane Williamson available for a large part of the *T20* campaign, so I fully expect an improvement in our fortunes.

Moving on to the Second Eleven, we used over 30 players during the season for a variety of reasons. Although the match results weren't particularly good it did mean that a number of young players were given an opportunity at a higher level, and we learned a great deal about them with the future in mind.

The Academy had another successful season, even though a number of senior players had been "released" to play league cricket elsewhere. They achieved a cup double — the Yorkshire League Knockout Cup and the Black Sheep Champion of Champions Trophy. A fantastic effort, and again a positive reflection on the excellent work being done by Ian Dews and Richard Damms.

As I've said before we have an outstanding group of coaches and support staff at the Club, and I would like to thank them all for their hard work, passion and commitment in providing the players with the best possible help in preparing them for competition.

We obviously now have Rich Pyrah on the coaching staff. He has been a loyal player who excelled in the one-day form of the game over many years. He has a great enthusiasm for coaching, and is already doing some good work across all age groups. He spent some time during the winter at the Big Bash with Jason, and Aaron Finch also arranged for him to work with the Melbourne Renegades for two weeks. This was a fantastic experience, and both he and Jason have learned things that can help us to improve.

It is a very exciting time to be involved in Yorkshire cricket. I have spoken about our various teams and cricket staff, but our staff off the field are doing great things. The Club is united, and is led brilliantly by our Chairman, Steve Denison, and CEO, Mark Arthur. They have a clear vision for the future of the Club and the development of Headingley. They will not allow complacency, as there are challenges ahead, but we are in a good position to continue our progress across all areas.

Thank you once again for your continued support. It means a great deal to the players and staff to know that we are the best supported county in the country and I hope that we can continue to provide you with success to enjoy.


MARTYN MOXON
Director of Professional Cricket
Yorkshire County Cricket Club

# MEMBERS' COMMITTEE
# CHAIRMAN'S REPORT

The following served on the Members' Committee during the year.

| | |
|---|---|
| Chairman: | **Mr S J Mann** |
| Elected Members: | **Mrs C Evers**<br>**Mr R Levin**<br>**Mr S J Mann**<br>**Mr E Stephens** |
| Appointed Members: | **Mr G Greenfield (from September 7, 2015)**<br>**Mr A Kilburn**<br>**Mrs. K Mathew (from February 23, 2015)**<br>**Mr R W Stott (to June 30, 2015)** |
| In Attendance: | **Mr R Smith,** Board Director<br>**Mr M Arthur,** Chief Executive<br>**Mr A Dawson,** Commercial Director |

There were six full committee meetings during 2015. As in previous years the minutes of these meetings are submitted to the main Board and included in papers for the Board meeting immediately thereafter. There were a number of changes to the committee during the year, specifically concerning appointed members.

After several years of committed and dedicated service Bob Stott, with considerable reluctance, stepped down in early summer. The committee were fortunate to be joined by Kathryn Mathew and Graeme Greenfield, who immediately made contributions of substance.

**STEPHEN MANN**

Two member forums were held during the year. At the first the new Chairman and the Chief Executive of the Club attended and detailed the Board's view on potential restructuring of the domestic game. At the second forum towards the end of the season the Director of Professional Cricket addressed the members and took questions. The format for the forums was changed for this year to ensure that there was a particular issue of debate and to ensure members were as informed as possible on the current and key topics. Feedback has shown that the changes were well received; indeed, attendance levels were over 120 for each gathering. As might be expected the same format will be followed in 2016.

The key issue dominating all others has been the ECB proposal to reduce first-class cricket through changes to the County Championship, changes to a structure that clearly works and is widely considered successful. The Club have been consistent and strong in reflecting the views of the membership that there should be no reduction in the programme.

Having reflected the concerns of many members regarding the preparedness and facilities at Scarborough in 2014, it is pleasing to record that the Scarborough club responded positively with the result that no issues of substance were raised in 2015. The issue of the Scarborough fixtures being too close together was raised as there seemed no doubt that such timing was having a detrimental impact on overall attendances, strong though they are. Pleasingly, the issue appears remedied for 2016.

Continuing the trend over the last few years the Club hosted two highly successful international matches. The management approach to staging such events deserves much credit, and Headingley is now one of the best grounds for watching international cricket in the country. The spectator experience coupled with more than reasonable pricing should make attendance at the Test a must for all members and their friends. The five-day ticket is incomparable in value to watch international sport. More importantly, the larger the crowd the greater the benefit to YCCC. Many members were able to attend in 2015 as the county were not involved in a Championship match. Hopefully, that will be repeated in 2016.

Administrative standards continue to improve, particularly in the area of membership services. Mistakes and omissions do arise from time to time, but such occurrences are rare when compared to recent years.

I would like to conclude by recording my sincere thanks to all my colleagues on the Members' Committee for their support during the year. They all give of their time freely, and several travel from the extreme boundaries of the county to meetings at their own expense. They are, without exception, committed to helping to enhance the well-being of the club, the members and the continuance of the membership concept.

I mentioned in my opening comments that Bob Stott had reluctantly resigned from the committee earlier in the year. This report would not be complete without a sincere expression of appreciation to Bob for his dedication and effort working for the Club and members over several years. He has given much time, not only to the Members' Committee, but also to chairing the committee that delivered a highly successful programme of events to celebrate the 150-year anniversary. I know members will join with me in saying to Bob quite simply: "Thank you."

STEPHEN MANN,
Chairman,
Members' Committee
Yorkshire County Cricket Club

# INDEPENDENT AUDITORS' REPORT

## TO THE MEMBERS OF THE YORKSHIRE
## COUNTY CRICKET CLUB

We have audited the financial statements of The Yorkshire County Cricket Club ("the Club") for the year ended December 31, 2015, set out on Pages 447 to 456. The financial reporting framework that has been applied in their preparation is applicable law and UK Accounting Standards (UK Generally Accepted Accounting Practice, including FRS102 The Financial Reporting Standard applicable in the UK and Republic of Ireland).

This report is made solely to the Club's members, as a body, in accordance with section 87 of the Co-operative and Community Benefit Societies Act 2014. Our audit work has been undertaken so that we might state to the Club's members those matters we are required to state to them in an auditor's report and for no other purpose. To the fullest extent permitted by law we do not accept or assume responsibility to anyone other than the Club and the Club's members, as a body, for our audit work, for this report, or for the opinions we have formed.

## Respective responsibilities of directors and auditor

As more fully explained in the Statement of Directors' Responsibilities set out on Page 445 the Club's directors are responsible for the preparation of financial statements which give a true and fair view. Our responsibility is to audit, and express an opinion on, the financial statements in accordance with applicable law and International Standards on Auditing (UK and Ireland). Those standards require us to comply with the Auditing Practices Board's Ethical Standards for Auditors.

### Scope of the audit of the financial statements

A description of the scope of an audit of financial statements is provided on the Financial Reporting Council's website at www.frc.org.uk/auditscopeukprivate.

## Opinion on financial statements

In our opinion the financial statements:

- give a true and fair view, in accordance with UK Generally Accepted Accounting Practice, of the state of the Club's affairs as at December 31, 2015, and of its surplus for the year then ended; and
- comply with the requirements of the Co-operative and Community Benefit Societies Act 2014.

## Matters on which we are required to report by exception

We have nothing to report in respect of the following.

Under the Co-operative and Community Benefit Societies Act 2014 we are required to report to you if, in our opinion:

- The Club has not kept proper books of account; or
- The Club has not maintained a satisfactory system of control over its transactions; or
- The financial statements are not in agreement with the Club's books of account; or
- We have not received all the information and explanations we need for our audit.

**MARCUS TYLDSLEY** for and on behalf of KPMG LLP, Statutory Auditor
Chartered Accountants
Leeds                                        FEBRUARY 12, 2016

# CORPORATE GOVERNANCE

The Board is accountable to the Club's members for good corporate governance, and this statement describes how the principles of governance are applied.

## THE BOARD

The Board is responsible for approving Club policy and strategy. It meets bi-monthly, or more frequently if business needs require, and has a schedule of matters specifically reserved to it for decision, including all significant commercial issues and all capital expenditure.

The Executive Management Team supply the Board with appropriate and timely information, and Board Members are free to seek any further information they consider necessary.

## NOMINATIONS COMMITTEE

The Nominations Committee is formally constituted with written terms of reference, which are defined in the Club Rules and reviewed regularly. It consists of the President, Secretary and two other Board members, currently S Denison and R A Smith.

## AUDIT COMMITTEE

The Audit Committee meets to provide oversight of the financial reporting process, the audit process, systems of internal controls and compliance with laws and regulations. It meets with the external auditors as part of this process. Members of the committee are S J Denison, S Willis and Professor P Smith.

## RELATIONS WITH MEMBERS

The Club encourages effective communication with its members, and a specific Committee, as defined in the Club Rules, is appointed for that purpose.

## INTERNAL CONTROL

The Board acknowledges its responsibility to maintain a sound system of internal control relating to operational, financial and compliance controls and risk management, to safeguard the members' interests and the Club's assets, and will regularly review its effectiveness. Such a system, however, is designed to manage and meet the Club's particular needs and mitigate the risks to which it is exposed, rather than eliminate the risk of failure to achieve business objectives, and can provide only reasonable and not absolute assurance against material mis-statement or loss.

The Club considers its key components to provide effective internal control and improve business efficiency are:

- Regular meetings with senior management to review and assess progress made against objectives and deal with any problems which arise from such reviews.

- A financial reporting system of annual budgets, periodic forecasts and detailed monthly reporting which includes cash-flow forecasts. Budgets and forecasts are reviewed and approved by the Board.
- A defined management and organisation structure with defined responsibilities and appropriate authorisation limits and short lines of communication to the Executive Chairman.
- A management and organisation structure exists with defined responsibilities and appropriate authorisation limits and short lines of communication to the Non-Executive Chairman.
- A Senior Independent Director is appointed by the Board whose role is to serve as a sounding board for the Chairman and act as an inter-mediary for other directors. The position is currently held by R A Smith.

## DIRECTORS' RESPONSIBILITIES

The directors are responsible for preparing the Annual Report and the Club's financial statements in accordance with applicable law and regulations. Co-operative and Community Benefit Society law requires the directors to prepare financial statements for each financial year. Under that law the directors have elected to prepare the financial statements in accordance with UK Accounting Standards including FRS102 the Financial Reporting Standard applicable in the UK and Republic.

The financial statements are required by law to give a true and fair view of the state of affairs of the Club and of its income and expenditure for that period. In preparing the Club's financial statements, the directors are required to:
- select suitable accounting policies and apply them consistently;
- make judgements and estimates that are reasonable and prudent;
- state whether Accounting Standards have been followed, subject to any material departures disclosed and explained in the financial statements, and
- prepare the financial statements on the going-concern basis unless it is inappropriate to presume that the Club will continue in business.

The directors are responsible for keeping proper books of account that disclose with reasonable accuracy at any time the financial position of the Club and enable them to ensure that its financial statements comply with the Co-operative and Community Benefit Societies Act 2014. They have general responsibility for taking such steps as are reasonably open to them to safeguard the assets of the Club and to prevent and detect fraud and other irregularities.

The directors are responsible for the maintenance and integrity of the corporate and financial information included on the Club's website. Legislation in the UK governing the preparation and dissemination of financial statements may differ from legislation in other jurisdictions.the maintenance and integrity of the corporate and financial information included on the Club's website. Legislation in the UK governing the preparation and dissemination of financial statements may differ from legislation in other jurisdictions.

# INCOME AND EXPENDITURE ACCOUNT
## for the year ended 31st December, 2015

| | Note | 2015 £ | 2014 £ |
|---|---|---|---|
| **Income** | | | |
| International ticket and hospitality revenue | | **2,440,612** | 2,181,135 |
| Domestic ticket and hospitality revenue | | **835,547** | 538,131 |
| Subscriptions | | **652,324** | 564,990 |
| England and Wales Cricket Board | | **2,480,607** | 2,194,791 |
| Commercial income | | **1,904,940** | 1,797,563 |
| Other income | | **51,683** | 30,588 |
| | | **8,365,713** | 7,307,199 |
| **Cost of sales** | | | |
| International match and hospitality expenditure | | **1,300,521** | 1,202,876 |
| Domestic match and hospitality costs (home fixtures) | | **421,390** | 348,286 |
| Retail | | **239,447** | 163,483 |
| Catering | | **31,518** | 31,678 |
| | | **(1,992,876)** | (1,746,323) |
| **Cricket expenses** | | | |
| Staff remuneration and employment expenses | | **2,563,753** | 2,205,459 |
| Match expenses (away fixtures) | | **238,265** | 215,808 |
| Development expenses | | **337,108** | 317,529 |
| Other cricket expenses | | **28,926** | 26,664 |
| | | **(3,168,052)** | (2,765,460) |
| **Overhead** | | | |
| Infrastructure and ground operations | | **943,772** | 807,500 |
| Commercial | | **767,982** | 672,324 |
| Administration | | **697,705** | 685,077 |
| Ticket and membership office | | **201,015** | 146,568 |
| | | **(2,610,474)** | (2,311,469) |
| **Earnings before interest, tax, depreciation and amortisation** | | **594,311** | 483,946 |
| **Below the line expenditure:** | | | |
| Loan Interest | | **(638,741)** | (1,050,437) |
| Depreciation | | **(434,768)** | (438,533) |
| Release of Capital Grants | | **177,382** | 178,265 |
| | | **(896,127)** | (1,310,705) |
| **(Deficit) before taxation and exceptional items** | | **(301,816)** | (826,758) |
| **Exceptional items \*1** | 8 | **781,106** | 500,000 |
| **Surplus before taxation** | | **479,290** | (326,758) |
| **Taxation** | 4 | **(110,877)** | — |
| **Surplus for the year after taxation** | | **368,413** | (326,758) |

\*1 2014 exceptional item — A one-off amount of £500,000 was received from the ECB and used to clear down part of an outstanding loan balance with the ECB.

# BALANCE SHEET

## as at 31st December, 2015

| | Note | 2015 £ | 2015 £ | 2014 £ | 2014 £ |
|---|---|---|---|---|---|
| **Assets employed:** | | | | | |
| Fixed Assets | 5 | | 29,259,590 | | 28,335,784 |
| | | | | | |
| **Current assets:** | | | | | |
| Stocks | | 112,770 | | 87,753 | |
| Debtors | 6 | 1,482,891 | | 1,311,146 | |
| Cash at bank and in hand | | 765,142 | | — | |
| | | 2,360,803 | | 1,398,899 | |
| | | | | | |
| **Creditors: amounts falling due within one year** | 7 | (4,153,629) | | (3,764,066) | |
| | | | | | |
| **Net current liabilities** | | | (1,792,826) | | (2,365,166) |
| | | | | | |
| **Total assets less current liabilities** | | | 27,466,764 | | 25,970,618 |
| | | | | | |
| **Funded by:** | | | | | |
| | | | | | |
| **Creditors: amounts falling due after more than one year** | 8 | | 25,160,683 | | 24,165,569 |
| | | | | | |
| **Deferred income — capital grants** | 9 | | 5,152,286 | | 5,019,668 |
| | | | 30,312,969 | | 29,185,237 |
| | | | | | |
| **Capital and Reserves** | | | | | |
| Called-up share capital | 11 | | 197 | | 199 |
| Capital redemption reserve | 12 | | 693 | | 691 |
| Income and expenditure account | 12 | | (2,847,095) | | (3,215,508) |
| | | | 2,846,205 | | (3,214,619) |
| | | | | | |
| | | | 27,466,764 | | 25,970,618 |

These accounts were approved by the Board on 12th February 2016

**S J DENISON, Chairman**

**R A SMITH, Director**

The accompanying notes form an integral part to these accounts. There were no other gains and losses in the current or preceding year other than those stated above.

# CASH FLOW STATEMENT
## for the year ended 31st December, 2015

| | Note | 2015 £ | 2014 £ |
|---|---|---|---|
| **Cash flows from operating activities** | | | |
| Profit/(loss) for the year | | 368,413 | (326,758) |
| **Adjustments for:** | | | |
| Deprecation of tangible assets | | 434,768 | 438,533 |
| Loan Interest payable | | 638,741 | 1,050,437 |
| Capital Grants Released | | (177,382) | (178,265) |
| Taxation | | 110,87 | — |
| Waiver of loan balance | | (907,000) | — |
| Adjustment to Debenture Debt | | (23,696) | — |
| (Increase)/decrease in trade and other debtors | | (282,622) | 554,270 |
| (Increase)/decrease in stocks | | (25,017) | (19,125) |
| Increase/(decrease) in creditors | | 493,291 | (547,622) |
| Tax Paid | | — | — |
| Interest Paid | | (638,741) | (1,050,437) |
| **Net cash inflow from operating activities** | | (8,367) | (78,967) |
| **Cash flows from investing activities** | | | |
| Purchase of tangible fixed assets | | (658,573) | (281,289) |
| Capital Grants Received | | 310,000 | 500,000 |
| **Net cash outflow from operating activities** | | (348,573) | 218,711 |
| **Cash flows from financing activities** | | | |
| Proceeds from new loans | | 13,765,400 | 1,524,321 |
| Repayment of borrowings | | (12,200,000) | (1,470,000) |
| Repayment of finance lease liabilities | | (138,549) | (197,585) |
| **Net cash outflow from financing activities** | | 1,426,851 | (143,264) |
| **Increase/(decrease) in cash in the period** | | 1,069,911 | (3,520) |
| Cash and cash equivalents at January1, 2015 | | (304,769) | (301,249) |
| Cash and cash equivalents at December 31, 2015 | | 765,142 | (304,769) |

## ANALYSIS OF NET DEBT

| | At 1 Jan 2015 £ | Cash flow 2015 £ | Other changes 2015 £ | At 31 Dec 2015 £ |
|---|---|---|---|---|
| Cash at bank and in hand | — | 765,142 | — | 765,142 |
| Overdraft - current | (304,769) | 304,769 | — | — |
| | (304,769) | 1,069,911 | — | 765,142 |
| **Debt due within one year:** | | | | |
| HSBC loan | (200,000) | 200,000 | — | — |
| Leeds City Council loan | (200,000) | 200,000 | — | — |
| Other loans ECB | (450,000) | (250,000) | — | (700,000) |
| Finance leases less than one year | (126,693) | 138,549 | (108,649) | (96,794) |
| **Debt due after one year:** | | | | |
| HSBC loan | (2,869,014) | (200,000) | — | (3,069,014) |
| Leeds City Council loan | (7,207,000) | 6,300,000 | 907,000 | — |
| Pride Appeal loan | (5,000) " | — | — | (5,000) |
| Graves Family Trusts loans | (5,600,000) | (13,307,000) | — | (18,907,000) |
| C J Graves loan | (5,500,000) | 5,500,000 | — | — |
| Debentures | (380,296) | ( 8,400) | 23,696 | ( 365,000) |
| Finance leases more than one year | (1,086,069) | — | (591,351) | (1,677,420) |
| | (23,624,072) | (1,426,851) | 230,696 | (24,820,228) |
| **Total** | 23,928,842) | (356,939) | 230,696 | (24,055,085) |

# NOTES TO THE ACCOUNTS

## for the year ended 31st December, 2015

### 1. Accounting policies

These financial statements were prepared in accordance with Financial Reporting Standard 102 The Financial Reporting Standard applicable in the UK and Republic of Ireland (FRS 102) as issued in August 2014. The amendments to FRS 102 issued in July 2015 and effective immediately have been applied. The presentation currency of these financial statements is sterling.

In the transition to FRS 102 from old UK GAAP the Club has made no measurement, and recognition adjustments.accounts have been prepared in accordance with applicable accounting standards and under the historical cost convention. The principal accounting policies of the Club have remained unchanged from the previous year.

**(a) Income**

All income is accounted for on an accruals basis except for donations, which are accounted for in the year of receipt.

Income represents amounts receivable from the Club's principal activities. Income is analysed between international ticket and hospitality revenue, domestic ticket and hospitality revenue, subscriptions, England and Wales Cricket Board, commercial and other income.

*Subscriptions*

Subscription income comprises amounts receivable from members in respect of the current season. Subscriptions received in respect of future seasons is treated as deferred income.

*Domestic-ticket and hospitality revenue*

Relate to amounts received from gate charges, ticket sales, hospitality and guarantees directly attributable to staging domestic cricket matches in Yorkshire.

*International-ticket and hospitality revenue*

Relate to amounts received from gate charges, ticket sales, hospitality and guarantees directly attributable to staging international cricket matches in Yorkshire.

*England and Wales Cricket Board (ECB)*

ECB income relates to fees receivable, including performance-related elements, in the current season distributed from central funds in accordance with the First Class Memorandum of Understanding. ECB fees received in respect of future seasons are treated as deferred income. ECB distributions receivable to fund capital projects are treated as deferred income, and are released to the Income and Expenditure Account by equal instalments over the expected useful lives of the relevant assets in accordance with accounting policy (b) Fixed assets and depreciation, as set out below.

*Commercial and other income*

Relates to amounts received, net of related expenditure, from ground advertising, catering guarantees, box lettings, facility hire, dinners and other events. Advertising income received in respect of future seasons is treated as deferred income. Other income relates to amounts received, net of related expenditure, from retail, Cricket Centre bar, Taverners' Club, fundraising activities and other sundry items.

**(b) Fixed assets and depreciation**

All expenditure in connection with the development of Headingley Carnegie Cricket Ground and the related facilities has been capitalised. Finance costs relating to and incurred during the period of construction were also capitalised. Depreciation is only charged once a discrete phase of the development is completed.

The periods generally applicable are:

Headingley Carnegie Cricket Ground and Cricket Centre

| | | |
|---|---|---|
| Buildings | Carnegie Pavilion | 125 years |
| | Other buildings | 50 years |
| Fixtures | | 4 years |
| Plant & Equipment | Between 4 and 10 years | |
| Office equipment | | |
| — telephone system | | 4 years |
| Computer equipment | | 2 years |
| Freehold land is not depreciated. | | |

450

All other expenditure on repairs to Headingley Carnegie Cricket Ground and other grounds is written off as and when incurred.

**(c) Carnegie Pavilion**

The Club's contribution towards the design and build cost of the Carnegie Pavilion is £3m, of which £1.5m is payable over 20 years under a 125-year lease agreement. The £3m, together with the associated legal, professional and capital fit-outs costs of the areas within the Pavilion that the Club occupies, have been capitalised and depreciated over the 125-year lease term. The £1.5m, payable under the lease agreement has been treated as a finance lease within the financial statements with the capital element reported within Creditors (Finance leases) and the interest element charged to the Income and Expenditure Account on a straight-line basis over the 20-year term.

**(d) Stocks**

Stocks represent goods for resale, and are stated at the lower of cost and net realisable value.

**(e) Grants**

Capital grants relating to the development of Headingley Carnegie Cricket Ground (including the Yorkshire Cricket Museum) and Cricket Centre are included within the Balance Sheet as deferred income, and are released to the Income and Expenditure Account by equal instalments over the expected useful lives of the relevant assets in accordance with accounting policy (b) Fixed assets and depreciation, as set out above.

Grants of a revenue nature are credited to the Income and Expenditure Account in the same period as their related expenditure.

**(f) Disclosure of information to Auditor**

The members of the Board who held office at the date of approval of the Annual Report and Accounts confirm that, so far as they are aware, there is no relevant information of which the Club's auditor is unaware; or each member has taken all the steps that he ought to have taken as a member to make himself aware of any relevant audit information or to establish that the Club's auditor is aware of that information.

## 2. Financial Position

The Club is in a net liability position of £2.7m (2014:£3.2m). This includes deferred income of £2.0m (2014:£1.8m). Details of the loan and overdraft maturity analysis which impact on the financial position can be found in Note 8. The Club is expecting minimal movement in the cash balance for 2016 before capital expenditure, so the Club will continue to pay creditors as they fall due. Due to this, the Board considers it appropriate to prepare the financial statements on a going-concern basis.

## 3. Directors' Remuneration and Staff Numbers and Costs

|  | 2015 | 2014 |
|---|---|---|
|  | £ | £ |
| Wages and salaries | 105,975 | — |
| Social security costs | 11715 | — |
| Pension costs | 8498 | — |
|  | 126,188 | — |

**Staff Numbers and Costs**

The average number of persons employed by the company (including directors) during the year, analysed by category, was as follows:

|  | 2015 | 2014 |
|---|---|---|
| Players (including Academy Players) | 37 | 29 |
| Non Playing Full Time Staff | 42 | 39 |
| Seasonal and Casual Staff | 13 | 8 |
|  | 92 | 76 |

The aggregate payroll costs of these persons were as follows:

|  | 2015 | 2014 |
|---|---|---|
| Wages and Salaries | 3,403,851 | 2,956,633 |
| Social Security Costs | 365,369 | 325,143 |
| Contribution to Pension Plans | 280,160 | 215,275 |
|  | 4,049,380 | 3,497,051 |

|  | 2015 | 2014 |
|---|---|---|
|  | £ | £ |
| **4. Taxation** | | |
| Profit/(loss) for the year | 368,413 | (326,758) |
| Total tax expense | 110,877 | — |
| Profit/(loss) excluding taxation | 479,290 | (326,758) |
| | | |
| Current tax at 20.25% (2014: 21.50%) | 97,056 | (70,253) |
| Reduction in tax rate on deferred tax balances | 88,454 | — |
| Expenses not deductible for taxation purposes | 84,523 | 61,864 |
| Non taxable income | (112,428) | (104,958) |
| Depreciation for the period in excess of capital allowances | 3,518 | 2,366 |
| Losses (utilised)/not utilised | (72,669) | 110,981 |
| Origination/(reversal) of timing differences | 66,661 | — |
| Adjustments in respect of prior periods | (44,238) | — |
| Total current tax charge (see above) | 110,877 | — |

The tax charge for the year represents deferred tax and such is a non-cash item, which has been fully recognised in the income and expenditure account. No charges have been recognised in other comprehensive income or directly in equity. In 2014 no tax charge was recognised in the income and expenditure account, other comprehensive income or directly in equity.

**5. Fixed assets (See next page)**

**6. Debtors**

|  | 2015 | 2014 |
|---|---|---|
|  | £ | £ |
| Trade debtors | 597,608 | 304,543 |
| Deferred tax asset (see Note 10) | 729,429 | 840,306 |
| Other debtors | 155,854 | 166,297 |
|  | 1,482,891 | 1,311,146 |

**7. Creditors: amounts falling due within one year**

|  | 2015 | 2014 |
|---|---|---|
|  | £ | £ |
| Leeds City Council loan | — | 200,000 |
| HSBC Bank Loan | — | 200,000 |
| Bank overdraft (secured) | — | 304,724 |
| ECB loans | 700,000 | 450,000 |
| Trade creditors | 684,254 | 175,157 |
| Finance leases | 96,794 | 126,693 |
| Social security and other taxes | 389,662 | 368,925 |
| Other creditors | 113,874 | 58,358 |
| Accruals | 197,639 | 111,774 |
| Deferred income | 1,971,406 | 1,768,389 |
|  | 4,153,629 | 3,764,066 |

|  | Cricket Centre | | Headingley Carnegie Cricket Ground | | | | | |
|  | Freehold Land and Buildings £ | Plant & Equipment £ | Freehold Land and Buildings £ | Plant and Equipment £ | Improvements to Leasehold Property £ | Assets in the Course of Construction £ | Office Equipment £ | Total £ |
|---|---|---|---|---|---|---|---|---|
| **Cost** | | | | | | | | |
| At January 1, 2015 | 601,124 | 773,176 | 25,329,216 | 4,921,743 | 4,453,421 | 370,828 | 395,179 | 36,844,687 |
| Additions | 7,500 | 6,918 | 1,289,685 | 32,536 | — | — | 21,934 | 1,358,573 |
| Adjustments | — | — | 370,828 | — | — | (370,828) | — | — |
| At December 31, 2015 | 608,624 | 780,094 | 26,989,729 | 4,954,279 | 4,453,421 | — | 417,113 | 38,203,260 |
| **Depreciation** | | | | | | | | |
| At January 1, 2015 | 139,239 | 762,639 | 2,615,492 | 4,413,677 | 197,130 | — | 380,725 | 8,508,902 |
| Provided in the year | 16,538 | 2,208 | 248,709 | 112,339 | 42,523 | — | 12,451 | 434,768 |
| At December 31, 2015 | 155,777 | 764,847 | 2,864,201 | 4,526,016 | 239,653 | — | 393,176 | 8,943,670 |
| **Net book value** | | | | | | | | |
| At January 1, 2015 | 452,847 | 15,247 | 24,125,528 | 428,263 | 4,213,768 | — | 23,935 | 29,259,590 |
| **At December 31, 2015** | **461,885** | **10,537** | **22,713,724** | **508,066** | **4,256,291** | **370,828** | **14,454** | **28,335,785** |

453

Improvements to Headingley Cricket Ground Freehold Land and Buildings include the floodlights, which were under construction at the end of 2014 and the Dickie Bird Players Balcony.

|  | **2015** | 2014 |
|  | **£** | £ |
| **8. Creditors: amounts falling due after more than one year** | | |
| Leeds City Council Loan | — | 7,207,000 |
| HSBC Bank Loan | **3,069,014** | 2,869,014 |
| Pride Appeal Loans | **5,000** | 5,000 |
| CJ and J Graves Accumulation and Maintenance Trusts Loans | **6,703,500** | 5,600,000 |
| J Graves Accumulation and Maintenance Trusts Loans | **6,703,500** | — |
| CJ Graves 1999 Settlement Trust Loan | **5,500,000** | — |
| C J Graves Loan | — | 5,500,000 |
| Debentures | **365,000** | 380,296 |
| Finance Leases | **1,677,424** | 1,086,069 |
| Deferred income | **1,137,245** | 1,518,190 |
|  | **25,160,683** | 24,165,569 |

| **Loan and overdraft maturity analysis:** | | |
| In one year or less or on demand | **796,794** | 1,281,462 |
| In more than one year but not more than two years | **803,096** | 6,075,000 |
| In more than two years but not more than five years | **22,214,270** | 6,925,000 |
| In more than five years | **1,006,073** | 9,647,379 |
|  | **24,820,233** | 23,928,841 |

**Exceptional Item**

The Graves family trusts have provided loans of £18.9m, which have allowed the previous loans from Colin Graves, the Graves family trusts and Leeds City Council to be repaid. As part of the refinancing we are grateful to Leeds City Council, who after reviewing the actual cost of interest that the council has incurred in servicing the debt which demonstrated that the cost to the council has been fully met by the Club, accepted £6.5m in settlement of the £7.4m capital outstanding on the loan. This gave rise to exceptional income, net of costs, of £781,106.

As part of the refinancing HSBC agreed to return any capital payments made in 2015, lower their interest rate to 2.5 per cent, and defer full capital repayment until October 1, 2018, in return for a First Legal Charge over the Cricket Centre and a Third Legal Charge over Headingley Cricket Ground in respect of the bank loan and overdrafts. HSBC Bank plc also has a fixed and floating charge over all of the assets of the Club, subject to the Legal Charges referred to above.

To enable the repayment of the Leeds City Council debt, further debt has been incurred. C J and J Graves Accumulation and Maintenance and J Graves Accumulation and Maintenance Trusts loans now stand at £6.7m, each bearing an interest rate of 4.625 per cent, and with initial capital repayments to be made in 2019 (£2m each Trust) and during 2020 (£1.5m each Trust) with the balance at December 31, 2020. The two Trusts have been granted by the Club joint First Legal Charge over Headingley Cricket Ground and joint Second Legal Charge over the Cricket Centre.

A further £5.5m of debt has also been incurred from the CJ Graves 1999 Settlement Trust, bearing an interest rate of 0 per cent. The Club has granted Second Legal Charge over Headingley Cricket Ground and Third Legal Charge over the Cricket Centre.

An additional loan was made available by the ECB towards the cost of installing the floodlights at Headingley Cricket Ground. The total available loan is £700,000, of which all was drawn down early in 2015. £200,000 has been repaid by a one-off fee payment from the ECB following the first floodlit televised games at Headingley Cricket Ground in 2015, and it is expected that the remainer will be repaid by further fee payments following floodlit televised games in 2016.

| **9. Deferred income -capital grants** | | |
| At January 1, 2015 | **5,019,668** | 4,697,933 |
| Received in year | **310,000** | 500,000 |
| Released to Income and Expenditure Account | **(177,382)** | (178,265) |
| At December 31, 2015 | **5,152,286** | 5,019,668 |

|  | 2015 £ | 2014 £ |
|---|---|---|
| **10. Provision for Liabilities** | | |
| **— Deferred Taxation Asset / (Liability)** | | |
| At January 1, 2015 | **(840,306)** | (840,306) |
| Charge to Income and Expenditure Account for the year | **455** | — |
| At December 31, 2015 | **(729,429)** | (840,306) |
| The elements of deferred taxation are as follows: | | |
| Difference between accumulated depreciation and capital allowances | **171,755** | 219,690 |
| Tax losses | **(901,184)** | (1,059,996) |
| | **(729,429)** | (840,306) |

**11. Share capital**

| | | |
|---|---|---|
| Allotted, called up and fully paid Ordinary shares of 5p each" | **197** | 199 |

During the year there was a net reduction in qualifying members of 49. The total number of qualifying members at December 31, 2015, was 3,924 (2014: 3,973). Each member of the Club owns one Ordinary share, and the rights attached thereto are contained within the Club's rules, which can be found on the Club's website or from the Secretary on request.

**12. Reserves.**

| | Income and Expenditure Account | Capital Redemption Reserve |
|---|---|---|
| At January 1, 2015 | **(3,215,508)** | 691 |
| Surplus for the year | **368,413** | — |
| Shares in respect of retiring members | **—** | 2 |
| At December 31, 2015 | **(2,847,095)** | 693 |

**13. Leasing commitments**

Finance lease liabilities are payable as follows:

| *Minimum Lease Payment* | 2015 | 2014 |
|---|---|---|
| In one year or less | **96,794** | 126,693 |
| Between two and five years | **966,351** | 300,000 |
| More than five years | **711,073** | 786,069 |
| | **1,774,218** | 1,212,762 |

The Club currently has two finance leases. One is with Leeds Beckett University relating to the Carnegie Pavilion. This lease is for 125 years, with lease payments being made for 20 years until 2030, after which a peppercorn rate is due. The second lease is with Investec in relation to the floodlights installed during 2015. This lease will be repaid in 2019, at which point ownership of the floodlights will revert to the Club.

Operating lease payments amounting to £41,704 (2014:£41,704) were recognised as an expense in the profit-and-loss account in respect of operating leases. Non cancellable operating lease rentals are payable as follows:

| *Minimum Lease Payment* | 2015 | 2014 |
|---|---|---|
| In one year or less | **41,704** | 41,704 |
| Between two and five years | **113,853** | 143,056 |
| In five years or more | **—** | 12,500 |
| | **155,557** | 197,260 |

### 14. Related Party Transactions

During the year Mr R A Smith was a Board member and Trustee of the Yorkshire Cricket Foundation (YCF). During 2014 the YCF awarded non-capital grants of £11,594 (2014:£20,083).

### 15. Pensions

The Club operates defined contribution pension schemes for the benefit of certain employees. The amounts paid during the year were £265,352 (2014:£236,334). The assets of these schemes are administered in funds independent from those of the Club.

### 16. Audit Fee

The Club paid its auditors £16,750 (2014:£16,750) in respect of the audit of these Financial Statements.

# Stop Press: Head heads for Headingley

The *Yearbook* was going to Press when it was learned that Yorkshire had signed Australian *T20* international Travis Head, left, as their replacement overseas player for 2016 when Kiwi Kane leaves the county in July.

Head, 22, captain of South Australia in first-class cricket, is an aggressive left-hand batsman and off-spin bowler. He will be available to play in all competitions for Yorkshire from July 18. During the winter he starred for Adelaide Strikers in the *Big Bash T20* competition under the guidance of Jason Gillespie and was the fifth leading scorer with 299 runs from nine matches.